BLMC Mini
Owners
Workshop
Manual

_221079_

D1465702

by J H Haynes
Member of the Guild of Motoring Writers
and B L Chalmers - Hunt
TEng(CEI), AMIMI, AMIRTE, AMVBRA
Foreword by Paddy Hopkirk

Models covered

Saloon Mk I and II. 848 cc and 998 cc
Countryman/Traveller. Mk I and II. 848 cc and 998 cc
Van and Pick-up. Mk I and II. 848 cc and 998 cc
Cooper and Cooper S. Mk I, II and III. 970 cc, 997 cc, 998 cc, 1071 cc and 1275 cc
Clubman Saloon. 998 cc and 1098 cc
Clubman Estate. 998 cc and 1098 cc
Clubman 1275 GT. 1275 cc
Riley Elf. Mk I, II and III. 848 cc and 998 cc
Wolseley Hornet. Mk I, II and III. 848 cc and 998 cc

Covers automatic and manual gearbox versions of above. Does not fully cover the Mini-Moke

ISBN 0 85696 213 9

Printed in England

HAYNES PUBLISHING GROUP
SPARKFORD YEOVIL SOMERSET ENGLAND
distributed in the USA by
HAYNES PUBLICATIONS INC
861 LAWRENCE DRIVE
NEWBURY PARK
CALIFORNIA 91320
USA

Mini 850

Mini 1275 GT

Foreword

When I first obtained my car driving licence at 17 years of age, I bought a 1935 Austin 7 which was almost a wreck - and completely rebuilt it myself with the indispensable aid of an old manual. Perhaps my affection for this car led to my eventual connection with the Mini, a car which I have rallied and raced all over the world, and a car for which I naturally have a great admiration and respect. Through the years I have acquired a very detailed knowledge of the mechanics of the Mini, but even now I make regular use of a workshop manual, and the so-called 'expert' who believes he doesn't need one does not impress me in the least. The Mini is a splendid car, providing it is properly serviced and repaired, and this Mini Owner's Workshop Manual is just the book to really help the owner who prefers to tackle his own repair and overhaul work.

Most of the work described in the manual has been carried out by the author and his team of assistance, and you are therefore getting the benefit of first hand knowledge gained through practical experience - so take advantage of it! There are over **449** photographs covering complete overhaul of the major components which, together with 245 line drawings, means that even the novice should have little difficulty in tackling the more complicated tasks.

Frequently ordinary tools can be used to make very effective repairs. On several occasions during major Rallies we have hit trouble and had to make use of the limited materials to hand, and always with the minimum of time available. During an Alpine Rally, the rear hub bearing on my Mini had gone, and when the mechanics were drawing it off, it disintegrated, leaving the inner ring on the stub axle. We therefore cracked it off by hitting it with one hammer, holding another hammer on the opposite side. This took only about ten minutes and was completely effective, but our late arrival at the check point (by only one minute!) cost us our 'Coupe Des Alpes'. In normal repair work time is not quite so important.

I wish you trouble-free motoring!

Acknowledgements

Thanks are due to BLMC Limited for their assistance in the supply of technical material and certain illustrations, to Castrol Limited for advice on lubrication, and the Champion Sparking Plug Company, who supplied the illustrations showing the various spark plug conditions. The bodywork repair photographs used in this manual were provided by Lloyds Industries Limited, who supply 'Turtle Wax', 'Dupli-Colour Holts', and other Holts range products.

Lastly, special thanks are due to all of those people at Sparkford who helped in the production of this manual. Particularly, Brian Horsfall, Les Brazier, Rod Grainger, Stanley Randolph, Ian Coomber, John Austin, John Rose and Lee Saunders.

About this manual

This, the second edition of the Haynes Mini Owner's Workshop Manual, retains many elements of the original widely acclaimed, and very popular publication. It is a completely revised book containing details of the latest Mini models, and information on the modifications made to the Mini during its many years of production.

We like to think that the Mini manual has matured over the years, along with the Mini, and that this manual, on the current Mini, is even better than the original.

This is a manual for the do-it-yourself minded Mini motoring enthusiasts. It shows how to maintain these cars in first class condition, and how to carry out repairs when components become worn or break. By doing all maintenance and repair work themselves owners will gain three ways: they will know the job has been done properly; they will have had the satisfaction of doing the job themselves; and they will have saved garage labour charges which, although quite fair bearing in mind the high cost of capital equipment and skilled men, can be very high. Regular and careful maintenance is essential if maximum reliability and minimum wear are to be achieved.

The author has stripped, overhauled, and rebuilt all the major mechanical and electrical assemblies and most of the minor ones as well. Only through working in this way can solutions be found to the sort of problems facing private owners. Other hints and tips are also given which can only be obtained through practical experience.

The step-by-step photographic strip and rebuild sequences show how each of the major components was removed, taken apart, and rebuilt. In conjunction with the text and exploded illustrations this should make all the work quite clear - even to the novice who has never previously attempted the more complex job.

Manufacturers' official manuals are usually splendid publications which contain a wealth of technical information. Because they are issued primarily to help the manufacturers' authorised dealers and distributors they tend to be written in very technical language, and tend to skip details of certain jobs which are common knowledge to garage mechanics. Haynes Owners' Workshop Manuals are different as they are intended primarily to help the owner, and therefore contain details of all sorts of jobs not normally found in official manuals.

Owners who intend to do their own maintenance and repairs should have a reasonably comprehensive tool kit. Some jobs require special service tools, but in many instances it is possible to get round their use with a little care and ingenuity. For example a jubilee clip makes a most efficient and cheap piston ring compressor.

Throughout this manual ingenious ways of avoiding the use of special equipment and tools are shown. In some cases the proper tool must be used. Where this is the case a description of the tool and its correct use is included.

When a component malfunctions garage repairs are becoming more and more a case of replacing the defective item with an exchange rebuilt unit. This is excellent practice when a component is thoroughly worn out. but it is a waste of good money when overall the component is only half worn, and requires the replacement of but a single small item to effect a complete repair. As an example, a non-functioning dynamo can frequently be repaired quite satisfactory just by fitting new brushes.

A further function of this manual is to show the owner how to examine malfunctioning parts; determine what is wrong; then how to make the repair.

Given the time, mechanical do-it-yourself aptitude, and a reasonable collection of tools this manual will show the enthusiastic owner how to maintain and repair his car really economically with minimum recourse to professional assistance and expensive tools and equipment.

Using this manual

The book is divided into thirteen Chapters, each of which covers a logical sub-division of the vehicle. Each Chapter is divided into numbered Sections which are headed in **bold type** between horizontal lines. Each Section consists of serially numbered paragraphs.

There are two types of illustration:

Figures: These are numbered according to Chapter, and sequence of occurrence in that Chapter. Thus, 'Fig. 2.8' is the eigth illustration in Chapter 2. Every figure has an individual caption.

Photographs: The majority of the photographs in this manual form complete dismantling and reassembly sequences - and can be used, as such, without reference to the text. If you are attempting a relatively major task for the first time, it may be better to use the text of the manual (which is more detailed), making occasional references to the relevant photographs.

Photographic and textual sequences may vary slightly, so it is best to stick to one or the other. Photographs which form a complete sequence are numbered serially, throughout the book. The remaining photographs have their reference numbers divided by a point (eg: 7.31). In this case the photograph numbers pinpoints the paragraph and Section number of the piece of text relevant to the photograph. Thus, the example quoted refers to paragraph 31/Section 7 of the Chapter in which the photograph occurs.

When the left or right-hand side of a car is mentioned it is as if one were looking in the forward direction of travel.

Although every care has been taken to ensure all the information in this manual is correct, no liability can be accepted by the authors or publishers for damage, loss, or injury caused by any errors in, or omissions from the information given.

Contents

Mini Clubman Estate

Buying
spare parts and vehicle identification numbers

Buying spare parts

Spare parts are available from many sources, for example: BLMC garages, other garages and accessory shops, and motor factors. Our advice regarding spare part sources is as follows:

Officially appointed BLMC garages - This is the best source of parts which are peculiar to your car and are otherwise not generally available (eg complete cylinder heads, internal gearbox components, badges, interior trim etc). It is also the only place at which you should buy parts if your car is still under warranty - non-BLMC components may invalidate the warranty. To be sure of obtaining the correct parts it will always be necessary to give the storeman your car's engine and chassis number, and if possible, to take the 'old' part along for positive identification. Remember that many parts are available on a factory exchange scheme - any parts returned should always be clean! It obviously makes good sense to go straight to the specialists on your car for this type of part for they are best equipped to supply you.

Other garages and accessory shops - These are often very good places to buy materials and components needed for the maintenance of your car (eg oil filters, spark plugs, bulbs, fan belts, oils and greases, touch-up paint, filler paste etc). They also sell general accessories, usually have convenient opening hours, charge lower prices and can often be found not far from home.

Motor factors - Good factors will stock all of the more important components which wear out relatively quickly (eg clutch components, pistons, valves, exhaust systems, brake cylinders/pipes/hoses/seals/shoes and pads etc). Motor factors will often provide new or reconditioned components on a part exchange basis - this can save a considerable amount of money.

Vehicle identification numbers

When ordering spare parts it is essential to give full details of your car to the storeman. He will want to know the commission, car, and engine numbers. When ordering parts for the transmission unit or body it is also necessary to quote the transmission casing and body numbers.

Commission number: Stamped on a plate fixed to the right-hand wing valance.

Car number: Located on a plate mounted between the radiator and the left-hand wing valance.

Engine number: Stamped on the cylinder block or on a metal plate fixed to the right-hand side of the cylinder block.

Transmission casing assembly: Stamped on a facing provided on the casting just below the starter motor.

Body number: Stamped on a metal plate fixed to the grille stopper.

Routine maintenance

The maintenance instructions listed below are basically those recommended by the manufacturer. They are supplemented by additional maintenance tasks which, through practical experience, the author recommends should be carried out at the intervals suggested.

The additional tasks are indicated by an asterisk and are primarily of a preventative nature in that they will assist in eliminating the unexpected failure of a component due to fair wear and tear.

When a new car is delivered the complete engine/transmission unit contains sufficient 'running-in' oil for the 'running-in' period. Provided the level is maintained between the "low" and "high" marks on the dipstick during this period, topping up is unnecessary. At the first 'Free Service', the 'running-in' oil is drained and the sump replenished to the level of the "high" mark on the dipstick.

Owners of early Minis may also use the tasks recommended provided that the overall mechanical condition of the car is good.

Weekly, before a long journey or every 250 miles (400 km)

1 Check oil level in engine/transmission unit and top-up if necessary.
2 Check battery electrolyte level and top-up if necessary with distilled water.
3 Check level of coolant in radiator and top-up if necessary.
4 Check level of water in windscreen washer reservoir and top-up if necessary.
5 Check tyre pressures and adjust as necessary. Also check the depth of tread on the tyres (minimum 1 mm) and also inspect for signs of damage to treads and side walls.
6 Check tightness of road wheel nuts.

Every 3,000 miles (5,000 km) or 3 months

Complete the service items in the weekly service check plus:
1 Check fan belt tension and adjust as necessary. (Fig. 1).
2 Check level of hydraulic fluid in clutch reservoir and top-up if necessary.
3 Check steering system generally for oil leaks.
4 Check steering unit joints for security, backlash and gaiter condition.
5 Visually check brake hydraulic pipes and unions for chafing, leaks and/or corrosion.
6 Check level of hydraulic fluid in brake reservoir and top up if necessary. (Fig. 2).
7 Check brake pedal travel and adjust if necessary. Check operation of handbrake.
8 Check correct operation of horns, direction indicators, windscreen wipers and all lights.
9 Check specific gravity of battery electrolyte with a hydrometer.
10 Check headlight beam alignment and reset as necessary.
11 Check condition of windscreen wiper blades and if worn renew. This should be done at least once a year in any case.

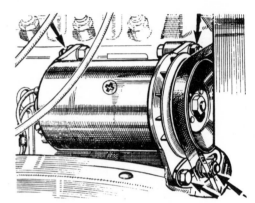

RM1. Generator mounting points to be slackened for fan belt adjustment

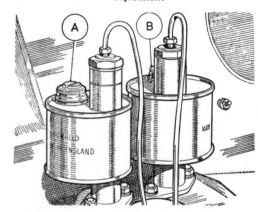

RM2. Brake (A) and clutch (B) master cylinder reservoirs

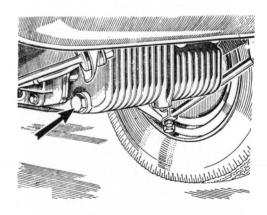

RM3. Engine/transmission unit drain plug

12 Visually, check the condition of the fuel and clutch pipes and unions for signs of chafing, leaks and/or corrosion.

13 Carefully inspect the exhaust system for leaks and its mountings for security.

14 Ensure that the tyres fitted are inflated to the manufacturer's specification.

15 Check condition and security of seat belts.

16 Ensure that the rear view mirror and exterior mirrors are clean, undamaged and are correctly adjusted.

17 Re-oil air cleaner elements - Cooper models.

Every 6,000 miles (10,000 km) or 6 months

Complete the service items in the 3000 mile service check plus:

1 Change engine/transmission unit oil. (Fig. 3).

2 Fit new engine oil filter.

3 Fit new air cleaner element (dusty areas only).

4 Top-up carburettor piston dashpot. (Fig. 4).

5 Check carburettor settings and adjust if necessary.

6 Carefully examine cooling system and heater system for leaks.

7 Lubricate accelerator control linkage, cable and pedal fulcrum.

8 Clean and reset spark plugs.

9 Check and adjust distributor contact breaker points gap.

10 Lubricate distributor. (Fig. 5 and 6).

11 Check ignition timing and automatic advance system, preferably using electronic equipment. If possible this should be left to the local BLMC garage.

12 Lubricate brake and clutch pedal fulcrum points.

13 Remove and clean the filters in the carburettor and fuel pump where these are fitted. (Fig. 7).

14 Check clearance at clutch lever return stop and adjust if necessary.

15 Check and if necessary tighten the door hinges and striker plate securing screws. (Fig. 8).

16 Repack rear hub bearings with grease.

17 Check front wheel alignment and adjust if necessary. Preferably this should be left to the local BLMC garage.

18 Check tightness of steering column clamp bolt.

19 Balance the front wheels to eliminate steering vibration. This is a job for the local BLMC garage.

20 Lubricate all grease nipples. (Figs. 9, 10 and 11).

a) Steering tie rod balljoints - one nipple on each shaft. These nipples are found on early models only, (total 2).

b) Inner driveshaft sliding joints: one nipple on each shaft. These nipples are found on early models only, (total 2).

c) Steering swivel knuckle. Two nipples, one upper and one lower on each side (total 4).

d) Upper suspension arm inner pivot: one nipple on each arm (total 2).

e) Rear suspension radius arm pivot: one nipple on each arm. To expose the nipples remove the rubber blanking plugs.

f) Handbrake cable swivel pivot on the underside of the rear radius arm pivot. No grease nipple is fitted but cover generously with grease to ensure smooth operation.

g) Handbrake cable guide channels located at the rear of the exhaust pipe tunnel. Grease each channel generously. (No grease nipple fitted).

21 Check the hydraulic damper mounting nuts, suspension nuts and steering nuts for tightness.

22 *If wished change the tyres round to equalize the wear. (Not when radials are fitted together with crossply tyres).

23 *Wax polish the body and also the chromium plating. Force wax polish into any joints in the bodywork to prevent rust formation.

24 Lubricate handbrake mechanical linkage and cables.

25 Grease both battery connections.

26 Lubricate dynamo rear bearing (no lubrication point for alternator).

27 Lubricate all door, bonnet and boot lid locks and hinges.

28 Carry out a road test to ensure correct and smooth operation of all controls.

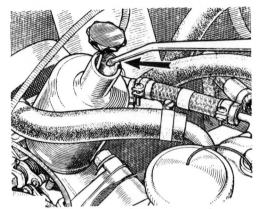

RM4. Carburettor dashpot oil level topping up

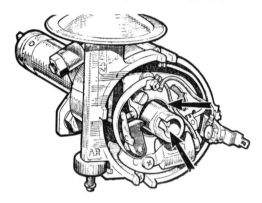

RM5. Distributor lubrication points

RM6. Distributor lubrication points

RM7. Early type fuel pump filter. Later models have mechanical fuel pump – see Chapter 3

Every 12,000 miles (20,000 km) or 12 months

Complete the service items in the 6,000 mile service check as applicable plus:

1 Fit new air cleaner element.
2 Fit new rocker cover oil filler cap and filter assembly.
3 Check valve rocker clearances and adjust as necessary.
4 Fit new spark plugs.
5 *Inspect the ignition HT leads for cracks and damage and replace as necessary.
6 *Examine the dynamo brushes; replace them if worn and clean the commutator. Full details will be found in Chapter 10.
7 *Steam clean underside of the body and clean the engine/ transmission exterior as well as the whole of the front compartment.
8 Remove the brake drums and check brake linings for wear. Also check the condition of the brake drums and renew as necessary. Remove all traces of dust. When disc brakes are fitted check pad thickness and disc condition.
9 Remove carburettor float chamber, empty any sediment present, check the condition of the needle valve, clean and refit.
10 Remove the speedometer cable, clean and lubricate the inner cable with grease. When reassembling, the inner cable should be withdrawn by 8 inches (203 mm) and the surface grease wiped off. This is done so that grease will not work its way into the speedometer head.
11 Later models with crankcase closed circuit breathing system: Strip and clean breather valve. (Fig. 12).
12 Early type servo: Remove five screws securing air valve cover and blow out filter chamber. (Fig. 13).
13 Lubricate water pump. (Early models only fitted with plug). Fig. 14).

Every 24,000 miles (40,000 km) or 18 months

Complete the service items in the 6,000 and 12,000 mile service check as applicable plus:

1 *Examine the hub bearings for wear and replace as necessary. Full information will be found in Chapter 11.
2 *Check the tightness of the battery earth lead on the bodywork.
3 *Renew the condenser in the distributor. See Chapter 4 for full information.
4 *Remove the starter motor, examine the brushes and replace as necessary. Clean the commutator and starter drive as described in Chapter 10.
5 *Test the cylinder compressions, and if necessary remove the cylinder head, decarbonise, grind-in the valves and fit new valve springs. Full information will be found in Chapter 1.
6 Completely drain the brake hydraulic fluid from the system. All seals and flexible hoses throughout the braking system should be examined and preferably renewed. The working surfaces of the master cylinder, wheel and caliper cylinders (disc brakes) should be inspected for wear or scoring and new parts fitted as considered necessary. Refill the hydraulic system with new hydraulic fluid.
7 *Check and adjust any loose play in the rack and pinion steering gear. Full information will be found in Chapter 11.
8 *Examine all balljoints and hub bearings for wear and replace as necessary. Full information will be found in Chapter 11.
9 *Examine the inner 'rubber' universal joints for wear and renew as necessary. (Early models only).

RM8. Door lock catch and striker attachment screws

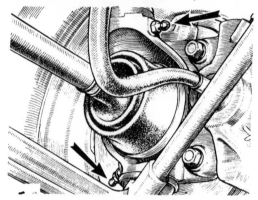

RM9. Swivel grease nipples

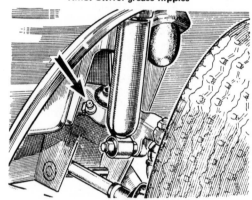

RM10. Upper suspension grease nipple

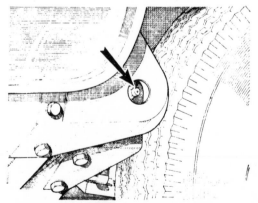

RM11. Rear suspension radius arm nipple

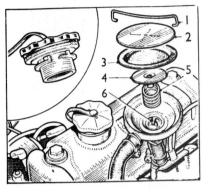

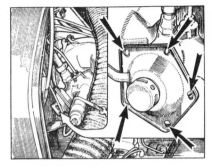

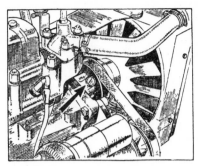

RM12. Crankcase closed circuit breathers

1 *Spring clip*
2 *Cover*
3 *Diaphragm*
4 *Metering needle*
5 *Spring*
6 *Cruciform guides*

RM13. Vacuum servo unit air valve attachment points

RM14. Water pump lubrication plug (early models only)

Every 36,000 miles (60,000 km) or 3 years

Complete the service items in the 6,000 and 12,000 miles

service check as applicable plus:

1 Renew the servo unit air filter. This is only applicable when a servo unit is fitted.

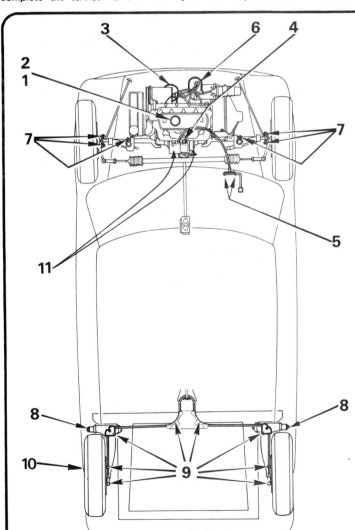

RM15 Lubrication chart
Every 3000 miles (5000 km) or 3 months
1 Engine and transmission - drain and refill with fresh multigrade engine oil if vehicle is normally used in severe or adverse conditions.

Every 6000 miles (10000 km) or 6 months
2 Engine and transmission - drain and refill with fresh multigrade engine oil
3 Renew oil filter cartridge/element
4 Top up carburettor piston damper with multi-grade engine oil
5 Lubricate accelerator control linkage and pedal fulcrum with multigrade engine oil
6 Lubricate distributor cam with general purpose grease, and contact breaker pivot, weights and drive spindle with multigrade engine oil
7 Lubricate steering joints with general purpose grease
8 Lubricate rear suspension radius arm pivots with general purpose grease
9 Lubricate the handbrake cable linkages and sector pivots with general purpose grease

Every 24000 miles (40000 km) or 18 months
10 Lubricate the rear hubs with general purpose grease
11 Lubricate the gear change shafts with general purpose grease

Chapter 1 Engine

Contents

Specifications

The engine originally fitted to the ADO15 Mini was of 848 cc and standard versions are still of this capacity. In 1961 the 997 cc Cooper was introduced, the increase in capacity being obtained by lengthening the stroke. In 1963 a 998 cc engine was introduced and was fitted originally to the Elf and Hornet. Although this engine was only 1 cc larger than the Cooper unit it was fundamentally different by having a nearly 'square' bore/stroke ratio. The 997 cc Cooper engine was superseded in January 1964 in favour of the 998 cc unit. In 1963 the first Cooper 'S' with 1,071 cc short stroke engine was introduced. This was followed in 1964 with the basically similar 970 cc and 1,275 cc 'S' models.

Engine specification & data - 848 cc Mini Mk I and Mk II (Types 8AM, 8AH, 8MB and 85H)

Engine (general):

Type	4 cylinder in-line transversely mounted with ohv pushrod operated
Bore	2.478 in. (62.94 mm)

Stroke	2.687 in. (68.26 mm)
Cubic capacity	848 cc (51.7 cu in.)
Compression ratio	8.3 : 1 (8.9 : 1 for 8AH engine)
Capacity of combustion chamber (valves fitted)	24.5 cc (1.49 cu in.)
Oversize bore	Max. 0.040 in. (1.016 mm)
	1st 0.010 in. (0.254 mm)
Maximum torque	44 lbf ft at 2,900 rpm (44 lbf ft at 2500 rpm for 8AH engine)
BMEP	128 lbs/sq in. (9 kg/cm^2) at 2,900 rpm (150 lbs/sq in (10.5 kg/cm^2) at 2,900 rpm for 8AH engine).
Firing order	1 3 4 2
Location of No. 1 cylinder	Next to radiator
Engine mountings	3-point suspension on rubber mountings

Camshaft and camshaft bearings:

The camshaft is driven from the crankshaft by a single roller chain. The camshaft is supported by three bearings, comprising a steel-backed white metal lined shell bearing at the front, while the centre and rear bearings run direct in the block.

Camshaft bearing clearance: Front	0.001 to 0.002 in. (0.0254 to 0.0508 mm)
Centre and rear	0.00125 to 0.00275 in. (0.032 to 0.07 mm)
Inside bearing diameter reamed when fitted:	
Front bearing	1.667 to 1.6675 in. (42.342 to 42.355 mm)
End float	0.003 to 0.007 in. (0.076 to 0.178 mm)
Journal diameters: Front	1.6655 to 1.666 in. (42.304 to 42.316 mm)
Centre	1.62275 to 1.62325 in. (41.218 to 41.231 mm)
Rear	1.3725 to 1.3735 in. (34.862 to 34.887 mm)
Clearance	0.001 to 0.002 in. (0.025 to 0.051 mm)

Connecting rods and big-end bearings:

Length between centres	5.75 in. (14.605 cm)
Big-end bearings	Steel-backed, lead-indium lined
Side clearance	0.008 to 0.012 in. (0.203 to 0.305 mm)
Bearing internal diameter clearance	0.001 to 0.0025 in. (0.025 to 0.063 mm)

Crankshaft and main bearings:

Main journal diameter	1.7505 to 1.7510 in. (44.46 to 44.47 mm)
Minimum main journal regrind diameter	1.7105 in. (43.45 mm)
Crankpin journal diameter	1.6254 to 1.6259 in. (41.28 to 41.30 mm)
Minimum crankpin regrind diameter	1.5854 in. (40.27 mm)
Main bearings	White metal, steel-backed liners - 3 shell type
End float	0.002 to 0.003 in. (0.051 to 0.076 mm)
Side thrust	Taken by thrust washers located on either side of centre main bearing
Undersizes available	−0.010 in. (−0.254 mm), −0.020 in. (−0.508 mm), −0.030 in. (−0.762 mm), −0.040 in. (−1.02 mm)

Cylinder block:

Type	Cylinder cast integral with top half of crankcase
Water jackets	Full length

Cylinder head:

Type	Cast iron with vertical valves. Siamised inlet ports, 2
Combustion chamber capacity with valves fitted	24.5 cc (1.49 cu in.)

Gudgeon pins:

Type	Semi-floating. Held by clamp bolt
Fit to piston	Hand push-fit −0.0001 to 0.00035 in. (0.0025 to 0.009 mm)
Fit in connecting rod	Hand push-fit −0.0001 to 0.0006 in. (0.0025 to 0.015 mm)
Diameter (outer)	0.6244 to 0.6246 in. (15.86 to 15.865 mm)

Lubrication system:

Type	Pressure feed. Pressure fed bearings: Main, camshaft and connecting rods. Reduced pressure to rocker shaft. Piston pin and cylinder wall lubrication - splash
Oil filter	Full-flow
Capacity of oil filter	1 pint (1.2 US pints. −0.57 litres)
Crankcase ventilation	Directed flow, via, road draught tube on left-hand side of engine
Transmission casing/sump capacity	7.5 pints
Transmission casing/sump and filter capacity	8.5 pints (10.2 US pints. −4.83 litres)
Oil pump, type	Eccentric rotor or vane
Oil pump relief pressure	60 lbs/sq in.
Oil pressure: Normal	30 to 60 lbs/sq in.
Idling	15 to 25 lbs/sq in.
Relief valve spring: Free length	2.859 in. (72.63 mm)
Fitted length	2.156 in. (54.77 mm)

Pistons:

Type		Split skirt, anodised aluminium alloy. 3 compression rings, 1 oil control ring
Clearance of piston:	Top of skirt	0.0026 to 0.0032 in. (0.066 to 0.081 mm)
	Bottom of skirt	0.0006 to 0.0012 in. (0.015 to 0.030 mm)
Piston oversizes available		+0.010 in. (+0.254 mm), +0.020 in. (+0.508 mm), +0.030 in. (+0.762 mm), +0.040 in. (+1.02 mm)

Piston rings:

Top compression ring	Plain
2nd and 3rd compression ring	Tapered
Fitted gap	0.007 to 0.012 in. (0.178 to 0.30 mm)
Groove clearance	0.0015 to 0.0035 in. (0.038 to 0.089 mm)
Oil control ring	Slotted scraper
Fitted gap	0.007 to 0.012 in. (0.178 to 0.30 mm)
Clearance in groove	0.0015 to 0.0035 in. (0.038 to 0.089 mm)

Tappets (cam followers):

Type	Bucket
Length	1.505 in. (38.23 mm)
Diameter	0.8120 in. (20.62 mm)

Valves:

Head diameter:	Inlet	1.093 to 1.098 in. (27.76 to 27.89 mm)
	Exhaust	1.000 to 1.005 in. (25.4 to 25.53 mm)
Valve lift		0.285 in. (7.24 mm)
Seat angle		Inlet and Exhaust: 45°
Valve clearance:		
Under normal conditions		0.012 in. (0.305 mm)
Stem diameter: Inlet		0.2793 to 0.2798 in. (7.094 to 7.107 mm)
Exhaust		0.2788 to 0.2793 in. (7.081 to 7.094 mm)
Valve stem to guide clearance:	Inlet	0.0015 to 0.0025 in. (0.038 to 0.063 mm)
	Exhaust	0.002 to 0.003 in. (0.051 to 0.076 mm)
Valve rocker bush bore (reamed)		0.5630 to 0.5635 in. (14.30 to 14.31 mm)

Valve guides:

Length: Inlet and Exhaust		1.687 in. (42.86 mm)
Diameter: Inlet and Exhaust:	Outside	0.4695 to 0.470 in. (11.92 to 11.94 mm)
	Inside	0.2813 to 0.2818 in. (7.145 to 7.177 mm)
Fitted height above head		0.594 in. (15.1 mm)

Valve timing:

Inlet valve:	Opens 5° btdc	Exhaust valve: Opens 40° bbdc
	Closes 45° abdc	Closes 10° atdc
Valve timing marks		Dimples on crankshaft and camshaft sprockets. Marks on flywheel
Chain pitch and No. of pitches		0.375 in. (9.52 mm) 52 pitches
Valve rocker clearance: timing		0.019 in. (0.48 mm)

Valve springs:

Type	Single valve springs
No. of coils	4½
Free length: Inlet and Exhaust	1.672 in. (42.47 mm) early models, 1.75 in (44.45 mm) late models
Valve spring pressure with valves open	70 lbf early models, 88 lbf late models
Valve spring pressure with valves closed	37.5 lbf early models, 55 lbf late models

Engine specification & data - Mini Cooper 997 cc (Type 9F)

The engine specification is identical to the type 8AM specification except for the differences detailed below.

Engine (general):

Type	9F
Bore	2.458 in. (62.43 mm)
Stroke	3.20 in. (81.28 mm)
Capacity	997 cc (60.87 cu in.)
Compression ratio: High	9 : 1
Low	8.3 : 1
BMEP High compression ratio	134 lb/sq in. at 3,500 rpm

Low compression ratio	129 lb/sq in. at 3,500 rpm
Maximum torque High compression ratio	54 lb/ft at 3,600 rpm
Low compression ratio	53 lb/ft at 3,500 rpm

Camshaft and camshaft bearings:
The camshaft is driven from the crankshaft by a single roller chain with tensioner. The camshaft is supported by 3 steel-backed white metal bearings.

Inside bearing diameter fitted and after reaming:
Front bearing	1.667 to 1.6675 in. (42.342 to 42.355 mm)
Centre bearing	1.6245 to 1.6255 in. (41.261 to 41.287 mm)
Rear bearing	1.3748 to 1.3755 in. (34.914 to 34.937 mm)

Connecting rods and big-end bearings:
Big-end bearing material	Steel-backed copper-lead; thin wall
Bearing length	0.875 in. (22.22 mm)

Crankshaft and main bearings:
Main bearing material	Steel-backed copper-lead; thin wall
Bearing length	1.0625 in. (26.99 mm)
Running clearance	0.001 to 0.0027 in. (0.025 to 0.069 mm)

Lubrication system:
Oil pump: type	'Hobourn-Eaton'
Relief valve opens	70 lb/sq in. (4.92 kg/cm^2)
Relief valve spring free length	2.609 in. (66.28 mm)
Oil pressure: Normal	70 lb/sq in. (4.92 kg/cm^2)

Pistons:
Type	Solid skirt, anodised aluminium alloy
Clearance: Bottom of skirt	0.0016 to 0.0022 in. (0.041 to 0.056 mm)

Piston rings:
Top compression ring	Plain, chrome faced
2nd and 3rd compression ring	Tapered

Valves:
Head diameter: Inlet	1.156 in. (29.4 mm)
Exhaust	1.000 in. (25.4 mm)
Throat diameter: Inlet	1.0312 in. (26.2 mm)
Exhaust	0.908 in. (23.06 mm)
Valve lift	0.312 in. (7.92 mm)

Valve timing:
Inlet valve:	Opens	16° btdc	Exhaust valve: Opens	51° bbdc
	Closes	56° abdc	Closes	21° atdc

Valve springs:
Free length: Inlet and Exhaust	1.750 in. (44.45 mm)
No. of coils	4½
Valve spring pressure with valves open	90 lbs (40.8 kg)
Valve spring pressure with valves closed	55 lbs (24.9 kg)

Engine specification & data - Mini Cooper 998 cc (Type 9FA)

The engine specification is identical to the type 9F specification except for the differences detailed below

Engine (general):
Type	9FA
Bore	2.543 in. (64.588 mm)
Stroke	3.000 in. (76.2 mm)
Cubic capacity	998 cc (60.96 cu in.)
Compression ratio: High	9 : 1
Low	7.8 : 1
BMEP: High compression ratio	142 lb/sq in. at 3,000 rpm
Low compression ratio	135 lb/sq in. at 3,000 rpm
Maximum torque: High compression ratio	57 lb/ft at 3,000 rpm
Low compression ratio	56 lb/ft at 2,900 rpm
Oversize bore: 1st	+0.010 in. (0.254 mm)
Max.	+0.020 in. (0.508 mm)

Gudgeon pin:

Type	Fully floating
Fit in piston	0.0001 in. (0.0025 mm) tight to 0.00035 in. (0.0089 mm) slack
Fit in small end	0.0002 in. (0.005 mm) slack, to size
Diameter	0.6244 in. (15.86 mm) to 0.6247 in. (15.867 mm))

Pistons:

Clearance: Bottom of skirt (pressure face)	0.0005 to 0.0011 in. (0.013 to 0.028 mm)

Piston rings:

Width (all rings)	0.0620 to 0.0625 in. (1.574 to 1.588 mm)
Thickness (all rings)	0.106 to 0.112 in. (2.692 to 2.835 mm)

Valves:

Head diameter: Inlet	1.219 in. (30.86 mm)
Exhaust	1.000 in. (25.4 mm)
Throat diameter: Inlet	1.172 in. (29.77 mm)
Exhaust	0.908 in. (23.06 mm)

Valve timing:

Inlet valve:	Opens	5⁰ btdc	Exhaust valve:	Opens	51⁰ bbdc
	Closes	45⁰ abdc		Closes	21⁰ atdc

Valve springs:

Type	Double valve springs
Free length: Inner spring	1.672 in. (42.47 mm)
Outer spring	1.75 in. (44.45 mm)
Valve spring pressure with valves open: Inner	30 lb (13.6 kg)
Outer	88 lb (39.9 kg)
Valve spring pressure with valves closed: Inner	18 lb (8.17 kg)
Outer	55.5 lb (25.13 kg)

Engine specification & data - Cooper 'S' 970 cc (Type 9FC), 1,071 cc (Type 10F), 1,275 cc (Type 12FA and 12H)

The engine specifications are identical to the type 9FA specification except for the differences listed below

Engine:

Bore (all models)	2.780 in. (70.6 mm)
Stroke: 970 cc	2.4375 in. (61.91 mm)
1,071 cc	2.687 in. (68.26 mm)
1,275 cc	3.200 in. (81.33 mm)
Cubic capacity	970 cc (59.1 cu in.), 1,071 cc (63.35 cu in.), 1,275 cc (77.9 cu in.)
Compression ratio: 970 cc	10 : 1
1,071 cc	9 : 1
1,275 cc	9.75 : 1
Combustion chamber capacity (spark plugs and valves fitted) 1	21.4 cc (1.306 cu in.)
BMEP: 970 cc	142 lb/sq in. at 4,500 rpm
1,071 cc	143 lb/sq in. at 4,500 rpm
1,275 cc	153 lb/sq in. at 3,000 rpm
Maximum torque: 970 cc	56 lb/ft at 4,500 rpm
1,071 cc	62 lb/ft at 4,500 rpm
1,275 cc	79 lb/ft at 3,000 rpm
Normal compression pressure at 500 rpm	190 to 200 lb/sq in.

Camshaft and camshaft bearings:

Rear journal diameter	1.372 to 1.373 in. (34.8 mm)
Rear journal inside diameter after reaming	1.374 to 1.375 in. (34.9 mm)
Rear bearing running clearance	0.001 to 0.002 in. (0.025 to 0.057 mm)
Rear bearing length	0.7656 ± .010 in. (19.45 ± .25 mm)

Connecting rods and big-end bearings:

Little end bore diameter	0.8110 to 0.8115 in. (20.60 to 20.61 mm)

Crankshaft and main bearings:

Main journal diameter	2.0005 to 2.0010 in. (50.81 to 50.82 mm)
Minimum main journal regrind diameter	1.9805 to 1.9810 in. (50.30 to 50.31 mm)
Main bearings	Steel-backed copper lead; thin wall
Running clearance	0.001 to 0.0027 in. (0.025 to 0.068 mm)
Main bearing length	1.000 in. (25.4 mm)

Gudgeon pin:

Type ...	Pressed-in connecting rod
Fit in piston ...	Hand push-fit
Fit in connecting rod	0.0008 to 0.0015 in. (0.020 to 0.038 mm) interference
Diameter: Outer ...	0.8123 to 0.8125 in. (20.63 to 20.64 mm)

Lubrication system:

Oil pressure: Normal	60 lb/sq in. at 70° C oil temperature

Pistons:

Clearance of piston: Top of skirt ...	0.025 to 0.0283 in. (0.63 to 0.72 mm)
Bottom of skirt ...	0.0019 to 0.0025 in. (0.048 to 0.063 mm)

Piston rings:

Fitted gap (all rings) ...	0.008 to 0.013 in. (0.20 to 0.33 mm)
Clearance in piston groove (all rings) ...	0.0015 to 0.0035 in. (0.04 to 0.09 mm)
Compression rings: Width ...	0.0459 to 0.0469 in. (1.16 to 1.19 mm)
Thickness ...	0.116 to 0.122 in. (29.4 to 30.9 mm)
Oil control ring: Width ...	0.1553 to 0.1563 in. (3.94 to 3.96 mm)
Thickness ...	0.116 to 0.122 in. (29.4 to 30.9 mm)

Valves:

Head diameter: Inlet ...	1.401 to 1.406 in. (35.58 to 35.71 mm)
Exhaust ...	1.214 to 1.219 in. (30.83 to 30.96 mm)
Valve lift ...	0.318 in. (8.08 mm)
Valve rocker clearance for checking timing only ...	0.021 in. (0.53 mm)
Valve rocker clearance for competition work only ...	0.015 in (0.38 mm)

Valve springs:

Type ...	Double valve springs
No. of coils: Inner springs ...	6.25
Outer springs ...	4.5
Free length: Inner spring ...	1.705 in. (43.31 mm)
Outer spring ...	1.740 in. (44.19 mm)
Valve spring pressure with valves open: Inner ...	46 lb (20.865 kg)
Outer ...	94 lb (42.638 kg)
Valve spring pressure with valves closed: Inner ...	26.6 lb (12.065 kg)
Outer ...	49.6 lb (22.498 kg)

Engine specification & data - Mini 1000 Mk II and Clubman 998 cc (Type 99H)

The Type 99H engine is fitted to the Mini Mk II and Clubman and is the same as the Type 9FA engine except for the following:

Engine (general):

Compression ratio ...	8.3 : 1
BMEP ...	130 lb/sq in. (9.14 kg/sq cm) @ 2,700 rpm
Torque ...	52 lb/ft (7.28 kg/cm) @ 2,700 rpm
Inlet valve throat diameter ...	0.969 in. (24.61 mm)
Valve lift ...	0.28 in. (7.14 mm)
Piston oversizes available ...	+010 in. (0.254 mm), +020 in. (0.508 mm)

Engine specification & data - 998 cc Automatic models (Types 9AG and 99H)

Specifications as per the standard 99H engine but compression ratio is 8.9 : 1

Engine specification & data - Mini Clubman GT 1275 cc (Type 12H)

The engine is similar to the Cooper 'S' 1275 cc Type 12H with the following differences:

Engine (general):

Compression ratio ...	8.8 : 1 HC or 8.0 : 1 LC
BHP ...	60 @ 5,250 rpm
Maximum torque ...	68.5 lbf ft at 3000 rpm
Carburettor ...	Single SU HS4

Torque wrench settings:

	lb f ft	kg fm
848 cc, 997 cc, 998 cc:		
Bottom cover retaining bolts ¼ in. diameter UNC (change speed tower)	6	0.83
Connecting rod big end bolts	35	4.8
Crankshaft pulley nut	70	9.68
Cylinder head nuts	40	5.5
Distributor clamp bolt: Fixed nut type	50	6.9
Fixed bolt type	30	4.15
First motion shaft nut	90	12.4
Flywheel centre bolt	110 to 115	15.2 to 15.9
Flywheel housing bolts and stud nuts	18	2.49
Gudgeon pin clamp bolts	25	3.4
Main bearing set bolts	60	8.30
Manifold nuts	15	2.07
Oil filter retaining nut	16	2.21
Oil pump retaining nuts	9	1.2
Rocker cover bolts	4	0.55
Rocker shaft bracket nuts	25	3.4
Set bolt, driving strap to flywheel	16	2.21
Set bolt, clutch spring housing to pressure plate	16	2.21
Tappet chest side cover bolt	2	0.3
Timing cover ¼ in. UNF bolts	6	0.83
Timing cover 5/16 in. UNF bolts	14	1.94
Third motion shaft nut	90	12.4
Transmission case studs 3/8 in. diameter UNC	8	1.11
Transmission case studs 5/16 in. diameter UNC	6	0.83
Transmission case stud nuts 3/8 in. UNF	25	3.4
Transmission case stud nuts 5/16 in. UNF	18	2.49
Transmission case to crankcase	6	0.83
Water outlet elbow nuts	8	1.11
Water pump nuts	17	2.35
970 cc, 1071 cc, 1275 cc Type 'S':	lb f ft	kg fm
Connecting rod big-end bolts	46	6.4
Cylinder head nuts (Qty. 10)	42	5.81
Cylinder head front bolts (Qty. 1)	25	3.4
Drive shaft nut	150	20.7
Main bearing set bolts (early type)	67	9.25
Main bearing nuts (later type)	57	7.85
Automatic transmission:	lb f ft	kg fm
Converter centre bolt	110 to 115	15.2 to 15.9
Converter (six central bolts)	22 to 24	3.0 to 3.3
Converter housing bolts	18	2.5
Oil filter bowl	10 to 15	1.4 to 2.0
Transmission to engine securing nut	12	1.6
5/16 in. UNF bolts	18 to 20	2.5 to 2.8
3/8 in. UNF bolts	30	4.1

1 General description

The Mini engine is a four-cylinder overhead valve type of 848, 997, 998, 970, 1,071, 1,098 or 1,275 cc, depending on the model and its year of manufacture.

The engine is supported by rubber mountings to reduce noise and vibrations.

Two valves per cylinder are mounted vertically in the cast iron cylinder head and run in pressed-in valve guides. They are operated by rocker arms and pushrods from the camshaft which is located at the base of the cylinder bores in the left-hand side of the engine (viewed from the clutch or torque converter end).

The cylinder head has all five inlet and exhaust ports on the left-hand side. Cylinders 1 and 2 share a siamised inlet port and also cylinders 3 and 4. Cylinders 1 and 4 have individual exhaust ports and cylinders 2 and 3 share a siamised exhaust port.

The cylinder block and the upper half of the crankcase are cast together. The bottom half of the crankcase consists of a combined transmission casing and oil sump.

The pistons are made from anodised aluminium alloy with either split or solid skirts, depending on the model: Three compression rings and a slotted oil control ring are fitted to all types. The gudgeon pin is retained in the little end of the connecting rod by a pinch bolt on 848 cc models; and by means of two circlips on later models, which have fully floating gudgeon pins. 'S' type models make use of gudgeon pins which are retained solely by interference fit in the little end. Renewable white metal, lead-indium, or lead-tin big end bearings are fitted.

At the front of the engine a single row chain drives the camshaft, via the camshaft and crankshaft chain wheels. On all models the chain is tensioned by two rubber rings either side of the gear wheel teeth. The camshaft is supported by three bearings, two being bored directly in the crankcase while a white metal bearing (which is renewable) is fitted at the chain wheel end.

On later model 998 cc engines and all the Cooper and Cooper 'S' units three steel-backed white metal camshaft bearings were fitted. The later 997 cc and 998 cc engines also had no water passages between cylinders 1 and 2, and 2 and 3 and 4. On the Cooper 'S' models all four cylinders are

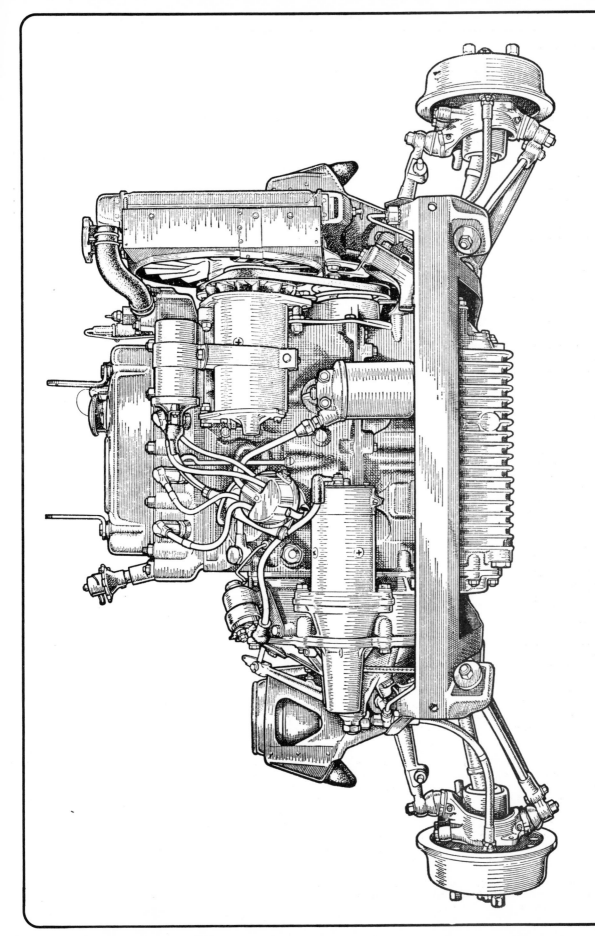

Fig. 1.1. Engine and front suspension assembly

siamised. This was achieved by moving the inner bores together 0.125 in. (3.175 mm) and the outer bores out 0.125 in. (3.175 mm).

The statically and dynamically balanced forged steel crankshaft is supported by three renewable main bearings. Crankshaft end-float is controlled by four semi-circular thrust washers, two of which are located on either side of the centre main bearing.

The centrifugal water pump and radiator cooling fan are driven together with the generator from the crankshaft pulley wheel by a rubber/fabric belt. The distributor is mounted towards the rear of the right-hand side of the cylinder block and advances and retards the ignition timing by mechanical and vacuum means. The distributor is driven at half crankshaft speed by a short shaft and skew gear from a skew gear on the camshaft. The oil pump is driven from the rear of the camshaft.

2   Major operations with engine in place

Not very many major operations can be carried out on the Mini engine with it in-situ because it is not possible to drop the sump as can be done with most cars. The following operations *are* possible however:
1   Removal and replacement of the cylinder head assembly.
2   Removal and replacement of the timing chain and gears.
3   Removal and replacement of the clutch/flywheel.
4   Removal and replacement of the engine mountings.

3   Major operations with engine removed

The following major operations can be carried out with the engine out of the body frame and on the bench or floor:
1   Removal and replacement of the main bearings.
2   Removal and replacement of the crankshaft.
3   Removal and replacement of the oil pump.
4   Removal and replacement of the big-end bearings.
5   Removal and replacement of the pistons and connecting rods.
6   Removal and replacement of the camshaft.

4   Methods of engine removal

There are two methods of engine removal. The engine can be removed from under the car complete with subframe, or the engine can be lifted out through the bonnet aperture.

In either instance the engine is removed complete with the transmission, and also the radiator.

It is easier to lift the engine/transmission assembly (weight approx. 330 lbs.) out of the engine compartment with the aid of a suitable block and pulley than to separate the subframe from the body, and lift the body up, using the rear wheels as a pivot. This is especially so with hydrolastic models. The subframe comprises the frame itself, the wheels, brakes, driveshafts, hubs, and suspension, complete except for dampers.

In either case it is necessary to raise and support the front of the car so that it can be worked on from underneath.

5   Engine - removal (manual transmission)

The engines on all Minis including Cooper, Riley and Wolseley variants, can be removed by the system detailed below. Where slight variations occur between one model and another, these are detailed at the end of this section.

Practical experience has proved that the engine can be removed easily in about 4½ hours (less with experience) by adhering to the following sequence of operations:
1   Turn on the water drain taps found at the bottom of the radiator and on the side of the cylinder block. Note: Do not drain the water in your garage or the place where you will remove the engine/transmission unit if receptacles are not available to catch the water.
2   Disconnect the battery by removing the earth lead.
3   With a suitable container in position unscrew the drain plug from the rear end of the transmission casing (under the clutch bellhousing) and drain off the oil. When the oil is drained screw the plug back in tightly to ensure it is not mislaid. If the engine, gearbox, or differential is to be stripped down, remove the oil filter and empty away the oil.
4   Remove the bonnet by undoing the two set bolts and spring washers from each of the bonnet hinges on the bonnet side of the hinge. Carefully lift the bonnet off and place it somewhere safe where it will not be scratched or damaged.
5   Jack up each side of the car in turn placing supporting blocks under each of the front wheels. Alternatively place the car over a pit or on ramps.
6   Disconnect the inlet and outlet water hoses to the heater/demister unit (where fitted) by undoing the securing clips.
7   Remove the fresh air heater/demister blower motor on models with it fitted under the bonnet. Free the air intake control cable, separate the wire to the unit at the snap connector, undo the clips holding the air trunking in place, disconnect the earth wire, undo the four securing nuts and lift the motor away. Remove the intake trunking completely, and tie back the delivery trunking out of the way.

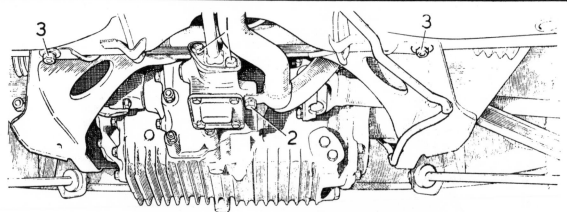

Fig. 1.2. Underside view of manual transmission unit and subframe

1   *Gearchange lever retaining bolts (early type)*   2   *Exhaust pipe retaining bolt*   3   *Two of the front subframe to body mounting bolts (the other two are at the front of the subframe)*

8 It frequently makes the job very much easier if the radiator grille is removed. Undo the eight screws/bolts which hold it in place and lift it out. On Clubman and 1275 GT models, the ignition shield will have to be removed.

9 On models fitted with a recirculatory heater inside the car, just release the air trunking from the front grille and tie the trunking back out of the way of the engine.

10 Pull the leads off the spark plugs, snap back the distributor cap securing clips, undo the HT lead to the centre of the cap, and lift off the distributor cap. If left in place it is easily broken when the engine is removed.

11 Remove the windscreen washer bottle and the bottle carrier on models where they are fitted on the wing valance.

12 Pull off the breather hose from the pipe on the rocker cover, loosen the clip which holds the air cleaner to the air intake pipe, and remove the air cleaner.

13 Undo the knurled nut which holds the speedometer cable to the rear of the speedometer, and release the cable from its securing clip on the bulkhead. Pull the cable through into the engine compartment. Alternatively, use the method outlined in paragraph 35, which we think is the better method.

14 Disconnect the choke linkage and the throttle cable at the carburettor end.

15 Undo the small nut which holds the distributor vacuum advance pipe to the carburettor, and also the union nut which secures the fuel pipe in place.

16 On early models, undo the two nuts which hold the carburettor in place and lift the carburettor away together with the metal plate.

17 Unscrew the bolts which hold the exhaust pipe clamp in place so separating the exhaust pipe from the exhaust manifold.

18 From underneath the car remove the bolt on the transmission casing which holds the exhaust pipe in place and then tie the pipe to the bulkhead to be out of the way.

19 Undo the hexagon plug from the gear change extension casing, and remove the anti-rattle spring, together with the plunger. On Cooper models and those later cars fitted with a remote control gear change, refer to the special notes at the end of this Section.

20 From inside the car pull up the rubber boot from the base of the gear lever, and through this hole undo the two set bolts on the gear lever retaining plate. Pull the gear lever away and place on one side.

21 Free the engine tie-rod from the cylinder block and pull the rod back against the bulkhead out of the way.

22 Disconnect the low tension lead to the distributor and the leads from the dynamo or alternator, starter motor, water temperature gauge (where fitted) and oil pressure warning bulb.

23 Disconnect the oil pressure pipe to the oil pressure gauge (where fitted) by loosening the retaining clip on the rubber connector pipe, and then pulling the pipe off.

24 Undo the bolt which holds the earth lead to the clutch cover.

25 In the case of models fitted with a tachometer either remove the reduction drive and cable from the rear of the dynamo or remove the drive cable from the timing gear cover. Note: Modified cars might make use of electronic tachometers. If this is the case check the wiring and disconnect as appropriate.

26 Undo the two bolts holding the clutch slave cylinder to the flywheel housing, detach the tension spring, and remove the pushrod from the slave cylinder. Tie the clutch slave cylinder back out of the way. **On no account depress the clutch pedal after this has been done.**

27 Disconnect the differential flexible drive flanges from the drive shafts by undoing the nuts from the two 'U' bolts on each side facing out which hold the rubber coupling to the drive shaft sliding joint onto the drive shaft, taking care not to damage the flexible rubber boot.

28 On models fitted with the starter motor solenoid switch mounted on a bracket on the flywheel housing, remove the switch and cables by undoing the two screws which hold the bracket in place. On some models the coil is fitted in this position and should be removed in the same way as the solenoid switch.

29 Remove the bolts securing the horn in place and disconnect the electrical wires at the snap connectors. Place the horn on one side.

30 To make the engine easier to lift, the starter motor, dynamo, and cylinder head can be removed if wished.

31 The engine can be removed by a sling placed round each end of the transmission casing, or by special lifting hooks available from most BLMC garages. There are five cylinder head studs on the front of the cylinder head. If lifting hooks are being used remove the nuts and washers from studs two and four, position the hooks over the studs and tighten down the securing nuts.

32 With lifting tackle connected to the lifting hooks or with slings round the engine as previously described, take the weight of the engine/transmission unit.

33 The engine mountings are lifted out together with the engine. They are released by undoing the two set bolts which hold each one to the front subframe.

34 The engine/transmission unit can now be lifted out. Tilt it slightly backwards as it comes up to allow the gear change extension to clear the body. Ensure that the drive shaft flexible couplings, the engine tie-rod, and the clutch slave cylinder are clear.

35 When the engine is halfway out disconnect the speedometer cable from the transmission casing. This is much easier than disconnecting it from the rear of the speedometer. **Do not forget to reconnect it when the engine is refitted.**

The instructions given in paragraphs 19 and 20 do not apply to Mini Coopers and other models fitted with the remote control gear change. Instead, apply the following instructions:

1 Undo the three nuts and bolts which secure the exhaust pipe and silencer and lower them to the ground. This will give unrestricted access to the remote control extension bracket.

2 The gear change mechanism is different to the ordinary models, being of remote control type. The instructions given in paragraphs 19 and 20 will therefore not apply.

3 Undo the three bolts which hold the remote control rear extension bracket to the underside of the floor.

4 Unscrew the knob from the gear lever and undo the screws which hold the gear lever rubber cover and plate in place.

5 Undo the four nuts which hold the remote control extension to the transmission casing and remove the extension.

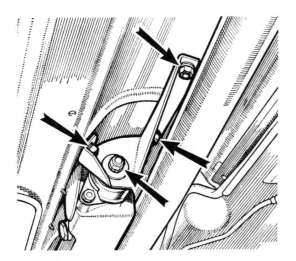

Fig. 1.3. Securing points for the remote control gear change extension (early type remote system)

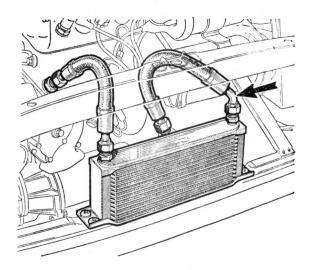

Fig. 1.4. The Cooper 'S' oil cooler
Note angled hose connection (arrowed)

6 Remove the vacuum servo unit which is fitted on 'S' type and some other models after first disconnecting the vacuum and hydraulic pipes.

7 Do not forget to disconnect the oil cooler pipes (when fitted).

6 Engine - removal with subframe (manual transmission)

For Hydrolastic suspension models, see Special Notes at end of this Section.

The engine/transmission unit can be removed from under the body, the body being lifted at the front by three or four strong men and then wheeled away; or the body can be lifted at the front with a block and tackle and the subframe and engine/transmission unit wheeled out from underneath by two men. The engine/transmission unit is removed together with the subframe, which together weigh 430 lb.

1 Presuming that the engine is to be separated from the transmission casing after removal, turn on the water drain taps found at the bottom of the radiator and on the side of the cylinder block, and drain into a suitable container.

2 Disconnect the battery by removing the earth lead.

3 With a container capable of holding no less than 1¼ gallons (5.58 litres) in position, unscrew the drain plug from the rear end of the transmission casing (under the clutch bellhousing), and drain off the oil. When the oil has all drained screw back the plug tightly to ensure it is not mislaid. Remove the hub caps and loosen the front wheel nuts.

4 Remove the bonnet by undoing the two set bolts and spring washers from each of the two bonnet hinges on the bonnet side of the hinge. Carefully lift the bonnet off and place it somewhere safe where it will not be scratched or damaged. Jack up the front of the car so as to be able to work underneath it and to later remove the front wheels.

Fig. 1.5. The body being lifted off power unit/subframe assembly
The arrows indicate the position from which the two bolts (or nuts on early models) must be removed. They hold the body (2) to the subframe towers (1). Also shown (3) are the holes through which the front two subframe to body bolts are removed

5 Disconnect the inlet and outlet water hoses to the heater/demister unit (where fitted) by undoing the securing clips. If a fresh air heater/demister blower unit is fitted under the bonnet, remove it, together with the front grille and air trunking as described in paragraphs 7 and 8 of the previous Section.

6 Pull the leads off the spark plugs, snap back the distributor cap securing clips, undo the HT lead to the centre of the cap, and lift off the distributor cap. If left in place it is easily broken when the engine is removed. On Clubman and 1275 GT models the ignition shield will have to be removed first.

7 Pull off the breather hose from the pipe on the rocker cover, loosen the clip which holds the air cleaner to the air intake pipe, and remove the air cleaner.

8 Undo the small nut which holds the distributor vacuum advance pipe to the carburettor, and also the union nut which secures the fuel pipe in place. On later models with a mechanical fuel pump, disconnect the pump inlet pipe and plug the end.

9 Disconnect the choke linkage and the throttle cable at the carburettor end, undo the two nuts which hold the carburettor in place and lift the carburettor away together with the metal plate.

10 Unscrew the bolts from the clamp which holds the exhaust manifold to the exhaust pipe.

11 From underneath the car remove the bolt on the transmission casing which holds the exhaust pipe in place. Also undo the two bolts on the rear subframe which support the rear of the exhaust system and lower the exhaust pipe and silencer to the ground.

12 On early models, undo the hexagon plug from the gear change extension casing and remove the anti-rattle spring together with the plunger. On Cooper models and those cars fitted with a remote control gear change system, refer to the Special Notes at the end of this Section.

13 From inside the car pull up the rubber boot from the floor at the base of the gear lever. This leaves an aperture through which the two set bolts retaining the gear lever retaining plate can be undone. Pull the gear lever out and place it on one side.

14 Free the engine tie-rod from the cylinder block and pull the rod back against the bulkhead out of the way.

15 Disconnect the low tension lead to the distributor and the leads from the dynamo, starter motor, water temperature gauge (where fitted), oil pressure warning bulb, and the stop light switch.

16 Disconnect the oil pressure pipe from the oil pressure gauge (where fitted) by loosening the retaining clip on the rubber connector pipe, and then pulling the pipe off.

17 Undo the bolt which holds the earth lead to the clutch cover.

18 In the case of models fitted with a tachometer either remove the reduction drive and cable from the rear of the dynamo, or remove the drive cable from the timing gear cover. Note: Some modified cars might use an electronic tachometer. If this is the case check the wiring and disconnect as appropriate.

19 Undo the two bolts holding the clutch slave cylinder to the flywheel housing, detach the tension spring and remove the pushrod from the slave cylinder. Tie the clutch slave cylinder back out of the way. On no account press the clutch pedal after the slave cylinder has been removed.

20 On models fitted with the starter motor solenoid switch mounted on a bracket on the flywheel housing, remove the switch and cables by undoing the two screws which hold the bracket in place.

21 Undo the knurled nut which holds the speedometer cable to the rear of the speedometer; release the cable from its securing clip on the bulkhead, and pull the cable through into the engine compartment.

22 Undo the hydraulic brake supply pipe to the front wheels at the three way union on the left-hand side of the engine bulkhead. Block the hole in the union with a rubber stop or a clean 3/8 in. UNF screw so as not to lose all the hydraulic fluid. On Cooper models undo the hydraulic brake pipe from the top of the intensifier cylinder.

23 The car should have already been jacked up and the wheel nuts loosened. Remove the wheelnuts and take off each of the front wheels.

24 Knock back the locking tabs from the nuts (some models use self-locking nuts) on the balljoints at the end of the steering tie-rods. Remove the nuts, and free the ball pins from the steering arm by impact hammering. (Use two hammers opposite each other on the sides of the eye of each steering arm).

25 The next step is to remove the dampers. For full information see Chapter 11.

26 Replace the front wheels and lower the car to the ground. Place suitable blocks underneath the transmission casing to support the engine.

27 From inside the car remove the front carpets to expose the four set bolts which hold the rear of the subframe to the front floor and undo them.

28 Undo the two nuts and bolts which hold the front of the subframe to the very front of the body below the grille.

29 Knock back the locking plate tabs from the two bolts (nuts and studs on some models) on either side of the engine compartment which hold the subframe uprights to the bulkhead crossmember.

30 Undo the bolts (or nuts), and note that where nuts are used it is advisable to screw the studs out to avoid damage when the body is lifted off.

31 Finally carefully lift the body up to clear the engine, taking care that the radiator matrix is not damaged, and that no wires or cables get caught between the body and the engine/transmission assembly.

32 Wheel the bodyshell away from the engine, or the subframe away from the bodyshell - whichever is most convenient. We prefer the former method.

Special Notes

The instructions given in paragraphs 12 and 13 do not apply to Mini Coopers and other models fitted with the remote control gearchange. Instead apply the instructions given below:

1 Undo the three bolts which hold the remote control rear extension bracket to the underside of the floor.

2 Remove the gear lever knob, unscrew the four screws holding the gear lever rubber boot retaining plate in position, and remove the plate and boot.

3 Undo the two bolts which hold the gear lever retainer to the remote control extension, and lift the gear lever out.

4 The gear lever remote control extension comes away with the engine/transmission unit in the subframe when the body is lifted out.

5 On Mini Cooper 'S' type and other models fitted with a vacuum servo unit it is necessary to disconnect the vacuum pipe from the inlet manifold.

6 On models fitted with Hydrolastic suspension it will be necessary to disconnect the suspension hoses from the suspension fluid pipes on the front bulkhead, after having depressurised the system by releasing the interconnecting pipe valve.

Note: The suspension will need evacuating, repressurising, and trimming, which involves the use of specialised equipment only found at officially approved BLMC garages, after the subframe has been replaced.

7 Engine - removal from subframe

Removal of the engine from the subframe is fairly straightforward and should take about 20 minutes. The engine/transmission unit can be lifted by using a block and tackle, or three strong men. If all the ancillaries such as the starter motor, dynamo, exhaust and inlet manifolding, etc., are removed, then two men can lift the unit.

1 Place supports under each of the subframe sidemembers.
Remove the radiator after undoing the hose clips, and the
bolts holding the top and bottom brackets in place.

2 Separate the drive shafts from the differential flanges by
undoing the four outside nuts on the two 'U' bolts on each
side of the differential. Pull the two 'U' bolts clear. Do not
touch the nuts on the other two 'U' bolts.

3 The drive shaft flange can then be pushed onto the drive
shaft - so separating the flexible coupling from the drive shaft
flange.

4 Undo the two bolts which hold each of the two engine
mountings to the subframe.

5 Lift the engine/transmission unit out using a sling, block
and pulley or three men, as already indicated.

6 Up to engine No. "4354" paper gaskets were fitted
between the engine mountings, the subframe, and the clutch
cover. Make sure these are renewed on reassembly and on no
account omit them. Replacement is a straight reversal of the
removal procedure.

8 Engine separation from transmission - flywheel removal (manual transmission)

Before the engine can be stripped right down it is essential
to separate the transmission casing from the cylinder block.
Until this is done it is not possible to remove the pistons,
connecting rods, or crankshaft. Before the transmission casing/
sump can be removed it is necessary to take off the clutch,
flywheel, and flywheel housing. The clutch and flywheel are
best removed together because of their unusual construction.

1 Remove the clutch cover, as described in Chapter 5.

2 Remove the clutch thrust plate by undoing the three
nuts/dowel bolts which hold it to the spring pressure plate.

3 Before removing the flywheel it is most important to turn
the crankshaft so that the mark ¼ on the flywheel periphery is
at tdc or the slot in the flywheel and crankshaft is in the
horizontal position. If this is done the 'C' washer which holds
the primary gear in place cannot drop. If this is not done and
the washer drops, serious damage can be caused to the flywheel
oil seal.

4 The flywheel is held in position on the tapered end of the
crankshaft by a single centre retaining bolt which will have
been tightened to a torque of 110 to 115 lb f. ft (15.2 - 15.9
kg fm). Knock back the tab on the lock washer, and if a
spanner large enough to undo the retaining bolt is not
available, then chisel it round three or four times using a
suitable cold chisel on the ends of the flats.

5 To pull the flywheel off the taper on the end of the crankshaft will involve the use of a special puller. This is BLMC
service tool "18G 304" which is used with adapter "18G
304L or N". It is hardly worth while making up this tool as it
involves drilling and cutting steel at least 0.5 in. (12.7 mm)
thick. It is far better to borrow this tool from your friendly
BLMC garage.

6 To operate the puller screw the three studs into the three
tapped holes in the flywheel. Place the puller plate over the
studs and then screw the nuts onto the studs keeping the plate
parallel with the flywheel. Screw in the short centre screw and
tighten till the flywheel breaks free from the crankshaft. If it
proves very difficult to break the flywheel from the taper, tap
the centre bolt with a hammer while the bolt is tightened
down hard. This will jar the flywheel loose.

7 As soon as the taper has been broken, remove the puller
tool, unscrew the retaining bolt and take off the flywheel.

8 On early models oil from the annulus at the rear of the
flywheel oil seal may run down the flywheel onto the clutch
driven plate, unless every care is taken to hold the flywheel/
clutch assembly quite upright. Should oil get onto the clutch
linings this could cause severe clutch slip. Later models use a
modified primary gear bush which allows the flywheel oil seal
to be omitted. **Note:** On early models there is a rubber cap in
the centre of the rear crankshaft boss. If oil is weeping from

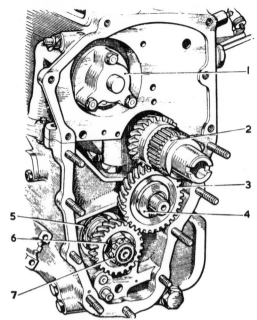

Fig. 1.6. End view of transfer gears with clutch, flywheel and housing removed

1 *Oil pump*	5 *First motion shaft bearing*
2 *Crankshaft primary gear*	6 *First motion shaft gear-*
3 *Idler or transfer gear*	*wheel*
4 *Thrust washer*	7 *Roller bearing*

this area, remove the rubber cap and knock the brass taper
plug further into the crankshaft with a drift. Fit a new rubber
cap. Later models make use of an improved brass taper and
the rubber cap is dispensed with.

9 Engine separation from transmission - flywheel housing removal (manual transmission)

With the flywheel and clutch removed the flywheel housing
(which is effectively the engine end plate) can be separated
from the transmission casing/engine as follows:

1 Knock back the tabs on the lock washers inside the
housing.

2 Undo and remove the nine nuts from the studs on the
transmission casing.

3 Undo and remove the six bolts from the cylinder block.
Note the positions from which the shorter bolts are removed.

4 The housing can now be carefully pulled off. The flywheel
housing oil seal should always be renewed when the housing is
removed. If for any reason this is not possible, then wrap tinfoil or adhesive tape round the primary gear splines before
pulling off the housing, so that the splines do not damage the
oil seal.

5 Undo and remove the transmission to cylinder block nuts
and setscrews and lift the engine vertically from the transmission unit.

10 Engine and automatic transmission - removal

1 For safety reasons, disconnect the battery.

2 Remove the bonnet by undoing and removing the two nuts
and washers from each of the bonnet hinges on the bonnet
side of the hinge. Carefully lift the bonnet off and place it
somewhere safe where it will not be scratched or damaged.

3 Jack up each side of the car in turn, placing supporting
blocks under each side of the subframe. To give better access,
remove the two front wheels. Alternatively, place the car over
a pit or on a ramp.

4 Suitably mark the drive flanges at the inboard ends and

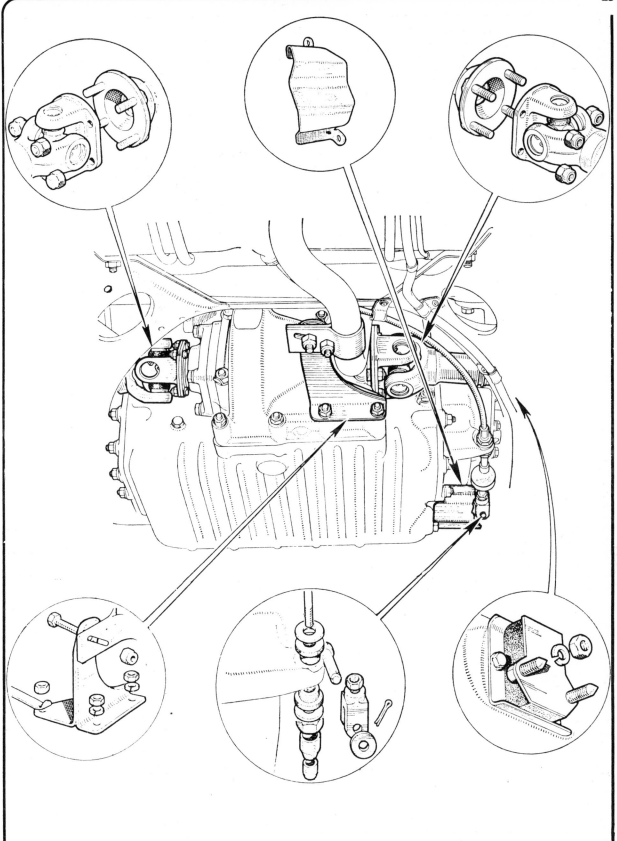

Fig. 1.7. Main components to be disconnected or removed from below the car before removing engine and automatic transmission unit

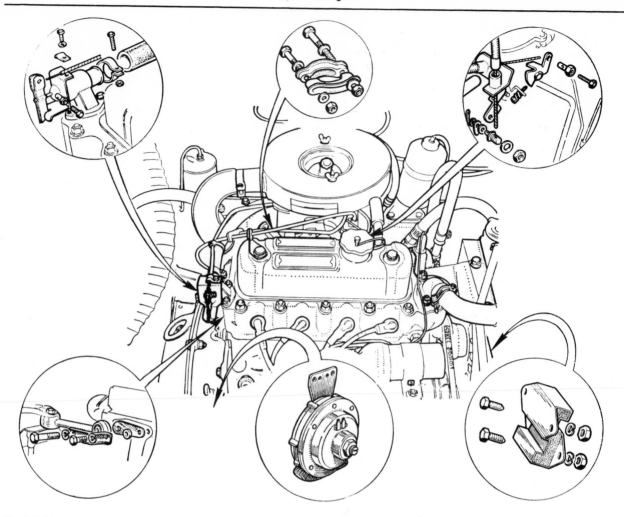

Fig. 1.8. Main components to be disconnected or removed from above the car before removing engine and automatic transmission unit

then undo and remove the securing nuts.

5 When a weather protection cover is fitted in front of the engine, this should be unclipped next and lifted away.

6 When a weather protection cover is fitted to the rear of the transmission unit this must next be removed. As an alternative a rubber sleeve may be fitted and in this case it should be pulled back.

7 Disconnect the gear selector cable by removing the clevis pin.

8 Slacken the yoke clamp nut and remove the yoke, nut, rubber ferrules and sleeve. Then remove the cable front adjusting nut from the outer cable and pull the cable clear of the transmission.

9 Remove the exhaust bracket from the final drive cover. Note that the larger nut is secured by a locking tab.

10 Refer to Chapter 2 and completely drain the cooling system.

11 Disconnect the heater hoses and water control valve cable from the engine.

12 Slacken the fixing clips on the heater fresh air tube connections on the grille and the wing valance. Swing the tube clear of the engine compartment.

13 Make a note of all electrical connections from the engine and then detach at the terminal connectors. Tuck the cables out of the way of the engine.

14 Detach the HT leads from the spark plugs having suitably marked each cable to ensure correct refitment. Also detach the HT lead from the centre of the ignition coil. Spring back the distributor cap retaining clips and lift away the distributor cap.

15 Refer to Chapter 3 and remove the air cleaner and carburettor installation.

16 Working at the rear of the speedometer head disconnect the speedometer cable.

17 Slacken the clip and detach the oil pressure gauge hose.

18 Make a note of the electrical connections to the horn/s and detach at the terminal connectors. Undo and remove the nuts and bolts securing the horn to the mounting and lift away the horn.

19 Release the exhaust manifold to downpipe clamp and detach the downpipe. Tie the exhaust downpipe hard up against the bulkhead.

20 Disconnect the engine tie-rod from the cylinder block and swing the rod away from the engine.

21 Undo the rocker cover securing nuts and carefully lift away the rocker cover.

22 Place lifting brackets onto the rocker cover securing studs and then using an overhead hoist or crane suitably support the weight of the complete power unit.

23 Undo and remove the setscrews and washers that secure each engine mounting to the subframe.

24 Lift the complete unit sufficiently to release the drive shafts from the driving flanges, and the speedometer cable from the drive pinion.

25 Check that all attachments, hoses, cables and controls, have been disconnected and tucked out of the way and then lift the unit up through the engine compartment and away from the front of the car. Carefully lower to the ground.

11 Engine separation from automatic transmission

1 Before commencing work in separating the engine from the automatic transmission unit, it should be noted that several special tools are required to do the job properly. Some users of this manual will have the facilities of a well equipped workshop so with a little thought etc., use of the majority of these special tools can be overcome. Read this Section carefully before commencing work, to ensure that the facilities available are sufficient for this task.

2 Refer to Section 10 and remove the complete power unit.

3 Remove the radiator mounting bracket from the transmission casing.

4 Undo and remove the two bolts and washers securing the starter motor. Lift away the starter motor.

5 Undo and remove the setscrews and washers securing the converter cover. Lift away the converter cover.

6 If not already done so, remove the transmission unit drain plug and drain the contents into a suitable container.

7 Knock back the lock washer on the converter centre bolt.

8 Stop the converter from turning with a large screwdriver inserted through the hole in the converter housing and using a large socket (or tool "18G 587") undo and remove the centre bolt. It is tight so a box spanner probably will not cope (Fig. 1.9.).

9 Knock back the locking tabs and remove the three equally spaced setscrews from the centre of the converter.

10 Turn the crankshaft until the slot in the end of the crankshaft is horizontal. The converter must now be drawn off the end of the crankshaft and for this a special tool "18G 1086" must be used. Ensure that the adaptor is correctly positioned. (Fig. 1.10).

11 When the converter has been released remove the service tool and refit the three setscrews.

12 The low pressure valve may next be removed from the converter housing.

13 Fit service tool "18G 1088" onto the converter output gear and remove the input gear self locking nut. (Fig. 1.11).

14 Remove the gear change bellcrank lever clevis pin and nut and lift off the bellcrank lever. Remove the bellcrank lever pivot.

15 Fit the nylon protective sleeve service tool "18G 1098" over the converter output gear or alternatively tape well with some 'sellotape'.

16 Undo and remove the nuts and setscrews that secure the converter housing to the transmission and lift away the housing.

17 Remove the converter oil outlet pipe from the housing.

18 Carefully lever the main oil feed pipe from the transmission and oil pump.

19 The idler gear, thrust washers and converter output gear assembly may be removed next. (Fig. 1.12).

20 Remove the oil filter assembly and disconnect the engine oil feed pipe, together with its rubber seal and spring washer. The last two items are fitted to early Minis only. (Fig. 1.13).

21 Undo and remove the nuts, setscrews and washers that secure the engine to the transmission unit.

22 The engine may now be lifted upwards and away from the transmission unit.

12 Dismantling the engine - general

It is best to mount the engine on a dismantling stand, but as this is frequently not available, then the engine should be stood on a strong bench at a comfortable working height. Failing this, it can be stripped down on the floor. During the dismantling process the greatest care should be taken to keep the exposed parts free from dirt. As an aid to achieving this aim, thoroughly clean down the outside of the engine, removing all traces of oil and congealed dirt. A good grease solvent such as 'Gunk' will make the job much easier, as, after

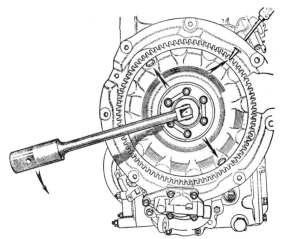

Fig. 1.9. Removal of converter centre bolt (automatic transmission
Converter drain plugs shown by arrows

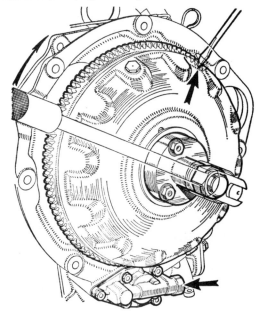

Fig. 1.10. Removal of converter using special tool 18G 1086
Arrow shows screwdriver inserted in starter ring gear (automatic transmission)

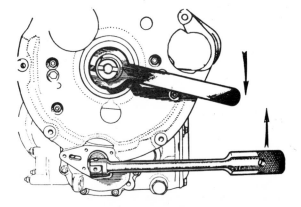

Fig. 1.11. Using special tool 18G 1088 to hold the converter output gear (automatic transmission)

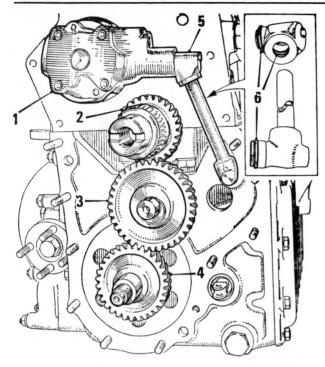

Fig. 1.12. Converter housing removed (automatic transmission)

1 Main oil pump   4 Input gear
2 Converter output gear   5 Oil feed pipe
3 Idler gear   6 Sealing rings

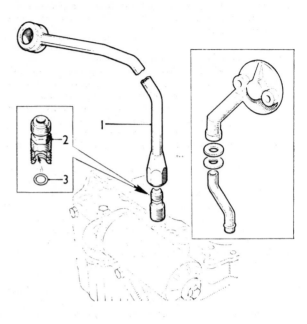

Fig. 1.13. Engine oil feed pipe (1), adaptor (2) with internal 'O' ring seal (3) (automatic transmission)
Inset shows early type pipe assembly

the solvent has been applied and allowed to stand for a time, a vigorous jet of water will wash off the solvent and all the grease and dirt. If the dirt is thick and deeply embedded, work the solvent into it with a wire brush.

Finally wipe down the exterior of the engine with a clean rag and only then, when it is finally quite free from dirt, should the dismantling process begin. As the engine is stripped, clean each part in a bath of paraffin or petrol. Never immerse parts with oilways in paraffin, ie., the crankshaft, but to clean wipe down carefully with a petrol damped rag. Oilways can be cleaned out with pipe cleaners. If an air line is present all parts can be blown dry and the oilways blown through as an added precaution.

A good way of cleaning black greasy nuts, bolts, and washers, and similar small components, is to wash them in a special tin. Knock or drill a number of small holes in the bottom of a tin. Place the parts to be cleaned in the tin and then dip it into a paraffin filled container. Shake the tin around so as to allow the paraffin to clean the parts. When the parts are clean lift the tin out allowing the paraffin to drain. You will not have had to grope around at the bottom of the paraffin container and none of the parts will be lost.

Re-use of old engine gaskets is false economy and can give rise to oil and water leaks - if nothing worse. To avoid the possibility of trouble after the engine has been reassembled always use new gaskets throughout. Do not throw the old gaskets away as it sometimes happens that an immediate replacement cannot be found and the old gasket is then very useful as a template. Hang up the old gaskets as they are removed on a suitable hook or nail.

To strip the engine it is best to work from the top down. The transmission case provides a firm base on which the engine can be supported in an upright position. When the transmission case/sump has to be removed the engine should be lifted up off the transmission casing.

Wherever possible, replace nuts and bolts and washers finger-tight from the original stud, bolt, or hole from which they were removed. This helps avoid later loss and muddle. If

they cannot be replaced then lay them out in such a fashion that it is clear from where they were removed, or keep them in clearly labelled boxes, tins or polythene bags.

13 Removing ancillary engine components

Before basic engine dismantling begins it is necessary to strip it of ancilliary components and these are as follows:
    Dynamo or alternator
    Distributor
    Thermostat
    Oil filter assembly and pipe
    Inlet manifold and carburettor/s
    Exhaust manifold

It is possible to strip all these items with the engine in the car if it is merely the individual items that require attention. Presuming the engine to be out of the car and on the bench, follow the procedure detailed below:

1 Slacken off the dynamo or alternator retaining bolts and remove the unit with its support brackets.
2 To remove the distributor first disconnect the manifold vacuum advance/retard pipe which leads from the small securing clip at the front of the cylinder head. Unscrew the clamp bolt at the base of the distributor and lift the distributor away from its base plate and drive shaft.
3 Remove the thermostat cover by releasing the three nuts and spring washers which hold it in position and then remove the gasket and lift out the thermostat unit.
4 Unscrew the bolts on the oil pipe leading from the filter to the block and remove the pipe. Mask over the hole left in the block with masking tape or block it with a clean piece of rag.
5 Remove the oil filter assembly by unscrewing the two retaining bolts which hold it to the block. The right-hand side of the engine is now stripped of all ancilliary equipment.
6 Inlet manifold and carburettors: Moving to the left-hand side of the engine, remove the inlet manifold complete with carburettor/s (if this item has not already been removed) by

unscrewing the brass nuts and washers holding both the inlet and exhaust manifolds to the cylinder head. The engine is now stripped of all ancilliary components and is ready for major dismantling to begin.

14 Cylinder head removal - engine on bench

1 Release the clips on the small bypass hose between the water pump and the cylinder head and remove the hose. This may prove very difficult, and providing a replacement hose is available, the hose can be cut away. Pull off the ignition leads from the spark plugs and remove the plugs.

2 Unscrew the two rocker cover bolts and lift the rocker cover and gasket away.

3 Unscrew the rocker pedestal nuts (four) and the nine main cylinder head nuts half a turn at a time in the order shown in Fig. 1.14 to avoid distortion of the head. On Mini Cooper 'S' and 1275 GT models the cylinder head is retained by ten nuts and one bolt. The head of the bolt has "300" stamped on it, is located at the front of the cylinder head, and must be released first. When all the nuts are no longer under tension they may be screwed off the cylinder head one at a time.

4 Remove the rocker assembly complete, and place it on one side.

5 Remove the pushrods, keeping them in the relative order in which they were removed. The easiest way to do this is to push them through a sheet of thick paper or thin card in the correct sequence.

6 The cylinder head can now be removed by lifting upwards. If the head is jammed, try to rock it to break the seal. Under no circumstances try to prise it apart from the block with a screwdriver or cold chisel as damage may be done to the faces of the head or block. If the head will not turn readily, turn the engine over by the flywheel as the compression in the cylinders will often break the cylinder head joint. If this fails to work, strike the head sharply with a plastic or wooden headed hammer, or with a metal hammer with an interposed piece of wood to cushion the blows. Under no circumstances hit the head directly with a metal hammer as this may cause the iron casting to fracture. Several sharp taps with the hammer at the same time pulling upwards should free the head. Lift the head off squarely and place on one side.

15 Cylinder head removal - engine in car

For models fitted with emission control equipment refer to the Special Notes at the end of this Section.

To remove the cylinder head with the engine still in the car first carry out the following before proceeding as above.

1 Disconnect the battery by removing the lead from the positive terminal.

2 Drain the water by turning the taps at the base of the radiator, and at the bottom left-hand corner of the cylinder block.

3 Loosen the clip at the thermostat housing end on the top

water hose, and pull the hose from the thermostat housing outlet pipe.

4 Undo the three bolts holding the radiator support bracket to the cylinder head.

5 Free the distributor vacuum advance pipe from its mountings on the front of the thermostat housing.

6 Undo the clamp which holds the exhaust manifold to the down pipe.

7 Remove the carburettor/s and exhaust and inlet manifolds by undoing the retaining nuts and washers. Lift away the manifolds and carburettor/s complete.

8 Remove the small water pump to cylinder head bypass hose.

9 Remove the heater/demister unit inlet hose by releasing the clip securing it to the cylinder head (on cars with heater/demister units).

10 The procedure is now the same as for removing the cylinder head when on the bench. One tip worth noting is that should the cylinder head refuse to free easily, the battery can be reconnected, and the engine turned over on the solenoid switch. Under no circumstances turn the ignition on where an SU electrical fuel pump is fitted unless the wire to the pump is disconnected, and ensure that the distributor cap is removed to prevent the engine firing.

Special Notes - emission control models

The following additional items will have to be disconnected when removing the cylinder head.

a) *When removing the air cleaner, disconnect the air temperature control valve unit.*

b) *Detach the hose from the check valve and the hose from the gulp valve, and place the diverter valve out of the way.*

c) *Unscrew and remove the number 1 spark plug.*

d) *Loosen the alternator pivot and air pump adjustment link bolt, and then extract the screw retaining the air pump adjusting bracket. Unscrew and remove the air pump pivot bolt, slacken the tension on the drivebelt and disconnect it. Remove the air pump.*

e) *Disconnect the purge pipe from the rocker cover pipe before removing the rocker cover.*

f) *Detach the lead from the manifold heater.*

16 Valve - removal

The valves can be removed from the cylinder head as follows:

1 With a pair of pliers remove the spring circlips holding the two halves of the split tapered collets together. Compress each spring in turn with a valve spring compressor until the two halves of the collets can be removed. Release the compressor and remove the spring, shroud, and valve.

2 If, when the valve spring compressor is screwed down, the valve spring retaining cap refuses to free and expose the split collet, do not continue to screw down on the compressor as there is a likelihood of damaging it. Gently tap the top of the tool directly over the cap with a light hammer. This will free the cap. To prevent the compressor jumping off the valve

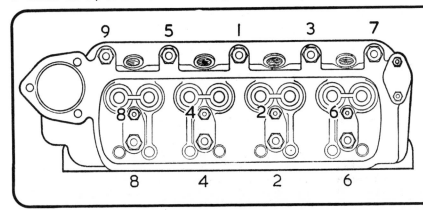

Fig. 1.14. Loosen and tighten the cylinder head nuts in the order shown

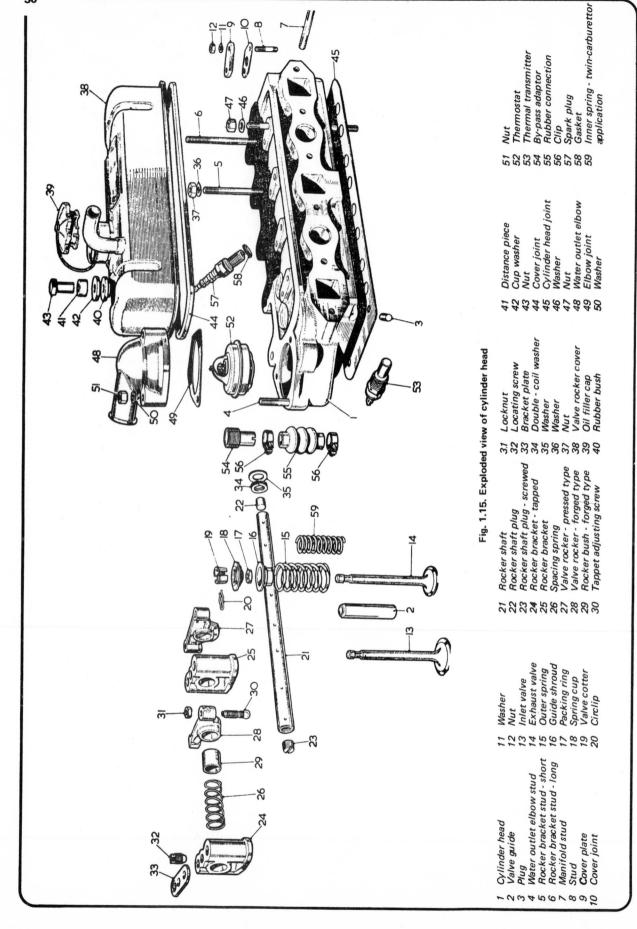

Fig. 1.15. Exploded view of cylinder head

1 Cylinder head	31 Locknut
2 Valve guide	32 Locating screw
3 Plug	33 Bracket plate
4 Water outlet elbow stud	34 Double - coil washer
5 Rocker bracket stud - short	35 Washer
6 Rocker bracket stud - long	36 Washer
7 Manifold stud	37 Nut
8 Stud	38 Valve rocker cover
9 Cover plate	39 Oil filler cap
10 Cover joint	40 Rubber bush
11 Washer	41 Distance piece
12 Nut	42 Cup washer
13 Inlet valve	43 Nut
14 Exhaust valve	44 Cover joint
15 Outer spring	45 Cylinder head joint
16 Guide shroud	46 Washer
17 Packing ring	47 Nut
18 Spring cup	48 Water outlet elbow
19 Valve cotter	49 Elbow joint
20 Circlip	50 Washer
21 Rocker shaft	51 Nut
22 Rocker shaft plug	52 Thermostat
23 Rocker shaft plug - screwed	53 Thermal transmitter
24 Rocker bracket - tapped	54 By-pass adaptor
25 Rocker bracket	55 Rubber connection
26 Spacing spring	56 Clip
27 Valve rocker - pressed type	57 Spark plug
28 Valve rocker - forged type	58 Gasket
29 Rocker bush - forged type	59 Inner spring - twin-carburettor
30 Tappet adjusting screw	application

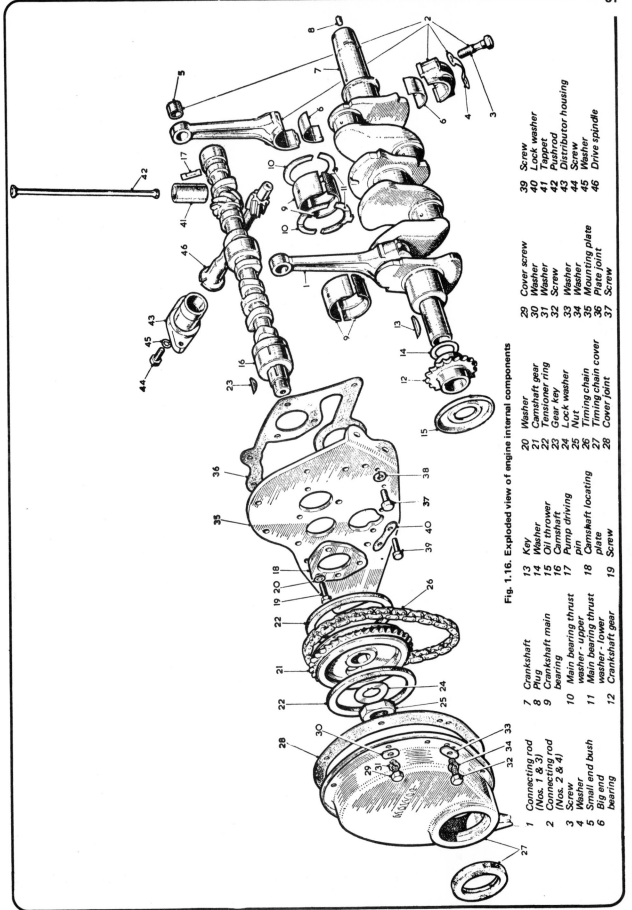

Fig. 1.16. Exploded view of engine internal components

1	Connecting rod (Nos. 1 & 3)	13	Key	29	Cover screw
2	Connecting rod (Nos. 2 & 4)	14	Washer	30	Washer
3	Screw	15	Oil thrower	31	Washer
4	Washer	16	Camshaft	32	Screw
5	Small end bush	17	Pump driving pin	33	Washer
6	Big end bearing	18	Camshaft locating plate	34	Washer
7	Crankshaft	19	Screw	35	Mounting plate
8	Plug	20	Washer	36	Plate joint
9	Crankshaft main bearing	21	Camshaft gear	37	Screw
10	Main bearing thrust washer - upper	22	Tensioner ring	39	Screw
11	Main bearing thrust washer - lower	23	Gear key	40	Lock washer
12	Crankshaft gear	24	Lock washer	41	Tappet
		25	Nut	42	Pushrod
		26	Timing chain	43	Distributor housing
		27	Timing chain cover	44	Screw
		28	Cover joint	45	Washer
				46	Drive spindle

spring retaining cap when it is tapped, hold the compressor firmly in position with one hand.

Slide the rubber oil control seal off the top of each valve stem and then drop out each valve through the combustion chamber.

3 It is essential that the valves are kept in their correct sequence unless they are so badly worn that they are to be renewed. If they are going to be kept and used again, place them in a sheet of card having eight holes numbered 1 to 8 corresponding with the relative positions the valves were in when fitted. Also keep the valve springs, washers, etc., in the correct order.

17 Valve guide - removal

If it is wished to remove the valve guides they can be removed from the cylinder head in the following manner. Place the cylinder head with the gasket face on the bench and with a suitable hard steel punch drift the guides out of the cylinder head.

18 Dismantling the valve rocker assembly

To dismantle the rocker assembly, release the rocker shaft locating screw, remove the split pins, flat washers, and spring washers from each end of the shaft and slide from the shaft the pedestals, rocker arms, and rocker spacing springs.

19 Timing cover, gears and chain - removal

The timing cover, gears, and chain can be removed with the engine in the car provided the radiator and fan belt are removed. (For radiator and fan belt removal see Chapter 2). The procedure for removing the timing cover, gears and chain is otherwise the same irrespective of whether the engine is in the car or on the bench, and is as follows:
1 Bend back the locking tab of the crankshaft pulley locking washer under the crankshaft pulley retaining bolt, prising it back with a cold chisel or screwdriver through the radiator grille in the wing if the engine is still in the car. With a large spanner remove the bolt and locking washer. This bolt is sometimes very difficult to shift and hitting the free end of the spanner with a heavy hammer is sometimes the only way to start it. If the engine is still in the car, put the car in top gear and apply the handbrake hard to prevent the engine from turning.
2 Placing two large screwdrivers behind the camshaft pulley wheel at 180° to each other, carefully lever the wheel off. It is preferable to use a proper pulley extractor if this is available, but large screwdrivers or tyre levers are quite suitable, providing care is taken not to damage the pulley flange.
3 Remove the woodruff key from the crankshaft nose with a pair of pliers and note how the channel in the pulley is designed to fit over it. Place the woodruff key in a glass jam jar as it is a very small part and can easily be mislaid.
4 Unscrew the bolts holding the timing cover to the block. **Note:** Four of the bolts are larger than the others, and each bolt makes use of a large flat washer as well as a spring washer.
5 Take off the timing cover and gasket. On 1275 GT engines detach the engine breather hose from the cover.
6 With the timing cover off, take off the oil thrower. **Note:** The concave side faces forward.
7 Bend back the locking tab on the washer under the camshaft retaining nut and unscrew the nut noting how the locking washer locating tag fits in the camshaft gear wheel keyway.
8 To remove the camshaft and crankshaft timing wheels complete with chain, ease each wheel forward a little at a time, levering behind each gear wheel in turn with two large screwdrivers at 180° to each other. If the gear wheels are locked solid then it will be necessary to use a proper gear

wheel and pulley extractor. With both gear wheels off, remove the woodruff keys from the crankshaft and camshaft with a pair of pliers and place them in a jam jar for safe keeping. **Note** the number of very thin packing washers behind the crankshaft gear wheel and remove them very carefully.

20 Camshaft - removal

The camshaft can be removed only with the engine on the bench. The timing cover, gears and chain, must be removed as detailed in the previous Section. It is also necessary to remove the distributor drive gear as detailed in the following Section. With the drive gear out of the way, proceed in the following manner:
1 Remove the three bolts and spring washers which hold the camshaft locating plate to the block. The bolts are normally covered by the camshaft gear wheel.
2 Remove the plate. The camshaft can now be withdrawn. Take great care to remove the camshaft gently, and in particular ensure that the cam peaks do not damage the camshaft bearings as the shaft is pulled forward.

21 Distributor drive - removal

To remove the distributor drive with the transmission casing still in position it is first necessary to remove one of the tappet cover bolts. With the distributor and the distributor clamp plate already removed, this is achieved as follows:
1 Unscrew the single retaining bolt and lockwasher to release the distributor housing.
2 With the distributor housing removed, with the casing still in position, screw into the end of the distributor drive shaft a 5/16 in. UNF bolt. A tappet cover bolt is ideal for this purpose. The drive shaft can then be lifted out, the shaft being turned slightly in the process to free the shaft skew gear from the camshaft skew gear.
3 If the gear casing has already been removed then it is a simple matter to push the drive shaft out from inside the crankcase.

22 Piston, connecting rod and big-end bearing - removal

The pistons, and connecting rods can be removed with the engine on the bench. Proceed as for removing the cylinder head with the engine on the bench. The pistons and connecting rods are drawn up out of the top of the cylinder bores.
1 Undo the 10 set bolts and the two nuts holding the transmission casing to the cylinder block, taking care to note the positions from which the shorter bolts are removed.
2 With the help of a friend lift the engine away from the transmission casing, or alternatively, use a block and tackle.
3 Knock back with a cold chisel the locking tabs on the big end retaining bolts, and remove the bolts and locking tabs. The 1275 GT engine does not have locking tabs and the big end caps are retained by bolts and special multi-sided nuts.
4 Remove the big end caps one at a time, taking care to keep them in the right order and the correct way round. Also ensure that the shell bearings are also kept with their correct connecting rods and caps unless they are to be renewed. Normally, the numbers 1 to 4 are stamped on adjacent sides of the big end caps and connecting rods, indicating which cap fits on which rod and which way round that cap fits. If no numbers or lines can be found then with a sharp screwdriver scratch mating marks across the joint from the rod to the cap. One line for connecting rod No. 1; two for connecting rod No. 2, and so on. This will ensure there is no confusion later as it is essential that the caps go back in the correct position on the connecting rods from which they were removed.
5 If the big-end caps are difficult to remove they may be gently tapped with a soft mallet.

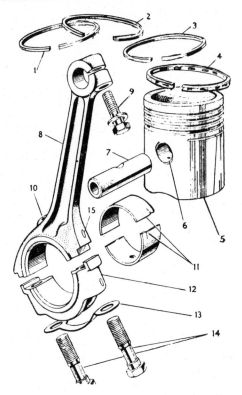

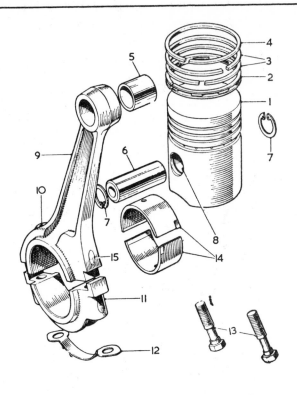

Fig. 1.17. Early type piston and connecting rod assembly

1 Piston ring - parallel
2 Piston ring - taper
3 Piston ring - taper
4 Piston ring - scraper
5 Piston
6 Gudgeon pin lubricating hole
7 Gudgeon pin
8 Connecting rod
9 Clamping screw and
   washer
10 Cylinder wall lubricating jet
11 Connecting rod bearings
12 Connecting rod cap
13 Lockwasher
14 Bolts
15 Connecting rod and cap marking

Fig. 1.18. Later type piston and connecting rod assembly

1 Piston
2 Piston ring - scraper
3 Piston rings - taper
4 Piston ring - parallel
5 Small - end bush
6 Gudgeon pin
7 Circlip
8 Gudgeon pin lubricating hole
9 Connecting rod
10 Cylinder wall lubricating jet
11 Connecting rod cap
12 Lockwasher
13 Bolts
14 Connecting rod bearings
15 Connecting rod and cap marking

6 To remove the shell bearings, press the bearing opposite the groove in both the connecting rod, and the connecting rod caps and the bearings will slide out easily.

7 Withdraw the pistons and connecting rods upwards and ensure they are kept in the correct order for replacement in the same bore. Refit the connecting rod caps and bearings to the rods if the bearings do not require renewal to minimise the risk of getting the caps and rods muddled.

23 Gudgeon pin - removal

Three different types of gudgeon pin retention are employed, depending on the type and cubic capacity of the engine.

On early 850 cc and 997 cc Minis and Mini Cooper models, to remove the gudgeon pin to free the piston from the connecting rod, it is merely necessary to remove the end bolt and lock washer. With the bolt removed the gudgeon pin should push out through either side of the piston. If it shows reluctance to move, then on no account force it out, as this could damage the piston. Immerse the piston in a pan of boiling water for three minutes. On removal the expansion of the aluminium should allow the gudgeon pin to slide out easily.

On 998 cc Mini Cooper and Elf/Hornet Mk 11 models, and the late model 850 cc, 1000 cc and 1098 cc engine models, fully floating gudgeon pins are fitted, these being retained in the pistons by a circlip at each end of the pin bore in the piston. To extract the pin, remove the circlips at one end and push the

pin out, immersing it in boiling water if it appears reluctant to move.
Make sure the pins are kept with the same piston for ease of refitting.

On all Mini Cooper 'S' and 1275 GT type engines the gudgeon pin is firmly held in the small end of the connecting rod by an interference fit. The bearing area being in the piston bosses.

Removal of the gudgeon pin calls for the use of a special BLMC service tool "18G 1002". In view of the high performance of 'S' type engine it is important that this job is done correctly, and the special tool **must** be used.

It is thought best for the private owner to take his connecting rod/piston assemblies to a good BLMC agent, and to allow a factory trained mechanic to withdraw the gudgeon pins. Use of the tool is fairly complex and it is easy to crush the piston if the work is done without previous experience.

24 Piston ring - removal

To remove the piston rings, slide them carefully over the top of the piston, taking care not to scratch the aluminium alloy. Never slide them off the bottom of the piston skirt. It is very easy to break the piston rings if they are pulled off roughly so this operation should be done with extreme caution. Special piston ring expanders are the best tools to use for the removal and refitting of piston rings; however, an old 0.020 in (0.508 mm) feeler gauge will do to assist with the removal of the rings if expanders are not readily available. Lift one end of the piston ring to be removed out of its groove and insert the end of the feeler gauge under it. Turn the feeler gauge slowly round the piston and as the ring comes out of its groove apply slight upward pressure so that it rests on the land above. It can then be eased off the piston using the feeler gauge to stop it slipping into any empty grooves if it is any but the top piston ring that is being removed.

25 Crankshaft and main bearing - removal

Removal of the crankshaft can only be attempted with the engine on the bench.

Drain the engine oil, remove the timing gears, the transmission casing and the big-end bearings, flywheel and flywheel housing as has already been described.

1 Release the locking tabs from the six bolts which hold the three main bearing caps in place.

2 Unscrew the bolts and remove them together with the locking plates.

3 Remove the two bolts which hold the front main bearing cap against the engine front plate.

4 Remove the main bearing caps and the bottom half of each bearing shell, taking care to keep the bearing shells in the right caps.

5 When removing the centre bearing cap, **Note** the bottom semi-circular halves of the thrust washers - one half lying on each side of the main bearing. Lay them with the centre bearing along the correct side.

6 Slightly rotate the crankshaft to free the upper halves of the bearing shells and thrust washers which should now be extracted and placed over the correct bearing cap.

7 Remove the crankshaft by lifting it away from the crankcase.

26 Lubrication system - general description

A forced feed system of lubrication is fitted with oil circulated round the engine from the transmission casing/sump. The level of engine oil in the sump is indicated on the dipstick which is fitted on the right-hand side of the engine. It is marked to indicate the optimum level which is the maximum mark. The level of oil in the sump should not be above or below this line. Oil is replenished, via, the filter cap on the front of the rocker cover.

The oil in the transmission casing/sump is also used to lubricate the gearbox and differential, the total capacity including the filter being 8.5 pints (4.83 litres).

The oil pump is mounted at the end of the crankcase and is driven by the camshaft. Three different types of oil pump have been fitted at different times. These are the 'Burman' rotary vane type, or the 'Hobourn-Eaton' or 'Concentric (Engineering) Ltd'. concentric rotor type. All are of the non-draining variety to allow rapid build-up when starting from cold.

Oil is drawn from the sump through a gauze screen in the oil strainer and is sucked up the pick-up pipe and drawn into the oil pump. From the oil pump it is forced under pressure along a gallery on the right-hand side of the engine, and through drillings to the big-end, main and camshaft bearings. A small hole in each connecting rod allows a jet of oil to lubricate the cylinder wall with each revolution.

From the camshaft front bearing oil is fed through drilled passages in the cylinder block and head to the front rocker pedestal where it enters the hollow rocker shaft. Holes drilled in the shaft allow for the lubrication of the rocker arms, and the valve stems and pushrod ends. This oil is at a reduced pressure to the oil delivered to the crankshaft bearings. Oil from the front camshaft bearing also lubricates the timing chain. Oil returns to the sump by various passages, the tappets being lubricated by oil returning, via, the pushrod drillings in the block.

On all models a full-flow oil filter is fitted, and all oil passes through this filter before it reaches the main oil gallery. The oil is passed directly from the oil pump across the block to an external pipe on the right-hand side of the engine which feeds into the filter head. Cooper 'S' models are fitted with an oil cooler. This is accessible after removing the front grille (see Fig 1.4).

27 Oil filter - removal and replacement

The full-flow oil filter fitted to all engines is located underneath the dynamo on the side of the engine facing the front of the car. It is removed by unscrewing the long centre bolt which holds the filter bowl in place. With the bolt released (use a 9/16AF spanner) carefully lift away the filter bowl which contains the filter and will also be full of oil. It is helpful to have a large basin under the filter body to catch the amount which is bound to spill.

Throw the old filter element away and thoroughly clean down the filter bowl, the bolts and associated parts with petrol and when perfectly clean wipe dry with a non-fluffy rag.

A rubber sealing ring is located in a groove round the head of the oil filter and forms an effective leak-proof joint between the filter head and the filter bowl. A new rubber sealing ring is supplied with each new filter element..

Carefully prise out the old sealing ring from the locating groove. If the ring has become hard and is difficult to move take great care not to damage the sides of the sealing ring groove.

With the old ring removed, fit the new ring in the groove at four equidistant points and press it home a segment at a time. Do not insert the ring at just one point and work round the groove pressing it home as, using this method, it is easy to stretch the ring and be left with a small loop of rubber which will not fit into the locating groove.

Reassemble the oil filter assembly by first passing up the bolt through the hole in the bottom of the bowl, with a steel washer under the bolt's head and a rubber or felt washer on top of the steel washer and next to the filter bowl.

Slip the spring over the bolt inside the bowl, then the other steel washer, the remaining rubber or felt washer and lastly the filter seating plate with the concave face downwards. Slip in a new filter element and with the bolt pressed hard up against the filter bowl body (to avoid leakage) three quarter fill the bowl with engine oil.

Offer up the bowl to the rubber sealing ring and before finally tightening down the centre bolt, check that the lip of the filter bowl is resting squarely on the rubber sealing ring and is not offset and off the ring. If the bowl is not seating properly, rotate it until it is. Run the engine and check the bowl for leaks.

28 Oil pressure relief valve - removal and replacement

To prevent excessive oil pressure - for example when the engine is cold - an oil pressure relief valve is built into the right-hand side of the engine at the rear just below the oil pressure unit take-off point.

The relief valve is identified externally by a large 9/16 in. domed hexagon nut. To dismantle the unit unscrew the nut and remove it, complete with the two fibre or copper sealing washers. The relief spring and the relief spring cup can then be easily extracted.

In position, the metal cup fits over the opposite end of the relief valve spring resting in the dome of the hexagon nut, and bears against a machining in the block. When the oil pressure exceeds 60 lb/sq.in. the cup is forced off its seat and the oil by-passes it and returns, via a drilling, directly to the sump.

Check the tension of the spring by measuring its length. If it is shorter than 2.875 in (73 mm) it should be replaced with a new spring. Reassembly of the relief valve unit is a reversal of the above procedure .

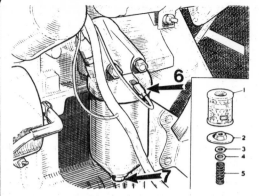

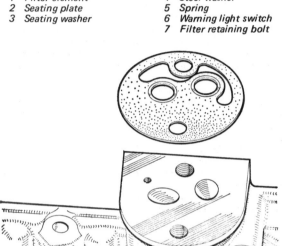

Fig. 1.19. Engine oil filter (manual transmission)

1 Filter element
2 Seating plate
3 Seating washer
4 Steel washer
5 Spring
6 Warning light switch
7 Filter retaining bolt

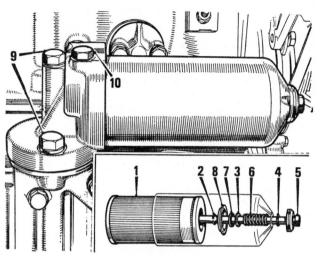

Fig. 1.20. Engine/automatic transmission oil filter
Inset shows filter components

1 Filter element
2 Circlip
3 Steel washer
4 Sealing ring
5 Centre bolt
6 Spring
7 Sealing washer
8 Sealing plate
9 Filter head retaining bolts
10 Oil pressure check plug

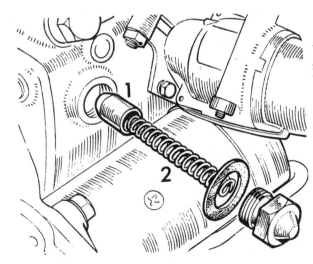

Fig. 1.21. Correct location of later type filter head/front cover joint washer (automatic transmission)

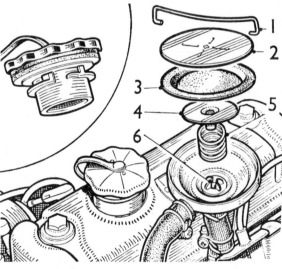

Fig. 1.22. Crankcase closed circuit breathing installation
Inset shows oil filler cap filter

1 Retaining clip
2 Cover
3 Diaphragm
4 Metering needle
5 Spring
6 Cruciform guides

Fig. 1.23. The oil pressure relief valve

1 Valve
2 Spring

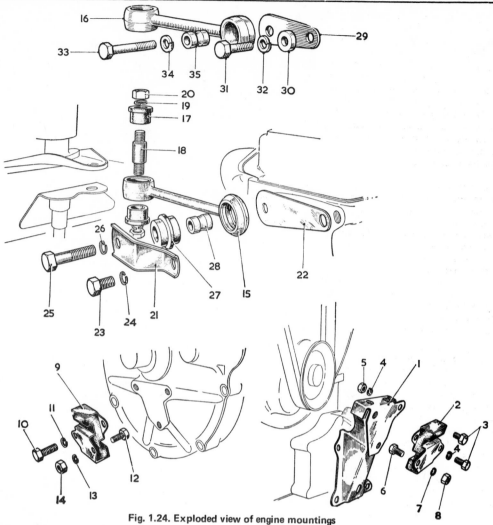

Fig. 1.24. Exploded view of engine mountings

1 Engine mounting bracket	10 Screw	18 Stud	28 Spacer
2 Rubber engine mounting	11 Spring washer	19 Spring washer	29 Packing strip
3 Mounting to bracket bolts	12 Mounting to frame bolt	20 Nut	30 Packing washer
4 Spring washer	13 Spring washer	21 Retaining bracket	31 Screw
5 Nut - bolt	14 Nut - bolt	22 Packing strip	32 Spring washer
6 Mounting to body bolt	15 Engine steady rod	23 Screw	33 Screw
7 Spring washer	(early)	24 Spring washer	34 Spring washer
8 Nut - bolt	16 Engine steady rod	25 Screw	35 Spacer
9 Rubber engine mounting	(late)	26 Spring washer	
flywheel end)	17 Rubber bush	27 Rubber bush	

29 Engine mountings - removal and replacement

The engine/transmission assembly is supported on two engine mountings. One is located under the timing chain (left-hand mounting), and the other under the clutch cover to which it is attached (right-hand mounting).

Should the mountings be worn or broken they can be replaced with the engine in place.

Place a jack under the same end of the transmission casing from which the engine is to be removed and take the weight of the engine. **Note:** Use a block of wood interposed between the transmission casing and the jack to spread the load on the transmission case.

If the right-hand mounting is to be removed proceed as follows:

1 Undo the nut securing the starter motor cable to the starter motor and remove the cable. Before removing the motor it is best to remove the front grille for easy access.

2 Undo the two bolts securing the starter motor in place and lift the motor out. If the grille has not been removed, then the motor must be worked along towards the radiator before it can be extracted.

3 Either the coil or the solenoid switch may be fitted to the top of the flywheel housing. Undo the bolts which secure them in place and disconnect the wires. On later models, the solenoid must be removed from the wing valance. On the 850 and 1000 models remove the coil from the cylinder head bracket.

4 With a pair of pliers pull out the split pin from the clutch lever pivot, disconnect the spring, undo the two securing bolts and lock washers that hold the slave cylinder in place and pull the clutch lever away.

5 Undo the engine tie rod, and undo the two nuts and bolts on the exhaust manifold pipe clamp.

6 Release the exhaust pipe mounting lug from its attachment

point on the gearlever extension by undoing the securing nut and bolt.

7 Undo the bolts which secure the radiator cowling steady bracket to the thermostat.

8 Undo and remove the two nuts, bolts and spring washers which hold the engine mountings to the subframe sidemember.

9 Undo and remove the nine bolts and washers which hold the clutch cover to the flywheel housing.

10 Jack up the engine just enough to be able to remove the clutch cover with engine mounting attached. While operating the jack frequently check that the fan blades are not fouling or damaging the radiator core.

11 Undo the three bolts holding the engine mounting to the clutch cover.

12 Replacement is a straight reversal of the above sequence.

Note: Prior to Engine No. 4354 paper gaskets were fitted between the engine mounting and clutch cover. These must be replaced on refitment.

If the left-hand mounting is to be removed proceed as below:

1 Remove the bonnet and the front grille.

2 Carefully remove the radiator as described in Chapter 2.

3 Undo and remove the two nuts, bolts and spring washers which hold the mounting to the subframe sidemember.

4 Undo and remove the two bolts which hold the mounting to the transmission casing and remove the mounting through the grille aperture.

5 Replacement is a straight reversal of the above sequence.

30 Oil pump - removal and dismantling

Oil pump removal is an operation which can only be carried out with the engine out of the car. Prior to removing the pump it is necessary to remove the clutch, flywheel, and flywheel housing. The oil pump engages, via a lip and slot, with the rear of the camshaft from which it is directly driven.

1 Bend back the locking tabs on the three securing bolts which hold the pump to the block

2 Unscrew the bolts and remove them complete with washers.

3 The oil pump cover can now be removed, complete with drive shaft and inner rotor.

4 To dismantle either the Burman or Hobourn Eaton type of pump, merely unscrew the two bolts holding the pump end plate in position.

5 The Concentric (Engineering) Ltd. pump must not be dismantled and if suspect must be exchanged for a rebuilt unit.

Note: A modified 'Hobourn-Eaton' oil pump was fitted to later engines and is fully interchangeable with the earlier type. The later type can be recognised by the words 'Hobourn Eaton' round the cover flange as opposed to round the cover centre. The new pump is identified by Part No. '2A 692' and is fully interchangeable with the old pump, identified by Part No. '2A 341'.

Before engine No. 194195 only the 'Hobourn-Eaton' concentric rotor pump was used. After this engine, either the Hobourn Eaton or the Burman rotary vane type may be fitted. If it is wished to remove the vanes from the rotor on the Burman pump it should be noted that the rotor sleeve is a press fit on the rotor and should be gently prised off when the vanes can be removed.

31 Engine examination and renovation - general

With the engine stripped down and all parts thoroughly cleaned, it is now time to examine everything for wear. The items in the following Sections should be checked, and where necessary, renewed or renovated.

32 Crankshaft - examination and renovation

Examine the crankpin and main journal surfaces for signs

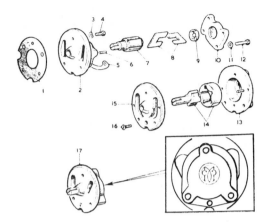

Fig. 1.25. Component parts of three types of oil pump which may be fitted

Burman Pump
1	Joint washer	11	Shakeproof washer
2	Pump body	12	Screw
3	Washer		
4	Set screw		Hobourn Eaton Pump
5	Lock plate	13	Body
6	Dowel	14	Rotor and shaft
7	Rotor	15	Cover
8	Vane	16	Screw
9	Sleeve	17	Concentric (engineering) Pump
10	Body cover		serviced as an assembly only

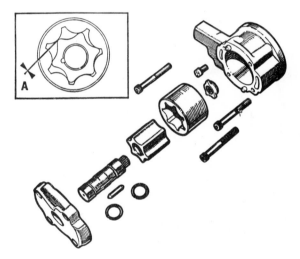

Fig. 1.26. Oil pump components (automatic transmission)
Inset 'A' shows lobe positions for checking clearances

of scoring or scratches. Check the ovality of the crankpins at different positions with a micrometer. If more than 0.001 in (0.0254 mm) out of round, the crankpins will have to be reground. They will also have to be reground if there are any scores or scratches present. Also check the journals in the same fashion. On highly tuned engines the centre main bearing has been known to break up. This is not always immediately apparent, but slight vibration in an otherwise normally smooth engine and a very slight drop in oil pressure under normal conditions are clues. If the centre main bearing is suspected of failure it should be immediately investigated by dropping the transmission casing and removing the centre main bearing cap. Failure to do this will result in a badly scored centre main

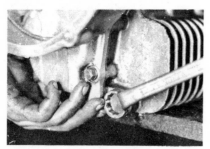

1 The first step is to drain the water by turning on the two taps, one at base of radiator, the other at bulkhead side of block. Then drain the oil after removing the drain plug

2 Disconnect the battery in the boot. Shown above are the two nuts and bolts which hold each bonnet hinge to the bonnet. Undo and extract them

3 The next step is to lift off the bonnet. It is not too heavy for one person to remove on his own

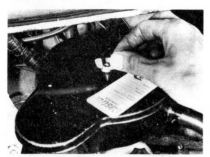

4 Release the rubber breather pipe from the air cleaner. Then undo the wing nut in the centre of the cleaner and lift it away from the carburettor intake flange

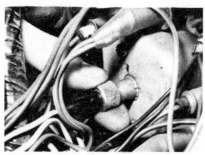

5 Undo the knurled nut which holds the speedometer cable to the rear of the speedometer head

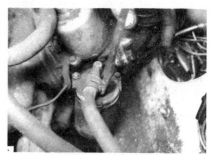

6 Next the clip on the carburettor fuel intake pipe must be slackened and the pipe removed from the float chamber

7 The bottom nut on the carburettor flange is rather difficult to get at and undo. A good tip is to use a normal open ended spanner cut in half

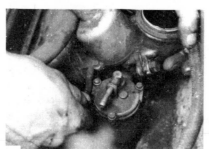

8 Next the accelerator cable connection, together with the choke cable and vacuum pipe must be freed from the carburettor

9 With both nuts removed from the studs on the inlet manifold the carburettor can be removed and placed on one side

10 The next step is to undo the two nuts and bolts from the clamp which holds the exhaust pipe to the exhaust manifold

11 Undo and remove the bolt which passes through the eye of the tie-rod and holds it to the block. Slacken the other bolt and move the tie-rod clear

12 Remove the three leads from the end of the coil and then unscrew the two nuts and washers holding the two electrical cables to the rear of the dynamo

13 Then remove the clutch return spring from the clutch operating lever with the aid of a pair of pliers

14 Undo and remove the two bolts holding the clutch operating cylinder to the flywheel casing. On no account push the clutch pedal after the operating cylinder is disconnected

15 Pull the HT leads off the spark plugs, spring back the two clips which hold the distributor cap in place, and remove the cap to prevent it getting damaged

16 Undo the clips holding the heater hoses to the take off points on the cylinder head (shown) and the bottom radiator hose. Undo the starter motor cable from the starter motor

17 Jack up the front of the car. Place load spreaders (short bits of plank) behind each front wheel arch and fit two supports. NEVER work under the car with only the jack holding it up

18 Release the exhaust pipe where it is held to the lug on the gearbox extension by undoing the nut and bolt

19 Undo the four inner nuts from the two 'U' bolts to each of the rubber universal joints. Leave the nuts on the driveshaft flange 'U' bolts in place

20 With the aid of a screwdriver lever out the two 'U' bolts which hold the rubber joint to the final drive flanges

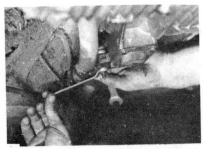

21 From inside the wheel arches remove the two nuts from each engine mounting. Then drive the bolts ....

22 .... through the subframe. There is just sufficient room between the subframe and mounting bracket to withdraw the bolts

23 Place a sling round the engine/transmission unit, or attach a lifting hook to the front centre cylinder head bolt and hoist the assembly complete with radiator out of the car

24 Typical view of empty Mini engine compartment

25 Lifting away water shield

26 Hinge attachment to bonnet. The nuts and washers have been removed

27 Lifting away bonnet

28 For safety reasons disconnect the battery

29 Removal of air cleaner assembly

30 Cylinder block drain plug

31 Disconnecting multi pin connector from rear of alternator

32 Disconnecting temperature sender unit terminal connector

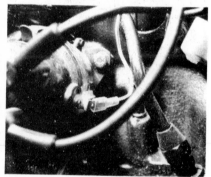

33 The LT lead on the side of the distributor body

34 Detach the HT lead from the spark plugs

35 Note location of cable connections on coil and then detach

36 Disconnect heater tap control cable

37 Detaching hose from heater tap

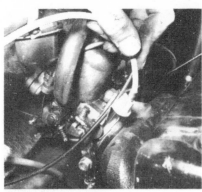

38 Disconnecting throttle control cable from side of carburettor

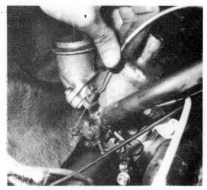

39 Disconnecting choke control cable from side of carburettor

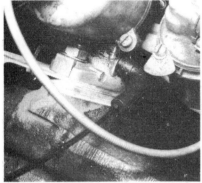

40 Distributor vacuum control pipe connected to carburettor

41 Side view of carburettor with all controls detached

42 Second heater hose to be detached

43 Removal of tie-rod securing bolt from side of cylinder block

44 Removal of tie-rod securing bolt from bulkhead mounting bracket

45 Removal of clutch slave cylinder. Do not forget to release return spring first

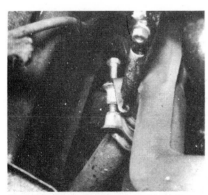

46 Removal of exhaust manifold to down-pipe securing clamp

47 Petrol outlet pipe detached from pump

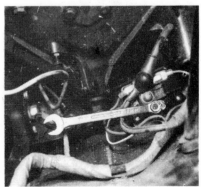

48 Releasing starter cable from solenoid mounted on inner wing panel

49 Lifting away solenoid

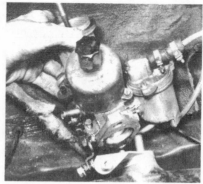

50 The carburettor should next be removed

51 Detaching exhaust pipe bracket from subframe mounting

52 Detaching second exhaust pipe bracket from mounting

53 Exhaust pipe clamp adjacent to driveshaft

54 Do not forget to detach engine earth cable

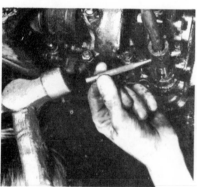

55 Drifting out selector shaft connection roll pin

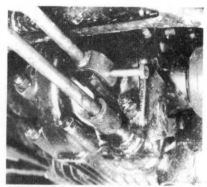

56 Removal of stay rod securing nut and bolt

57 Detaching steering tie-rod to steering arm

58 Detaching balljoint from upper suspension arm

59 Latest type driveshaft detached from final drive

60 Detach the air intake duct from inner wing panel

61 The intake duct is retained by raised lips

62 Removal of second air duct

63 Removal of rocker cover

64 Lifting chains fitted to rocker cover retaining studs

65 Starter solenoid tucked away on inner wing panel

66 Engine and transmission unit partially raised

67 Make sure all control cables, electric cables are tucked out of the way before lifting too high

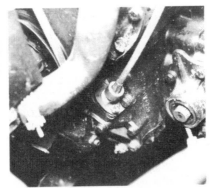
68 Do not forget to detach the speedometer cable from the transmission unit

69 The complete power unit raised ready for drawing from over engine compartment

70 This photo shows the spring ring that retains the driveshaft constant velocity joint

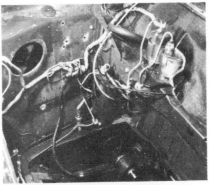
71 Side view of engine compartment. Before refitting the power unit spend a little time on cleaning down

journal. The following is the standard crankpin and main journal diameter with the regrind sizes available;

	850 cc, 997 cc and 1098 cc models
Crankpin diameter (Standard)	1.6254 to 1.6259 in or 41.285 to 41.298 mm.
Regrind sizes	-0.010 in (0.254 mm) -0.020 in (0.508 mm) -0.030 in (0.762 mm) -0.040 in (1.016 mm)
Main journal diameter (Standard)	1.7505 to 1.751 in. (44.46 to 44.47 mm)
Main journal diameter	Mini Cooper 'S' Models, 970 cc, 1071 cc and 1275 cc 2.0005 to 2.001 in (50.81 to 50.82 mm)
Minimum main journal	1.9805 to 1.9810 in (50.30 to 50.31 mm)

Regrind sizes are the same as for crankpin regrind sizes. The crankpin and main journal diameters for both engines should not be ground less than as listed below. If it is necessary to grind below the permitted diameters a new crankshaft should be fitted.

Minimum crankpin regrind diameter	1.5854 in. (40.27 mm)
Minimum main journal regrind diameter	1.7105 in. (43.45 mm)

On early 848 cc engines clutch slip frequently occured because of oil from an oilway hole in the crankshaft under the primary gear finding its way past the flywheel sealing ring onto the clutch. On models produced after January, 1963 the oil hole was blocked and a new primary gear fitted which made use of self-lubricating bushes. From engine Nos. "8AM-FA-U-H 450359," "8AM-U-H 452354," and "9F-SA-H 15633," the flywheel oil seal was omitted. It is possible to block the oil hole on the early type crankshaft and fit a modified primary gear. Details are given in Chapter 6.

33 Big-end and main bearings - examination and renovation

Big-end bearing failure is accompanied by a noisy knocking from the crankcase, and a slight drop in oil pressure. Main bearing failure is accompanied by vibration which can be quite severe as the engine speed rises and falls, and a drop in oil pressure.

Bearings which have not broken up, but are badly worn will give rise to low oil pressure and some vibration. Inspect the big-ends, main bearings, and thrust washers for signs of general wear, scoring, pitting, and scratches. The bearings should be matt grey in colour. With lead-indium bearings should a trace of copper colour be noticed the bearings are badly worn as the lead bearing material has worn away to expose the indium underlay. Renew the bearings if they are in this condition or if there is any sign of scoring or pitting.

Main bearings are not interchangeable between the 848 cc and 998 cc engines as the main journals are of a different length. The undersizes available are designed to correspond with the regrind sizes, ie., -0.010 bearings are correct for a crankshaft reground -0.010 undersize. The bearings are in fact, slightly more than the stated undersize as running clearances have been allowed for during their manufacture.

Very long engine life can be achieved by changing big-end bearings at intervals of 30,000 miles and main bearings at intervals of 50,000 miles, irrespective of bearing wear. Normally, crankshaft wear is infinitesimal and regular changes

of bearings will ensure mileages of between 100,000 and 150,000 miles before crankshaft regrinding becomes necessary. Crankshafts normally have to be reground because of scoring caused by bearing failure.

34 Cylinder bores - examination and renovation

The cylinder bores must be examined for taper, ovality, scoring and scratches. Start by carefully examining the top of the cylinder bores. If they are at all worn a very slight ridge will be found on the thrust side. This marks the top of the piston ring travel. The owner will have a good indication of the bore wear prior to dismantling the engine, or removing the cylinder head. Excessive oil consumption accompanied by blue smoke from the exhaust is a sure sign of worn cylinder bores and piston rings.

Measure the bore diameter just under the ridge with a micrometer and compare it with the diameter at the bottom of the bore, which is not subject to wear. If the difference between the two measurements is more than .006in, then it will be necessary to fit special piston rings or to have the cylinders rebored and fit oversize pistons and rings. If no micrometer is available remove the rings from a piston and place the piston in each bore in turn about ¾in, (17 mm) below the top of the bore. If an 0.010 feeler gauge can be slid between the piston and the cylinder wall on the thrust side of the bore then remedial action must be taken. Oversize pistons are available dependent on the bore, diameter, and the respective sizes available are given in the Specifications Section.

These are accurately machined to just below these measurements so as to provide correct running clearances in bores bored out to the exact oversize dimensions.

If the bores are slightly worn but not so badly worn as to justify reboring, then special oil control rings can be fitted to the existing pistons which will restore compression and stop the engine burning oil. Several different types are available and the manufacturer's instructions concerning their fitting must be followed closely, but the pistons must obviously be in good condition, and they may have to be machined to suit the oversize rings.

35 Pistons and piston rings - examination and renovation

If the old pistons are to be refitted, carefully remove the piston rings and then thoroughly clean them. Take particular care to clean out the piston ring grooves. At the same time do not scratch the aluminium in any way. If new rings are to be fitted to the old pistons then the top ring must be of the stepped type so as to clear the ridge left above the previous top ring. If a normal but oversize new ring is fitted, it will hit the ridge and break, because the new ring will not have worn in the same way as the old, which will have worn in unison with the ridge.

Before fitting the rings on the pistons each should be inserted approximately 3 in. (76 mm) down the cylinder bore and the gap measured with a feeler gauge. This should be between 0.006 in. and 0.010 in (0.152 and 0.254 mm). It is essential that the gap should be measured at the bottom of the ring travel, as if it is measured at the top of a worn bore and gives a perfect fit, it could easily seize at the bottom. If the ring gap is too small rub down the ends of the ring with a very fine file until the gap, when fitted, is correct. To keep the rings square in the bore for measurement, line each up in turn by inserting an old piston in the bore upside down, and use the piston to push the ring down about 3 in. (76 mm). Remove the piston and measure the piston ring gap.

When fitting new pistons and rings to a rebored engine the piston ring gap can be measured at the top of the bore as the bore will not now taper. It is not necessary to measure the

Fig. 1.27. Piston markings

side clearance in the piston ring grooves with the rings fitted as the groove dimensions are accurately machined during manufacture. When fitting new oil control rings to old pistons it may be necessary to have the grooves widened by machining to accept the new wider rings. In this instance the manufacturer's representative will make this quite clear and will supply the address to which the pistons must be sent for machining.

When new pistons are fitted, take great care to fit the exact size best suited to the particular bore of your engine. BLMC go one stage further than merely specifying one size of piston for all standard bores. Because of very slight differences in cylinder machining during production it is necessary to select just the right piston for the bore. Five different sizes are available for the standard bores as well as the four oversize dimensions already shown.

Examination of the cylinder block face will show adjacent to each bore a small diamond shaped box with a number stamped in the metal. Careful examination of the piston crown will show a matching diamond and number. These are the standard piston sizes and will be the same for all four bores. If standard pistons are to be refitted or standard low compression pistons changed to standard high compression pistons, then it is essential that only pistons with the same number in the diamond are used. With larger pistons, the amount oversize is stamped in an ellipse in the piston crown.

On engines with tapered second and third compression rings, the top narrow side of the rings is marked with a 'T'. Always fit this side uppermost and carefully examine all rings for this mark before fitting.

36 Camshaft and camshaft bearings - examination and renovation

Carefully examine the camshaft bearings for wear. **Note:** On early engines only the front camshaft bearing is renewable. If the bearings are obviously worn or pitted or the metal underlay is showing through, then they must be renewed. This is an operation for your local BLMC garage or the local engineering works as it demands the use of specialised equipment. The bearings are removed with a special drift, after which, new bearings are pressed in, care being taken to ensure the oil holes in the bearings line up with those in the block. With a special tool the bearings are then reamed in position.

The camshaft itself should show no signs of wear, but if very slight scoring on the cams is noticed, the score marks can

be removed by very gentle rubbing down with very fine emery cloth. The greatest care should be taken to keep the cam profiles smooth.

37 Valves and valve seats - examination and renovation

Examine the heads of the valves for pitting and burning, especially the heads of the exhaust valves. The valve seatings should be examined at the same time. If the pitting on valve and seat is very slight the marks can be removed by grinding the seats and valves together with coarse, and then fine, valve grinding paste. Where bad pitting has occurred to the valve seats it will be necessary to recut them and fit new valves. If the valve seats are so worn that they cannot be recut, then it will be necessary to fit new valve seat inserts. These latter two jobs should be entrusted to the local BLMC garage or engineering works. In practice it is very seldom that the seats are so badly worn that they require renewal. Normally, it is the valve that is too badly worn for replacement, and the owner can easily purchase a new set of valves and match them to the seats by valve grinding.

Valve grinding is carried out as follows:
1 Place the cylinder head upside down on a bench, with a block of wood at each end to give clearance for the valve stems. Alternatively, place the head at 45° to a wall with the combustion chambers facing away from the wall.
2 Smear a trace of coarse carborundum paste on the seat face and apply a suction grinder tool to the valve head. With a semi-rotary motion, grind the valve head to its seat, lifting the valve occasionally to distribute the grinding paste. When a dull matt even surface finish is produced on both the valve seat and the valve; then wipe off the paste and repeat the process with fine carborundum paste, lifting and turning the valve to re-distribute the paste as before. A light spring placed under the valve head will greatly ease this operation.
3 When a smooth unbroken ring of light grey matt finish is produced, on both valve and valve seat faces, the grinding operation is completed.
4 Scrape away all carbon from the valve head and the valve stem. Carefully clean away every trace of grinding compound, taking great care to leave none in the ports or in the valve guides. Clean the valves and valve seats with a paraffin soaked rag then with a clean rag, and finally, if an air line is available, blow the valves, valve guides and valve ports clean.

38 Timing gears and chain - examination and renovation

Examine the teeth on both the crankshaft gear wheel and the camshaft gear wheel for wear. Each tooth forms an inverted 'V' with the gear wheel periphery, and if worn the side of each tooth under tension will be slightly concave in shape when compared with the other side of the tooth, ie, one side of the inverted 'V' will be concave when compared with the other. If any sign of wear is present the gear wheels must be renewed.

Examine the links of the chain for side slackness and renew the chain if any slackness is noticeable when compared with a new chain. It is a sensible precaution to renew the chain at about 60,000 miles and at a lesser mileage if the engine is stripped down for a major overhaul. The actual rollers on a very badly worn chain may be slightly grooved. 'S' type engines use duplex chains.

39 Valve rockers and rocker shafts - examination and renovation

Remove the threaded plug with a screwdriver from the end of the rocker shaft and thoroughly clean out the shaft. As it acts as the oil passage for the valve gear, clean out the oil holes and make sure they are quite clear. Check the shaft for straightness by rolling it on the bench. It is most unlikely that it will deviate from normal, but, if it does, then a judicious attempt must be made to straighten it. If this is not successful, purchase a new shaft. The surface of the shaft should be free from any worn ridges caused by the rocker arms. If any wear is present, renew the shaft. Wear is only likely to have occurred if the rocker shaft oil holes have become blocked.

Check the rocker arms for wear of the rocker bushes, for wear at the rocker arm face which bears on the valve stem, and for wear of the adjusting ball ended screws. Wear in the rocker arm bush can be checked by gripping the rocker arm tip and holding the rocker arm in place on the shaft, noting if there is any lateral rocker arm shake. If shake is present, and the arm is very loose on the shaft, remedial action must be taken. Pressed steel valve rockers cannot be renovated by renewal of the rocker arm bush. It is necessary to fit new rocker arms. Forged rocker arms which have worn bushes may be taken to your local BLMC garage or engineering works to have the old bush drawn out and a new brush fitted. Forged rockers and pressed steel rockers are interchangeable in sets of eight, but, where one or two pressed steel rockers only require renewal it is not advised to replace them with the forged type.

Check the tip of the rocker arm where it bears on the valve head for cracking or serious wear on the case hardening. If none is present re-use the rocker arm. Check the lower half of the ball on the end of the rocker arm adjusting screw. On high performance Mini engines wear on the ball and top of the pushrod is easily noted by the unworn 'pip' which fits in the small central oil hole on the ball. The larger this 'pip' the more wear has taken place to both the ball and the pushrod. Check the pushrods for straightness by rolling them on the bench. Renew any that are bent.

40 Tappets (cam followers) - examination and renovation

Examine the bearing surface of the tappets (cam followers) which lie on the camshaft. Any indentation in this surface or any cracks indicate serious wear and the tappets should be renewed. Thoroughly clean them out, removing all traces of sludge. It is most unlikely that the sides of the tappets will prove worn, but, if they are a very loose fit in their bores and can readily be rocked, they should be exchanged for new units. It is very unusual to find any wear in the tappets, and any wear present is likely to occur only at very high mileages.

41 Flywheel starter ring - examination and renovation

If the teeth on the flywheel starter ring are badly worn, or if some are missing, then it will be necessary to remove the ring. This is achieved by splitting the ring with a cold chisel. The greatest care should be taken not to damage the flywheel during this process.

To fit a new ring, heat it gently and evenly with an oxy-acetylene flame until a temperature of approximately 350° C is reached. This is indicated by a light metallic blue surface colour. With the ring at this temperature, fit it to the flywheel with the the front of the teeth facing the flywheel register. The ring should be tapped gently down onto its register and left to cool naturally when the contraction of the metal on cooling will ensure that it is a secure and permanent fit. Great care must be taken not to overheat the ring, as if this happens the temper of the ring will be lost.

Alternatively, your local BLMC garage or local engineering works may have a suitable oven in which the flywheel can be heated. The normal domestic oven will only give a temperature of about 250° C at the very most and, although it may just be possible to fit the ring with it at this temperature, it is unlikely and no great force should have to be used.

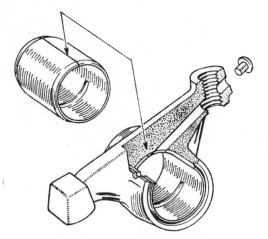

Fig. 1.28. Forged type valve rocker

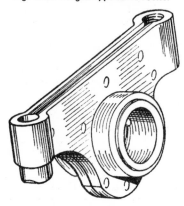

Fig. 1.29. Pressed steel type valve rocker

42 Oil pump - examination and renovation

It is unlikely that the oil pump will be worn, but if the engine is fully stripped down it is only sensible to check the pump for wear. With the 'Hoburn-Eaton' pump dismantled check the rotor internally and also the drive shaft lobes for any signs of excessive wear or scoring. If wear is found, renew the worn components.

If it is the 'Burman' pump, examine the inside of the pump body in which the vanes rotate and also the edges of the vanes for signs of scoring. If any is found renew the worn components.

The 'Concentric Engineering' pump, if suspect, cannot be dismantled and should be exchanged for a reconditioned unit.

43 Cylinder head - decarbonisation

This can be carried out with the engine in or out of the car. With the cylinder head off, carefully remove (with a wire brush and blunt scraper) all traces of carbon deposits from the combustion spaces and ports. The valve head stems and valve guides should also be freed from any carbon deposits. Wash the combustion spaces and ports down with petrol and scrape the cylinder head surface free of any foreign matter with the side of a steel rule, or a similar article.

Clean the pistons and tops of the cylinder bores. If the pistons are still in the block then it is essential that great care is taken to ensure that no carbon gets into the cylinder bores as this could scratch the cylinder walls or cause damage to the pistons and ring. To ensure this does not happen, first turn the crankshaft so that two of the pistons are at the top of their bores. Stuff rag into the other two bores or seal them off with paper and masking tape. The waterways should also be covered with small pieces of masking tape to prevent particles of carbon entering the cooling system and damaging the water pump.

There are two schools of thought as to how much carbon should be removed from the piston crown: one school recommends that a ring of carbon should be left round the edge of the piston and on the cylinder bore wall as an aid to low oil consumption. Although this is probably true for early engines with worn bores, on later engines the second school recommends that for effective decarbonisation all traces of carbon should be removed.

If all traces of carbon are to be removed, press a little grease into the gap between the cylinder walls and the two pistons which are to be worked on. With a blunt scraper carefully scrape away the carbon from the piston crown, taking great care not to scratch the aluminium. Also scrape away the carbon from the surrounding lip of the cylinder wall. When all carbon has been removed, scrape away the grease which will now be contam inated with carbon particles, taking care not to press any into the bores. To assist prevention of carbon build-up the piston crown can be polished with a proprietary metal polish such as 'Brasso'. Remove the rags or masking tape from the other two cylinders and turn the crankshaft so that the two pistons which were at the bottom are now at the top. Place rag or masking tape in the cylinders which have been decarbonised and proceed as before.

If a ring of carbon is going to be left round the piston then this can be helped by inserting an old piston ring into the top of the bore to rest on the piston and ensure that carbon is not accidentally removed. Check that there are no particles of carbon in the cylinder bores. Decarbonising is now complete.

44 Valve guides - examination and renovation

Examine the valve guides internally for wear. If the valves are a very loose fit in the guides and there is the slightest suspicion of lateral rocking, then new guides will have to be fitted. If the valve guides have been removed compare them internally by visual inspection with a new guide as well as testing them for rocking with the valves.

45 Engine reassembly - general

To ensure maximum life with minimum trouble from a rebuilt engine, not only must everything be correctly assembled, but everything must be splotlessly clean, all the oilways must be clear; locking washers and spring washers must always be fitted where indicated and all bearing and other working surfaces must be thoroughly lubricated during assembly. Before assembly begins renew any bolts or studs, the threads of which are in any way damaged, and whenever possible use new spring washers. Apart from your normal tools, a supply of clean rag, an oil can filled with engine oil (an empty plastic detergent bottle thoroughly cleaned and washed out, will invariably do just as well), a new supply of assorted spring washers, a set of new gaskets, and preferably a torque spanner, should be collected together.

46 Crankshaft - replacement

Ensure that the crankcase is thoroughly clean and that all oilways are clear. A thin-twist drill is useful for cleaning them out. If possible, blow them out with compressed air. Treat the crankshaft in the same fashion, and then inject engine oil into the crankshaft oilways.

Commence work on rebuilding the engine by replacing the crankshaft and main bearings:

1 If the old main bearing shells are to be replaced, (a false economy unless they are virtually as new), fit the three upper halves of the main bearing shells to their location in the crankcase, after wiping the locations clean.

2 **Note:** At the back of each bearing is a tab which engages in locating grooves in either the crankcase or the main bearing cap housings.

3 If new bearings are being iftted, carefully clean away all traces of the protective grease with which they are coated.

4 With the three upper bearing shells securely in place, wipe the lower bearing cap housings and fit the three lower shell bearings to their caps ensuring that the right shell goes into the right cap if the old bearings are being refitted.

5 Wipe the recesses either side of the centre main bearings which locate the upper halves of the thrust washers.

6 Generously lubricate the crankshaft journals and the upper and lower main bearing shells and carefully place the crankshaft in position.

7 Introduce the upper halves of the thrust washers (the halves without tabs) into their grooves on each side of the centre main bearing, rotating the side of the centre main bearing, rotating the crankshaft in the direction towards the main bearing tabs (so that the main bearing shells do not slide out). At the same time feed the thrust washers into their locations with their oil grooves facing outwards away from the bearing.

8 Ensure that all six tubular locating dowels are firmly in place, one on each side of the upper halves of the three main bearings, and then fit the main bearing caps in position ensuring they locate properly on the dowels. The mating surfaces must be spotlessly clean or the caps will not seat properly.

9 When replacing the centre main bearing cap, ensure the thrust washers, generously lubricated, are fitted with their oil grooves facing outwards, and the locating tab of each washer is in the slot in the bearing cap.

10 Replace the one-piece locking tabs over the main bearing caps and replace the main bearing cap bolts screwing them up finger-tight.

11 Test the crankshaft for freedom of rotation. Should it be very stiff to turn or possess high spots a most careful inspection must be made, preferably by a qualified mechanic with a micrometer to get to the root of the trouble. It is very seldom that any trouble of this nature will be experienced when fitting the crankshaft.

12 Tighten the main bearing bolts to the torque given in the Specifications and turn up the locking tabs with a cold chisel.

47 Oil pump - reassembly and replacement

The oil pump must be fitted before the flywheel housing on all models.

To reassemble the 'Hobourn-Eaton' oil pump replace the outer rotor, inner rotor and drive shaft in the pump body and secure the end cover in place with the two bolts and spring washers.

To reassemble the 'Burman' oil pump, replace the vanes in the rotor and fit the rotor to the pump body. Secure the pump end cover in place with the two bolts and spring washers.

To replace either oil pump or the 'Concentric (Engineering) Ltd' oil pump to the crankcase, fill the pump being fitted with engine oil; place the paper gasket in its correct position on the pump body flange, ensuring that the gasket does not cover the inlet or exhaust ports, and firmly bolt the pump unit to the crankcase using a spring washer under the head of each bolt, which should be tightened to the torque given in the Specifications.

Because of the disposition of the three bolt holes it is impossible to fit the oil pump the wrong way round.

48 Piston and connecting rod - reassembly

If the same pistons are being used, then they must be mated to the same connecting rod with the same gudgeon pin. If new pistons are being fitted it does not matter which connecting rod they are used with, but, the gudgeon pins should be fitted on the basis of selective assembly.

This involves trying each of the pins in each of the pistons in turn and fitting them to the ones they fit best, as described below.

Because aluminium alloy, when hot has a greater co-efficient of expansion than steel, the gudgeon pin may be a very tight fit in the piston when they are cold, particularly on the variety which use a small-end clamp bolt. To avoid any damage to the piston it is best to heat in boiling water before fitting the pin, which will then slide in easily.

Lay the correct piston adjacent to each connecting rod and remember that the same rod and piston must go back into the same bore. If new pistons are being used it is only necessary to ensure that the right connecting rod is placed in each bore.

To assemble the pistons to the connecting rods or engines where the gudgeon pin is held in the small-end by a clamp bolt, proceed as follows:

1 Locate the small end of the connecting rod in the piston with the marking "FRONT" on the piston crown towards the front of the engine, and the hole for the gudgeon pin bolt in the connecting rod towards the camshaft.

2 **Note** the indentation in the centre of the gudgeon pin and insert the pin in the connecting rod so that the indentation lines up with the clamp bolt hole in such a way that the bolt will pass through without touching the gudgeon pin.

3 For the gudgeon pin to fit correctly it should slide in three-quarters of its travel quite freely and for the remaining quarter have to be tapped in with a plastic or wooden headed hammer. If the piston is heated in water then the pin will slide in the remaining quarter easily.

4 Fit a new spring washer under the head of the connecting rod bolt and screw it into position using a torque figure of 25 lb f ft. (3.4 kg. fm).

To assemble the piston to the connecting rod on engines where the gudgeon pin is fully floating proceed as follows:

1 Fit a gudgeon pin circlip in position at one end of the gudgeon pin hole in the piston.

2 Locate the connecting rod in the piston with the marking "FRONT" on the piston crown towards the front of the engine, and the connecting rod caps towards the camshaft side of the engine.

3 Slide the gudgeon pin in through the hole in the piston and through the connecting rod small-end until it rests against the previously fitted circlip. **Note:** The pin should be a push fit.

4 Fit the second circlip in position. Repeat this procedure for all four pistons and connecting rods.

49 Piston ring - replacement

Check that the piston ring grooves and oilways are thoroughly clean and unblocked. Piston rings must always be fitted over the head of the piston and never from the bottom. If ring expanders are not available the easiest method to use when fitting rings is to wrap a 0.020 in. (0.508 mm) feeler gauge round the top of the piston and place the rings one at a time, starting with the bottom oil control ring, over the feeler gauge.

The feeler gauge, complete with ring, can then be slid down the piston over the other piston ring grooves until the correct groove is reached. The piston ring is then slid gently off the feeler gauge into the groove.

An alternative method is to fit the rings by holding them slightly open with the thumbs and both of your index fingers. This method requires a steady hand and great care as it is easy to open the ring too much and break it.

50 Piston - replacement

The pistons, complete with connecting rods, can be fitted to the cylinder bores in the following sequence:

1 With a wad of clean rag wipe the cylinder bores clean.

2 The pistons, complete with connecting rods, are fitted to their bores from above.

3 As each piston is inserted into its bore ensure that it is the correct piston/connecting rod assembly for that particular bore and that the connecting rod is the right way round, and that the front of the piston is towards the front of the bore, ie towards the front of the engine.

4 The piston will only slide into the bore as far as the oil control ring. It is then necessary to compress the piston rings in a clamp and to gently tap the piston into the cylinder bore with a wooden or plastic hammer. If a proper piston ring clamp is not available then a suitable 'Jubilee' clip does the job very well.

5 Lubricate each cylinder bore and piston with clean engine oil prior to fitting.

51 Connecting rod to crankshaft - reassembly

As the big-ends on the connecting rods are offset it will be obvious if they have been inserted the wrong way round as they will not fit over the crankpins. The centre two connecting rods should be fitted with the offset part of the rods adjacent, and the connecting rods at each extremity of the engine should have the offset part of the rods facing outwards.

1 Wipe the connecting rod half of the big-end bearing cap and the underside of the shell bearing clean, and fit the shell bearing in position with its locating tongue engaged with the corresponding groove in the connecting rod.

2 If the old bearings are nearly new and are being refitted then ensure they are replaced in their correct locations on the correct rods.

3 Generously lubricate the crankpin journals with engine oil, and turn the crankshaft so that the crankpin is in the most advantageous position for the connecting rod to be drawn onto it.

4 Wipe the connecting rod bearing cap and back of the shell bearing clean and fit the shell bearing in position ensuring that the locating tongue at the back of the bearing engages with the locating groove in the connecting rod cap.

5 Generously lubricate the shell bearing and offer up the connecting rod bearing cap to the connecting rod.

6 Fit the connecting rod bolts with the one-piece locking tab under them and tighten the bolts with a torque spanner to the figure given in the specifications. With a cold chisel knock up the locking tabs against the bolt head.

7 When all the connecting rods have been fitted, rotate the crankshaft to check that everything is free, and that there are no high spots causing binding.

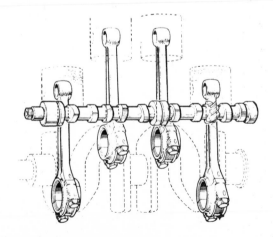

Fig. 1.30. The correct positions of the offsets on the connecting rod big ends when assembled to the crankshaft

52 Flywheel housing oil seal - removal

If the sharp edges of the oil seal in the flywheel housing are at all damaged it is a simple matter to carefully prise it out. Keep it on one side to assist with the replacement of the new seal.

53 Flywheel housing oil seal - replacement

The new seal goes into position from the flywheel side of the flywheel housing. Ensure it enters the housing tensioning spring side first. Keep the oil seal square in the housing, and use the old seal to protect the new one as it is tapped or pressed gently into position.

54 Replacing the engine on the transmission casing - flywheel housing replacement (manual transmission)

Carefully scrape away all traces of the old gaskets from the crankcase to transmission case joint and the engine/transmission to flywheel housing joints. **Note**: If it has been necessary to fit new transfer gears then it is essential to check the end float of the idler-gear in the transmission casing before proceeding any further. See Chapter 6 for details.

1   Fit a new front bearing cork oil seal and position the crank-case to transmission casing gaskets carefully. Ensure the 'O' ring on the top transmission casing flange is in place.

2   Lower the engine onto the transmission casing and ensure the cork oil seal and the gaskets do not slip.

3   Replace and tighten down the 10 set bolts and 2 nuts which hold the transmission casing to the engine. Use a torque of 6 lb f ft. (0.83 kg fm).

4   Ensure that the primary gear thrust washer is fitted next to the crankshaft with its bevelled edge against the crankshaft flange. Replace the 'C' washer which locks the primary gear in place. Measure the primary gear end float which should be between 0.003 in. and 0.006 in. (0.0762 and 0.1524 mm). If this is incorrect, measure the gap without the thrust washer in position. The width of the gap will determine the washer that should be used to give the ideal clearance of 0.0045 in. (0.1016 mm).

Gap width	Washer Part No.	Washer thickness
0.1295 to 0.1315 in. (3.27 to 3.34 mm.)	22A 83	0.125 to 0.127 in. (3.17 to 3.22 mm.)
0.1315 to 0.1335 in. (3.34 to 3.39 mm.)	22A 238	0.127 to 0.129 in. (3.22 to 3.27 mm.)
0.1335 to 0.1345 in. (3.39 to 3.42 mm.)	22A 239	0.129 to 0.131 in (3.27 to 3.32 mm.)

On older models, perhaps suffering from clutch slip, it is desirable to fit the modified primary gear bearing. Details are given in Chapter 6.

5   Before fitting the flywheel housing make sure that a flywheel housing oil seal has been fitted, and cover the splines of the crankshaft primary gear with the special thin sleeve used by BLMC garages (BLMC special tool No. "18G 570"). Alternatively, wrap a piece of tinfoil, or waxed paper tightly over the splines so that no damage will be done to the oil seal by the sharp edges on the splines. Lubricate the seal prior to refitting the housing.

6   Fit a new BLMC gasket in position on the end of the engine/transmission casing. **Note** the cut out on the outer edge; this is to allow a measurement to be taken with a feeler gauge when the housing bolts/nuts have been fully tightened-down. This is to check that the gasket has compressed to the correct thickness of 0.030 in. (0.762 mm).

7   Carefully fit the housing in position. If the small roller bearing on the outer end of the first motion shaft will not enter the housing, on no account try to force the housing on. Turn the bearing a quarter of a turn and try again. The rollers can be held in position with grease if wished. The second or third attempts are invariably successful.

8   Fit new locking tabs, and tighten down the nine nuts and six bolts evenly to a torque of 18 lb f ft. (2.49 kg fm). Make certain that the correct short bolt is fitted in the top right-hand position. Too long a bolt may damage the main oil gallery in the cylinder block.

55 Flywheel - replacement

1   Turn the crankshaft so that cylinders 1 and 4 are at tdc and the grooves in the sides of the crankshaft are vertical.

2   Check that the curved portion of the 'C' washer which holds the primary gear in place is at the top of the crankshaft, and that the sides of the washer fit in the crankshaft grooves.

3   Carefully clean the mating tapers in the flywheel and on the end of the crankshaft and make quite certain there are no traces of oil, grease, or dirt present. Sparingly lubricate the edges of the oil seal, where an oil seal is fitted - early models only.

4   Replace the flywheel on the end of the crankshaft with the ¼ tdc markings at the top and then replace the driving washer which positively locates the flywheel.

5   Fit a new lockwasher under the head of the flywheel securing bolt. Insert the bolt in the centre of the flywheel and tighten it to 110 to 115 lb f ft. (15.2 - 15.9 kg fm).

6   Tap down the side of the lockwasher against the driving plate, and tap up the other side of the washer against the retaining bolt head.

7   Fit the thrust plate. Use new tab washers under the heads of the nuts. Tighten the nuts down firmly and knock up the tabs of the washers. **Note**: On models with diaphragm clutches the thrust plate is held by a circular retaining spring.

56 Camshaft - replacement

With the transmission casing in position the engine can be stood upright and the following operations, including camshaft replacement, will be found easier with the engine in this position.

Wipe the camshaft bearing journals clean and lubricate them generously with engine oil.

Insert the camshaft into the crankcase gently taking care not to damage the camshaft bearings with the cams.

With the camshaft inserted into the block as far as it will go, rotate it slightly to ensure that the slot in the oil pump drive has mated with the camshaft flange. If it has not yet mated the camshaft will go a further 0.25 in. (6.35 mm) into the block as the flange and slot line up.

Replace the camshaft locating plate and tighten down the three retaining bolts and washers. Check the camshaft endfloat which should be 0.003 to 0.007 in (0.076 to 0.178 mm).

57 Timing gears, chain and cover - replacement

Before reassembly begins check that the packing washers are in place on the crankshaft nose. If new gearwheels are being fitted it may be necessary to fit additional washers (see paragraph 6). These washers ensure that the crankshaft gearwheel lines up correctly with the camshaft gearwheel.

1   Replace the Woodruff keys in their respective slots in the crankshaft and camshaft and ensure that they are fully seated. If their edges are burred they must be cleaned with a fine file.

2   Lay the camshaft gearwheels on a clean surface so that the two timing dots are adjacent to each other. Slip the timing chain over them and pull the gearwheels back into mesh with the chain so that the timing dots, although further apart are still adjacent to each other.

3   Rotate the crankshaft so that the Woodruff key is at top

dead centre. (The engine should be standing upright on its transmission casing).

4   Rotate the camshaft so that when viewed from the front the Woodruff key is at the two o'clock position.

5   Fit the timing chain and gearwheel assembly onto the camshaft and crankshaft, keeping the timing marks adjacent. If the camshaft and crankshaft have been positioned accurately it will be found that the keyways on the gearwheels will match the position of the keys, although it may be necessary to rotate the camshaft a fraction to ensure accurate lining-up of the camshaft gearwheel.

6   Press the gearwheels into position on the crankshaft and camshaft as far as they will go. **Note:** If new gearwheels are being fitted they should be checked for alignment before being finally fitted to the engine. Place the gearwheels in position without the timing chain and place the straight edge of a steel ruler from the side of the camshaft gear teeth to the crankshaft gearwheel, and measure the gap between the steel rule and the gearwheel. If a gap exists a suitable number of packing washers must be placed on the crankshaft nose to bring the crankshaft gearwheel onto the same plane as the camshaft gearwheel.

7   Fit the oil thrower to the crankshaft with the concave side forward.

8   Fit the locking washer to the camshaft gearwheel with its locating tab in the gearwheel keyway.

9   Screw on the camshaft gearwheel retaining nut and tighten securely.

10 Bend up the locking tab of the locking washer to hold the camshaft retaining nut securely.

11 Generously oil the chain and gearwheels.

12 Ensure the interior of the timing cover and the timing cover flange is clean. Examine the condition of the timing cover oil seal and replace it if damaged or worn. Then, with a new gasket in position, fit the timing cover to the block.

13 Screw in the timing cover retaining bolts with the flat washer next to the cover flange and under the spring washer. Tighten the respective bolts to the recommended torque given in the specifications.

14 Fit the crankshaft pulley to the nose of the crankshaft ensuring that the keyway engages with the Woodruff key.

15 Fit the crankshaft retaining bolt locking washer in position and screw in the crankshaft pulley retaining bolt. Tighten to the torque given in the specifications.

58 Valve and valve spring - reassembly

1   Rest the cylinder head on its side, or if the manifold studs are still fitted, with the side facing the cylinder block downwards.

2   Fit each valve and valve spring in turn, wiping down and lubricating each valve stem as it is inserted into the same valve guide from which it was removed.

3   As each valve is inserted slip the oil control rubber ring into place just under the bottom of the cotter groove. A much larger oil seal is used in Mini Cooper 'S' and 1275 GT engines. This should be fitted over the top of the valve guide.

4   Move the cylinder head towards the edge of the work bench if it is facing downwards and slide it partially over the edge of the bench so as to fit the bottom half of the valve spring compressor to the valve head.

5   Slip the valve spring, shroud and cap over the valve stem.

6   With the base of the valve compressor on the valve head compress the valve spring until the cotters can be slipped into place in the valve grooves. Gently release the compressor and fit the circlip in position in the grooves in the cotters.

7   Repeat this procedure until all eight valves and valve springs are fitted.

59 Rocker shaft - reassembly

To reassemble the rocker shaft fit the split pin, flat washer and spring washer at the rear end of the shaft and then slide on the rocker arms, rocker shaft pedestals, and spacing springs in the same order in which they were removed.

With the front pedestal in position, screw in the rocker shaft locating screw and slip the locating plate into position. Finally, fit to the front of the shaft the spring washer, plainwasher, and split pin, in that order.

60 Tappets (cam followers) and pushrods - replacement

Generously lubricate the tappets (cam followers) internally and externally and insert them in the bores from which they were removed through the tappet chest.

With the cylinder head in position fit the pushrods in the

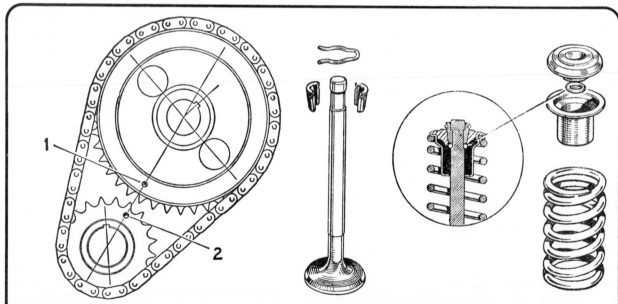

Fig. 1.31. The timing gears correctly assembled into the chain so the two timing marks (1, 2) are opposite and adjacent

Fig. 1.32. Exploded view of the valve assembly
NOTE the position of the oil seal (arrowed)

same order in which they were removed. Ensure that they locate properly in the stems of the tappets, and lubricate the pushrod ends before fitment.

61 Cylinder head - replacement

After checking that both the cylinder block and cylinder head mating faces are perfectly clean, generously lubricate each cylinder with engine oil.

1 Always use a new cylinder head gasket as the old gasket will be compressed and not capable of giving a good seal. It is also easier at this stage to refit the small hose from the water pump to the cylinder head.

2 Never smear grease on the gasket, as when the engine heats-up, the grease will melt and may allow compression leaks to develop. It should not be necessary to use gasket cement as if a new gasket is used and the head and block faces are 'true' there should be no requirement for it. (The most successful racing engines never use gasket cement).

3 The cylinder head gasket is marked "FRONT" and "TOP" and should be fitted in position according to the markings.

4 With the gasket in position carefully lower the cylinder head onto the cylinder block.

5 With the head in position fit the cylinder head nuts and washers finger tight to the five cylinder head holding down studs, which remain outside the rocker cover. It is not possible to fit the remaining nuts to the studs inside the rocker cover until the rocker assembly is in position.

6 Fit the pushrods as detailed in the previous section.

7 The rocker shaft assembly can now be lowered over its eight locating studs. Take care that the rocker arms are the right way round. Lubricate the balljoints , and insert the rocker arm balljoints in the pushrod cups. Note: Failure to place the balljoints in the cups can result in the ball joints seating on the edge of a pushrod or outside it when the head and rocker assembly is pulled down tight.

8 Fit the four rocker pedestal nuts and washers, and then the four cylinder head stud nuts and washers which also serve to hold down the rocker pedestals. Pull the nuts down evenly, but without tightening them right up.

9 When all is in position, the nine cylinder head nuts and the four rocker pedestal nuts can be tightened down in the order shown in Fig. 1.14. Turn the nuts a quarter of a turn at a time and tighten the four rocker pedestal nuts to the recommended torque as given in the Specifications.

Note: Mini Cooper 'S' and 1275 GT type engines make use of ten cylinder head nuts and one cylinder head bolt. (Identified by the figures '300' stamped on the bolt head). The cylinder head nuts should be tightened to a torque of 42 lb f ft (5.81 kg fm). The cylinder head bolt should be tightened last to a torque of 25 lb f ft (3.4 kg fm). On no account exceed this figure because of the risk of stripping the thread in the cylinder block.

62 Rocker arm/valve clearance - adjustment

The valve adjustments should be made with the engine cold. The importance of correct rocker arm/valve stem clearances cannot be overstressed as they vitally affect the performance of the engine. If the clearances are set too open, the efficiency of the engine is reduced as the valves open late and close earlier than was intended. If, on the other hand the clearances are set too close there is a danger that the stems will expand upon heating and not allow the valves to close properly which will cause burning of the valve head and seat and possible warping. If the engine is in the car access to the rockers is by removing the two holding down studs from the rocker cover, and then lifting the rocker cover and gasket away.

It is important that the clearance is set when the tappet of the valve being adjusted is on the heel of the cam, (ie opposite the peak). This can be ensured by carrying out the adjustments in the following order (which also avoids turning the crankshaft

more than necessary).

Valve fully open	Check and Adjust
Valve No. 8	Valve No. 1
" " 6	" " 3
" " 4	" " 5
" " 7	" " 2
" " 1	" " 8
" " 3	" " 6
" " 5	" " 4
" " 2	" " 7

The correct valve clearance of 0.012 in. (0.305 mm) is obtained by slackening the hexagon locknut with a spanner while holding the ball pin against rotation with a screwdriver. Then, still pressing down with the screwdriver, insert a feeler gauge in the gap between the valve stem head and rocker arm and adjust the ball pin until the feeler gauge will just move in and out without nipping. Then, still holding the ball pin in the correct position, tighten the locknut. An alternative method is to set the gaps with the engine running, and although this may be faster it is no more reliable, and not recommended to the novice.

63 Distributor and distributor drive - replacement

It is important to set the distributor drive correctly as otherwise the ignition timing will be totally incorrect. It is possible to set the distributor drive in apparently the right position, but, in fact, 180° out, by omitting to select the correct cylinder which must not only be at tdc but must also be on its firing stroke with both valves closed. The distributor drive should therefore not be fitted until the cylinder head is in position and the valves can be observed. Alternatively, if the timing cover has not been replaced, the distributor drive can be replaced when the dots on the timing wheels are adjacent to each other.

1 Rotate the crankshaft so that No. 1 piston is at tdc and on its firing stroke (the dots in the timing gears will be adjacent to each other). When No. 1 piston is at tdc the inlet valve on No. 4 cylinder is just opening and the exhaust valve closing.

2 When the marks "1/4" on the flywheel are at tdc, then Nos. 1 and 4 pistons are at tdc.

3 Screw the tappet cover bolt into the head of the distributor drive (any 5/16 in. UNF bolt will do if it is not less than 3 in. (76.2 mm) long.

4 Hold the distributor drive so that the slot is as shown in Fig. 1.33 inset A. Insert the drive into its housing. As the gear on the

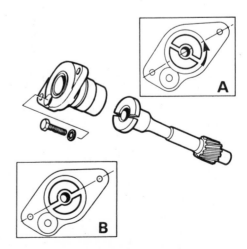

Fig. 1.33. Distributor drive shaft installation
The large offset is uppermost

72 After removing the flywheel casing, by undoing the casing to crankcase bolts the crankcase is separated from the gearbox casing

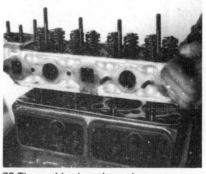

73 Thoroughly clean the engine externally before stripping it down. Take off the rocker cover, tappet chest covers, rocker gear, and pushrods and lift off the head

74 The crankshaft fan belt pulley wheel can be gently eased off after the retaining bolt has been removed

75 The crankshaft can be prevented from turning by placing a length of wood such as a hammer handle between the crankshaft and the side of the block

76 The gearwheels can be removed by judicious levering with spanners or broad screwdrivers as illustrated. Move each wheel a little in turn so as not to strain the chain

77 The next step is to thoroughly clean the block internally. Check that the oilways are clean, and remove all traces of old gaskets

78 The camshaft is inserted from the front of the block. Make sure the peaks of the cams do not damage the white metal bearings

79 A vane-type oil pump may be found on a few very early models. 1 pump body. 2 vanes and rotor. 3 cover plate. 4 securing bolts and lockwashers

80 The vanes and rotor seat in the recess in the cover. They should be fitted first to the pump body

81 Make sure a new gasket is properly positioned between the pump and the block. The slot in the rotor engages a raised lip in the end of the camshaft

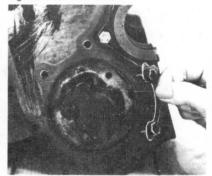

82 With the pump in place, fit the securing bolts and remember to turn up the tabs on the lockwasher

83 The pump is now securely fitted and the next step is to carefully examine the reciprocating components

84 Carefully examine the rings for wear. In this instance replacement of the complete piston is essential as the top ring has completely broken up

85 Measure the wear in the cylinder bore with a micrometer. Your local engineering works will be able to do this for you

86 If the bores are badly worn they must be rebored

87 A few very early models made use of a clamped little end. Make sure the cutout in the gudgeon pin lines up with the little end bolt. Circlips are used in 95% of models

88 When tightening the little end pinch bolt (where fitted) prevent the piston from turning by inserting a metal rod into the hollow bore of the gudgeon pin

89 In this illustration the rods are correctly fitted to the pistons with the offsets the right way round

90 This timing chain is badly worn. Note how it deflects inwards when pressed. If in good condition it should deflect not more than approx. ¼ in.

91 Examine the shell bearings for wear. This one is in dreadful condition. The surface is worn and has actually started to break up

92 If a bearing begins to disintegrate it will soon mark the crankshaft. The ridges on the journals can be easily seen and also felt with a fingernail

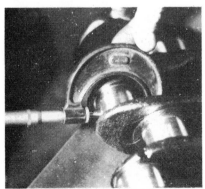

93 Check the diameter of the crankshaft journals with a micrometer. If the journals are oval the crank must be reground

94 Another item to check is the flywheel starter ring. The teeth may be badly worn in one or two places. If so the ring must be removed and a new one fitted

95 If the block is to be rebored and the crankshaft reground it is a false economy not to renew the front timing chain cover oil seal as well

96 The next step is to fit the distributor drive. This can be inserted and removed by hand providing the sump is off

97 The lower end of the drive fits into a recess in the block and the skew gear meshes with a similar gear on the camshaft

98 The drive head should initially be in this position to allow for rotation when fitted. **The larger segment should be at the top.**

99 With the drive fully home the slots should be in the 'twenty to two' position. **The larger segment should be at the top**

100 Next the distributor drive retaining plate is placed in position with the recessed hole lining up with the threaded hole in the flange on the block

101 Screw in the retaining bolt and lock washer to secure the plate

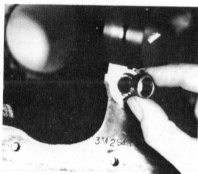

102 Before fitting the main bearings and crankshaft make sure the bearing cap locating dowels are in place

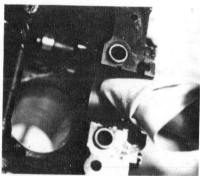

103 Thoroughly clean the bearing housings and the oilways in the block

104 The shell bearing on the left is worn and scored. Compare it with the condition of the new bearing on the right! Renew the bearing if worn

105 The next step is to fit the main bearing so that the lip on each shell engages with the machined slot in each bearing housing

106 With the new shells fitted to the block, lubricate them generously with engine oil. An old plastic detergent bottle makes a handy oil can

107 Next place a thrust washer, grooves facing outwards, on either side of the centre main bearing housing. Hold the washer to the block by a dab of oil

108 Check that everything is scrupulously clean. Lubricate the main journals with engine oil before fitting the crankshaft to the crankcase

109 With the crankshaft in place the next job is to fit the main bearing caps

110 The three main bearing caps are each different. The one on the right is fitted at the front, and the other two at the middle and rear, respectively

111 Thoroughly clean the main bearing cap and fit the shell bearing so the notch lies in the groove in the cap

112 With the shell bearing in place in the centre main bearing cap, fit the lower halves of the thrust washer, grooves facing outwards

113 With the main bearing caps fitted check the crankshaft endfloat between the thrust washers and the crank with a feeler gauge. 0.003 in. (0.075 mm) endfloat is correct

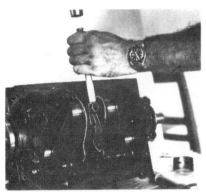

114 With all six main bearing bolts tightened down to the specified torque, lock the bolts by knocking up the locking tabs

115 If the original crankshaft is being fitted check the washers are in place on the crankshaft nose. They ensure the gearwheels lie in the same plane

116 The next step is to thoroughly clean the face of the block and fit a new front end plate gasket

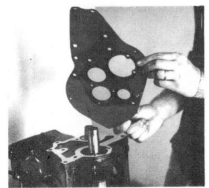

117 The front end plate must be carefully cleaned and then fitted to the block. Hold it in place with several bolts screwed in finger tight

118 With the front end plate in place the camshaft retaining plate can be fitted

119 Fit the locking tab to the end plate as shown, and fit the two bolts. Turn up the tabs on the locking plate

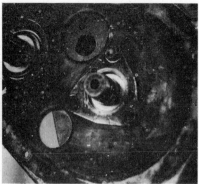

120 Fit and tighten down the three camshaft retaining plate bolts. Remember to fit spring washers

121 When refitting the chain round the gear wheels and to the engine, the two 'dots' must be adjacent to each other on an imaginary line passing through each wheel centre

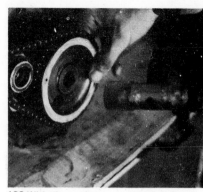

122 With the engine on its side, set the crankshaft and camshaft so the Woodruff keys are at 2 o'clock and 4 o'clock respectively

123 Next, place the camshaft locking washer with its tag in the gearwheel keyway. Then fit the securing nut

124 Tighten the camshaft gearwheel nut, holding the crankshaft stationary with a spanner as shown. Make sure plenty of rag is placed between the spanner and the crankshaft

125 The gearwheels and timing chain are now in place and correctly positioned

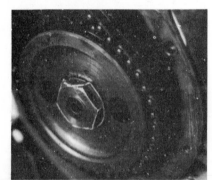

126 Next bend back the camshaft locking washer to lock the camshaft gearwheel nut in place

127 The flange on the timing gear case must be carefully cleaned and scraped and a new gasket laid on the front endplate

128 Place the oil thrower, concave side down, on the nose of the crankshaft. Remember to position the thrower so it fits over the crankshaft key

129 Replace the timing chain cover over the chain and gearwheels. Fit the retaining bolts and washers and tighten securely. Smear the edge of the oil seal with oil

130 Next fit the crankshaft pulley wheel. Note that the wheel will only go on in one position with the crankshaft key entering the pulley groove

131 Although correctly lined up, when a new oil seal has been fitted it is sometimes necessary to drive the wheel into place as shown

132 With the crankshaft pulley wheel in place fit the lockwasher so the tab locks into the pulley wheel groove

133 Next screw in the pulley wheel bolt. This is the largest bolt on the engine and it may be necessary to borrow a 1 ¼ in. A.F. socket

134 Hold the crankshaft from turning by inserting a square section bar or similar in the slot at the flywheel end. Then tighten the bolt to a torque of 70 lb f ft (9.68 kg/fm)

135 When the bolt is correctly tightened knock up the lockwasher against one of the flats on the bolt

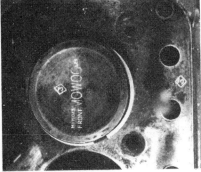

136 Each piston is clearly marked "FRONT". Fit it this way round. The '3' in the diamond stamped on the block and piston crown indicates the grade of piston fitted

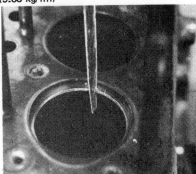

137 Measure each piston ring gap in turn, with a feeler gauge, with the rings fitted in the bore. The gap should be 0.007 to 0.012 in. (0.177 to 0.305 mm)

138 Cylinder head studs can be removed and replaced by locking together on a stud two cylinder head nuts and then turning the stud out (or in)

139 When compressing the piston rings there is no need to use an expensive piston ring compressor. A jubilee clip is just as good

140 When all the pistons have been returned to the same bores from which they were removed, the connecting rods can be attached to the crankshaft

141 The connecting rod big end cap must be perfectly clean. The bearing shell can then be fitted with its lip locating in the groove in the rod

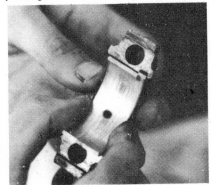

142 Fit the big end cap bearing shell in the same way and make sure you replace the big end cap to the same connecting rod from which it was removed

143 The next step is to tighten the big end bolts to a torque of 35 lb f ft (4.8 kg fm) and then knock up the tab on the locking washer

144 On later models there is no oil hole for primary gear lubrication. This is because on early models clutch slip frequently developed due to oil leakage

145 It is well worthwhile fitting the later self lubricating primary gear to early models. A special conversion kit exists. Block the oil hole with the pin supplied

146 Drive the pin down flush with the top of the crankshaft. If necessary file any projection off the pin

147 The oil seal MUST be removed from the centre of the flywheel. If the old seal is not removed the new gear (on right) will not fit

148 The next step is to fit the valves and valve springs to the cylinder head. Start by fitting the valve guide shroud in place

149 Next fit each valve, oil seal and valve spring. Compress the spring with a compressor and make sure the head of the compressor does not slip

150 Now fit the split collets. A trace of grease will help hold them to the valve stem recess. This job calls for care as the items are small and easily dropped

151 Slacken off the spring compressor until the collets are firmly held by the valve spring cup. Fit a circlip to the collets to make sure they stay together

152 This is what the completed built-up valve and valve spring assembly should look like

153 The next step is to thoroughly clean the face of the block and cylinder head. Fit a new cylinder head gasket with the side marked 'top' upwards

154 The cylinder head can now be fitted. Keep the head and block parallel to each other so the head does not bind on the cylinder head studs

155 Make sure the oil holes in the tappets are clear, and replace them through the tappet chest apertures

156 Next fit the push rods with the mushroom shaped end fed into the block first. Make sure the push rods seat properly in the tappets

157 Next reassemble the rocker gear on the rocker shaft and fit to the cylinder head. Make sure that the oil holes are clear in the rocker shaft

158 Make sure that the rocker pedestal locking plate is fitted before replacing the rocker pedestal and cylinder head nuts

159 The cylinder head and rocker bracket washers and nuts are now fitted. Tighten the cylinder head nuts to a torque of 40 lb f ft (5.5 kg fm) in the order shown in Fig. 1.14

160 The next step is to set the valve clearance to 0.015 in. (0.381 mm). Unlock the nut and screw the tappet adjusting screw up or down until the arm just nips the blade

161 Clean the thermostat housing flange and then fit a new gasket in place

162 Then fit the thermostat and thermostat cover and replace the spring washer and do up the three nuts

163 The oil pressure relief valve fits into the threaded hole on the right-hand side of the engine at the rear

164 The next step is to clean the tappet chest flanges and refit the tappet chest covers using a new cork gasket. Tighten the bolts to 2 lb f ft (0.3 kg fm)

165 Make sure the hole at the rear of the cylinder head is covered by the heater take off (or flat plate) and remember to fit a new gasket

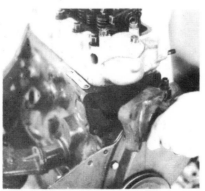

166 Now fit the water pump to the front of the engine, Make sure the mating surfaces are clean and that a new gasket is fitted

167 Fit the by-pass hose at the same time as the pump is fitted. It is very difficult to fit the hose after the pump is in place

end of the drive meshes with the skew gear on the camshaft the drive will turn anti-clockwise. When it is fully home, the upper part of the slot should be in the 'two o'clock' position, as shown in the inset B (Fig. 1.33).

5   Remove the tappet cover bolt from the drive shaft.

6   Replace the distributor housing and lock it in position with the single bolt and lockwasher.

7   The distributor can now be replaced and the two securing bolts and spring washers which hold the distributor clamping plate to the distributor housing, tightened. If the clamp bolt on the clamping plate was not previously loosened and the distributor body was not turned in the clamping plate, then the ignition timing will be as previously. If the clamping bolt has been loosened, then it will be necessary to re-time the ignition as shown in Chapter 4.

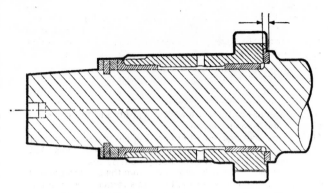

Fig. 1.34. Converter output gear. Measure gap indicated and fit appropriate thrust washer

64 Engine fitment to transmission casing and torque converter replacement - (automatic transmission)

1   Before refitting the engine to the transmission unit certain parts must be checked for wear. First make sure that the oil rings fitted to the main oil pipe, oil filter, transmission to engine oil feed pipes and the main oil strainer pipe are in perfect condition. Ideally new oil rings should always be fitted.

2   Ensure that all joint faces are free from burrs and any old jointing compound. A new set of gaskets must be used during reassembly.

3   Carefully inspect the idler gear bearings and if worn they must be renewed. A special tool is usually required to draw out the old bearings from the casings so take the relevant parts to the local BLMC garage for them to do the work or carefully dismantle the old bearings using a very sharp chisel.

4   Inspect the input gear bearing and renew if necessary by removing the circlip and drifting the bearing from the housing.

5   Check the main oil seals and renew if necessary. To renew the converter output gear oil seal it is necessary to remove the rear case assembly. Lubricate the new seal well before refitting.

6   To refit the engine to the transmission unit first immerse the front main bearing cap moulded rubber oil seal in oil and refit with the lip facing the rear of the engine.

7   Fit the rubber sealing ring onto the main oil strainer pipe and fit new gaskets to the transmission casing.

8   Carefully lower the engine onto the transmission unit ensuring that the moulded rubber seal is correctly located. Tighten the securing set screws, nuts and washers in a progressive manner as the engine is being finally positioned on the transmission unit.

9   Refit the transmission to engine oil feed pipe, with the spring beneath the rubber seal and refit the oil filter assembly.

10 Refit the main oil pump to transmission unit oil pipe.

11 Using a sharp knife trim off any excess transmission joint from the rear of the unit.

12 Clean the surfaces and fit a new converter housing gasket.

13 Refit the converter output gear. There must be a running clearance of 0.0035 - 0.0065 in. (0.089 - 0.165 mm) between the inner thrust washer and converter output gear. (Fig. 1.34). Should the clearance be outside these limits, select and fit the appropriate washer with the chamfered inner edge of the washer to free the crankshaft. Thrust washers are available in the following sizes:

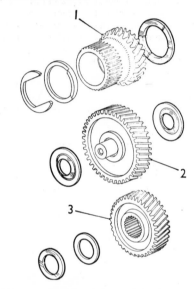

Fig. 1.35. Converter output (1) idler (2) and input gear (3) with their respective thrust washers (early type)

> 0.112 - 0.114 in. (2.848 - 2.898 mm)
> 0.114 - 0.116 in. (2.898 - 2.949 mm)
> 0.116 - 0.118 in. (2.949 - 3.0 mm)
> 0.118 - 0.120 in. (3.0 - 3.051 mm)

14 **Important:** Two types of input gears have been used. Those fitted to earlier units have two thrust washers whereas the later gears (which have an increased hub thickness) have a number of thin shims fitted to the outer hub face of the gear for adjustment.

15 It is necessary to adjust the idler gear and input gear but for this special tools are required. These cannot be made at home as

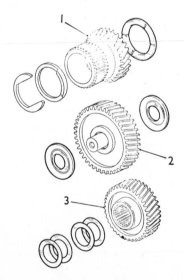

Fig. 1.36. Converter output (1) idler (2) and input gear (3) with their respective thrust washers and shims (later type)

they are setting gauges which are accurately set during manu-
-facture. From the authors experience if the original thrust
washers/shims are used then in the majority of cases this will be
sufficient. However, for the perfectionist the author
recommends that this subject be discussed with the local BLMC
garage.

16 With the gears in position, refit and align the converter outlet
pipe.

17 Fit a new converter housing joint washer and refit the
converter housing. Tighten the securing nuts and set screws in a
diagonal and progressive manner.

18 Refit the input gear shaft nut and tighten to a torque wrench
setting of 70 lb f ft (9.6 kg fm). For this, service tools "18G
1088" and "18G 592" (large socket) should be used.

19 Remove each pair of bolts in turn from the converter and fit
new locking plates. Tighten the bolts to a torque wrench setting
of 22 - 24 lb f ft (3.0 - 3.3 kg fm). **Do not** remove all six screws
from the converter at any one time.

20 Lubricate the converter oil seal well and refit the converter.
Refit the washer (offset pegs) and the centre bolt with its lockwasher. Tighten the bolt to a torque wrench setting of 110 - 115
lb f ft (15.2 - 15.9 kg fm). Secure by bending up the lockwasher.

21 Refit the low pressure valve and gasket.

22 Refit the gear selector bellcrank lever, clevis pin and rubber
boot.

23 The converter cones, starter motor and rear engine mounting
may now be refitted.

24 The complete power unit may now be refitted to the car. For
further information see Section 68.

65 Engine - final assembly

The rocker cover can now be fitted, using a new cork gasket.
Fit the two tappet cover plates, using new gaskets, and tighten
the tappet chest bolts to a torque of 2 lb f ft (0.3 kg fm). Do not
exceed this figure or the covers will distort and leak oil. Reconnect the ancilliary components to the engine in the reverse
order to which they were removed.

It should be noted that in all cases it is best to reassemble the
engine as far as possible before refitting it to the car. This means
that the inlet and exhaust manifolds, carburettor, dynamo, water
thermostat, oil filter, distributor and engine mounting brackets,
should all be in position. Ensure that the oil filter is filled with
engine oil, as otherwise there will be a delay in the oil reaching
the bearings while the oil filter refills.

66 Engine - replacement (manual transmission)

Although the engine can be replaced by one man using a
suitable winch, it is easier if two are present: one to lower the
engine into the engine compartment and the other to guide the
engine into position and to ensure it does not foul anything.
Generally speaking, engine replacement is a reversal of the
procedures used when removing the engine. The sequence is not
quite the same however, and the following will be found the
easiest and quickest order to follow:

1 Refit the radiator, and radiator hoses. Always use new hoses
if the old hoses show any signs of internal or external cracking or
general deterioration. The bottom hose is especially susceptible
because of the heater take-off portion which tends to crack and
leak first.

2 Connect lifting tackle to the lifting hooks or place suitable
slings round each end of the transmission casing.

3 Raise the engine and if using a fixed hoist, roll the car under
it. Jack up the front of the car securely so it can be worked on
from underneath. Lower the engine/transmission unit into the
engine compartment. Stop halfway in and reconnect the speedometer cable to the transmission casing.

4 Keep the sliding joints pushed well back on the drive shafts
and ensure that nothing is fouling as the engine is lowered into
place. Take particular care to make sure that the radiator matrix

is not damaged during this operation.

5 To line up the mounting bracket holes it may be necessary to
move the engine about slightly and this will be found much
easier to do if the slings are still in position and taking most of
the weight. Replace the nuts, bolts, and spring washers
engine mounting brackets and tighten them finger tight. To
avoid vibration it is most important to position the mountings
correctly as described below.

6 Refit the exhaust manifold to the exhaust pipe, replace the
clamp and secure the joint loosely with the two clamp bolts. It is
essential to fit the exhaust properly as otherwise the exhaust
downpipe may fracture, or the mounting lug may break away
from the pipe due to the rocking motion of the engine on its
mountings.

7 Check that the engine tie-bar bush is in good condition and
attach the bar to the engine. It may be necessary to move the
engine slightly so that the hole in the tie-rod lines up with the
engine attachment hole. Under no circumstances should the
engine mountings be tightened before the tie-rod holes are
aligned. Insert and do up the tie-rod bolt.

8 Remove the sling from the engine and let the full weight of
the power unit onto the engine mounting brackets. The nuts and
bolts may now be tightened down securely.

9 Check the gap between the exhaust pipe mounting clip and
the fixing point on the gearbox extension. Fill the gap with
washers and insert and tighten loosely the securing nut and bolt.
On early models the hole in the extension was threaded and a set
bolt used to secure the pipe. It is best to drill out this hole (use
an 8 mm. drill), and replace the set bolt with 5/16 in UNF nut,
bolt and spring washer.

10 Do up the manifold clamp securing bolts tightly, followed by
the gearbox extension to exhaust pipe clip bolt, and the tail pipe
support clips.

11 Replace the horn and the starter motor solenoid switch
where this is mounted on the flywheel housing.

12 Pull the sliding joints into contact with the flexible coupling,
and insert the two 'U' bolts. **Note:** The sides of the 'U' bolts
tend to spread apart when removed from the couplings. Nip them
gently in a vice, taking care not to damage the threads before
refitment. This will ease their replacement considerably. Tighten
up the 'U' bolt securing nuts. See Chapter 7 for later models.

13 Refit the clutch slave cylinder to the flywheel housing, and
reconnect the earth lead.

14 On models fitted with a tachometer, refit the tachometer
drive.

15 Refit the carburettor to the inlet manifold.

16 Reconnect the fuel inlet pipe to the carburettor/s.

17 Refit the distributor cap and reconnect the high tension leads
to the appropriate spark plugs.

18 Reconnect the high tension lead from the centre of the distributor cap to the coil and the low tension lead from the
terminal 'C' on the coil to the terminal on the side of the distributor.

19 Reconnect the leads to the dynamo. The different sized
terminals ensure that no mistake can be made. Also reconnect
the starter motor cable to the starter motor.

20 Reconnect the accelerator and choke cables and replace the
air cleaner/s on the carburettor/s.

21 Reconnect the oil pressure sender unit, or the oil pressure
gauge pipe line to the threaded take off point at the right-hand
near side of the engine.

22 If the small bypass hose between the cylinder head and the
water pump was not replaced when the head was refitted then
this must be done now. This can sometimes be a difficult
operation but should be carried out fairly easily if the small
'Jubilee' clips are slipped over each end of the tube which is then
squeezed in a vice, and is quickly fitted before the hose has time
to expand to its normal length again.

23 Refit the blower motor and heater hose where this is under
the bonnet. Always use new hoses if the old hoses show signs of
internal or external cracking or flaking.
Reconnect the distributor vacuum advance.

24 Reconnect the water temperature gauge sender unit where a

water temperature gauge is fitted.

25 Reconnect the distributor vacuum advance pipe and refit the front grille if previously removed.

26 Replace the gearlever in the gearbox extension and refit the rubber boot at the base of the gearlever.

27 Replace the windscreen washer bottle and carrier if previously removed.

28 Replace the bonnet (easier with two people).

29 Reconnect the battery.

30 Check that the drain taps are closed or the plugs refitted and refill the cooling system with water and the engine with the correct grade of oil.

67 Engine - replacement with subframe (manual transmission)

The procedure for replacing the engine and subframe together as a unit is very similar to replacing the engine as described in the previous section.

Generally, replacement is a reversal of the removal sequence, but as an aid to rapid refitment, the following notes are made:

1 Either wheel the subframe into position under the body, or wheel the body over the subframe as preferred and depending on whether a hoist is available from which to suspend the front of the bodyshell.

2 When replacing the subframe in the body take great care not to get the brake pipes, battery cables, or main electrical leads, nipped between the body and the subframe.

3 Replace the nuts and bolts securing the subframe to the bodyshell but do **not** tighten them right down until they are all in position. This ensures that the subframe is properly aligned with the bodyshell.

4 Reconnect the steering tie-rods to the steering arms and tighten balljoint nuts to a torque wrench setting of 25 lb f ft (3.4 kg fm).

5 Reconnect the shock absorbers to the suspension.

6 To help ensure lack of engine vibration and to help prevent the exhaust downpipe fracturing or the clip breaking, it is wisest to fit the tie-rod before securing the exhaust system, and to loosen the engine mounting bolts to move the engine slightly if the alignment between the tie bar hole and the engine mounting hole is not perfect. This is described in detail in paragraphs 6 and 7 of the previous section.

7 After the hydraulic brake pipe to the front brakes is connected up it will be necessary to bleed the braking system.

68 Engine and automatic transmission - replacement

1 Refitting the complete power unit is the reverse sequence to removal. For any additional information which is similar to that for the manual transmission application refer to Section 66. The following information should be borne in mind, being applicable to the automatic transmission unit.

2 Lower the power unit in the engine compartment to a position where the driveshafts can engage the driving flange studs. Screw on the securing nuts by approximately four threads.

3 It will be necessary to check and, if necessary, adjust the gear selector rod and cable. Full information will be found in Chapter 6.

69 Engine - initial start up after overhaul or major repair.

1 Make sure that the battery is fully charged and that the oil, water and fuel are replenished.

2 If the fuel system has been dismantled it will require several revolutions of the engine on the starter motor to get the petrol up to the carburetttor. An initial prime by pouring a small amount of petrol into the carburettor orifice will help the engine to fire quickly thus relieving the load on the battery.

3 As soon as the engine fires and runs, keep it going at a fast tickover only (not faster) and bring it up to normal working temperature.

4 As the engine warms up there will be odd smells and some smoke from parts getting hot and burning off oil deposits. The signs to look for are leaks of oil or water which will be obvious, if serious. Check also the clamp connections of the exhaust pipes to the manifolds as these do not always 'find' their exact gas tight position until the warmth and vibration have acted on them and it is almost certain that they will need tightening further. This should be done, of course, with the engine stopped.

5 When normal running temperature has been reached adjust the idling speed as described in Chapter 3.

6 Stop the engine and wait a few minutes to see if any lubricant or coolant is dripping out when the engine is stationary.

7 Road test the car to check that the timing is correct and giving the necessary smoothness and power. Do not race the engine - when new bearings and/or pistons and rings have been fittted it should be treated as a new engine and run in at reduced revolutions for the first 500 miles.

70 Fault diagnosis - engine

Symptom	Reason/s	Remedy
Engine fails to turn over when starter operated	Discharged or defective battery	Charge or replace battery. Push-start car.
	Loose battery leads	Tighten both terminals and earth ends of earth lead.
	Defective starter solenoid or switch or broken wiring	Run a wire direct from the battery to the starter motor or by-pass the solenoid.
	Engine earth strap disconnected	Check and retighten strap.
	Jammed starter motor drive pinion	Place car in gear and rock from side to side. Alternatively, free exposed square end of shaft with spanner.
	Defective starter motor	Remove and recondition.
Engine turns over, but will not start	Ignition system damp or wet	Wipe dry the distributor cap and ignition leads.
	Ignition leads to spark plugs loose	Check and tighten at both spark plug and distributor cap ends.
	Shorted or disconnected low tension leads	Check the wiring on the CB and SW terminals of the coil and to the distributor.
	Dirty, incorrectly set, or pitted contact breaker points.	Clean, file smooth, and adjust.
	Faulty condenser	Check contact breaker points for arcing, remove and fit new.

	Defective ignition switch	By-pass switch with wire.
	Ignition leads connected wrong way round	Remove and replace leads to spark plugs in correct order.
	Faulty coil	Remove and fit new coil.
	Contact breaker point spring earthed or broken	Check spring is not touching metal part of distributor. Check insulator washers are correctly placed. Renew points if the spring is broken.
	No petrol in petrol tank	Refill tank!
	Vapour lock in fuel line (In hot conditions or at high altitude)	Blow into petrol tank, allow engine to cool, or apply a cold wet rag to the fuel line.
	Blocked float chamber needle valve	Remove, clean, and replace.
	Fuel pump filter blocked	Remove, clean, and replace.
	Choked or blocked carburettor jets	Dismantle and clean.
	Faulty fuel pump	Remove, overhaul, and replace.
	Too much choke allowing too rich a mixture to wet plugs	Remove and dry spark plugs or with wide open throttle, push-start the car.
	Float damaged or leaking or needle not seating	Remove, examine, clean and replace float and needle valve as necessary.
	Float lever incorrectly adjusted	Remove and adjust correctly.
Engine stalls and will not re-start	Ignition failure - sudden	Check over low and high tension circuits for breaks in wiring.
	Ignition failure - misfiring precludes total stoppage	Check contact breaker points, clean and adjust. Renew condenser if faulty.
	Ignition failure - In severe rain or after traversing water splash	Dry out ignition leads and distributor cap.
	No petrol in petrol tank	Refill tank.
	Petrol tank breather choked	Remove petrol cap and clean out breather hole.
	Sudden obstruction in carburettor(s)	Check jet, filter, and needle valve in float chamber for blockage.
	Water in fuel system	Drain tank and blow out fuel lines.
	Ignition leads loose	Check and tighten as necessary at spark plug and distributor cap ends.
	Battery leads loose on terminals	Check and tighten terminal leads.
	Battery earth strap loose on body attachment point	Check and tighten earth lead to body attachment point.
Engine misfires or idles unevenly	Engine earth lead loose	Tighten lead.
	Low tension leads to SW and CB terminals on coil loose	Check and tighten leads if found loose.
	Low tension lead from CB terminal side to distributor loose	Check and tighten if found loose.
	Dirty, or incorrectly gapped plugs	Remove, clean, and regap.
	Dirty, incorrectly set, or pitted contact breaker points	Clean, file smooth, and adjust.
	Tracking across inside of distributor cover	Remove and fit new cover.
	Ignition too retarded	Check and adjust ignition timing.
	Faulty coil	Remove and fit new coil.
	Mixture too weak	Check jets, float chamber needle valve, and filters for obstruction. Clean as necessary. Carburettor incorrectly adjusted.
	Air leak in carburettor	Remove and overhaul carburettor.
	Air leak at inlet manifold to cylinder head, or inlet manifold to carburettor	Test by pouring oil along joints. Bubbles indicate leak. Renew manifold gasket as appropriate.
	Incorrect valve clearances	Adjust to take up wear.
	Burnt out exhaust valves	Remove cylinder head and renew defective valves.
	Sticking or leaking valves	Remove cylinder head, clean, check and renew valves as necessary.
	Weak or broken valve springs	Check and renew as necessary.
	Worn valve guides or stems	Renew valve guides and valves.
	Worn pistons and piston rings	Dismantle engine, renew pistons and rings.
Lack of power and poor compression	Burnt out exhaust valves	Remove cylinder head, renew defective valves.
	Sticking or leaking valves	Remove cylinder head, clean, check, and renew valves as necessary.

	Worn valve guides and stems	Remove cylinder head and renew valves and valve guides.
	Weak or broken valve springs	Remove cylinder head, renew defective springs.
	Blown cylinder head gasket (Accompanied by increase in noise)	Remove cylinder head and fit new gasket.
	Worn pistons and piston rings	Dismantle engine, renew pistons and rings.
	Worn or scored cylinder bores	Dismantle engine, rebore, renew pistons and rings.
	Ignition timing wrongly set. Too advanced or retarded.	Check and reset ignition timing.
	Contact breaker points incorrectly gapped	Check and reset contact breaker points.
	Incorrect valve clearances	Check and adjust.
	Incorrectly set spark plugs	Remove, clean and regap.
	Carburation too rich or too weak	Tune carburettor for optimum performance.
	Dirty contact breaker points	Remove, clean, and replace.
	Fuel filters blocked causing top end fuel starvation	Dismantle, inspect, clean, and replace all fuel filters.
	Distributor automatic balance weights or vacuum advance and retard mechanisms not functioning correctly	Overhaul distributor.
	Faulty fuel pump giving top end fuel starvation	Remove, overhaul, or fit exchange reconditioned fuel pump.
Excessive oil consumption	Badly worn perished or missing valve stem oil seals.	Remove, fit new oil seals to valve stems.
	Excessively worn valve stems and valve guides	Remove cylinder head and fit new valves and valve guides.
	Worn piston rings	Fit oil control rings to existing pistons or purchase new pistons.
	Worn pistons and cylinder bores	Fit new pistons and rings, rebore cylinders.
	Excessive piston ring gap allowing blow-up	Fit new piston rings and set gap correctly.
	Piston oil return holes choked	Decarbonise engine and pistons.
	Leaking oil filter gasket	Inspect and fit new gasket as necessary.
	Leaking tappet cover gasket	Inspect and fit new gasket as necessary.
	Leaking tappet chest gasket	Inspect and fit new gasket as necessary.
	Leaking timing case gasket	Inspect and fit new gasket as necessary.
	Leaking sump gasket	Inspect and fit new gasket as necessary.
	Loose sump plug	Tighten, fit new gasket if necessary.
Unusual noises from engine	Worn valve gear (Noisy tapping from top cover)	Inspect and renew parts as necessary.
	Worn big end bearing (Regular heavy knocking)	Drop sump, if bearings broken up, clean out oil pump and oilways, fit new bearings. If bearings not broken but worn fit bearing shells.
	Worn chain and gear (Rattling from front of engine)	Remove timing cover, fit new timing wheels and timing chain.
	Worn main bearings (Rumbling and vibration)	Remove crankshaft, if bearings worn but not broken up, renew. If broken up strip oil pump and clean out oilways.
	Worn crankshaft (Knocking, rumbling and vibration)	Regrind crankshaft, fit new main and big end bearings.

Chapter 2 Cooling system

Contents

Specifications

Type	Pump and fan with pressurised radiator
Thermostat type:	Bellows or wax type
Thermostat settings:	
Standard	82º C (180º F)
Hot climates	74º C (165º F); 77º C (170º F) for some 1275 GT models
Cold climates	88º C (188º F)
Radiator cap pressure:	
Early models only	7 lb/sq in. (0.49 kg/cm^2)
Later models	13 lb/sq in. (0.91 kg/cm^2) or 15 lb/sq in. (1.05 kg/cm^2)
Fan belt tension	0.5 in. (12.70 mm) free movement midway between water pump and dynamo (or alternator) pulleys
Capacity (coolant):	
Less heater	5.25 pints (3 litres)
With heater	6.25 pints (3.55 litres)

Torque wrench settings:	**lb f ft**	**kg fm**
Water pump to cylinder block bolts	17	2.3

1 General description

The engine cooling water is circulated by a thermo-syphon, water pump assisted system, and the coolant is pressurised. This is both to prevent the loss of water down the overflow pipe with the radiator cap in position and to prevent premature boiling in adverse conditions. The radiator cap is pressurised to 7 lb/sq. in. (0.49 kg/cm^2) and increases the boiling point to 226ºF. On later models the pressure was increased to 13 lb sq in. (0.91 kg/cm^2) the pressure in the system forces the internal part of the cap off its seat, thus exposing the overflow pipe down which the steam from the boiling water escapes thus relieving the pressure. It is, therefore, important to check that the radiator cap is in good condition and that the spring behind the sealing washer has not weakened. Most garages have a special machine in which radiator caps can be tested.

The cooling system comprises the radiator, top and bottom water hoses, bypass hose to return water to the block when the thermostat is closed, heater hoses (if heater/demister fitted), the impeller water pump, (mounted on the front of the engine it carries the fan blades and is driven by the fan belt), the thermostat and the two drain taps or drain plugs.

The system functions in the following manner: Cold water in the bottom of the radiator circulates up the lower radiator hose to the water pump where it is pushed round the water passages in the cylinder block, helping to keep the cylinder bores and pistons cool.

The water then travels up into the cylinder head and circulates round the combustion spaces and valve seats absorbing more heat. Then, when the engine is at its proper operating temperature, the water travels out of the cylinder head, past the open thermostat into the upper radiator hose, and so into the radiator header tank. The water travels down the radiator where it is rapidly cooled by the rush of cold air through the radiator core. As the radiator is mounted in the wheel arch the fan PUSHES cold air through the radiator matrix. The water, now cool, reaches the bottom of the radiator, when the cycle is repeated.

When the engine is cold the thermostat (which is a valve which opens and closes according to the temperature of the water) maintains the circulation of the same water in the engine by returning it, via the bypass hose to the cylinder block. Only when the correct minimum operating temperature has been reached, as shown in the specification, does the thermostat begin to open, allowing water to return to the radiator.

2 Cooling system - draining

With the car on level ground drain the system as follows:

1 If the engine is cold remove the filler cap from the radiator by turning the cap anticlockwise. If the engine is hot having just been run, then turn the filler cap very slightly until the pressure in the system has had time to disperse. Use a rag over the cap to protect your hand from escaping steam. If, with the engine very hot, the cap is released suddenly the drop in pressure can result in water boiling. With the pressure released the cap can be removed.

2 If antifreeze is in the radiator drain it into a clean bowl for re-use.

3 Open the two drain taps or remove the drain plugs as applicable. When viewed from the side the radiator drain tap or plug is on the bottom right-hand side of the radiator, and the engine drain tap or plug is halfway down the rear right-hand side of the cylinder block. A short length of rubber tubing over the radiator drain tap nozzle will assist draining the coolant into a container without splashing. **Note:** On some later models a drain plug is fitted at the bottom of the radiator, rather than a drain tap.

4 When the water has finished running, probe the drain tap orifices with a short piece of wire to dislodge any particles of rust or sediment which may be blocking the taps and preventing all the water draining out.

3 Cooling system - flushing

With time the cooling system will gradually lose its efficiency as the radiator becomes choked with rust, scale deposits from the water, and other sediment. To clean the system out, remove the radiator filler cap and drain plug and leave a hose running in the filler cap neck for ten to fifteen minutes.

In very bad cases the radiator should be reverse flushed. This can be done with the radiator in position. The cylinder block-plug is refitted and a hose with a suitable tapered adaptor placed in the drain plug hole. Water under pressure is then forced through the radiator and out of the header tank filler cap neck.

It is recommended if the engine is cool, to place some polythene over the engine to stop water finding its way into the ignition system.

The hose should now be removed and placed in the radiator cap filler neck and the radiator washed out in the usual manner.

4 Cooling system - filling

1 Close the two drain taps or refit the drain plugs as applicable.

2 Fill the system slowly to ensure that no air locks develop. If a heater unit is fitted, check that the valve to the heater unit is open, otherwise an air lock may form in the heater. The best type of water to use in the cooling system is rain water, so use this whenever possible.

3 Do not fill the system higher than within 0.5 in. (12.7 mm) of the filler orifice. Overfilling will merely result in wastage which is especially to be avoided when antifreeze is in use.

4 Only use antifreeze mixture with a glycerine or ethylene glycol base.

5 Replace the filler cap and turn it firmly clockwise to lock in into position.

5 Radiator - removal, inspection and cleaning

The radiator on Mini Cooper models is removed in a slightly different manner to that on other models. The radiator on standard models is removed by different methods depending on whether a one or two piece cowling is fitted.

1 Undo and remove the two bolts and spring washers from the bonnet side of each of the two hinges. Carefully lift the bonnet off and place it to one side.

2 Drain the engine as previously described.

3 Models up to car No. "3940" had a one piece cowling, which is removed with the radiator as below:

a) Undo and remove the cowling upper support bracket, and take off the two bolts which hold the bottom of the cowling to the bracket on the engine mounting.

b) Unscrew the clip on the upper radiator hose at the thermostat housing outlet pipe, and remove the hose off the pipe.

c) The bottom water hose incorporates a bonded-in take-off tube which carries water to the heater (where fitted). Disconnect this tube and then completely remove the bottom hose by unscrewing the clips at each end.

d) Undo and remove the four bolts which hold the cowling to the radiator, and lift the radiator and cowling out.

4 The two piece cowling was fitted from car No. "3941" and is removed with the radiator as described below:

a) Undo the bolts holding the radiator support bracket to the thermostat housing.

b) Undo the clip holding the top hose to the radiator, pull off

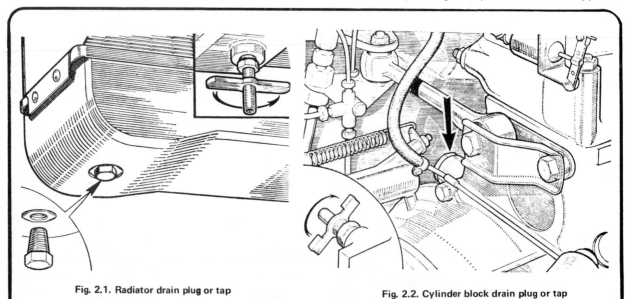

Fig. 2.1. Radiator drain plug or tap   Fig. 2.2. Cylinder block drain plug or tap

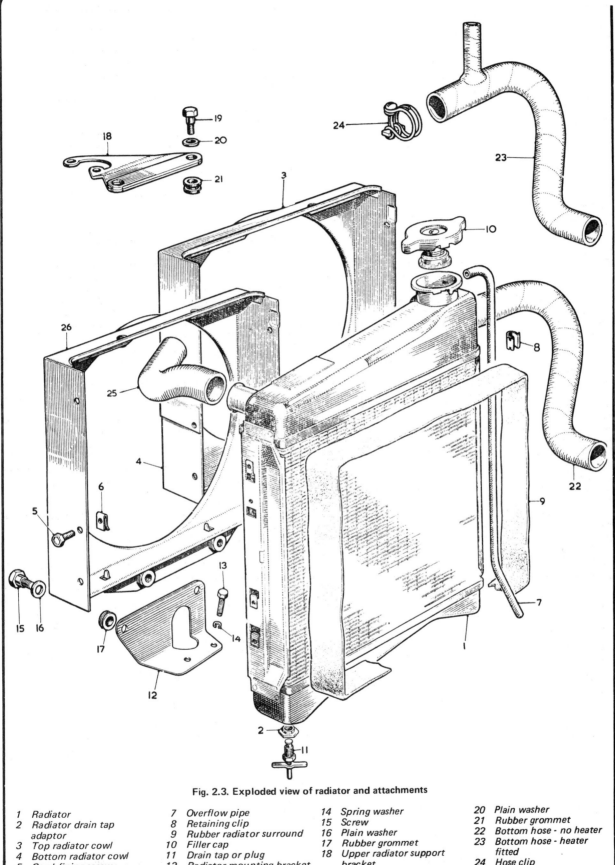

Fig. 2.3. Exploded view of radiator and attachments

1	Radiator	7	Overflow pipe	14	Spring washer	20	Plain washer
2	Radiator drain tap	8	Retaining clip	15	Screw	21	Rubber grommet
	adaptor	9	Rubber radiator surround	16	Plain washer	22	Bottom hose - no heater
3	Top radiator cowl	10	Filler cap	17	Rubber grommet	23	Bottom hose - heater
4	Bottom radiator cowl	11	Drain tap or plug	18	Upper radiator support		fitted
5	Cowl fixing screw	12	Radiator mounting bracket		bracket	24	Hose clip
6	Nut	13	Screw	19	Screw	25	Top hose

the hose, undo and remove the six bolts which hold the top half of the cowling to the radiator and remove the top half of the cowling.

c) Undo and remove the two bolts holding the cowling to the bracket on the engine mounting.

d) Undo the clip holding the lower hose to the water pump, and pull the hose outside the bottom half of the cowling. NOTE: Disconnect the heater hose from its take off to the lower hose (where fitted).

e) Lift the radiator and bottom part of the cowling out of the car.

5 The Mini Cooper radiator is removed as at '4' above, after undoing the eight crosshead screws which hold the front grille in place, and removing the grille. Before the radiator is lifted out of the car, it is also advised to remove the fan. Pull the radiator back against the wind valance, undo the four bolts and washers which hold the fan in place, and remove the fan.

6 With the radiator out of the car any leaks can be soldered up or repaired with a substance such as 'cataloy'. Clean out the inside of the radiator by flushing as detailed in the Section before last. When the radiator is out of the car it is advantageous to turn it upside down for reverse flushing. Clean the exterior of the radiator by hosing down the radiator matrix with a strong jet of water to clear away road dirt, dead flies, etc.

7 Inspect the radiator hoses for cracks, internal or external perishing, and damage caused by over-tightening of the securing clips. Replace the hoses as necessary. Examine the radiator hose securing clips and renew them if they are rusted or distorted. The drain taps should be renewed if leaking, but ensure the leak is not because of a faulty washer behind the tap. If the tap is suspected try a new washer to see if this clears the trouble first.

6 Radiator - replacement

To replace the radiator proceed as follows:

1 Fit the radiator bottom hose to the bottom pipe (except on cars before No. "3941") but do not tighten the clip completely.

2 Fit the top hose in position on the thermostat outlet pipe. Do not tighten completely.

3 Replace the radiator and bottom cowling. (Complete cowling in the case of cars before No. "3941". Replace the fan on Mini Cooper models).

4 Fit the lower hose to the input side of the water pump (fit the lower hose to the radiator outlet pipe as well on pre- "3941" models), fit and do-up the engine mounting to radiator support bracket, and tighten the lower hose clips.

5 Reconnect the heater hose to its take off on the bottom hose (where applicable).

6 Replace the top half of the radiator cowling and do-up the securing bolts.

7 Refit the top radiator support bracket to the thermostat housing.

8 Fit the top hose in position on the top radiator pipe and tighten the clips at each end of the hose.

9 Replace the bonnet.

10 In the case of Mini Cooper models refit the radiator grille.

11 Fill the system with water. Start the engine to pressurise the system, and check for leaks.

7 Thermostat - removal, testing and replacement

1 Partially drain the cooling system (usually 4 pints (2.27 litres) is enough), loosen the upper radiator hose at the thermostat elbow and ease the hose from the elbow.

2 Unscrew the three bolts and spring washers securing the thermostat housing and the two bolts and spring washers from the radiator cowling.

3 Lift away the radiator support bracket and also the advance and retard pipe clip.

4 Lift away the thermostat housing and recover the paper gasket.

5 The thermostat may now be withdrawn from the cylinder head.

6 Test the thermostat for correct functioning by suspending it on a string in a saucepan of cold water together with a thermometer. Heat the water and note the temperature at which the thermostat begins to open. This should be 82° C (180° F) - standard setting. It is advantageous in winter to fit a thermostat that does not open too early. Continue heating the water until the thermostat is fully open. Then let it cool down naturally.

7 If the thermostat does not fully open in boiling water, or does not close down as the water cools, then it must be discarded and a new one fitted. Should the thermostat be stuck open when cold this will be apparent when removing it from the housing.

8 Refitting the thermostat is the reverse sequence to removal. Always ensure that the thermostat housing and cylinder head mating faces are clean and flat. If the housing is badly corroded and eaten away, fit a new housing. Always use a new paper joint.

9 If a new winter thermostat is fitted, provided the summer one is still functioning correctly, it can be placed on one side and refitted in the spring. Thermostats should last for two to three years, at least, before renewal.

8 Water pump - removal and replacement

1 Refer to Section 2 and drain the cooling system.

2 Remove the top radiator support bracket by undoing the bolts securing it to the radiator and thermostat housing. Remove the top half of the cowling.

3 Either remove the top and bottom radiator hoses and remove the radiator and cowling completely as previously described (Section 5) or just remove the two bolts which hold the bottom of the radiator and cowling to the support bracket and pull the radiator back against the wing valance to give clearance.

4 Loosen the dynamo or alternator securing bolts and remove the fan belt. **Note:** On later, post August 1961, engines fitted with sixteen blade fans it is recommended that the four bolts holding the fan to the pulley are undone and the fan and pulley removed. The easiest way to remove these bolts is to hold the head of a bolt with a spanner, and then to rotate the fan clockwise.

5 Undo the clips on the by-pass hose and the clip holding the lower radiator hose to the water pump inlet pipe.

6 Unscrew the four bolts which hold the pump to the front of the cylinder block and lift the water pump away.

7 Recover the water pump gasket.

8 Refitting the water pump is the reverse sequence to removal but the following additional points should be noted:

a) Regrease the bearing by pushing a small amount of grease into the greaser and then screwing in the greasing screw. Under no circumstances should grease be applied under pressure as it could ruin the efficiency of the oil seal.

b) The bypass hose should always be replaced at the same time as the pump. It is very difficult to replace the hose after the pump is in position. It can, however, be done, and the trick here is to slip the securing clip over each end of the tube, compress the tube in a vice, and then quickly fit the hose before it has time to expand to its normal length again.

c) The fan belt tension must be correct when all is reassembled. If the belt is too tight undue strain will be placed on the water pump and dynamo bearings, and if the belt is too loose it will slip and wear rapidly as well as giving rise to low electrical output from the dynamo.

9 Water pump - dismantling and overhaul

If the water pump starts to leak (make certain it is not the bypass hose) the pump can be dismantled and rebuilt, or an exchange reconditioned pump fitted. To dismantle the pump proceed as follows:

1 Undo and remove the four bolts and spring washers which

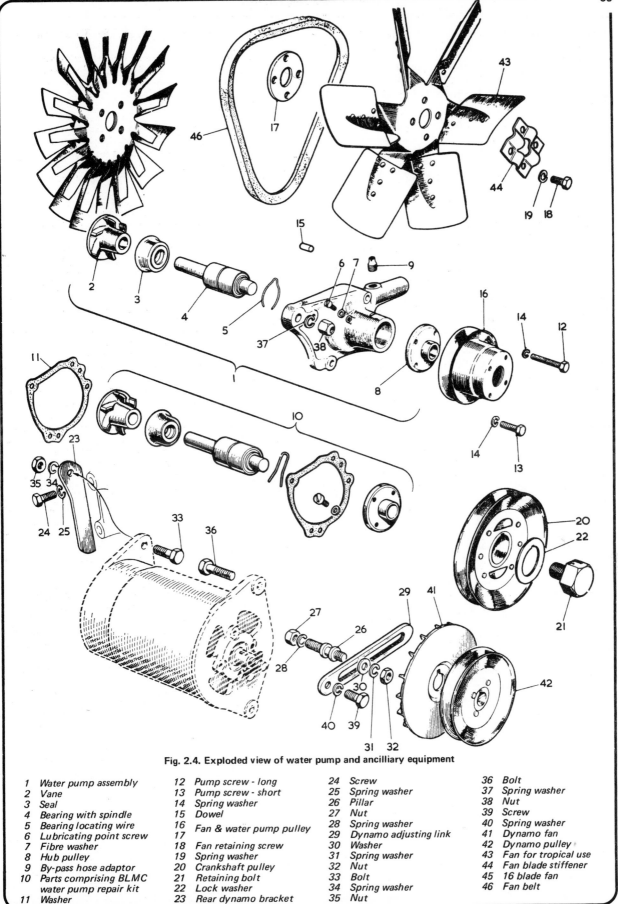

Fig. 2.4. Exploded view of water pump and ancilliary equipment

1	Water pump assembly	12	Pump screw - long	24	Screw	36	Bolt
2	Vane	13	Pump screw - short	25	Spring washer	37	Spring washer
3	Seal	14	Spring washer	26	Pillar	38	Nut
4	Bearing with spindle	15	Dowel	27	Nut	39	Screw
5	Bearing locating wire	16	Fan & water pump pulley	28	Spring washer	40	Spring washer
6	Lubricating point screw	17		29	Dynamo adjusting link	41	Dynamo fan
7	Fibre washer	18	Fan retaining screw	30	Washer	42	Dynamo pulley
8	Hub pulley	19	Spring washer	31	Spring washer	43	Fan for tropical use
9	By-pass hose adaptor	20	Crankshaft pulley	32	Nut	44	Fan blade stiffener
10	Parts comprising BLMC	21	Retaining bolt	33	Bolt	45	16 blade fan
	water pump repair kit	22	Lock washer	34	Spring washer	46	Fan belt
11	Washer	23	Rear dynamo bracket	35	Nut		

hold the fan blades and fan pulley in place. With these removed, pull or tap off the hub from the end of the spindle, taking great care not to damage it.

2   Carefully pull out the bearing retaining wire.

3   The spindle and bearing assembly are combined (and are only supplied as a complete unit), and should now be gently tapped out of the rear of the water pump.

4   The oil seal assembly and the impeller will also come out with the spindle and bearing assembly.

5   The impeller vane is removed from the spindle by judicious tapping and levering, or preferably, to ensure no damage and for ease of operation, with a universal three leg puller. The oil seal assembly can then be slipped off. Reassembly of the water pump is a reversal of the above sequence. The following additional points should however be noted:

a) If the oil seal assembly shows any sign of damage or wear it should be renewed, and the gasket between the water pump and the cylinder block should be renewed every time the pump is removed.

b) There is a small hole in the bearing body cover. When assembled it is vital that this hole lines up with the lubrication hole in the pump body. To check that this is so, prior to reassembly remove the greasing screw and check visually that the hole is in the correct position directly below the greasing aperture.

10 Fan belt - removal and replacement

If the fan belt is worn or has stretched unduly it should be replaced. The most usual reason for replacement is that the belt has broken in service. It is therefore recommended that a spare belt is always carried.

1   Loosen the two dynamo or alternator pivot bolts and the nut on the adjusting link and push the dynamo or alternator in towards the engine. Remove the old belt if still in place.

2   Fit the belt by manoeuvring it over each fan blade in turn, through the small gap at the top front side of the radiator.

3   Slip the belt over the crankshaft, dynamo or alternator and water pump pulleys.

4   Adjust the belt as detailed in the following section and tighten the dynamo or alternator mounting nuts. **Note:** After fitting a new belt it will require adjustment 250 miles (400 km) later.

11 Fan belt - adjustment

It is important to keep the fan belt correctly adjusted and although not listed by the manufacturer, it is considered that this should be a regular maintenance task performed every 6,000 miles (10,000 km). If the belt is too loose it will slip, wear rapidly, and cause the dynamo and water pump to malfunction. If the belt is too tight the dynamo or alternator and water pump bearings will wear rapidly causing premature failure of these components.

The fan belt tension is correct when there is 0.5 in (12.7 mm) of lateral movement at the midpoint position of the belt between the dynamo pulley wheel and the water pump pulley wheel.

To adjust the fan belt, slacken the dynamo or alternator securing bolts and move the dynamo either in or out until the correct tension is obtained. It is easier if the dynamo or alternator bolts are only slackened a little so it requires some force to move the dynamo or alternator. In this way the tension of the belt can be arrived at more quickly than by making frequent adjustments. If diffiuclty is experienced in moving the dynamo or alternator away from the engine a long spanner placed behind the dynamo or alternator and resting against the block serves as a very good lever and can be held in position while the dynamo or alternator bolts are tightened.

12 Antifreeze mixture

1   In circumstances where it is likely that the temperature will drop below freezing it is essential that some of the water is

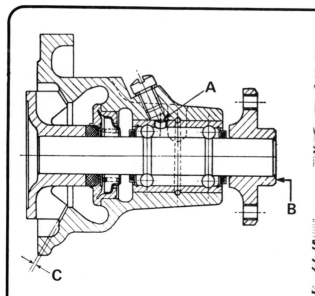

Fig. 2.5. Cross section through water pump showing the location of the components. When assembled, the hole (A) in the bearing must coincide with the lubricating hole in the water pump. The face of the hub (B) must be flush with the end of the spindle.
C = 0.020 — 0.030 in. (0.508 — 0.762 mm)

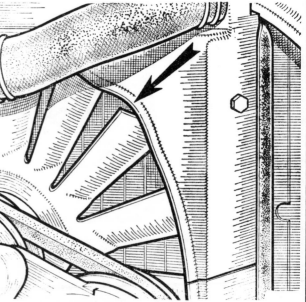

Fig. 2.6. Remove and refit the fan belt through the special gap (arrowed)

drained and an adequate amount of ethylene glycol antifreeze such as Castrol Antifreeze is added to the cooling system.

2 If Castrol Antifreeze is not available, any antifreeze which conforms with specifications "BS 3151" or "BS 3152" can be used. Never use an antifreeze with an alcohol base as evaporation is too high.

3 Castrol Antifreeze with an anti-corrosion additive can be left in the cooling system for up to two years, but after six months it is advisable to have the specific gravity of the coolant checked at your local garage, and thereafter once every three months.

4 The table below gives the amount of antifreeze and the degree of protection.

5 Never use antifreeze in the windscreen washer reservoir as it will cause damage to the paintwork.

Antifreeze	Commences to freeze		Frozen solid		Amount of antifreeze
%	°C	°F	°C	°F	Pints (litres)
25	-13	9	-26	-15	1.5 (0.85)
33.1/3	-19	-2	-36	-33	2 (1.2)
50	-36	-33	-48	-53	3.25(1.8)

13 Fault diagnosis - cooling system

Symptom	Reason/s	Remedy
Overheating	Insufficient water in cooling system	Top up radiator.
	Fan belt slipping (Accompanied by a shrieking noise on rapid engine acceleration)	Tighten fan belt to recommended tension or replace if worn.
	Radiator core blocked or radiator grille restricted	Reverse flush radiator, remove obstructions.
	Bottom water hose collapsed, impeding flow	Remove and fit new hose.
	Thermostat not opening properly	Remove and fit new thermostat.
	Ignition advance and retard incorrectly set (Accompanied by loss of power and perhaps, misfiring)	Check and reset ignition timing.
	Carburettors incorrectly adjusted (mixture too weak)	Tune carburettor(s).
	Exhaust system partially blocked	Check exhaust pipe for constrictive dents and blockages.
	Oil level in sump too low	Top up sump to full mark on dipstick.
	Blown cylinder head gasket (Water/steam being forced down the radiator overflow pipe under pressure)	Remove cylinder head, fit new gasket.
	Engine not yet run-in	Run-in slowly and carefully.
	Brakes binding	Check and adjust brakes if necessary.
Engine does not reach normal operating temperature	Thermostat jammed open	Remove and renew thermostat.
	Incorrect grade of thermostat fitted allowing premature opening of valve	Remove and replace with new thermostat which opens at a higher temperature.
	Thermostat missing	Check and fit correct thermostat.
Coolant leakage	Loose clips on water hoses	Check and tighten clips if necessary.
	Top or bottom water hoses perished and leaking.	Check and replace any faulty hoses.
	Radiator core leaking	Remove radiator and repair.
	Thermostat gasket leaking	Inspect and renew gasket.
	Pressure cap spring worn or seal ineffective	Renew pressure cap.
	Blown cylinder head gasket (Pressure in system forcing water/steam down overflow pipe	Remove cylinder head and fit new gasket.
	Cylinder wall or head cracked	Dismantle engine, dispatch to engineering works for repair.

Chapter 3 Fuel system and carburation

Contents

Specifications

Air cleaner:

All Mini models (except Cooper, Cooper S and Mini
1275GT):

Early models	Dry type cleanable air filter
Later models	Renewable paper element

Mini Cooper 997 & 998 cc:

Early models	Oil wetted gauze
Later models	Renewable paper elements

Mini Cooper 'S', Mk I, II and III: ... ... Renewable paper elements. Adjustable air intake

Mini 1275GT and Clubman: ... ... Renewable paper element. Adjustable air intake

Fuel pump:

Make and type (up to 1969)

Early models	SU electric PD
Later models	SU electric SP or AUF 201
Make and type (from 1969)	SU mechanical or AUF 705

Delivery rate:

PD	45 pints/hr (25.5 litres/hr)
SP and AUF 201	56 pints/hr (32 litres/hr)

Delivery pressure:

PD	$2 - 3$ lb/in^2 ($0.14 - 0.21$ kg/cm^2)
SP and AUF 201	$2.5 - 3$ lb/in^2 ($0.17 - 0.21$ kg/cm^2)
AUF 705	3 lb/in^2 (0.21 kg/cm^2)

Carburettor/s (all models except Cooper):

	Mini Mk I and Mk II Mini 850 848 cc	Mini Mk II and Mini 1000 998 cc	Mini Mk I and II Automatic 848 cc	Mini Mk II, Mini 1000 and Clubman Automatic 998 cc	Mini Clubman
	1959 on	1967 on	1965 - 69	1967 on	1969
Type	HS2	HS2	HS4	HS4	HS2
Piston spring	Red	Red	Red	Red	Red
Jet size	0.090 in. (2.29 mm)	0.090 in. (2.29 mm)	0.090 in. (2.29 mm)	0.090 in. (2.29 mm)	0.090 in. (2.29 mm)
Needle:					
Standard	EB	GX	AN	AC	GX
Rich	M	M	H6	MI	M
Weak	GG	GG	EB	HA	GG
Idle speed	500 rpm	500 rpm	650 rpm	650 rpm	500 rpm
Fast idle speed	900 rpm	900 rpm	1050 rpm	1050 rpm	900 rpm

Carburettor/s (Cooper model):

	Mini Cooper 997 cc	Mini Cooper 998 cc	Mini Cooper 'S' 970 and 1071 cc	Mini Cooper 'S' Mk I, II, III	Mini 1275GT
	1961 - 64	1964 - 69	1963 - 65	1964 on	1969
Type	Twin HS2	Twin HS2	Twin HS2	Twin HS2	Twin HS4
Piston spring	Red	Blue	Red	Red	Red
Jet size	0.090 in. (2.29 mm)	0.090 in. (2.29 mm)	0.090 in. (2.29 mm)	0.090 in. (2.29 mm)	0.090 in. (2.29 mm)
Needle:					
Standard	GZ	GY	970 1071 AN H6	M	AC, DZ or ABB
Rich	—	M	—	AH2	BQ
Weak	—	GG	—	EB	HA or CF
Idle speed	500 rpm	500 rpm	600 rpm	600 rpm	650 rpm
Fast idle speed	900 rpm	900 rpm	1000 rpm	1000 rpm	1050 rpm

Fuel tank capacity:

Mini Saloon (except Cooper 'S' Mk II and III) and 1275 GT up to July 1974	5.5 gallons (25 litres)
Clubman Estate	6 gallons (27.3 litres)
Van and Pick-up	6 gallons (27.3 litres)
Traveller and Countryman:	
Early models	6.5 gallons (29.6 litres)
Later models with under floor tank	6 gallons (27.3 litres)
Twin tank (Cooper 'S' Mk II and III)	11 gallons (50 litres)
1275 GT after July 1974	7.5 gallons (34 litres)

1 General description

The fuel systems on all Minis comprise a fuel tank at the rear, an electric or mechanical fuel pump and single or twin SU carburettors. Full information on each component of the fuel system will be found in the relevant Section of this Chapter.

2 Air cleaner - removal and replacement

Early air cleaners made use of a composite filter which could be removed and cleaned. However, later air cleaners made use of a disposable paper element.

Initially gauze type air cleaners were fitted to Mini Cooper models and these have now been replaced by a disposable paper element type.

Early type composite filter:

1 Undo and remove the wing nut from the top of the cover and lift away the cover.
2 Recover the filter element.
3 Carefully wipe the inside of the cleaner body. Tap the element to loosen the dust and then blow it out from the inside with an air line - this is most easily done at the local garage.
4 Refitting the element and cover is the reverse sequence to removal.

Later type disposable paper element:

1 This section is not applicable to Cooper models.
2 Undo and remove the wing nut and washer from the top of the cover and lift away the cover. Note on models fitted with automatic transmission two wing nuts are used. It will also be necessary to detach the breather hose.
3 Recover the filter element.
4 Carefully wipe the inside of the cleaner body. Do not attempt to clean the element but always renew it at the recommended mileages.
5 Refitting the element and cover is the reverse sequence to removal.
6 To avoid carburettor icing in winter the air cleaner intake should be positioned close to the exhaust manifold. For the best performance in summer the intake should be moved as far away from the exhaust manifold as possible.

Gauze filter (Cooper models):

1 Disconnect the breather pipe from the front filter and then undo and remove the four retaining bolts.
2 Lift away the air filter assemblies.
3 Wash the filters in petrol and allow to drip dry.
4 Re-oil the gauze inserts with engine oil.
5 Check the condition of the gaskets; obtain new if necessary, and refit the air filter assemblies - this being the reverse sequence to removal. Do not forget to reconnect the breather pipe.

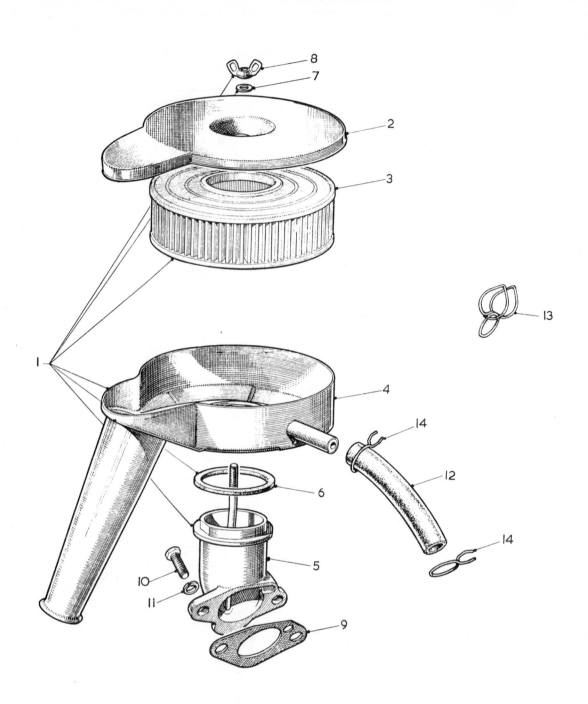

Fig. 3.1. Exploded view of standard air cleaner

1	Air cleaner and silencer assembly	4 Air cleaner body	8 ¼ in. U.N.C. wing nut	12 Air cleaner to rocker cover tube
2	Lid	5 Downpipe casting	9 Joint gasket	13 Rocker cover end clip
3	Element	6 Rubber washer	10 Bolt	14 Air cleaner end clip
		7 Fibre washer	11 Spring washer	

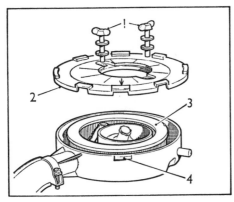 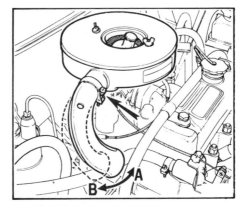

Fig. 3.2. Air cleaner fitted to Mini Clubman

1 Wing nuts	*2 Top cover*	*3 Element*	*4 Cover to body alignment marks*
	A Cold winter setting	*B Summer setting*	

Disposable paper element (Cooper and all late models)

1 Undo and remove the two wing nuts and washers securing the cover to the body. Prise free and lift away the cover.

2 Withdraw the filter element.

3 Carefully wipe the inside of the air cleaner body. Do not attempt to clean the element but always renew it at the recommended mileages.

4 The filter body may be removed if necessary by first detaching the throttle lever return spring and breather hose (if fitted) and then carefully manoeuvreing it over the carburettors.

5 Refitting the body, element and cover is the reverse sequence to removal. If the body has been removed ensure that the air manifold rubber seals are in good order and seating correctly.

3 Electric fuel pump - general description

Several types of electric fuel pumps have been fitted to Mini models covered by this manual. Basically, these pumps were fitted up to the time when the negative earth electrical systems were introduced to these models.

The PD pump is fitted to pre-1962 models and the SP AUF 201 to later models. The PD pump is unusual in that the diaphragm is operated by light mineral oil which is displaced by a metal plunger. The main part of the pump is therefore sealed, and the pump cannot be completely dismantled for repair.

The main portion comprises an oil filled brass tube which also contains a steel plunger with an insulated distance piece, a permanent magnet with two pole pieces and a coil spring. Each end of the tube is hermetically sealed by a diaphragm.

With the ignition off the plunger, magnet and pole pieces are at the bottom of their travel and the contacts closed because of the contact breaker rocker. On switching on the ignition the plunger, magnet and pole pieces move upwards magnetically. As the fluid in the brass tube is hermetically sealed the bottom diaphragm also moves upwards so sucking in fuel from the petrol tank through the inlet valve.

When the plunger is almost at the top of its stroke the rocker mechanism allows the contacts to open, so breaking the magnetic circuit. The plunger, magnet, and pole pieces are then forced down by the coil spring and the action of the lower diaphragm is reversed, which expels the fuel through the outlet valve to the carburettor. The points then close and the whole cycle is repeated.

The SP and AUF pumps are so similar it is quite possible that a non-standard one has been fitted on an exchange basis, and for this reason the differences between them will be listed in the text as they occur so that if a later type of pump has been fitted it will create no difficulty. The following can be taken to apply equally to both types of pump except where otherwise stated.

The SU 12 volt electric fuel pump consists of a long outer body casing housing the diaphragm, armature and solenoid assembly, with at one end the contact breaker assembly protected by a bakelite cover, and at the other end a short casting containing the inlet and outlet ports, filter, valves, and pumping chamber. The joint between the bakelite cover and the body casing is protected with a rubber sheath.

The pump operates in the following manner. When the ignition is switched on current travels from the terminal on the outside of the bakelite cover through the coil located round the solenoid core which becomes energised and acting like a magnet draws the armature towards it. The current then passes through the points to earth.

When the armature is drawn forward it brings the diaphragm with it against the pressure of the diaphragm spring. This creates sufficient vacuum in the pump chamber to draw in fuel from the tank through the fuel filter and non-return inlet valve.

As the armature nears the end of its travel a 'throw over' mechanism operates which separates the points so breaking the circuit.

The diaphragm return spring then pushes the diaphragm and armature forwards into the pumping chamber so forcing the fuel in the chamber out to the carburettor through the non-return outlet valve. When the armature is nearly fully forward the throw over mechanism again functions, this time closing the points and re-energising the solenoid, so repeating the cycle.

4 Electric fuel pump - removal and replacement

All models except Moke:

1 Disconnect the earth lead from the battery. (Positive terminal).

2 Disconnect the earth and the supply wires from their terminals on the pump body.

3 Prepare to squeeze the rubber portion of the petrol pipe leading from the tank with a mole wrench to ensure the minimum of fuel is lost when the inlet pipe is removed from the pump. Alternatively, have a suitable container handy into which the fuel can drain.

4 Remove the fuel inlet and outlet pipes by undoing the union nuts or the clip screws. (Remove the vent pipe connector where fitted, at this stage).

5 Unscrew the two bolts and spring washers which hold the pump bracket in position and remove the pump.

6 Replacement of the pump is a reversal of the above process. Two particular points to watch are that:

a) The fuel inlet and outlet pipes are connected up the right way round.

b) A good electrical earth connection is made.

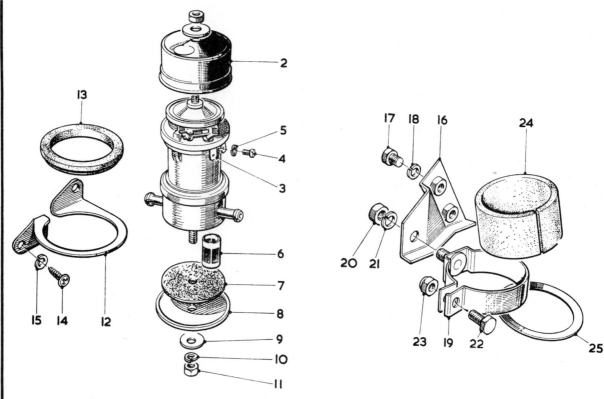

Fig. 3.3. Exploded view of PD type fuel pump and bracket

1 Fuel pump
2 Top cover
3 Lucar connector
4 Earth lead screw
5 Spring washer
6 Filter
7 Cork sealing disc
8 Bottom cover
9 Dished washer
10 Spring washer
11 Nut
12 Bracket
13 Pump mounting
14 Bracket to subframe screw
15 Spring washer
16 Fuel pump bracket
17 Screw
18 Spring washer
19 Fuel pump mounting clip
20 Nut
21 Spring washer
22 Screw
23 Nut
24 Strap
25 Abutment washer

Fig. 3.4. PD type fuel pump
Inset shows location of filter

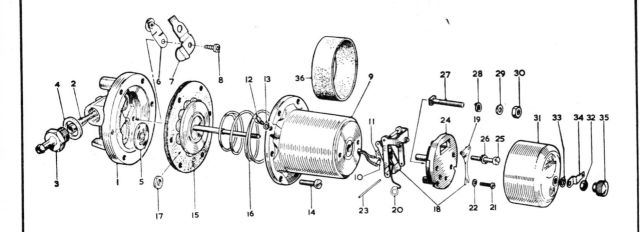

Fig. 3.5. Exploded view of SP type fuel pump

1 Body
2 Filter
3 Nozzle inlet
4 Washer for nozzle
5 Outlet valve
6 Inlet valve
7 Valve retainer
8 Screw for retainer
9 Coil housing
10 5 B.A. terminal tag
11 2 B.A. terminal tag
12 Earth screw
13 Spring washer
14 Housing to body screw
15 Diaphragm assembly
16 Spring
17 Roller
18 Rocker and blade
19 Blade
20 2 B.A. terminal tag
21 Screw for blade
22 Dished washer
23 Spindle for contact breaker
24 Pedestal
25 Pedestal to housing screw
26 Spring washer
27 Screw for terminal
28 Spring washer
29 Lead washer for screw
30 Nut for screw
31 End cover
32 Nut for cover
33 Shakeproof washer
34 Lucar connector
35 Terminal knob
36 Rubber sleeve

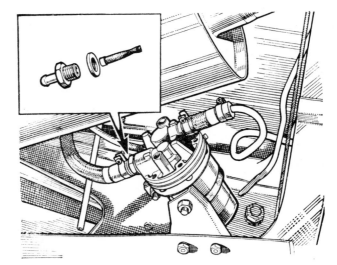

Fig. 3.6. SP type fuel pump mounted on subframe
Inset shows location of filter

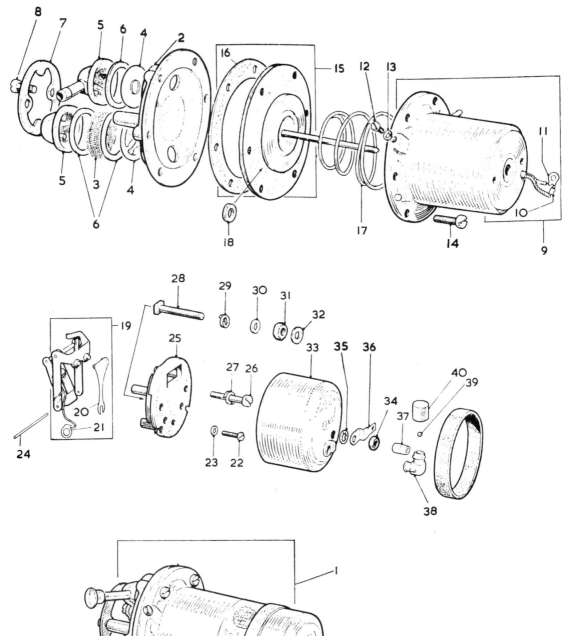

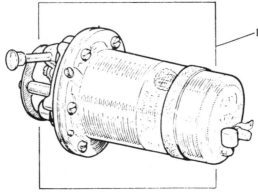

Fig. 3.7. Exploded view of AUF type fuel pump

1	Pump assembly	11	2 B.A. terminal tag	21	Tag terminal 2 B.A.	31	Recessed nut
2	Pump body	12	Earth screw	22	Blade screw	32	Washer
3	Filter	13	Spring washer	23	Dished washer	33	End cover
4	Valves	14	Screw	24	Contact breaker spindle	34	Cover nut
5	Inlet and outlet nozzles	15	Diaphragm	25	Pedestal	35	Shakeproof washer
6	Sealing washer	16	Diaphragm sealing washer	26	Screw	36	Lucar connector
7	Clamp plate	17	Armature spring	27	Spring washer	37	Insulating sleeve
8	Plate screw	18	Roller	28	Terminal screw	38	Ventilator valve
9	Coil housing	19	Rocker & blade assembly	29	Spring washer	39	Valve ball
10	5 B.A. terminal tag	20	Blade	30	Lead washer	40	Sealing ring

Moke:

1 Disconnect the earth lead from the battery. (Positive terminal).
2 Release the two quick release fasteners retaining the left-hand pannier side cover, lift away the side cover.
3 Disconnect the lead from the pump terminal.
4 Slacken the clips and pull the hose from the delivery pipe and then the suction hose from the pump.
5 Undo and remove the two nuts and washers securing the mounting bracket to the body. Lift away the pump assembly.
6 Refitting the pump is the reverse sequence to removal. Do not forget to secure the earth lead to one of the mounting bracket nuts.

5 Electric fuel pump - dismantling

1 The filter and inlet and outlet arrangements differ between the three pumps and for this reason it is necessary to deal with them individually at this stage:

   a) Type SP. Remove the inlet nozzle by unscrewing it, and take out the filter from the inlet port. **Note** the fibre washer under the nozzle head. The outlet nozzle is pressed into the end casting and cannot be removed.

   b) Type AUF. Release the inlet and outlet nozzles, valves, sealing washers, and filter by unscrewing the two screws from the spring clamp plate which hold them all in place.

   c) Type PD. The filter is at the bottom of the pump under the cover plate. To remove the cover plate undo the retaining nut, and take off the spring washer, dished washer, cover plate, and cover plate cork gasket. The bakelite cover can be removed from the top of the pump to give access to the contacts. It is not possible to dismantle the pump any further and the following instructions refer to the SP and AUF pumps only.

2 Mark the flanges adjacent to each other and separate the housing holding the armature and solenoid assembly from the pumping chamber casting, by unscrewing the six screws holding both halves of the pump together. Take great care not to tear or damage the diaphragm as it may stick to either of the flanges as they are separated. On the SP pump, remove the pan-headed screw which holds the valve retainer in place to the floor of the pumping chamber, and remove the retainer and the inlet and outlet valves which have already been removed on the AUF pump.
3 The armature spindle which is attached to the armature head and diaphragm is unscrewed anticlockwise from the trunnion at the contact breaker end of the pump body. Lift out the armature, spindle, and diaphragm, and remove the impact washer from under the head of the armature. (This washer quietens the noise of the armature head hitting the solenoid core), and the diaphragm return spring.
4 Slide off the protective rubber sheath and unscrew the terminal nut, connector (where fitted), and washer from the terminal screw, and remove the bakelite contact breaker cover.
5 Unscrew the 5 BA screws which hold the contact spring blade in position and remove it with the blade and screw washer.
6 Remove the cover retaining nut on the terminal screw, and cut through the lead washer under the nut on the terminal screw with a pocket knife.
7 Remove the two bakelite pedestal retaining screws complete with spring washers which hold the pedestal to the solenoid housing, remove the braided copper earth lead, and the coil lead from the terminal screw.
8 Remove the pin on which the rockers pivot by pushing it out sideways and remove the rocker assembly. The pump is now fully dismantled. It is not possible to remove the solenoid core and coil and the rocker assembly must not be broken down, as it is only supplied on exchange as a complete assembly.

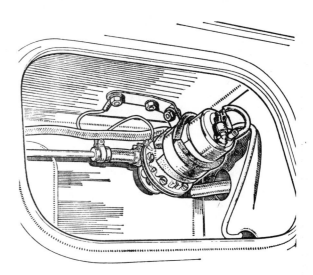

Fig. 3.8. Location of fuel pump in left-hand side member (Moke)

6 Electric fuel pump - inspection and servicing

1 Although not given in the official manufacturer's servicing recommendations it is considered a very sound scheme to service the SU fuel pump every 12,000 miles (20,000 Km) to minimise the possibility of failure.
2 Remove the filter as has already been detailed and thoroughly clean it in petrol. At the same time clean the points by gently drawing a piece of thin card between them. Do this very carefully so as not to disturb the tension of the spring blade. If the points are burnt or pitted they must be renewed and a new blade and rocker assembly fitted. The cork gasket on the PD pump should be renewed as a matter of course. If this gasket leaks the pump will work rapidly and fuel starvation is likely. If, after having cleaned the contacts and the filter, the PD pump still refuses to function, it should be exchanged for the later SP type complete with modified mounting bracket.
3 On any of the three pumps fuel starvation combined with rapid operations is indicative of an air leak on the suction side. To check whether this is so, undo the fuel line at the top of the float chamber, and immerse the end of the pipe in a jam jar half filled with petrol. With the ignition on and the pump functioning, should a regular stream of air bubbles emerge from the end of the pipe, air is leaking in on the suction side.
4 If the filter is coated with gum-like substance very like varnish, serious trouble can develop in the future unless all traces of this gum (formed by deposits from the fuel) are removed.
5 To do this boil all steel and brass parts in a 20% solution of caustic soda, and then dip them in nitric acid and clean them in boiling water. Alloy parts can be cleaned with a clean rag after they have been left to soak for a few hours in methylated spirits.
6 With the pump stripped right down, wash and clean all the parts thoroughly in paraffin and renew any that are worn, damaged, fractured, or cracked. Pay particular attention to the gaskets and diaphragm.

7 Electric fuel pump - reassembly

1 Fit the rocker assembly to the bakelite pedestal and insert the rocker pivot pin. The pin is case hardened and wire or any other substitute should never be used if the pin is lost.
2 Place the spring washer, wiring tag from the short lead from the coil, a new lead washer, and the nut on the terminal screw, and tighten the nut down.

3 Attach the copper earth wire from the outer rocker immediately under the head of the nearest pedestal securing screw, and fit the pedestal to the solenoid housing with the two pedestal securing screws and lockwashers. It is unusual to fit an earth-wire immediately under the screw head but in this case the spring washer has been found not to be a particularly good conductor.

4 Fit the lockwasher under the head of the spring blade contact securing screw, then the last lead from the coil, and then the spring blade so that there is nothing between it and the bakelite pedestal. It is important that this order of assembly is adhered to. Tighten the screw lightly.

5 The static position of the pump when it is not in use is with the contact points making firm contact and this forces the spring blade to be bent slightly back. Move the outer rocker arm up and down and position the spring blade so that the contacts on the rocker or blade wipe over the centre line of the other points. When open the blade should rest against the small ledge on the bakelite pedestal just below the points. The points should come into contact with each other when the rocker is halfway forward. To check that this is correct press the middle of the blade gently so that it rests against the ridge with the points just having come into contact. It should now be possible to slide a 0.030 in (0.762 mm) feeler gauge between the rocker rollers and the solenoid housing. If the clearance is not correct bend the tip of the blade very carefully until it is (Fig. 3.10).

On the AUF and SP pumps with the outer rocker against the coil housing and the spring blade contact resting against the pedestal, the gap between the points should be 0.030 in (0.762 mm).

6 Tighten down the blade retaining screw, and check that with AUF and SP models a considerable gap exists between the underside of the spring blade and the pedestal ledge, with the rocker contact bearing against the blade contact and the rocker fully forward in the normal static position. With the rocker arm down, ensure that the underside of the blade rests on the ledge of the pedestal. If not, remove the blade and very slightly bend it until it does.

7 Place the impact washer on the underside of the armature head, fit the diaphragm return spring with the wider portion of the coils against the solenoid body, place the brass rollers in position under the diaphragm and insert the armature spindle through the centre of the solenoid core, and screw the spindle into the rocker trunnion.

8 It will be appreciated that the amount the spindle is screwed into the rocker trunnion will vitally affect the functioning of the pump. To set the diaphragm correctly, turn the steel blade to one side, and screw the armature spindle into the trunnion until, if the spindle was screwed in a further sixth of a turn, the throw-over rocker would not operate the points closed to points open position. Now screw out the armature spindle four holes (2/3 of a turn) to ensure that wear in the points will not cause the pump to stop working. Turn the blade back into its normal position (Fig. 3.11).

9 Reassembly of the valves, filters, and nozzles into the pumping chamber is a reversal of the dismantling process. Use new washers and gaskets throughout.

10 With the pumping chamber reassembled, replace it carefully on the solenoid housing, ensuring that the previously made mating marks on the flanges line up with each other. Screw the six screws in firmly.

11 Fit the bakelite cover and replace the shakeproof washer, lucar conductor, cover nut, and terminal knob to the terminal screw. Then, replace the terminal lead and cover nut, so locking the lead between the cover nut and the terminal nut. Assembly of all three types is now complete.

8 Mechanical fuel pump - general description

The mechanical pump is fitted to all post 1969 models. It is mounted on the rear left-hand side of the crankcase and is driven from the crankshaft.

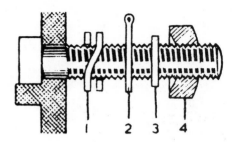

Fig. 3.9. Components of the terminal screw assembled in the correct order

1 Spring washer   *3 Lead washer*
2 Wiring tag   *4 Recessed nut*

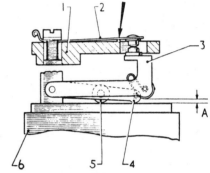

Fig. 3.10. The contact gap setting 'A' on early type rocker assemblies should be 0.030 in. (0.8 mm)

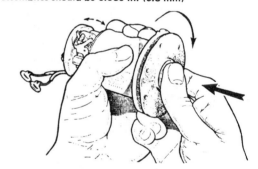

Fig. 3.11. Screw in diaphragm until rocker throw-over stops

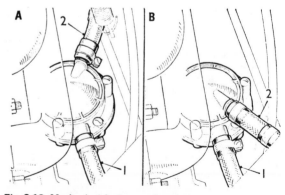

Fig. 3.12. Mechanical fuel pump locations

A 1275 GT   *B 850/1000 and Clubman*
1 Inlet connection   *2 Outlet connection*

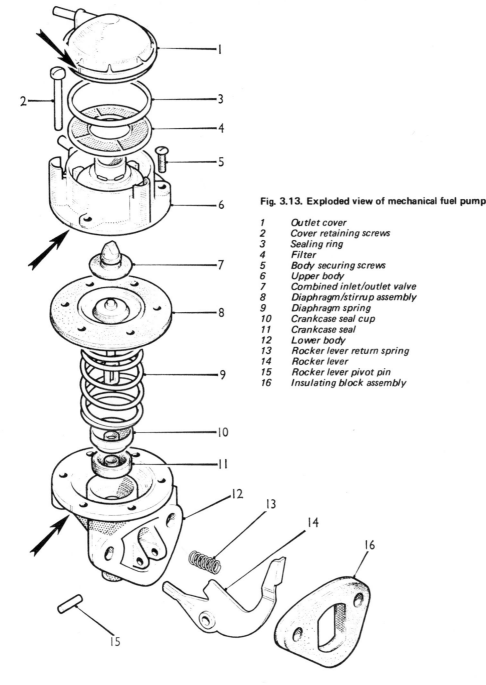

Fig. 3.13. Exploded view of mechanical fuel pump

1	Outlet cover
2	Cover retaining screws
3	Sealing ring
4	Filter
5	Body securing screws
6	Upper body
7	Combined inlet/outlet valve
8	Diaphragm/stirrup assembly
9	Diaphragm spring
10	Crankcase seal cup
11	Crankcase seal
12	Lower body
13	Rocker lever return spring
14	Rocker lever
15	Rocker lever pivot pin
16	Insulating block assembly

The camshaft lobe operates the rocker lever drawing the pump diaphragm downwards creating suction on the fuel inlet pipe from the fuel tank. This draws fuel through the filter into the diaphragm chamber (upper body), via the two way valve.

The outer seat lifts to allow fuel to pass into the diahragm chamber. The spring then takes over the return stroke and forces fuel back through the centre seat of the two way valve (which now lifts) up through the central tube of the upper body through the outlet cover to the carburettor.

When the carburettor float valve is closed against the pump delivery the diaphragm of the pump stays in the down position line pressure holding the spring compressed. The rocker lever idles free in these instances.

As soon as the carburettor float chamber valve opens the pressure in the outlet line from the pump decreases and the normal fuel delivery continues.

9 Mechanical fuel pump - removal and replacement

1 Disconnect the battery for safety reasons.

2 Remove the carburettor air cleaner for ease of access.

3 Slacken the pipe clip screw on the outlet pipe connection and draw it off. Have a small container handy to collect what little fuel may drain from the pipe.

4 In all saloon models, if the tank is more than half full, the fuel will drain from the tank under gravity when the fuel pump inlet pipe is disconnected, so provide for this situation by fitting a suitable clip or bung in the pipe if necessary. On estate models the tank is below the pump. Slacken the pipe clip screw on the inlet pipe connection and draw it off.

5 Slacken the two nuts which hold the pump to the crankcase on two studs through the lower body.

6 Draw the pump off a little way and loosen the insulating block and its two sealing washers. Take care not to damage these if it is necessary to use a little leverage with a screwdriver. Then draw off the pump and insulating block.

7 Replacement of the pump is a reversal of this procedure paying particular attention that :-

The insulating block and the two washers are replaced exactly as taken off. If damage requires any replacement it is essential that the total original thickness of block and washers is maintained. Any change would affect the stroke of the rocker lever and consequent malfunctioning or damage to the pump.

10 Mechanical fuel pump - dismantling

1 Clean any dirt off the whole of the assembly and work on a bench covered with a clean sheet of paper.

2 Mark the relationship between the outlet cover, upper body and lower body which must reassemble the same way.

3 Remove the three top cover retaining screws which clamp the lip of the cover.

4 The sealing ring should have come off with the outlet cover but if not, carefully lift it away from the upper body and remove the filter disc.

5 Remove the three screws holding the upper body to the lower body and lift it off.

6 Take out the inlet/outlet valve. This is a press fit and care is needed to avoid damage to the edge of the outer (inlet) seat.

7 To remove the diaphragm and spring the rocker lever needs to be removed. Press the diaphragm and spring down sufficiently to take the pressure off the rocker lever pivot pin which can be removed by a light tap with a long nosed punch. Withdraw the lever from the diaphragm stirrup and watch for the spring flying out. Put a little oil on the diaphragm stirrup to prevent damage to the gland and then carefully draw the diaphragm and spring from the lower body.

8 It should not normally be necessary to replace the crankcase seal in the lower body but if it should and a replacement is definitely available, it can be prised and hooked out. This will damage the old seal, so if the old seal is going to be reused then service tool "18G 1119" is needed to draw it out.

11 Mechanical fuel pump - inspection and servicing

1 Although no recommended service/inspection interval is indicated by the manufacturer a 12000 mile (20,000 km) check is preferable to a roadside failure. Ensure that the filter is clean and undamaged, check the diaphragm for signs of cracking and perforation and examine the seats of the inlet/outlet valve for chipping or wear on the seats. The sealing ring in the outlet cover is best renewed anyway but does not have to be. If in doubt about any of these items, replace them.

2 Gummy deposits should be cleaned off as described in Section 6.

12 Mechanical fuel pump - reassembly

The reverse of the dismantling procedure is required noting the following points.

1 If the crankcase seal is to be renewed replace it using, if available, tool "18G 1119". Otherwise press the seal in using a suitably sized mandrel.

2 If a new diaphragm is being fitted ensure that there are no sharp edges or burrs on the spindle or stirrup slot. Oil the spindle lightly and replace it with the stirrup slot positioned correctly for engagement with the rocker lever.

3 Replacing the rocker lever is best done with two pairs of hands. The diaphragm spring needs depressing sufficiently to introduce the end of the lever and the lever in turn has to be positioned with its own return spring compressed. The pin is then replaced. If another pair of hands is not available tie the

diaphragm spring in the compressed position with a piece of string around the body. (Do not put the string over the diaphragm).

4 Replace the inlet/outlet valve carefully ensuring that the groove registers in the housing and that the fine edge of the inlet valve seats evenly.

5 Place upper body over the lower, lining up the screw holes with each other and the diaphragm and replace the three short screws, holding the diaphragm flat by depressing the rocker lever. Do not tighten the short screws.

6 Replace the filter, sealing washer and outlet cover and the three long screws. Then tighten all six screws evenly.

7 To test the pump is functioning correctly hold a finger over the inlet nozzle and operate the rocker lever through three full strokes when suction should be heard and felt. Similarly for the outlet nozzle, one stroke of the rocker lever should give maintained pressure for 15 seconds. Never use compressed air for blowing through the pump as it is usually at a pressure far greater than the pump is designed to withstand.

13 SU carburettor- general description

The variable choke SU carburettor is a relatively simple instrument and is basically the same irrespective of its size and type. It differs from most other carburettors in that instead of having a number of various sized fixed jets for different conditions, only one variable jet is fitted to deal with all possible conditions.

Although the alterations are few, it is interesting to know the differences between the early H2 type SU carburettor fitted to the 'A' series engine from which the Mini engine was developed. SU carburettors are very reliable and last for a long time. It is, therefore, as well to also know how to recognise the H2 from the HS2 type, especially if twin carburettors have been fitted to a standard Mini. The H2 carburettor has a thimble gauze filter in

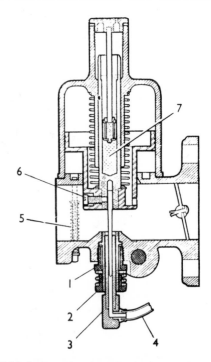

Fig. 3.14. Cross section through carburettor body

1   Jet locking nut   5   Piston lifting pin
2   Jet adjusting nut   6   Needle securing screw
3   Jet head   7   Piston damper oil well
4   Nylon fuel pipe

the float chamber inlet union, the fuel is carried from the float chamber to the jet in a casting which is part of the float chamber, and the float chamber is secured to the carburettor body by a float chamber holding up bolt which passes through the float chamber extension casting, and is surrounded on either side with rubber grommets. (These grommets frequently wear, allowing fuel to leak. Regular renewal is recommended at intervals of 12,000 miles (20,000 km). Under the head of the holding-up bolt is a metal washer. The jet bearings are in two halves and are held apart with a spring.

The HS2 carburettor is a simplified version of the H2 type. As well as modifications to the mixture control and ignition control advance and retard pipe, there is no gauze filter in the float chamber inlet union, the fuel is carried from the float chamber to the base of the jet head by a nylon pipe, the float chamber is secured to the carburettor body by a horizontally positioned bolt with rubber cushioning washers and grommets, and the jet bearing assembly is far simpler, consisting of one long bearing.

These alterations result in a more reliable and efficient carburettor with less likelihood of developing faults.

Air passing rapidly through the carburettor choke draws petrol from the jet so forming the petrol/air mixture. The amount of petrol drawn from the jet depends on the position of the tapered carburettor needle, which moves up and down the jet orifice according to engine load and throttle opening, thus effectively altering the size of the jet so that exactly the right amount of fuel is metered for the prevailing road conditions.

The position of the tapered needle in the jet is determined by engine vacuum. The shank of the needle is held at its top end in a piston which slides up and down the dashpot in response to the degree of manifold vacuum. This is directly controlled by the position of the throttle.

With the throttle fully open, the full effect of inlet manifold vacuum is felt by the piston which has an air bleed into the choke tube on the outside of the throttle. This causes the piston to rise fully, bringing the needle with it. With the acceleration

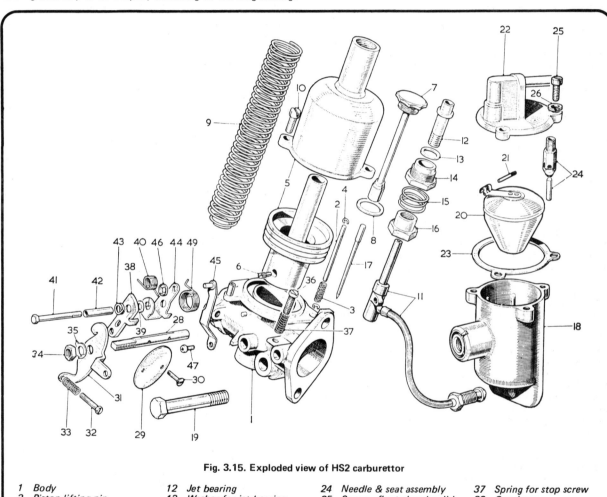

Fig. 3.15. Exploded view of HS2 carburettor

1 Body	12 Jet bearing	24 Needle & seat assembly	37 Spring for stop screw
2 Piston lifting pin	13 Washer for jet bearing - brass	25 Screw - float chamber lid to body	38 Cam lever
3 Spring for pin	14 Lock screw for jet bearing	26 Spring washer	39 Washer
4 Circlip for pin	15 Lock spring	27 Baffle - overflow	40 Cam lever spring
5 Suction chamber & piston assembly	16 Jet adjusting screw	28 Throttle spindle	41 Cam lever pivot bolt
6 Needle locking screw	17 Jet needle	29 Throttle disc	42 Pivot blot tube
7 Piston damper assembly	18 Float chamber body	30 Screw - throttle disc	43 Spring washer
8 Washer for damper cap - fibre	20 Float & lever assembly	31 Throttle lever	44 Pick-up lever assembly
9 Piston spring	21 Lever hinge pin	32 Cam stop screw	45 Jet link
10 Screw - suction chamber to body	22 Float chamber lid assembly	33 Spring for stop screw	46 Jet link retaining clip
11 Jet assembly	23 Washer for lid	34 Throttle spindle nut	47 Jet link securing screw
		35 Tab washer for nut	48 Bush
		36 Idling stop screw	49 Spring for pick-up lever

partially closed only slight inlet manifold vacuum is felt by the piston (although, of course, on the engine side of the throttle the vacuum is now greater), and the piston only rises a little, blocking most of the jet orifice with the metering needle.

To prevent the piston fluttering, and to give a richer mixture when the accelerator is suddenly depressed, an oil damper and light spring are fitted inside the dashpot.

The only portion of the piston assembly to come into contact with the piston chamber or dashpot is the actual central piston rod. All the other parts of the piston assembly, including the lower choke portion, have sufficient clearances to prevent any direct metal to metal contact which is essential if the carburettor is to work properly.

The correct level of the petrol in the carburettor is determined by the level of the float in the float chamber. When the level is correct the float rises and by means of a lever resting on top of it closes the needle valve in the cover of the float chamber. This closes off the supply of fuel from the pump. When the level in the float chamber drops as fuel is used in the carburettor the float sinks. As it does, the float needle comes away from its seal so allowing more fuel to enter the float chamber and restore the correct level.

In the specifications it will be seen that models fitted with automatic transmission use an HS4 carubrettor instead of the HS2 type. Dismantling and reassembly of this carburettor is basically identical to that described for the HS2. The major difference will be found in adjusting the carburettor and this is described in a separate Section.

14 SU carburettor - removal and replacement

Manual transmission. Single and twin application:

1 Release the clip which secures the breather hose to the rocker cover, and pull the hose from the rocker cover pipe.
2 Unscrew the union which holds the vacuum advance pipe to the carburettor body.
3 Remove the air cleaner complete by releasing the two securing bolts and lockwashers from the carburettor flange.
4 Unscrew the union or clip securing the fuel inlet pipe to the float chamber and pull away the pipe.
5 Remove the choke and accelerator cables from the carburettor linkages.
6 Remove the two nuts and lockwashers which hold the SU carburettor to the inlet manifold. The bottom nut is sometimes difficult to unscrew, but merely requires patience. Lift the carburettor away from the inlet manifold together with the inlet manifold gasket. If twin carburettors are being removed then the procedure is exactly the same as above but both carburettors will have to be lifted off together as they are joined by a common spindle.

To replace the carburettor/s reverse the above procedure using new gaskets where required. Do not omit to fit the spring washers.

Automatic transmission application:

1 Refer to Section 2, and remove the air cleaner assembly.
2 Disconnect the mixture (choke) and throttle control cables from the linkage on the side of the carburettor.
3 Detach the suction advance pipe and the fuel inlet hose from the carburettor.
4 Disconnect the governor control rod fork end from the throttle lever.
5 Undo and remove the two securing nuts and spring washers and carefully draw the carburettor from the two studs.
6 Remove the cable abutment plate.
7 Refitting the carburettor is the reverse sequence to removal. Always fit new joint washers between the manifold face and the abutment plate and the carburettor flange.

15 SU carburettor - dismantling and reassembly

The SU carburettor with only two (normally) moving parts - the throttle valve and the piston assembly - makes it a straightforward instrument to service, but at the same time it is a delicate unit and clumsy handling can cause much damage. In particular it is easy to knock the finely tapering needle out of true, and the greatest care should be taken to keep all the parts associated with the dashpot scrupulously clean.

1 Remove the oil dashpot plunger nut from the top of the dashpot.
2 Unscrew the two set screws holding the dashpot to the carburettor body, and lift away the dashpot, light spring, and piston and needle assembly.
3 To remove the metering needle from the choke portion of the piston unscrew the sunken retaining screw from the side of the piston choke and pull out the needle. When replacing the needle ensure that the shoulder is flush with the underside of the piston.
4 Release the float chamber from the carburettor by releasing the clamping bolt and sealing washers from the carburettor base. (The bolt is removed from the side in the case of the H2 type).
5 Normally it is not necessary to dismantle the carburettor further, but if because of wear or for some other reason it is wished to remove the jet, this is easily accomplished by removing the clevis pin holding the jet operating lever to the jet head, and then removing the jet by extracting it from the base of the carburettor. The jet adjusting screw can then be unscrewed together with its locking spring.
6 If the larger jet locking screw above the jet adjusting screw is removed, then the jet will have to be recentred when the carburettor is reassembled. With the jet screws removed on HS2 carburettors, it is a simple matter to release the jet bearing. On the H2 type of carburettor, dismantling is more complex. With the jet locking screw removed, take out the sealing washer, jet gland spring, brass gland washer, gland washer, and the top half of the jet bearing in this order.
7 To remove the throttle and actuating spindle release the two screws holding the throttle in position in the slot in the spindle, slide the throttle out of the spindle and then remove the spindle.
8 Reassembly is a straightforward reversal of the dismantling sequence.

16 SU carburettor, float chamber - dismantling, examination and reassembly

To dismantle the float chamber, first disconnect the inlet pipe from the fuel pump at the top of the float chamber cover. The float chamber cover is held in place by three set screws. Undo them and lift the cover off. **Note:** There is a fibre gasket between the float chamber cover and the float chamber.

If it is not wished to remove the float chamber completely and the carburettor is still attached to the engine, carefully insert a thin piece of bent wire under the float and lift the float out. To remove the float chamber from the carburettor body release the bolt which runs horizontally through the carburettor. On Mini Cooper models the crosshead screw which holds the jet operating link to the jet head must be undone first, before access can be gained to the float chamber bolt. **Note:** To avoid damage to the jet head, counterbalance the pressure of the screwdriver by supporting the other side of the head. Undo the union nut at the base of the float chamber and pull the feed pipe to the jet assembly clear. If the float chamber is removed completely it is a simple matter to turn it upside down to drop the float out. Check that the float is not cracked or leaking. If it is it must be repaired or renewed.

The float chamber cover contains the needle valve assembly which regulates the amount of fuel which is fed into the float chamber.

One end of the float lever rests on top of the float, rising and falling with it, while the other end pivots on a hinge pin which is held by two lugs. On the float cover side of the float lever is a needle which rises and falls in its brass seating according to the movement of the lever.

With the cover in place the hinge pin is held in position by the walls of the float chamber. With the cover removed the pin is easily pushed out so freeing the float lever and the needles.

Examine the tip of the needle and the needle seating for wear. Wear is present when there is a discernible ridge in the chamfer of the needle. If this is evident then the needle and seating must be renewed. This is a simple operation and the hexagon head of the needle housing is easily screwed out. The needle and the seating should be renewed together as otherwise it will not be possible to get a fuel tight joint.

Clean the fuel chamber out thoroughly. Reassembly is a reversal of the dismantling procedure detailed above. Before replacing the float chamber cover, check that fuel level setting is correct.

17 SU carburettor float chamber - fuel level adjustment

It is essential that the fuel level in the float chamber is always correct as otherwise excessive fuel consumtion may occur. On reassembly of the float chamber check the fuel level before replacing the float chamber cover, in the following manner: Invert the float chamber so that the needle valve is closed. It should just be possible to place a 0.32 in (7.937 mm) - early models or 0.125 in (3.175 mm) - later models, bar parallel to the float lever hinge pin and in the centre of the float chamber cover without fouling the float. If the bar lifts the float, or if the float stands proud of the bar then it is necessary to bend the float lever very slightly until the clearance is correct.

18 SU carburettor - examination and repair

The SU carburettor generally speaking, is most reliable, but even so it may develop one of several faults which may not be readily apparent unless a careful inspection is carried out. The common faults the carburettor is prone to are:

1 Piston sticking.
2 Float needle sticking.
3 Float chamber flooding.
4 Water and dirt in the carburettor.

In addition the following parts are susceptible to wear after long mileages and as they vitally affect the economy of the engine should be checked and renewed, where necessary, every 24,000 miles (40,000 km).

a) The carburettor needle: If this has been incorrectly assembled at some time so that it is not centrally located in the jet orifice, then the metering needle will have a tiny ridge worn on it. If a ridge can be seen then the needle must be renewed. SU carburettor needles are made to very fine tolerances and should a ridge be apparent no attempt should be made to rub the needle down with fine emery paper. If it is wished to clean the needle it can be polished lightly with metal polish.

b) The carburettor jet: If the needle is worn it is likely that the rim of the jet will be damaged where the needle has been striking it. It should be renewed as otherwise fuel consumption will suffer. The jet can also be badly worn or ridged on the outside from where it has been sliding up and down between the jet bearings everytime the choke has been pulled out. Removal and renewal is the only answer here as well.

c) Check the edges of the throttle and the choke tube for wear. Renew if worn.

d) The washers fitted to the base of the jet, to the float chamber, and to the petrol inlet union may all leak after a time and can cause much fuel wastage. It is wisest to renew them automatically when the carburettor is stripped down.

e) After high mileages the float chamber needle and seat are bound to be ridged. They are not an expensive item to replace and should be renewed as a set. They should never be renewed separately.

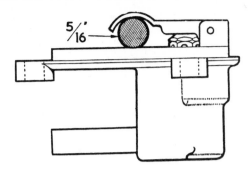

Fig. 3.16. Method of setting the correct clearance of the float lever (early cars)

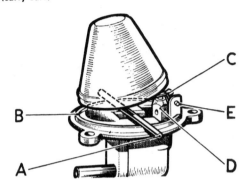

Fig. 3.17. Method of setting the correct clearance of the float lever (later cars)

A 0.125 in. (3.18 mm)
B 0.1875 in. (4.76 mm)
C Angle of float lever
D Float needle and seat assembly
E Lever hinge pin

19 SU carburettor - piston sticking

The hardened piston rod which slides in the centre guide tube in the middle of the dashpot is the only part of the piston assembly (which comprises the jet needle, suction disc, and piston choke) that should make contact with the dashpot. The piston rim and the choke periphery are machined to very fine tolerances so that they will not touch the dashpot or the choke tube walls.

After high mileages wear in the centre guide tube (especially on semi-downdraught SU's) may allow the piston to touch the dashpot wall. This condition is known as sticking.

If piston sticking is suspected or it is wished to test for this condition, rotate the piston about the centre guide tube at the same time sliding it up and down inside the dashpot. If any portion of the piston makes contact with the dashpot wall then that portion of the wall must be polished with metal polish until clearance exists. In extreme cases, fine emery cloth can be used.

The greatest care should be taken to remove only the minimum amount of metal to provide the clearance, as too large a gap will cause air leakage and will upset the functioning of the carburettor. Clean down the walls of the dashpot and the piston rim and ensure that there is no oil on them. A trace of oil may be judiciously applied to the piston rod.

If the piston is sticking under no circumstances try to clear it by trying to alter the tension of the light return spring.

20 SU carburettor - float needle sticking

If the float needle sticks the carburettor will soon run dry and the engine will stop despite there being fuel in the tank.

The easiest way to check a suspected sticking float needle is to remove the inlet pipe at the carburettor, and where a mechanical fuel pump is fitted, turn the engine over on the starter motor by pressing the solenoid. Where an electrical fuel pump is fitted turn on the ignition. If fuel spurts from the end of the pipe (direct it towards the ground or into a wad of cloth or jar), then the fault is almost certain to be a sticking float needle.

Remove the float chamber, dismantle the valve and clean the housing and float chamber out thoroughly.

21 SU carburettor - float chamber flooding

If fuel emerges from the small breather hole in the cover of the float chamber this condition is known as flooding. It is caused by the float chamber needle not seating properly in its housing; normally this is because a piece of dirt or foreign matter is jammed between the needle and the needle housing. Alternatively the float may have developed a leak or be maladjusted so that it is holding open the float chamber needle valve even though the chamber is full of petrol. Remove the float chamber cover, clean the needle assembly, check the setting of the float as described in Section 17 and shake the float to verify if any petrol has leaked into it.

22 SU carburettor - water and dirt in carburettor

Because of the size of the jet orifice, water or dirt in the carburettor is normally easily cleared. If dirt in the carburettor is suspected, lift the piston assembly and flood the float chamber. The normal level of fuel should be about 1/16 in below the top of the jet, so that on flooding the carburettor the fuel should well up out of the jet hole.

If very little or no petrol appears, start the engine (the jet is never completely blocked) and with the throttle fully open, blank off the air intake. This will create a partial vacuum in the choke tube and help to suck out any foreign matter from the jet tube. Release the throttle as soon as the engine starts to race. Repeat this procedure several times, stop the engine, and then check the carburettor as detailed in the first paragraph.

If this has failed to do the trick then there is no alternative but to remove and blow out the jet.

23 SU carburettor - needle replacement

1 Should it be found necessary to fit a new needle, first remove the piston and suction chamber assembly, marking the chamber for correct reassembly in its original position.
2 Slacken the needle clamping screw and withdraw the needle from the piston.
3 Upon refitting a new needle it is important that the shoulder on the shank is flush with the underside of the piston. Use a straight edge such as a metal rule for the adjustment. Refit the piston and suction chamber and check for freedom of piston movement. (Fig. 3.18).

24 SU carburettor - jet centering

The carburettor metering needle is used as a pilot for centering the jet. The piston should therefore be in position, with the dashpot in place, before the jet is centred. Remove the link between the jet head and lever. Remove the union holding the nylon feed tube to the base of the jet, together with the jet and jet adjusting nut securing spring.

Replace the jet and nylon feed tube and press them up under the head of the large hexagonal jet locking nut. Unscrew this nut slightly until the jet bearing can be turned.

Remove the damper securing nut and damper from the top of the dashpot and push the piston assembly right down so that the metering needle enters fully into the jet.

Tighten the jet locking nut and test the piston assembly to check that the needle is still quite free to slide in the jet orifice. Lift the piston and then release it. The piston should hit the inside jet bridge with a soft metallic click, and the intensity of the click should be the same whether the jet is in its normal position or is fully lowered.

If the sound is different when the jet is fully lowered, then the jet is not properly centralised and the process must be repeated.

When all is correct, remove the jet, replace the jet adjusting nut securing spring, the adjusting nut and jet, and the link between the jet head and lever.

25 SU carburettor - adjustment and tuning

Important: Models fitted with automatic transmission refer to Section 27 first

To adjust and tune the SU carburettor proceed in the following manner: Check the colour of the exhaust at idling speed with the choke fully in. If the exhaust tends to be black, and the tailpipe interior is also black it is a fair indication that the mixture is too rich. If the exhaust is colourless and the deposit in the exhaust pipe is very light grey it is likely that the mixture is too weak. This condition may also be accompanied by intermittent misfiring, while too rich a mixture will be associated with 'hunting'. Ideally the exhaust should be colourless with a medium grey pipe deposit.

The exhaust pipe deposit should only be checked after a good run of at least 20 miles. Idling in city traffic and stop/start motoring is bound to produce excessively dark exhaust pipe deposits.

Once the engine has reached its normal operating temperature, detach the carburettor/s air intake cleaner. With twin carburettors disconnect the throttle linkage between them by loosening the throttle shaft levers on the throttle shaft.

Only two adjustments are provided on the SU carburettor. Idling speed is governed by the throttle adjusting screw, and the mixture strength by the jet adjusting screw. The SU carburettor is correctly adjusted for the whole of its engine revolution range when the idling mixture strength is correct.

Idling speed adjustment is effected by the idling adjusting screw. To adjust the mixture set the engine to run about 1,000 rpm by screwing in the idling screw. If twin SU carburettors are fitted repeat this procedure for each instrument in turn.

Check the mixture strength by lifting the piston of the carburettor approximately 1/32 in (8 mm) with the piston lifting pin so as to disturb the airflow as little as possible. If:
a) The speed of the engine increases appreciably the mixture is too rich.
b) The engine speed immediately decreases the mixture is too weak.
c) The engine speed increases very slightly the mixture is correct.

To enrich the mixture rotate the adjusting screw, which is the screw at the bottom of the carburettor, in an anticlockwise direction, ie downwards. To weaken the mixture rotate the jet adjusting screw in a clockwise direction ie upwards. Only turn the adjusting screw a flat at a time and check the mixture strength each turn. It is likely that there will be a slight increase or decrease in rpm after the mixture adjustment has been made so the throttle idling adjusting screw should now be turned so that the engine idles at between 600 and 700 rpm.

26 Synchronisation of twin SU carburettors

First ensure that the mixture is correct in each instrument. With twin SU carburettors, in addition to the mixture strength being correct for each instrument the idling suction must be equal on both. It is best to use a vacuum synchronising device such as the Motor Meter synchro tester. If this is not available it

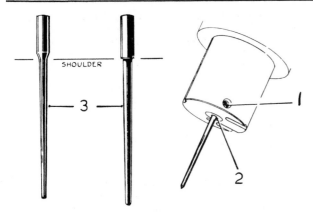

Fig. 3.18. Needle fitting into piston

1 *Needle securing screw*
2 *Needle shoulder flush with bottom of piston*
3 *Needle (two types of shoulder are in use)*

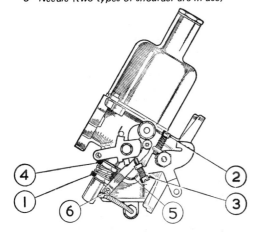

Fig. 3.19. Carburettor adjustment screws (HS2)

1 *Jet adjusting nut*	4 *Jet locking nut*
2 *Throttle adjusting screw*	5 *Float chamber bolt*
3 *Fast-idle adjustment screw*	6 *Jet link securing screw*

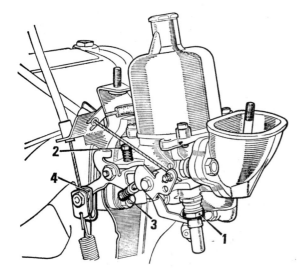

Fig. 3.20. Carburettor adjustment points (HS4)

1 *Jet adjustment nut*	3 *Fast idle adjustment screw*
2 *Throttle adjustment screw*	4 *Governor control rod*

is possible to obtain fairly accurate synchronisation by listening to the hiss made by the air flow into the intake throats of each carburettor.

The aim is to adjust the throttle butterfly disc so that an equal amount of air enters each carburettor. Loosen the throttle shaft levers on the throttle shaft which connects the two throttle disc splines. Listen to the hiss from each carburettor and if a difference in intensity is noticed between them, then unscrew the throttle adjusting screw on the other carburettor until the hiss from both the carburettors is the same.

With vacuum synchronisation device all that it is necessary to do is to place the instrument over the mouth of each carburettor in turn and adjust the adjusting screws until the reading on the gauge is identical for both carburettors.

Tighten the levers on the interconnecting linkage to connect the throttle disc of the two carburettors together, at the same time holding down the throttle adjusting screws against their idling stops. Synchronisation of the two carburettors is now complete.

27 SU carburettor adjustment and tuning - automatic transmission models

The method of adjusting the jet and slow running for the HS4 carburettor is basically identical to that for the HS2 but the following additional points should be noted.

1 To obtain accuracy it is desirable to fit an electric tachometer to the ignition system.

2 Move the selector to the "N" position and apply the handbrake.

3 Start the engine and run until it reaches normal operating temperature.

4 Adjust the jet position as described in Section 25.

5 Adjust the throttle adjustment screw (Fig. 3.20) until a maximum engine idle speed of 650 rpm is obtained.

6 Pull out the choke control knob to the maximum fast idle position. Check, and adjust if necessary, the fast idel adjustment screw so as to obtain a maximum fast idle speed of 1050 rpm.

7 Push in the choke control again and recheck the engine idle speed.

8 The governor control rod should now be adjusted. Refer to Chapter 6 for further information.

28 Fuel tank - removal and replacement

Boot fuel tank:

1 Disconnect the earth lead from the battery and remove the petrol gauge wires from their attachments to the fuel gauge sender unit mounted in the side of the tank.

2 Remove the filler cap and, on early models, undo the clip holding the flexible pipe from the tank to the fuel pump inlet nozzle and drain the fuel tank contents into a suitable container. Later models are fitted with a combined drain plug and tube. From under the car undo the drain plug three turns, with a 7/16 in box spanner at least 5 in long, and let all the fuel run into a suitable container. **Note:** The drain plug operates on the same principle as a brake bleed nipple. When the tank is empty remove the drain plug and tube completely. Latest models do not have a drain plug so it will be necessary to syphon any petrol from the tank.

3 On later models, undo the clip holding the flexible fuel pipe to the inlet side of the fuel pump and pull the pipe off the nozzle of the pump.

4 Undo and remove the bolt from the tank retaining strap, free the vent pipe from the clip on the rear seat panel, and carefully manoeuvre the tank from the boot.

5 On replacing the tank ensure that the fuel tank locating plate is in position with the tongue secure in the slot in the floor of the boot, before the retaining strap bolt is tightened down.

6 Also ensure that the drain plug and washer are securely

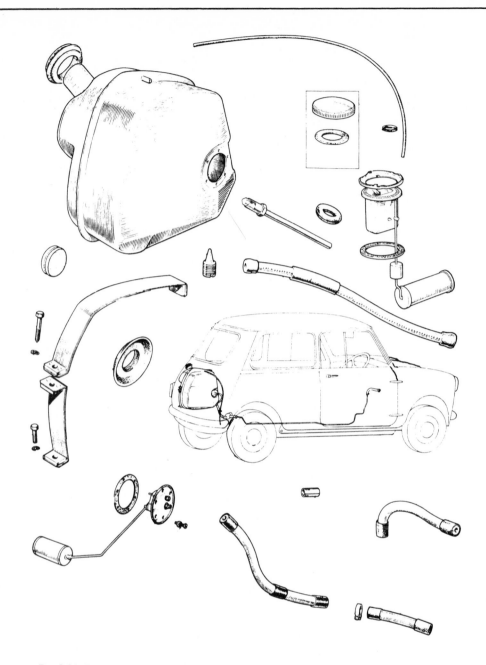

Fig. 3.21. Fuel tank and fittings — Saloons Mk I, Elf, Hornet Mk I, Cooper and 'S' Mk I

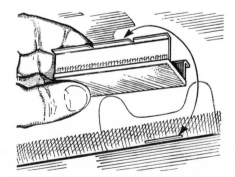

Fig. 3.22. The tongue of the fuel tank locating plate must be secured in the slot in the luggage compartment floor

replaced and make a good seal with the body so that water cannot leak through, and that the rubber ferrule beneath the filler cap makes an efficient seal with the body.

7   The drain tube and plug should not be refitted until the tank is back in position.

Under floor fuel tank:

1   Remove the filler cap and from underneath the car unscrew the drain plug from the tank, draining the contents into a suitable container. When drained, replace the plug and washer securely.

2   While still underneath the car disconnect the fuel outlet pipe from the tank connection.

3   Disconnect the earth lead from the battery (positive terminal) and remove the petrol gauge wires from their attachments to the fuel gauge sender unit mounted in the side of the tank.

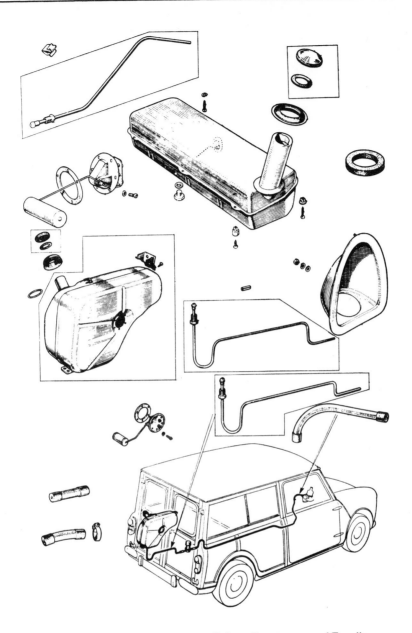

Fig. 3.23. Fuel tank and fittings — Van, Pick-up, Countryman and Traveller

4 Unscrew the six screws which hold the tank unit in place and remove the tank. Note the nylon spacers under the flange and take care not to damage them. At this stage it is sometimes helpful to position a jack under the tank so that it does not pull away as the bolts are released. It may be found easier to move the tank partially before releasing the sender gauge unit leads, as, with the tank half removed, they are more accessible.
Note: On early Countryman and Traveller models paragraph 4 above does not apply. Here it is necessary to remove the trim from the side of the body above the tank; to remove the luggage platform floor; and to remove the bolts which hold the tank to its support brackets. The removal procedure is otherwise the same.

Replacing the tank is a reversal of the above process. Four particular points to watch are:
a) The nylon spacers are correctly in place.

b) The drain plug and washer are securely replaced.
c) The rubber ferrule beneath the filler cap makes an efficient seal with the body.
d) The end of the breather pipe is held well clear of the exhaust pipe, with the aid of a rubber clip.

Moke:

1 The fuel tank is located in the left-hand sidemember.
2 Remove the forward pannier side cover and disconnect the lead from the fuel gauge sender unit terminal.
3 Working under the sidemember and through the access hole drain the fuel tank (Fig. 3.24).
4 Slacken the clip and disconnect the suction hose from the fuel pump.

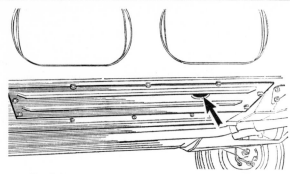

Fig. 3.24. Access point for draining fuel tank (Moke)

5 Undo and remove the screws securing the bottom cover plate from the sidemember.

6 Undo and remove the fuel tank retaining screw from the top face of the sidemember.

7 Remove the support bracket and carefully lower the fuel tank.

8 Refitting the fuel tank is the reverse sequence to removal.

Cooper 'S' twin fuel tank:

1 Working in the rear luggage compartment remove the trimmed floor panel.

2 For safety reasons, disconnect the battery earth cable.

3 Lift out the spare wheel.

4 Remove the fuel filler caps.

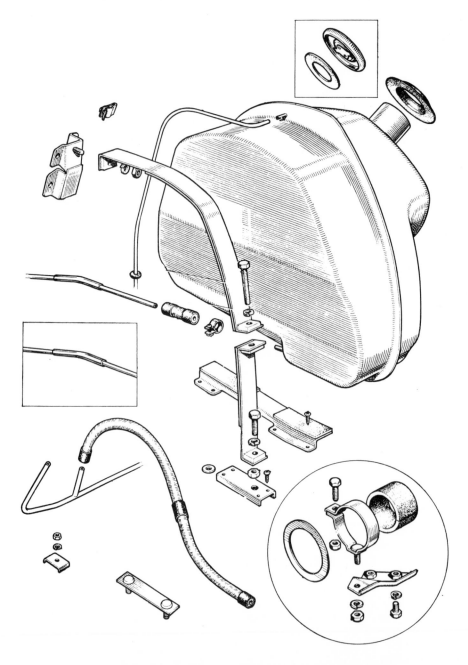

Fig. 3.25. Fuel tank and fittings — Saloons Mk II, Elf and Hornet Mk III

5 Unscrew the left-hand fuel tank drain plug three turns and allow fuel to drain from both tanks.
Left-hand tank: (for right-hand tank proceed to paragraph 10).

6 Disconnect the electrical connectors from the sender unit.
7 Remove the tank strap securing bolt.
8 Detach the flexible pipe and the vent pipe from the fuel tank.
9 Carefully ease the fuel tank towards the centre of the luggage compartment and lift away from the rear of the car.

Right-hand tank:

10 Completely remove the battery.
11 Remove the tank strap securing bolt.
12 Detach the flexible hose from the left-hand tank.
13 Move the tank slightly from its mountings taking extreme care not to damage the flexible fuel pipes.
14 The fuel tank will still contain a small amount of petrol which should be drained into a small container when the flexible fuel pipe is disconnected.
15 Disconnect the flexible fuel pipe.
16 Finally detach the vent pipe from the tank and lift away the tank from the rear of the car.
17 Refitting the fuel tank is the reverse sequence to removal. Make sure that the seal around the drain plug housing is watertight.

29 Fuel tank - cleaning

With time it is likely that sediment will collect in the bottom of the fuel tank. Condensation, resulting in rust and other impurities, will usually be found in the fuel tank of any car more than three or four years old.

When the tank is removed it should be vigorously flushed out and turned upside down, and if facilities are available, steam cleaned.

30 Fuel tank sender unit - (fuel level gauge) - removal and replacement

All models, except Moke:

1 Disconnect the earth lead from the battery (positive terminal) and remove the petrol gauge wires from their attachments to the fuel gauge sender unit mounted in the side of the tank.

2 *Early models*: Unscrew the screws which hold the gauge unit to the tank carefully, and lift the complete unit away, ensuring that the float lever is not bent or damaged in the process.

3 *Later models*: Using crossed screwdrivers remove the fuel gauge sender unit by turning the locking ring through 30° and lifting away. Carefully lift the unit from the tank ensuring the float lever is not bent or damaged in the process.
4 Replacement of the unit is a reversal of the above process. To ensure a fuel tight joint, scrape both the tank and sender gauge mating flanges clean, and always use a new joint washer and a suitable gasket cement.

Moke:

1 Refer to Section 28, and remove the fuel tank.
2 Removal is now similar to that described for all other Mini models.

31 Exhaust emission control system - general description

Certain models of the Mini, in particular those exported to the USA are fitted with an exhaust emission control system that conforms to the various laws governing the amount of carbon monoxide and hydrocarbons emitted from the exhaust outlet.

The system fitted to the Mini allows a maximum of 4.5% of carbon monoxide to be emitted.

Fig. 3.26 shows a typical layout of the system which works in the following way.

A rotary vane air pump (5) which is mounted on the front of the cylinder head and is belt driven from the water pump pulley, pumps air through a manifold (1) to the exhaust ports in the cylinder head. The air entering the pump is cleaned in a dry element replaceable air cleaner (4). At high engine revolutions more air may be pressurised in the pump than is required at the exhaust ports, so this is allowed to escape through a relief valve (6). Gases from the exhaust ports are prevented from coming back along the manifold into the pump by a non-return check valve (3). Should the belt driving the pump break or the airflow from the pump fail for any other reason the valve will automatically close.

A gulp valve (9) fitted in the pump line to the inlet manifold controls the amount of air being passed to the inlet manifold on engine over-run, a condition that normally causes a rich mixture to enter the inlet ports. By allowing extra air to be fed into the manifold on over-run, the gulp valve thus ensures a more complete burn of the fuel/air mixture.

The special SU HS4 carburettor fitted to emission controlled

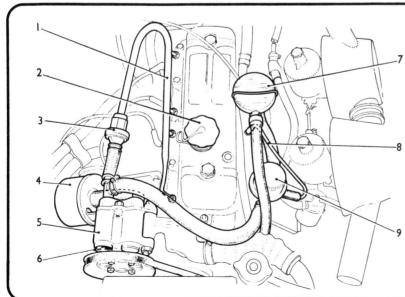

Fig. 3.26. View of engine emission control layout

1 Air manifold
2 Filtered oil filler cap
3 Non-return check valve
4 Air pump air filter
5 Air pump
6 Relief valve
7 Crankcase emission control valve
8 Gulp valve signal pipe
9 Gulp valve

models is balanced to provide maximum performance with a near perfect fuel/air mixture at all engine speeds. Under no circumstances must it be changed for any other type of carburettor or parts interchanged as it is manufactured to very fine tolerances.

On some models a line fuel filter is fitted. On models with electrical fuel pumps this is fitted between the pump and the carburettor. On later models with a mechanical fuel pump it is fitted between the tank and the fuel pump. This filter acts as an added safeguard against dirt reaching the carburettor and disturbing the very critical settings.

Note: It is not advisable for the private owner to attempt to service or repair any components of the exhaust emission control system except the line fuel filter replacement which is detailed below. As the adjustments and settings are so critical it is better to entrust the work to your local BLMC garage.

32 Fuel line filter - removal and replacement

1 The line fuel filter must be replaced every 12,000 miles (20,000 km).
2 To remove the filter check that the ignition is off, (in the case of models with an electrical fuel pump) unscrew the clips at either end of the filter and pull off the fuel pipes.
3 Discard the old filter and fit a new one.
4 With electrical fuel pumps, having fitted the new filter, switch on the ignition and check for leaks. Start the engine and check for leaks again. With a mechanical fuel pump start the engine, rev it up and check for leaks.

33 Crankcase emission control valve - general description

The crankcase emission control valve enables fumes created in

the crankcase to be fed into the inlet manifold where they are carried in with the fuel/air mixture and burnt in the cylinders. The crankcase outlet connection incorporates an oil separator to prevent any oil being pulled over with the fumes from the crankcase. A filtered, restricted hole 9/16 in diameter in the oil filler cap provides a supply of fresh air to the crankcase as fumes are withdrawn by inlet manifold depression.

34 Crankcase emission control valve - special servicing

1 Every 12,000 miles (20,000 km) a new oil filter cap must be fitted and the crankcase emission control valve serviced.
2 Referring to Fig. 3.27 remove all the connecting pipes, remove the spring clip (6) and cover plate (5) and lift out the rubber diaphragm (4) noting the correct fitting position of its top face.
3 Remove the metering valve (3) and the spring (2) then clean all components in petrol or methylated spirits.
4 Renew the diaphragm if this appears to be damaged in any way and reassemble in the reverse order to the above procedure.

35 Crankcase emission control valve - testing

1 Start the engine and allow it to warm up to its normal operating temperature.
2 With the engine running at its normal idling speed, remove the oil filler cap. If the crankcase emission control valve is working correctly, this action will result in an audible increase in the engine speed.
3 If the engine speed does not increase service the valve as described in Section 34.

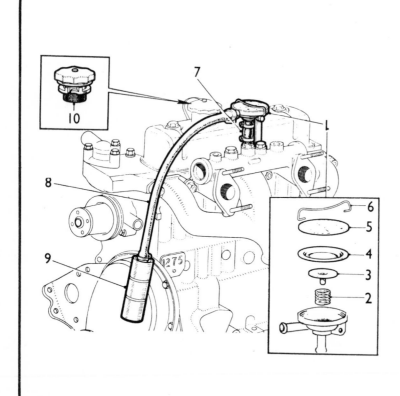

Fig. 3.27. View of crankcase emission
        control system

1 Emission control valve
2 Valve spring
3 Metering valve
4 Diaphragm
5 Cover plate
6 Spring clip
7 Manifold connection
8 Breather hose
9 Oil separator
10 Filtered oil filler cap

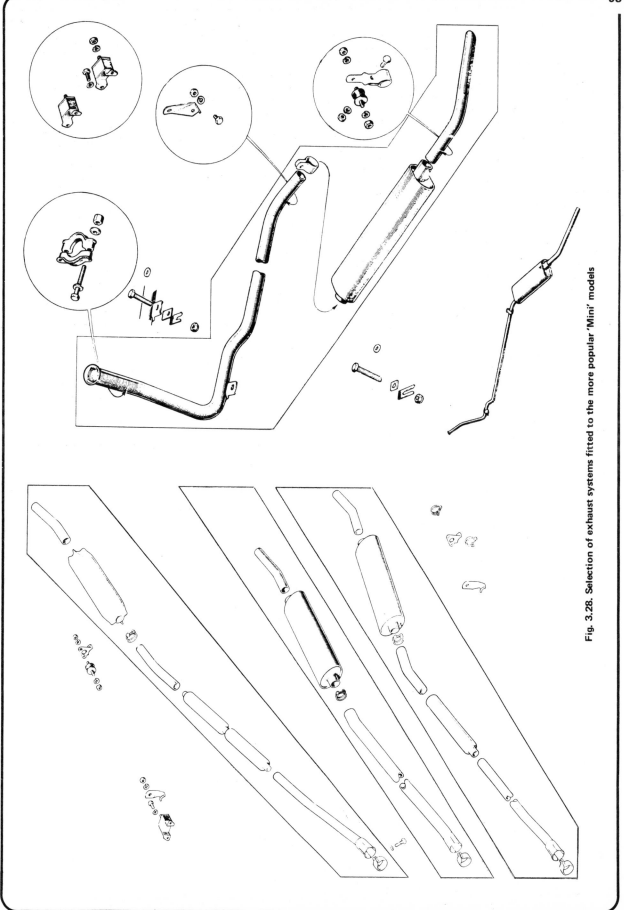

Fig. 3.28. Selection of exhaust systems fitted to the more popular 'Mini' models

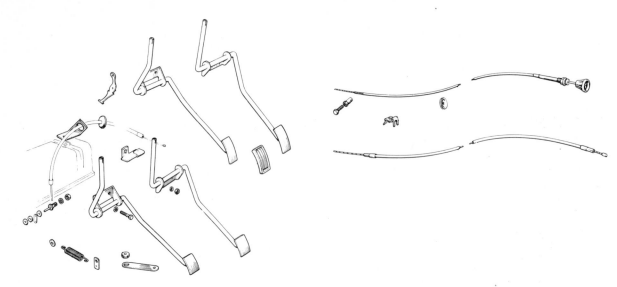

Fig. 3.29. Choke cable, accelerator cable and pedal assemblies

36 Fault diagnosis - carburation

Symptom	Reason/s	Remedy
Fuel consumption excessive	Air cleaner choked and dirty giving rich mixture	Remove, clean and replace air cleaner.
	Fuel leaking from carburettor, fuel pumps, or fuel lines	Check for and eliminate all fuel leaks. Tighten fuel line union nuts.
	Float chamber flooding	Check and adjust float level.
	Generally worn carburettor	Remove, overhaul and replace.
	Distributor condenser faulty	Remove, and fit new unit.
	Balance weights or vacuum advance mechanism in distributor faulty	Remove, and overhaul distributor.
	Carburettor incorrectly adjusted, mixture too rich	Tune and adjust carburettor.
	Idling speed too high	Adjust idling speed.
	Contact breaker gap incorrect	Check and reset gap.
	Valve clearances incorrect	Check clearances and adjust as necessary.
	Incorrectly set spark plugs	Remove, clean, and regap.
	Tyres under-inflated	Check tyre pressures and inflate if necessary.
	Wrong spark plugs fitted	Remove and replace with correct units.
	Brakes dragging	Check and adjust brakes.
Insufficient fuel delivery or weak mixture	Petrol tank air vent restricted	Remove petrol cap and clean out air vent.
	Partially clogged filters in pump and carburettor	Remove and clean filters.
	Dirt lodged in float chamber needle housing	Remove and clean out float chamber and needle valve assembly.
	Incorrectly seating valves in fuel pump	Remove, dismantle, and clean out fuel pump.
	Fuel pump diaphragm leaking or damaged	Remove, and overhaul fuel pump.
	Gasket in fuel pump damaged	Remove, and overhaul fuel pump.
	Fuel pump valves sticking due to petrol gumming	Remove, and thoroughly clean fuel pump.
	Too little fuel in fuel tank (Prevalent when climbing steep hills)	Refill fuel tank.
	Union joints on pipe connections loose	Tighten joints and check for air leaks.
	Split in fuel pipe on suction side of fuel pump	Examine, locate, and repair.
	Inlet manifold to block or inlet manifold to carburettor gasket leaking	Test by pouring oil along joints - bubbles indicate leak. Renew gasket as appropriate.

Chapter 4 Ignition system

Contents

Specifications

Spark plugs:

Mini 1000/Clubman/1275 GT/Cooper 'S' engines	Champion N9Y
848 cc Automatic, 997 and 998 cc Cooper engines	Champion N5
Other engines	N5 or N9Y
Size	14 mm
Gap	0.024 - 0.026 in (0.61 - 0.66 mm)

Firing order ... ...   1 - 3 - 4 - 2 (no. 1 cylinder next to radiator)

Coil:

All models - excluding Cooper models	Lucas LA12
Cooper models	Lucas HA12
Primary resistance at 20°C (68°F):	
Lucas LA12	3.2 - 3.4 ohms (cold)
Lucas HA12	3.0 - 3.4 ohms (cold)
Consumption (ignition on)	3.9 amps

Automatic advance:

All models except 1275 engine	Centrifugal and vacuum
1275 engine	Centrifugal only

Distributor:

Type:	
Early models	Lucas DM2P4 or DM2
Later models	Lucas 23D4, 24D4, 25D4 or 45D4
Contact breaker gap	0.014 - 0.016 in. (0.35 - 0.40 mm)
Rotational direction of rotor	Anticlockwise
Dwell angle	60° ± 3° (51° ± 5° for the 45D4 type)
Condenser capacity	0.18 - 0.24 mf
Serial Numbers:	
Lucas DM2P4 or DM2	
a) Premium fuel distributor (Mini 850)	40768 or 41026
b) Regular fuel distributor (Mini 850)	40767 or 41007
Lucas 23 D4, 24 D4 or 25 D4	
c) 998 cc (1967 on)	40931 or 41030 (25 D4)
d) 848 cc (Mini 850 Mk 1 and Mk 11 automatic, 1965 - 69)	41134, 41242 or 41251 (25 D4)
e) 998 cc (Mini 1000 and Clubman Automatic, 1967 on) ...	41134 or 41242 (25 D4)
997 cc (Mini Cooper, 1961 - 64)	
f) High compression	40774 (25 D4)
g) Low compression	40873 (25 D4)
998 cc (Mini Cooper, 1964 - 69)	
h) High compression	40955 or 41032 (24 D4)
i) Low compression	40958 or 41031 (24 D4)
j) 970 and 1071 cc (Mini Cooper 'S', 1963 - 1965) ...	40819 (23 D4)
k) 1275 cc (Mini Cooper 'S' Mk I, II and III, 1964 on) ...	40819 or 41033 (23 D4)
l) 998 cc (Mini Clubman, 1969)	41030 (25 D4)
m) 1275 cc (Mini 1275 GT, 1969)	41257 (25 D4)

Lucas 45 D4
   n) Mini 1000 (later models) and Clubman   41418
   p) Mini 1275 GT...   41419
   q) Mini 850 (later models)   41417

Centrifugal and vacuum advance (crankshaft degrees and rpm):
Note - Centrifugal advance figures quoted are with the vacuum pipe disconnected

a) **Centrifugal advance**   **Vacuum advance**
   30° to 34° at 3400 rpm   Starts ...   ...   7 in (17.7 cm) Hg
   24° to 28° at 2500 rpm   Finishes   ... 10° at 13 in (33 cm) Hg
   16° to 20° at 1300 rpm
   9° to 15° at 900 rpm
   1° to 7° at 700 rpm
   No advance below 500 rpm

b) **Centrifugal advance**   **Vacuum advance**
   22° to 26° at 5000 rpm   Starts ...   ...   5 in (12.7 cm) Hg
   15° to 19° at 3900 rpm   Finishes   ... 16° at 11 in (27.9 cm) Hg
   1° to 5° at 1700 rpm
   No advance below 850 rpm

c) **Centrifugal advance**   **Vacuum advance**
   22° to 26° at 5000 rpm   Starts ...   ...   5in (12.7 cm) Hg
   16° to 20° at 3400 rpm   Finishes   ... 14° at 11 in (27.9 cm) Hg
   9° to 13° at 1600 rpm
   6° to 10° at 1300 rpm
   0° to 4° at 900 rpm
   No advance below 600 rpm

d) **Centrifugal advance**   **Vacuum advance**
   26° to 30° at 5500 rpm   Starts ...   ...   3 in (7.62 cm) Hg
   24° to 28° at 4800 rpm   Finishes   ... 18° at 15 in (38.1 cm) Hg
   15° to 19° at 1800 rpm
   12° to 16° at 1600 rpm
   0° to 4° at 800 rpm
   No advance below 600 rpm

e) **See (d)**

f) **Centrifugal advance**   **Vacuum advance**
   16° to 22° at 1600 rpm   Starts ...   ...   3 in (7.62 cm) Hg
   2° to 8° at 1000 rpm   Finishes   ... 14° at 8 in (20.3 cm)
   0° to 3° at 800 rpm
   No advance below 600 rpm

g) **Centrifugal advance**   **Vacuum advance**
   26° to 30° at 2600 rpm   Starts ...   ...   4 in (10.1 cm) Hg
   21° to 25° at 2000 rpm   Finishes   ... 14° at 7 in (17.8 cm) Hg
   15° to 19° at 1200 rpm
   8° to 12° at 900 rpm
   0° to 5° at 600 rpm
   No advance below 300 rpm

h) **Centrifugal advance**   **Vacuum advance**
   30° to 34° at 6000 rpm   Starts ...   ...   3 in (7.62 cm) Hg
   28° to 32° at 4500 rpm   Finishes   ... 14° at 8 in (20.32 cm) Hg
   24° to 28° at 4200 rpm
   18° to 22° at 2300 rpm
   12° to 16° at 1800 rpm
   1° to 5° at 800 rpm
   No advance below 300 rpm

i) **Centrifugal advance**   **Vacuum advance**
   28° to 32° at 5500 rpm   Starts ...   ...   3 in (7.62 cm) Hg
   26° to 30° at 4400 rpm   Finishes   ... 16° at 7 in (17.7 cm) Hg
   22° to 26° at 2200 rpm
   16° to 20° at 1800 rpm
   3° to 9° at 1000 rpm
   0° to 3° at 600 rpm
   No advance below 400 rpm

j) **Centrifugal advance**   **Vacuum advance**
   28° to 32° at 7000 rpm   Nil
   22° to 26° at 5200 rpm
   10° to 14° at 1600 rpm
   6° to 12° at 1000 rpm

0° to 3° at 600 rpm
No advance below 450 rpm

k) **Centrifugal advance**
28° to 32° at 7000 rpm
22° to 20° at 5200 rpm
10° to 14° at 1600 rpm
6° to 12° at 1000 rpm
0° to 3° at 600 rpm
No advance below 450 rpm

Vacuum advance
Nil

l) **Centrifugal advance**
22° to 26° at 5000 rpm
16° to 20° at 3400 rpm
9° to 13° at 1600 rpm
6° to 10° at 1300 rpm
0° to 4° at 900 rpm
No advance below 600 rpm

Vacuum advance
Starts ...   ...   5 in (12.7 cm) Hg
Finishes   ...   14° at 11 in (27.9 cm) Hg

m) **Centrifugal advance**
18° to 22° at 4000 rpm
11° to 15° at 2800 rpm
0° to 10° at 2000 rpm
4° to 8° at 1600 rpm
0° to 3° at 800 rpm
No advance below 300 rpm

Vacuum advance
Starts ...   ...   3 in (7.62 cm) Hg
Finishes   ...   18° to 22° at 10 in (25.4 cm) Hg

n) **Centrifugal advance**
14° to 18° at 4000 rpm
9° to 13° at 2400 rpm
6° to 10° at 1500 rpm
0° to 1° at 900 rpm
No advance below 800 rpm

Vacuum advance
Starts ...   ...   6 in (15.2 cm) Hg
Finishes   ...   16° at 14 in (35.6 cm) Hg

p) **Centrifugal advance**
18° to 22° at 4000 rpm
11° to 15° at 2800 rpm
6½° to 10° at 2100 rpm
4° to 8° at 1600 rpm
0° to 3° at 800 rpm
No advance below 300 rpm

Vacuum advance
Starts ...   ...   3 in (7.6 cm) Hg
Finishes   ...   20° at 10 in (25.4 cm) Hg

q) **Centrifugal advance**
24° to 28° at 4800 rpm
18° to 22° at 2800 rpm
12° to 16° at 1600 rpm
0° to 4° at 800 rpm
No advance below 300 rpm

Vacuum advance
Starts ...   ...   3 in (7.6 cm) Hg
Finishes   ...   18° at 15 in (38.1 cm) Hg

Ignition timing:

									970 cc	1071
a)	Static	...	...	...	...	...	...	...	tdc	
	Strobe at 600 rpm	...	...	...	...	...	...	3° btdc	
b)	Static	...	...	...	...	...	...	...	7° btdc	
	Strobe at 600 rpm	...	...	...	....	...	...	10° btdc	
c)	Static	...	...	...	...	...	...	...	5° btdc	
T	Strobe at 600 rpm	...	...	...	...	...	...	8° btdc	
d)	Static	...	...	...	...	...	...	...	3° btdc	
	Strobe at 600 rpm	...	...	...	...	...	...	6° btdc	
e)	Static	...	...	...	...	...	...	...	4° btdc	
	Strobe at 600 rpm	...	...	...	...	...	...	6° btdc	
f)	Static	...	...	...	...	...	...	...	7° btdc	
	Strobe at 600 rpm	...	...	...	...	...	...	9° btdc	
g)	Static	...	...	...	...	...	...	...	5° btdc	
	Strobe at 600 rpm	...	...	...	...	...	...	7° btdc	
h)	Static	...	...	...	...	...	...	...	5° btdc	
	Strobe at 600 rpm	...	...	...	...	...	...	7° btdc	
i)	Static	...	...	...	...	...	...	...	5° btdc	
	Strobe at 600 rpm	...	...	...	...	...	...	7° btdc	
j)	Static	...	...	...	...	...	...	...	12° btdc	3° btdc
	Strobe at 600 rpm	...	...	...	...	...	...	14° btdc	5° btdc
k)	Static	...	...	...	...	...	...	...	2° btdc	
	Strobe at 600 rpm	...	...	...	...	...	...	4° btdc	
l)	Static	...	...	...	...	...	...	...	5° btdc	
	Strobe at 600 rpm	...	...	...	...	...	...	8° btdc	
m)	Static	...	...	...	...	...	...	...	8° btdc	

								998	1098
Strobe at 600 rpm	...	...	...	...	...	...	10º btdc		
n) Strobe at 1000 rpm	...	...	...	...	...	...		7º	12º
p) Strobe at 1000 rpm	...	...	...	...	...	...	13º btdc		
q) Strobe at 1000 rpm	...	...	...	...	...	...	7º btdc		

Timing marks   ...   .   Dimples on timing wheels, marks on flywheel or converter (Automatic transmission)

Torque wrench settings

							lbf ft	kgf m
Spark plugs							30	4.15
Distributor to plate							2.5	0.35
Distributor clamp bolt								
Fixed nut type							5.0	0.576
Fixed bolt type							3.0	0.345

1 General description

In order that the engine can run correctly it is necessary for an electrical spark to ignite the fuel/air mixture in the combustion chamber at exactly the right moment in relation to engine speed and load. The ignition system is based on feeding low tension voltage from the battery to the coil where it is converted to high tension voltage. The high tension voltage is powerful enough to jump the spark plug gap in the cylinders many times a second under high compression pressures; providing that the system is in good condition and that all adjustments are correct.

The ignition system is divided into two circuits. The low tension circuit and the high tension circuit.

The low tension (sometimes known as the primary) circuit consists of the battery, lead to the control box, lead to the ignition switch, lead from the ignition switch to the low tension or primary coil windings (terminal SW), and the lead from the low tension coil windings (coil terminal CB) to the contact breaker points and condenser in the distributor.

The high tension circuit consists of the high tension or secondary coil windings, the heavy ignition lead from the centre of the coil to the centre of the distributor cap, the rotor arm, and the spark plug leads and spark plugs.

The system functions in the following manner. Low tension voltage is changed in the coil into high tension voltage by the opening and closing of the contact breaker points in the low tension circuit. High tension voltage is then fed, via the carbon brush in the centre of the distributor cap, to the rotor arm of the distributor. The rotor arm revolves inside the distributor cap and each time it comes in line with one of the former metal segments in the cap, which are connected to the spark plug leads, the opening and closing of the contact breaker points causes the high tension voltage to build up and jump the gap from the rotor arm to the appropriate metal segment. The voltage then passes, via the spark plug lead, to the spark plug, where it finally jumps the spark plug gap, before going to earth.

The ignition is advanced and retarded automatically, to ensure the spark occurs at just the right instant for the particular load at the prevailing engine speed.

The ignition advance is controlled both mechanically and by a vacuum operated system (mechanical only on Cooper 'S' models). The mechanical governor mechanism comprises two leadweights, which move out from the distributor shaft, due to centrifugal force, as the engine speed rises. As they move outwards they rotate the cam relative to the distributor shaft, and so advance the spark. The weights are held in position by two light springs and it is the tension of the springs which is largely responsible for correct spark advancement.

The vacuum control consists of a diaphragm, one side of which is connected, via a small bore tube, to the carburettor, and the other side to the contact breaker plate. Depression in the inlet manifold and carburettor, which varies with engine speed and throttle opening, causes the diaphragm to move, so moving the contact breaker plate, and advancing or retarding the spark.

A fine degree of control is achieved by a spring in the vacuum assembly.

2 Contact breaker points - adjustment

1 To adjust the contact breaker points so that the correct gap is obtained, first release the two clips securing the distributor cap to the distributor body, and lift away the cap. Clean the inside and outside of the cap with a dry cloth. It is unlikely that the four segments will be badly burned or scored, but if they are the cap must be renewed. If only a small deposit is on the segments it may be scraped away using a small screwdriver.

2 Push in the carbon brush, located in the top of the cap, several times to ensure that it moves freely. The brush should protrude by at least 0.25 in (6.35 mm).

3 Gently prise the contact breaker points open to examine the condition of their faces. If they are rough, pitted or dirty, it will be necessary to remove them for resurfacing, or for replacement points to be fitted.

4 Presuming the points are satisfactory, or that they have been cleaned or replaced, measure the gap between the points by turning the engine over until the contact breaker arm is on the peak of one of the four cam lobes. A 0.015 in (0.381 mm) feeler gauge should now just fit between the points.

5 If the gap varies from this amount, slacken the contact plate securing screw and adjust the contact gap by inserting a screwdriver in the notched hole at the end of the plate, turning clockwise to decrease, and anticlockwise to increase, the gap. Tighten the securing screw and check the gap again.

6 Replace the rotor arm and distributor cap and clip the spring blade retainers into position.

3 Contact breaker points - removal and replacement

1 If the contact breaker points are burned, pitted or badly worn, they must be removed and either replaced or their faces must be filed smooth.

2 To remove the points, unscrew the terminal nut (Fig. 4.1) and remove it together with the washer under its head. Remove the flanged nylon bush, the condenser lead and the low tension lead from the terminal pin. Lift off the contact breaker arm and remove the large fibre washer from the terminal pin.

3 The adjustable contact breaker plate is removed by unscrewing one holding down screw and removing it, complete with spring and flat washer.

4 To reface the points, rub the face on a fine carborundum stone, or on fine emery paper. It is important that the faces are rubbed flat and parallel to each other so that there will be complete face to face contact when the points are closed. One of the points will be pitted and the other will have deposits on it.

5 It is necessary to remove completely the built up deposits, but unnecessary to rub the pitted point right to the stage where all the pitting has disappeared, though obviously if this is done it will prolong the time before the operation of refacing the points

Measuring plug gap. A feeler gauge of the correct size (see ignition system specifications) should have a slight 'drag' when slid between the electrodes. Adjust gap if necessary

Adjusting plug gap. The plug gap is adjusted by bending the earth electrode inwards, or outwards, as necessary until the correct clearance is obtained. Note the use of the correct tool

Normal. Grey-brown deposits lightly coated core nose. Gap increasing by around 0.001 in (0.025 mm) per 1000 miles (1600 km). Plugs ideally suited to engine and engine in good condition

Carbon fouling. Dry, black, sooty deposits. Will cause weak spark and eventually misfire. Fault: over-rich fuel mixture. Check: carburettor mixture settings, float level and jet sizes; choke operation and cleanliness of air filter. Plugs can be re-used after cleaning

Oil fouling. Wet, oily deposits. Will cause weak spark and eventually misfire. Fault: worn bores/piston rings or valve guides; sometimes occurs (temporarily) during running-in period. Plugs can be re-used after thorough cleaning

Overheating. Electrodes have glazed appearance, core nose very white - few deposits. Fault: plug overheating. Check: plug value, ignition timing, fuel octane rating (too low) and fuel mixture (too weak). Discard plugs and cure fault immediately

Electrode damage. Electrodes burned away; core nose has burned, glazed appearance. Fault: initial pre-ignition. Check: as for 'Overheating' but may be more severe. Discard plugs and remedy fault before piston or valve damage occurs

Split core nose (may appear initially as a crack). Damage is self-evident, but cracks will only show after cleaning. Fault: pre-ignition or wrong gap-setting technique. Check: ignition timing, cooling system, fuel octane rating (too low) and fuel mixture (too weak). Discard plugs, rectify fault immediately

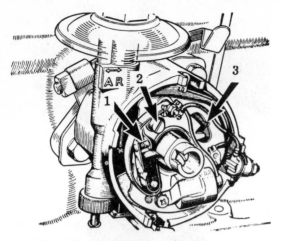

Fig. 4.1. The DM2 type distributor with cover and rotor arm
removed

1   *Contact breaker points*
2   *Securing screw*
3   *Slot for screwdriver to adjust points gap*

has to be repeated.

6 To replace the points, first position the adjustable contact
breaker plate, and secure it with its screw, spring and flat washer.
Fit the fibre washer to the terminal pin and fit the contact
breaker arm over it. Insert the flanged nylon bush with the condenser lead immediately under its head, and the low tension lead
under that, over the terminal pin. Fit the steel washer and screw
on the securing nut.

7 The points are now reassembled and the gap should be set as
detailed in the previous Section.

4 Condenser - removal, testing and replacement

1 The purpose of the condenser (sometimes known as a capac-
itor) is to ensure that when the contact breaker points open
there is no sparking across them which would waste voltage and
cause wear.

2 The condenser is fitted in parallel with the contact breaker
points. If it develops a short circuit, it will cause ignition failure,
as the points will be prevented from interrupting the low tension
circuit.

3 If the engine becomes very difficult to start, or begins to miss
after several miles running, and the breaker points show signs of
excessive burning, then the condition of the condenser must be
suspect. A further test can be made by separating the points by
hand with the ignition switched on. If this is accompanied by a
flash it is indicative that the condenser has failed.

4 Without special test equipment, the only sure way to diagnose
condenser trouble is to replace a suspected unit with a new one
and note if there is any improvement.

5 To remove the condenser from the distributor, remove the
distributor cap and the rotor arm. Unscrew the contact breaker
arm terminal nut, remove the nut, washer and flanged nylon
bush and release the condenser. Replacement of the condenser is
simply a reversal of the removal process. Take particular care
that the condenser lead does not short circuit against any
portion of the breaker plate.

5 Distributor - lubrication

1 It is important that the distributor cam is lubricated with
petroleum jelly at the specified mileages, and that the breaker
arm, governor weights and cam spindle are lubricated with
engine oil once every 6,000 miles (10,000 km). In practice it

will be found that lubrication every 3,000 miles (5,000 km) is
preferable although this is not recommended by the manufacturers.

2 Great care should be taken not to use too much lubricant, as
any excess that might find its way onto the contact breaker
points could cause burning and misfiring.

3 To gain access to the cam spindle, lift away the rotor arm.
Drop no more than two drops of engine oil onto the screw head.
This will run down the spindle when the engine is hot and
lubricate the bearings. No more than **one** drop of oil should be
applied to the pivot post.

6 Distributor - removal and replacement

1 To remove the distributor from the engine, start by pulling
the terminals off each of the spark plugs. Release the nut
securing the low tension lead to the terminal on the side of the
distributor and unscrew the high tension lead retaining cap from
the coil and remove the lead.

2 Unscrew the union holding the vacuum tube to the distributor
vacuum housing.

3 Remove the distributor body clamp bolts which hold the distributor clamp plate to the engine and remove the distributor.
Note: If it is not wished to disturb the timing then under no
circumstances should the clamp pinch bolt, which secures the
distributor in its relative position in the clamp, be loosened.
Providing the distributor is removed without the clamp being
loosened from the distributor body and the engine is not rotated
whilst the distributor is out, the timing will not be lost.

4 Replacement is a reversal of the above process providing that
the engine has not been turned in the meantime. If the engine
has been turned it will be best to retime the ignition. This will
also be necessary if the clamp pinch bolt has been loosened.

7 Distributor - dismantling

1 With the distributor removed from the car and on the bench,
remove the distributor cap and lift off the rotor arm. If very
tight, lever it off gently with a screwdriver.

2 Remove the points from the distributor as detailed in Section
3.

3 Remove the condenser from the contact breaker plate by
releasing its securing screw.

4 Unhook the vacuum unit spring from its mounting on the
moving contact breaker plate.

5 Remove the contact breaker plate.

6 Unscrew the two screws and lockwashers which hold the
contact breaker base plate in position and remove the earth lead
from the relevant screw. Remember to replace this lead on reassembly.

7 Lift out the contact breaker base plate.

8 **Note** the position of the slot in the rotor arm drive in
relation to the offset drive dog at the opposite end of the distributor. It is essential that this is reassembled correctly as otherwise the timing may be 180° out.

9 Unscrew the cam spindle retaining screw, which is located in
the centre of the rotor arm drive, and remove the cam spindle.

10 Lift out the centrifugal weights together with their springs.

11 To remove the vacuum unit (where applicable), spring off
the small circlip which secures the advance adjustment nut
which should then be unscrewed. With the micrometer adjusting
nut removed, release the spring and micrometer adjusting nut
lock spring clip. This is the clip that is responsible for the
'clicks' when the micrometer adjuster is turned, and it is small
and easily lost, as is the circlip, so put them in a safe place.
Do not forget to replace the lock spring clip on reassembly.

12 It is only necessary to remove the distributor drive shaft or
spindle if it is thought to be excessively worn. With a thin punch
drive out the retaining pin from the driving tongue collar on the
bottom end of the distributor drive shaft. The shaft can then be
removed. The distributor is now completely dismantled.

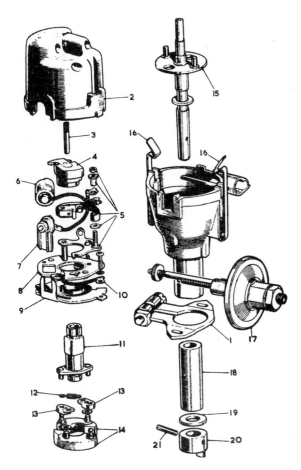

Fig. 4.2. Component parts of DM2 P4 distributor

1	Clamping plate	11	Cam
2	Moulded cap	12	Automatic advance springs
3	Brush and spring	13	Toggles
4	Rotor arm	14	Weight assembly
5	Contacts (set)	15	Shaft and action plate
6	Capacitor	16	Cap retaining clips
7	Terminal and lead	17	Vacuum unit
	(low tension)	18	Bush
8	Moving contact breaker	19	Thrust washer
	plate	20	Driving dog
9	Contact breaker base plate	21	Taper pin
10	Earth lead		

8 Distributor - inspection and repair

1 Thoroughly wash all mechanical parts in petrol and wipe dry using a clean non-fluffy rag.

2 Check the points that have already been described previously. Check the distributor cap for signs of tracking, indicated by a thin black line between the segments. Replace the cap if any signs of tracking are found.

3 If the metal portion of the rotor arm is badly burned or loose, renew the arm. If slightly burnt, clean the arm with a fine file. Check that the carbon brush moves freely in the centre of the distributor cover.

4 Examine the fit of the breaker plate on the bearing plate and also check the breaker arm pivot for looseness, or wear, and renew as necessary.

5 Examine the centrifugal weights and pivot pins for wear, and renew the weights or cam assembly if a degree of wear is found.

6 Examine the shaft and the fit of the cam assembly on the shaft. If the clearance is excessive compare the items with new units and renew either, or both, if they show excessive wear.

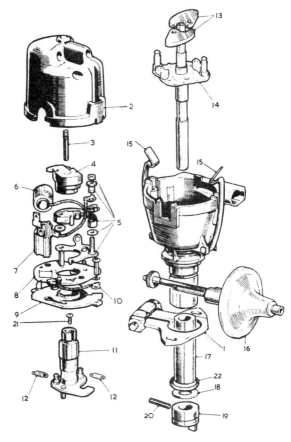

Fig. 4.3. Component parts of 24 D4 distributor

1	Clamping plate	11	Cam
2	Moulded cap	12	Automatic-advance springs
3	Brush and spring	13	Weight assembly
4	Rotor arm	14	Shaft and action plate
5	Contacts (set)	15	Cap - retaining clips
6	Capacitor	16	Vacuum unit
7	Terminal and lead (low	17	Bush
	tension)	18	Thrust washer
8	Moving contact - breaker	19	Driving dog
	plate	20	Parallel pin
9	Contact - breaker base	21	Cam screw
	plate	22	'O' ring oil seal (when
10	Earth lead		fitted)

7 If the shaft is a loose fit in the distributor bushes and can be seen to be worn, it will be necessary to fit a new shaft and bushes. The old bushes in the early distributor, or the single bush in the later ones, are simply pressed out. **Note**: Before inserting new bushes they should be immersed in engine oil for 24 hours.

8 Examine the length of the balance weight springs and compare them with a new spring. If they have stretched they should be renewed.

9 Distributor - reassembly

1 Reassembly is a reversal of the dismantling process, but there are several points which should be noted in addition to those already given in Section 7.

2 Lubricate the balance weights and other parts of the mechanical advance mechanism, the distributor shaft, and the portion of the shaft on which the cam bears, with SAE 20 engine oil, during reassembly. Do not oil excessively but ensure these parts are adequately lubricated.

3 On reassembling the cam driving pins with the centrifugal

weights, check that they are in correct poisition so that when viewed from above, the rotor arm should be at 'six o'clock' position, and the small offset on the driving dog must be on the right.

4 Check the action of the weights in the fully advanced and fully retarded positions and ensure they are not binding.

5 Tighten the micrometer adjusting nut to the middle position on the timing scale.

6 Finally, set the contact breaker gap to the correct clearance of 0.015 in (0.381 mm).

10 Ignition timing

1 If the clamp plate pinch bolt has been loosened on the distributor and the static timing lost, or if for any other reason it is wished to set the ignition timing, proceed as follows:

2 Undo the two bolts from the inspection plate on the top of the flywheel housing and remove the plate. The timing marks can now be checked with the help of a small mirror. The static advance is checked at the exact moment of opening of the points relative to the position of the timing marks on the flywheel, in relation to the pointer in the flywheel housing inspection hole. The 1/4 mark on the flywheel indicates tdc and the marks 5, 10 and 15 indicate 5°, 10° and 15° advance before tdc respectively.

3 Check the 'Ignition specification' for the correct position of the flywheel when the points should be just beginning to open. This is shown as the 'static setting'.

4 Having determined whether your engine possesses a high or low compression ratio (by checking the engine number) turn the engine over so that No 1 piston is coming up to tdc on the compression stroke. (This can be checked by removing No 1 spark plug and feeling the pressure being developed in the cylinder, or by removing the rocker cover and noting when the valves in No 4 cylinder are rocking ie the inlet valve just opening and exhaust valve just closing. If this check is not made it is all too easy to set the timing 180° out, as both No 1 and 4 cylinders come up to tdc at the same time but only one is on the firing stroke.

5 Continue turning the engine until the pointer in the flywheel or torque converter (automatic transmission) inspection hole is in line with the correct timing mark on the flywheel periphery.

6 Remove the distributor cover, slacken off the distributor body clamp bolt, and with the rotor arm pointing towards the No 1 terminal (check this position with the distributor cap and lead to No 1 spark plug), insert the distributor into the distributor housing. The dog on the drive shaft should match up with the slot in the distributor driving spindle.

7 Insert the two bolts holding the distributor in position.

8 With the engine set in the correct position and the rotor arm opposite the correct segment for No 1 cylinder, turn the advance/retard knob on the distributor until the contact points are just beginning to open. Eleven clicks of the knurled micrometer adjuster nut represent 1^O of timing movement. **Note**: Because of the absence of a vacuum advance unit on Cooper 'S' type models adjustment can only be made by slackening the pinch bolt on the distributor clamp and turning the distributor body.

9 If the range of adjustment provided by this adjustment is not sufficient then, if the clamp bolt is not already slackened, it will be necessary to slacken it and turn the distributor body half a graduation as marked on the adjusting spindle barrel. (Each graduation represents 5° timing movement or 55 clicks of the micrometer adjuster). Sufficient adjustment will normally be found available using the distributor micrometer adjuster. When this has been achieved the engine is statically timed.

10 Difficulty is sometimes experienced in determining exactly when the contact breaker points open. This can be ascertained most accurately by connecting a 12 volt bulb in parallel with the contact breaker points (one lead to earth and the other from the distributor low tension terminal). Switch on the ignition, and turn the advance and retard adjuster until the bulb lights up indicating that the points have just opened.

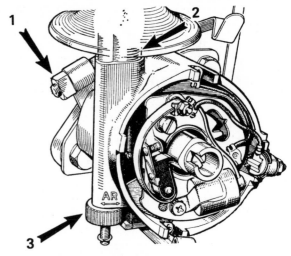

Fig. 4.4. Distributor timing points

1   Distributor pinch bolt   3   Fine adjuster
2   Vernier scale

Fig. 4.5. Ignition timing marks (manual transmission)
It is easier to align the timing marks with the aid of a mirror once the plate has been removed

Fig. 4.6. Ignition timing marks (automatic transmission)
The hole in the converter housing (see inset) may be used for inserting a suitable tool to turn the converter

11 If a stroboscopic timing light is being used, attach one lead to No 1 spark plug, and attach the other lead into the free end of No 1 plug ignition cable leading from the distributor. Start the engine and shine the light on the flywheel periphery and timing indicators. If the engine idles at more than 600 rpm then the correct static timing will not be obtained as the centrifugal weights will have started to advance.

12 If the light shows the pointer in the flywheel inspection hole to be to the right of the timing marks, then the ignition is too far retarded. If the pointer appears to the left of the timing marks, then the ignition is too far advanced. Turn the distributor body or micrometer adjuster until the timing pointer appears in just the right position in relation to the timing marks.

13 Tighten the clamp bolt and recheck that the timing is still correct, making any small correction necessary with the micrometer adjuster.

11 Spark plugs and HT leads

1 The correct functioning of the spark plugs is vital for the proper running and efficiency of the engine.

2 At intervals of 6000 miles (10,000 km) the plugs should be removed, examined, cleaned, and if worn excessively, replaced. The condition of the spark plug will also tell much about the general condition of the engine.

3 If the insulator nose of the spark plug is clean and white, with no deposits, this is indicative of a weak mixture, or too hot a plug (a hot plug transfers heat away from the electrode slowly - a cold plug transfers heat away quickly).

4 The plugs fitted as standard are detailed in the specifications at the beginning of this Chapter. If the top and insulator nose is covered with hard black looking deposits, then this is indicative that the mixture is too rich. Should the plug be black and oily, then it is likely that the engine is fairly worn, as well as the mixture being too rich.

5 If the insulator nose is covered with light tan to greyish brown deposits, then the mixture is correct, and it is likely that the engine is in good condition.

6 If there are any traces of long brown tapering stains on the outside of the white portion of the plug, then the plug will have to be renewed, as this shows that there is a faulty joint between the plug body and the insulator, and compression is being allowed to leak away.

7 Plugs should be cleaned by a sand blasting machine, which will free them from carbon more than by cleaning by hand. The machine will also test the condition of the plugs under compression. Any plug that fails to spark at the recommended pressure should be renewed.

8 The spark plug gap is of considerable importance, as, if it is too large or too small the size of the spark and its efficiency will be seriously impaired. The spark plug gap should be set to 0.025 in (0.38 mm) for the best results.

9 To set it, measure the gap with a feeler gauge, and then bend open, or close, the outer plug electrode until the correct gap is achieved. The centre electrode should never be bent as this may crack the insulation and cause plug failure, if nothing worse.

10 When replacing the plugs, remember to use new washers and replace the leads from the distributor in the correct firing order which is 1 3 4 2, cylinder No 1 being nearest the fan.

11 The HT leads require no routine maintenance other than being kept clean and wiped over regularly. At intervals of 6000 miles (10,000 km) however, pull each lead off the plug in turn and remove them from the distributor. Water can seep down these joints giving rise to a white corrosive deposit which must be carefully removed from the end of each cable.

12 Fault symptoms - ignition system

There are two main symptoms indicating ignition faults. Either the engine will not start, or fire, or the engine is difficult to start and misfires. If it is regular misfire, ie the engine is only running on two or three cylinders, the fault is almost sure to be in the secondary, or high tension, circuit. If the misfiring is intermittent, the fault could be in either the high or low tension circuits. If the engine stops suddenly, or will not start at all, it is likely that the fault is in the low tension circuit. Loss of power and overheating, apart from faulty carburation settings, are normally due to faults in the distributor, or incorrect ignition timing.

13 Fault diagnosis - engine fails to start

If the engine fails to start it is likely that the fault is in the low tension circuit. The way the starter motor spins over will indicate whether there is a good charge in the battery. If the battery is evidently in good condition, then check the distributor.

Remove the distributor cap and rotor arm, and check that the contact points are not burnt, pitted or dirty. If the points are badly pitted or burnt or dirty, clean and reset them as has already been described in Section 3.

If the engine still refuses to fire check the low tension circuit further. Check the condition of the condenser as described in Section 4. Switch on the ignition and turn the crankshaft until the contact breaker points have fully opened. With either a voltmeter or bulb, and length of wire, connect the contact breaker plate terminal to earth on the engine. If the bulb lights, the low tension circuit is in order, and the fault is in the points. If the points have been cleaned and reset, and the bulb still lights, then the fault is in the high tension circuit.

If the bulb fails to light, connect it to the ignition coil terminal CB and earth. If it lights, it points to a damaged wire or loose connection in the cable from the CB terminal to the terminal on the contact breaker plate.

If the bulb fails to light, connect it between the ignition coil terminal SW and earth. If the bulb lights, then the fault is somewhere in the switch, or wiring and control box. Check further as follows:

a) Check the white cable leading from the control "A 3" terminal to the ignition switch. If the bulb fails to light, then this indicates that the cable is damaged, or one of the connections loose, or that there is a fault in the switch.

b) Connect the bulb between the ignition switch white terminal cable and earth. If the bulb fails to light, this indicates a fault in the switch or in the wiring leading from the control box.

c) Connect the bulb to the other ignition switch terminal and then to earth. If the bulb fails to light, this indicates a fault or loose connection in the wiring leading from the control box.

d) Connect the bulb between the lighting and ignition terminal in the control box, and then to earth. If the bulb fails to light this indicates a faulty control box.

e) Connect the bulb from the fuse unit terminal to earth. If the bulb fails to light this indicates a fault or loose connection in the wire leading from the starter solenoid to the control box.

f) Connect the bulb from the input terminal of the solenoid switch to earth. If the bulb fails to light then there is a fault in the cable from the battery to the solenoid switch, or the earth lead of the battery is not properly earthed, and the whole circuit is dead.

g) When an alternator is fitted refer to the relevant wiring diagram and trace the ignition circuit, this basically being identical to that for models fitted with a dynamo.

If the fault is not in the low tension circuit check the high tension circuit. Disconnect each plug lead in turn at the spark plug end and hold the end of the cable about 3/16 in (4.5 mm) away from the cylinder block. Spin the engine on the starter motor by pressing the rubber button on the starter motor solenoid switch (under the bonnet). Sparking between the end of the cable and the block should be fairly strong with a regular blue spark. (Hold the lead with rubber to avoid electric shocks).

Should there be no spark at the end of the plug leads, disconnect the lead at the distributor cap, and hold the end of the lead about ¼ in (6.0 mm) from the block. Spin the engine as before, when a rapid succession of blue sparks between the end of the lead and the block, indicate that the coil is in order, and that either the distributor cap is cracked, or the carbon brush is stuck or worn, or the rotor arm is faulty.

Check the cap for cracks and tracking, and the rotor arm for cracks or looseness of the metal portion and renew as necessary.

If there are no sparks from the end of the lead from the coil, then check the connections of the lead to the coil and distributor head, and if they are in order, and the low tension side is without fault, then it will be necessary to fit a replacement coil.

14 Fault diagnosis - engine misfires

If the engine misfires regularly, run it at a fast idling speed, and short out each of the plugs in turn by placing a short screwdriver across from the plug terminal to the cylinder. Ensure that the screwdriver has a **wooden** or **plastic insulated handle.**

No difference in engine running will be noticed when the plug in the defective cylinder is short circuited. Short circuiting the working plugs will accentuate the misfire.

Remove the plug lead from the end of the defective plug and hold it about 3/16 in (4.5 mm) away from the block. Restart the engine. If the sparking is fairly strong and regular the fault must lie in the spark plug.

The plug may be loose, the insulation may be cracked, or the points may have burnt away giving too wide a gap for the spark to jump. Worse still, one of the points may have broken off. Either renew the plug, or clean it, reset the gap, and then test it.

If there is no spark at the end of the plug lead, or if it is weak and intermittent, check the ignition lead from the distributor to the plug. If the insulation is cracked or perished, renew the lead. Check the connections at the distributor cap.

If there is still no spark, examine the distributor cap carefully for tracking. This can be recognised by a very thin black line running between two or more electrodes, or between an electrode and some other part of the distributor. These lines are paths which now conduct electricity across the cap thus letting it run to earth. The only answer is a new distributor cap.

Apart from the ignition timing being incorrect, other causes of misfiring have already been dealt with under the section dealing with the failure of the engine to start. To recap - these are that:

a) The coil may be faulty giving an intermittent misfire.
b) There may be a damaged wire or loose connection in the low tension circuit.
c) The condenser may be short circuiting.
d) There may be a mechanical fault in the distributor (Broken driving spindle or contact breaker spring).

If the ignition is too far retarded, it should be noted that the engine will tend to overheat, and there will be a quite noticeable drop in power. If the engine is overheating and the power is down, and the ignition timing is correct, then the carburettor should be checked, as it is likely that this is where the fault lies. See Chapter 3 for further details on this.

Chapter 5 Clutch

Contents

Specifications

Make:

Early	BLMC
Later	Borg and Beck

Type:

Early	Single dry plate
Later	Diaphragm spring

Diameter:

Early	7.25 in. (184.15 mm)
Later	7.125 in. (180.9 mm)

Facing material:

All except Cooper 'S'	Wound yarn
Cooper 'S'	Wound yarn, riveted

Pressure springs (early type clutch only):

Number	6
Spring colour code:	
Mini Mk I and II, 848 cc, Mk II 998 cc, and Clubman ...	Red spot
Mini Cooper (997 and 998 cc)	Black enamel with white spot
Mini Cooper 'S':	
Inner	Green spot
Outer	White spot

Diaphragm spring (later type clutch only):

Diaphragm spring colour code:	
Mini Mk 1 and 11, 848 cc and late 998 cc	Brown
Mini Mk II 998 cc, and Clubman	Light green
Mini Cooper (997 and 998 cc)	Light green
Cooper 'S'	Light green
Mini 1275 GT	Green/blue or dark blue

Clutch release lever clearance	0.020 in (0.508 mm)
Slave cylinder diameter	0.875 in (22.2 mm)
Master cylinder diameter	0.75 in (19.05 mm)

Torque wrench settings:

	lb f ft	kg fm
Clutch spring housing to pressure plate bolts	16	2.2
Driving strap to flywheel setscrew	16	2.2
Flywheel centre bolt	110 to 115	15.2 to 15.9

1 General description

Initially a BLMC single dry plate clutch of 7.25 in (184.15 mm) diameter was fitted. In 1964 an improved Borg and Beck diaphragm clutch of 7.125 in (180.9 mm) diameter was introduced. Both types of clutch are very unusual because there are major parts of the clutch assembly on both the **inside** and the **outside** of the flywheel.

The main parts of the clutch assembly on the outside of the flywheel comprise the spring housing (18), (see Fig. 5.3) the thrust plate (27), the release bearing (30), the 6 pressure springs (16), (double springs in the case of Cooper 'S' models), and the three driving straps (10)

The main parts of the clutch assembly on the inside of the flywheel are the clutch disc (2), and the pressure plate (1).

The spring housing (18), is firmly bolted to the pressure plate (1) by 3 bolts and spring washers (19, 20). The spring housing is held to the flywheel (8) by driving straps (10) which are held a little way away from the outer clutch face by spacing washers (9). The clutch disc is free to slide along the splines of the primary gear which is fitted to the end of the crankshaft.

Friction lining material is riveted to the clutch disc (2) which has a segmented hub to help absorb transmission shocks and to ensure a smooth take-off.

The clutch is actuated hydraulically. The pendant clutch pedal is connected to the clutch master cylinder and hydraulic fluid reservoir by a short pushrod. The master cylinder and hydraulic reservoir are mounted on the engine side of the bulkhead in front of the driver.

Depressing the clutch pedal moves the piston in the master cylinder forwards, so forcing hydraulic fluid through the clutch hydraulic pipe to the slave cylinder.

The piston in the slave cylinder moves forward on the entry of the fluid and actuates the clutch operating lever by means of a short pushrod. The opposite end of the operating lever (43), slots, by means of a ball joint, into a throw-out plunger (40).

As the pivoted operating lever (43) moves backwards it bears against the release bearing (30) pushing it forwards. This in turn bears against the clutch thrust pate (27), the spring housing (18) and the pressure plate (1), which all move forward slightly so disengaging the pressure plate face from the clutch disc (2).

When the clutch pedal is released, the pressure plate springs (16) force the pressure plate spring housing (18) outwards, which, because it is attached to the pressure plate (1) brings the pressure plate into contact with the high friction linings on the clutch disc. At the same time the disc is forced firmly against the inner face of the flywheel and so the drive is taken up.

As the friction linings of the clutch disc wear, the clearance between the clutch thrust race and the clutch ring will decrease.

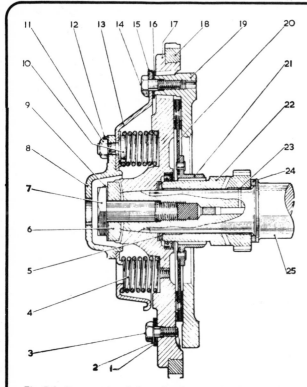

Fig. 5.1. Cross sectional view of early type clutch assembly

1	Driving strap and spacing washer	13	Pressure spring housing
2	Lockwasher	14	Driving bolt
3	Driving pin	15	Lock washer
4	Pressure spring	16	Driving strap
5	Circlip	17	Flywheel
6	Keyed washer	18	Starter ring
7	Flywheel screw	19	Pressure plate
8	Thrust plate	20	Clutch disc
9	Locking washer	21	Driven plate hub
10	Pressure spring housing	22	Crankshaft primary gear
11	Guide nut	23	Primary gear bearing
12	Lock washer	24	Thrust washer
		25	Crankshaft

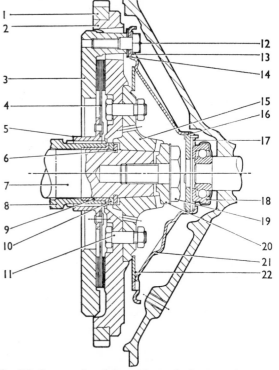

Fig. 5.2. Cross sectional view of later, diaphragm spring type clutch assembly

1	Starter ring	12	Driving pin
2	Flywheel	13	Lock washer
3	Pressure plate	14	Driving strap
4	Driven plate	15	Flywheel hub
5	Driven plate hub	16	Thrust plate
6	Circlip	17	Plate retaining spring
7	Crankshaft	18	Thrust bearing
8	Crankshaft primary gear	19	Flywheel screw
9	Primary gear bearing	20	Keyed washer
10	Thrust washer	21	Cover
11	Flywheel hub bolt	22	Diaphragm spring

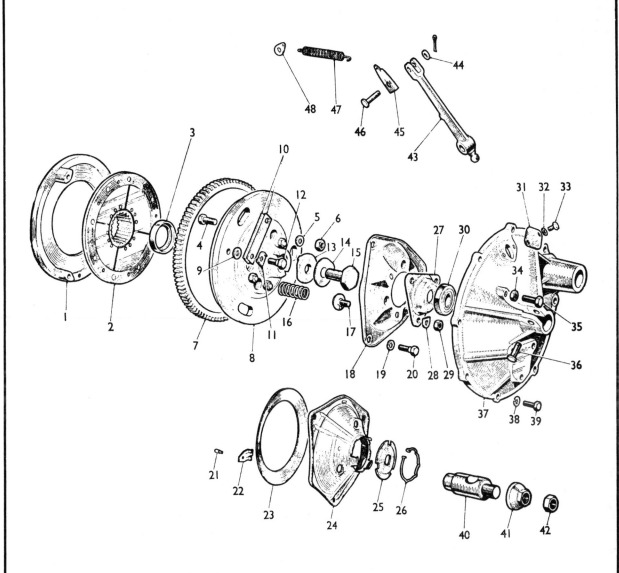

Fig. 5.3. Exploded view of flywheel and clutch assembly

1	Pressure plate	18	Spring housing	33	Screw
2	Clutch disc	19	Washer	34	Locknut
3	Flywheel oil seal	20	Pressure plate bolt	35	Screw
4	Hub screw		Diaphragm spring type	36	Lever pin
5	Lockwasher	21	Rivet dowel	37	Clutch cover
6	Nut	22	Retaining clip	38	Washer
7	Starter ring	23	Diaphragm spring	39	Cover screw
8	Flywheel assembly	24	Spring housing	40	Throw-out plunger
9	Washer	25	Thrust plate	41	Throw-out stop
10	Driving strap	26	Plate retaining spring	42	Stop locknut
11	Lockwasher		Coil spring type	43	Clutch operating lever
12	Strap bolts	27	Clutch thrust plate	44	Washer
13	Key	28	Lock washer	45	Spring anchor (lever)
14	Lockwasher	29	Nut	46	Pushrod pin
15	Flywheel bolt	30	Release bearing	47	Lever pull-off spring
16	Pressure spring	31	Cover plate	48	Spring anchor (cylinder)
17	Thrust plate screw	32	Washer		

The pressure plate will move in closer to the clutch disc to compensate for wear, and unless the wear is taken up by adjustment at the adjustable stop located between the clutch housing and the operating lever, clutch slip will result. See Section 2 for details.

2 Clutch adjustment

As the friction linings of the clutch disc wear, the distance between the clutch release bearing and the clutch thrust plate will decrease. The pressure plate moves in closer to the clutch disc to compensate for wear. Unless the wear is taken up by adjustment of the stop located between the clutch housing and the operating lever, the clutch will start to slip.

1 Unhook the release spring from the clutch operating lever.
2 Pull the lever back until **all the FREE** movement is taken up. Hold the operating lever in this position and check the gap between the lever and the adjustable stop with a feeler gauge. (Fig. 5.4).
3 On early models the gap should be 0.060 in (1.5 mm). If this is not so, slacken the adjusting stop lock bolt and screw the bolt in or out till the clearance is correct. Tighten the lock bolt, and replace the release spring. On later models with the shouldered stop this clearance is reduced to 0.020 in. (0.50 mm). **Note:** On later models after a clutch overhaul the throw out stop fitted in the centre of the flywheel cover boss must be reset. (Fig. 5.5).
a) Slacken fully the locknut and the throw-out stop in the middle of the clutch cover.
b) Press down the clutch pedal, and holding the pedal in this position, screw the throw-out stop up to the cover boss.
c) Release the clutch pedal and screw in the stop a further 0.007 to 0.010 in (0.20 to 0.25 mm) (about 1 flat of the locknut). Tighten the locknut and check the clearance between the operating lever and the stop screw which should be reset to 0.020 in (0.50 mm) if not already correct.

3 Clutch overthrow

The purpose of adjusting the clutch as above is to prevent clutch slip, and to ensure that clutch overthrow does not overload the crankshaft thrust bearings. Even with the stop adjustment correct, clutch overthrow can occur if the clutch operating lever spring or the clutch pressure springs have weakened or the operating mechanism is stiff. Test for overthrow as follows:
1 Start the engine and allow it to warm up to its usual running temperature.
2 With the engine idling at no more than 500 rpm press the clutch pedal three or four times rapidly.
3 If the engine slows down much or stalls overthrow is occurring.
4 Increase the distance between the operating lever and the stop bolt to 0.075 in (2.0 mm).
5 If there is no improvement check the lever for stiffness.
6 If overthrow is still present replace the operating lever pull off spring with a stronger one.
7 Should no improvement be noticed then the clutch must be dismantled and new pressure plate springs or diaphragm spring assembly fitted.

4 Clutch hydraulic system - bleeding

1 Gather together a clean jam jar, a 9 in. (300 mm) length of rubber tubing which fits tightly over the bleed nipple in the slave cylinder and a tin of hydraulic brake fluid. The services of an assistant will also be required.
2 Check that the master cylinder is full and if not fill it, and cover the bottom inch of the jar with hydraulic fluid.
3 Remove the rubber dust cap from the bleed nipple on the slave cylinder and with a suitable spanner open the bleed nipple one turn.

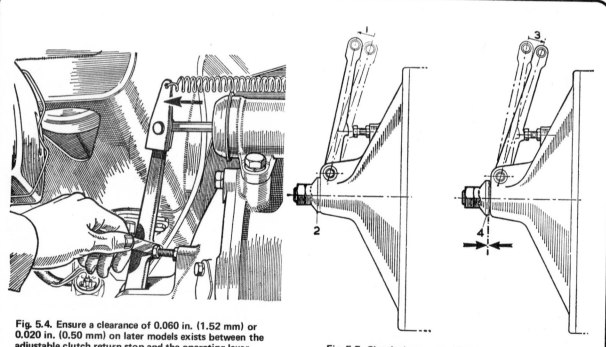

Fig. 5.4. Ensure a clearance of 0.060 in. (1.52 mm) or 0.020 in. (0.50 mm) on later models exists between the adjustable clutch return stop and the operating lever

Fig. 5.5. Clutch throw-out adjustment

1 Clutch fully released
2 Throw-out stop screwed up to the cover boss
3 Clutch fully engaged
4 Screw up the stop a further 1 flat of the lock nut

4 Place one end of the tube securely over the nipple and insert the other end in the jam jar so that the tube orifice is below the level of the fluid.

5 The assistant should now pump the clutch pedal up and down slowly until air bubbles cease to emerge from the end of the tubing. He should also check the reservoir frequently to ensure that the hydraulic fluid does not disappear so letting air into the system.

6 When no more air bubbles appear, tighten the bleed nipple on the downstroke.

7 Replace the rubber dust cap over the bleed nipple. Allow the hydraulic fluid in the jar to stand for at least 24 hours before using it, in order that all the minute air bubbles may escape.

5 Clutch slave cylinder - removal and replacement

1 Wipe the area around the bleed nipple on the slave cylinder, unscrew the nipple and attach a bleed tube. Place the other end in a clean jam jar.

2 Pump the pedal and empty the clutch hydraulic fluid from the system.

3 Carefully unscrew the clutch hydraulic pipe.

4 Disconnect the pushrod from the clutch lever.

5 Undo and remove the two clutch slave cylinder securing bolts and spring washers and lift away from the flywheel housing.

6 Refitting the clutch slave cylinder is the reverse sequence to removal. It will be necessary to bleed the clutch hydraulic system as described in Section 4.

6 Clutch slave cylinder - dismantling, examination and reassembly

1 Clean the cylinder down externally with a clean rag until it is free from dirt.

2 Pull off the rubber boot or dust cap, remove the pushrod, and release the circlip with a pair of long-nosed pliers. Tap or shake out the piston, piston cup, cup filler and the small spring. (Fig. 5.6).

3 Clean all the components thoroughly with hydraulic fluid or methylated spirits and then dry them off.

4 Carefully examine the rubber components for signs of swelling, distortion, splitting or other wear, and check the piston and cylinder wall for wear and score marks. Replace any parts that are found faulty.

5 Reassembly of the slave cylinder is the reverse sequence to dismantling. As the parts are refitted they should be lubricated with fresh hydraulic fluid.

7 Clutch master cylinder - removal and replacement

1 Drain the clutch hydraulic system as described in Section 5, paragraphs 1 and 2.

2 Spring off the circlip from the end of the clevis pin which holds the clutch pushrod to the clutch pedal. Slide out the clevis pin.

3 Unscrew the union nut from the end of the hydraulic pipe where it enters the clutch master cylinder and gently pull the pipe clear.

4 Unscrew the two nuts and spring washers holding the clutch

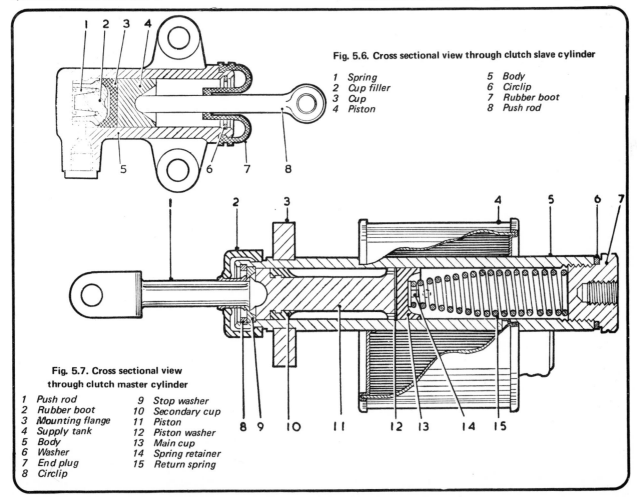

Fig. 5.6. Cross sectional view through clutch slave cylinder

1	Spring	5	Body
2	Cup filler	6	Circlip
3	Cup	7	Rubber boot
4	Piston	8	Push rod

Fig. 5.7. Cross sectional view through clutch master cylinder

1	Push rod	9	Stop washer
2	Rubber boot	10	Secondary cup
3	Mounting flange	11	Piston
4	Supply tank	12	Piston washer
5	Body	13	Main cup
6	Washer	14	Spring retainer
7	End plug	15	Return spring
8	Circlip		

cylinder mounting flange to the mounting bracket.
5   Remove the master cylinder and reservoir assembly.
6   Refitting the clutch slave cylinder is the reverse sequence to removal. It will be necessary to bleed the clutch hydraulic system as described in Section 4.

8 Clutch master cylinder - dismantling, examination and re-assembly

1   Remove the rubber boot or dust cover, and extract the circlip from the end of the body with a pair of long-nosed pliers. (Fig. 5.7).
2   Pull out the pushrod and stop washer and shake out the piston, secondary cup, copper piston washer, the primary or main cup, and the spring and spring washer.
3   Clean all the components thoroughly with hydraulic fluid or methylated spirits and then dry them off.
4   Carefully examine the parts, especially the rubber primary and secondary cups for signs of swelling, distortion, or splitting, and check the piston and cylinder wall for wear and score marks. Replace any parts that are faulty.
5   Reassembly is a straight reversal of the dismantling procedure, but note the following points:
a) As the components are returned to the cylinder barrel, lubricate them with the correct grade of hydraulic fluid.
b) Insert the return spring into the barrel with its broader base first.

9 Clutch pedal - removal and replacement.

1   From underneath the facia take off the circlip which retains the fulcrum pin or pedal cross-shaft in position. Slip off the hooked ends of the arms of the springs bearing against the pedal levers and push the cross-shaft out.
2   Remove the small circlip from the end of the clevis pin fitted to the end of the pushrod and slide out the clevis pin.
3   The pedal is now free and can be lifted out.
4   Replacement is a straight reversal of the above procedure.

10 Clutch and flywheel assembly - removal and replacement (early type)

The clutch can be removed with the engine in the car or with the engine on the bench. If the engine is in the car proceed as follows:
1   Place a jack under the offside end of the transmission casing and take the weight of the engine. **Note**: Use a block of wood interposed between the transmission casing and the jack to spread the load on the transmission case.
2   Remove the front grille for easy access to the starter motor. Undo the nut securing the starter motor and pull the cable away. Undo the two bolts securing the starter motor in place and lift the motor out. If the front grille was not removed then the motor will have to be worked along towards the radiator before it can be extracted.
3   Either the coil or the solenoid switch may be fitted to the top of the flywheel housing. Undo the bolts which hold either in place and disconnect the wires.
4   Undo and remove the two bolts and spring washers which hold the offside engine mounting to the subframe sidemember.
5   Undo the bolt from the engine tie-rod and pull the tie-rod back against the bulkhead.
6   Loosen the two nuts and bolts on the exhaust pipe to exhaust manifold clamp. Undo and remove the bolt which holds the clip on the exhaust pipe to the gearlever casing extension.
7   Undo and remove the bolts which hold the top radiator steady bracket in place and remove the bracket.
8   Remove the slave cylinder return spring, undo and remove the two bolts which hold the slave cylinder to the top of the flywheel housing, and pull the cylinder off the short pushrod which is attached to the top of the clutch operating lever.

9   Undo and remove the nine bolts and spring washers, which hold the clutch cover to the flywheel housing.
10 Jack up the engine just enough to be able to remove the clutch cover (which comes away with the engine mounting attached to it). While operating the jack frequently check that the fan blades are not damaging or fouling the radiator core.
11 Because the clutch is spread out on both sides of the flywheel, it is necessary to remove the flywheel before access can be gained to the pressure plate and the clutch disc.
12 Knock back the tabs which secure the three nuts to the three thrust plate screws. Pull off the clutch thrust plate.
13 Knock back the tab on the lockwasher which securely holds the flywheel bolt and undo the bolt three turns.
14 The flywheel is held firmly in place on the end of the crankshaft by means of a taper. A special puller will have to be borrowed to break this seal. See Chapter 1 for details. **Note**: If the engine is on the bench it is only necessary to carry out the operations described in paragraphs 9 and 11 to 14.
15 To refit the flywheel and clutch assembly first place the flywheel/clutch assembly on the rear of the crankshaft as described in Chapter 1.
16 Replace the clutch cover to the flywheel housing and insert and tighten up the nine bolts and washers which hold it in place.
17 Lower the engine and secure the offside engine mounting to the side of the subframe. Do not yet tighten the two bolts fully.
18 Replace and reconnect the slave cylinder. Adjust the clutch as described in Section 2.
19 Line up the hole in the tie-rod with the hole in the block so that the minimum strain will be placed on the rod and the engine mountings. It may be necessary to move the engine about ¼inch (6½ mm) before the holes line up.
20 Tighten the engine mounting and tie-rods. Tighten the exhaust pipe manifold clamp. Insert sufficient washers between the exhaust pipe clip and the mounting lug on the gearlever extension to take up any gap. Refit the clip to mounting lug nut and bolt.
21 Refit the coil or solenoid switch, the starter motor and the front grille.
22 Release the jack from under the car.

11 Clutch and flywheel assembly - removal and replacement (diaphragm spring type)

1   To enable this work to be carried out satisfactorily, it is preferable to remove the complete engine/transmission unit as described in Chapter 1.
2   Undo and remove the bolts and spring washers securing the clutch cover to the flywheel housing. Lift away the clutch cover.
3   Suitably mark the pins and cover to ensure that the parts are refitted in their original positions.
4   Slacken (but do not remove) the three clutch driving pins evenly to release the spring pressure.
5   Replace the pins as they are removed one at a time with three 5/16 in UNF x 2 in studs so as to prevent the pressure plate moving out of alignment.
6   Next the cover and spring assembly may be removed.
7   Slowly rotate the crankshaft until nos. 1 and 4 pistons are at their tdc position. This will prevent the primary gear 'C' washer falling and being wedged behind the flywheel. With the crankshaft in any other position this could happen and result in damage as the flywheel is withdrawn.
8   Carefully knock up the locking washer and remove the flywheel retaining screw using a large socket.
9   Lift away the keyed washer and insert the plug from the special puller (18G304N) in the screw hole.
10 Using the special puller (18G304N) plus adaptors (18G304N) remove the flywheel assembly. Screw the three adaptor screws into the flywheel and fit the large plate of the tool over the screws with the retaining nuts screwed on evenly to keep the plate parallel with the flywheel. Screw in the large centre bolt and holding the flywheel tighten the centre bolt fully. This will

release the flywheel from the crankshaft taper.

11 To refit the assembly, if the driving straps have been removed from the flywheel ensure that the spacing washers are fitted between the straps and flywheel face.

12 Refer to paragraph 7, and set pistons 1 and 4 to tdc.

13 Locate the cover and spring assembly with the clutch balance mark 'A' adjacent to the ¼ timing mark on the flywheel.

14 Fit the driving pins in their original positions, tightening each a turn at a time to a final torque wrench setting of 16 lb f ft (2.2 kg fm)

15 Make sure that the dowel portions of the driving pins have entered the holes in each pair of driving straps. Incorrect assembly will probably cause clutch judder.

16 Refit and tighten the flywheel retaining screw to a torque wrench setting of 110-115 lb f ft (15.2 - 15.9 kg fm). Lock the screw by bending up the lock washer.

17 Replace the clutch cover and secure with the bolts and spring washers.

18 The engine/transmission unit may now be replaced.

12 Clutch - dismantling (coil pressure spring type)

1 With the flywheel and clutch removed take great care to keep the assembly upright until any oil in the flywheel annulus has been mopped away.

2 To ensure that the clutch will still be evenly balanced on reassembly mark all the component parts of the clutch/flywheel unit so they can be replaced in their same relative positions. On most units the letters 'A' have been stamped on the edge of the pressure plate, and on the corner of the thrust plate and spring housing. Ensure the laminated driving straps are also marked.

3 Screw into the flywheel through the holes in the spring housing, three 2½ in. 3/8 in. UNF bolts, or the three studs of Service tool "18G 304 M". Tighten down the bolts (or nuts on the studs) finger tight. Then tighten them a further turn at a time until the load is completely taken from the three pressure plate bolts. Undo and remove the pressure plate bolts and their washers. **Note**: When dismantling the diaphragm spring clutch there is no need to use the bolts or the special studs of the service tool referred to above.

4 Undo and remove the clutch strap bolts and unscrew the bolts

or nuts on the special screws a turn at a time until the clutch springs are fully released. The clutch is now fully dismantled.

13 Clutch - inspection (coil pressure spring type)

Examine the clutch disc friction linings for wear and loose rivets and the disc for rim distortion, cracks, and worn splines.

It is always best to renew the clutch disc as an assembly to preclude further trouble, but, if it is wished to merely renew the linings, the rivets should be drilled out and not knocked out with a punch. The manufacturer's do not advise that only the linings are renewed and personal experience dictates that it is far more satisfactory to renew the disc complete than to try and economise by only fitting new friction linings.

Check the machined faces of the flywheel and the pressure plate. If either is badly grooved it should be machined until smooth. If the pressure plate is cracked or split it must be renewed.

Check the thrust plate for cracks and renew it if any are found.

Renew any clutch pressure springs that are broken or shorter than standard.

Examine the holes in the spring housing through which the pressure plate bolts pass, and if any of the holes are elongated the housing should be renewed.

Also examine the shoulders of the pressure plate bolts for ridges or signs of wear, and the driving straps for distortion or hole elongation. **Note**: If any of the bolts or straps require renewal they should be renewed as a set. Failure to do this will result in the clutch being thrown out of balance.

14 Clutch - reassembly (coil pressure spring type)

1 During clutch reassembly ensure that all the components are placed in their correct relative positions.

2 It is most important that no oil or grease gets on the clutch disc friction lining, or the pressure plate and flywheel faces. It is advisable to rebuild the clutch with clean hands and to wipe down the pressure plate and flywheel faces with a clean dry rag before assembly begins.

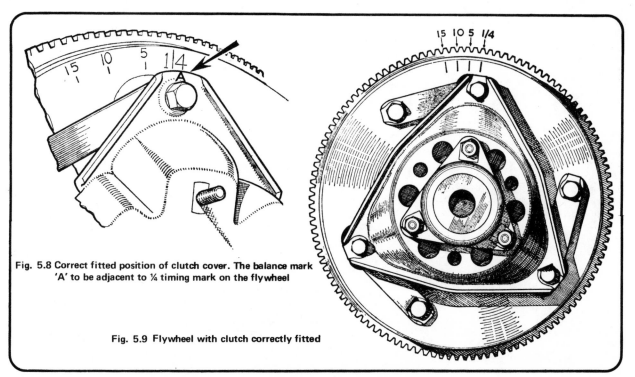

Fig. 5.8 Correct fitted position of clutch cover. The balance mark 'A' to be adjacent to ¼ timing mark on the flywheel

Fig. 5.9 Flywheel with clutch correctly fitted

1 Undo the bolts holding the clutch cover in place and remove the cover. The clutch is unusual in that it is spread out on both sides of the flywheel

2 The next step is to undo the three nuts which hold the thrust plate in position and lift away the plate

3 Because part of the clutch is on the inside of the flywheel, this must be removed. Knock back the tab washer from the flywheel retaining bolt and undo the bolt three turns

4 Then screw down fingertight three 3/8 in. UNF bolts, or three studs from BLMC tool 18G304M (early type) or 18G304N (later type) into the flywheel through the three holes in the spring housing

5 If bolts are used this plate must be placed under their heads. If studs are being used tighten the nuts down evenly

6 Prevent the engine from rotating by a screwdriver jammed against a tooth on the flywheel and the casing. Tighten the large centre bolt to break the flywheel to crankshaft seal

7 With the seal broken and the flywheel now loose on the crankshaft taper remove the special plate, undo the retaining bolt completely, and lift the flywheel away from the engine

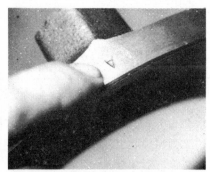

8 Generally, dismantling the flywheel is a reversal of the assembly sequence shown in the following paragraphs. Make sure all the parts marked 'A' line up with the ¼ mark on the flywheel

9 Support the pressure plate so it is raised at least 2 in. off the ground and then fit the clutch driven plate with the long splined centre position facing downwards

10 Then gently replace the flywheel making sure the '¼' mark on the flywheel rim is adjacent to the 'A' mark on the pressure plate

11 Then replace the clutch pressure springs and the thrust plate screws as shown. The next step is to carefully lower the spring housing into place

12 If a clutch compressing tool is not to hand carefully standing on the housing will compress the springs enough for the bolts to be fitted

13 With the flywheel back on the crank-shaft replace the flywheel retaining bolt. Stop the flywheel from turning by inserting a cold chisel in the position shown

14 Tighten the flywheel retaining bolt to a torque of 115 lb ft (15.9 kg fm)

15 Knock back the tab of the lock washer with the aid of a drift. The clutch housing can also be fitted with the flywheel in place as shown in the next 4 photos

16 Either a diaphragm or a coil spring housing may be fitted. In either case ensure the mark "A" lines up with the ¼ mark on the flywheel

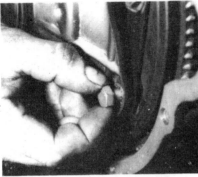

17 Then replace the three bolts and washers which hold the spring housing to the pressure plate

18 The next step is to replace the thrust plate which is simply held in place with a retaining spring on diaphragm clutches

19 In this photograph the retaining spring and thrust plate have been replaced and the method of attachment can be clearly seen

20 The next step is to fit the starter motor switch is held in place with two bolts

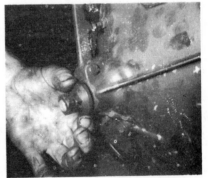

21 Then refit the clutch cover and adjust the clutch throw-out stop as follows: Screw the locknut and stop as far out from the cover as possible

22 Pull and hold out the clutch lever as far as it will go and then do up the throw-out stop until it touches the cover boss

23 Release the clutch lever and turn the throw-out stop a further 0.007 to 0.010 in (0.2 to 0.25 mm) clockwise (approximately one flat). Then tighten the locknut

24 Then check the clearance of the clutch lever against the adjustable bolt on the casing and screw the bolt in or out to give a gap of 0.020 in. (0.508 mm)

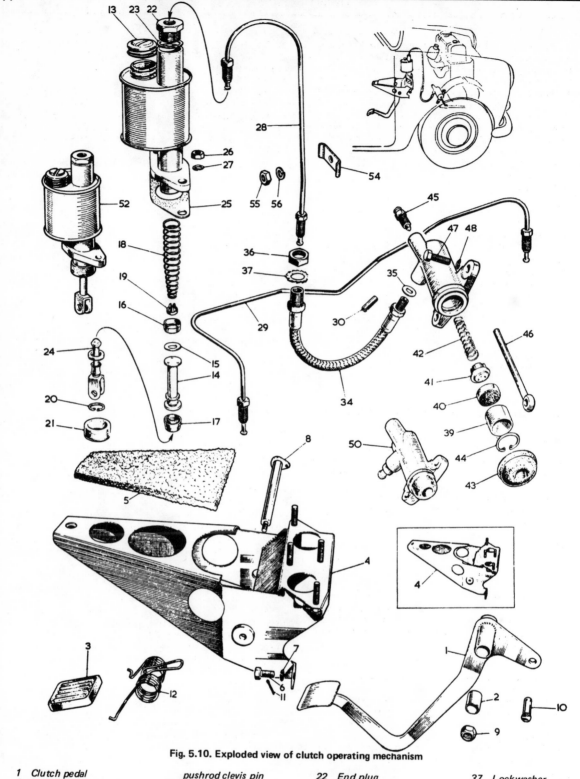

Fig. 5.10. Exploded view of clutch operating mechanism

1 Clutch pedal	pushrod clevis pin	22 End plug	37 Lockwasher
2 Pedal bush	11 Split pin	23 Gasket	39 Piston
3 Pedal pad	12 Return spring	24 Pushrod	40 Piston cup
4 Clutch & brake pedal	13 Filler cap	25 Sealing washer	41 Piston cup filler
bracket	14 Piston	26 Nut	42 Filler cup spring
5 Felt	15 Washer	27 Spring washer	43 Rubber boot
6 Screw	16 Main cup	28 12 in. (305 mm) pipe	44 Circlip
7 Spring washer	17 Secondary cup	29 29 in. (736 mm) pipe (lhd)	45 Bleed screw
8 Clutch and brake pedal	18 Return spring	30 Rubber pipe (lhd)	46 Pushrod
shaft	19 Retainer spring	34 Clutch hose	47 Screw
9 Nut	20 Circlip	35 Gasket	48 Spring washer
10 Clutch pedal to	21 Rubber boot	36 Locknut	

3 Renew the oil seal in the flywheel where one is fitted (see Chapter 1 for details). Reassemble the driving straps to the flywheel and ensure the spacing washers are in position.

4 Place the pressure plate, lugs facing upwards, on two blocks of wood on the assembly bench so there is about 1.5 in (38·1mm) clearance between the centre of the pressure plate and the bench.

5 Place the clutch disc in the exact centre of the pressure plate using the polished working area on the pressure plate face as an accurate guide if the special centralising tool BLMC part No. "18G 571" is not available. Ensure that the longer end of the splined hub faces the bench away from the flywheel.

6 Carefully place the flywheel on the clutch disc so as not to disturb the position of the disc on the pressure plate. Also ensure the flywheel is in its correct relative position.

7 Stand the clutch pressure springs in their recessed holes in the flywheel.

8 Hold the spring housing in its correct relative position about 1 foot above the flywheel and note which springs lie underneath the elongated holes in the spring housing.

9 Place the three thrust plate bolts on top of the springs which will lie under the elongated holes and lower the spring housing over them. Ensure the flat flanks of the bolts register properly in the holes in the housing.

10 Compress the springs with the aid of the three 5/16 in. UNF bolts or the special tool. (Not necessary with diaphragm clutches).

11 Replace and do up the three pressure plate bolts, using new washers under their heads and tighten them down to a torque of 16 lb f ft (2.2 kg fm).

12 Ensure the bolts which hold the driving straps to the flywheel are also tightened down to a torque of 16 lb f ft (2.2 kg fm) and that the tabs of the locking washer are turned up.

15 Clutch - inspection (diaphragm spring type)

1 Refer to Section 13 and follow the inspection sequence as applicable.

2 Inspect the cover for elongation of the driving pin holes.

3 Inspect the driving pins for ridging and wear. Obtain three new pins if any are worn.

4 Inspect the driving straps and if any are worn a new set must be obtained.

16 Clutch faults

There are four main faults which the clutch and release mechanism are prone to. They may occur by themselves or in conjunction with any of the other faults. They are clutch squeal, slip, spin and judder.

17 Clutch squeal - diagnosis and cure

1 If on taking up the drive or when changing gear, the clutch squeals, this is a sure indication of a badly worn clutch release bearing. As well as regular wear due to normal use, wear of the clutch release bearing is much accentuated if the clutch is ridden, or held down for long periods in gear, with the engine running. To minimise wear of this component the car should always be taken out of gear at traffic lights and for similar hold-ups.

2 The clutch release bearing is not an expensive item.

18 Clutch slip - diagnosis and cure

1 Clutch slip is a self-evident condition which occurs when the clutch friction plate is badly worn, the release arm free travel is insufficient, oil or grease have got onto the flywheel or pressure plate faces, or the pressure plate itself is faulty.

2 The reason for clutch slip is that, due to one of the faults listed above, there is either insufficient pressure from the pressure plate, or insufficient friction from the friction plate to ensure solid drive.

3 If small amounts of oil get onto the clutch they will be burnt off under the heat of clutch engagement, in the process gradually darkening the linings. Excessive oil on the clutch will burn off leaving a carbon deposit which can cause quite bad slip, or fierceness, spin and judder.

4 If clutch slip is suspected, and confirmation of this condition is required, there are several tests which can be made:

a) With the engine in second or third gear and pulling lightly up a moderate incline, sudden depression of the accelerator pedal may cause the engine to increase its speed without any increase in road speed. Easing off on the accelerator will then give a definite drop in engine speed without the car slowing.

b) Drive the car at a steady speed in top gear and braking with the left leg, try and maintain the same speed by pressing down on the accelerator. Providing the same speed is maintained a change in the speed of the engine confirms that slip is taking place.

c) In extreme cases of clutch slip the engine will race under normal acceleration conditions.

5 If slip is due to oil or grease on the linings a temporary cure can sometimes be effected by squirting carbon tetrochloride into the clutch. The permanent cure, of course, is to renew the clutch driven plate and trace and rectify the oil leak.

19 Clutch spin - diagnosis and cure

1 Clutch spin is a condition which occurs when there is a leak in the clutch hydraulic actuating mechanism where this system of actuation is used, the release arm free travel is excessive, there is an obstruction in the clutch either on the primary gear splines, or in the operating lever itself, or the oil may have been partially burnt off the clutch linings and have left a resinous deposit which is causing the clutch disc to stick to the pressure plate or flywheel.

2 The reason for clutch spin is that due to any, or a combination of, the faults just listed, the clutch pressure plate is not completely freeing from the centre plate even with the clutch pedal fully depressed.

3 If clutch spin is suspected, the condition can be confirmed by extreme difficulty in engaging first gear from rest, difficulty in changing gear, and very sudden take-up of the clutch drive at the fully depressed end of the clutch pedal travel as the clutch is released.

4 Check the operating lever free travel. If this is correct examine the clutch master and slave cylinders and the connecting hydraulic pipe for leaks. Fluid in one of the rubber boots fitted over the end of either the master or slave cylinders, where fitted, is a sure sign of a leaking piston seal.

5 If these points are checked and found to be in order then the fault lies internally in the clutch, and it will be necessary to remove the clutch for examination.

20 Clutch judder - diagnosis and cure

1 Clutch judder is a self-evident condition which occurs when the gearbox or engine mountings are loose or too flexible, when there is oil on the faces of the clutch friction plate, or when the clutch pressure plate has been incorrectly adjusted.

2 The reason for clutch judder is that due to one of the faults just listed, the clutch pressure plate is not freeing smoothly from the friction disc, and is snatching.

3 Clutch judder normally occurs when the clutch pedal is released in first or reverse gears, and the whole car shudders as it moves backwards or forwards.

4 The only cure available is to disassemble the clutch and check for the symptoms just given. Replace parts as necessary.

Chapter 6 Gearbox and automatic transmission

Contents

Specifications

Manual gearbox

Early				4 speed, synchromesh on top 3 gears	
Later				4 speed, synchromesh on all 4 gears	
Final drive type:				Helical gears and differential	

Ratios	Top	Third	Second	First	Reverse
Mini Mk I and II (848), Mk II (998)					
3 speed synchromesh					
Gearbox	1.000	1.412	2.172	3.627	3.627
Overall	3.765	5.317	8.176	13.657	13.657
4 speed synchromesh					
(From engine number 8AM-WE-H101)					
Gearbox	1.000	1.43	2.21	3.52	3.54
Overall	3.76	5.40	8.32	13.25	13.30
(From engine numbers 99H-159-H101 and 99H-251-H101)					
Gearbox	1.000	1.43	2.21	3.52	3.54
Overall	3.444	4.93	7.63	12.13	12.19
Final drive ratio standard all models		3.765 : 1 (3.444 : 1 alternative saloon only)			
Cooper (997 and 998)					
Gearbox	1.000	1.357	1.916	3.20	3.20
Overall	3.765	5.11	7.213	12.05	12.05
Overall alternative	3.444	4.674	6.598	11.03	11.03
Final drive ratio standard		3.765 : 1 (3.444 : 1 available as service item only)			
Cooper 'S' Mk I (970 & 1071), Cooper 'S' Mk II (1275)					
3 speed synchromesh					
Gearbox	1.000	1.357	1.916	3.200	3.200
Overall (970 and 1071)	3.765	5.11	7.21	12.05	12.05
Overall (1275)	3.444	4.67	6.60	11.02	11.02
Overall alternative ...	3.939	5.34	7.54	12.06	12.06
Overall alternative ...	4.133	5.61	7.92	13.27	13.27
Overall alternative ...	4.267	5.79	8.18	13.65	13.65
3 speed synchro close ratio					
Gearbox	1.000	1.242	1.178	2.57	2.57
Overall (1275)	3.444	4.28	6.13	8.84	8.84
Overall alternative ...	3.647	4.53	6.49	9.37	9.37
Overall (970 and 1071) ...	3.765	4.68	6.70	9.66	9.66
Overall alternative ...	3.939	4.89	7.02	10.12	10.12
Overall alternative ...	4.133	5.13	7.35	10.61	10.61
Overall alternative ...	4.267	5.30	7.61	10.90	10.90
Overall alternative ...	4.350	5.4	7.74	10.18	10.18
Cooper 'S' Mk III (1275) and 1275 GT (before July 1974)					
Gearbox	1.000	1.35	2.07	3.3	3.35

Overall (3.65 : 1)	3.65	4.93	7.56	12.04	12.21

Final drive ratio   3.65 : 1 (alternative on Cooper 'S' Mk III only 3.939 4.267 4.35)

Mini 850/1000 Saloon, Van and Pick-up (4 speed synchromesh)

848 engine

Gearbox	1.000	1.43	2.21	3.52	3.54
Overall	3.76	5.40	8.32	13.25	13.30

Final drive ratio   3.76 : 1

998 engine (Note: Van and Pick-up data see Mini 848)

Gearbox	1.000	1.43	2.21	3.52	3.54
Overall	3.44	4.93	7.63	12.13	12.19

Final drive ratio   3.44 : 1

Mini Clubman

Gearbox	1.00	1.43	2.21	3.52	3.54
Overall	3.44	4.93	7.63	12.13	12.19

Final drive ration   3.44 : 1

Speedometer drive ratio 6/17

Lubricant capacity:

    Transmission casing (inc. filter)   ... ...   8.5 pints (4.83 litres)

Automatic transmission

Torque converter:

Type	3 element
Ratio	2 : 1 maximum
Converter output gear ratio	1.15 : 1
Converter endfloat	0.0035 — 0.0065 in. (0.089 — 0.164 mm)

Ratios (gearbox):

Top	1.0 : 1
Third	1.46 : 1
Second	1.845 : 1
First	2.69 : 1
Reverse	2.69 : 1

Overall ratios:

Top	3.76 : 1
Third	5.49 : 1
Second	6.94 : 1
First	10.11 : 1
Reverse	10.11 : 1

Speedometer drive ratio: 7/17

Lubricant capacity:

Transmission casing (inc. filter)	13 pints (7.38 litres)
Refill capacity (approx)	9 pints (5 litres)

Torque wrench settings:	**lb f ft**	**kg f m**
Manual gearbox		
Flywheel housing nuts and bolts	18	2.5
First motion shaft nut (early gearboxes)	90	12.0
(later gearboxes)	150	20.7
Third motion shaft nut (early gearboxes)	90	12.0
(later gearboxes)	150	20.7
Transmission case to crankcase	6	0.8
Transmission drain plug	40 to 50	5.5 to 6.9
Transmission case studs 3/8 in. UNC	8	1.1
Transmission case studs 5/16 in. UNC	6	0.8
Transmission case stud nuts 3/8 in. UNF	25	3.4
Transmission case stud nuts 5/16 in. UNF	18	2.5
Bottom cover setscrews 1/4 in. UNC (change speed tower) ...	6	0.8
Speedometer drive housing nuts	18	2.5
Automatic transmission		
Converter centre bolt	110 to 115	15.2 to 15.9
Converter (six central bolts)	22 to 24	3.0 to 3.3
Converter drain plugs	18 to 20	2.5 to 2.8
Converter housing bolts	18	2.5
Differential drive flange securing bolts	40 to 45	5.5 to 6.2
Kickdown control assembly to transmission casing (on nyloc housing)	5	7
Oil filter bowl	10 to 15	1.4 to 2
Transmission to engine securing nut	12	1.6

1 General description

The manual gearbox fitted to the Mini contains four forward gears and reverse. It is housed in the engine sump and forms a single unit with the differential.

On earlier models second, third and top gears were fitted with synchromesh action but this was changed on Cooper 'S' and later models and all synchromesh gearboxes were fitted. There have been several modifications to these gearboxes and where these occur full information is given in the text.

Drive from the gearbox is passed to the drive shafts through a pair of spur gears located behind the mainshaft. All transmissions have separate synchroniser rings. The countershaft gear cluster bearings and the mainshaft pilot bearings are of the needle roller type and the gear cluster endfloat is adjusted by selective-fit thrust washers fitted each end.

Automatic transmission was available as a factory fitted optional extra on all Mk II models with the exception of the Mini Cooper. Further information on the automatic transmission will be found later in this chapter.

2 Gearbox - removal and replacement

The gearbox is removed from the car together with the engine and differential assembly as described in Chapter 1. It will then be necessary to separate the gearbox from the engine: again, full information will be found in Chapter 1.

3 Gearbox - dismantling

Place the gearbox on a strong bench so it is at a comfortable working height and quite accessible. If a bench is not available then lay the gearbox on the floor, but make sure the latter is clean and dirt free and preferably covered with paper.

To make the dismantling and rebuilding sequence as easy as possible, the text has been keyed to Fig. No. 6.1 except where otherwise stated. Throughout the text the numbers in brackets, ie., (15) refer to the parts shown in this illustration. Strip the gearbox in the following sequence:

1 Undo the hexagon cap from the gear change extension and remove the gear change lever, anti-rattle spring and plunger.

2 Undo the four bolts and washers (3), holding the bottom cover plate to the underside of the gearchange extension (See Fig. 6.2).

3 Unscrew the clamping bolt (131) which secures the lever (130) to the remote control shaft (129) in the rear of the transmission casing, and slide the shaft out. On early models a nylon cup and spring were fitted to the bottom of the shaft. On later models the cup and spring were omitted. If found during overhauls discard the nylon cup and also the spring. This helps to give a positive and easier gearchange.

4 Remove the spring plug (135), the plug washer (136), the spring (134) and the reverse check plunger (133) which serves to locate the gearchange shaft (120).

5 Take off the intermediate gear (43) together with its thrust washers (44) from the rear of the transmission casing. Make sure that the washers are kept in their correct relative position either side of the gear.

6 Undo the bolt (97) on the speedometer pinion housing and take off the pinion housing cover (95). Pull out the speedometer pinion (93). Undo the two bolts and washers (103, 104), from the front cover (137), and remove the end plate, joint gasket, and speedometer gear (101,102,100).

7 Unscrew the clamp bolt and washer (124, 125) from the selector lever (122) and remove the gearchange shaft (120), the selector lever (122), and the oil seal (121), from the transmission casing (1). **Note:** There is a woodruff key (123) fitted to the lower end of the gearchange shaft (120). Ensure this key is extracted before removing the shaft.

8 Undo and remove the bolts, nuts and spring washers

Fig. 6.1. Exploded view of early type transmission

No.	Part	No.	Part	No.	Part
1	Transmission cover	55	Locating plate	106	Reverse fork rod
2	Control shaft bush	56	Bearing	107	Ford rod selector
3	Differential cover stud	57	Distance piece	108	1st & 2nd gear shifter fork
4	Differential cover stud	58	Retaining ring	109	1st & 2nd gear shifter rod
5	Differential cover dowel	59	Thrust washer - rear	110	3rd & 4th gear shifter fork
6	Differential cover joint washer - upper	60	Thrust washer - front	111	3rd & 4th gear shifter rod
7	Differential cover joint washer - lower	61	1st motion shaft	112	Selector screw
8	Differential cover stud nut	62	1st motion shaft roller bearing	113	Nut
9	Washer	63	1st motion ball bearing	114	Locknut
10	Washer	64	Circlip	115	Plunger
12	Differential cover stud nut	65	Mainshaft	116	Plunger spring
13	Washer	66	Mainshaft bearing	117	Plug
14	Flywheel housing stud	67	Circlip	118	Plug washer
15	Flywheel housing stud	68	1st gear	119	Change speed gate
16	Front cover stud - long	69	Synchroniser ball	120	Gear change shaft
17	Front cover stud - short	70	Spring	121	Oil seal
18	Front cover dowel	71	2nd speed synchroniser plunger	122	Selector lever
19	Flywheel housing dowel	72	Baulk ring	123	Key
20	Idler gear bearing	73	2nd gear thrust washer	124	Clamp bolt
21	Bearing circlip	74	2nd gear	125	Washer
22	Operating lever pin	75	2nd gear bush	126	Operating shaft lever
23	Exhaust pipe bracket	76	Interlocking ring	127	Clamp bolt
24	Drain plug	77	3rd gear	128	Washer
25	Plug washer	78	3rd gear bush	129	Remote - control shaft
26	Oil strainer	79	3rd motion shaft thrust washer	130	Shaft lever
27	Sealing ring	80	Thrust washer peg	131	Lever bolt
28	Strainer bracket	81	Spring	132	Washer
29	Screw to strainer	82	3rd/top synchroniser	133	Reverse check plunger
30	Washer	83	Ball	134	Plunger spring
31	Screw to casing	84	Spring	135	Spring plug
32	Locking	85	Baulk ring	136	Plug washer
33	Oil suction pipe	86	Bearing retainer	137	Front cover
34	Joint gasket	87	Lockwasher	138	Cover gasket
35	Pipe blanking plate	88	Bolt	139	Cover bolt
36	Joint gasket	89	Bearing shim	140	Washer
37	Pipe screw	90	Final drive pinion	141	Mounting adaptor stud
38	Washer	91	Nut	142	Washer
39	Sealing ring	92	Washer	143	Nut
40	Primary gear	93	Speedometer pinion	144	Crankcase joint washer RH
41	Gear bush - front	94	Bush	145	Crankcase joint washer LH
42	Gear bush - rear	95	Pinion housing cover	146	Bearing cap oil seal
43	Intermediate gear	96	Joint	147	Transmission to crankcase screw
44	Intermediate gear	97	Speedometer pinion housing bolt	148	Transmission to crankcase screw - long
45	1st motion shaft gear	98	Washer	149	Transmission to crankcase stud
46	Nut	99	Spring washer	150	Nut
47	Lockwasher	100	Speedometer spindle & gear	151	Washer
48	Reverse gear	101	End plate	152	Lubricator differential cover
49	Bush	102	Joint gasket	153	Lubricator differential cover washer
50	Reverse gear shaft	103	Bolt		
51	Reverse operating lever	104	Washer		
52	Pivot pin circlip	105	Reverse fork		
53	Layshaft				
54	Laygear				

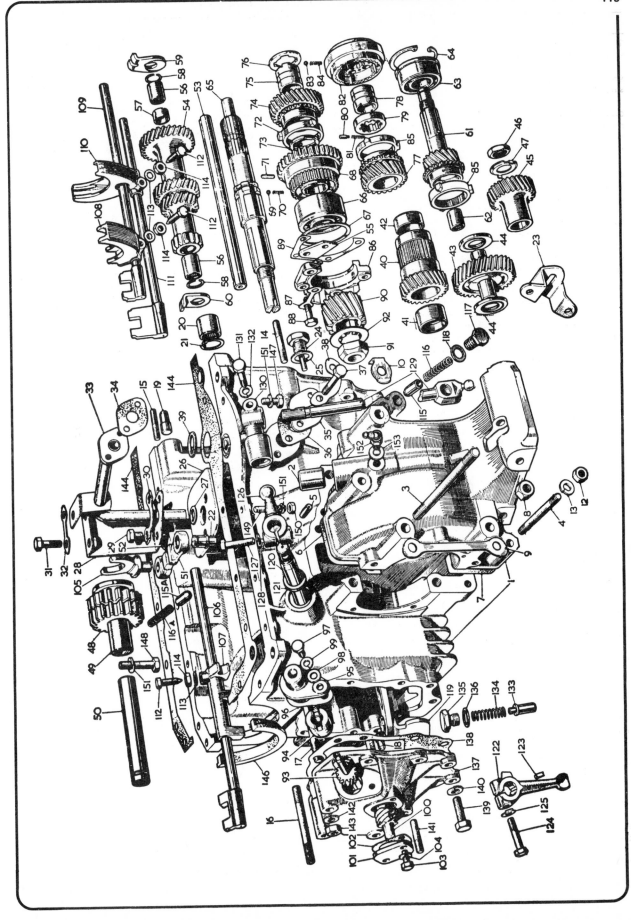

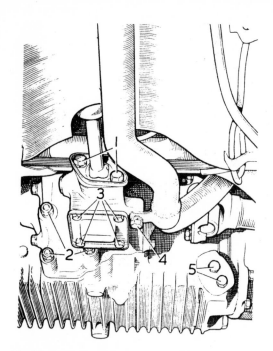

Fig. 6.2. Underside view of early type transmission unit

1 Gear lever retaining bolts
2 3 of the 4 differential stud nuts
3 Extension cover plate bolts
4 Exhaust pipe front fixing point
5 Plugs, interlocking plungers and springs

(139,143,142,140) which hold the front cover in position. Pull the cover (137). and gasket (138) from the transmission casing.

9 Knock back the tab of the lock washer (32) from the bolt (31) which holds the oil suction pipe support bracket to the lug on the gearbox casing. Undo the two bolts (37) which hold the oil pipe flange (33) to the casing, and remove the suction pipe (33) and joint gasket (34). The oil strainer (26) cannot yet be removed.

10 Knock back the tabs of the locking washers (87) and undo the bolts (88) which hold the mainshaft bearing retainer (86) to the web in the centre of the casing. Take off the retainer (86) and remove the bearing shim (89).

11 Lock together two gears by pressing the shifter fork rods in. This will prevent the mainshaft from turning.

12 Undo and remove the nut and washer (91,92) which holds the final drive pinion (90) to the mainshaft (65). Pull the pinion off the mainshaft.

13 Remove the circlip and roller bearing from the end of the first motion shaft, unlock the lock washer (47), undo the nut (46), and take off the driving gear (45). The locked gears may now be freed.

14 Measure the endfloat of the laygear (54) with a feeler gauge. If the endfloat exceeds 0.006 in. (0.1524 mm) or is less than 0.002 in. (0.0508 mm) then new thrust washers must be fitted on reassembly. A single locating plate (55) holds both the layshaft (53), and the reverse shaft (50) in place by means of slots in the ends of the shafts into which the plate fits. Remove the plate from the centre web so freeing the shafts.

15 Tap the layshaft out of the transmission casing and lift the laygear (54) together with the thrust washers (59,60) out of the gearbox.

16 Unscrew the 2 plugs (117) from the transmission housing (1) and remove the plungers (115) and plunger springs which locate in the 1st and 2nd, and 3rd and 4th gear shifter rods.

17 Remove the circlip (64) from the transmission housing, and carefully tap out the first motion shaft ball bearing (63).

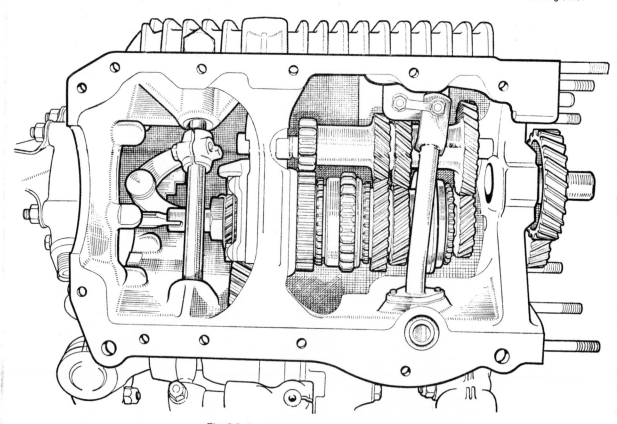

Fig. 6.3. Four speed synchromesh transmission assembly

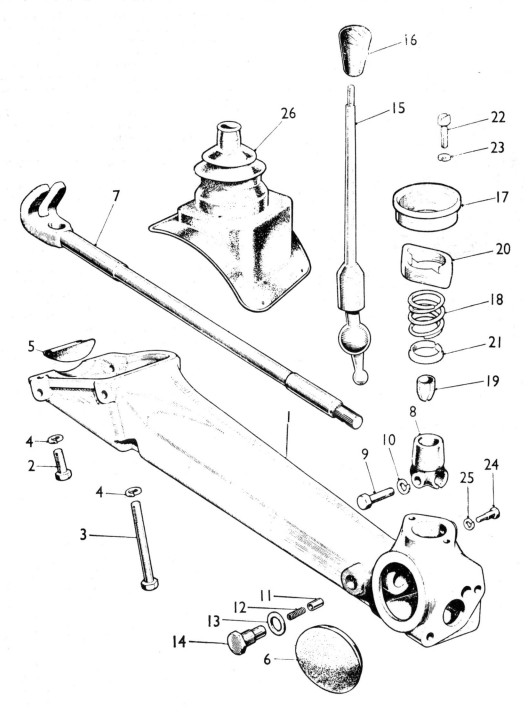

Fig. 6.4. Exploded view of early type remote control

1	Housing	9	Screw lever	18	Spring
2	Securing screw - short	10	Spring washer	19	Bush - split
3	Securing screw - long	11	Damper plunger	20	Distance piece
4	Spring washers	12	Plunger spring	21	Flange
5	Rubber plug	13	Washer	22	Retainer to housing screw
6	Rubber dust cover	14	Cap nut - spring retainer	23	Spring washer
7	Primary shaft	15	Change speed lever	24	Locating pin
8	Primary shaft lever	16	Lever knob	25	Spring washer
		17	Retainer	26	Gaiter - change speed lever

18 Release the locknut (114) from the 1st and 2nd gear shifter fork (108), unscrew the shifter fork bolt (112) and remove the 1st and 2nd gear shift rod (109). Lift the shifter fork out of the transmission casing.

19 With a suitable drift drive the mainshaft (65), about 1 in. (25 mm) to the rear of the transmission casing. Because the mainshaft bearing is held with a circlip against the forward edge of the centre web it will be prevented from emerging on the other side of the web with the mainshaft. Insert the BLMC special tool "18G 613" in the gap now created between the 1st speed gear (68) and the mainshaft bearing (66).

20 Drive the mainshaft forward towards the front of the casing, taking care not to damage the shifter forks until the bearing is nearly clear of the centre housing. Carefully lever the bearing off. If the special tool "18G 613" is not used the splines or shoulder of the 1st gear may damage the centre web. Note: Two thick metal packing pieces may be used instead of the tool if available.

21 Remove the bearing, the mainshaft and the associated parts from the transmission casing.

22 Knock back the other tab on the lockwasher (32), unscrew the remaining bolt (31) from the strainer bracket (28) and lift the strainer (6) and bracket out of the gearbox casing.

23 Loosen the locknut (114) from the 3rd and 4th gear shifter fork (110), unscrew the shifter fork bolt (112) and remove the gear shifter rod (111). Lift the shifter fork (110) out of the transmission casing. Repeat this operation with the reverse gear shifter rod (106) and shifter fork (107).

24 Remove the reverse gear shaft (50), the reverse gear (48), and the reverse gear shifter fork (105). Remove the plunger (115), and the plunger spring (116).

25 Remove the circlip (52) from the top of the reverse gear shifter lever (51) and extract the lever from the casing, together with the lever pin (22).

26 The gearbox is now completely stripped. The component parts should now be examined for wear as detailed later, and the layshaft, first motion shaft, and mainshaft broken down further as shown in Section 4.

4 Gearbox - examination and renovation

Carefully examine all the component parts starting with the synchronising cones or baulk rings. The cones are copper in colour and are shrunk onto the sides of the second, third and fourth speed gears. If the ridges are badly worn, or if the cones are loose on their gears, or if the cones are cracked or broken, they must be renewed. It is normal practice to purchase new gears and synchronising cones complete.

If engineering facilities are available it is possible to shrink on new cones to existing gearwheels, and then machine the cones to the correct dimensions. This is highly skilled work, it is most unlikely that the private owner, or the majority of garages, have the necessary equipment, and the saving is not really sufficient to make it worthwhile. It is altogether better to purchase either a complete reconditioned mainshaft or new gears and synchronising units and fit them to the mainshaft yourself.

Examine the gearwheels for excessive wear and chipping of the teeth and renew them as necessary.

If the laygear endfloat is above the permitted tolerance (see paragraph 14 in Section 3) the thrust washers must be renewed.

Measure the distance between the larger gearwheel and the side of the casing, immediately below the layshaft. If the gap is 0.125 to 0.127 in. (3.18 to 3.22 mm). fit the BLMC part no. "22A 48". If 0.128 to 0.130 in. (3.25 to 3.30 mm). fit part no. "22A 49". If 0.131 to 0.133 in. (3.32 to 3.37 mm) fit part no. "22A 50". If 0.134 in. (3.41 mm) fit part no. "22A 52".

A needle roller bearing is fitted internally to each end of the laygear. To examine them, prise out the retaining clips from each end, and with a finger pull out the outer race, needle rollers, and inner race. At the end of the laygear with the smaller gear, also extract the distance piece and the inner spring rings from both ends. Renew the roller bearings and races, if worn.

Dealing first with the smaller end of the laygear, place it upright with the smaller end at the top and fit the inner spring ring, the distance piece, and slide the new roller bearing, into position. Slip the spring retaining ring into the groove. Repeat this procedure for the larger end of the laygear, turning the laygear round, and omitting, of course, the distance piece.

Examine the condition of the main ball bearings, one on the first motion shaft, and the other on the mainshaft. If there is looseness between the inner and outer races the bearings must be renewed.

If it is wished to renew the synchronisers, or to examine the second and third gear bushes or needle roller bearings the third motion shaft must be dismantled in the following sequence which will ensure the job is done rapidly, correctly and easily.

If new bushes are being fitted they must be first heated to about 19C°C. Expansion will allow them to slide on the mainshaft easily and as they cool the subsequent contraction will ensure they fit securely on the mainshaft.

5 Mainshaft (early type) - dismantling and reassembly

1 Slide the synchroniser hub (82) for third/top gears from off the rear of the mainshaft. Note: the plain part of the hub faces towards the rear of the transmission casing.

2 With an electricians screwdriver or piece of thin rod, press down the spring loaded plunger (80,81), and turn the splined thrust washer (79) so that a spline holds the plunger down, and the thrust washer is so positioned, that it can slide forward off the rear of the mainshaft. Now slide the baulk ring synchroniser (85) and the third gear (77) off the mainshaft in the same manner.

3 Remove the now exposed plunger and spring (80,81) and take off the third gear bush (78), (or needle roller bearings) and the interlocking ring (76).

4 Remove the second gear (74) together with the baulk ring synchroniser (72) and the second gear bush (75). Note: in post 1965 models a needle roller bearing replaces the bush. Take off the thrust washer (73).

5 Slide the first gear and hub (68) off the front of the mainshaft.

6 If it is wished to remove the hubs from the centre of gearwheels, ensure a rag is placed round the assembly to catch the three spring loaded balls (69, 70) contained in each hub.

7 On reassembly of the gearwheel to the hub ensure that the cut-away on the spline in the gearwheel lines up with the hole for the plunger. Also ensure that the teeth on the first gear are on the cone side of the first gear hub.

8 Replace the second gear thrust washer (73) and slide the second gear bush (75), or needle roller bearing, onto the rear of the mainshaft so the smooth end of the bush abuts the thrust washer. Oil the bearings.

9 Fit the second gear and synchroniser (72,74) over the second gear thrust washer and slide on the interlocking ring (76) so that two of the cutouts mate with the two protrusions on the end of the second gear bush (75).

10 Replace the first gear and hub assembly (68) on the front of the mainshaft (65), pushing it firmly up to the second gear (74). Ensure that the flat end of the hub assembly (68) will abut the roller bearing (66) when the latter is replaced.

11 Moving to the rear of the mainshaft, fit the third gear bush (78) ensuring that the two protrusions slide into the two remaining slots in the inter-locking ring (76).

12 Slide the third gear (77) onto the rear of the mainshaft, flat side first, and drop the spring (81) and locking plunger (80) into the mainshaft drilling.

13 Press down the plunger (80), slide the thrust washer (79) up the splines of the mainshaft over the depressed plunger, and rotate the washer in the circular mainshaft groove one spline width. Turning the thrust washer in this way allows the plunger to spring up into one of the internal spline grooves, so locking the washer in place.

14 Measure the endfloat of the second and third speed gears

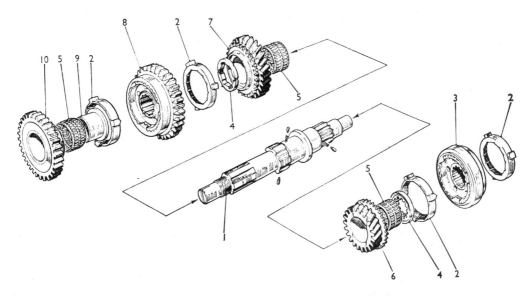

Fig. 6.5. Exploded view of the mainshaft assembly on four speed synchromesh gearboxes

1	Main shaft	4	Thrust washers
2	Baulk rings	5	Needle roller bearings
3	3rd & 4th speed synchro hub	6	Third gear

7	Second gear	9	Needle roller bearing journal
8	Reverse mainshaft gear and 1st & 2nd synchro hub	10	First gear

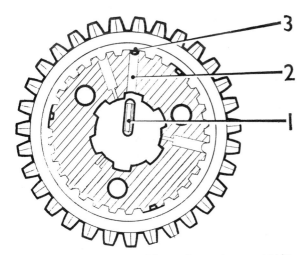

Fig. 6.6. Cross section of first and second gear assembly (later type transmission)

1	Plunger	3	Cut-away tooth
2	Drilling in hub		

which should be between 0.0035 and 0.0055 in. (0.09 and 0.13 mm).

15 Replace the synchroniser hub (82) for third/top gears with the plain side facing the rear of the transmission casing. Mainshaft assembly is now complete.

---

6 Mainshaft (later type) - dismantling and reassembly

1 Slide the synchroniser hub for third/top gears from off the rear of the mainshaft. **Note:** the plain part of the hub faces towards the rear of the transmission casing.
2 With an electricians screwdriver or piece of thin rod, press down the spring loaded plunger and turn the splined thrust washer so that a spline holds the plunger down, and the thrust washer is so positioned, that it can slide forward off the rear of the mainshaft. Now slide the baulk ring synchroniser and the third gear off the mainshaft in the same manner.
3 Slide the first gear off the shaft followed by the baulk ring.
4 Remove the needle roller bearing and journal
5 Slide off the reverse mainshaft gear together with the synchromesh unit hub for 1st and 2nd gears.
6 Remove the 2nd gear baulk ring.
7 Depress and twist the thrust washer so that it lines up with the splines on the shaft and then draw it off.
8 Finally remove the 2nd gears and the needle roller bearing.
9 Reassembly of the mainshaft is the reverse sequence to dismantling as described in paragraphs 3 to 8 inclusive. Then the following additional points should be noted:
a) Slide the third gear onto the rear of the mainshaft, flat side first, and drop the spring and locking plunger into the mainshaft drilling.
b) Press down the plunger, slide the thrust washer up the splines of the mainshaft over the depressed plunger, and rotate the washer in the circular mainshaft groove one spline width. Turning the thrust washer in this way allows the plunger to spring up into one of the internal spline grooves, so locking the washer in place.
c) Measure the end float of the second and third speed gears which should be between 0.0035 and 0.0055 in. (0.09 and 0.13 mm).

---

7 Gearbox - reassembly

Thoroughly clean down the gearbox casing, and scrape all traces of old gaskets off the gearbox flanges. Clean in paraffin, and, if possible blow dry with an airline, the internal components of the gearbox. Reassembly should proceed as follows:
1 Press the reverse lever operating pin (22) into its bore in the bottom of the casing with the groove in the pin uppermost.
2 Press the reverse operating lever (51) into place on the operating pin (22), and fit operating lever retaining circlip (52)

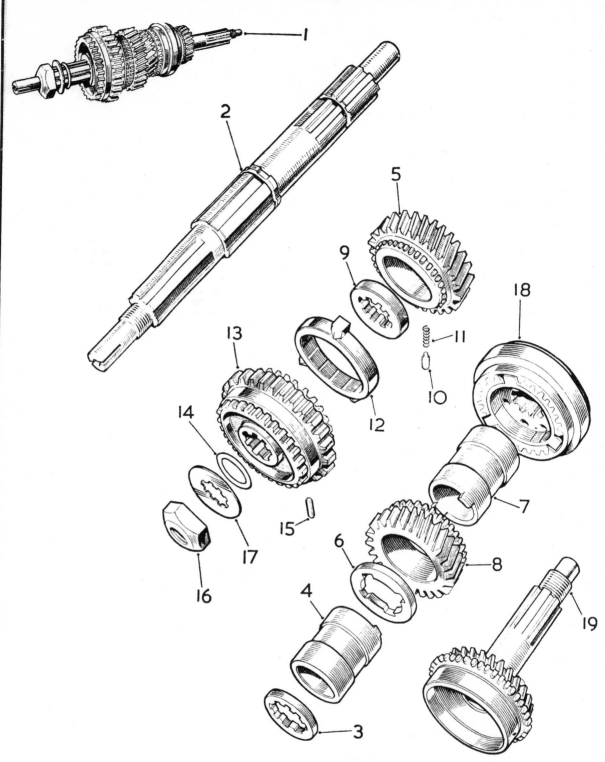

Fig. 6.7. Exploded view of the baulk ring conversion kit.
Gearboxes with cone synchromesh can be converted to baulk ring by fitting the parts supplied
in the kit

1 Assembled baulk ring conversion kit	5 2nd gear	10 Thrust washer peg
2 Mainshaft	6 2nd & 3rd gear inter- locking ring	11 Thrust washer spring
3 2nd gear thrust washer	7 Bush for 3rd gear	12 Baulk ring
4 Bush for 2nd gear	8 3rd gear	13 1st gear with 2nd gear synchroniser
	9 Thrust washer	14 Spacing washer

15 Plunger
16 Final drive pinion nut
17 Lockwasher
18 3rd and 4th gear synchroniser
19 1st motion shaft

to the operating pin (22).

3 Replace the reverse fork (105) in the hole in the reverse operating lever (51). Ensure the cut-out on the fork faces the front of the gearbox.

4 Place the reverse gear and bush (48,49) in position so the flange on the end of the gear slides over the prongs of the reverse fork (105).

5 Oil the reverse gear shaft (50) and pass it through the centre web of the transmission case, into the reverse gear (49), with the slotted end of the shaft (50) facing towards the front of the casing.

6 Fit and hold the reverse gear shifter rod spring (116A) and plunger (115A) in place, and then slide in the reverse fork rod (106) from the front of the casing so the fork rod selector (107) picks up the reverse fork.

7 Place the third and fourth gear shifter fork (110) in the casing and push the third and fourth gear shifter rod (111) in from the front of the casing so the rod enters the lower hole in the fork (110).

8 Place the first and second gear shifter fork (108) in the casing and push the first and second gear shifter rod (109) in from the front of the casing so the rod enters the locating hole in the first and second gear selector fork (108) and also passes through the clearance hole in the third and fourth gear shifter fork (110).

9 Line up the indentations in the rods (106,111,109) with the holes in the forks (107,110,108) and insert and tighten down the selector screws (112), lockwashers (113), and locknuts (114). Make certain the locknuts (114) are properly tightened down, and on no account omit the lockwashers (113). As the selectors lie in the bottom of the transmission casing if one works loose the whole gearbox must be stripped to tighten it.

10 Place the oil strainer sealing ring (27) in the recess in the oil strainer (26), and lightly grease the ring to help the oil pipe pass through easily when it is fitted later. Attach the oil strainer bracket (28) to the oil strainer (26), fit the lockwasher (30), and insert and tighten the two bolts (29) securely. Turn up the tabs on the lockwasher. Place the strainer in position in the bottom of the casing. Do not yet insert the bolts (31) which hold the bracket to the lugs on the casing.

11 Replace the mainshaft assembly with the forked end of the shaft (65) facing the front of the gearbox casing and with the synchroniser hubs in place over the shifter forks.

12 Press the first motion shaft ball bearing (63) onto the end of the first motion shaft (61) and insert the assembly into the casing.

13 Place the circlip (67) in the retaining groove of the mainshaft bearing (66); ensure that both the mainshaft and the first motion shaft are correctly aligned and then carefully drift both bearings into position in the casing. **Note:** When drifting in the bearings ensure the load is spread over both the inner and outer ball race cases. Oil both bearings.

14 With a pair of circlip pliers replace the circlip (64) retaining the first motion shaft ball bearing (63) in its housing.

15 Replace the first and second and third and fourth gear selector rod plungers (115) into their drillings on the outside of the casing, and follow them up with their locating springs (116), plugs and plug washers (117, 118). If possible use new plug washers, and on no account omit them or oil leaks will develop.

16 Fit the final drive pinion (90), a new locking washer (92), and screw on the pinion retaining nut. Tighten the nut down to a torque of 90 lb f ft (12.4 kg fm) early models; later models 150 lb f ft (20.7 kg fm). Turn up the edge of the lockwasher.

17 Place the first motion shaft gearwheel (45) on the locating splines at the front of the first motion shaft (61); fit a new lockwasher (47), making sure that two protrusions on the washer locate in the two holes in the gearwheel; and tighten down the securing nut (46) to a torque of 90 lb f ft (12.4 kg fm) early models; later models 150 lb f ft (20.7 kg fm). Turn up the edge of the lockwasher.

18 Early gearboxes:

a) Place a thrust washer (60) in position (hold it with a dab of grease) and carefully fit the laygear (54) taking care not to disturb the washer. Oil the layshaft (53) and by judicious

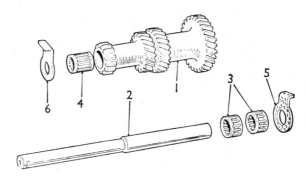

Fig. 6.8. Exploded view of the four speed synchromesh laygear

1	Laygear	5	Large standard thrust washer
2	Stepped layshaft		
3	Needle roller bearings	6	Small selective thrust washer
4	Needle roller bearing		

manipulation insert it through the hole in the centre web, through the thrust washer (60) to the far end of the laygear (54). Then fit the second thrust washer (59) and push the layshaft right home in the housing. **Note:** The slot in the side of the layshaft must be towards the front of the gearbox casing.

b) Measure the end clearance which should be between 0.002 in. and 0.006 in. (0.0508 and 0.1524 mm) as already described. Thrust washers sized from 0.121 to 0.132 in. (3.0734 to 3.3528 mm) are available to compensate for wear.

19 Later gearboxes:

a) The thrust washers on the lay gear differ from the earlier types with synchromesh on three speeds only. On the three speed synchromesh models the smaller thrust washer was standard and the larger one selective. On the four speed synchromesh the larger one is standard and the smaller one selective.

b) Endfloat should be between 0.002 and 0.006 ins. (0.0508 and 0.1524 mm).

c) With the standard washer fitted and the gap between the end of the lay gear and the casing measured, the selective washer can be decided upon. The table below gives the part numbers for the appropriate selective washers, based on the measured gap with the standard washer fitted. Column 'A' is for gearboxes with synchromesh on three speeds and Column 'B' for synchromesh on four speeds.

When gap is	A	B
0.125 to 0.127 in (3.18 to 3.22mm)	88G 325	22G 856
0.128 to 0.130 in. (3.25 to 3.30 mm)	88G 326	22G 857
0.131 to 0.133 in (3.32 to 3.37 mm)	88G 327	22G 858
0.134 in. (3.41 mm)	88G 328	22G 859

20 Do not yet fit the mainshaft bearing retainer shim (89) in position, but fit the bearing retainer (86). Turn the slots in the sides of the layshaft (53), and the reverse gear shaft (50), until they are at approximately 90° to each other and then refit the locating plate (55), which fits **between** the shim (89) (not yet fitted) and the retainer (86).

21 Replace the two tab lockwashers (87), tighten down the four bolts (88), and then with a feeler gauge measure the gap between the mainshaft bearing retainer, and the wall of the housing as indicated in Fig. 6.9. Use the table below to determine the correct thickness of shim to use.

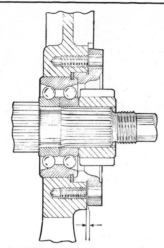

Fig. 6.9. Cross section view of third motion shaft bearing. Measure the gap between mainshaft bearing and retainer with a feeler gauge

Measured Gap	Fit shims totalling
0.005 to 0.006 in. (0.127 to 0.152 mm)	0.005 in. (0.127 mm)
0.006 to 0.008 in. (0.152 to 0.203 mm)	0.007 in. (0.178 mm)
0.008 to 0.010 in. (0.203 to 0.254 mm)	0.009 in. (0.229 mm)
0.010 to 0.012 in. (0.254 to 0.304 mm)	0.011 in. (0.279 mm)
0.012 to 0.014 in. (0.304 to 0.356 mm)	0.013 in. (0.330 mm)
0.014 to 0.015 in. (0.356 to 0.381 mm)	0.015 in. (0.381 mm)

22 Remove the retainer (86), fit the appropriate shims under the locating plate (55), and replace and tighen down the bolts holding the retainer and locating plate in position. Knock up the tabs of the locking washers (87).

23 Lightly grease the end of the oil suction pipe (33) and insert it into the hole in the centre of the oil strainer (26) taking care not to dislodge the rubber sealing ring (27).

24 The top flange on the bracket (28) lies under the lug on the side of the gearbox casing. The oil pipe bracket lies on top of the lug. Position the lockwasher (32), and insert the two bolts (31) through the two holes in the lug into the the fixed nuts under the bracket flange (28). Place a new joint gasket (36) between the pipe blanking plate (35) and the flange on the outside of the casing, and a new gasket (34) between the oil pipe flange (33) and the inside of the casing. Fit a new lockwasher (38) and tighten up the two pairs of bolts (37,31). Turn up the tabs on both lockwashers (32,38).

25 Refit the change speed gate (119); fit a new front cover gasket (138) to the flange on the front of the casing; fit the front cover (137) and insert and tighten up the bolts (139), nuts (143) and springwashers (140,142) as appropriate.

26 Replace the oil seal (121), and partially insert the gear change shaft (120) into the transmission casing. Refit the woodruff key (123) to the shaft, position the selector lever in the casing, making sure its lower end engages with the change speed gate (119) and push the gear change shaft (120) through the hole in the lever (122) so the Woodruff key (123) mates with the slot in the selector lever (122). Push the shaft (120) right into its housing in the transmission case, and line up the cutout in the shaft (120) with the hole for the clamp bolt in the lever (122). Insert and tighten the clamp bolt (124), and turn up the tab on the lockwasher (125).

27 Replace the reverse check plunger (133), and the plunger spring (134) in the hole in the casing; make sure the washer (136) is under the head of the spring plug (135) and tighten the plug securely.

28 Insert the speedometer spindle and gear (100), through the front cover (137) so the spindle engages the slot in the end of the mainshaft (65). Replace the joint gasket (102), end plate (101), and tighten down the two securing bolts and lockwashers (103,104).

29 Replace the speedometer pinion (93) in the side of the front cover (137), and carefully fit the brush (94), the joint gasket (96), and the pinion housing cover (95). Insert and tighten down the speedometer pinion housing bolt, flat and spring washers (98,99).

30 Refit the differential assembly to the gearbox casing as described in Chapter 8.

31 Refit the remote control shaft (129) and the lever (130) in place. **Note:** Leave off the nylon cup and spring if previously fitted. Replace the bottom cover plate on the underside of the gear change extension and refit the anti-rattle spring, plunger and hexagon cap. The gearbox is now completely assembled with the exception of the intermediate gear which is dealt with under Section 9.

8 Transfer gears - description

Drive is transmitted from the clutch to the gearbox by means of three transfer gears. On the end of the crankshaft is the primary gear. When the clutch pedal is depressed the primary gear remains stationary while the crankshaft revolves inside it. On releasing the clutch pedal the drive is taken up and the primary gear revolves with the crankshaft at crankshaft speed.

On early models the bearing inside the primary gear was lubricated from an oilway drilled in the crankshaft. In practice oil frequently found its way past the flywheel oil seal, onto the friction face of the clutch. Self-lubricating primary gear bearings were therefore fitted to later models and the oil hole in the crankshaft blocked. As owners of early models may wish to modify their crankshafts to the later specification details of how to block the oilway and fit a modified primary gear are given later in the Chapter.

Drive is taken from the primary gear, through an intermediate gear, to the first motion shaft drive gear which is a splined fit on the nose of the first motion shaft.

9 Transfer gears - removal and replacement

Removal and replacement of the primary gear (40) has already been covered in Chapter 1. To remove the first motion shaft gear knock back the locking tab on the lockwasher (47), undo the retaining nut (46), and pull off from the end of the first motion shaft, the first motion shaft gearwheel (45). Replacement is a straight reversal of this procedure.

The intermediate gear (43) is removed by pulling it out of its housing on the rear end of the gearbox casing. Make sure the thrust washers (one on each side) are kept in their correct relative positions. Replacement is a straight reversal of this process. **Note:** It is important to check the endfloat as described below, and to also ensure the thrust washers are replaced with the chamfered bores against the gear face.

Make sure the mating flanges of the flywheel housing and gearbox casing are thoroughly clean and fit a new flywheel housing gasket in place.

Fit the bearing rollers on the end of the first motion shaft with a trace of grease to hold them in place, replace the circlip, and carefully refit the flywheel housing to the transmission casing. The usual reason for the housing not mating properly first time, is that one of the roller bearings has tilted, so causing an obstruction. Never use force to fit the flywheel housing.

Tighten down the flywheel housing nuts to the correct torque and measure the endfloat of the intermediate gear between the side of the gear and the casing. Endfloat should be between 0.003 in. and 0.008 in. (0.076 and 0.203 mm). Thrust washers from 0.132 to 0.139 in. (3.34 to 3.54 mm) are available to correct any deficiency.

Undo the flywheel housing nuts, and pull the housing away from the transmission casing. The engine and gearbox may now be fitted together and the flywheel housing replaced. **Always** use a **new** uncompressed flywheel housing gasket, and never the one used to take the intermediate gear endfloat measurement. The

Manual gearbox (early type) dismantling and reassembly sequence. Photos 1 to 120
Note - All the numbers in brackets refer to Fig. 6.1. Later gearbox covered in text

1 The first step in dismantling the gearbox is to remove the flywheel housing, and lift away the engine. The gears etc. are then exposed as above

2 Then undo the clamp bolt (127) from the operating shaft lever (126). NOTE the spring washer (128) under the head of the clamp bolt

3 Remove the differential unit from the gearbox casing as described in detail in Chapter 8

4 Undo the nuts, bolts, and spring washers (142, 143, 139, 140) holding on the front cover (137) and carefully knock the cover off with length of wood as shown above

5 Take the intermediate gear (43), together with its thrust washers (44) off the rear of the transmission casing

6 Lock the gearbox solid by knocking in two of the three selector rods as shown in the above illustration

7 Then knock back the tab of the lock washer (47) and undo the nut (46) off the end of the first motion shaft

8 The first motion shaft gear (45) is then removed off the splines on the first motion shaft

9 With a pair of circlip pliers pinch together the enlarged ends of the circlip (64) and remove the clip from the transmission casing

10 Then lock up the gearbox again by driving in the two selectors with the aid of a screwdriver

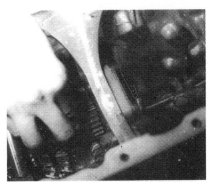

11 Before the nut (91) which holds the final drive pinion (90) in place can be undone knock back the tab of the lockwasher (92)

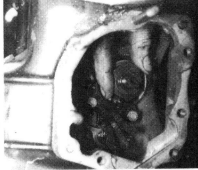

12 Loosen the final drive pinion nut (90) and then unscrew it as shown above

13 Then remove the lockwasher (92) and pull the final drive pinion (90) off the end of the mainshaft

14 Free the gearbox by lining up the selector rod cut-outs

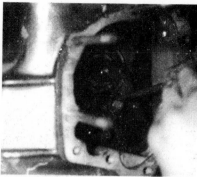

15 The next step is to knock back the tabs of the locking washers (87) which hold the bearing retainer (86) in place

16 Undo the bolts (88) which hold the bearing retainer (86) in position and lift the retainer out

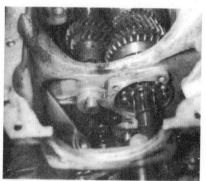

17 With the bearing retainer removed the position of the locating plate (55) which engages in the slots on the layshaft (53) reverse shaft (50) can be clearly seen

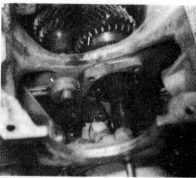

18 Carefully remove the plate, noting which way round it is fitted

19 The next step is to knock back the tabs on the lockwasher (32) and undo the two bolts (31) holding the oil suction pipe in place

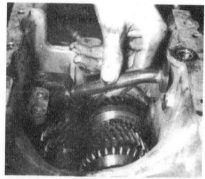

20 Undo the two bolts (37) which hold the oil suction pipe flange to the gearbox casing and then lift the pipe out of the gearbox

21 Measure and note the laygear end float and then tap the layshaft (53) out of the laygear (54). Lift the laygear from the gearbox

22 Carefully tap out the first motion shaft and bearing. Remove the circlip (67). Loosen the shifter forks, drive the mainshaft 1 inch rearwards and then drift out the mainshaft bearing (66)

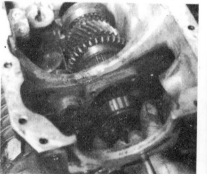

23 The mainshaft bearing can then be removed from the end of the mainshaft. Make a note of which way round it was fitted

24 Now pull back the mainshaft assembly so as to clear the hole in the centre web

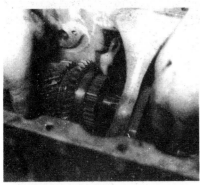

25 Move the mainshaft assembly back as far as possible as shown above

26 The mainshaft assembly can now be lifted out of the transmission casing

27 With the mainshaft removed examine the gearwheel teeth carefully for chipping and wear. First gear (68) in this case is badly worn

28 On removal of the hubs from the gearwheels it is vital that a rag is placed round the assembly to prevent loss of the three spring loaded balls (69, 70)

29 On hub reassembly the three spring loaded balls must enter the cut-outs arrowed

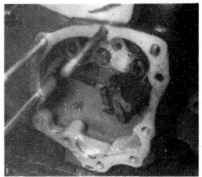

30 Under normal circumstances there is no need to remove the selector rods. If it is wished to extract them undo the selector screws and locknuts (112, 114)

31 It is vital that the selector screws and locknuts are tightened securely on reassembly. If a gear shifter fork comes loose the whole gearbox has to be stripped

32 The selector screw and locknut for the first and second gear shifter fork can be tightened through the hole for the differential unit

33 The reverse shifter fork selector screw and locknut rests in the bottom of the gearbox casing facing upwards

34 Before replacing the gears the oil strainer must be placed in position as above and then turned through 90º to rest under the lug

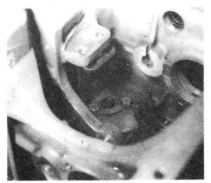

35 This shows the strainer in position but not yet secured to the lug. Smear the oil sealing ring (27) with grease

36 Now replace the mainshaft assembly with the forked end of the shaft (65) facing the front of the gearbox casing, and with the synchroniser hubs in the shifter forks

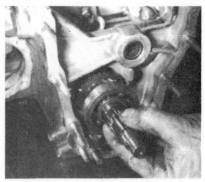

37 Carefully fit the mainshaft bearing (66) drifting it into place and then secure it with the circlips (67)

38 This is how the gearbox should now look. The roller bearing on the right runs inside the first motion shaft (61) which is fitted next

39 With the first motion shaft ball bearing (63) in place on the shaft fit the first motion gear so it engages with the mainshaft

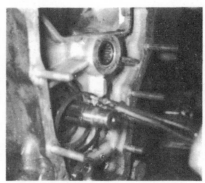
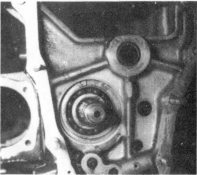

40 It may be necessary to drift the assembly into place especially when the ball bearing (63) meets the gearbox casing

41 With the first motion shaft properly in position replace the circlip (64) which holds the bearing in place

42 Make sure that the circlip fits properly into its recess as shown in the above photograph

43 If the first motion shaft has been correctly fitted to the mainshaft the assembly will now look like this

44 Replace the distance piece (57) in the end of the laygear (54)

Then fit the needle roller bearing (56) into the smaller end of the laygear (54) and secure it with the retaining ring (58)

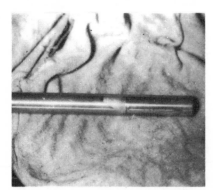

46 New bearings and layshaft were fitted to the laygear in this instance because the old layshaft case hardening had collapsed

47 Place the new thrust washers (47) at each end of the casing so they rest on the lugs between which the laygear fits

48 Drop the laygear (54) into position with the larger end adjacent to the gearbox end casing as shown above

49 Then fit the layshaft carefully pushing it through the centre of the laygear until the retaining slot emerges through the hole in the centre web

50 With the laygear in place and layshaft fitted the gearbox should now look like this. The laygear endfloat should be 0.002 to 0.006 in. (0.0508 to 0.1524 mm) (later type - see text)

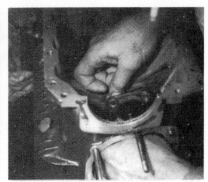

51 Now fit the appropriate mainshaft bearing shims (89), replace the locating plate (55) so it enters the notches on the two shafts (50, 53) and fit the bearing retainer (86)

52 Fit new lockwashers (87) and then insert and do up the four retaining bolts (88)

53 Turn up the tabs of the lockwashers to firmly secure the bolts

54 Then fit the pinion (90) onto the splines on the end of the mainshaft

55 It may be necessary to drift the pinion into place. To ensure the pinion slides on squarely tap each side of the gear in turn

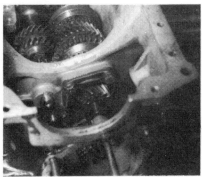

56 With the pinion firmly in place fit a new lockwasher. This is vital

57 The next step is to screw the pinion retaining nut (91) onto the end of the mainshaft

58 This shows the ends of two of the selector rods in the unlocked position. Lock the gearbox up by first punching in the lower rod

59 Punch in the top selector rod. This engages two gears at once and prevents the gears inside the box from turning when either the mainshaft or first motion shaft nuts are tightened

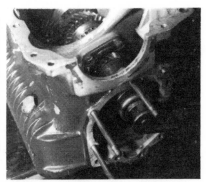

60 Tighten up the pinion retaining nut (91) on the mainshaft with a torque wrench to 150 lb f ft (20.7 kg fm)

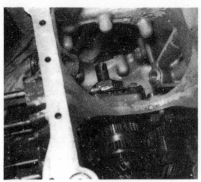

61 Knock over the edge of the lock-washer (92) to securely hold the nut (91) from working loose

62 Moving to the clutch end of the gearbox casing fit the first motion shaft gear (45) over the splines of the first motion shaft (61) as shown above

63 Then fit a new lockwasher (47) so the two lips engage in the two holes in the gearwheel (45)

64 Now fit the nut (46) on the end of the first motion shaft

65 Tighten up the first motion shaft gearwheel nut (46) with a torque spanner to 90 lb f ft (11.0 kg fm), Later gearboxes 150 lb f ft (20.7 kg fm)

66 The next step is to lock the nut in place by bending over the edge of the lockwasher

67 Now fit the oil suction pipe (33) to the oil strainer (26) and secure the pipe flange to the casing by doing up the two

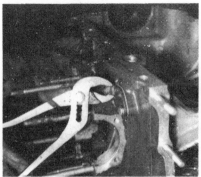

68 Make sure new joint gaskets (34, 36) are fitted and remember to turn up the lips of the one-piece lockwasher

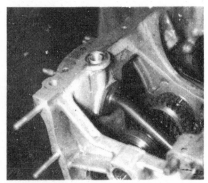

69 The bolts actually register in a thread cut in the flange shown, so holding it to the side of the casing

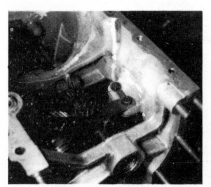

70 Then insert the two bolts holding the oil strainer bracket (28) in place, inserting them through the lug on the casing. Turn up the lockwasher tabs

71 Moving to the other end of the gearbox casing fit a new oil seal (121) in the recess after greasing it

72 Very carefully slide in the gear change shaft (120) so as not to damage the oil seal

73 Fit the selector lever (122) over the end of the gear change shaft so the woodruff key enters the flange and the cut-out lies parallel with the hole for the bolt

74 Position the cut-out in the gear change shaft inside the selector lever so that the clamp bolt (124) can be inserted

75 Remember to fit a lockwasher (125) under the head of the clamp bolt and tighten the latter firmly

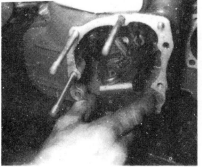

76 The next step is to fit the change speed gate (119) so the jaws lie in the selector rod cut-outs with the selector lever between the two jaw points

77 In this photograph the change speed gate (119) is shown correctly assembled to the gearbox casing

78 Fit a new cover gasket (138) in place after making sure that all traces of the old gasket have been removed

79 The next step is to fit the front cover (137) in position as shown

80 Make sure the end of the speedometer spindle engages the slot in the end of the mainshaft

81 Replace the speedometer pinion (93) and then the joint gasket (96), and the pinion housing cover (95)

82 At the other end of the transmission casing fit a new roller bearing over the nose of the first motion shaft. The old bearing can be used if unworn

83 With a pair of circlip pliers fit the circlip which holds the bearing in place

84 Then fit the differential unit in place. For full details see Chapter 8

85 The next step is to fit the intermediate gear (43) with a thrust washer (44) on either side of the gear

86 Make sure the grooves on the thrust washers face outwards from the intermediate gear

87 Fit a new gearbox to transfer gearcase gasket and carefully fit the gear case to the gearbox. Make sure the roller bearing on the first motion shaft enters its recess cleanly

88 Tighten down the nuts holding the transfer gear case in place to a torque of 18 lb ft

89 Then measure with a feeler gauge the intermediate gear end float which should be between 0.003 to 0.008 in (0.762 to 0.2032 mm). If incorrect different size thrust washers are available

90 Fit a new "O" rubber sealing ring in the circular groove in the gearbox casing flange. On no account use the old ring as it may leak resulting in low oil pressure

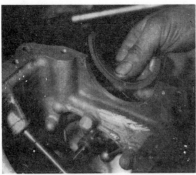

91 Clean the gearbox casing front cut-out in preparation for fitting a new gasket. When fitted it should stand not more than 0.0625 in. (1.588 mm)

92 The gearbox is now rebuilt and ready to be mated with the engine

93 Lightly grease the two halves of the crankcase to gearbox casing gasket and place them in position on the crankcase flanges

94 Fit a new seal at the front of the engine having previously checked it for correct fitting in the gearbox casing front cut-out

95 Carefully lower the engine onto the gearbox casing making sure that the locating dowels enter their corresponding holes cleanly

96 Then refit the gearbox casing to crankcase bolts, tightening them to a torque of 6 lb f ft (0.8 kg fm)

97 Next place the primary gear thrust washer, bevelled side away from the gear-wheel, on the crankshaft and follow it with the crankshaft primary gear

98 Then fit the outer thrust washers (not fitted on early models) so the raised portion lies at the bottom of the crank-shaft

99 Turn the crankshaft so Nos. 1 and 4 pistons are at T.D.C. Fit the horseshoe or "C" ring so it engages the two slots cut into the crankshaft

100 Then measure the primary gear end-float which should be between 0.0035 to 0.0065 in, (0.0762 to 0.1524 mm). Different sized thrust washers are available from your local BLMC dealer

101 With the intermediate gear and thrust washers fitted all is now ready to fit the flywheel housing or transfer gear case

102 Fit a new gasket in place. Do not re-use the gasket used to get the intermediate gear end float measurement

103 Then offer up the flywheel housing to the cylinder block and gearbox end-faces

104 With the flywheel housing in place next fit a new tab washer

105 Then replace the flywheel housing nuts and bolts and tighten them up to a torque of 18 lb f ft (2.5 kg fm)

106 Turn up the tabs of the lockwashers to secure the nuts and bolts

107 A new oil seal can be fitted with the primary gear either on or off the crank-shaft. The procedure involved is identical in both cases

108 It is necessary to protect the new seal from the splines on the primary gear. Either use the special sleeve shown above or bind the splines with masking tape

109 Push the seal over the sleeve until it abuts the gearwheel and then remove the sleeve

110 If the primary gear was removed for the new seal to be fitted it should now be replaced

111 To press the seal into position either use the special tool shown above or a short length of suitably sized tubing

112 If using the special tool, the bolt shown above screws into the end of the crankshaft. As the bolt is tightened the sleeve slides forward, pressing in the seal

113 With the primary gear, thrust washers, and "C" ring back in place all is now ready for replacement of the flywheel/clutch assembly

114 With the crankshaft set so pistons Nos. 1 and 4 are at T.D.C. replace the pressure plate with the lugs facing outwards and the mark "A" at T.D.C.

115 Then fit the clutch disc with the longer side of the boss facing towards the pressure plate

116 Press the clutch disc firmly home against the pressure plate. Always renew the disc if linings are worn or oil saturated

117 Then fit the flywheel after making certain that the area which contacts the clutch lining is perfectly clean

118 Ensure the ¼ mark on the flywheel periphery lines up with the "A" mark on the pressure plate lug

119 The next step is to replace the locking key followed by the lock washer shown in the next photograph

120 Then replace the flywheel bolt etc. as shown in Chapter 5 which deals with the clutch.

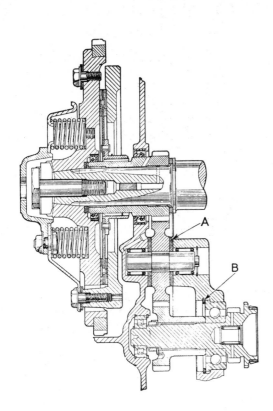

Fig. 6.10. Cross section view of intermediate gear and related components
Measure the intermediate gear end float 'A' with a feeler gauge (0.003 - 0.008 in . (0.762 - 0.2032 mm) is correct
Measure B and use circlip 2A3710 if gap 0.096 - 0.098 in.
(2.438 - 2.489 mm)
or circlip 2A3711 if gap is 0.098 - 0.100 in.
(2.489 - 2.54 mm)

flywheel housing gasket contains a small cutout on its outer edge. When assembled the gasket should be compressed to 0.030 in (0.762 mm) which can be measured at the area round the cutout with a feeler gauge.

10 Flywheel housing bearing - removal and replacement

If the intermediate gear bearing in the flywheel housing is worn and requires replacement it can be removed and refitted as follows:
1 Heat the flywheel housing in boiling water. On no account apply a direct flame to the housing. If a receptacle large enough to hold the flywheel housing is not available slowly pour boiling water over the area round the bearing.
2 Remove the retaining ring (where fitted) and carefully prise the bearing out of the casing taking great care not to damage the bearing housing. If possible use BLMC service tool "18G 582".
3 When fitting a new bearing carefully drift it into position (having previously heated the housing as described above) until it is just clear of the retaining ring recess (where fitted). On no account press the bearing right into the recess in the housing, as this would mask the bearing oil supply hole which is at the rear of the recess.
4 If the outer race of the first motion shaft roller bearing requires renewal use the system described above but if possible borrow BLMC service tool "18G 617".

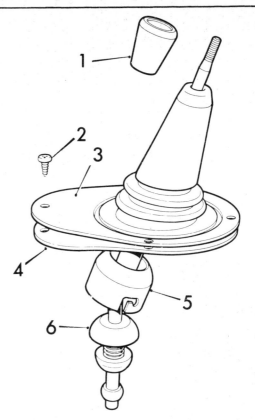

Fig. 6.11. Gear change lever assembly (latest type)

1 Knob	4 Gaiter
2 Screw	5 Bayonet cap
3 Gaiter retaining ring	6 Gear change lever

11 Primary gear (modified type) - fitting

From 1963 a self lubricating type of primary gear was fitted. If wished this gear can be fitted to pre- 1963 models and the crankshaft oil hole blocked. A kit of parts is available through BLMC dealers. The use of a new primary gearwheel with the old intermediate gear is likely to result in a noticeable increase in transmission noise. This is of no mechanical importance.
1 Remove the clutch/flywheel assembly as described in Chapter 5, and take off the flywheel housing and primary gearwheel as described in Chapter 1.
2 Block the hole in the crankshaft by driving in the tapered brass plug supplied in the kit. Ensure the head of the plug lies 0.045 in. (1.143 mm) below the crankshaft bearing surface.
3 If the plug cannot be driven fully in, remove it and cut off the excess length.
4 Fit the new primary gear and thrust washer and note the endfloat should be between 0.0035 and 0.0050 in. (0.076 and 0.127 mm). Various sized thrust washers are available.
5 The splines on the new primary gear finish at the forward edge of the gearwheel. On the older primary gear assembly, to allow for the flywheel sealing ring, the splines stopped about 0.25 in (6.35 mm) short. Therefore the oil seal in the centre of the flywheel **must** be removed. Otherwise the flywheel will not seat properly on the rear of the crankshaft.
6 Replace the clutch/flywheel assembly.

12 Gear change lever (latest type) - removal and replacement

1 Unscrew the knob from the gear change lever (Fig. 6.11).
2 Remove the front floor carpeting.

3 Undo and remove the gaiter retaining ring screws and draw the gaiter up the lever.
4 Press down and turn the bayonet cap fixing to release the lever from the remote control assembly.
5 The gear change lever may now be lifted up and away from the remote control assembly.
6 Refitting the gear change lever is the reverse sequence to removal.

13 Gear change remote control assembly (latest type) - removal and replacement

1 Refer to Section 12 and remove the gearchange lever.
2 Using a suitable diameter parallel pin punch drift out the roll pin retaining the extension rod to the selector rod at the final drive housing.
3 Undo and remove the nut and bolt that secures the remote control steady rod to the final drive housing on the gearbox.
4 Undo and remove the one nut and bolt that secures the remote control housing to the mounting bracket.
5 The remote control assembly may now be lifted away from the underside of the car.

14 Gear change remote control assembly (latest type) - dismantling and reassembly

1 Refer to Section 13 and remove the gearchange remote control assembly.
2 Suitably hold the assembly in a vice, and then undo and remove the bottom cover plate securing screws. Lift away the cover plate noting which way round it is fitted.
3 The steady rod securing nut and washer should next be removed. Withdraw the steady rod.
4 Move the extension rod eye rearwards and remove the roll pin that secures the extension rod to the rod eye using a suitable diameter parallel pin punch.
5 The extension rod may now be removed.
6 Move the extension rod eye forwards and remove the roll pin that retains the support rod to the extension rod eye.
7 The support rod should now be drifted out.
8 Recover the extension rod eye.
9 Wash all parts and inspect for wear. If evident new parts must be obtained.
10 Reassembly of the gear change remote control assembly is the reverse sequence to dismantling. The following parts should be lubricated with Duckham Laminoid O grease.
a) The hemispherical fulcrum surface in the housing.
b) The selector rod eye.
c) Two selector rod bearing locations.
d) The inner surface of the bottom cover plate and in particular the reverse lift plate.

15 Gear change remote control assembly mountings (latest type) - removal and replacement.

1 Remove the front floor carpeting.
2 Undo and remove the nuts and spring washers securing the remote control mountings to the tunnel panel. Lower the assembly from the underside of the floor panel.
3 Undo and remove the nuts and spring washers that secure the mounting to the support bracket .
4 Lift away the mountings.
5 Refitting the mountings is the reverse sequence to removal.

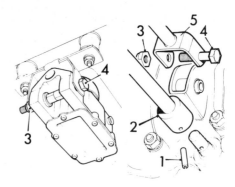

Fig. 6.12. Remote control attachments (latest type)

1	Roll pin	4	Bolt
2	Selector rod	5	Steady rod
3	Nut		

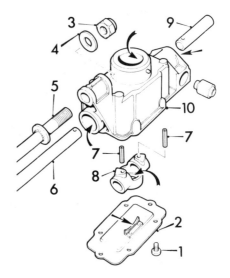

Fig. 6.13. Exploded view of remote control assembly

1	Screw	6	Selector rod
2	Cover plate	7	Roll pin
3	Nut	8	Extension rod eye
4	Washer	9	Extension rod
5	Steady rod	10	Housing

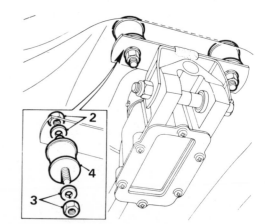

Fig. 6.14. Remote control assembly mountings

16 Automatic transmission - general description

The automatic transmission fitted as an optional extra to Mini models incorporates a three element fluid torque converter with a maximum conversion ratio of 2:1 coupled to a bevel gear train assembly.

The final drive is transmitted from a drive gear to a conventional type differential unit, which in turn transmits engine torque through two flange type coupling drive shafts - employing constant velocity joints, to the road wheels.

The complete gear train assembly, including the reduction gears and differential units, runs parallel to, and below, the crankshaft and is housed in the transmission casing which also serves as the engine sump.

The system is controlled by a selector lever within a gated quadrant marked with seven positions and mounted centrally on the floor of the car. The reverse, neutral, and drive positions are for normal automatic driving, with the first, second, third, and fourth positions used for manual operation or override as required. This allows the system to be used as a fully automatic four speed transmission, from rest to maximum speed with the gears changing automatically according to throttle position and load. If a lower gear is required to obtain greater acceleration, an instant full throttle position ie., 'kick-down' on the accelerator, immediately produces the change.

Complete manual control of all four forward gears by use of the selector lever provides rapid changes. However, it is very important that downward changes are effected at the correct road speeds otherwise serious damage may result in to the automatic transmission unit. The second, third and top gears provide engine braking whether driving in automatic or manual

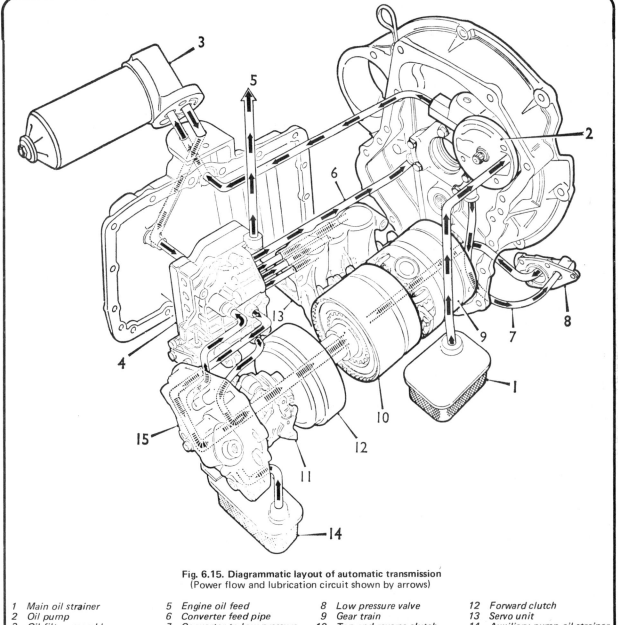

Fig. 6.15. Diagrammatic layout of automatic transmission
(Power flow and lubrication circuit shown by arrows)

1 Main oil strainer	5 Engine oil feed	8 Low pressure valve	12 Forward clutch
2 Oil pump	6 Converter feed pipe	9 Gear train	13 Servo unit
3 Oil filter assembly	7 Converter to low pressure	10 Top and reverse clutch	14 Auxiliary pump oil strainer
4 Valve block	valve feed	11 Governor	15 Auxiliary pump

conditions. In first gear a free wheel condition exists when decelerating. Manual selection to third or second gear gives engine braking and also allows the driver to stay in a particular low gear to suit road conditions or when descending steep hills.

Due to the complexity of the automatic transmission unit, if performance is not up to standard, or overhaul is necessary, it is imperative that this be left to the local main agents who will have the special equipment for fault diagnosis and rectification.

The intent of the following Sections, is therefore, confined to supplying general information and any service information and instruction that can be used by the owner.

17 Automatic transmission - removal and replacement

The automatic transmission is removed from the car together with the engine and differential assembly as described in Chapter 1. It will then be necessary to separate the gearbox from the engine; again, full information will be found in Chapter 1.

18 Starter inhibitor switch (auto transmission) - adjustment

1 The starter inhibitor switch is located on the rear of the gear selector housing. It has four terminals, two of which are connected through the ignition/starter circuit. This ensures that the engine will only start when the gear selector lever is in the 'N' position. (Fig. 6.16).
2 The switch terminals marked '2' and '4' are used in the ignition/starter circuit and both the electrical leads are interchangeable to the '2' and '4' positions of the switch.
3 When a reversing light is fitted terminals '1' and '3' are used for this light.
4 Before making any adjustments to the switch ensure that the gear change cable and selector rod adjustment is correct as described in Section 19.
5 To adjust the switch just move the selector lever to the 'N' position..
6 Disconnect the electrical connections from the rear of the switch.
7 Slacken the locknut and screw out the switch as far as possible.
8 Connect a test light and battery across the switch terminals numbered '2' and '4'.
9 Screw the switch into the housing until the circuit is made and mark the switch body.
10 Continue screwing in the switch and note the number of turns required until the circuit breaks.
11 Remove the test equipment and unscrew the switch from the housing half the number of turns counted.
12 Tighten the locknut and refit the electrical leads to the appropriate terminals.
13 Check that the starter motor only operates when the gear selector lever is in the 'N' position. When a reverse light is fitted check that it only comes on when 'R' position is selected.

19 Gear change cable and selector rod (auto transmission) - adjustment

1 Refer to Fig. 6.17 and pull back the rubber boot.
2 Extract the split pin and remove the washer and clevis pin.
3 Make sure the selector rod is screwed in tightly and push it fully into the transmission case.
4 **Warning: Do not attempt to start the engine with the selector rod disconnected.**
5 Refit the clevis pin into the selector rod yoke and check the measurement 'A' which should be 0.781 in. (20 mm) (Fig. 6.17).
6 If the measurement obtained is not correct make any adjustment by slackening the yoke locknut and turning the yoke in or out until the required dimension is obtained.
7 Tighten the locknut and ensure that the yoke is set squarely to the bellcrank lever arm.

Fig. 6.16. Starter inhibitor switch

a   Arrow denotes locknut
b   Inset shows numbering sequence of terminals

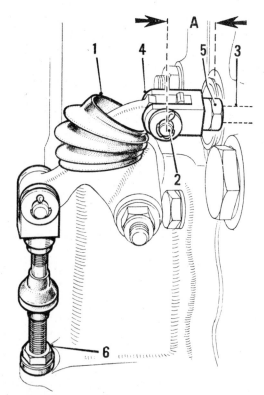

Fig. 6.17. Gear change cable and selector rod adjustment

1   Rubber boot
2   Clevis pin
3   Selector rod
4   Selector rod yoke
5   Selector rod yoke locknut
6   Cable adjusting nuts

A = 0.781 in. (20 mm)

8 Select 'N' in the transmission unit by pulling the selector rod fully out and then pushing it back in by one detent. The measurement at 'A' should now be 1.45 in (37 mm).

9 Select 'N' on the quadrant with the gear selector and adjust the outer cable using the adjustment nut. Adjustment is considered correct when the clevis pin can be easily refitted.

10 Before finally reconnecting ensure that the yoke ends on the selector cable and rod are square to the bellcrank lever.

11 To test the gear change cable and selector rod adjustment first start the engine and move the gear lever to the 'R' position. Check that reverse is engaged. Slowly move the lever back towards the 'N' positon, checking that the gear is disengaged just before or as soon as the lever drops into the 'N' position on the quadrant.

12 Repeat the test procedure for the first gear '1' position.

13 If necessary re-adjust the outer cable slightly to obtain the correct operating condition.

14 Make sure that all adjustment and locknuts are tight and the clevis pins are secure.

15 Pack the rubber boots with 'Duckhams Lammol' grease and refit. When a weather protection shield is used it should now be refitted.

20 Governor control rod (auto transmission) - adjustment

1 For this adjustment a tachometer is needed.

2 Start the engine and run it until it reaches normal operating temperature.

3 Refer to Chapter 3 and ensure that the carburettor settings are correct.

4 Disconnect the governor control rod at the carburettor.

5 Insert a 0.25 in (6.4 mm) diameter rod through the hole in the governor control rod bellcrank lever and into the hole in the transmission casing (Fig. 6.18).

6 Slacken the locknut and adjust the length of the rod to suit the carburettor linkage in the tickover position.

7 Reconnect the governor control rod to the carburettor. Tighten the ball joint locknut and remove the checking rod from the bellcrank lever.

21 Gear change lever housing and cable (auto transmission) - removal and replacement

1 Remove the weather protection cover from the convertor housing if one is fitted.

2 Pull back the rubber sleeve and disconnect the gear change cable by removing the clevis pin.

3 Slacken the yoke clamp nut and remove the yoke, nut, rubber ferrules, and sleeve.

4 Remove the adjustment nuts from the outer cable and pull the cable clear of the transmission.

5 Release the cable clip from the floor panel.

6 Remove the front floor covering.

7 Make a note of their relative positions, then, disconnect the electrical leads from the inhibitor switch.

8 Undo and remove the four screws and spring washers that secure the gear change lever housing. Carefully pull the cable through the rubber dust excluder and remove the housing and cable assembly.

9 Refitting the gear change lever housing and cable is the reverse sequence to removal. Adjust the cable and selector rod as described in Section 19 and the inhibitor switch as described in Section 18.

22 Gear change lever housing and cable (auto transmission) - dismantling and reassembly

1 Remove the assembly as described in Section 21.

2 Hold the assembly in a vice and then undo and remove the set screws that secure the quadrant to the housing.

3 Release the reverse return spring from the base of the housing and remove the quadrant and lever assembly.

4 Unscrew the cable securing nuts from the front of the housing; pull the cable from the housing and release it from the gear change lever plunger.

5 Wash all parts and inspect moving parts for wear. Obtain new parts as necessary.

6 Reassembling the gear change lever housing and cable is the reverse sequence to removal. Thoroughly lubricate all moving parts with grease.

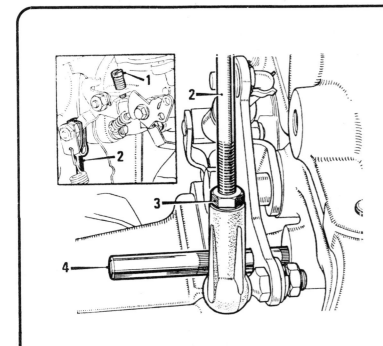

Fig. 6.18. Governor control rod adjustment

1   Throttle adjustment screw
2   Governor control rod
3   Locknut
4   0.25 in. (6.4 mm) diameter rod

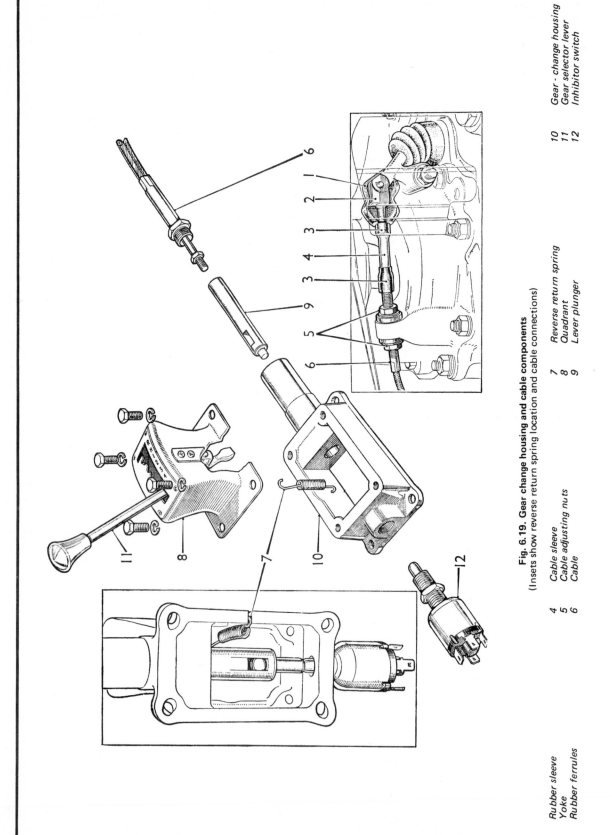

Fig. 6.19. Gear change housing and cable components
(Insets show reverse return spring location and cable connections)

1	Rubber sleeve	4	Cable sleeve	7	Reverse return spring	10	Gear - change housing
2	Yoke	5	Cable adjusting nuts	8	Quadrant	11	Gear selector lever
3	Rubber ferrules	6	Cable	9	Lever plunger	12	Inhibitor switch

23 Fault diagnosis - manual gearbox

Symptom	Reason/s	Remedy
Weak or ineffective synchromesh	Synchronising cones worn, split or damaged	Dismantle and overhaul gearbox. Fit new gear wheels and synchronising cones.
	Baulk ring synchromesh dogs worn, or damaged	Dismantle and overhaul gearbox. Fit new baulk ring synchromesh.
Jumps out of gear	Broken gear change fork rod spring	Dismantle and replace spring.
	Gearbox coupling dogs badly worn	Dismantle gearbox. Fit new coupling dogs.
	Selector fork rod groove badly worn	Fit new selector fork rod.
	Selector fork rod securing screw locknut loose	Remove gearbox and tighten.
Excessive noise	Incorrect grade of oil being used	Drain complete unit and refill with correct grade of oil.
	Brush or needle roller bearings worn or damaged	Dismantle and overhaul gearbox. Renew bearings.
	Gear teeth excessively worn or damaged	Dismantle and overhaul gearbox. Renew gear wheels.
	Laygear thrust washers worn allowing excessive end play	Dismantle and overhaul gearbox. Renew thrust washers.
Excessive difficulty in engaging gear	Clutch pedal adjustment incorrect	Adjust clutch pedal movement (Chapter 5).

24 Fault diagnosis - automatic transmission reason/s

Important: Before the automatic transmission is removed for repair of a suspected malfunction it is imperative that the cause be traced and confirmed. To do this requires the use of a pressure gauge, tachometer and special adaptors. It is recommended that if a fault is suspected the car be taken to the local main agents for their inspection and report.

To act as a guide a change speed chart is given and also a Fault diagnosis chart, together with rectification details. Some of the information given will be outside the confines of this Owners Workshop Manual.

Change speed chart

Selector position	Throttle position	Gear change	mph	kph
"D"	Light	1—2	10—14	16—22
		2—3	15—19	24—30
		3—4	20—24	32—39
"D"	Kick-down	1—2	25—33	40—53
		2—3	37—45	60—72
		3—4	49—57	78—91
"D"	Kick-down	4—3	43—39	70—64
		3—2	35—31	56—50
		2—1	22—18	35—29
"D"	Closed (roll out)	4—3	20—16	32—26
		3—2	14—10	22—16
		2—1	8—4	12—6

See next page for 'Fault diagnosis and rectification chart'.

Fault diagnosis

Diagnosis and rectification sequence number

Faulty gear selection, possibly with tie-up in "D" position on kick-down	1
Slip or no drive in forward gears	2, 3
Slip in reverse	4, 5, 6
Slip or no drive in all gears	7, 8, 13, 20, 23
Difficult or bumpy selection and shifts possibly with squawk on selection and with lubrication warning light on or low gauge pressure	7, 8, 9, 13, 20
Erratic automatic shifts	7, 10
Incorrect shift speeds	11
Excessive creep or engine stalls when selecting gear	12
Unable to tow start	13, 14
Gear whine consistent with road speed but not in 'top' gear (4)	15
Continual whine consistent with engine speed	16
No drive in 'first' gear (1) automatic and manual	17, 18
Slip or no drive in 'second' gear (2) automatic and manual	19
No drive in "2", "3" or "4" positions manual but drives in these gears on automatic "D"	13
No drive in "2", "3" or "4" automatic "D" positions, but drives in these gears on manual selection	13
Poor acceleration	21
Reduced maximum speed in all gears with servo converter overheating	22

Diagnosis and rectification chart

1	Check gear change cable and selector rod adjustment
2*	Check the fitting of forward clutch feed pipe
3*	Check the forward clutch and/or the shaft rings
4*	Check the reverse gear band adjustment or remove the valve block and check the reverse servo feed pipe 'O' ring seals
5*	Remove the valve block and clean; regulator valve or reverse booster piston faulty
6*	Check the top and reverse clutch booster piston or shut-off valve
7	Check engine/transmission oil level
8*	Carry out pressure check
9	Check oil filter head 'O' ring seals or fitting of joint washer
10*	Remove and examine governor unit for sticking
11	Check governor control rod adjustment
12	Check carburettor adjustment - incorrect idle speed
13*	Remove and clean valve block
14*	Check auxiliary pump, pipes and seals
15*	Check gear train adjustment
16	Check converter housing bush
17*	Check free wheel support dowel bolt - sheared?
18*	Check the one-way clutch unit
19*	Remove the valve block and check the servo feed pipe 'O' ring seals and check the second gear band adjustment
20*	Check main oil pump and flow valve, the supply and feed pipe seals, and main oil strainer seals
21*	Carry out stall speed check
22	Change the torque converter unit
23	Check the low pressure valve

*   *Not within the scope of this manual.*
Refer to local main agent.

Chapter 7 Drive shaft and universal joints

Contents

Specifications

Type: ... ... Solid shaft reverse spline with rubber bush, Hardy Spicer or constant velocity inner joint - depending on model and year of production. Constant velocity outer joint.

Torque wrench settings:

	lb f ft	kg fm
Front hub nut (drive shaft)	60	8.3

1 General description

Drive is transmitted from the differential to the front wheels by means of two driveshafts. Fitted at each end of each shaft are universal joints which allow for vertical movement of the front wheels. Fore-and-aft movement is absorbed by a sliding spline on the inner ends of the shafts.

The outer universal joints are of the Birfield constant velocity type and are manufactured by Hardy Spicer. The driveshaft fits inside the circular outer cv joint which is also the driven shaft. Drive is transmitted from the driveshaft to the driven shaft by six steel balls which are located in curved grooves machined in line with the axis of the shaft on the inside of the driven shaft and outside of the driveshaft. This allows the driven shaft to hinge freely on the driveshaft, but at the same time keeps them together.

Enclosing the cv joint is a rubber boot.

The inner universal joints have been the subject of several modifications. The first type used was of the rubber bushed type made by Dunlop. The second type used was that of the Hardy-Spicer design as usually found at the ends of a conventional propeller shaft. The third type uses constant velocity joints which are mounted on the ends of the differential gears. Note that a small rubber boot covers the joint between the flange and shaft and on early driveshafts a grease nipple was fitted to the flange and covered by the rubber boot.

Before commencing work identify which type is fitted to the car and ensure that spare parts are available if overhaul is necessary.

2 Driveshaft - removal and replacement

1 Remove the wheel trim from the wheel from which the drive shaft is to be removed. **Note**: If this proves difficult thread a

1 Latest type drive shaft with inboard constant velocity joint

2 Nylon dust/water shield which must always be in good condition

small strip of cloth in through one of the slots in the trim and out through another. Then give a quick pull holding both ends. This is a much better system of removal than damaging the trim by trying to remove it by prising it off.

2 Place the car in gear and apply the handbrake firmly. Extract the split pin from the hub nut, and undo and remove the nut.

3 Loosen the front roadwheel securing nuts and jack up the car on the same side.

4 As it will be necessary to work underneath the car, supplement the jack with a stand or support blocks. This will minimise the danger should the jack collapse.

5 Remove the roadwheel.

6 Undo the self-locking nut from the balljoint on the end of the steering tie-rod three turns. Free the tapered balljoint pin from the steering arm with either a balljoint extractor or by hitting the opposite sides of the steering arm eye at the same time, until the balljoint pin is free. Remove the nut (which was kept in place to protect the balljoint threads from accidental damage) and pull the balljoint pin from the steering arm.

7 Because the inner end of the shaft is a sliding fit on the flange it will now be possible to partially free the end of the driveshaft from the centre of the hub. With a soft drift and hammer tap the end of the shaft until it is seen to move inwards slightly.

8 Undo the securing nuts which hold the upper and lower suspension arms to the steering swivel, and disconnect the arms.

9 Undo and remove the nut and washer from the lower suspension arm inner hinge pin, and tap the pin clear to release the arm.

10 Having previously started separating the driveshaft from the hub swivel axle and brake assembly it should now be fairly easy to pull the latter off. Rest the hub assembly on a wooden block or similar to ensure no strain is placed on the flexible brake hose. On no account allow the hub assembly to hang freely on the hydraulic hose.

11 The procedure now differs depending on the type of driveshaft fitted.

12 *Early type:*

a) Mark the drive flange and flexible joint so on reassembly they can be placed in the same relative positions.

b) Undo and remove the four outside nuts from the 'U' bolts holding the driveshaft flange to the flexible rubber coupling. The shaft can now be extracted from the car through the wheelarch.

13 *Hardy Spicer universal joint type:*

a) Mark the drive flanges so on reassembly they can be placed in the same relative positions.

b) Undo and remove the four nuts, bolts and washers that secure the two drive flanges together, part the two flanges and withdraw the driveshaft through the wheelarch.

14 *Constant velocity type:*

a) Refer to Figs. 7.1, 7.2 and using a metal lever as shown carefully detach the driveshaft from the differential. It is possible to use two large screwdrivers to release the constant velocity joint from the spring clip on the differential gearshaft but extreme care must be taken.

b) Lift away the complete driveshaft assembly.

15 Replacement of the driveshaft assembly is the reverse sequence to removal but the following additional points should be noted.

16 *Early type*

a) Replace the driveshaft in the car in its correct relative position to the flexible rubber coupling. Before replacing the 'U' bolts, thread their nuts on a few turns and lightly nip the prongs of the 'U' bolt in a vice. They tend to 'spread' when removed from the coupling and nipping them in this way will greatly ease their replacement.

b) Replace the 'U' bolts and tighten down the nuts. **Note:** Do not overtighten.

c) Replace the hub, swivel axle and brake assembly on the end of the driveshaft.

d) Refit the lower suspension arm hinge pin. **Note:** If an early type left-hand side driveshaft with a lubricating nipple on the inner flange is being replaced with the later type fitted

with the rubber boot it will be necessary to fit a cranked lower arm pivot pin to ensure adequate clearance between the driveshaft and the pin. (Fig. 7.3).

e) Refit the upper and lower suspension arms to the steering swivel, and refit the balljoint to the steering arm. Tighten the balljoint nut to a torque of 25 lb f ft (3.4 kg fm).

f) Replace and tighten down the hub nut; replace the split pin.

17 *Hardy Spicer universal joint type*

a) A new rubber boot must be fitted and refilled with ¾ oz (21 gms) Duckhams M - B Grease.

18 *Constant velocity type*

a) Make sure that the chamfers on the end of the shaft and the shaft splines are free from damage or burrs before entering the shaft into the differential unit.

b) Should any difficulty be found in engaging the shaft pulley into the differential circlip, try fitting a 3½ in (89 mm) diameter 'Jubilee' clip round the pot joint housing and applying an even and sustained pressure by hand onto the shaft. Use a drift located on the 'Jubilee' clip to drive the shaft into its full engagement position.

3 Constant velocity joint rubber boot - removal and replacement

If a rubber boot on one of the cv joints has split or been damaged it should be replaced with the minimum of delay. Although it is necessary to remove the driveshaft before the boot can be removed, speedy action will ensure that a large bill for a new driveshaft is avoided.

1 Remove the driveshaft as described in the previous section.

2 Undo the wire securing the smaller rubber boot in place, and pull the flange and boot off the end of the driveshaft.

3 Undo the clips or wires holding the larger boot in place on the cv joint and pull the boot off the inner splined end of the shaft.

4 Carefully clean all traces of rubber from both ends of the shaft and the flange, and wipe all traces of the old grease from the cv joint. **Note:** If grit is present in the grease then it is essential that the cv joint is thoroughly cleaned out.

5 Fit the new boot from the inner splined end and carefully slide it down the driveshaft.

6 Lubricate the cv joint and repack the rubber boot with about 1 oz of "Duckhams Q5795" grease. It is important not to use any other type.

7 Carefully pull the boot over the joint so that the moulded lips of the boot fit on the shallow machined depression in the outer circumference of the joint, and on the shaft.

8 Secure the rubber boot to the shaft with two turns of soft iron wire. Twist the ends together and turn them to face away from the direction of forward rotation of the shaft. **Note:** Ensure the wires are correctly located on the area of the boot directly over the shallow depressions.

9 Moving to the inner end of the shaft fit the smaller rubber boot, sliding it up the shaft until the moulded lip fits in the shallow machined depression about 2 in (50.8 mm) beyond the end of the splines.

10 Fill the cavity in the joint flange with "Duckhams Q5795" grease up to the old grease nipple hole (now blocked with a bolt).

11 Slide the flange onto the end of the shaft, and pull the larger lip of the rubber boot over the end of the flange.

12 Secure the rubber boot to the flange with two turns of soft iron wire. Twist the ends together and turn them away from the direction of forward rotation (Fig. 7.4).

13 When clips are to be used in securing rubber gaiter pull clip tight and clinch in order shown in Fig. 7.5.

14 Place the driveshaft in a vice and push the flange fully onto the shaft. At the same time, hold the lip of the boot off the shaft with a screwdriver to allow surplus grease to escape. diameter of the rubber boot bellows does not exceed 1¾ in

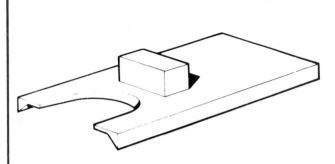

Fig. 7.1. Tool to be used for detaching inner constant velocity joint (latest type)

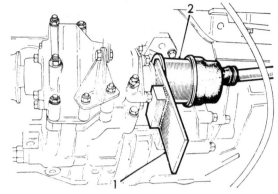

Fig. 7.2. Use of tool to detach inner constant velocity joint (latest type)

1   Special tool
2   Constant velocity joint

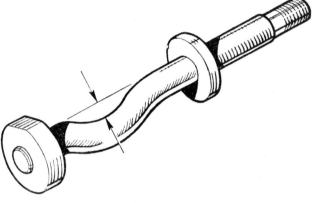

Fig. 7.3. Lower arm pivot pin
Measurement at location shown must be 0.312 in. (7.9 mm) to accommodate rubber boot of later type driveshaft assemblies

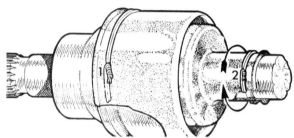

Fig. 7.4. When securing the rubber boot with retaining wire ensure the ends the wire (1, 2) are bent away from the direction of rotation (arrowed)

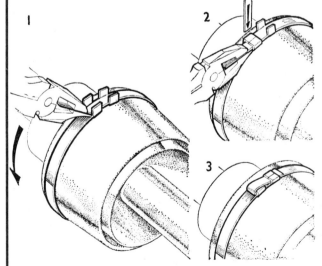

Fig. 7.5. When clips are to be used in securing rubber gaiter pull clip tight and clinch in order shown. Arrow shows normal direction of rotation

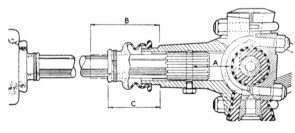

Fig. 7.6. Pack the hollow portion of the flange with the amount of grease shown at 'A'. Adjust the flange and shaft to 2.5 in. (63.5 mm) as shown at 'B' before securing the boot to the shaft. 'C' represents the correct measurement of 1.875 in. (47.625 mm) from the flange shoulder to the end of the boot when the shaft is adjusted to 'B'

(44.45 mm). If in excess of this figure, squeeze grease out of the boot until correct. If this not done the life of the boot will be considerably shortened.

16 Secure the rubber boot to the shaft with two turns of soft iron wire as previously described.

4 Outer constant velocity joint - dismantling, overhaul and reassembly

On early models up to 1961 it is not possible to dismantle the outer cv joints. If badly worn they must be replaced with the later type and this also means renewing the hub flange. On post 1961 models the driveshafts can be dismantled as follows:

1 Remove the driveshaft from the car, and the rubber boot from the cv joint as previously described.

2 Mount the shaft vertically in a vice with the cv joint facing downwards.

3 Before the joint can be dismantled it must be removed from the driveshaft. This is easily done by firmly tapping the outer edge of the cv joint with a hide or plastic headed hammer. The cv joint is held to the shaft by an internal circular section circlip ("B" in Fig. 7.8) and tapping the joint in the manner described forces the circlip to contract into a groove so allowing the joint to slide off.

4 Carefully note which way round the joint was fitted to the shaft. With the joint now free, the inner race can tilt sufficiently for the six balls to be released one at a time. Mark the relative positions of the balls, inner race and cage, and the outer race. This will ensure the same mating surfaces are adjacent on reassembly.

5 Remove and separate the inner race and cage. The cv joint is now completely dismantled.

6 Thoroughly clean all the component parts of the joint by washing in paraffin.

7 Examine each ball in turn for cracks, flat spots, or signs of surface pitting.

8 The cage which fits between the inner and outer races must be examined for wear in the ball cage windows and for cracks which are especially likely to develop across the narrower portions between the outer rims and the holes for the balls.

9 Wear is most likely to be found in the ball tracks on the inner and outer race. If the tracks have widened the balls will no longer be a tight fit and, together with excessive wear in the ball cage windows, will lead to the characteristic 'knocking' on full lock described previously.

10 If wear is excessive then all the parts must be renewed as a matched set.

11 Reassemble the inner race into the cage, and then the cage into the outer race. Tilt the cage and replace the balls one at a time.

12 Pack the joint with the contents of a tube of special "Duckhams M-B" grease.

13 Fit the cv joint onto the shaft the correct way round and with the joint pressing against the circlip. Contract the circlip right into its groove in the shaft with the aid of two screwdrivers, so the inner race of the cv joint will slide over it. It may be necessary to tap the outside end of the joint smartly with a soft faced hammer in order to close the circlip completely. Tap the joint till it is fully home with the inner race resting against the large retaining clip "A". The circlip "B" should now have expanded inside the joint.

14 Replace the rubber boot, and refit the driveshaft to the car as described in Section 2.

5 Inner constant velocity joint - dismantling, overhaul and reassembly

The principle of dismantling, overhaul and reassembly is basically identical to that for the outer constant velocity joint as described in Section 4.

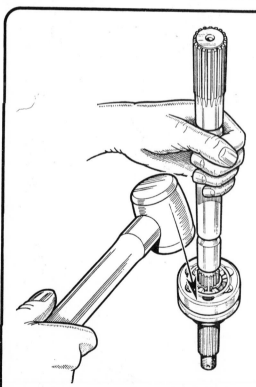

Fig. 7.7. Firmly tap the outer edge of the cv joint with a hide hammer to drive the joint off the shaft

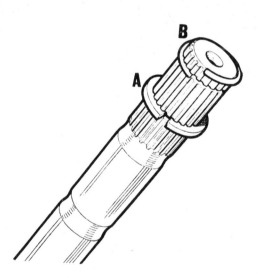

Fig. 7.8. Detail of driveshaft end

A   Spring ring
B   Round section circlip

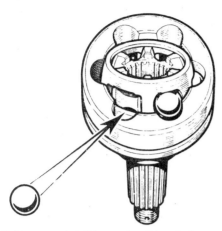

Fig. 7.9. Extract each ball in turn by tilting the inner race as illustrated

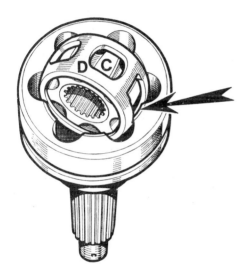

Fig. 7.10. With all the balls removed the cage and inner race can be removed as illustrated. Then remove the inner race 'C' from the cage 'D'

6 Inner Hardy Spicer type joint - inspection

Wear in the needle roller bearings is characterised by vibration in the transmission, 'clonks' on taking up the drive, and in extreme cases of lack of lubrication, metallic squeaking, and ultimately grating and shrieking as the bearings break up.

It is easy to check if the needle roller bearings are worn with the driveshaft in position, by trying to turn the shaft with one hand, the other hand holding the drive coupling flange. Any movement between the drive shaft and the half coupling is indicative of considerable wear. If worn, the old bearings and spiders will have to be discarded and a repair kit, comprising new universal joint spiders, bearings, oil seals, and retainers purchased. Check also by trying to lift the shaft and noticing any movement in the joints.

Examine the driveshaft splines for wear. If worn it will be necessary to purchase a new half coupling, or if the yokes are badly worn, a new or exchange driveshaftt will be required. It is not possible to fit oversize bearings and journals to the trunnion bearing holes.

7 Inner Hardy Spicer type joint - dismantling, overhaul and reassembly

1 Clean away all traces of dirt and grease from circlips located on the ends of the spiders, and remove the clips by pressing their open ends together with a pair of pliers and lever them out with a screwdriver. **Note**: If they are difficult to remove tap the

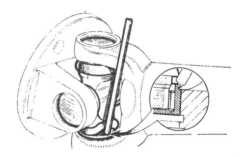

Fig. 7.11. Universal joint bearing removal using a small diameter rod. To be used if bearing cup is really tight

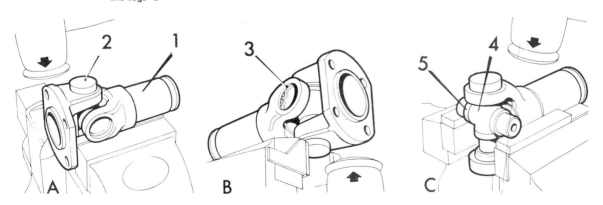

Fig. 7.12. Alternative sequence of operations to be used when removing needle bearing from universal joint

1 Yoke
2 Needle bearing race
3 Retaining circlip
4 Journal spider
5 Rubber seal

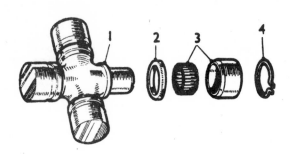

Fig. 7.13. Universal joint component parts

1   *Journal spider*
2   *Rubber seal*
3   *Needle rollers and bearing cup*
4   *Circlip*

bearing face resting on top of the spider with a mallet which will ease the pressure on the circlip.

2   Hold the joint assembly in one hand and remove the bearing cups and needle rollers by tapping the yoke at each bearing with a copper or hide faced hammer. As soon as the bearings start to emerge they can be drawn out with your fingers. If the bearing cup refuses to move then place a thin bar against the inside of the bearing and tap it gently until the cup starts to emerge.

3   With the bearings removed it is relatively easy to extract the spiders from their yokes. If the bearings and spider journals are thought to be badly worn this can easily be ascertained visually with the universal joints dismantled.

4   Thoroughly clean out the yokes and journals.

5   Fit new rubber seals and retainers on the spider journals, place the spider on the shaft yoke, and assemble the needle rollers in the bearing races with the assistance of some thin grease.

6   Pack the bearing cup ends with 0.125 in. (3 mm) of grease and refit onto the spider. Tap the bearings home so that they lie squarely in position.

7   Replace the circlips and ensure complete freedom of movement. If necessary tap the bearings and yoke to settle the bearing cups.

Chapter 8 Differential unit

Contents

Specifications

The differential unit on all Mini variants with manual transmission is identical with the exception of the ratio which varies from one model to another. A different differential unit is used for models with automatic transmission.

Model:	Ratio
848 cc:	
Manual	3.765 : 1
Automatic	3.27 : 1
997 cc and 998 cc:	
Standard	3.765 : 1
Optional	3.444 : 1 (available as service item only)
998 cc (automatic)	3.27 : 1
998 cc Van and Pick-up	3.444 : 1
970 cc and 1071 'S' models	3.765 : 1
1098 cc	3.44 : 1
1275 cc 'S' type models	3.444 : 1
Clubman	3.44 : 1
Cooper 'S' Mk III (1275) & 1275 GT	3.65 : 1

Alternative ratios are available for Cooper 'S' type Mk III models;

These are:	3.939 : 1
	4.267 : 1
	4.35 : 1

Differential bearing preload:

Early bearings	0.001 – 0.002 in. (0.0254 – 0.0508 mm)
Later 'thrust' bearings	0.004 in. (0.1016 mm)

Torque wrench settings:	lb f ft	kg fm
Manual transmission		
End cover bolts	18	2.5
Driven gear to differential case	60	8.3
Nut, driving flange to differential:		
early models	85	11.75
late models	70	9.7
Automatic transmission		
Differential driving flange securing bolts	40 to 45	5.5 to 6.2

1 General description

The differential is located on the bulkhead side of the engine/transmission unit and is held in place by nuts and studs. The crownwheel or drive gear together with the differential gears are mounted in the differential unit. The drive pinion is mounted on the end of the mainshaft in the gearbox.

All repairs can be carried out to the component parts of the differential unit, only after the engine/transmission unit has been removed from the car. If it is wished to attend to the pinion it will be necessary to separate the transmission casing from the engine.

2 Differential unit - removal and replacement (manual transmission)

1 Remove the engine/transmission assembly as described in Chapter 1.
2 Undo the four bolts which hold the cover plate to the underside of the gearchange extension and remove the plate.
3 Undo and remove the bolt which holds the shaft lever to the remote control shaft and then withdraw the shaft.
4 A split pin locks each of the driveshaft flange securing nuts. Remove the pins and, holding the flange stationary (by means of a screwdriver inserted through one of the holes in the drive

flange) undo each nut in turn and pull the flanges from off the gearshafts.

5 Undo and remove the five bolts and spring washers which hold the end covers in place. Take off the end covers together with their cover gaskets. Carefully note the number of shims fitted between the drive gear bearing and the end cover housing.

6 Undo the seven nuts which secure the differential casing to the main transmission casing. On later models tap the lockwasher tabs straight and then undo the retaining nuts.

Withdraw the selector shaft detent spring, sleeve and ball on the later models.

7 Pull the differential casing up off the transmission casing studs and then lift out the differential assembly.

8 To refit the differential assembly place in the transmission casing with the drive gear furthest away from, but with a bias towards, the clutch end.

9 Ensure the differential casing flanges are clean and free from all traces of the old gasket. Fit a new gasket, and then carefully lower the casing over the studs.

10 Refit the seven nuts and washers and tighten them down lightly so that, although the drive gear bearings are firmly held, they can still be moved slightly together with the differential unit.

11 Clean the end cover flanges, fit a new right-hand end cover gasket and replace the right-hand end cover. Ensure the holes in the cover flange and the tapped hole in the transmission casing and differential housing are correctly aligned.

12 Screw in the five bolts and spring washers an equal amount so that the inner face of the cover bears evenly on the differential bearing outer race. As the bolts are tightened a little at a time the differential assembly will move away from the flywheel end of the casing, so centralising the assembly in the differential housing.

13 Now fit the left-hand end cover but **omit** the gasket. Tighten the bolts so that the cover register just seats the bearing outer race. Do not overtighten the bolts or the end cover flange will be distorted.

14 Measure the gap between the end cover and the differential casing in several places to ensure the end cover is seating squarely on the differential assembly. Variations in measurement indicate that the bolts have been tightened unevenly so pulling the differential assembly out of alignment. Alternatively the end cover flange may be distorted. Adjust the tension on the bolts accordingly.

15 The correct gap necessary to give the required preload to the bearings without the gasket fitted is 0.008 to 0.009 in (0.2032 to 0.2286 mm). As the gasket when compressed is 0.007 in. (0.1778 mm) thick, the correct gap with the gasket fitted is 0.001 in. to 0.002 in. (0.0254 to 0.0508 mm) before the bolts are finally tightened down.

16 Any deviation from 0.008 to 0.009 in (0.2032 to 0.2286 mm) must be rectified by fitting appropriate shims between the register on the inside of the end cover and the bearing outer race.

Measured gap (No gasket) - see lower table for shim thickness
a) Zero to 0.001 in.   (Zero to 0.0254 mm)
b) 0.001 to 0.002 in.   (0.0254 to 0.0508 mm)
c) 0.002 to 0.003 in.   (0.0508 to 0.0762 mm)
d) 0.003 to 0.004 in.   (0.0762 to 0.1016 mm)
e) 0.004 to 0.005 in.   (0.1016 to 0.1270 mm)
f) 0.006 to 0.007 in.   (0.1524 to 0.1778 mm)
g) 0.007 to 0.008 in.   (0.1778 to 0.2032 mm)
h) 0.008 to 0.009 in.   (0.2032 to 0.2286 mm)

Shim thickness
a) 0.008 in.   (0.2032 mm)
b) 0.006 to 0.007 in.   (0.1524 to 0.1778 mm)
c) 0.005 to 0.006 in.   (0.1270 to 0.1524 mm)
d) 0.004 to 0.005 in.   (0.1016 to 0.1270 mm)
e) 0.003 to 0.004 in.   (0.0762 to 0.1016 mm)
f) 0.002 to 0.003 in.   (0.0508 to 0.0762 mm)
g) 0.001 to 0.002 in.   (0.0254 to 0.0508 mm)
h) None necessary

17 Remove the end cover. Fit the necessary shims. Replace the cover complete with gasket, and tighten down the securing bolts evenly to a torque of 18 lb f ft (2.5 kg fm).

18 Tighten the differential housing nuts; refit the driving flanges, replace the driving flange washers and nuts and tighten to 85 lb/ft (11.75 kg fm). (Turn the slotted nut as necessary to align with the next split pin hole). Insert new split pins.

19 Refit the remote control shaft, the shaft lever, and the extension cover plate. Replace the engine/transmission unit in the car as described in Chapter 1.

3 Differential unit - dismantling, examination and reassembly (manual transmission)

1 With the aid of a bearing extractor or universal puller pull off the two bearings from the right and left-hand gearshafts. The bearings on some models are marked 'Thrust' on the outside face.

2 Mark the differential case and the drivegear so that they can be reassembled in their original positions.

3 Knock back the tabs of the three lockwashers and unscrew the six set bolts which hold the drivegear to the differential case.

4 Remove the drivegear complete with the left gearshaft. Pull the drivegear off the shaft together with the thrust washer.

5 Gently tap out the tapered peg roll pin which holds the centre pin in place.

6 Remove the centre pin and the component parts of the differential case. The differential case can now be removed from the right gearshaft.

7 Check the bearings for side play and the rollers and races for general wear. Examine the centre pin, the thrust block, and the thrust washers for score marks, and pitting, and renew these components as necessary.

8 Examine the teeth of the drivegear for pitting, score marks, chipping and general wear. If a new drivegear is required a mated drivegear and drive pinion must be fitted. It is asking for trouble to renew one without the other. Examine the oil seals in the end flanges and renew them if worn.

9 Reassembly is a straight reversal of the above sequence. **Note**: When replacing the differential gear thrust washers ensure the slightly chamfered bores rest against the machined faces of the differential gears. The six drivegear bolts should be tightened to a torque of 60 lb f ft (8.3 kg fm) each.

4 Final drive pinion - removal and replacement (manual transmission)

Remove the differential unit as described. Separate the engine from the transmission casing as described in Chapter 1. Now proceed as follows:

1 Undo the plug on the forward facing side of the transmission casing. This plug holds the change speed reverse detent plunger in place. Remove the plug, washer, spring and plunger.

2 Undo the clamp screw from the selector lever and the Woodruff key from the end of the gearchange operating shaft.

3 Pull the gearchange operating shaft up out of the transmission casing.

4 Undo the speedometer pinion housing bolt, remove the housing and extract the pinion. Undo the two bolts which hold the speedometer gear retaining plate to the transmission case front cover, remove the plate and then the speedometer spindle and gear.

5 Knock back the securing tag of the lockwasher which holds the drive pinion securing nut in place, and undo and remove the nut.

6 The final drive pinion can then be pulled off the splines on the mainshaft.

7 Replacement is a straightforward reversal of the removal sequence. Use a new pinion lockwasher and tighten the pinion securing nut to 90 lb f ft (12.0 kg fm) (150 lb f ft (20.7 kg fm) on Mini Cooper 'S' models).

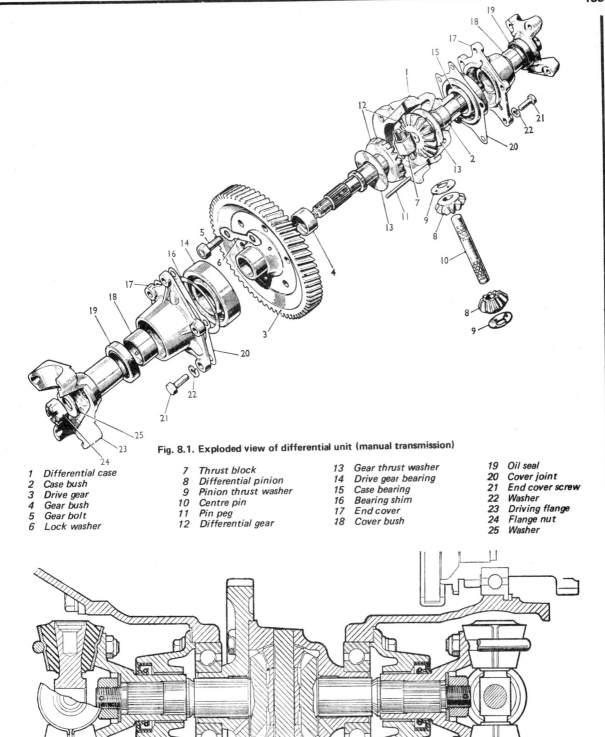

Fig. 8.1. Exploded view of differential unit (manual transmission)

1 Differential case	7 Thrust block	13 Gear thrust washer	19 Oil seal
2 Case bush	8 Differential pinion	14 Drive gear bearing	20 Cover joint
3 Drive gear	9 Pinion thrust washer	15 Case bearing	21 End cover screw
4 Gear bush	10 Centre pin	16 Bearing shim	22 Washer
5 Gear bolt	11 Pin peg	17 End cover	23 Driving flange
6 Lock washer	12 Differential gear	18 Cover bush	24 Flange nut
			25 Washer

Fig. 8.2. With the left-hand drive cover fitted without its joint washer, measure the gap at point 'A' and fit shims between the bearing and cover to obtain the required pre-load

Differential unit removal and replacement sequence (early type shown). Photographs 1 to 24

1 The differential assembly can be removed without having to separate the gearbox and the engine, although this has been done in this instance. Undo the remaining "U" bolt nuts

2 Remove the "U" bolts and the rubber universal joints. If the universal joints are worn they must be replaced

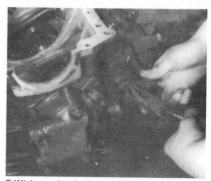

3 With a pair of pliers remove the split pins from the castellated nuts on either side of the differential unit

4 BLMC mechanics have the use of a special spanner which engages with the four "U" bolt holes on the driving flanges and prevents them from turning when undoing the flange nuts

5 The driving flange can normally be locked in place with a couple of steel rods jammed against the casing. Remove the nuts and pull the flanges off the gear shafts

6 Next undo the end cover bolts and remove them from the differential unit together with the split washers

7 Pull the end covers away from the differential unit and place on one side

8 The differential cover is removed next from the gearbox casing. Undo the retaining nuts and remove them together with the washers

9 In this photograph the nuts have been removed from the differential cover studs and it can be seen that the end covers have also been removed

10 Carefully lift the differential cover away from the gearbox casing

11 The differential assembly can now be lifted straight out as shown. To remove the pinion it is necessary to take off the gearbox end cover

12 Thoroughly clean all traces of the old gasket from the gearbox and differential flanges

13 Refit the differential assembly and drive gear and fit new gaskets as shown

14 Remember to replace the differential bearing shims. These might have to be changed if the correct clearance with the cover flanges cannot be obtained (see text)

15 Prise out the old cover flange oil seals unless they are obviously nearly new

16 Carefully press in new end cover flange oil seals. This will help ensure no oil leaks develop from the transmission casing

17 Refit the driving flanges to the end covers on the bench. This is much easier than fitting the flanges after the end covers have been fixed to the differential casing

18 Refit the driving flanges without a gasket, gently tighten down the cover bolts (do not overtighten or the flange will distort) and measure the gap as described in the text

19 When the gap of 0.008 to 0.009 in. (0.2032 to 0.2286 mm) is even all the way round fit a new gasket, and replace the end cover

20 Fit the end cover bolts and washers and tighten them down to a torque of 18 lb f ft (2.49 kg fm)

21 Replace the differential cover and do up the retaining nuts. One is actually inside the gearchange extension and difficult to reach as shown

22 Now fit the flange washer and then the flange nut. Holding the flange securely tighten the nut to 85 lb f ft (11.75 kg fm)

23 Turn the castellated nut on so the next slot lines up with the hole in the gear shaft and fit a new split pin

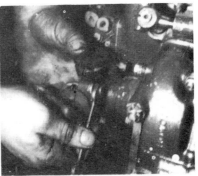

24 Finally refit the rubber universal joints. It will be found helpful to gently nip the ends of the "U" bolts (after replacing the nuts) in a vice prior to refitting

25 Spring ring clip that retains the inner constant velocity joint (latest type driveshaft)

5 Differential unit - removal and replacement (automatic transmission)

1 Remove the engine/transmission assembly as described in Chapter 1.
2 Hold the driving flange using a wrench or screwdriver and undo and remove the drive flange to splined shafts securing bolts and washers.
3 The flanges may now be withdrawn from the splined shafts.
4 Tap back the lockwashers and undo and remove the nuts from the final drive housing.
5 Undo and remove the securing screws and pull the kickdown linkage assembly clear of the transmission case.
6 Undo and remove the two set screws that secure the end cover to the transmission case and lift away the final drive and housing assembly.
7 Undo and remove the remaining securing bolts from the end cover and remove the cover and adjustment shims.
8 To refit the differential unit to the transmission casing first push into position and move the assembly towards the converter. The slot in the spacer must be in alignment with the dowel in the transmission case.
9 Smear a new joint washer with a little "Hylomar" jointing compound and fit into position.
10 Make sure the oil seal is pressed squarely against the face of the spacer and refit the differential housing. Fit new locking plates and lightly tighten the securing nuts.

11 It is now necessary to adjust the bearing preload. Refit the end cover, less the joint washer, but with the original adjustment shims.
12 Tighten the cover securing bolts evenly and sufficiently only for the cover register to nip the bearing outer race. Overtightening will distort the flange.
13 Make several feeler gauge measurements between the side cover flange and the differential housing. Any variations in measurement will indicate that the cover bolts are not evenly tightened and they must be reset.
14 The compressed thickness of a new cover joint washer is 0.007 in (0.178 mm) and the required preload on the bearings is 0.002 in (0.051 mm). The correct gap must be 0.009 in (0.229 mm) and any deviation from this reading must be made up by adding or subtracting shims.
15 Remove the end cover and fit the required thickness of shims and refit the cover with a new joint washer coated with "Hylomar" jointing compound. Tighten the differential housing nuts and cover bolts.
16 Tap up the locking plate tabs, except the one nut which accepts the exhaust pipe bracket.
17 Lubricate the driving flange oil seal and refit the flanges making sure that the split collets are correctly located inside the flanges.
18 Fit new rubber seals to the central securing bolts and refit to the splined shafts.
19 Suitably hold the flanges and tighten the flange bolts.
20 Refit the governor control linkage to the transmission case with a new washer. Make sure the lever is positioned correctly.

6 Differential unit - dismantling, examination and reassembly (automatic transmission)

1 Remove the differential unit from its casing and then withdraw the oil seal housing and remove the bearings using a universal puller.
2 Carefully knock back the locking plate tabs and remove the bolts that secure the driving gear to the cage.
3 Mark the gear and cage so that they can be refitted in their original positions.
4 Separate the driving gear from the cage and remove the differential gear and thrust washer from the driving gear.
5 Using a suitable parallel pin punch tap out the roll pin and lift away both pinions and thrust washers, pinion spacer and the other differential gear and thrust washer.
6 Refer to Section 2, and examine the various parts as described in paragraphs 7 and 8.
7 Reassembly is a straight reversal of the above sequence. Ensure that the differential gear thrust washers are refitted with their chamfered bores against the machined faces of the differential gears. All components must be refitted in their original positions.

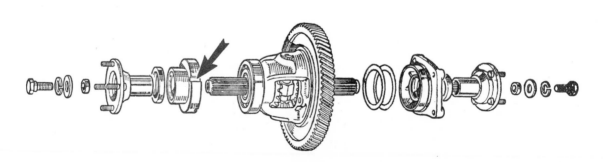

Fig. 8.3. Exploded view of differential unit (automatic transmission)

Chapter 9 Braking system

Contents

Specifications

All models 848 cc pre-September 1964

Make	Lockheed
Footbrake	Hydraulic on all 4 wheels
Handbrake (on rear wheels only)	Mechanical
Type of brakes: Front and Rear	Single leading shoe
Drum diameter	7 in. (17.8 cm)
Lining dimensions: Front and Rear	6.75 in. by 1.25 in. (17.14 cm by 3.17 cm)
Lining material	Don 202
Total lining area per brake drum	33.75 sq in. (217.7 cm^2)
Minimum lining thickness	0.313 in. (0.794 mm)

All models 848 cc post September 1964. Riley Elf and Wolseley Hornet from March 1963.
As for pre-September 1964 models with the alterations and differences listed below:

Type of brakes: Front	Two leading shoes
Rear	Single leading shoe
Drum diameter	7 in. (17.8 cm)
Lining dimensions: Front	6.75 in. by 1.5 in.
Rear	6.75 in. by 1.25 in.

997 cc Mini Cooper models

Make	Lockheed
Footbrake	Hydraulic on all 4 wheels
Handbrake (on rear wheels only)	Mechanical
Type of brakes: Front	Disc 7 in. (17.8 cm) diameter
Rear	Drum 7 in. (17.8 cm) diameter

Disc pad material	...	...	...	...	...	...	...		DA3
Lining material	...	...	...	...	...	...	...		Don 202
Minimum disc pad thickness	...	...	...	...	...	...			0.063 in. (1.6 mm)

998 cc, 970 cc, 1071 cc & 1275 'S' type Mini Cooper models (Mk I and II)

Make	...	...	...	...	...	...	...	...	Lockheed; with vacuum servo
Footbrake	...	...	...	...	...	...	...	...	Hydraulic on all 4 wheels
Handbrake (on rear wheels only)			...	...	...	...	...	...	Mechanical
Type of brakes: Front	...	...	...	...	...	...	...	...	Disc - 7.5 in. (190.5 mm) diameter
Rear	...	...	...	...	...	...	...	...	Drum 7 in. (177.8 mm) diameter
Disc pad material	...	...	...	...	...	...	...		DA6
Drum lining material	...	...	...	...	...	...			Mintex M.32 or Don 202

Mini 1275 GT Clubman (up to July 1974) and Cooper 'S' Mk III

Make	...	...	...	...	...	...	...	...	Lockheed; with vacuum servo type 6

Torque wrench settings:

	lb f ft	kg fm
Caliper retaining bolts	35 to 40	4.8 to 5.5
Bleed screw	4 to 6	0.5 to 0.8
PDWA valve - electrical switch	2 to 2.5	0.28 to 0.35
Tie-rod balljoint nut	25	3.5
Front hub nut	55 to 60	7.6 to 8.3
Servo shell bolts (later type)	17	2.35
Disc to drive flange	42	5.8
Backplate to radius arm bolts	20	2.8
Master cylinder reservoir screws	5	0.7
Pressure failure switch	14	1.9
Pressure failure switch body end plug	26	3.6
Inertia valve plug	45	6.4

1 General description

The four wheel drum brakes fitted are of the internal expanding type and are operated by means of the brake pedal, which is coupled to the brake master cylinder and hydraulic fluid reservoir mounted on the front bulkhead.

The front and rear brakes of pre-September 1964 models (excluding Cooper and Cooper 'S' variants and Mk II Riley Elf and Wolseley Hornet models) are of the single leading shoe-type, with one brake cylinder per wheel for both shoes. Attached to each of the rear wheel operating cylinders is a mechanical expander operated by the handbrake lever through a cable which runs from the brake lever to the backplate brake levers. This provides an independent means of rear brake application.

The front brakes on post September 1964 models (excluding Cooper and Cooper 'S' variants) are of the two leading shoe-type, with a separate cylinder for each shoe. The ends of each shoe are able to slide laterally in small grooves in the ends of the brake cylinders, so ensuring automatic centralisation when the brakes are applied.

Drum brakes have to be adjusted periodically to compensate for wear in the linings. It is unusual to have to adjust the handbrake system as the efficiency of this system is largely dependent on the condition of the brake linings and the adjustment of the brake shoes. The handbrake can, however, be adjusted separately to the footbrake operated hydraulic system.

The hydraulic brake system functions in the following manner: On application of the brake pedal, hydraulic fluid under pressure is pushed from the master cylinder to the brake operating cylinder at each wheel, by means of a four way union and steel pipe lines and flexible hoses. Pressure to the rear brakes is limited by a pressure relief valve fitted in the rear brake pipe line. This reduces the tendency of the rear wheels to lock when braking heavily and weight transfers from the rear wheels to those at the front. When the pressure in the brake line reaches a certain predetermined figure the valve closes and all the additional pressure is transferred to the front wheel cylinders.

The hydraulic fluid moves the pistons out so pushing the brake shoes into contact with the brake drums. This provides an equal degree of retardation on all four wheels in direct proportion to the pressure applied to the brake pedal. Return springs between each pair of brake shoes draw the shoes together when the brake pedal is released.

When disc brakes are fitted to the front wheels they are of the rotating disc and static caliper type, the latter containing two piston operated friction pads, which on application of the footbrake pinch the disc rotating between them.

Application of the foot brake creates hydraulic pressure in the master cylinder and fluid from the cylinder travels, via steel and flexible pipes, to the cylinder in each half of the calipers, the fluid so pushing the friction pads - which are in contact with the caliper piston - into contact with each side of each disc.

Two rubber seals are fitted to the mouth of the operating cylinders. The outer seal prevents moisture and dirt from entering the cylinder, while the inner seal (which is retained in a groove just inside the cylinder) prevents fluid leakage, and provides a running clearance for the pad irrespective of how worn it is, by moving the pad back a fraction when the brake pedal is released.

As the friction pad wears, so the pistons move further out of the cylinders and the level of the fluid in the hydraulic reservoir drops; disc pad wear is thus taken up automatically, and eliminates the need for periodic adjustments by the owner.

2 Drum brakes - adjustment

1 Jack up one side of the car to attend to the brakes on that side.

2 The brakes on all models are taken up by turning a square headed adjuster on the rear of each backplate. The edges of the adjuster are easily burred if an ordinary spanner is used. Use a square headed brake adjusting spanner if possible (BLMC part No 18G419). **Note** When adjusting the rear brakes make sure the handbrake is off.

3 Up to September 1964 one square headed brake adjuster was fitted in each backplate. After this date on models fitted with twin leading shoes two adjusters per backplate were used. (Front wheels only).

4 Turn the adjuster a quarter of a turn at a time until the wheel is locked. Then turn back the adjuster one notch so the wheel will rotate without binding.

5 Spin the wheel and apply the brakes hard to centralise the shoes. Recheck that it is not possible to turn the adjusting screw

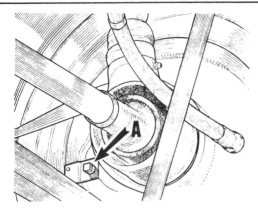

Fig. 9.1. On Mini models with a single leading brake shoe arrangement, one square headed adjuster 'A' is found on each backplate

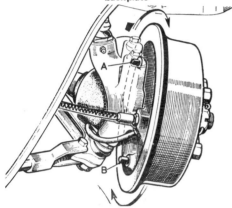

Fig. 9.2. On Mini models with twin leading shoes on the front wheels, two adjusters 'A' and 'B' are provided. To tighten the brakes turn the adjusters clockwise (nearside brake) or anti-clockwise (offside brake)

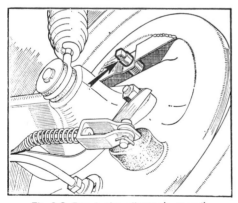

Fig. 9.3. Rear brake adjuster (arrowed)

further without locking the shoe. **Note:** A rubbing noise when the wheel is spun is usually due to dust in the brake drum. If there is no obvious slowing of the wheel due to brake binding there is no need to slacken off the adjusters until the noise disappears. Better to remove the drum and blow out the dust.
6 Repeat this process to the other three brake drums. A good tip is to paint the head of the adjusting screws white which will facilitate future adjustment by making the adjuster heads easier to see.

3 Braking system - bleeding

Gather together a clean jam jar, a 9 in 230 mm) length of

tubing which fits tightly over the bleed nipples, and a tin of the correct brake fluid. Then proceed as follows:
1 Fill the master cylinder and the bottom inch of the jam jar with hydraulic fluid. **Note:** On Cooper models fitted with a front brake intensifier, bleed this unit before bleeding the wheel cylinders. Loosen the bleeder screw at the top of the intensifier and pump the brake pedal slowly up and down until air-free hydraulic fluid emerges. With the pedal held down tighten the bleed screw, top-up the master cylinder, and bleed the brakes as normal.
2 On the wheel furthest away from the master cylinder, remove the rubber dust cap from the bleed nipples and with a suitable spanner unscrew the nipple three quarters of a turn.
3 Place one end of the tube over the wheel cylinder nipple and insert the other open end in the jam jar so that it is covered by the fluid.
4 An assistant should now pump the brake pedal up and down, slowly, replenishing the master cylinder as necessary, until all air bubbles cease to emerge with the fluid from the end of the tube.
5 Tighten the bleed nipple during the next down stroke, and replace the rubber dust cap.
6 Repeat this process with the other three bleed nipples, finishing up at the nipple nearest the brake master cylinder. **Note:** Never use immediately the fluid bled from the hydraulic system to top-up the hydraulic reservoir. The fluid should be left to stand for at least 24 hours to allow the minute air bubbles to escape. Better still, discard all used brake fluid.

4 Drum brake shoes - inspection, removal and replacement

After high mileages it will be necessary to fit replacement brake shoes with new linings. Refitting new brake linings to old shoes is not always satisfactory, but if the services of a local garage or workshop with brake lining equipment are available, then there is no reason why your own shoes should not be successfully relined.
1 Remove the hub cap, loosen off the wheel nuts, securely jack up the car, and remove the road wheel. Mark the relative position of the hub to the drum.
2 Completely slacken off the brake adjustment and take out the two set screws, which hold the drum in place. Remove the brake drum. If it proves obstinate tap the rim gently with a soft-headed hammer. The shoes are now exposed for inspection.
3 The brake linings should be renewed if they are so worn that the rivet heads are flush with the surface of the lining. If bonded linings are fitted they must be removed when the material has worn down to 1/32 in. (1 mm) at its thinnest point. On early models fitted with a single leading shoe it will be found that the linings do not wear evenly. On no account should the shoes be swapped around in an attempt to obtain even wear.
4 Detach the shoes and return springs by pulling one end of the shoes away from the slot in the closed end of one of the brake cylinders and in the case of rear wheel brakes pull the ends of both shoes out of the pivot post. Carefully note the holes in the brake shoes into which the return springs fit, and that the springs are fitted so that they are on the inside of the shoes facing the backplate. Allow the return spring to pull the free end of the brake shoe down the side of the brake cylinder. Repeat this process at the other brake cylinder (where fitted) and then lift both brake shoes away.
5 Thoroughly clean all traces of dust from the shoes, backplates, and brake drums with a dry paintbrush and compressed air, if available. Brake dust can cause squeal and judder, and it is therefore important to clean out the brakes thoroughly.
6 Check that the pistons are free in their cylinders and that the rubber dust covers are undamaged and in position and that there are no hydraulic fluid leaks. Secure the pistons with wire or string. On no account press the brake pedal while the brake drum is off, as this would force the pistons out of the brake cylinders resulting in complete loss of hydraulic fluid.
7 Prior to reassembly, smear a trace of white brake grease to all sliding surfaces. The shoes should be quite free to slide on the closed end of the cylinder and the piston anchorage point. It is

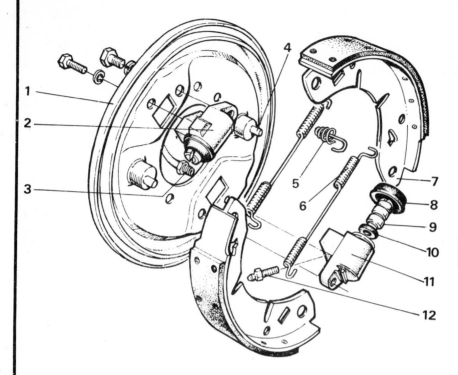

Fig. 9.4. Front drum brake assembly (later type)

1 Backing plate
2 Wheel cylinder
3 Fluid pipe
4 Adjuster
5 Spring hook
6 Pull-off spring
7 Brake shoe
8 Rubber boot
9 Piston
10 Seal
11 Cylinder body
12 Bleed screw

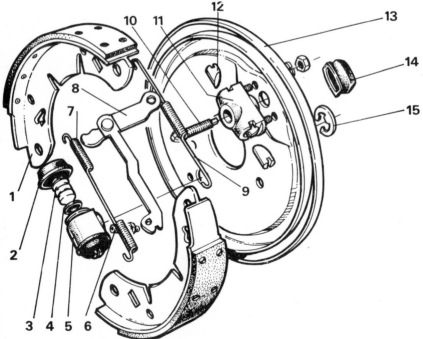

Fig. 9.5. Rear drum brake assembly

1 Brake shoe
2 Rubber boot
3 Piston
4 Seal
5 Cylinder body
6 Bleed screw
7 Lower (divided) spring
8 Parking brake lever
9 Upper spring
10 Adjuster wedge
11 Adjuster body
12 Adjuster peg
13 Backing plate
14 Rubber boot
15 Washer

1 Remove the wheel trim and loosen the wheel nuts before jacking up the car

2 Jack up the car, undo the wheel nuts placing them in the hub cap for safe keeping, and remove the road wheel

3 On Mini models a single adjustment is provided by means of a square headed adjuster on the backplate. On later models two adjusters are fitted

4 To remove a brake drum to inspect the condition of the brake shoe linings, undo the two screws holding the drum in place

5 Fully slacken off the brake adjuster and pull the drum off evenly. A little judicious tapping with a rawhide mallet will help if the drum is obstinate

6 Carefully remove all traces of brake dust by wiping the drum and linings with a clean cloth. Excessive brake dust can cause squeal and judder

7 If it is wished to remove the brake shoes for relining or replacement lift one end of the shoe with a screwdriver and slide out the adjacent end of the opposite shoe

8 Moving to the opposite end of the brake shoes repeat the process

9 Both shoes can now be lifted out. Note the holes into which each hook of the two springs fit

10 Under no account must the brake pedal be pressed when the brake drum is off. Clean the backplate and ensure the adjuster is working properly

11 When replacing the brake shoes ensure the coil portion of the pull off springs face the backplate

12 Carefully manoeuvre the shoes into place, then replace the drum, and tighten the adjuster

Rear brake shoe removal sequence. Photographs 1 to 5

1 Fully slacken off the brake adjuster and pull the drum off evenly

2 The brake assembly with drum removed

3 Removal of brake shoes

4 Correct location of the top and bottom pull off springs

5 Handbrake lever end that engages with brake shoe web

vital that no grease or oil comes in contact with the brake drums or the brake linings.

8 Replacement is a straight reversal of the removal procedure, but note the following points:

a) Check that the adjusters are backed right off.

b) Ensure that the return springs are in their correct holes in the shoes and lie between them and the backplate.

5 Flexible hose - removal and replacement

Inspect the condition of the flexible hydraulic hoses leading from the chassis mounted metal pipe to the brake backplates. If any are swollen, damaged, cut, or chaffed, they must be renewed.

1 Unscrew the metal pipe union nut from its connection to the hose, and then holding the hexagon on the hose with a spanner, unscrew the attachment nut and washer.

2 The chassis end of the hose can now be pulled from the chassis mounting bracket and will be quite free.

3 Disconnect the flexible hydraulic hose at the backplate by unscrewing it from the brake cylinder. **Note:** When releasing the hose from the backplate, the chassis end must always be freed first.

4 Replacement is a straight reversal of the above procedure.

6 Slave cylinders (drum brakes) - removal, dismantling, re-assembly and replacement

If hydraulic fluid is leaking from one of the brake cylinders it will be necessary to dismantle the cylinder and replace the piston rubber sealing ring. If brake fluid is found running down the side of the wheel, or it is noticed that a pool of liquid forms along-side one wheel and the level in the master cylinder has dropped,

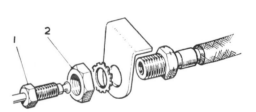

Fig. 9.6. Never try to undo the flexible hose before unscrewing the union nut '1'. Follow this with attachment nut '2'

proceed as follows:

1 Remove the brake drums and brake shoes as detailed in Section 4.

2 Ensure that all the other wheels and drums are in place and where two brake operating cylinders are fitted to one backplate, as on the front wheels, securely wire the piston in the cylinder which is not leaking. Remove the piston, piston rubber and seal from the leaking cylinder by applying gentle pressure to the foot brake. On early models fitted with one wheel cylinder per brake drum, take off the dust seals from each end of the cylinder and remove both pistons. Place a quantity of rag under the backplate or a tray to catch the hydraulic fluid as it pours out of the cylinder.

3 Inspect the inside of the cylinder for score marks caused by impurities in the hydraulic fluid. If any are found the cylinder and piston will require renewal.

4 If the cylinder is sound, thoroughly clean it out, with fresh hydraulic fluid.

5 The old rubbers will probably be swollen and visibly worn. Smear the new rubbers with hydraulic fluid and reassemble in the cylinder in the case of twin leading shoes the spring, cup filler, cup, piston, sealing ring and dust cover, in that order. On

early models fitted with single leading shoes fit new seals to the recesses in the piston and replace both pistons in the operating cylinder.

6 Replenish the brake fluid, replace the brake shoes and brake drum, and bleed the hydraulic system as previously detailed.

7 If the cylinder is scored and is to be renewed, remove the flexible hose as detailed in Section 5.

8 In the case of twin leading shoe front brakes disconnect the pipe between the two brake cylinders and remove complete with the banjo adaptors. Unscrew from the backplate the two set bolts and spring washers which retain each cylinder in place. The cylinders are now free. Replacement is a direct reversal of this process.

9 In the case of single leading shoes unscrew the bleed screw, remove the circlip and the dished washer from off the wheel cylinder boss which protrudes through the brake backplate. Remove the wheel cylinder. Reassembly is a direct reversal of this process.

10 In the case of the rear brake assembly, remove the hydraulic pipe, the flexible cable, bleed screw, and circlip from the cylinder boss which protrudes through the backplate. With the brake drum and brake shoes removed the cylinder can now be released. Reassembly is a direct reversal of this process.

7 Backplate (drum brakes) - removal and replacement

1 In the case of the front brakes the backplate can be removed after disconnecting the flexible pipe and the wheel hub, by removing the four backplate securing bolts and washers.

2 In the case of the rear brakes the backplate securing bolts can be removed and the backplate lifted away after
a) The road wheels, brake drum, handbrake lever rod, and hydraulic pipe have been disconnected.
b) The hub assembly has been removed.

3 Replacement in both cases is a straight reversal of the above.

8 Disc brake friction pads - inspection, removal and replacement

1 Remove the front wheels and inspect the amount of lining material left on the friction pads. The pads must be renewed when the thickness of the material has worn down to 0.063 in. (1.588 mm).

2 Press down on the pad retaining spring and extract the retaining spring split pins. On later type calipers the spring is not used. (See Fig. 9.9).

3 Take off the spring clip and with a slight rotational movement, remove the friction pads and anti-squeal shims, using a pair of sharp-nosed pliers if necessary.

4 Carefully clean the recesses in the caliper in which the friction pad assemblies lie, and the exposed face of each piston from all traces of dirt and dust.

5 Remove the cap from the hydraulic fluid reservoir and place a large rag underneath the unit. Press the pistons in each half of the caliper right in - this will cause the fluid level in the reservoir to rise and possibly to spill over the brim onto the protective rag.

6 After checking that the cutaway face of each piston is facing upwards, fit the new friction pads into the calipers and position the anti-squeal shims between the friction pad and the piston.

7 Check that the new friction pad assemblies move freely in the caliper recesses and remove any high spots on the edge of the pressure plate by careful filing.

8 Check that the retaining spring clips show no sign of damage or loss of tension and then, if sound, replace them, press them down and insert the split pins.

9 Replace the road wheels and remove the jacks. Press the brake pedal several times to adjust the brakes. Top-up the master cylinder as required. **Note:** Different type calipers are fitted from car Nos "CA2S4 382852"; "KA2S4 382183" (rhd), and "CA2S4 383843", "KA2S4 379926", (lhd). Although similar in construction and operation to the early type calipers, these later

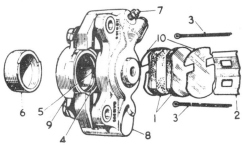

Fig. 9.7. Exploded view of caliper assembly (early type)

1 Friction pads
2 Pad retaining spring
3 Retaining split pins
4 Piston dust seal
5 Piston fluid seal
6 Piston, showing cut-away at top
7 Bleeder screw
8 Mounting half caliper
9 Rim half caliper
10 Anti-squeak shim

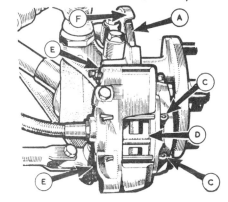

Fig. 9.8. Disc brake assembly (early type)

A Brake disc
C Split pins
D Pad retaining spring
E Caliper mounting bolts
F Dust cover

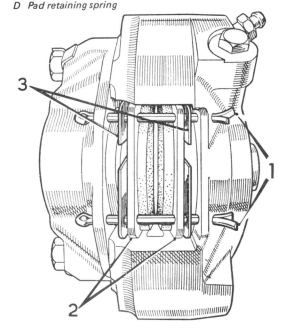

Fig. 9.9. Modified disc brake caliper assembly

1 Pad retaining split pins
2 Brake pads
3 Anti-squeak shims

types differ in that the pads are a different shape and are held directly by the split pins. These pins pass directly through both the pads, as well as the caliper. The spring retaining clip is therefore dispensed with. The disc brake pads fitted on these later models are not interchangeable with the earlier type.

9 Disc brake calipers - removal and dismantling

1 Jack up the car, remove the roadwheel, and prise back the locking tabs and unscrew the nut which holds the tie-rod balljoint to the steering arm.
2 Undo the two nuts and screws which hold the locking plate to the disc brake dust cover.
3 Remove the disc brake friction pads and anti-squeal shims as previously detailed.
4 Unscrew the two caliper mounting bolts and lockwashers and remove the caliper assembly from the disc, together with the top and bottom halves of the dust cover.
5 Meticulously clean the caliper, and place the caliper on a block or similar support, or ask a friend to hold it to avoid it hanging on the hydraulic hose which could damage the latter.
6 Clamp the piston in either the mounting half or the rim half of the caliper with wire or a suitable clamp, depending on which side of the caliper the piston is to be removed from first.
7 Gently apply the footbrake so forcing the unclamped piston out of the caliper until it is in a position where it can be removed by hand.
8 Gently prise the dust seal retainer from the cylinder by carefully inserting a penknife blade between the dust seal retainer and the dust seal, and then extract the seal.
9 Remove the inner hydraulic fluid seal from its groove in the caliper cylinder with a blunt nosed tool. **Note:** Great care should be taken not to damage or scratch the cylinder bore or fluid seal groove.
10 After the piston and rubber seals in one side of the caliper have been checked and replaced as necessary, and the piston reassembled to the caliper as detailed in Section 10, the piston in the other half of the caliper can be removed by clamping the rebuilt piston assembly in place and then repeating the process used to remove the first piston.

10 Disc brake calipers - reassembly and replacement

1 Coat a new rubber fluid seal with hydraulic brake fluid and fit the seal to the groove in the cylinder.
2 Slacken the bleed screw in the caliper one turn.
3 Lubricate the piston with hydraulic fluid and press the piston into the cylinder carefully, with the undercut portion facing upwards, and out. Press the piston in squarely until approximately 0.25 in 6.35 mm) protrudes from the cylinder.
4 Smear a new dust seal with hydraulic fluid and fit it to its retainer.
5 Place the dust seal assembly with the seal resting on the raised portion of the piston and press the piston and seal home with a suitable clamp. Tighten the bleed screw. Repeat this procedure with the remaining cylinder in the other half of the caliper.
6 Refit the caliper to the disc. Replace the two screws which hold the dust cover to the tie-rod end nut locking plate. Tighten down the tie-rod balljoint nut to a torque of 25 lb f ft (3.4 kg fm) and knock up the securing tabs on both sides of the lockwasher. Fit a new lockwasher if either of the tabs are broken or cracked. Tighen the caliper to a torque of 35-40 lb f ft (4.8 - 5.5 kg fm).
7 Fit the anti-squeal plates and disc brakes friction pads as previously described and bleed the hydraulic system. Assembly is now complete.

11 Brake discs - removal and replacement

1 To remove a disc first refer to Section 9 and remove the brake caliper.
2 Carefully prise off the hub bearing cover, then extract the split pin, unscrew the hub nut, and pull off the hub flange and disc.
3 If the disc is to be separated from the hub flange, mark the relative positions of the disc and hub flange so that they may be refitted in their original positions, and separate the two parts.
4 Thoroughly clean the disc and inspect for signs of deep scoring or excessive corrosion. If these are evident, the disc may be re-ground, but no more than a maximum total of 0.060 in (1.524 mm) may be removed. It is, however, desirable to fit a new disc if at all possible.
5 Refitting the disc is the reverse sequence to removal. The hub nut must be tightened to a torque wrench setting of 55-60 lb f ft (7.6 to 8.3 kg fm).
6 Measure the run out at the outer periphery of the disc by means of feeler gauges positioned between the inside of the caliper and the disc. If the run out of the friction faces exceeds 0.009 in (0.2286 mm) remove the disc and reposition it on the drive plate. Should the run out be really bad, the disc is probably distorted due to overheating and a new one must be fitted.

12 Handbrake - adjustment

If the handbrake requires adjustment it is more than likely that the footbrake will require adjustment also. Excess travel in the footbrake is compensated by adjusting the brake shoes, this automatically compensates for excess travel in the handbrake lever also.

Never try to adjust the handbrake to compensate for wear on the rear brake linings. It is very seldom that the handbrake will require adjustment, and that only after very high mileage due to slight stretching of the cable. Usually it is badly worn rear brake linings that lead to excessive handbrake travel. If the rear brake linings are in good condition or have been recently renewed and the handbrake tends to reach the end of its ratchet travel before the brakes come on, adjust the handbrake as follows:
1 Lock the rear brake shoes by rotating the adjustment screw as far as it will turn clockwise.
2 Apply the handbrake on the fourth notch of its ratchet.
3 Remove the slackness in the cable by adjusting the nuts at the handbrake lever trunnion. **Do not overtighten** the cables or the rear brakes will bind.
4 Release the handbrake and check that neither of the rear wheels are binding.

13 Handbrake cable - removal and replacement

If the handbrake cables have stretched to the extent where adjustment is no longer possible or if they are badly corroded or worn, they can be replaced as follows:
1 Remove the hub cap and loosen the four securing nuts on the rear road wheel on the side from which the cable is to be removed.
2 Place the car in bottom gear, and with a jack under the rear sub-frame raise the rear of the car, and remove the roadwheel.
3 Undo the cable adjusting nuts on the handbrake lever trunnion and take off the cable fairlead which is positioned in the middle of the floor towards the rear of the front seats.
4 From underneath the floor of the car pull the cable out from inside the body and free the cable from its guide channel on the rear subframe crossmember.
5 Prise off the guide tube from the clip on the radius arm, and then pull it away from its securing hole in the radius arm boss. (Note: Later models are fitted with a cable swivel which is pinched to the cable and released from the radius arm by undoing the securing nut).
6 Free the cable from the handbrake actuating lever on the brake backplate, and pull the cable through the subframe and remove complete in the case of later models with the cable swivel.

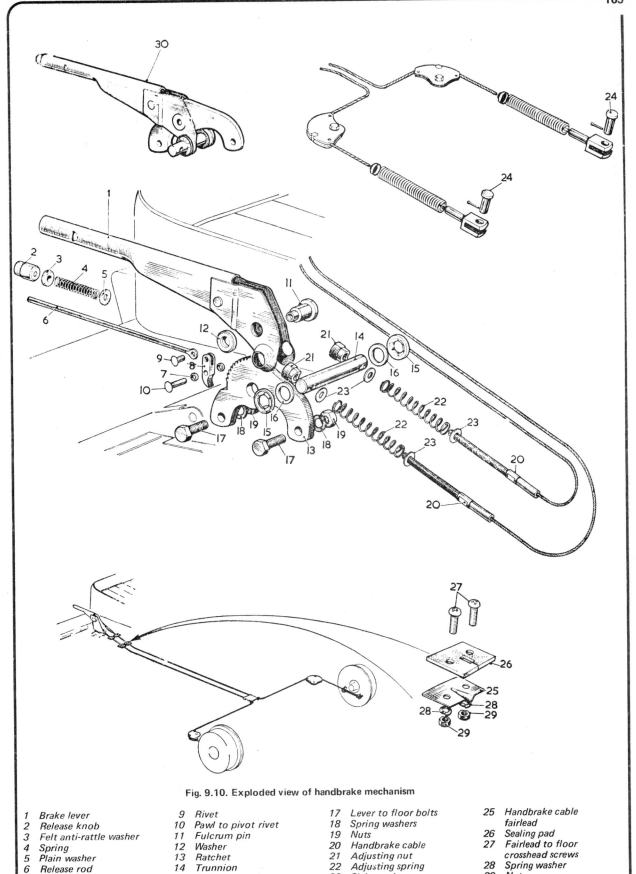

Fig. 9.10. Exploded view of handbrake mechanism

1	Brake lever	9	Rivet	17	Lever to floor bolts	25	Handbrake cable
2	Release knob	10	Pawl to pivot rivet	18	Spring washers		fairlead
3	Felt anti-rattle washer	11	Fulcrum pin	19	Nuts	26	Sealing pad
4	Spring	12	Washer	20	Handbrake cable	27	Fairlead to floor
5	Plain washer	13	Ratchet	21	Adjusting nut		crosshead screws
6	Release rod	14	Trunnion	22	Adjusting spring	28	Spring washer
7	Plain washer	15	Trunnion washer	23	Plain washer	29	Nut
8	Pawl	16	Trunnion	24	Clevis pin	30	Handbrake lever assembly

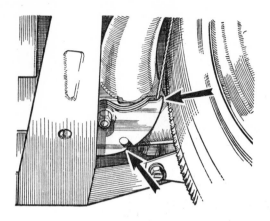

Fig. 9.11. The handbrake cable sector mounted on underside of radius arm. To retain the cable it must be nipped at the corners

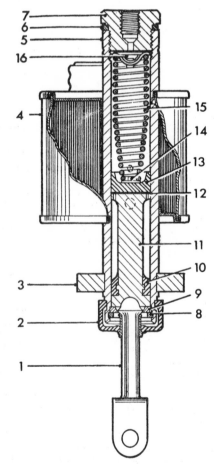

Fig. 9.12. Cross section through brake master cylinder

1	Push rod	9	Stop washer
2	Rubber boot	10	Secondary cup
3	Mounting flange	11	Piston
4	Supply tank	12	Piston washer
5	Body	13	Main cup
6	Seal	14	Spring retainer
7	End plug	15	Return spring
8	Circlip	16	Non - return valve

7 Replacement is a direct reversal of the above procedure but the following two points should be noted:
a) Always ensure that the guide channel is well lubricated and that on early models the guide tube is pushed right into its anchorage hole and held by the securing clip.
b) The handbrake should be adjusted as described in Section 12.

14 Brake pedal - removal and replacement

The brake pedal is removed in an identical manner to removing the clutch pedal. Full information will be found in Chapter 5.

15 Master cylinder - removal, dismantling and replacement

1 Spring off the circlip from the end of the clevis pin which holds the brake pushrod to the brake pedal. Slide out the clevis pin.
2 Unscrew the union nut from the end of the hydraulic pipe where it enters the brake master cylinder and gently pull the pipe clear.
3 Unscrew the two nuts and spring washers holding the brake cylinder mounting flange to the mounting bracket.
4 Remove the master cylinder and reservoir, unscrew the filler cap, and drain the hydraulic fluid into a clean container.
5 Remove the rubber boot or dust cover, and extract the circlip from the end of the body with a pair of long nosed pliers.

6 Pull out the pushrod and stop washer and shake out the piston, secondary cup, copper piston washer, the primary or main cup, and the spring retainer, spring and non-return valve.
7 Clean all the components thoroughly with hydraulic fluid or methylated spirits and then dry them off.
8 Carefully examine the parts, especially the rubber primary and secondary cups for signs of swelling, distortion, or splitting, and check the piston and cylinder wall for wear and score marks. Replace any parts that are faulty.
9 Reassembly is a straightforward reversal of the dismantling procedure, but **note** the following points:
a) As the components are returned to the cylinder barrel, lubricate them with the correct grade of hydraulic fluid.
b) Insert the return spring into the barrel with its broader base first.
c) On completion of assembly top up the reservoir tank with the correct grade of hydraulic fluid and bleed the system.

16 Master cylinder pushrod to piston clearance - adjustment

It is unlikely that the master cylinder pushrod to piston clearance will have to be reset, unless the adjusting nuts have been disturbed. If they have, then reset the nuts to give 0.156 in (3.96 mm) clearance at the foot pedal before the piston begins to move. If the pedal is depressed by hand the point when the piston begins to move is quite obvious by the greatly increased pressure required to depress the pedal further.

17 Brake intensifier - general description

Certain Mini Cooper models make use of a brake intensifier. This is a special cylinder which increases the hydraulic pressure available at the front brakes, without a corresponding increase in pedal pressure. On later models the brake intensifier was discontinued and a new master cylinder with a different bore fitted.
The intensifier is secured to the right-hand wing valance of the engine compartment. The hydraulic pipe from the master cylinder is connected to its lower end, while the pipe which emerges from its upper end runs to the disc brake calipers on the front wheels.
The intensifier consists of a cylinder (6) (All numerical

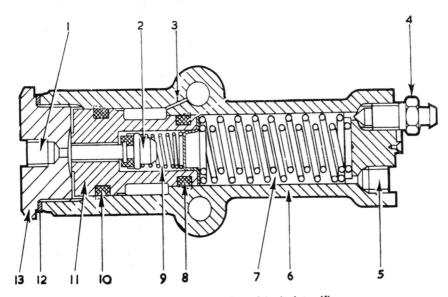

Fig. 9.13. Cross section through brake intensifier

1 Fluid inlet	4 Bleed screw	7 Piston return spring	10 Piston seal - large
2 Valve	5 Fluid outlet	8 Piston seal - small	11 Piston
3 Air relief passage	6 Intensifier cylinder body	9 Valve return spring	12 Copper gasket
			13 Hexagon end plug

references in brackets refer to Fig. 9.13 with a two diameter bore into which a stepped piston (11) is fitted.

The piston has a rubber seal at each end (8, 10), and at rest is held against the lower end of the bore by the piston return spring (7).

The centre of the piston is machined to accommodate a valve (2), and valve return spring (9), and when there is no pressure in the inlet hydraulic pipeline, the valve is held open against the pressure of the spring by the valve stem which rests against the end of the intensifier cylinder (6).

On applying the brakes hydraulic fluid from the master cylinder enters the brake intensifier through the fluid inlet (1); passes up inside the piston (11); round the valve (2); into the smaller but longer intensifier bore; and out to the disc brake calipers through the fluid outlet hole (5).

As soon as the disc pads have moved out into contact with the brake disc the hydraulic pressure rises in the system as the brake pedal continues to be pressed.

The hydraulic pressure now becomes great enough to move the piston (11) slightly forward so overcoming both the pressure from the coil return spring (7) and the pressure on the small diameter of the piston.

As soon as the stepped piston (11) moves forward the valve closes (the stem is no longer able to hold it open) and the hydraulic fluid in both the larger and smaller bores of the cylinder is effectively separated.

As the brake pedal is depressed further, the hydraulic pressure against the large face of the piston increases, so forcing it forward. so creating an even greater pressure on the brake fluid in the smaller cylinder bore. In this way a greater pressure can be applied at the calipers.

On releasing the brake pedal the return spring (7) forces the piston (11) back, so opening the valve (2), in preparation for the sequence of events to begin again.

An air release passage is drilled from the area between the two diameters of the piston into one of the mounting holes in the intensifier body. The flange of this bolt hole is specially machined to allow the air to escape and on no account must be filed flat or obstructed. The correct diameter fixing bolt must also always be fitted to prevent the air hole becoming blocked.

18 Brake intensifier - removal, dismantling, reassembly and replacement

1 Lay some rag or cotton waste under the intensifier to catch any hydraulic fluid which may be spilt.
2 Loosen the top brake pipe union, and from inside the wheel arch, undo the two nuts and spring washers, and pull out the two intensifier mounting bolts.
3 Remove the top pipe union and then undo and remove the bottom union and pull away the outlet and inlet pipes.
4 Carefully secure the intensifier in a vice and then undo the large hexagon plug.
5 Remove the piston seal assembly and the return springs from the bore of the intensifier. Thoroughly clean the parts in methylated spirits.
6 Examine the condition of the rubber seals. If they are worn, damaged. or deteriorated the piston assembly must be renewed complete with seals as a unit.
7 Reassemble the components of the intensifier in the reverse order to that in which they were removed.
8 Replacement is a straight reversal of the removal procedure.

19 Pressure regulating valve - removal, dismantling, reassembly and replacement

1 Thoroughly clean all dirt away from the body of the valve (located under the floor on the rear subframe front cross-member) and from the brake line unions to ensure no dirt enters the system on removal of the unit.
2 Undo the three nuts which hold the brake pressure pipes to the valves and pull the pipes clear of the unit. Loosen the large end plug.
3 Undo and remove the nut and washer which secures the valve to the crossmember and lift away the valve assembly.
4 Remove the end plug together with its sealing washer and extract the valve piston, and the return spring.
5 Examine the rubber seals on the piston. If they are worn or

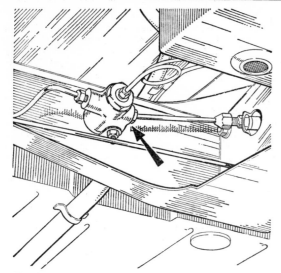

Fig. 9.14. Location of hydraulic pressure regulating valve (arrowed)

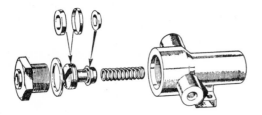

Fig. 9.15. Exploded view of hydraulic brake pressure regulating valve

perished new seals will have to be fitted.

6 Carefully clean the interior of the valve body and lubricate the bore with clean brake fluid prior to reassembly of the piston.

7 Fit new taper and piston seals and make certain that the taper seal is fitted so that the smaller diameter enters the valve bore first.

8 Insert the return spring first, followed by the piston assembly, followed by the sealing washer and end plug.

9 Replace the valve assembly to the subframe, tighten the end plug, reconnect the three brake pressure pipes and finally bleed the system as described in in Section 3.

20 Vacuum servo unit (early type) - general description

All early Mini Cooper 'S' models are fitted with a vacuum servo unit, which greatly reduces the pressure necessary at the brake pedal to stop the car.

The system relies on the difference in pressure between engine vacuum and atmosphere. The main components comprise a control valve; booster diaphragm; slave cylinder; and a non-return valve.

The system operates in the following manner. With the brakes off and the engine running, the servo is at rest (Fig. 9.16). The vacuum in chambers '1' '2' '3' and '4' is the same as that in the inlet manifold. The air valve (6) is closed because of the pressure differential across it, and also because of the spring behind it.

When the brakes are applied hydraulic fluid under pressure enters, via the inlet hole (13) from the master cylinder and reacts upon the rear face of the valve piston (7) which moves the diaphragm (10) until the stem meets the air valve (5). Chambers '1' and '4' are now isolated from the vacuum in the inlet manifold.

Continuing pressure on the brake pedal results in the diaphragm stem lifting the air valve (5) to the atmosphere. The

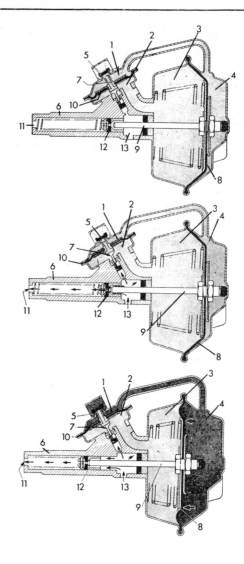

Fig. 9.16. Vacuum servo unit operation (earlier type)

1	Chamber 1	8	Booster diaphragm
2	Chamber 2	9	Push rod
3	Cnamber 3	10	Diaphragm
4	Chamber 4	11	Fluid outlet to brakes
5	Air valve	12	Cup
6	Slave cylinder	13	Fluid inlet from master
7	Valve piston		cylinder

air admitted into chambers '1' and '4' (Fig. 9.16) drives the booster diaphragm to the left against the pressure of the spring, because of the partial vacuum present in chambers '2' and '3'.

At the same time the pushrod (9) first seals the centre hole in the cup (12), and continuing the movement, applies pressure on what is now a locked 'line' of hydraulic fluid to the wheel cylinders and disc brake calipers.

When the necessary degree of retardation is achieved the master cylinder pressure acting against the valve piston (7) balances the control valve diaphragm, (10) which deflects back to its position in Fig. 9.16 so allowing the air valve (5) to shut. This prevents the entry of further air. In this position the booster diaphragm is static and the boost held. If further pressure is applied to the brake pedal the air valve (5) will again open allowing more air into chambers '1' and '4' so causing the pushrod (9) to move slightly and increase the pressure on the brakes. When the pressure in the master cylinder balances the control valve diaphragm the air valve (5) will again close and so the brakes are held on steadily.

When the brakes are released the hydraulic pressure is removed from the underside of the valve piston (7) and the diaphragm (10) returns to its normal position. This allows all four chambers to be subject to the same degree of vacuum from the inlet manifold, and the large spring behind the booster diaphragm helps it return to its normal position as in Fig. 9.16. As the booster diaphragm moves to the right it pulls the pushrod with it, so releasing the pressure of the hydraulic fluid in the brake linings, the fluid reversing towards the master cylinder because of the action of the rubber seals and pull-off springs which release the brakes.

21 Vacuum servo air filter (early type) - removal and replacement

1 Free the outer end of the heater air intake hose.
2 Undo the five screws which hold the air valve cover in place and remove the valve cover.
3 Press the air valve in the centre of the underside of the cover off its seat, and blow compressed air at a low pressure into the filter chamber to clean it out. Never lubricate the filter or try and remove it from the air valve cover.
4 Replacement is a straightforward reversal of the removal sequence.

22 Vacuum servo unit (early type) - removal and replacement

1 Remove the front end of the interior heater hose from the grille; remove the clip which holds the hose to the slave cylinder and tie the hose back out of the way to give easy access to the servo unit.
2 Disconnect the two hydraulic pipes from the servo unit and carefully plug their open ends to prevent the excessive loss of fluid.
3 Free the rubber pipe which carries the vacuum from the non-return valve on the servo unit.
4 Undo the two nuts and spring washers which hold the servo unit to its rear mounting bracket. **Note:** One of the nuts holds the securing clip for the vacuum pipe.
5 Free the servo unit from its front mounting bracket and then lift the unit from the car.
6 Replacement presents no problems and is a direct reversal of the removal procedure. When everything is reconnected it will be necessary to bleed the brake system. **Note:** To stop the servo from operating pump the pedal rapidly to destroy the vacuum during this operation.

23 Vacuum servo unit (early type) - dismantling, examination and reassembly

To make dismantling and reassembly instructions as clear as possible all numbers in brackets refer to Fig. 9.17 and will be used throughout this section.
1 With the servo unit on the bench unscrew the five screws (1) which hold the air valve cover (2) in place and remove the cover and control valve diaphragm (4).
2 Undo the four screws (5) and lift out the valve housing (6) together with the housing gasket (7).
3 Try and shake the valve piston (8) out of the slave cylinder body. Alternatively apply an air line at the smaller hole on the side of the body and blow the piston (8) out together with its rubber cup (9).
4 Unscrew the nut and washer (25, 26) from the end of the clamping bolt (24) and remove the bolt (24) from the clamping ring (20).
5 Take off the end cover (23), clamping ring (20), and the diaphragm assembly, at the same time freeing the return spring

(16) from the locking plates (14) inside the vacuum shell (12).
6 Hold the pushrod (15) by the fixed hexagon immediately behind the fixed plate (17). Take the greatest care not to damage the finely machined pushrod end as this is responsible for sealing the hydraulic fluid. Remove the rubber buffer (22) and unscrew the fixing nut for the diaphragm assembly (21). Separate the small plate (10), diaphragm (18), and the large plate (17).
7 Bend back the tags on the locking plates (14) and unscrew the four bolts (27) holding the vacum shell to the slave cylinder body (10).
8 Dismantle the slave cylinder (10). Extract the guide piece and the rod cup (29), cup spreader (30), and spring (31). With a piece of 5/16 in diameter rod press down the piston (35) and then remove the circlip (32) with a pair of long nosed pliers.
9 Gently release the rod from the piston and extract the remaining parts from the slave cylinder body.
10 Unscrew the non-return valve from the side of the slave cylinder.
11 Clean all the component parts (except the air valve cover which should be blown clean with compressed air at low pressure), in methylated spirits. Dry them thoroughly prior to inspection.
12 Examine the metal parts and replace any that are worn or damaged. Renew the end cover assembly if the pipe in the vacuum shell cover is loose. Renew the rubber seals, cups, and gaskets throughout the unit. If the vacuum non-return valve is faulty a new assembly must be fitted.
13 To reassemble the unit first fit the spring retainer (39), to one end of the spring (38), and the spring guide (37) to the other. Place the spring in the bore of the slave cylinder spring retainer end (39) first.
14 Lubricate the bore with hydraulic fluid and fit the cup (36) taking great care not to turn or buckle the lip.
15 Replace the piston (35) flat side first. Carefully push the piston down the bore with the 5/16 in diameter rod until the groove in the bore is well exposed. Then fit the distance piece (34), washer (23), and the circlip (32). This is a fiddly job and great care must be taken not to score or damage the bore when fitting the circlip (32).
16 Next place the spring (31) in the bore, and then the cup spreader (30) concave side first. Carefully fit the pushrod cup (29) so the concave portion fits the cup spreader (30). Fit the guide piece flat side first.
17 Fit the slave cylinders (10) to the vacum shell (12) using a new gasket (11), and insert the four bolts (27) through the locking plates (14) and the adjustment plate (13) to secure the slave cylinder. Tighten down the four bolts (27) and turn up the tabs on the locking plates (14).
18 Replace the diaphragm components (17, 18, 19) on the pushrod (15) in the order shown in the illustration and tighten up the securing nut (21). Secure the nut in position by punching the thread in two opposite positions. Replace the rubber buffer (22).
19 Secure the small end of the return spring (16) to the locking plate tabs (14) and refit the pushrod and diaphragm assembly. Ensure the pushrod (15) enters the hole in the slave cylinder, and hold the rod in position while refitting the end cover (23).
20 Replace the clamping ring (20) and refit, but do not tighten the clamping bolt (24) nut and washer (25,26). Ensure the pipe in the cover is roughly aligned with the inclined face of the slave cylinder.
21 Fit the cup (9) onto the valve piston (8) and fit the valve piston (8) into the central hole in the inclined face of the slave cylinder body.
22 Replace the gasket (7) and the valve housing (6) and tighten down the four valve housing screws (5).
23 Place the diaphragm (4) on the valve housing (6) with the diaphragm stem passing through the contral hole.
24 Fit the rubber pipe (3) to the end of the metal pipe on the air valve cover (2) and fit the cover to the slave cylinder (10) at the same time engaging the rubber elbow (3) with the vertical pipe from the diaphragm end cover (23).
25 Fit and tighten the five air valve cover screws (1) and position

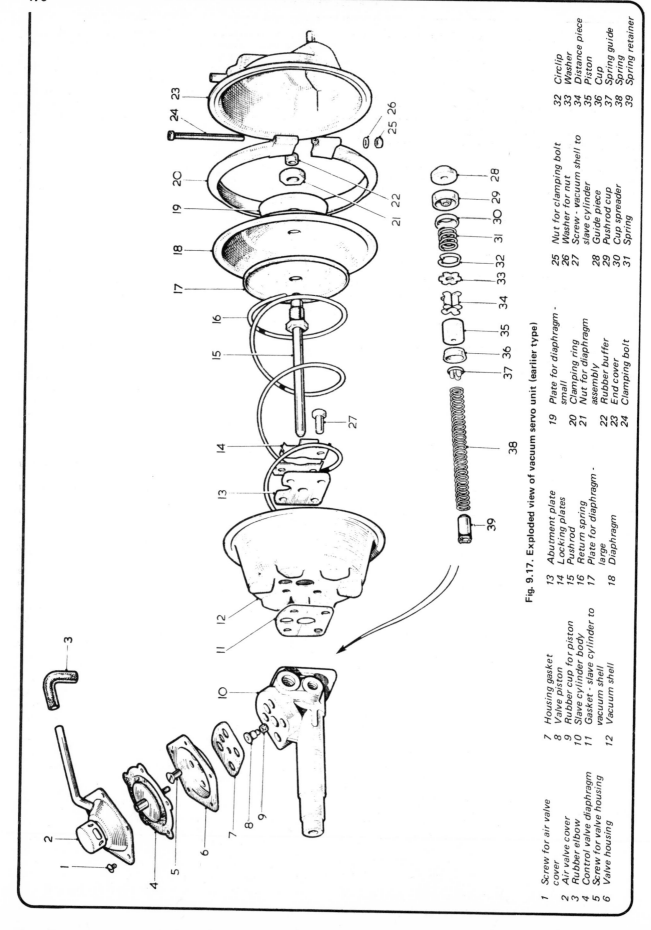

Fig. 9.17. Exploded view of vacuum servo unit (earlier type)

1 Screw for air valve cover
2 Air valve cover
3 Rubber elbow
4 Control valve diaphragm
5 Screw for valve housing
6 Valve housing
7 Housing gasket
8 Valve piston
9 Rubber cup for piston
10 Slave cylinder body
11 Gasket - slave cylinder to vacuum shell
12 Vacuum shell
13 Abutment plate
14 Locking plates
15 Pushrod
16 Return spring
17 Plate for diaphragm - large
18 Diaphragm
19 Plate for diaphragm - small
20 Clamping ring
21 Nut for diaphragm assembly
22 Rubber buffer
23 End cover
24 Clamping bolt
25 Nut for clamping bolt
26 Washer for nut
27 Screw - vacuum shell to slave cylinder
28 Guide piece
29 Pushrod cup
30 Cup spreader
31 Spring
32 Circlip
33 Washer
34 Distance piece
35 Piston
36 Cup
37 Spring guide
38 Spring
39 Spring retainer

the end cover so that the rubber elbow (3) is in proper alignment with both the air valve cover (2) and the end cover pipe (23).

26 Finally, tighten down the clamping bolt (24) and the nut and washer (25, 26).

24 Vacuum servo unit (later models) - general description

The vacuum servo unit fitted to previous Cooper 'S' models has been superseded by the 'Lockheed Type' 6 servo unit which is now fitted to the 1275 GT Clubman and the Cooper 'S' Mk 111. The principle of operation of the complete unit is exactly the same as for the previous type. The main difference is in the dssign of the fitting together of the vacuum servo shell (10) (Fig.9.18) and the end cover (11). The main diaphragm (14) is also supported over a much greater area (15) and in a different configuration.

25 Vacuum servo unit (later type) - removal and replacement

1 First remove the heater hose from the intake unit by pulling it from beneath the right-hand front wing. Then withdraw the intake unit from inside the engine compartment.

2 Disconnect the vacuum pipe from the non-return valve connection of the unit (12, 13).

3 Remove securing bracket from the end of the servo and disconnect the two hydraulic brake lines. Plug the ends of these lines to minimise fluid wastage.

4 Remove the units securing the servo (by the end cover) to the mounting bracket and draw it off.

5 Replace the servo by reversing the procedure in paragraphs 1

6 Bleed the hydraulic system using clean new fluid and discarding the old fluid bleed out.

26 Vacuum servo unit (later type) - dismantling examination and reassembly)

1 Grip the servo unit in a well padded vice by the slave cylinder body (1) (Fig. 9.18) with the air valve (23) uppermost.

2 Remove the rubber pipe (29) from the end cover connection.

3 Undo the screws securing the plastic air valve cover and lift off the cover assembly complete, which comprises the filter and valve. If the air valve is suspect a new assembly which is part of the complete repair kit will have to be obtained. (i.e. individual parts cannot be obtained separately).

3a The dome containing these items is a snap fit into the air valve cover.

4 Remove the rubber diaphragm and its plastic support, and the three valve housing securing screws will then be revealed. Undo these and take off the housing and joint washer.

5 To get the air control valve piston (28) out of its cylinder will require a low pressure inside the slave cylinder. This can be done by blocking one of the two hydraulic fluid unions on the slave cylinder with a finger and applying air pressure from a foot pump to the other. When it is out remove the rubber cup from the piston (for replacement).

6 The non-return valve (12) which is mounted in a rubber grommet (13) can be pushed out by thumb pressure. Remove the grommet also.

7 It is now necessary to remove the end cover (11) from the main servo shell (10). This is a twist fit bayonet type of connection and to remove it calls for an anti-clockwise twist as far as the stops in the cover will permit, when it will come off. Although there is a special tool for this (C2030) one can achieve the same result by remounting the servo on the car mounting bracket by the three end cover studs and gripping the shell and twisting it anti- clockwise. The end cover can be left on the mounting bracket.

8 Put the unit back into the vice as before. To remove the diaphragm it is not necessary to free the retaining key (16) from the pushrod (17).

Turn the diaphragm support (15) so that the retaining key

(16) points downwards. Then supply light fluctuating pressure to the backplate against the main return spring (18) and the retaining key will drop out.

9 Hold on to the diaphragm support and take it and the diaphragm and the return spring from the servo shell.

10 The bolts (19) holding the servo shell to the slave cylinder are now exposed. Bend back the locking plate table (20) from the bolt heads and remove the bolts, locking plate (20) and abutment plate (21).

11 The shell can now be taken from the slave cylinder. Retrieve the washer between the two.

12 The pushrod (17) can now be drawn from the slave cylinder together with piston assembly.

13 Slide the bearing (8) cup (7) and spacer (6) off the pushrod noting the order and position in which they came off.

14 Prise the rubber seal (4) off the slave piston (3).

15 If the rod is to be detached from the piston the following action will be required but a new retaining clip (9) will be needed. It should not normally be necessary to separate them. Open up the retaining clip (5) by twisting a small screwdriver in the join and this will expose the connection pin (9) which can be pushed out. This disconnects the slave piston fom the connection rod. This unit is now completely dismantled.

16 Examine all rubber cups and seals for wear and replace as necessary. If the air valve unit is in good condition and it is only necessary to clean the filter, blow it through with a tyre foot pump. Do not use any cleaning fluids or lubricants on the filter.

17 Wash all slave cylinder components in clean hydraulic fluid, and remove any deposits from the slave cylinder walls in the same way. If the slave cylinder is scored then it must be replaced.

18 Reassembly must be done in very clean conditions as a single speck of grit in the wrong place can cause total malfunction. It is best to wash your hands, get new clean cloths and lay out all the components on a sheet of clean white paper. 5 minutes extra attention now could save you another complete dismantling operation later.

19 Use clean hydraulic fluid as a lubricant when reassembling the hydraulic components.

20 If the piston and pushrod were separated push the rod into the rear of the piston against the spring until the connection pin hole is open. Fit the pin followed by the retaining clip. It is important to ensure that the clip fits snugly in its groove. Any protrusions will score the cylinder wall.

21 Refit the rubber seal (4) to the slave piston (3) using only the fingers ensuring that the lips of the seal face away from the pushrod.

22 Lubricate (with hydraulic fluid only) the cylinder bore and insert the piston. Then replace in correct order, over the pushrod the spacer (6) cup (7) and bearing (8) into the mouth of the slave cylinder. Ensure that each item placed into the cylinder has its sealing lips neither bent nor turned back and that each is bedded individually in turn.

23 The servo shell is now refitted in the reverse order as given in paragraph 10. If the locking plate (20) has been used more that once before (ie. if the servo has already been twice dismantled) a new one should be fitted. Tighten the bolts evenly to a torque figure of 17lb ft (2.35 kg fm) and tap up the locking plate tabs.

24 To replace the diaphragm, support and spring tap pull out the pushrod as far as possible. Fit the spring and diaphragm support ensuring that the spring ends are correctly located over the abutment plate (21) and the diaphragm support boss.

25 Press the diaphragm support over the pushrod with the key slot facing upwards and when the groove in the pushrod and the slot in the diaphragm are lined up insert the key.

26 Ensuring that the support and diaphragm are quite clean and dry fit the diaphragm to the support, gently stretching the inner edge to ensure that it seats properly in the groove of the support.

27 Smear the outer edge of the diaphragm with disc brake lubricant (not grease or hydraulic oil). This prevents it from binding when the lid cover is refitted to the servo shell.

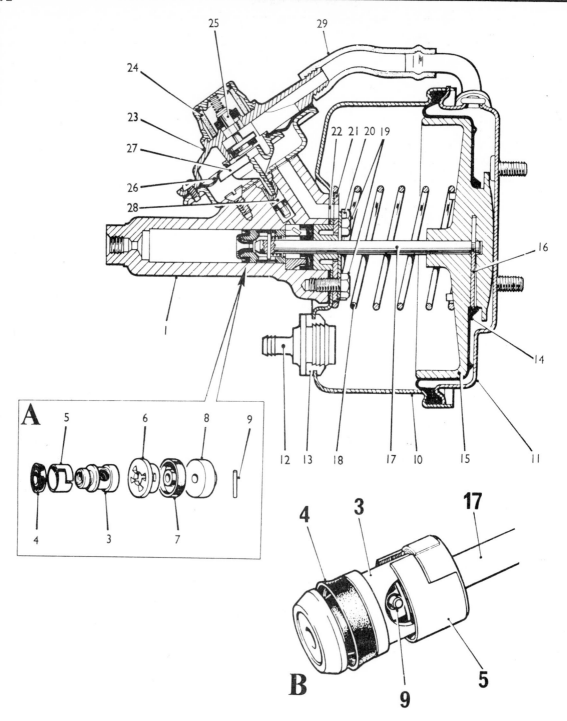

Fig. 9.18. Cross sectional view of vacuum servo unit (later type)
Inset 'A' shows exploded view of the slave piston
Inset 'B' shows the slave piston with the retaining clip withdrawn
to expose the connecting pin

1	Slave cylinder	9	Connecting pin	16	Retaining key	22	Joint washer
3	Slave piston	10	Servo shell	17	Push rod	23	Air valve cover
4	Piston seal	11	End cover	18	Main return spring	24	Air filter
5	Retaining clip	12	Non-return valve	19	Servo shaft retaining	25	Air valve
6	Spacer	13	Rubber mounting		bolts	26	Air valve diaphragm
7	Cup	14	Main servo diaphragm	20	Locking plate	27	Diaphragm support
8	Bearing	15	Diaphragm support	21	Abutment plate	28	Air valve piston
						29	Rubber pipe

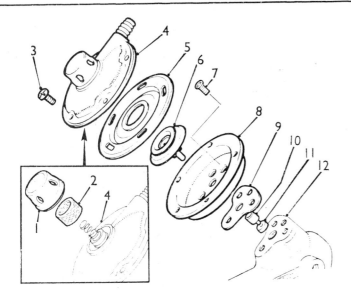

Fig. 9.19. Exploded view of servo unit air valve

1   Domed cover for filter
2   Air filter
3   Air valve cover securing screws
4   Air valve cover
5   Diaphragm
6   Diaphragm support
7   Valve housing securing screws
8   Valve housing
9   Joint washer
10 Piston
11 Piston cup
12 Slave cylinder

28 If no service tool is available fix the end cover onto the vehicle mounting bracket, (if you did not leave it there when taking it off) using the normal mounting units. Offer up the servo unit to the end cover so that when twisted clockwise the pipe will line up with the elbow on the end cover when the turn is completely up to the stops.

29 With the unit back on the bench replace the non-return valve and its mounting grommet.

30 To replace the air valve assembly first fit the rubber piston cup (11) (Fig.9.19) to the spigot of the piston (10) ensuring that the lips face away from the spigot shoulder. Lubricate the cup with a little hydraulic fluid and insert it into the slave cylinder taking care that the lips do not get bent back.

31 Fit the joint washer (9) and valve housing (8) to the slave cylinder (12) using the three securing screws (7).

32 Fit the diaphragm support (6) into the diaphragm (5) and make sure that the inner ring fits snugly into the groove in the support. Then place the spigot of the support into the hole in the air valve piston. Use no lubricants.

33 Line up the screw holes in the diaphragm (5) and the valve housing (8).

34 If the air filter, and dome have been removed (1 and 2) now is the time to snap the complete assembly back into the air valve cover (4).

35 Place the valve cover over the diaphragm so that the projection in the cover engage the slots in the diaphragm. Replace all five securing screws (3) finger tight. Tighten them down firmly, but not overtight, in a progressive and diagonal manner. This tightening sequence is important as the air valve must seat evenly and precisely. Any leak renders the whole servo inoperative.

36 Refit the rubber pipe from the valve cover port to the end cover elbow.

27 Hydraulic pipes and hoses - general

1 Periodically examine all brake pipes, pipe connections and unions thoroughly and carefully.

2 First examine for signs of leakage where the pipe unions occur. Then examine the flexible hoses for signs of chafing and fraying and, of course, leakage. This is only a preliminary part of the flexible hose inspection, as exterior condition does not necessarily indicate the interior condition, which will be considered later.

3 The steel pipes must be examined carefully and methodically. They must be cleaned off and examined for any signs of dents, or other damage and corrosion. Corrosion should be scraped off and, if the depth of pitting in the pipes is significant, they will need renewing. This is particularly likely in those areas under the car body where the pipes are exposed to road and weather conditions.

4 If any section of pipe is to be taken off, first wipe and then remove the fluid reservoir cap and place a piece of polythene over the reservoir neck. Refit the cap. This will stop syphoning during subsequent operations.

5 Rigid pipe removal is usually quite straightforward. The unions at each end are undone, the pipe and union pulled out, and the centre sections of the pipe removed from the body clips. Where the pipe unions are exposed to full force of road and weather they can sometimes be locked by corrosion. As one can only use an open ended spanner and the unions are not large burring of the flats is not uncommon when attempting to undo them. For this reason a selflocking grip wrench ('Mole') is often the only way to remove a stubborn union.

6 Removal of flexible hoses is described in Section 5.

7 With the flexible hose removed, examine the internal bore. If it is blown through first, it should be possible to see through it. Any specks of rubber which come out, or signs of restriction in the bore, means that the rubber lining is breaking up and the pipe must be renewed.

8 Rigid pipes which need renewing can usually be purchased at any garage where they have the pipe, unions and special tools to make them up. All they need to know is the total length of the pipe, the type of flare used at each end with the union, and the length and thread of the union. It is as well to take the old pipe to them.

9 Replacement of a pipe is a straightforward reversal of the removal procedure. If the rigid pipes have been made up it is best to get all the 'sets' (bends) in them before trying to install them. Also if there are any acute bends, ask your supplier to put these in for you on a special tube bender. Otherwise you may kink the pipe and thereby decrease the bore area and fluid flow.

10 With the pipe replaced, remove the polythene from the reservoir cap and bleed the hydraulic .

28 Dual line braking system - general description

For special model or market applications a dual line braking system is used. With this system the front brakes have a separate hydraulic system to that of the rear brakes so that if a failure occurs in either circuit half of the braking system is still operative. The information given in the remaining Sections of this Chapter is applicable to this braking system.

29 Brake system (dual line) - bleeding

1 Remove the reservoir cap and top up the fluid level. During the bleed operation it is important that the fluid level never drops by more that 0.5 in (1.25 m).

2 Wipe the nipples and attach bleed tubes to the front and rear bleed nipples on the drivers side of the car.

3 Submerge the open end of each bleed tube in a small quantity of clean brake fluid in the bottom of a clean jam jar.

4 Open both bleed screws one half of a turn.

5 An assistant should now depress the brake pedal and hold it down.

6 Close both bleed screws and allow the brake pedal to return slowly.

7 Repeat the operations in paragraphs 4-6 until no more air bubbles are seen; then repeat the operations a further four times.

8 With the brake pedal depressed tighten the bleed nipples to a torque wrench setting 4-6lb ft (0.5 - 0.8 kg fm).

9 Remove the bleed tubes and attach these to the front and rear bleed nipples on the opposite side of the car.

10 Repeat the previous operations for this side of the car.

30 Inertia valve (dual line braking system) - description, removal and replacement

An inertia valve is fitted into the hydraulic pipe to the rear brakes. It replaces the pressure regulating valve which is fitted to the standard braking system. (Section 19) although it is located in the same position on the rear subframe crossmember. It operates in the following manner. The angle at which the valve is mounted allows the steel ball inside the body to hold the valve in the open position. This means that hydraulic fluid may pass to the rear brakes. Upon heavy braking conditions the weight transfer to the front of the car will cause the ball to move away from the valve which is now closed by a light spring. Further pressure is thus prevented from reaching the rear brakes and all additional pressure is transferred to the front brakes.

1 To remove the inertia valve first wipe the top of brake master cylinder and remove the cap. Place a piece of polythene over the reservoir neck and replace the cap. This will stop syphoning of hydraulic fluid during subsequent operations.

2 Wipe all dust and dirt from the valve and hydraulic pipe.

3 Undo the brake pipe union nuts and detach the brake pipes.

4 Undo and remove the two fixing bolts and spring washers and lift away the inertia valve.

5 Refitting the inertia valve is the reverse sequence to removal

but the following additional points should be noted:
a) Ensure the valve is fitted the correct way round as denoted by the arrow and word "FRONT".
b) Bleed the hydraulic system as described in Section 29.
c) Road test the car and then inspect the valve and pipe unions for leaks.

31 Inertia valve (dual line braking system) - dismantling and re-assembly

1 With the exterior clean, undo and remove the end plug and washer.

2 Carefully tip out the steel ball.

3 Clean all parts in brake fluid or methylated spirits. Wipe dry and inspect all parts for wear, corrosion or damage. Any suspect part must be renewed.

4 Reassembly of the inertia valve is the reverse sequence to removal.

32 Pressure failure switch (dual line braking system) - description, removal and replacement

The pressure failure switch replaces the three-way brake pipe connection which is located on the right-hand side of the engine bulkhead crossmember.

1 To remove the switch; first, wipe the top of the brake master cylinder and remove the cap. Place a piece of polythene over the reservoir neck and replace the cap. This will stop syphoning of hydraulic fluid during subsequent operations.

2 Detach the electrical connector off the nylon switch.

3 Wipe the switch assembly and pipes free of dust.

4 Undo the brake pipe union nuts and detach the brake pipes.

5 Undo and remove the one retaining bolt and spring washer and lift away the pressure failure switch.

6 Refitting the switch is the reverse sequence to removal. It will be necessary to bleed the brake hydraulic system as described in Section 29.

33 Pressure failure switch (dual line braking system) - dismantling and reassembly

1 With the exterior clean unscrew and remove the end plug and discard the copper washer. **Note:** A new washer will be needed during reassembly.

2 Unscrew and lift away the nylon switch.

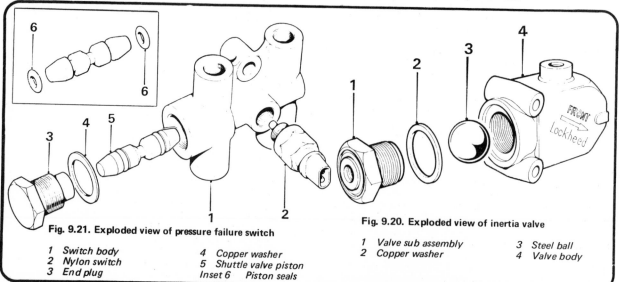

Fig. 9.21. Exploded view of pressure failure switch

1 Switch body	4 Copper washer
2 Nylon switch	5 Shuttle valve piston
3 End plug	Inset 6 Piston seals

Fig. 9.20. Exploded view of inertia valve

1 Valve sub assembly	3 Steel ball
2 Copper washer	4 Valve body

3 Shake out the shuttle valve piston assembly from the bore. If it is stubborn use an air line to free the piston.

4 Remove the two piston seals from the piston.

5 Clean all parts in brake fluid or methylated spirits. Wipe dry and inspect all parts for wear, corrosion or damage. Any suspect part must be renewed. If the bore is not in perfect condition the complete assembly must be renewed. Test the function of the switch using a test light and battery.

6 Reassembly of the switch is the reverse sequence to removal. Wet all parts with clean hydraulic fluid before inserting into the bore. It will be necessary to bleed the brake hydraulic system as described in Section 29.

34 Tandem master cylinder (dual line braking system) - removal and replacement

1 To remove the master cylinder first wipe the top of the brake master cylinder and remove the cap. Place a piece of polythene over the reservoir neck and replace the cap. This will stop loss of fluid from the reservoir until the master cylinder is away from the car.

2 Wipe the exterior or the master cylinder and pipe connections free from dust.

3 Unscrew the brake pipe union nuts and detach the brake pipes.

4 Undo and remove the two nuts and spring washers securing the master cylinder to the bulkhead.

5 Carefully lift away the master cylinder leaving the pushrod still attached to the brake pedal.

6 Refitting the master cylinder is the reverse sequence to removal. It will be necessary to bleed the hydraulic system as described in Section 29.

35 Tandem master cylinder (dual line braking system) - dismantling and reassembly

1 With the exterior clean, remove the reservoir cap and drain out any hydraulic fluid.

2 Slide off the rubber boot and mount the cylinder body between soft faces in a bench vice. The open end of the bore should face upwards.

3 Compress the return spring and using a small screwdriver remove the 'Spirolex' ring from its groove in the primary piston. Take care not to distort the coils of the ring or score the bore of the cylinder.

4 Using a pair of circlip pliers remove the piston retaining circlip.

5 Carefully move the piston up-and-down in the bore so as to free the nylon guide bearing and cap seal. Lift away the guide bearing seal.

6 Lift away the plain washer.

7 Using a pair of circlip pliers remove the inner circlip.

8 The primary and secondary piston assembly, complete with the stop washer may now be withdrawn from the cylinder bore.

9 Lift away the stop washer.

10 Compress the spring that separates the two pistons and then, using a small diameter parrellel pin punch, drive out the roll pin that retains the piston link.

11 Inspect and note the location of the rubber cups (look for the moulded indentations) and then remove the cups and washers from the pistons.

12 Undo and remove the four bolts that secure the plastic reservoir to the body and lift away the reservoir.

13 Recover the two reservoir sealing rings.

14 Unscrew and remove the hydraulic pipe connection adaptors, discard the copper gaskets and then recover the spring and trap valves.

15 Wash all parts in clean hydraulic fluid or methylated spirits and wipe dry.

16 Examine the bore of the cylinder carefully for any signs of scores or ridges. If this is found to be smooth all over new seals

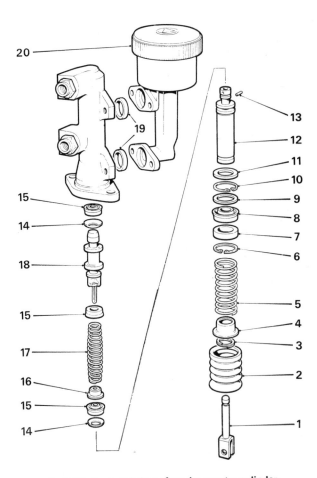

Fig. 9.22. Exploded view of tandem master cylinder

1	Push rod	11	Stop washer
2	Rubber boot	12	Primary piston
3	Spirolox ring	13	Roll pin
4	Spring retainer	14	Piston washer
5	Spring	15	Main cup
6	Circlip	16	Pin retainer
7	Nylon guide bearing	17	Spring
8	Secondary cup	18	Secondary piston
9	Washer	19	Reservoir seal
10	Circlip	20	Fluid reservoir

can be fitted. If, however, there is any doubt of the condition of the bore, then a new cylinder must be obtained and fitted.

17 If examination of the seals shows them to be apparently oversize, or swollen, or very loose on the plungers, suspect oil contamination in the system. Oil will swell these rubber seals, and if one is found to be swollen, it is reasonable to assume that all seals in the braking system will need attention.

18 Reassembly of the master cylinder is the reverse sequence to removal but the following additional points should be noted:

a) All components should be assembled wet by dipping in clean brake fluid.

b) Locate the piston washer over the head of the secondary piston, convex surface first, and then carefully ease the secondary cup over the piston and seat it with its flat surface against the washer.

c) Fit new copper gaskets to the connection adaptors.

d) The master cylinder is now ready for refitting to the car. Bleed the complete hydraulic system and road test the car.

36 Fault diagnosis - braking system

Symptom	Reason/s	Remedy
Pedal travels almost to the floor before brakes operate	Brake fluid level too low	Top up master cylinder reservoir. Check for leaks.
	Wheel cylinder or caliper leaking	Dismantle wheel cylinder or caliper, clean fit new rubbers and bleed brakes.
	Master cylinder leaking (Bubbles in master cylinder fluid)	Dismantle master cylinder, clean, and fit new rubbers. Bleed brakes.
	Brake flexible hose leaking	Examine and fit new hose if old hose leaking Bleed brakes.
	Brake line fractured	Replace with new brake pipe. Bleed brakes.
	Brake system unions loose	Check all unions in brake system and tighten as necessary. Bleed brakes.
	Linings over 75% worn	Fit replacement shoes and brake linings.
	Drum brakes badly out of adjustment	Jack up car and adjust rear brakes.
	Master cylinder pushrod out of adjustment, causing too much pedal free movement	Reset to manufacturer's specifications.
Brake pedal operation feels 'springy'	New linings not yet bedded-in	Use brakes gently until springy pedal feeling leaves.
	Brake drums or discs badly worn and weak or cracked	Fit new brake drums or discs.
	Master cylinder securing nuts loose	Tighten master cylinder securing nuts. Ensure spring washers are fitted.
Brake pedal operation feels 'spongy' & 'soggy'	Wheel cylinder or caliper leaking	Dismantle wheel cylinder or caliper, clean, fit new rubbers, and bleed brakes.
	Master cylinder leaking (Bubbles in master cylinder reservoir)	Dismantle master cylinder, clean, and fit new rubbers and bleed brakes. Replace cylinder if internal walls scored.
	Brake pipe line or flexible hose leaking	Fit new pipe line or hose.
	Unions in brake system loose	Examine for leaks, tighten as necessary.
Brake operation uneven - car pulls to one side	Linings and brake drums or discs contaminated with oil, grease, or hydraulic fluid	Ascertain and rectify source of leak, clean brake drums, fit new linings.
	Tyre pressures unequal	Check and inflate as necessary.
	Radial ply tyres fitted at one end of car only	Fit radial ply tyres of the same make to all four wheels.
	Brake backplate caliper or disc loose	Tighten backplate caliper or disc securing nuts and bolts.
	Brake shoes or pads fitted incorrectly	Remove and fit shoes or pads correct way round.
	Different type of linings fitted at each wheel	Fit the linings specified by the manufacturer's all round.
	Anchorages for front or rear suspension loose	Tighten front and rear suspension pick-up points including spring locations.
	Brake drums or discs badly worn, cracked or distorted	Fit new brake drums or discs.
Brakes tend to bind, drag or lock-on	Brake shoes adjusted too tightly	Slacken off rear brake shoe adjusters two clicks.
	Handbrake cable over-tightened	Slacken off handbrake cable adjustment.
	Master cylinder pushrod out of adjustment giving too little brake pedal free movement	Reset to manufacturer's specifications.
	Reservoir vent hole in cap blocked with dirt	Clean and blow through hole.
	Master cylinder by-pass port restricted - brakes seize in 'on' position	Dismantle, clean, and overhaul master cylinder. Bleed brakes.
	Wheel cylinder seizes in 'on' position	Dismantle, clean and overhaul wheel cylinder. Bleed brakes.
	Rear brake shoe pull off springs broken, stretched or loose	Examine springs and replace if worn or loose.
	Rear brake shoe pull off springs fitted wrong way round, omitted, or wrong type used	Examine, and rectify as appropriate.
	Handbrake system rusted or seized in the 'on' position	Apply 'Plus Gas' to free, clean and lubricate.

Chapter 10 Electrical system

Contents

Specifications

Battery:

Make ...	...	...	...	...	...	...	...	...	Lucas	
Type ...	...	...	...	...	...	...	...		BLT7A, BLTZ7A, BT7A, BTZ7A	
									CL7, CLZ7, C9, CZ9 (depending on model and date of manufacture)	

Capacity:									
BLT7A ...	...	...	...	...	...	...	...	34 amp hour at 20 hour rate
BLTZ7A	...	...	...	...	...	...	...	34 amp hour at 20 hour rate
BT7A ...	...	...	...	...	...	...	...	43 amp hour at 20 hour rate
BTZ7A ...	...	...	...	...	...	...	...	43 amp hour at 20 hour rate
CL7 ...	...	...	...	...	...	...	...	34 amp hour at 20 hour rate
CLZ7 ...	...	...	...	...	...	...	...	34 amp hour at 20 hour rate
C9 ...	...	...	...	...	...	...	...	43 amp hour at 20 hour rate
CZ9 ...	...	...	...	...	...	...	...	43 amp hour at 20 hour rate

Dynamo:

Make ...	...	...	...	...	...	...	...	...	Lucas
Type ...	...	...	...	...	...	...	...	...	C40/1
Max. output (current)	...	...	...	...	...	...			22 amps at 2250 rpm

Max. output (voltage) ... ...   13.5 volts
Cut-in speed ... ...   1450 rpm at 13.5 volts
Field resistance ... ...   6.0 ohms

Starter motor:
   Make ... ...   Lucas
   Type:
     Early models ... ...   M35G inertia
     Later models ... ...   M35J inertia

   M35G:
     Brush spring tension ... ...   15 — 25 oz. (425 — 709 gms)

   M35J:
     Brush spring tension ... ...   28 oz. (794 gms)
     Light running current ... ...   65 amps at 8,000 - 10,000 rpm)
     Lock torque ... ...   7 lb f ft (0.97 kg fm) with 350 — 375 amps

Control box:
   Make ... ...   Lucas
   Type ... ...   RB 106/2
   Cutout:
     Cut-in voltage ... ...   12.7 — 13.3 volts
     Drop off voltage ... ...   8.5 — 11.0 volts
     Reverse current ... ...   3 — 5 amps

   Regulator (at 3,000 rpm dynamo speed) open circuit setting
   at 20º C (68º F) ... ...   16.0 — 16.6 volts

Alternator:
   Make ... ...   Lucas
   Type ... ...   11 AC or 16ACR

   11AC:
     Maximum output ... ...   43 amps
     Rotor windings:
     Resistance ... ...   3.8 $\pm$ 0.2 ohms at 20º C (68º F)
     Current ... ...   3.2 amps at 12 volts
     Minimum brush length ... ...   0.156 in (3.969 mm)
     Brush spring pressure:
       0.781 in (19.85 mm) compressed length ... ...   4 — 5 oz (113 — 142 gms)
       0.406 in. (10.32 mm) compressed length ... ...   7.5 — 8.5 oz (212 — 241 gms)
     Control unit:
       Make ... ...   Lucas
       Type 4TR
       Voltage setting at 3000 alternator rpm ... ...   13.9 — 14.3 volts
       Circuit resistance (max.) ... ...   0.1 ohm
     Field isolating relay ... ...   Lucas 6RA
     Warning light control ... ...   Lucas 3AW

   16ACR:
     Maximum output ... ...   34 amps at 6000 rpm (engine - 2800 rpm)
     Nominal system voltage ... ...   14.2 volts at 20% max. output
     Max. continuous speed ... ...   12,500 rpm
     Resistance of rotor winding ... ...   4.33 ohms $\pm$ 5% at 20º C (68º F)
     Brush spring tension ... ...   7 — 10 oz. (198 — 283 gms)

Windscreen wiper:
   Type:
     Early models and Moke ... ...   Single speed
     Later models ... ...   14w Single or two speed
   Single speed:
     Normal running current ... ...   2.0 — 3.1 amps at 12 volts
     Armature resistance ... ...   0.28 — 0.35 ohms
     Field resistance ... ...   8.0 — 9.5 ohms
   Two speed:
     Light running speed (rack disconnected): ... ...
       Normal speed ... ...   46 — 52 rpm
       High speed ... ...   60 — 70 rpm
     Light running current:
       Normal speed ... ...   1.5 amps
       High speed ... ...   2.0 amps
     Brush spring pressure ... ...   5 — 7 oz. (140 — 200 gms)

Min. brush length	0.187 in. (4.8 mm)	
Armature end float	0.002 − 0.008 in. (0.05 − 0.2 mm)	
Max. pull to move rack in tube	6 lb (2.7 kg)	
Windscreen wiper arm spring pressure	7 − 9 oz. (200 − 255 gms)	

Bulbs:

Replacement bulbs:	*Voltage*	*Wattage*
Headlamps, LHD (except Europe - dip right)	12	50/40
Headlamps, Europe (except France - dip vertical)	12	45/40
Headlamps, France (dip vertical)	12	45/40
Direction indicators	12	21
Sidelamps and flasher repeaters	12	6
Number plate lamp (Saloon)	12	6
Number plate lamp (Estate)	12	6
Tail and stop lamps	12	21/6
Interior lamp	12	6
Panel and warning lamps	12	2.2

Sealed beam light units:		
Headlamps (UK only - dip left)	12	60/45
Headlamps (RHD - not UK)	12	60/50
Headlamps (N. America)	12	60/45
Headlamps (LHD - dip right)	12	60/50

Torque wrench settings:	**lb f ft**	**kg f m**
Alternator (11AC)		
Brush box fixing screws	10	1.38
Through bolts	45 − 50	6.22 − 6.9
Diode heat sink fixings	25	3.4
Alternator (16ACR)		
Shaft nut	25 − 30	3.5 − 4.2

1 General description

The electrical system is of the 12 volt type. The major components comprise a 12 volt battery, a voltage regulator and cutout, a Lucas dynamo or alternator which is fitted to the front right-hand side of the engine and is driven from the pulley on the front of the crankshaft; and a starter motor which is mounted on the rear right-hand side of the engine.

The battery supplies a steady current for the ignition, lighting and other electrical circuits, and provides a reserve of electricity when the current consumed by the electrical equipment exceeds that being produced by the dynamo or alternator.

The dynamo is of the brush type and works in conjunction with the voltage regulator and cutout. It is cooled by a multi-bladed fan mounted behind the dynamo pulley, which blows air through cooling holes in the dynamo end brackets. The output of the dynamo is controlled by the voltage regulator; this ensures a high output if the battery is in a low state of charge or the demand from the electrical system is high, and a low output if the battery is fully charged and there is little demand from the electrical equipment.

Later Minis were fitted with an alternator and further information on this unit will be found later on in this Chapter. At the same time the negative terminal of the battery was earthed instead of the positive terminal.

When fitting electrical accessories to cars with a negative earth system it is important (if they contain silicon diodes or transistors) that they are connected correctly, otherwise serious damage may result to the component concerned. Items such as radios, tape players and electronic tachometers, should all be checked for correct polarity before fitment.

It is also important that the battery leads are disconnected when the battery is boost charged or if body repairs are to be carried out using electric arc welding equipment - otherwise serious damage can be caused to the more delicate instruments.

2 Battery - removal and replacement

1 The battery is fitted in a recess in the right-hand side of the floor of the boot in saloon models; beneath the loading platform on the Countryman and Traveller; and behind the passenger seat on the van. Disconnect the positive and then the negative leads from the battery terminals by slackening the retaining nuts and bolts, or by unscrewing the retaining screws if these are fitted (photo).

2 Remove the battery clamp and carefully lift the battery out of its compartment. Hold the battery vertical to ensure that

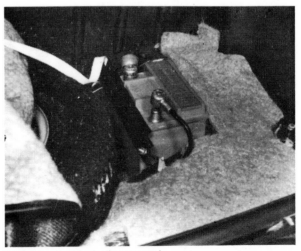

2.1 Battery terminals disconnected

none of the electrolyte is spilled.

3 Replacement is a direct reversal of this procedure. **Note**: Replace the negative lead before the positive lead and smear the terminals with petroleum jelly (vaseline) to prevent corrosion. **Never** use an ordinary grease as applied to other parts of the car.

3 Battery - maintenance and inspection

1 Normal weekly battery maintenance consists of checking the electrolyte level of each cell to ensure that the separators are covered by ¼ in (5 mm) of electrolyte. If the level has fallen, top up the battery using distilled water only. Do not overfill. If the battery is overfilled or any electrolyte spilled, immediately wipe away the excess as electrolyte attacks and corrodes any metal it comes into contact with very rapidly.

2 As well as keeping the terminals clean and covered with petroleum jelly, the top of the battery, and especially the top of the cells, should be kept clean and dry. This helps prevent corrosion and ensures that the battery does not become partially discharged by leakage through dampness and dirt.

3 Once every three months remove the battery and inspect the battery securing bolts, the battery clamp plate, tray, and battery leads for corrosion (white fluffy deposits on the metal which are brittle to touch). If any corrosion is found, clean off the deposits with ammonia and paint over the clean metal with an anti-rust/anti-acid paint.

4 At the same time inspect the battery case for cracks. If a crack is found, clean and plug it with one of the proprietary compounds marketed by firms such as 'Holts' for this purpose. If leakage through the crack has been excessive then it will be necessary to refill the appropriate cell with fresh electrolyte as detailed later. Cracks are frequently caused to the top of the battery cases by pouring in distilled water in the middle of winter **after** instead of **before** a run. This gives the water no chance to mix with the electrolyte and so the former freezes and splits the battery case.

5 If topping up the battery becomes excessive and the case has been inspected for cracks that could cause leakage, but none are found, the battery is being overcharged and the voltage regulator will have to be checked and reset.

6 With the battery on the bench at the three monthly interval check, measure its specific gravity with a hydrometer to determine its state of charge and condition of the electrolyte. There should be very little variation between the different cells and if a variation in excess of 0.025 is present it will be due to either:

a) Loss of electrolyte from the battery at some time caused by spillage or a leak resulting in a drop in the specific gravity of the electrolyte, when the deficiency was replaced with distilled water instead of fresh electrolyte.

b) An internal short circuit caused by buckling of the plates or a similar malady pointing to the likelihood of total battery failure in the near future.

7 The specific gravity of the electrolyte for fully charged conditions at the electrolyte temperature indicated, is listed in Table "A". The specific gravity of a fully discharged battery at different temperatures of the electrolyte is given at Table "B".

TABLE A

Specific Gravity - Battery fully charged

1.268 at 100°F or 38°C electrolyte temperature
1.272 at 90°F or 32°C   ''   ''
1.276 at 80°F or 27°C   ''   ''
1.280 at 70°F or 21°C   ''   ''
1.284 at 60°F or 16°C   ''   ''
1.288 at 50°F or 10°C   ''   ''
1.292 at 40°F or 4°C   ''   ''
1.296 at 30°F or -1.5°C   ''   ''

TABLE B

Specific Gravity - Battery fully charged

1.098 at 100°F or 38°C electrolyte temperature
1.102 at 90°F or 32°C   ''   ''
1.106 at 80°F or 27°C   ''   ''
1.110 at 70°F or 21°C   ''   ''
1.114 at 60°F or 16°C   ''   ''
1.118 at 50°F or 10°C   ''   ''
1.122 at 40°F or 4°C   ''   ''
1.126 at 30°F or -1.5°C   ''   ''

4 Battery - electrolyte replenishment

If the battery is in a fully charged state and one of the cells maintains a specific gravity reading which is 0.025 or more lower than the others, and a check of each cell has been made with a voltage meter to check for short circuits (a four to seven second test should give a steady reading of between 1.2 to 1.8 volts), then it is likely that electrolyte has been lost from the cell with the low reading at some time.

Top the cell up with a solution of 1 part sulphuric acid to 2.5 parts of water. If the cell is already fully topped up draw some electrolyte out of it with a pipette. The total capacity of each cell is 0.75 pint (0.427 litre). When mixing the sulphuric acid and water **never add water to sulphuric acid** - always pour the acid slowly onto the water in a glass container. **If water is added to sulphuric acid it will explode**. Continue to top up the cell with the freshly made electrolyte and then recharge the battery and check the hydrometer readings.

5 Battery charging

In winter time when heavy demand is placed upon the battery, such as when starting from cold, and much electrical equipment is continually in use, it is a good idea to occasionally have the battery fully charged from an external source at the rate of 3.5 to 4 amps. Continue to charge the battery at this rate until no further rise in specific gravity is noted over a four hour period. Alternatively a trickle charger charging at the rate of 1.5 amps can be safely used overnight. Specially rapid 'boost' charges which are claimed to restore the power of the battery in 1 to 2 hours are dangerous as they can cause serious damage to the battery plates through overheating. While charging the battery note that the temperature of the electrolyte should never exceed 100°F (37.8°C) Do not forget to disconnect the battery from the car's electrical system (if an alternator is fitted) before connecting up the charger.

6 Dynamo - maintenance

1 Routine maintenance consists of checking the tension of the fan belt, and lubricating the dynamo rear bearing once every 6,000 miles (10,000 km).

2 The fan belt should be tight enough to ensure no slip between the belt and the dynamo pulley. If a shrieking noise comes from the engine when the unit is accelerated rapidly then it is likely that it is the fan belt slipping. On the other hand, the belt must not be too taut or the bearings will wear rapidly and cause dynamo failure or bearing seizure. Ideally 0.5 in (12.7 mm) of total free movement should be available at the fan belt midway between the fan and the dynamo pulley. To adjust the fan belt tension slightly slacken the three dynamo retaining bolts, and swing the dynamo on the upper two bolts outwards to increase the tension, and inwards to lower it. It is best to leave the bolts fairly tight so that considerable effort has to be used to move the dynamo; otherwise it is difficult to get the correct setting. If the dynamo is being moved outwards to increase the tension and the bolts have only been slackened a little, a long spanner acting as a

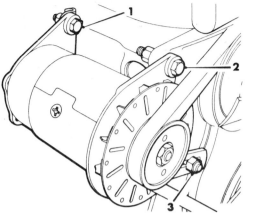

Fig. 10.1. Dynamo (left) and alternator (right) mountings

1 Securing nut and bolt (rear)   *2 Securing nut and bolt (front)*   *3 Adjustment link fixings*

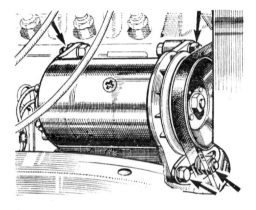

Fig. 10.2. Fan belt adjustment
Slacken the four nuts and bolts and move the dynamo in or out to adjust the fan belt tension

lever placed behind the dynamo with the lower end resting against the block works very well in moving the dynamo outwards. Retighten the dynamo bolts and check that the dynamo pulley is correctly aligned with the fan belt.
3 Lubrication on the C40 dynamo consists of inserting three drops of engine oil in the small oil hole in the centre of the commutator end bracket. This lubricates the rear bearing. The front bearing is pre-packed with grease and requires no attention.

7 Dynamo - testing in position

1 If, with the engine running no charge comes from the dynamo, or the charge is very low, first check that the fan belt is in place and is not slipping. Then check that the leads from the control box to the dynamo are firmly attached and that one has not come loose from its terminal. The lead from the 'D' terminal on the dynamo should be connected to the 'D' terminal on the control box, and similarly the 'F' terminals on the dynamo and control box should also be connected together.
2 Disconnect the leads from terminals 'D' and 'F' on the dynamo and then join the terminals together with a short length of wire. Attach to the centre of this length of wire the negative clip of a 0-20 volts voltmeter and run the other clip to earth. Start the engine and allow it to idle at approximately 750 rpm. At this speed the dynamo should give a reading of about 15 volts on the voltmeter. There is no point in raising the engine speed above a fast idle as the reading will then be inaccurate.
3 If no reading is recorded then check the brushes and brush

connections. If a very low reading of approximately 1 volt is observed then the field winding may be suspect. On early dynamos it was possible to remove the dynamo cover band and check the dynamo and brushes in position. With the Lucas C40 windowless yoke dynamo, fitted to all models, the dynamo has to be removed and dismantled before the brushes and commutator can be attended to.
4 If the voltmeter shows a good reading then with the temporary link still in position connect both leads from the control box to 'D' and 'F' on the dynamo ('D' to 'D' and 'F' to 'F'). Release the lead from the 'D' terminal at the control box end and clip one lead from the voltmeter to the end of the cable, and the other lead to a good earth. With the engine running at the same speed as previously, an identical voltage to that recorded at the dynamo should be noted on the voltmeter. If no voltage is recorded then there is a break in the wire. If the voltage is the same as recorded at the dynamo then check the 'F' lead in similar fashion. If both readings are the same as at the dynamo then it will be necessary to test the control box.

8 Dynamo - removal and replacement

1 Slacken the two dynamo retaining bolts, and the nut on the sliding link, and move the dynamo in towards the engine so that the fan belt can be removed.
2 Disconnect the two leads from the dynamo terminals. **Note:** If the ignition coil is mounted on top of the dynamo, remove the high tension wire from the centre of the coil by unscrewing the knurled nut, and unscrew the nuts holding the two low tension wires in place.
3 Remove the nut from the sliding link bolt, and remove the two upper bolts. The dynamo is then free to be lifted away from the engine.
4 Replacement is a reversal of the above procedure. Do not finally tighten the retaining bolts and the nut on the sliding link until the fan belt has been tensioned correctly.
5 If it is wished to fit a replacement dynamo, check the identification marks which will be found on the yoke, and quote these to your local BLMC garage or Lucas agent prior to handing the dynamo in to ensure a replacement is available.

9 Dynamo - dismantling and reassembly

1 Remove the dynamo pulley after unscrewing the nut and lockwasher which retains it to the armature shaft. (It is not necessary to do this if only the brushes and commutator are to be examined).
2 From the commutator end bracket remove the nuts, spring, and flat washers from the field terminal post. (Not necessary

where LUCAR connectors are fitted).

3 Unscrew the two through bolts and remove them together with their spring washers.

4 Take off the commutator end bracket, and remove the driving end bracket complete with the armature.

5 Lift the brush springs and draw the brushes out of the brush holders. Unscrew the screws and lockwashers holding the brush leads to the commutator end bracket.

6 The bearings need not be removed, or the armature shaft separated from the drive end bracket unless the bearings or the armature are to be renewed. If it is wished to remove the armature shaft from the drive end bracket and bearing (and this is necessary for bearing renewal) then the bearing retaining plate must be supported securely, and with the Woodruff key removed the shaft pressed out of the end bracket.

7 When a new armature is fitted or the old one replaced, it is most important that the inner journal of the ball bearing is supported by a steel tube of suitable diameter so that no undue strain is placed on the bearing as the armature shaft is pressed home.

8 Reassembly is a straight reversal of the above process. A point worth noting is that when fitting the commutator end plate with brushes attached, it is far easier to slip the brushes over the commutator if the brushes are raised in their holders and held in this position by the pressure of the springs resting against their flanks rather than on their heads.

10 Dynamo - inspection and repair

1 First check the brushes for wear. Any brush less than 0.5 in (12.7 mm) long on the C40 unit, must be replaced. Check that the brushes move freely and easily in their holders by removing the retaining springs and then pulling gently on the wire brush leads. If either of the brushes tend to stick in their holders clean the brushes with a petrol moistened rag and if still stiff, lightly polish the sides of the brush with a very fine file until the brush moves quite freely and easily in its holder.

2 If the brushes are but little worn and are to be used again then ensure that they are placed in the same holders from which they were removed. Check the tension of the brush springs with a spring balance. The tension of the springs when new was 26 oz

falling to 18 oz when the brush was sufficiently worn to warrent replacement.

3 Check the condition of the commutator, If the surface is dirty or blackened, clean it with a petrol dampened rag. If the commutator is in good condition the surface will be smooth and quite free from pits or burnt areas, and the insulated segments clearly defined.

4 If, after the commutator has been cleaned, pits and burnt spots are still present, then wrap a strip of glass paper round the commutator and rotate the armature.

5 In extreme cases of wear the commutator can be mounted in a lathe and with the lathe turning at high speed, a very fine cut may be taken off the commutator. Then polish the commutator with glass paper. If the commutator has worn so that the insulators between the segments are level with the top of the segments, then undercut the insulators to a depth of 0.0313 in (0.79 mm). The best tool to use for this purpose is half a hacksaw blade ground to the thickness of the insulator, and with the handle end of the blade covered in insulating tape to make it comfortable to hold. On later models using generators of the moulded type, the commutator should not be undercut more than 0.020 in (0.508 mm) deep, or 0.040 in (1.016 mm) wide.

6 Check the armature for open or short circuited windings. It is a good indication of an open circuited armature when the commutator segments are burnt. If the armature has short circuited the commutator segments will be very badly burnt, and the overheated armature windings badly discoloured. If open or short circuits are suspected then test by substituting the suspect armature for a new one.

7 Check the resistance of the field coils. To do this, connect an ohmmeter between the field terminal and the yoke and note the reading on the ohmmeter which should be about 6 ohms. If the ohmmeter reading is infinity this indicates an open circuit in the field winding. If the ohmmeter reading is below 5 ohms this indicates that one of the field coils is faulty and must be replaced.

8 Field coil replacement involves the use of a wheel operated screwdriver, a soldering iron, caulking and riveting and this operation is considered to be beyond the scope of most owners. Therefore, if the field coils are at fault either purchase a rebuilt dynamo, or take the casing to a reputable electrical engineering works for new field coils to be fitted.

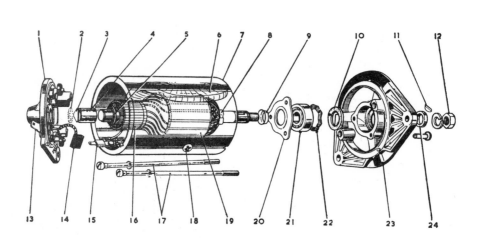

Fig. 10.3. The Lucas C40/1 dynamo

1 Commutator end bracket	7 Yoke	13 Output terminal 'D'	19 Armature
2 Felt ring	8 Shaft collar	14 Brushes	20 Bearing retaining plate
3 Felt ring retainer	9 Shaft collar retaining cup	15 Field terminal 'F'	21 Ball bearing
4 Bronze bush	10 Felt ring	16 Commutator	22 Corrugated washer
5 Thrust washer	11 Shaft key	17 Through bolts	23 Driving end bracket
6 Field coils	12 Shaft nut	18 Pole shoe securing screws	24 Pulley spacer

11 Dynamo bearings - inspection, removal and replacement

With the dynamo partially stripped down, check the condition of the bearings. They must be renewed when wear has reached such a state that they allow visible side movement of the armature shaft. A bush bearing is fitted to the commutator end bracket and a ball bearing to the drive end bracket. To renew the bush bearing proceed as follows:

1 With a suitable extractor pull out the old bush from the commutator end bracket. Alternatively screw a 5/8 in tap into the C40 bush and pull out the bush together with the tap.

2 **Note:** When fitting the new bush bearing, it is of the porous bronze type, and it is essential that it is allowed to stand in engine oil for at least 24 hours before fitment.

3 Carefully fit the new bush into the end plate, pressing it in until the end of the bearing is flush with the inner side of the end plate. If available press the bush in with a smooth shouldered mandrel the same diameter as the armature shaft. To renew the ball bearing fitted to the drive end bracket remove the armature from the end bracket, as detailed in Section 9, and then proceed as follows:

4 Drill out the rivets which hold the bearing retainer plate to the end bracket and lift off the plate.

5 Press out the bearing from the end bracket and remove the corrugated washer and felt washer from the bearing housing.

6 Thoroughly clean the bearing housing, and the new bearing and pack with high melting-point grease.

7 Place the felt washer and corrugated washer in that order in the end bracket bearing housing, and then press in the new bearing.

8 Replace the plate and fit new rivets opening out the rivet ends to hold the plate securely in position. **Note:** On the C40 dynamo the rivets are fitted from the outer face of the end bracket.

12 Control box - general description

The control box comprises the voltage regulator and the cut-out. The voltage regulator controls the output from the dynamo depending on the state of the battery and the demands of the electrical equipment, and ensures that the battery is not over-charged. The cutout is really an automatic switch and connects the dynamo to the battery when the dynamo is turning fast enough to produce a charge. Similarly it disconnects the battery from the dynamo when the engine is idling or stationary so that the battery does not discharge through the dynamo.

13 Cutout and regulator contacts - maintenance

1 Every 12,000 miles (20,000 km) check the cutout and regulator contacts. If they are dirty or rough or burnt, place a piece of fine glass paper (do not use emery paper or carborundum paper) between the cutout contacts, close them manually and draw the glass paper through several times.

2 Clean the regulator contacts in exactly the same way, but use emery or carborundum paper and not glass paper. Carefully clean both sets of contacts from all traces of dust with a rag moistened in methylated spirits.

14 Voltage regulator - adjustment

If the battery is in sound condition, but is not holding its charge, or is being continually overcharged, and the dynamo is in sound condition, then the voltage regulator in the control mox must be adjusted.

Check the regulator setting by removing and joining together the cables from the control box terminals 'A1' and 'A'. Then connect the negative lead of a 20 volt voltmeter to the 'D' terminal on the dynamo and the positive lead to a good earth. Start the engine and increase its speed until the voltmeter needle flicks and then steadies. This should occur at about 2,000 rpm. If the voltage at which the needle steadies is outside the limits listed below, then remove the control box cover and turn the adjusting screw clockwise, a quarter of a turn at a time to raise the setting and a similar amount, anticlockwise, to lower it (Fig. 10.5).

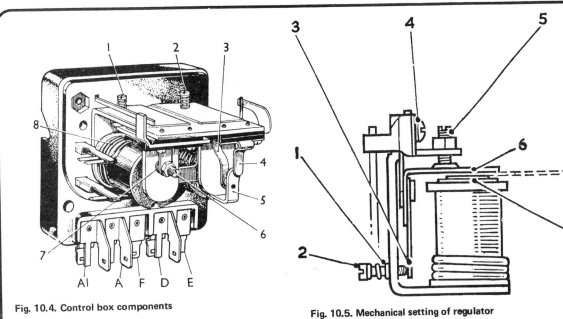

Fig. 10.4. Control box components

1 *Regulator adjusting screw*	5 *Armature tongue and moving contact*
2 *Cut-out adjusting screw*	6 *Regulator fixed contact screw*
3 *Fixed contact blade*	7 *Regulator moving contact*
4 *Stop arm*	8 *Regulator series windings*

Fig. 10.5. Mechanical setting of regulator

1 *Locknut*	5 *Fixed contact adjustment screw*
2 *Voltage adjusting screw*	6 *Armature*
3 *Armature tension spring*	7 *Core face and shim*
4 *Armature securing screws*	8 *0.021 in. (0.533 mm)*

Air Temperature	Type RB 106/2 Open circuit voltage
10°C or 50°F	16.1 to 16.7
20°C or 68°F	16.0 to 16.6
30°C or 86°F	15.9 to 16.5
40°C or 104°F	15.8 to 16.4

It is vital that the adjustments be completed within 30 seconds of starting the engine as otherwise the heat from the shunt coil will affect the readings.

15 Cutout - adjustment

Check the voltage required to operate the cutout by connecting a voltmeter between the control box terminals 'D' and 'E'. Remove the control box cover, start the engine and gradually increase its speed until the cutouts close. This should occur when the reading is between 12.7 and 13.3 volts. If the reading is outside these limits turn the cutout adjusting screw a fraction at a time clockwise to raise the voltage, and anticlockwise to lower it. To adjust the drop off voltage bend the fixed contact blade carefully. The adjustment to the cutout should be completely within 30 seconds of starting the engine as otherwise heat build-up from the shunt coil will affect the readings (Fig. 10.6).

If the cutout fails to work, clean the contacts and, if there is still no response, renew the cutout and regulator unit.

16 Alternator - general description

Although not standard yet on all models the Lucas 11AC alternator/4TR control unit and, more lately, the 16ACR alternator with control unit incorporated, may be found fitted on late models of all Minis in place of the standard C40 dynamo. The 11AC/4TR type was quickly superseded by the 16ACR which will form the basis of the following information. Alternators are a sophisticated means for electrical generation, incorporating the fruits of modern techinal research into the fields of semi-conductors and micro circuitry technique. With the exception of one or two items there is little that the average owner can hope to achieve in the case of difficulties or failure. Some components are hermetically sealed and the test equipment alone to check the circuitry would be rarely found in the most enthusiastic owner's workshop. The present high cost of alternators (about 4-5 times that of the dynamo) also discourages non-specialist repair.

The main advantage of the alternator lies in its ability to provide a high charge at slow revolutions. Driving slowly in heavy traffic with a dynamo invariably means no charge is reaching the battery. In similar conditions even with the wipers, heater, lights and perhaps radio switched on, an alternator will ensure a charge reaches the battery.

An important feature of the alternator is a built-in output control regulator, based on 'thick film' hybrid integrated micro-circuit technique, which results in this alternator being a self contained generating and control unit.

The system provides for direct connection of a charge light, and eliminates the need for a field switching relay and warning light control unit, necessary with former systems.

The alternator is of the rotating field ventilated design and comprises principally, a laminated stator on which is wound a star connected 3 - phase output winding; a twelve pole rotor carrying the field windings - each end of the rotor shaft runs in ball race bearings which are lubricated for life; natural finish aluminium die cast end brackets, incorporating the mounting lugs; a rectifier pack for converting the AC output of the machine to DC for battery charging; and an output control regulator.

The rotor is belt driven from the engine through a pulley

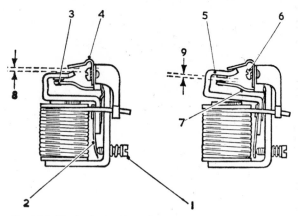

Fig. 10.6. Mechanical setting of cutout

1 Cutout adjusting screw	5 Armature tongue and
2 Armature tension spring	moving contact
3 'Follow through' - 010 to	6 Armature securing screws
.020 in (.25 to .51 mm)	7 Fixed contact blade
4 Stop arm	8 0.030 in (0.76 mm)
	9 0.01 to 0.02 in (0.25 to
	0.51 mm)

keyed to the rotor shaft. A pressed steel fan adjacent to the pulley draws cooling air through the machine. This fan forms an integral part of the alternator specification. It has been designed to provide adequate air flow with a minimum of noise, and to withstand the high stresses associated with maximum speed. Rotation is clockwise viewed on the drive end. Maximum continuous rotor speed is 12,500 rpm.

Rectification of alternator output is achieved by six silicon diodes housed in a rectifier pack and connected as a 3-phase full-wave bridge. The rectifier pack is attached to the outer face of the slip ring end bracket and contains also three 'field' diodes. At normal operating speeds, rectified current from the stator output windings flows through these diodes to provide self-excitation of the rotor field, via brushes bearing on face type slip rings.

The slip rings are carried on a small diameter moulded drum attached to the rotor shaft outboard of the rotor shaft axle, while the outer ring has a mean diameter of 0.75 in (19.05 mm). By keeping the mean diameter of the slip rings to a minimum, relative speeds between brushes and rings, and hence wear, are also minimal. The slip rings are connected to the rotor field winding by wires carried in grooves in the rotor shaft.

The brush gear is housed in a moulding screwed to the outside of the slip ring end bracket. This moulding thus encloses the slip ring and brush gear assembly, and, together with the shielded bearing, protects the assembly against the entry of dust and moisture.

The regulator is set during manufacture and requires no further attention. Briefly the 'thick film' regulator comprises resistors and conductors screen printed onto a 1 inch square alumina substrate. Mounted on the substrate are Lucas semiconductors consisting of three transistors, a voltage reference diode and a field recirculation diode, and also two capacitors. The internal connections between these components and the substrate are made by Lucas patented connectors. The whole assembly is 1/16 inch thick, and is housed in a recess in an aluminium heat sink, which is attached to the slip ring end bracket. Complete hermetic sealing is achieved by a silicon rubber encapsulant to provide environmental protection.

Electrical connections to external circuits are brought out to Lucar connector blades, these being grouped to accept a moulded connector socket which ensures correct connections.

17 Alternator - routine maintenance

1 The equipment has been designed for the minimum amount of maintenance in service, the only items subject to wear being

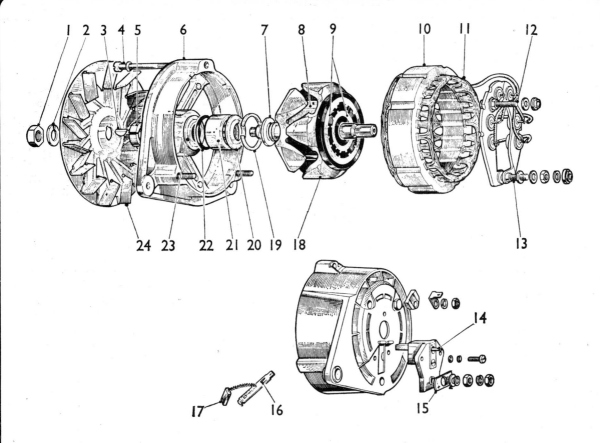

Fig. 10.7. Lucas 11AC alternator

1	Shaft nut	7 Jump ring shroud	14 Field terminal blade	19 Bearing circlip
2	Spring washer	8 Rotor (field) winding	15 Output terminal plastic	20 Bearing retaining plate
3	Key	9 Slip rings	strip	21 Ball bearing
4	Through bolt	10 Stator laminations	16 Terminal blade retaining	22 'O' ring oil seal
5	Distance collar	11 Stator windings	tongue	23 'O' ring retaining washer
6	Drive end bracket	12 Warning light terminal	17 Brush	24 Fan
		13 Output terminal	18 Rotor	

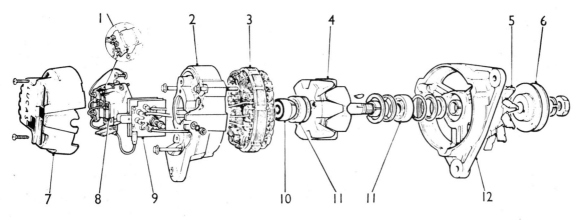

Fig. 10.8. Lucas 16 ACR alternator

1 Regulator pack	4 Rotor	7 End cover	10 Slip rings
2 Slip ring end bracket	5 Fan	8 Brush box moulding	11 Rotor bearings
3 Stator	6 Pulley	9 Rectifier pack	12 Drive end bracket

the brushes and bearings.

2 Brushes should be examined after 60.000 miles (100,000 km) and renewed if necessary. This is a job best left to an auto electrician.

3 The bearings are pre-packed with grease for life, and should not require any further attention.

18 Alternator - special procedures

1 A replacement alternator must always be checked to ensure that polarity connections are correct. They are clearly marked and wrong connection can damage the equipment.

2 Never reverse battery connections. The rectifiers could be damaged.

3 Always connect up the battery earth terminal first.

4 Disconnect the alternator/control unit whenever the battery is being charged in position, as a safety precaution.

5 Never disconnect the battery with the engine running, nor run the alternator with the output cable disconnected anywhere, or any other alternator circuits disconnected.

6 The cable between battery and alternator is always "live". Take care not to short it to earth.

19 Alternator - removal and replacement

1 Withdraw the connector terminal block from the alternator terminal output in the end cover.

2 Remove the bolt holding the fan belt tensioning link to the alternator.

3 Slacken the alternator mounting bolts and slip the fan belt over the pulley.

4 Remove the mounting bolts completely and take out the alternator.

5 Refitting the alternator is the reverse sequence to removal. The fan belt should be correctly adjusted so that a deflection of 0.5 in (12.7 mm) is possible (finger pressure) in the centre of its longest run.

20 Alternator (16ACR) brush - inspection, removal and replacement

1 Referring to Fig. 10.8 remove the end cover by undoing the

screws.

2 To inspect the brushes correctly the brush holder moulding should be removed completely by undoing the two bolts and disconnecting the 'Lucar' connection to the diode plates.

3 With the brush holder moulding removed and the brush assemblies still in position check that they protrude from the face of the moulding by at least 0.2 in (5 mm). Also check that when depressed, the spring pressure is 7-10 oz when the end of the brush is flush with the face of the brush moulding. To be done with any accuracy this requires a push type spring gauge.

4 Should either of the foregoing requirements not be fulfilled the spring assemblies should be replaced.

5 This can be done simply by renewing the holding screws of each assembly and replacing them.

6 With the brush holder moulding removed the slip rings on the face end of the rotor are exposed. These can be cleaned with a petrol soaked cloth and any signs of burning may be removed very carefully with fine glass paper. On no account should any other abrasive be used or any attempt at machining be made.

When the brushes are refitted they should slide smoothly in their holders. Any sticking tendency may first be rectified by wiping with a petrol soaked cloth, or if this fails, by carefully polishing with a very fine file where any binding marks may appear.

8 Reassemble in the reverse order of dismantling. Ensure that leads which may have been connected to any of the screws are reconnected correctly.

21 Alternator light control - general description

With an alternator the ignition warning light control feed comes from the centre point of a pair of diodes in the alternator via a control unit similar in appearance to an indicator flasher unit. Should the warning light indicate lack of charge check this unit by substitution before moving to the alternator. If suspect replace it.

22 Starter motor - general description

Two models of starter motor have been fitted to Mini models but they are both of the inertia type. Both starter motors are interchangeable and engage with a common starter ring gear. The relay for the starter motor is mounted on the inner wing panel.

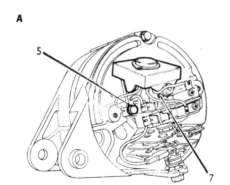
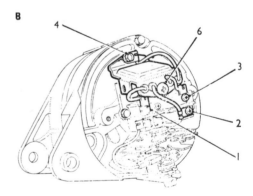

Fig. 10.9. View of the alternator regulator connections

A 11 TR regulator
1 B+
2 Positive (+)

3 Field (F)
4 Earth (−)

B 8 TR regulator
5 Earth (−)
6 Mounting screw

7 Mounting screw and spacer

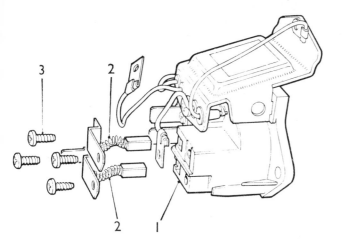

Fig. 10.10. Exploded view of alternator brush and spring assembly

1   Brush box mounting   *3   Four retaining screws*
2   Brush and spring assembly

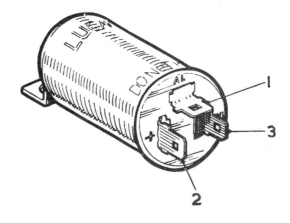

Fig. 10.11. View of ignition warning light control contacts

1   Alternator contact (A C)   *3   Warning light contact (WL)*
2   Positive contact (+)

The principle of operation of the inertia type starter motor is as follows: When the ignition switch is turned, current flows from the battery to the starter motor solenoid switch which causes it to become energised. Its internal plunger moves inwards and closes an internal switch so allowing full starting current to flow from the battery to the starter motor. This creates a powerful magnetic field to be induced into the field coils which causes the armature to rotate.

Mounted on helical splines is the drive pinion which, because of the sudden rotation of the armature, is thrown forwards along the armature shaft and so into engagement with the ring gear. The engine crankshaft will then be rotated until the engine starts to operate on its own and, at this point, the drive pinion is thrown out of mesh with the ring gear.

23 Starter motor (M35G) - testing on engine

1   If the starter motor fails to operate then check the condition of the battery by turning on the headlamps. If they glow brightly for several seconds and then gradually dim, the battery is in an uncharged condition.
2   If the headlamps continue to glow brightly and it is obvious that the battery is in good condition, then check the tightness of the battery wiring connections (and in particular the earth lead from the battery terminal to its connection on the bodyframe). Check the tightness of the connections at the relay switch and at the starter motor. Check the wiring with a voltmeter for breaks or shorts.
3   If the wiring is in order then check that the starter motor switch is operating. To do this, press the rubber covered button in the centre of the relay switch under the bonnet. If it is working the starter motor will be heard to 'click' as it tries to rotate. Alternatively check it with a voltmeter.
4   If the battery is fully charged, the wiring in order, and the switch working and the starter motor fails to operate then it will have to be removed from the car for examination. Before this is done, however, ensure that the starter pinion has not jammed in mesh with the ring gear. Check by turning the square end of the armature shaft with a spanner. This will free the pinion if it is stuck in engagement with the flywheel teeth.

24 Starter motor (M35G) - removal and replacement

1   Disconnect the earth lead from the battery for safety reasons.
2   Disconnect the starter motor cable from the terminal on the

starter motor end plate.
3   Unscrew the two starter motor bolts.
4   Lift the starter motor out of engagement with the teeth on the ring gear and pull it forward towards the radiator until it can be lifted clear.
5   Replacement is a straight reversal of removal procedure.

25 Starter motor (M35G) - dismantling and reassembly

1   With the starter motor on the bench, loosen the screw on the cover band and slip the cover band off. With a piece of wire bent into the shape of a hook, lift back each of the brush springs in turn and check the movement of the brushes in their holders by pulling on the flexible connectors. If the brushes are so worn that their faces do not rest against the commutator, or if the ends of the brush leads are exposed on their working face, they must be renewed (Fig. 10.12).
2   If any of the brushes tend to stick in their holders then wash them with a petrol moistened cloth and, if necessary, lightly polish the sides of the brush with a very fine file, until the brushes move quite freely in their holders.
3   If the surface of the commutator is dirty or blackened, clean it with a petrol dampened rag. Secure the starter motor in a vice and check it by connecting a heavy gauge cable between the starter motor terminal and a 12 volt battery.
4   Connect the cable from the other battery terminal to earth in the starter motor body. If the motor turns at high speed it is in good order.
5   If the starter motor still fails to function or if it is wished to renew the brushes, then it is necessary to further dismantle the motor.
6   Lift the brush springs with the wire hook and lift all four brushes out of their holders one at a time.
7   Remove the terminal nuts and washers from the terminal post on the commutator end bracket.
8   Unscrew the two through bolts which hold the end plates together and pull off the commutator end bracket. Also remove the driving end bracket which will come away complete with the armature.
9   At this stage if the brushes are to be renewed, their flexible connectors must be unsoldered and the connectors of new brushes soldered in their place. Check that the new brushes move freely in their holders as detailed above. If cleaning the commutator with petrol fails to remove all the burnt areas and spots, then wrap a piece of glass paper round the commutator and rotate the armature. If the commutator is very badly worn,

remove the drive gear as detailed in the following section. Then mount the armature in a lathe and with the lathe turning at high speed, take a very fine cut out of the commutator and finish the surface by polishing with glass paper. DO NOT UNDERCUT THE MICA INSULATORS BETWEEN THE COMMUTATOR SEGMENTS.

10 With the starter motor dismantled, test the four field coils for an open circuit. Connect a 12 volt battery with a 12 volt bulb in one of the leads between the field terminal post and the tapping point of the field coils to which the brushes are connected. An open circuit is proven by the bulb not lighting.

11 If the bulb lights, it does not necessarily mean that the field coils are in order, as there is a possibilty that one of the coils will be earthing to the starter yoke or pole shoes. To check this, remove the lead from the brush connector and place it against a clean portion of the starter yoke. If the bulb lights the field coils are earthing. Replacement of the field coils calls for the use of a

wheel operated screwdriver, a soldering iron, caulking and riveting operations and is beyond the scope of the majority of owners. The starter yoke should be taken to a reputable electrical engineering works for new field coils to be fitted. Alternatively, purchase an exchange Lucas starter motor.

12 If the armature is damaged this will be evident after visual inspection. Look for signs of burning, discolouration, and for conductors that have lifted away from the commutator. Re-assembly is a straight reversal of the dismantling procedure.

26 Starter motor drive (M35G) - removal and replacement

1 Extract the split pin from the shaft nut on the end of the starter drive.

2 Holding the squared end of the armature shaft at the commutator end bracket with a suitable spanner, unscrew the shaft

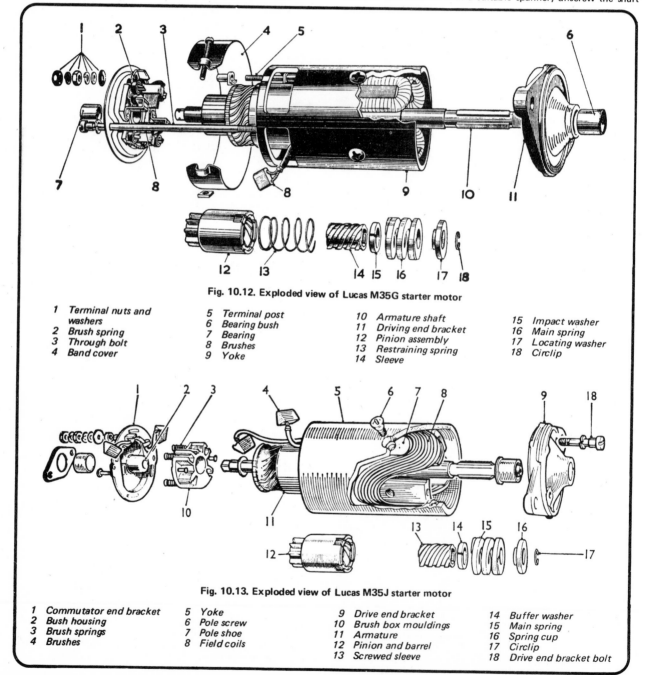

Fig. 10.12. Exploded view of Lucas M35G starter motor

1	Terminal nuts and washers	5	Terminal post	10	Armature shaft	15	Impact washer
2	Brush spring	6	Bearing bush	11	Driving end bracket	16	Main spring
3	Through bolt	7	Bearing	12	Pinion assembly	17	Locating washer
4	Band cover	8	Brushes	13	Restraining spring	18	Circlip
		9	Yoke	14	Sleeve		

Fig. 10.13. Exploded view of Lucas M35J starter motor

1	Commutator end bracket	5	Yoke	9	Drive end bracket	14	Buffer washer
2	Bush housing	6	Pole screw	10	Brush box mouldings	15	Main spring
3	Brush springs	7	Pole shoe	11	Armature	16	Spring cup
4	Brushes	8	Field coils	12	Pinion and barrel	17	Circlip
				13	Screwed sleeve	18	Drive end bracket bolt

nut which has a right-hand thread, and pull off the mainspring.

3 Slide the remaining parts with a rotary action off the armature shaft.

4 Reassembly is a straight reversal of the above procedure. Ensure that the split pin is refitted. **Note**: It is most important that the drive gear is completely free from oil, grease and dirt. With the drive gear removed, clean all the parts thoroughly in paraffin. **Under no circumstances oil the drive components.** Lubrication of the drive components could easily cause the pinion to stick.

27 Starter motor bushes (M35G) - inspection, removal and replacement

1 With the starter motor stripped down check the condition of the bushes. They should be renewed when they are sufficiently worn to allow visible side movement of the armature shaft.

2 The old bushes are simply driven out with a suitable drift and the new bushes inserted by the same method. As the bearings are of the phosphor bronze type it is essential that they are allowed to stand in engine oil for at least 24 hours before fitment.

28 Starter motor (M35J - testing on engine

The sequence for testing is basically identical to that for the M35G type. Refer to Section 23 for full information.

29 Starter motor (M35J) - removal and replacement

The sequence for removal and replacement of the M35J starter motor is identical to that for the M35G. Refer to Section 24 for full information.

30 Starter motor (M35J) - dismantling and reassembly

1 With the starter motor on the bench, first mark the relative positions of the starter motor body to the two end brackets.

2 Undo and remove the two screws and spring washers securing the drive end bracket to the body. The drive end bracket complete with armature and drive, may now be drawn forwards from the starter motor body (Fig. 10.14).

3 Lift away the thrust washer from the commutator end of the armature shaft.

4 Undo and remove the two screws securing the commutator end bracket to the starter motor body. The commutator end bracket may now be drawn back about an inch allowing sufficient access so as to disengage the field bushes from the bracket. Once these are free, the end bracket can be completely removed.

5 With the motor stripped, the brushes and brush gear may be inspected. To check the brush spring tension, fit a new brush into each holder in turn and, using an accurate spring balance, push the brush on the balance tray until the brush protrudes approximately 0.0625 in (1.59 mm) from the holder. Make a note of the reading which should be approximately 28 ounces. If the spring pressures vary considerably the commutator end bracket must be renewed as a complete assembly.

6 Inspect the brushes for wear and fit new brushes if the old brushes are nearing the minimum length of 0.375 in (9.525 mm). To renew the end bracket brushes, cut the brush cables from the terminal posts and, with a small file or hacksaw, slot the head of the terminal posts to a sufficient depth to accommodate the new leads. Solder the new brush leads to the posts.

7 To renew the field winding brushes, cut the brush leads approximately 0.25 in (6.35 mm) from the field winding junction and carefully solder the new brush leads to the remaining stumps, making sure that the insulation sleeves provide adequate cover.

8 If the commutator surface is dirty or blackened, clean it with

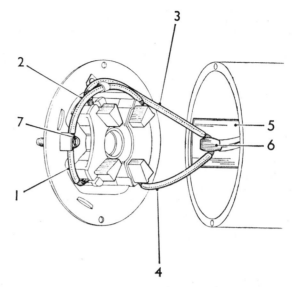

Fig. 10.14. Commutator end bracket assembly (M35J)

1 Short brush-flexible com-mutator end bracket	4 Short brush-flexible, field winding
2 Long brush-flexible com-mutator end bracket	5 Yoke insulation piece
3 Long brush-flexible field winding	6 Field winding junction
	7 Terminal post

a petrol dampened rag. Carefully examine the commutator for signs of excessive wear, burning or pitting. If evident it may be reconditioned by having it skimmed at the local engineering works or BLMC dealer, both of whom should possess a centre lathe. The thickness of the commutator must not be less than 0.08 in (2.032 mm). For minor reconditioning, the commutator may be polished with glass paper. **Do not undercut the mica insulators between the commutator segments.**

9 With the starter motor dismantled, test the field coils for open circuit. Connect a 12 volt battery with a 12 volt bulb in one of the leads between each of the field brushes and a clean part of the body. The lamp will light if continuity is satisfactory between the brushes, windings and body connection.

10 Replacement of the field coils calls for the use of a wheel operated screwdriver, a soldering iron, caulking and riveting operations and is beyond the scope of the majority of owners. The starter motor body should be taken to an automobile electrical engineering works for new field coils to be fitted. Alternatively purchase an exchange Lucas starter motor.

11 Check the condition of the bushes and they should be renewed when they are sufficiently worn to allow visible side movement of the armature shaft.

12 To renew the commutator end bracket bush, drill out the rivets securing the brush box moulding and remove the moulding, bearing seal retaining plate and felt washer seal.

13 Screw in a ½ in tap and withdraw the bush with the tap.

14 As the bush is of the phosphor bronze type it is essential that it is allowed to stand in engine oil for at least 24 hours before fitment. Alternatively, soak in oil at 100°C for 2 hours.

15 Using a suitable diameter drift, drive the new bush into position. Do not ream the bush as its self lubricating properties will be impaired.

16 To remove the drive end bracket bush it will be necessary to remove the drive gear as described in paragraphs 18 and 19.

17 Using a suitable diameter drift remove the old bush and fit a new one as described in paragraphs 14 and 15.

18 To dismantle the starter motor drive, first use a press to push the retainer clear of the circlip which can then be removed. Lift away the retainer and main spring.

19 Slide off the remaining parts with a rotary action of the armature shaft.

20 It is most important that the drive gear is completely free from oil, grease and dirt. With the drive gear removed, clean all parts thoroughly in paraffin. **Under no circumstances oil the drive components.** Lubrication of the drive components could easily cause the pinion to stick.

21 Reassembly of the starter motor drive is the reverse sequence to dismantling. Use a press to compress the spring and retainer sufficiently to allow a new circlip to be fitted to its groove on the shaft. Remove the drive from the press.

22 Reassembly of the starter motor is the reverse sequence to dismantling.

31 Starter motor solenoid - removal and replacement

1 Disconnect the battery.

2 Carefully ease back the rubber covers to gain access to the terminals.

3 Make a note of the Lucar terminal connectors and detach these terminals.

4 Undo and remove the heavy duty cable terminal connection nuts and spring washers. Detach the two terminal connectors.

5 Undo and remove the two securing screws and lift away the solenoid.

6 Refitting is the reverse sequence to removal.

32 Flasher unit and circuit - fault tracing and rectification

Early type:

The actual flasher unit is enclosed in a small cylindrical metal container located in the engine compartment. The unit is actuated by the direction indicator switch.

If the flasher unit fails to operate, or works very slowly or very rapidly, check-out the flasher indicator circuit as detailed below, before assuming there is a fault in the unit itself.

1 Examine the direction indicator bulbs front and rear for broken filaments.

2 If the external flashers are working but the internal flasher warning light has ceased to function check the filament of the warning bulb and replace as necessary.

3 With the aid of the wiring diagram check all the flasher circuit connections if a flasher bulb is sound but does not work.

4 In the event of total direction indicator failure, check the A3 - A4 fuse.

5 With the ignition turned on check that current is reaching the flasher unit by connecting a voltmeter between the "plus" or "B" terminal and earth. If this test is positive connect the "plus" or "B" terminal and the "L" terminal and operate the flasher switch. If the flasher bulb lights up the flasher unit itself is defective and must be replaced as it is not possible to dismantle and repair it.

Later type:

The flasher unit is enclosed in a small retangular container and is actuated by the direction indicator switch. Access to the unit on Clubman models in through an aperture in the facia parcel shelf.

Fault tracing and rectification is basically identical to that of the earlier type.

33 Fuses - general

The fuses are located on a block which is mounted on the right-hand wing valance and is covered by a plastic push-on cover. Upon inspection it will be seen that there are two main fuses and two spare fuses.

Before any fuse that has blown is renewed, it is important to find the cause of the trouble and for it to be rectified, as a fuse acts as a safety device and protects the electrical system against expensive damage should a fault occur.

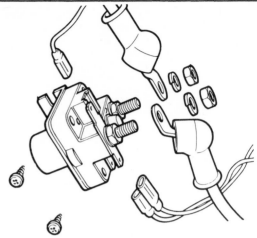

Fig. 10.15. Starter motor solenoid (later type)

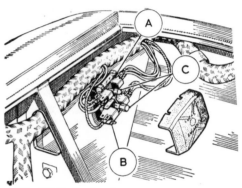

Fig. 10.16. The fuse box

A   35 amp fuse   C   Spare fuses
B   35 amp fuse

Fuse Connecting Function

1-2   The auxiliary units are protected by this fuse and are the interior light and horn which will operate without the ignition switched on. The fitting of additional accessories which are required to operate independently of the ignition circuit should be connected to the '2' terminal.

3-4   This fuse protects the auxiliary units which operate only when the ignition is switched on. The units connected into the circuit are the direction indicators, windscreen wiper motor, heater blower and stop lights. The fitting of additional accessories which are required to operate only when the ignition is switched on, should be connected to the '4' terminal.

Line fuses

A line fuse is fitted to protect an individual unit or circuit. To change a line fuse hold one end of the container, press and twist off the other end. Line fuses will be found in the following positions:

Side and tail lights	Located adjacent to the wiring connectors on the engine bulkhead
Hazard flasher	Located adjacent to the main fuse unit
Radio	Locate in the main feed line.

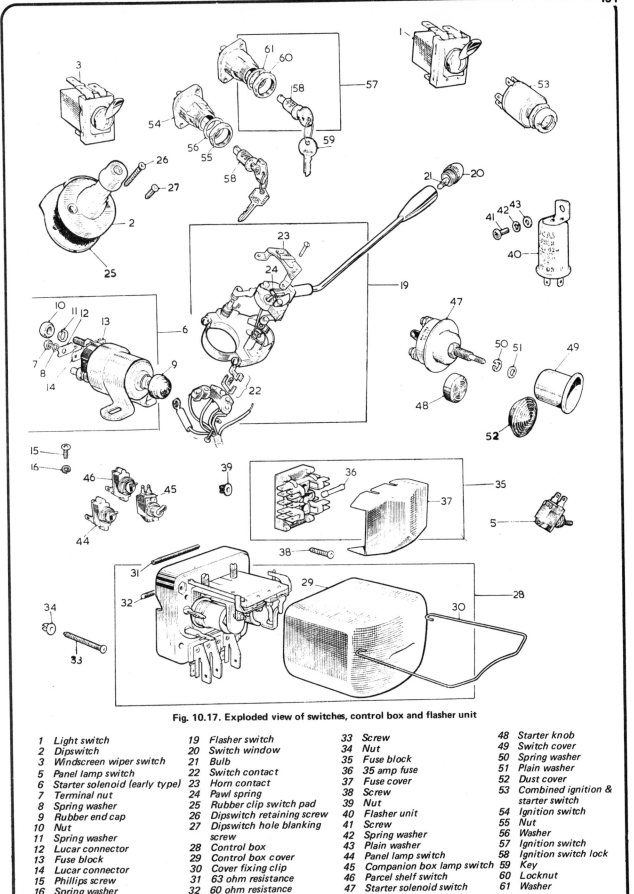

Fig. 10.17. Exploded view of switches, control box and flasher unit

1	Light switch	19	Flasher switch
2	Dipswitch	20	Switch window
3	Windscreen wiper switch	21	Bulb
5	Panel lamp switch	22	Switch contact
6	Starter solenoid (early type)	23	Horn contact
7	Terminal nut	24	Pawl spring
8	Spring washer	25	Rubber clip switch pad
9	Rubber end cap	26	Dipswitch retaining screw
10	Nut	27	Dipswitch hole blanking
11	Spring washer		screw
12	Lucar connector	28	Control box
13	Fuse block	29	Control box cover
14	Lucar connector	30	Cover fixing clip
15	Phillips screw	31	63 ohm resistance
16	Spring washer	32	60 ohm resistance

33	Screw	48	Starter knob
34	Nut	49	Switch cover
35	Fuse block	50	Spring washer
36	35 amp fuse	51	Plain washer
37	Fuse cover	52	Dust cover
38	Screw	53	Combined ignition &
39	Nut		starter switch
40	Flasher unit	54	Ignition switch
41	Screw	55	Nut
42	Spring washer	56	Washer
43	Plain washer	57	Ignition switch
44	Panel lamp switch	58	Ignition switch lock
45	Companion box lamp switch	59	Key
46	Parcel shelf switch	60	Locknut
47	Starter solenoid switch	61	Washer

34 Windscreen wiper arms - removal and replacement

1 Before removing a wiper arm, turn the windscreen wiper switch on and off, to ensure the arms are in their normal parked position with the blades parallel to the bottom of the windscreen.

2 To remove the arm, pivot the arm back and pull the wiper arm head off the splined drive, at the same time easing back the clip with a screwdriver.

3 When replacing an arm, place it so it is in the correct relative parked position and then press the arm head onto the splined drive until the retaining clip clicks into place.

35 Windscreen wiper mechanism - fault diagnosis and rectification

1 Should the windscreen wipers fall, or work very slowly, then check the terminals for loose connections, and make sure the insulation of the external wiring is not cracked or broken. If this is in order then check the current the motor is taking by connecting up an ammeter in the circuit and turning on the wiper switch. Consumption should be between 2.3 and 3.1 amps.

2 If no current is passing through check the A3 - A4 fuse. If the fuse has blown replace it after having checked the wiring of the motor and other electrical circuits serviced by this fuse for short circuits. If the fuse is in good condition check the wiper switch.

3 If the wiper motor takes a very high current check the wiper blades for freedom of movement. If this is satisfactory check the gearbox cover and gear assembly for damage and measure the armature endfloat which should be between 0.009 and 0.012 in. (0.20 and 0.30 mm). The endfloat is set by the adjusting screw. Check that excessive friction in the cable connecting tubes caused by too small a curvature is not the cause of the high current consumption.

4 If the motor takes a very low current ensure that the battery is fully charged. Check the brush gear after removing the commutator end bracket and ensure that the brushes are bearing on the commutator.

5 If not, check the brushes for freedom of movement and if necessary, renew the tension spring. If the brushes are very worn they should be replaced with new ones. The brush levers should be quite free on their pivots. If stiff, loosen them by moving them backwards and forwards by hand and by applying a little thin machine oil. Check rhe armature by substitution if this unit is suspected.

6 On some later Minis two-speed wipers were fitted. Should the wipers not operate at both speeds or not park automatically the fault will probably lie in the limit switch assembly and this should be replaced. It is connected to the bush gear by three wires which must be unsoldered from it. (photo)

36 Windscreen wiper motor, gearbox and wheelbox - removal and replacement

Single speed type:

1 Remove the windscreen wiper arms by lifting the blades, carefully raising the retaining clip and then pulling the arms off the splined drive shafts.

2 Disconnect the electrical cables from the wiper motor and release the outer cable from the gearbox housing.

3 Carefully prise back the body trimming from the left-hand side of the scuttle panel above the parcel tray, and unscrew and remove the three nuts and spring washers which hold the wiper motor in position.

4 Remove the cable rack from the motor and gearbox. First undo the pipe union nut. Then remove the gearbox cover, and the retaining washer from the crankpin and final gearwheel. The connecting link can now be lifted out and the wiper motor removed.

35.6   Later type, 14w windscreen wiper motor

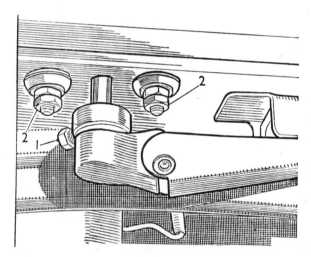

Fig. 10.18. Windscreen wiper arm and motor attachments (Moke)

1   Arm locking screw   *2   Motor mountings*

5 The windscreen wiper arm wheelboxes are located immediately underneath the splined drive shafts over which the wiper arms fit. To remove these wheelboxes release the cable rack outer casings by slackening the wheelbox cover screws. Remove the external nut, bush, and washer from the base of the splines and pull out the wheelboxes from under the facia.

6 Replacement is a straight reversal of the above sequence but take care that the cable rack emerges properly and that the wheelboxes are correctly lined up.

Twin speed type

1 For safety reasons disconnect the battery.

2 Withdraw the electrical cable terminal connector from the motor and then detach the earth cable from the wing valance.

3 Refer to Section 34 and remove the windscreen wiper arms.

4 Unscrew the union on the Bundy tube at the gearbox and release the strap from the mounting bracket.

5 Carefully withdraw the assembly pulling the cable rack from the Bundy tube.

6 The windscreen wiper arm wheelboxes are located immediately underneath the splined driveshafts over which the

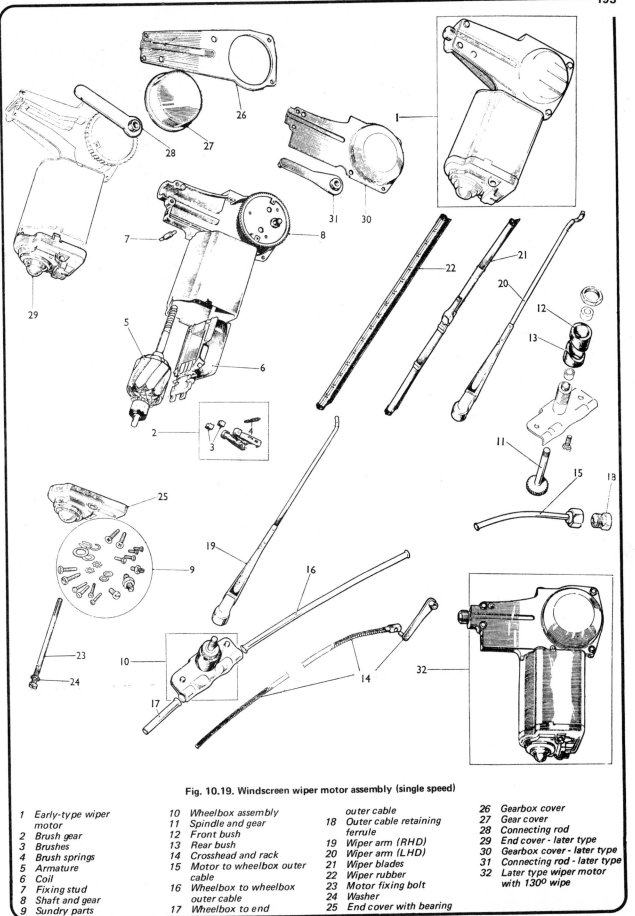

Fig. 10.19. Windscreen wiper motor assembly (single speed)

1	Early-type wiper motor	10	Wheelbox assembly
2	Brush gear	11	Spindle and gear
3	Brushes	12	Front bush
4	Brush springs	13	Rear bush
5	Armature	14	Crosshead and rack
6	Coil	15	Motor to wheelbox outer cable
7	Fixing stud	16	Wheelbox to wheelbox outer cable
8	Shaft and gear	17	Wheelbox to end
9	Sundry parts		

outer cable
18 Outer cable retaining ferrule
19 Wiper arm (RHD)
20 Wiper arm (LHD)
21 Wiper blades
22 Wiper rubber
23 Motor fixing bolt
24 Washer
25 End cover with bearing

26 Gearbox cover
27 Gear cover
28 Connecting rod
29 End cover - later type
30 Gearbox cover - later type
31 Connecting rod - later type
32 Later type wiper motor with 130° wipe

wiper arms fit. Removal is similar to that for the single speed
type as described in paragraph 5 (single speed type).

7 Replacement of the assembly is the reverse sequence to
removal. It is important that the wheelbox covers are left slack
until after the cable rack has been inserted and the motor
secured. Do not refit the wiper arms until the wheelboxes have
been checked.

37 Windscreen wiper motor (early type) - dismantling, inspection and reassembly

1 Undo the four screws holding the gearbox cover in place and
remove the cover.

2 Undo and remove the two through bolts from the commutator end bracket. Pull out the connector and free the end
bracket from the yoke.

3 Carefully remove the brush gear as a unit from the commutator and then withdraw the yoke.

4 Clean the commutator and brush gear and if worn fit new
brushes. The resistance between adjacent commutator segments
should be 0.34 to 0.41 ohm.

5 Carefully examine the internal wiring for signs of chafing,
breaks or charring which would lead to a short circuit. Insulate
or replace any damaged wiring.

6 Measure the value of the field resistance which should be

between 12.8 to 14 ohms. If a lower reading than this is
obtained it is likely that there is a short circuit and a new field
coil should be fitted.

7 Renew the gearbox gear teeth if they are damaged, chipped or
worn.

8 Reassembly is a straightforward reversal of the dismantling
sequence, but ensure the following items are lubricated:

a) Immerse the self aligning armature bearing in engine oil for 24
hours before assembly.

b) Oil the armature bearings in engine oil.

c) Soak the felt lubricator in the gearbox with engine oil.

d) Grease, generously, the worn wheel bearings, crosshead, guide
channel, connecting rod, crankpin, worm, cable rack and
wheelboxes and the final gearshaft.

38 Windscreen wiper motor (14w) - dismantling, inspection and reassembly

The only repair which can be effectively undertaken by the
diy mechanic to a wiper motor is brush replacement. Anything
more serious than this will mean exchanging the complete motor
or having a repair done by an auto electrician. Spare part avail-
ability is really the problem. Brush replacement is described
here.

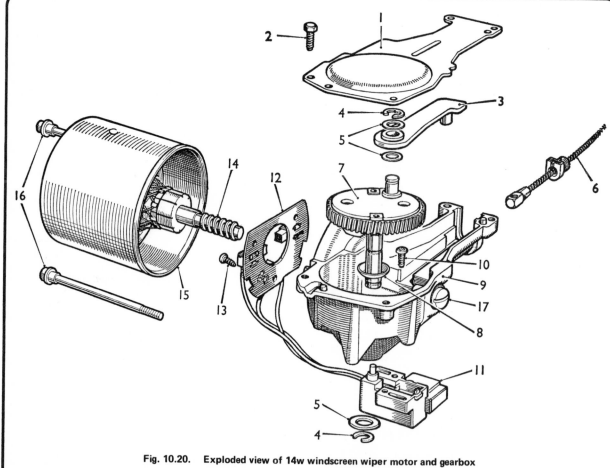

Fig. 10.20.   Exploded view of 14w windscreen wiper motor and gearbox

1	Gearbox cover	5	Plain washers	9	Gearbox	13	Screw for brush gear
2	Screw for cover	6	Crosshead and rack	10	Screw for limit switch	14	Armature
3	Connecting rod	7	Shaft and gear	11	Limit switch assembly	15	Yoke assembly
4	Circlip	8	Dished washer	12	Brush gear	16	Yoke bolts
						17	Armature thrust screw

1   Refer to Fig. 10.20 and remove the four gearbox cover retaining screws and lift away the cover. Release the circlip and flat washer securing the connecting rod to the crankpin on the shaft and gear. Lift away the connecting rod followed by the second flat washer.

2   Release the circlip and flat washer securing the shaft and gear to the gearbox body.

3   De-burr the gearshaft and lift away the gear making a careful note of the location of the dished washer.

4   Scribe a mark on the yoke assembly and gearbox to ensure correct reassembly and unscrew the two yoke bolts from the motor yoke assembly. Part the yoke assembly including armature from the gearbox body. As the yoke assembly has residual magentism ensure that the yoke is kept well away from metallic dust.

5   Unscrew the two screws securing the brush gear and the terminal and switch assembly and remove both the assemblies.

6   Inspect the brushes for excessive wear. If the main brushes are worn to a limit of 3/16 in (4.763 mm) or the narrow section of the third brush is worn to the full width of the brush fit a new brush gear assembly. Ensure that the three brushes move freely in their boxes.

7   Reassembly at this stage is a straight reversal of dismantling.

39 Horns - fault tracing and rectification

1   If a horn works badly or fails completely, first check the wiring leading to it for short circuits and loose connections. Also check that the horn is firmly secured and that there is nothing lying on the horn body.

2   The horn is protected by the A1 - A2 fuse and if this has blown the circuit should be checked for short circuits. Further information will be found in Section 33.

3   The horn should never be dismantled, but it is possible to adjust it. This adjustment is to compensate for wear of the moving parts only and will not affect the tone. To adjust the horn proceed as follows:

a) There is a small adjustment screw on the broad rim of the horn nearly opposite the two terminals. Do not confuse this with the large screw in the centre.

b) Turn the adjustment screw anticlockwise until the horn just fails to sound. Then turn the screw a quarter of a turn clockwise which is the optimum setting.

c) It is recommended that if the horn has to be reset in the car, the A1 - A2 fuse should be removed and replaced with a piece of wire, otherwise the fuse will continually blow due to the high current required for the horn in continual operation.

d) Should twin horns be fitted, the horn which is not being adjusted should be disconnected while adjustment of the other takes place.

40 Headlight units - removal and replacement

1   Sealed beam or renewable bulb light units are fitted.

2   The method of gaining access to the light unit for replacement is basically identical for all types of light units and bulbs - see also photographs.

3   Undo and remove the outer rim securing screw/s and ease the bottom of the outer rim forwards. Lift it up from the retaining lugs at the top of the light (early models). On later models simply lift away outer rim.

4   Unscrew the three inner rim retaining screws and remove the inner rim.

5   The light unit may now be drawn forwards.

6   *Sealed beam unit:* Withdraw the three pin connector from the rear of the reflector and lift away the complete unit. If it is necessary to remove the headlight pilot bulb it may be detached from the holder. A bayonet or capless type bulb may be fitted depending on year of manufacture.

7   *Spring clip type bulb holder:* Withdraw the three pin connector from the reflector and disengage the spring clip from

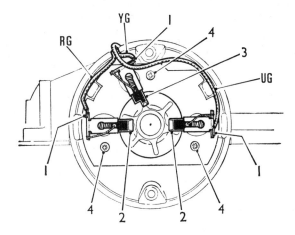

Fig. 10.21. View of windscreen wiper motor brush gear

1   *Soldered brush box connections*
2   *Main brushes*
3   *Fast-speed brush (2-speed version only)*
4   *Brush gear assembly securing screws*

RG —   *Red with green*
UG —   *Blue with green*
YG —   *Yellow with green*

the reflector lugs. Lift away the bulb. Note the locating pip on the reflector and mating indentation in the bulb rim. If it is necessary to remove the headlight pilot bulb from the reflector detach the bulb holder and then press and turn the bulb anticlockwise. Withdraw it from the holder.

8   *Cap type bulb holder:* Push and turn the cap anticlockwise. Lift off the cap and withdraw the bulb. Note the locating pip on the reflector and the mating indentation in the bulb rim. Renewal of the pilot light bulb is as described in paragraph 7.

9   Refitting in all cases is the reverse sequence to removal. Where a bulb is fitted make sure that the locating clip or slot in the bulb correctly registers in the reflector.

41 Headlight beam - adjustment

The headlights may be adjusted for both vertical and horizontal beam positions by the two screws. For vertical movement the upper spring loaded screw should be used and for horizontal movement the side spring loaded screw.

They should be set so that on full or high beam, the beams are set slightly below parallel with a level road surface. Do not forget that the beam position is affected by how the car is normally loaded for night driving, and set the beams with the car loaded to this position.

Although this adjustment can be approximately set at home, it is recommended that this be left to a local garage who will have the necessary equipment to do the job more accurately.

42 Front flashing direction indicator bulb - removal and replacement

1   To renew a bulb fold back the rubber flange and remove the plated rim and light glass. Only the fingers should be used to feed back the rubber flange.

2   When replacing a bulb note that the locating pins are offset to ensure correct replacement.

3   When replacing the light glass ensure that the chromium rim is secured, all round, by the rubber flange.

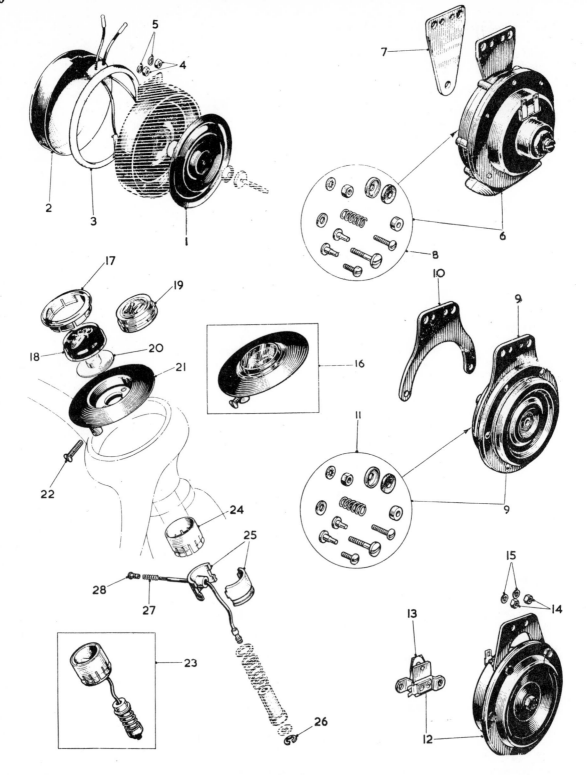

Fig. 10.22. Various types of horn assemblies fitted to Mini models

1	Horn tone disc	8	Set of sundry parts	15	Spring washers	22	Control retaining screw
2	Horn cover	9	Horn	16	Horn push assemblies	23	Slip ring assembly
3	Cover sealing ring	10	Bracket	17	Retaining knob ring	24	Slip ring
4	Nuts	11	Set of sundry parts	18	Horn push knob - Austin	25	Top & bottom half of rotor
5	Spring washers	12	Alternative horn	19	Horn push knob - Morris		with cable
6	Windhorn for Super &	13	Contact	20	Top contact	26	Circlip
	De Luxe models	14	Nuts	21	Lower cover & contact	27	Spring
7	Bracket						

1 Undo the screw at the bottom of the chrome ring, slightly turn and then carefully prise the ring off

2 The ring comes away exposing the headlamp adjusting and release screws

3 Shown above is one of the three adjustment/release screws. Adjustment to the beam is made by screwing each screw in or out

4 To remove the headlamp press it in towards the wing with the palms of your hands at the same time turning the unit slightly anti-clockwise

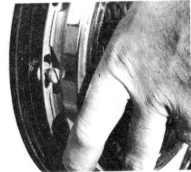

5 The enlarged portions of the headlamp rim slots are turned under the heads of the screws. The rim will then pass over them

6 With the headlamp free twist and pull out the bulb holder and remove the bulb. Later models have a multi-connector plug which is pulled straight out

7 To remove a front direction indicator bulb, first ease back the outer rubber lip with the aid of a screwdriver, and lift out the chrome ring

8 Then ease back the inner portion of the rubber lip and pull out the bulb glass cover

9 With the glass cover removed the bulb can be taken out and replaced in the normal manner

10 To replace a rear light or stop light bulb just undo the three Phillips screws holding the two section covers in place

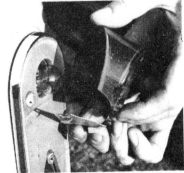

11 Take off both halves of the cover, also the separating plate and remove the bulb in the normal fashion

12 Should one of the rear number plate bulbs fail they are easily renewed after undoing the screw which holds the chrome cover and glass in place

1 Removal of outer rim securing screws

2 Lifting away outer rim

3 Removal of inner rim securing screws

4 Lifting away inner rim and sealed beam light unit

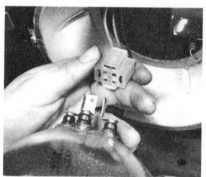

5 Detaching connector from rear of sealed beam light unit

6 Removal of rear combination light lens — all late models

43 Front side and direction indicator bulb (combination type) - removal and replacement

1 Undo and remove the two screws that secure the lens to the light body. Carefully lift away the lenses.
2 Either bulb is retained by a bayonet fixing so to remove a bulb push in slightly and rotate in an anticlockwise direction.
3 Refitting is the reverse sequence to removal. Take care not to tighten the two lens retaining screws as the lenses can be easily cracked.

44 Stop, tail and rear direction indicator light bulb - removal and replacement

1 When it is necessary to renew a bulb, withdraw the three screws to release the light lenses.
2 The flashing indicator bulb is fitted in the top and the stop-/tail bulb in the lower compartment.
3 The latter is of the double filament type giving a marked increase in illumination on brake application to provide a stop warning. This bulb also has offset locating pins to ensure correct replacement.
4 Both bulbs have bayonet fixings so to remove push in slightly, and rotate, in an anticlockwise direction.
5 Refitting is the reverse sequence to removal. Take care not to overtighten the lens securing screws as the lenses can easily be cracked.
6 On Elf and Hornet models, to gain access to the bulbs, open the boot lid and working at the rear of the light unit pull out the appropriate bulb holder. Detach the bulb which is of the conventional bayonet fixing type.

45 Number plate light bulb - removal and replacement

Three types of number plate lights are fitted depending on the model or date of manufacture.

Glass dome type
1 Remove the lens by depressing and turning through 90 degrees. Lift away the lens.
2 The bulb may be removed by pushing in slightly and rotating in an anticlockwise direction.

Metal cover - plastic lens - downward illumination
1 Undo and remove the two lens securing screws and carefully ease the lens and bulb holder from the light.
2 The festoon type bulb may now be detached from the contact blades.

Reassembly: Refitting the bulb and reassembling the number plate light is the reverse sequence to removal in all cases.

46 Interior light bulb - removal and replacement

1 To gain access to the bulb, carefully squeeze the two sides of the plastic lens together until the retaining lugs of the lens are clear of the sockets in the light base.
2 Draw the lens from the light base.

3 The festoon bulb may now be detached from the contact blades.
4 Refitting the bulb and lens is the reverse sequence to removal.

47 Warning and panel light bulbs - removal and replacement

All, except Elf, Clubman and 1275 GT
1 Access to the warning lights for ignition, headlight beam, lubrication, and speedometer illumination bulbs is effected under the bonnet by withdrawing the push in type holders from the rear of the speedometer.
2 On some models it may be found helpful to remove the air cleaner assembly (see Chapter 2).
3 To remove the bulbs from the oil and temperature gauges unscrew the four small crosshead screws visible on the instrument panel inside the car and withdraw the panel cover and shroud, so as to expose the gauges. The bulb holders can then be pulled out from the rear of the gauges.
4 On some Cooper models it may be found that it is not necessary to remove the panel cover and shroud to gain access to the oil and temperature gauge bulbs; instead simply pull the felt sound insulation blanket from the speedometer aperture.

Elf models
1 To renew the bulbs open the glovebox lid on the appropriate side of the instrument panel.
2 Pull back the glovebox lining from the side of the instrument panel and push the lining to one side to expose the rear of the instrument panel.
3 Pull out the appropriate bulb holder and remove the bulb.
4 Refitting the bulb and holder is the reverse sequence to removal.
5 Refitment is the reverse sequence to removal. Make sure that when the shroud is being fitted, the panel light switch is positioned to avoid the switch terminals coming into contact with the oil gauge pipe and causing a short circuit in the electrical system.

48 Bi-metallic resistance instrumentation

The bi-metallic resistance equipment for temperature and fuel gauges comprises an indicator head and transmitter unit connected to a common voltage stabilizer. In both applications the indicator head operates on a thermal principle, using a bimetallic strip surrounded by a heated winding, and the transmitter unit is of a resistance type. The system by which the equipment functions is voltage sensitive and the voltage stabilizer, which serves one or more gauges, is necessary to ensure a constant supply of a pre-determined voltage to the equipment.

Fault finding

Gauges: Check for continuity between the terminals with the wiring disconnected. The gauges must **not** be checked, by short circuiting to earth. If the gauge is faulty a new one should be fitted.
Transmitter: Check for continuity between the terminal and body with the lead disconnected. If the transmitter is faulty a new one should be fitted.
Voltage stabilizer: Check the average voltage between the output terminal "1" and earth. This should be 10 volts. If the voltage stabilizer is faulty a new one should be fitted. When replacing the voltage stabilizer terminals "B" and "E" must be uppermost and the unit must not be more than 20 degrees from the vertical plane.

49 Instrument cluster (early models) - removal and replacement

1 The information in this Section is applicable to the early Mini saloon, van and pick-up models fitted with the composite type

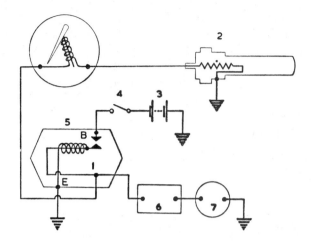

Fig. 10.23. Bi-metallic resistance instrumentation circuit

1 *Temperature gauge*	4 *Ignition switch*
2 *Temperature gauge*	5 *Voltage stabilizer*
transmitter	6 *Fuel gauge*
3 *Battery*	7 *Fuel gauge transmitter*

instrument cluster.
2 For safety reasons, disconnect the battery.
3 Working at the rear of the speedometer head carefully detach the speedometer cable.
4 To remove the cluster undo and remove the four screws and washers securing the instrument cluster cover to the dash. Note that one of the screws secures the windscreen washer pipe clip.
5 The instrument cluster may now be detached by undoing and removing the two side located screws.
6 To remove the fuel gauge undo and remove the two securing screws and spring washers. Disconnect the electrical terminal connectors and lift away the fuel gauge.
7 Reassembly and refitting of the instrument cluster is the reverse sequence to dismantling and removal.

50 Instrument cluster (Super Deluxe models) - removal and replacement

1 The information in this Section is applicable to the Super De Luxe Cooper, Traveller, Countryman and Hornet models.
2 For safety reasons, disconnect the battery.
3 Undo and remove the four crosshead screws that are located on the front of the instrument panel shroud. Carefully withdraw the shroud.
4 Disconnect the panel light switch leads and also the pipe union at the rear of the oil pressure gauge.
5 Detach the electrical leads from the temperature and oil pressure gauges.
6 Undo and remove the four countersunk crosshead screws from the front of the instrument panel and draw the panel and instruments away from the dash.
7 Unscrew and remove the two knurled nuts that secure the oil and temperature gauges and lift away the instruments.
8 Undo and remove the two screws that secure the instrument panel brackets, and speedometer, to the speedometer cowling.
9 Working under the bonnet unscrew the knurled nut that secures the speedometer cable to the rear of the speedometer head. Detach the cable from the instrument.
10 Carefully pull the four bulb holders from the rear of the speedometer head. Detach the electrical lead from the rear of the fuel gauge.
11 The speedometer head and fuel gauge may now be drawn forwards into the engine compartment.
12 Reassembly and refitting the instruments and panel is the reverse sequence to dismantling and removal.

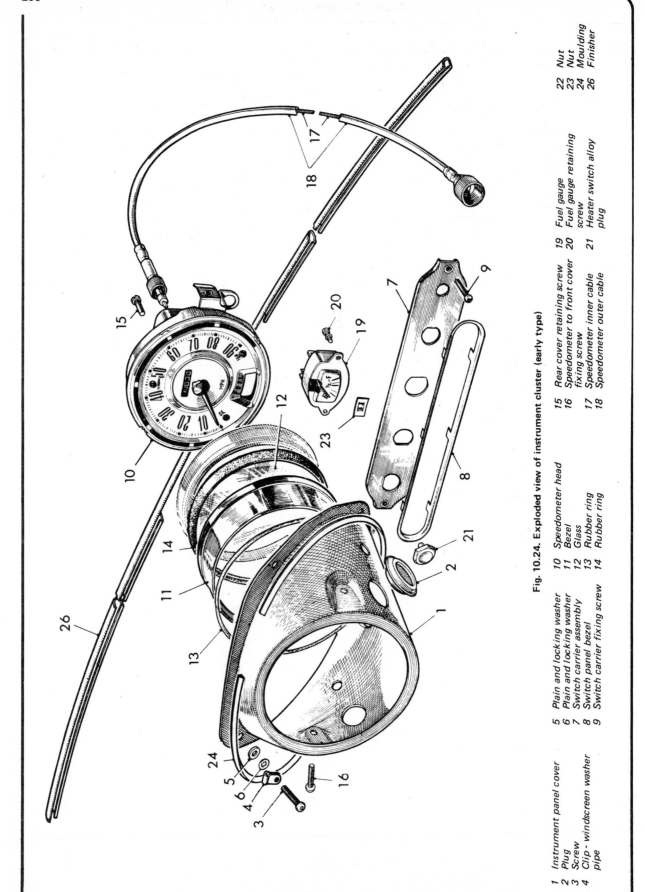

Fig. 10.24. Exploded view of instrument cluster (early type)

1 Instrument panel cover
2 Plug
3 Screw
4 Clip - windscreen washer pipe
5 Plain and locking washer
6 Plain and locking washer
7 Switch carrier assembly
8 Switch panel bezel
9 Switch carrier fixing screw
10 Speedometer head
11 Bezel
12 Glass
13 Rubber ring
14 Rubber ring
15 Rear cover retaining screw
16 Speedometer to front cover fixing screw
17 Speedometer inner cable
18 Speedometer outer cable
19 Fuel gauge
20 Fuel gauge retaining screw
21 Heater switch alloy plug
22 Nut
23 Nut
24 Moulding
26 Finisher

51 Instrument cluster (Riley Elf) - removal and replacement

1 For safety reasons, disconnect the battery.
2 Working inside the gloveboxes, undo and remove the three nuts, shakeproof and plain washers that secure the glovebox lids and frames to their brackets.
3 Carefully remove the glovebox lid and frame assemblies.
4 Undo and remove the screws that secure the speedometer housing to each side of the instrument panel brackets.
5 Undo and remove the two screws that secure the instrument panel to each support bracket. Pull the panel rearwards and detach the electrical leads and bulb holders from the rear of the instruments and also from the panel light switch.
6 Detach the pipe from the rear of the oil pressure gauge.
7 The complete panel assembly complete with gauges may now be lifted away.
8 Refitting the instrument cluster and panel assembly is the reverse sequence to removal.

52 Instrument panel (Clubman and 1275 GT) - removal and replacement

1 Disconnect the battery earth (negative).
2 Remove the air ventilation louvre at the side of the panel as described in Chapter 12.
3 Release the portion of the door seal which is glued to the facia trim liner and withdraw and remove the liner from behind the side of the panel.
4 Release the trim liner on the other side of the panel likewise but do not remove it. The four securing screws are now all accessible - two at each side.
5 Remove the screws and draw the panel out a little way.
6 The speedometer cable is held into the speedometer head by a simple clip connection on the end of the cable. Release the speedometer cable by depressing the catch and drawing it off.
7 Then pull out the multiplug wiring connector also the tachometer connections, if fitted.
8 The panel can then be lifted clear.

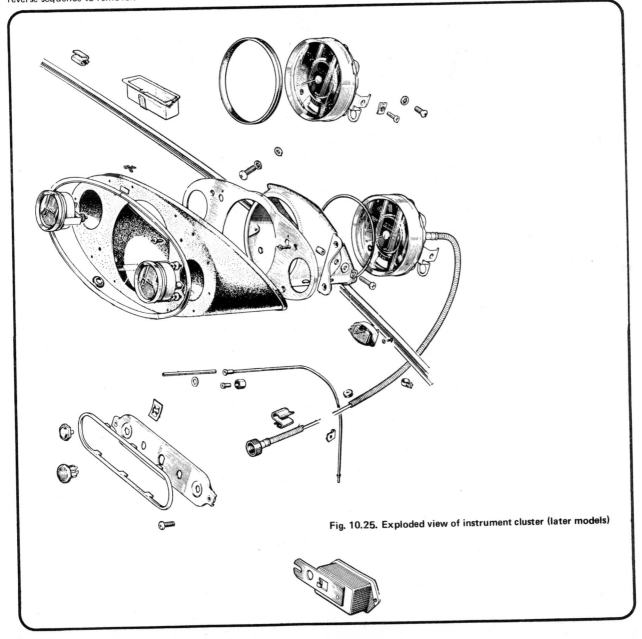

Fig. 10.25. Exploded view of instrument cluster (later models)

Removal of Clubman instrument panel

1 Removal of outer moulding

2 Removing upper securing screw

3 Removing lower securing screw

4 Drawing away instrument panel

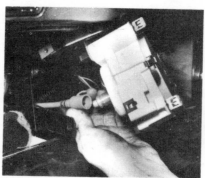

5 Disconnecting speedometer cable

6 The printed circuit. Take care as it is very fragile

7 The multi-pin connector that plugs into the printed circuit

Fig. 10.26. Instrument panel screws and connections (Clubman and 1275 GT)

1   Panel securing screws
2   Speedometer cable release lever
3   Multi-plug wiring connector
4   Tachometer connection   )   1275 GT
5   Tachometer connection   )   1275 GT

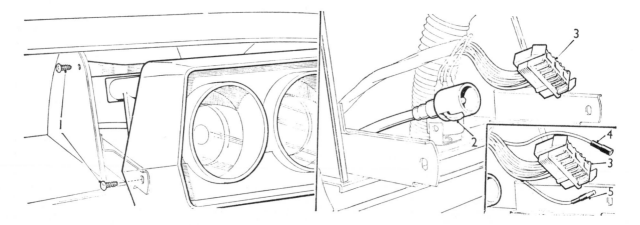

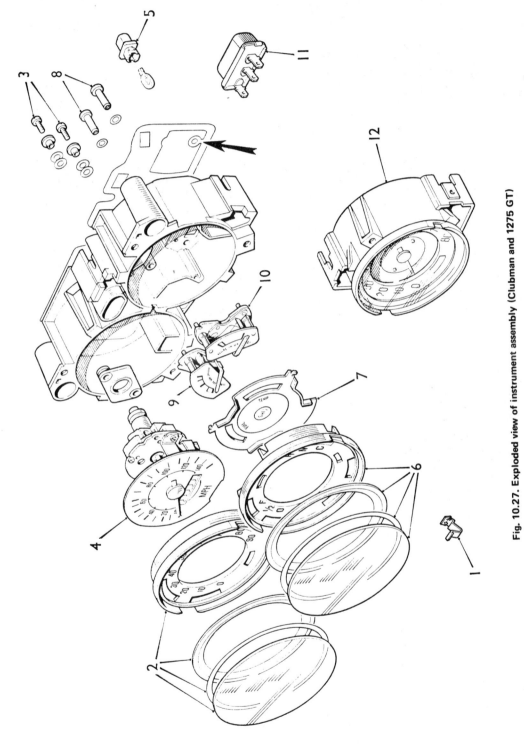

Fig. 10.27. Exploded view of instrument assembly (Clubman and 1275 GT)

1 Instrument lens securing clips
2 Speedometer dial and lens assembly
3 Speedometer securing screws
4 Speedometer unit
5 Panel lamp bulb and holder
6 Fuel/temperature gauge dial and lens assembly
7 Fuel/temperature gauge sub-dial
8 Fuel/temperature gauge securing screws
9 Fuel gauge
10 Temperature gauge
11 Voltage stabilizer
12 Tachometer assembly

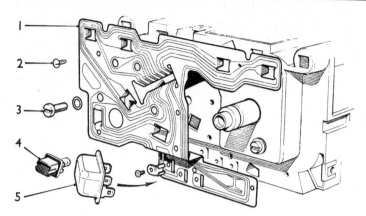

Fig. 10.28. Instrument panel printed circuit connections (Clubman and 1275 GT)

1   Printed circuit
2   Printed circuit securing stud
3   Fuel and temperature gauge securing screws
4   Panel light
5   Voltage stabiliser

9 Replacement is the exact reverse of the removal procedure. Ensure the speedometer cable is fully engaged when replacing it.
10 Care should be exercised when refitting the trim liners. The door seal will need to be fixed with adhesive. Use a good impact adhesive such as Evostik and take care to use it sparingly and only where it should go. Nothing spoils an interior trim appearance more than unslightly spots or misapplied glue.

53 Instruments (Clubman and 1275 GT) - removal and replacement

1 Refer to Section 52, and remove the instrument panel.
2 Should the speedometer or fuel and temperature gauges need replacement remove the complete unit from the panel by unscrewing the appropriate securing screws. Then take off the lens securing clips and remove the components of the lens assembly and sub dial. New instruments are fitted in the reverse order.
3 For the tachometer to be removed (1275 GT) first detach the printed circuit earth connection (arrowed) and remove the light bulb holder from the tachometer. The tachometer should not be dismantled any further as it is replaceable as a complete unit which should not be removed from its casing.

54 Printed circuit (Clubman and 1275 GT) - removal and replacement

1 Refer to Section 52 and remove the instrument panel.
2 Withdraw all bulb holders, noting where they come from and pull off the voltage stabilizer. Take off the three voltage stabilizer terminals which are fixed to the printed circuit by three small screws. Referring to Fig. 10.28 ease out the securing pins; the circuit can then be withdrawn.
3 Replacement of the printed circuit is a direct reversal process. Ensure that contacts on the printed circuit are bent into each bulb holder recess when they are put back.

55 Speedometer drive cable - removal and replacement

1 The speedometer cable must first be detached from the rear of the speedometer head. On models with access from the engine compartment detach the cable by unscrewing the knurled nut. On later models, it will be necessary, to remove the instrument panel first and then detach the speedometer cable. Where a knurled nut is not used, the cable may be released by depressing

55.2 Easing speedometer cable through bulkhead. Note the rubber grommet

the release lever and withdrawing the cable.
2 Carefully pull the cable into the engine compartment, taking care to release the rubber grommet (photo).
3 Working under the car disconnect the cable from the transmission unit. To gain access work through the aperture above the left-hand driveshaft.
4 Should the cable securing nut be tight to turn by hand, remove the set screw that secures the speedometer drive and withdraw the cable complete with the drive assembly. The cable may then be detached from the drive assembly.
5 Refitting the speedometer cable is the reverse sequence to removal but the following additional points should be noted:
a) If the speedometer drive was removed always fit a new joint washer.
b) To lubricate the inner cable, withdraw the inner cable and lightly grease it except for 8 in (200 mm) at the speedometer end. Refit the inner cable and wipe away any surplus grease.
c) Ensure that there is approximately 0.75 in (10 mm) projection of the inner cable beyond the outer casing at the speedometer end.

Fig. 10.29. Wiring diagram — Super, Super de-luxe, Countryman, Traveller and Cooper (up to 1964)

1   LH flasher lamp
2   LH headlamp & pilot lamp
3   RH headlamp & pilot lamp
4   RH flasher lamp
5   Distributor
6   Ignition coil
7   Voltage regulator & cut-out
8   Horn
9   Thermo element
10 Dynamo
11 Thermo gauge illumination light
12 Panel illumination lights
13 Stop lamp switch
14 Thermo gauge
15 Main beam warning light
16 Fuel gauge
17 Ignition warning light
18 Oil gauge illumination light
19 Oil gauge
20 Flasher unit
21 35-amp fuses
22 Panel light switch
23 Wiper motor
24 Heater motor
25 Heater switch
26 Wiper switch
27 Ignition & starter switch
28 Lighting switch
29 Starter motor
30 Interior lamp
31 Horn-push
32 Starter solenoid
33 Tank unit
34 Direction indicator switch
35 Direction indicator warning light
36 Dipper switch
37 12-volt battery
38 Fuel pump
39 LH stop, tail & flasher lamp
40 No. plate illumination lamp
41 RH stop, tail & flasher lamp
42 Earth connection
43 Connect to terminal 6 for North America

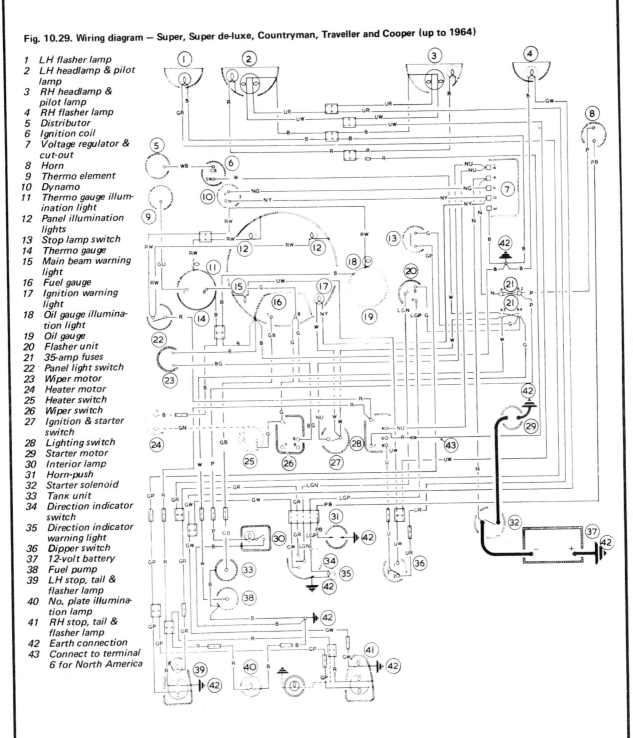

Note: On Export models the pilot lamps are combined with the flasher lamps

CABLE COLOUR CODE

When a cable has two colour code letters the first denotes the main colour and the second denotes the tracer colour

B Black	N Brown	P Purple	S Slate	Y Yellow	D Dark
U Blue	G Green	R Red	W White	L Light	M Medium

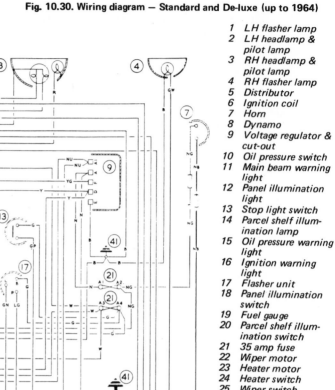

Fig. 10.30. Wiring diagram — Standard and De-luxe (up to 1964)

1 LH flasher lamp
2 LH headlamp & pilot lamp
3 RH headlamp & pilot lamp
4 RH flasher lamp
5 Distributor
6 Ignition coil
7 Horn
8 Dynamo
9 Voltage regulator & cut-out
10 Oil pressure switch
11 Main beam warning light
12 Panel illumination light
13 Stop light switch
14 Parcel shelf illumination lamp
15 Oil pressure warning light
16 Ignition warning light
17 Flasher unit
18 Panel illumination switch
19 Fuel gauge
20 Parcel shelf illumination switch
21 35 amp fuse
22 Wiper motor
23 Heater motor
24 Heater switch
25 Wiper switch
26 Ignition switch
27 Lighting switch
28 Starter motor
29 Tank unit
30 Horn push
31 Starter switch
32 Fuel pump
33 Companion box switch & lamp
34 Indicator switch & warning light
35 Dipper switch
36 12-volt battery
37 LH stop, tail & flasher lamp
38 No. plate illumination lamp
39 RH stop, tail & flasher lamp
40 Connect to No. 6 terminal for U.S.A.
41 Earth connection

CABLE COLOUR CODE

When a cable has two colour code letters the first denotes the main colour and the second denotes the tracer colour

B	Black	N	Brown	P	Purple	W	White	L	Light	M	Medium
U	Blue	G	Green	R	Red	Y	Yellow	D	Dark		

Fig. 10.31. Wiring diagram — Saloon, Van and Pick-up (1964 to 1967)

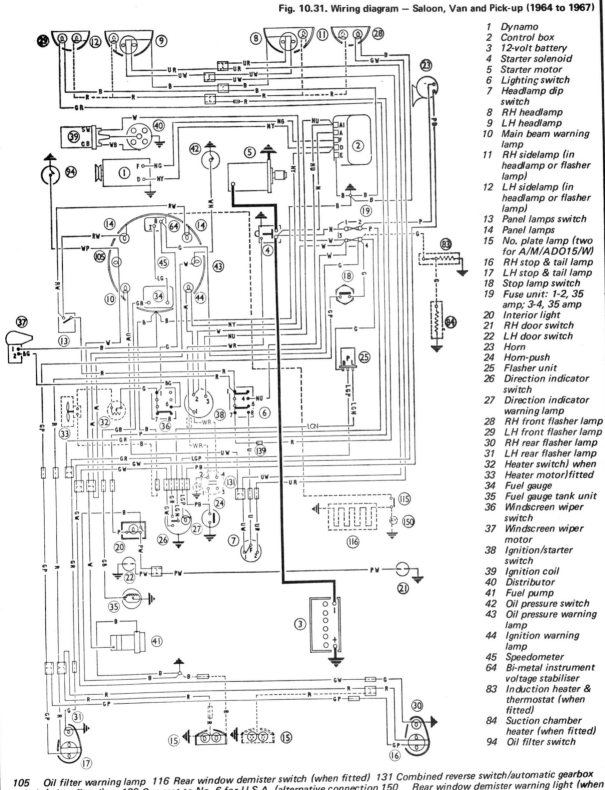

1 Dynamo
2 Control box
3 12-volt battery
4 Starter solenoid
5 Starter motor
6 Lighting switch
7 Headlamp dip switch
8 RH headlamp
9 LH headlamp
10 Main beam warning lamp
11 RH sidelamp (in headlamp or flasher lamp)
12 LH sidelamp (in headlamp or flasher lamp)
13 Panel lamps switch
14 Panel lamps
15 No. plate lamp (two for A/M/ADO15/W)
16 RH stop & tail lamp
17 LH stop & tail lamp
18 Stop lamp switch
19 Fuse unit: 1-2, 35 amp; 3-4, 35 amp
20 Interior light
21 RH door switch
22 LH door switch
23 Horn
24 Horn-push
25 Flasher unit
26 Direction indicator switch
27 Direction indicator warning lamp
28 RH front flasher lamp
29 LH front flasher lamp
30 RH rear flasher lamp
31 LH rear flasher lamp
32 Heater switch) when
33 Heater motor) fitted
34 Fuel gauge
35 Fuel gauge tank unit
36 Windscreen wiper switch
37 Windscreen wiper motor
38 Ignition/starter switch
39 Ignition coil
40 Distributor
41 Fuel pump
42 Oil pressure switch
43 Oil pressure warning lamp
44 Ignition warning lamp
45 Speedometer
64 Bi-metal instrument voltage stabiliser
83 Induction heater & thermostat (when fitted)
84 Suction chamber heater (when fitted)
94 Oil filter switch

105 Oil filter warning lamp 116 Rear window demister switch (when fitted) 131 Combined reverse switch/automatic gearbox switch (when fitted) 139 Connect to No. 6 for U.S.A. (alternative connection 150 Rear window demister warning light (when fitted)

CABLE COLOUR CODE

When a cable has two colour code letters the first denotes the main colour and the second denotes the tracer colour

B	Black	N	Brown	P	Purple	W	White	LG	Light Green
U	Blue	G	Green	R	Red	Y	Yellow		

Fig. 10.32. Wiring diagram — Cooper, Cooper 'S', Countryman, Traveller and Super de-luxe (1964 to 1967)

1　Dynamo
2　Control box
3　12-volt battery
4　Starter solenoid
5　Starter motor
6　Lighting switch
7　Headlamp dip switch
8　RH headlamp
9　LH headlamp
10　Main beam warning
11　RH sidelamp (in headlamp or flasher lamp)
12　LH sidelamp (in headlamp flasher lamp)
13　Panel lamps switch
14　Panel lamps
15　No. plate lamp (two for A/M/ADO15/W
16　RH stop & tail lamp
17　LH stop & tail lamp
18　Stop lamp switch
19　Fuse unit; 1-2, 35 amp; 3-4, 35 amp
20　Interior light
21　RH door switch
22　LH door switch
23　Horn
24　Horn-push
25　Flasher unit
26　Direction indicator switch
27　Direction indicator warning lamp
28　RH front flasher lamp
29　LH front flasher lamp
30　RH rear flasher lamp
31　LH rear flasher lamp
32　Heater switch)when
33　Heater motor)fitted
34　Fuel gauge
35　Fuel gauge tank unit
36　Windscreen wiper switch
37　Windscreen wiper motor
38　Ignition/starter switch
39　Ignition coil
40　Distributor
41　Fuel pump
42　Oil pressure switch
43　Oil pressure warning lamp
44　Ignition warning lamp
45　Speedometer
46　Temperature gauge
47　Temperature gauge transmitter
64　Bi-metal instrument voltage stabiliser
83　Induction heater & thermostat (when fitted)
84　Suction chamber heater
94　Oil filter switch

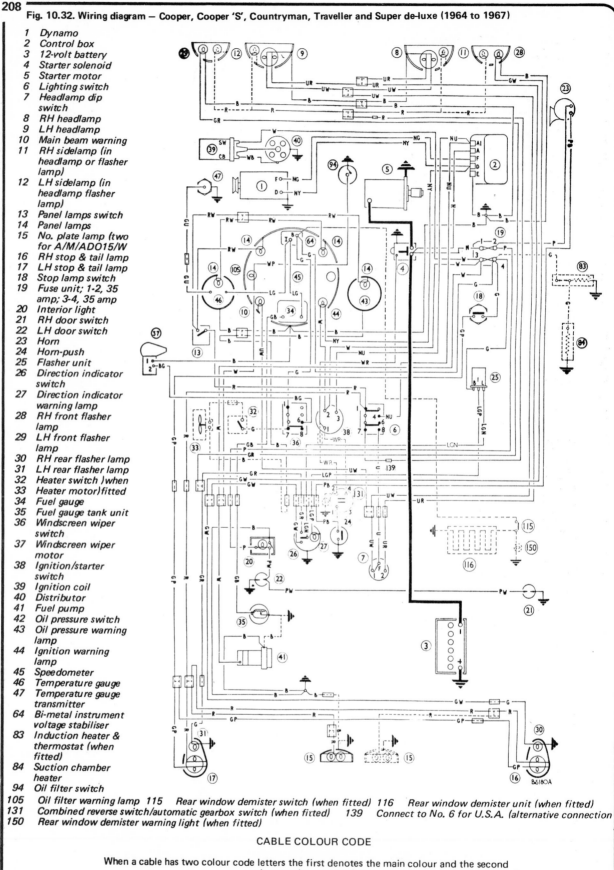

105　Oil filter warning lamp　115　Rear window demister switch (when fitted)　116　Rear window demister unit (when fitted)
131　Combined reverse switch/automatic gearbox switch (when fitted)　139　Connect to No. 6 for U.S.A. (alternative connection
150　Rear window demister warning light (when fitted)

CABLE COLOUR CODE

When a cable has two colour code letters the first denotes the main colour and the second denotes the tracer colour

B	Black	N	Brown	P	Purple	W	White	LG	Light Green
U	Blue	G	Green	R	Red	Y	Yellow		

Fig. 10.33. Wiring diagram - Mini Moke (up to 1967)

No.	Description
1	Dynamo
2	Control box
3	12-volt battery
4	Starter solenoid
5	Starter motor
6	Lighting switch
7	Headlamp dipswitch
8	RH headlamp
9	LH headlamp
10	Main beam warning lamp
11	RH sidelamp
12	LH sidelamp
14	Panel lamps
15	Number plate illumination lamp
16	RH stop and tail lamp
17	LH stop and tail lamp
18	Stop lamp switch
19	Two-way fuse unit
	1-2, 35 amp, 3-4, 35 amp
23	Horn
24	Horn push
25	Flasher unit
26	Direction indicator switch
27	Direction indicator
	warning lamp
28	RH front flasher lamp
29	LH front flasher lamp
30	RH rear flasher lamp
31	LH rear flasher lamp
34	Fuel gauge
35	Fuel gauge tank unit
36	Windscreen wiper switch
37	Windscreen wiper motor
38	Ignition starter switch
39	Ignition coil
40	Distributor
41	Fuel pump
42	Oil pressure switch
43	Oil pressure warning light
44	Ignition warning light
45	Speedometer
64	Bi-metallic instrument
	voltage stabilizer
83	Induction heater and
	thermostat
84	Suction chamber heater
94	Oil filter switch
105	Oil filter warning lamp

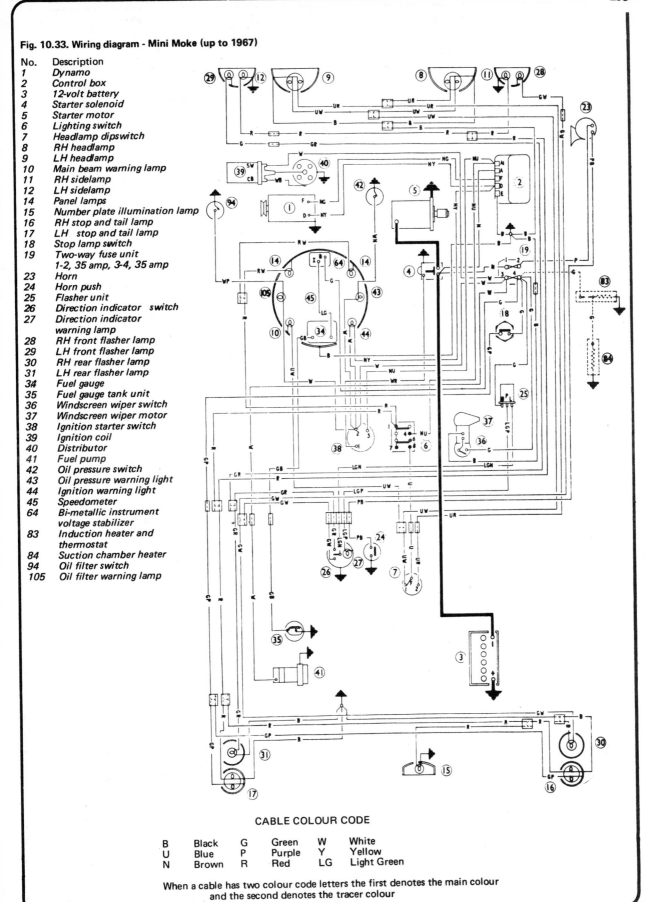

CABLE COLOUR CODE

B	Black	G	Green	W	White
U	Blue	P	Purple	Y	Yellow
N	Brown	R	Red	LG	Light Green

When a cable has two colour code letters the first denotes the main colour
and the second denotes the tracer colour

Fig. 10.34. Wiring diagram - Super de-luxe, Countryman, Traveller, Cooper and Cooper 'S' Mark II

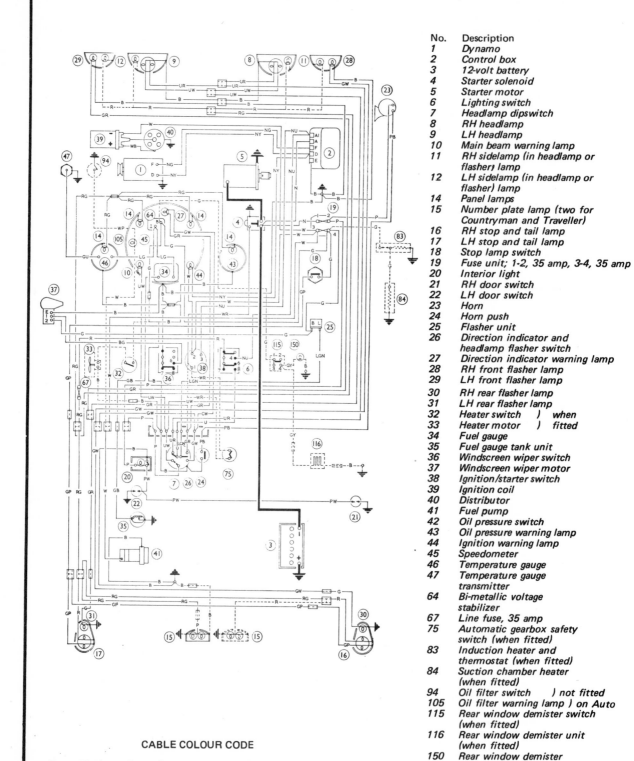

No.	Description
1	Dynamo
2	Control box
3	12-volt battery
4	Starter solenoid
5	Starter motor
6	Lighting switch
7	Headlamp dipswitch
8	RH headlamp
9	LH headlamp
10	Main beam warning lamp
11	RH sidelamp (in headlamp or flasher) lamp
12	LH sidelamp (in headlamp or flasher) lamp
14	Panel lamps
15	Number plate lamp (two for Countryman and Traveller)
16	RH stop and tail lamp
17	LH stop and tail lamp
18	Stop lamp switch
19	Fuse unit; 1-2, 35 amp, 3-4, 35 amp
20	Interior light
21	RH door switch
22	LH door switch
23	Horn
24	Horn push
25	Flasher unit
26	Direction indicator and headlamp flasher switch
27	Direction indicator warning lamp
28	RH front flasher lamp
29	LH front flasher lamp
30	RH rear flasher lamp
31	LH rear flasher lamp
32	Heater switch) when
33	Heater motor) fitted
34	Fuel gauge
35	Fuel gauge tank unit
36	Windscreen wiper switch
37	Windscreen wiper motor
38	Ignition/starter switch
39	Ignition coil
40	Distributor
41	Fuel pump
42	Oil pressure switch
43	Oil pressure warning lamp
44	Ignition warning lamp
45	Speedometer
46	Temperature gauge
47	Temperature gauge transmitter
64	Bi-metallic voltage stabilizer
67	Line fuse, 35 amp
75	Automatic gearbox safety switch (when fitted)
83	Induction heater and thermostat (when fitted)
84	Suction chamber heater (when fitted)
94	Oil filter switch) not fitted
105	Oil filter warning lamp) on Auto
115	Rear window demister switch (when fitted)
116	Rear window demister unit (when fitted)
150	Rear window demister warning light (when fitted)

CABLE COLOUR CODE

B	Black	G	Green	W	White
U	Blue	P	Purple	Y	Yellow
N	Brown	R	Red	LG	Light Green

When a cable has two colour code letters the first denotes the main colour and the second denotes the tracer colour

Fig. 10.35. Wiring diagram - Standard saloon, Van and Pick-up Mark II

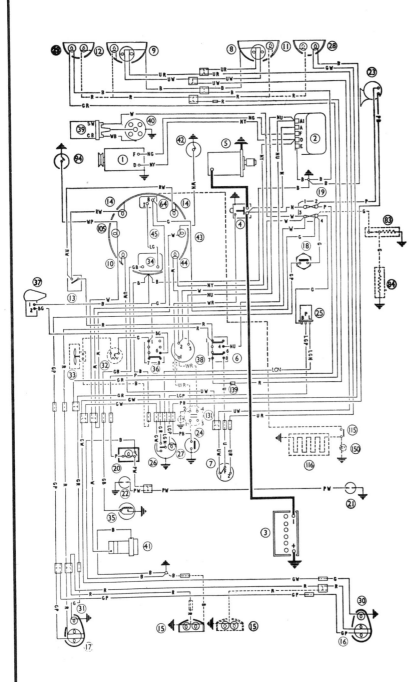

No.	Description
1	Dynamo
2	Control box
3	12-volt battery
4	Starter solenoid
5	Starter motor
6	Lighting switch
7	Headlamp dipswitch
8	RH headlamp
9	LH headlamp
10	Main beam warning light
11	RH sidelamp (in headlamp or flasher) lamp
12	LH sidelamp (in headlamp or flasher) lamp
14	Panel lamps
15	Number plate lamp (two for Van)
16	RH stop and tail lamp
17	LH stop and tail lamp
18	Stop lamp switch
19	Fuse unit; 1-2, 35 amp 3-4, 35 amp
20	Interior light
21	RH door switch
22	LH door switch
23	Horn
24	Horn push
25	Flasher unit
26	Direction indicator and headlamp flasher switch
27	Direction indicator warning lamp
28	RH front flasher lamp
29	LH front flasher lamp
30	RH rear flasher lamp
31	LH rear flasher lamp
32	Heater switch) when
33	Heater motor) fitted
34	Fuel gauge
35	Fuel gauge tank unit
36	Windscreen wiper switch
37	Windscreen wiper motor
38	Ignition/starter switch
39	Ignition coil
40	Distributor
41	Fuel pump
42	Oil pressure switch
43	Oil pressure warning lamp
44	Ignition warning lamp
45	Speedometer
64	Bi-metallic instrument voltage stabilizer
67	Line fuse, 35 amp
75	Automatic gearbox safety switch (when fitted)
83	Induction heater and thermostat (when fitted)
84	Suction chamber heater (when fitted)
94	Oil filter switch) not fitted
105	Oil filter warning lamp) on Auto
115	Rear window demister switch (when fitted)
116	Rear window demister unit (when fitted)
150	Rear window demister warning light (when fitted)

CABLE COLOUR CODE

B	Black	G	Green	W	White
U	Blue	P	Purple	Y	Yellow
N	Brown	R	Red	LG	Light Green

When a cable has two colour code letters the first denotes the main colour
and the second denotes the tracer colour

Fig. 10.36. Wiring diagram - Mini Moke Mark II

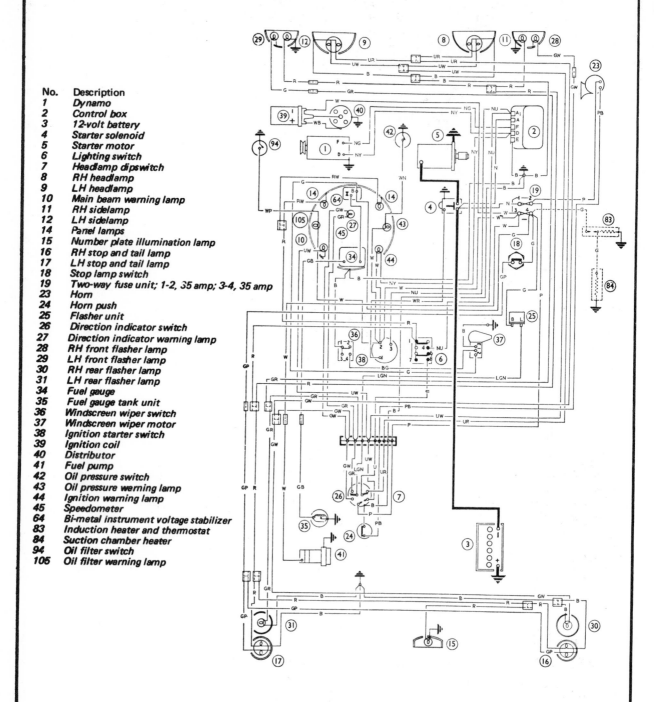

No.	Description
1	Dynamo
2	Control box
3	12-volt battery
4	Starter solenoid
5	Starter motor
6	Lighting switch
7	Headlamp dipswitch
8	RH headlamp
9	LH headlamp
10	Main beam warning lamp
11	RH sidelamp
12	LH sidelamp
14	Panel lamps
15	Number plate illumination lamp
16	RH stop and tail lamp
17	LH stop and tail lamp
18	Stop lamp switch
19	Two-way fuse unit; 1-2, 35 amp; 3-4, 35 amp
23	Horn
24	Horn push
25	Flasher unit
26	Direction indicator switch
27	Direction indicator warning lamp
28	RH front flasher lamp
29	LH front flasher lamp
30	RH rear flasher lamp
31	LH rear flasher lamp
34	Fuel gauge
35	Fuel gauge tank unit
36	Windscreen wiper switch
37	Windscreen wiper motor
38	Ignition starter switch
39	Ignition coil
40	Distributor
41	Fuel pump
42	Oil pressure switch
43	Oil pressure warning lamp
44	Ignition warning lamp
45	Speedometer
64	Bi-metal instrument voltage stabilizer
83	Induction heater and thermostat
84	Suction chamber heater
94	Oil filter switch
105	Oil filter warning lamp

CABLE COLOUR CODE

B	Black	G	Green	W	White
U	Blue	P	Purple	Y	Yellow
N	Brown	R	Red	LG	Light Green

When a cable has two colour code letters the first denotes the main colour
and the second denotes the tracer colour

Master Key to Wiring diagrams
(Figures 10.37, 10.38, 10.39, 10.40, 13.33, 13.34, 13.35, 13.36, 13.37)
Some of the components listed in this key may not be fitted to individual models

1	Dynamo or alternator
2	Control box
3	Battery (12-volt)
4	Starter solenoid
5	Starter motor
6	Lighting switch
7	Headlamp dip switch
8	RH headlamp
9	LH headlamp
10	Main beam warning lamp
11	RH sidelamp/parking lamp
12	LH sidelamp/parking lamp
14	Panel lamps
15	Number plate lamp(s)
16	RH stop and tail lamp
17	LH stop and tail lamp
18	Stop lamp switch
19	Fuse block
20	Interior light
21	RH door switch(es)
22	LH door switch(es)
23	Horn(s)
24	Horn push
25	Flasher unit
26	Direction indicator, headlamp flasher, and dip switch
27	Direction indicator warning lamp(s)
28	RH front flasher lamp
29	LH front flasher lamp
30	RH rear flasher lamp
31	LH rear flasher lamp
32	Heater or fresh-air blower switch
33	Heater or fresh-air blower
34	Fuel gauge
35	Fuel gauge tank unit
36	Windscreen wiper switch
37	Windscreen wiper motor
38	Ignition/starter switch
39	Ignition coil
40	Distributor
41	Fuel pump
42	Oil pressure switch

43	Oil pressure gauge or warning lamp
44	Ignition warning lamp
45	Speedometer (headlamp flasher switch on Canadian Mini 1000)
46	Water temperature gauge
47	Water temperature transmitter
49	Reverse lamp switch
50	Reverse lamp
64	Bi-metallic instrument voltage stabilizer
67	Line fuse (35 amp)
75	Automatic transmission safety switch (when fitted)
83	Induction heater and thermostat
84	Suction chamber heater
95	Tachometer
110	RH repeater flasher
111	LH repeater flasher
115	Rear window demister switch
116	Rear window demister unit
139	Alternative connections for two-speed wiper motor and switch
150	Rear window demist warning lamp
153	Hazard warning switch
154	Hazard warning flasher unit
158	Printed circuit instrument panel
159	Brake pressure warning lamp and lamp test switch
160	Brake pressure failure switch
164	Ballast resistor
168	Ignition key audible warning buzzer
170	R.H. front side-marker lamp
171	L.H. front side-marker lamp
172	R.H. rear side-marker lamp
173	L.H. rear side-marker lamp
198	Driver's seat belt switch
199	Passenger's seat belt switch
200	Passenger's seat switch
201	Seat belt warning gearbox switch
202	Seat belt warning lamp
203	Seat belt warning diode

CABLE COLOUR CODE

N	Brown	P	Purple	W	White
U	Blue	G	Green	Y	Yellow
R	Red	LG	Light Green	B	Black
O	Orange	K	Pink		

When a cable has two colour code letters the first denotes the main colour
and the second denotes the tracer colour

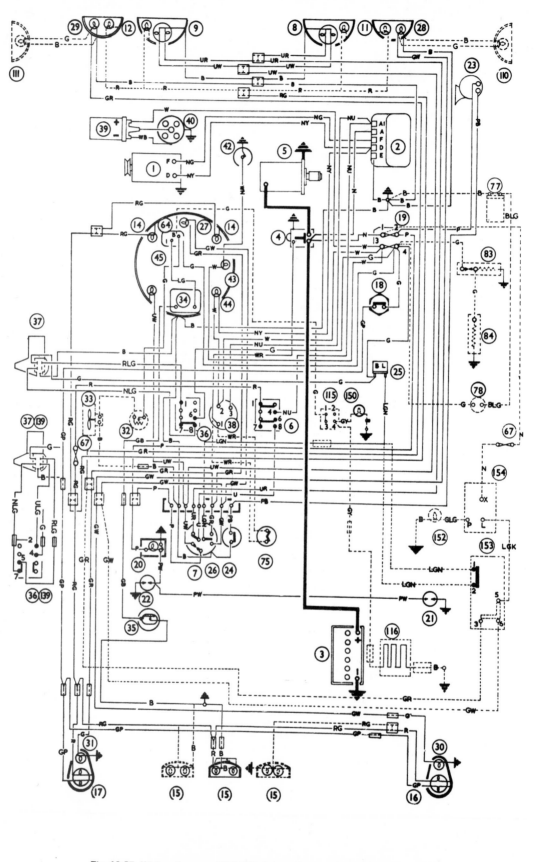

Fig. 10.37. Wiring diagram - Mini 850 de-luxe Saloon, Van and Pick-up
(For 'Key' see page 213)

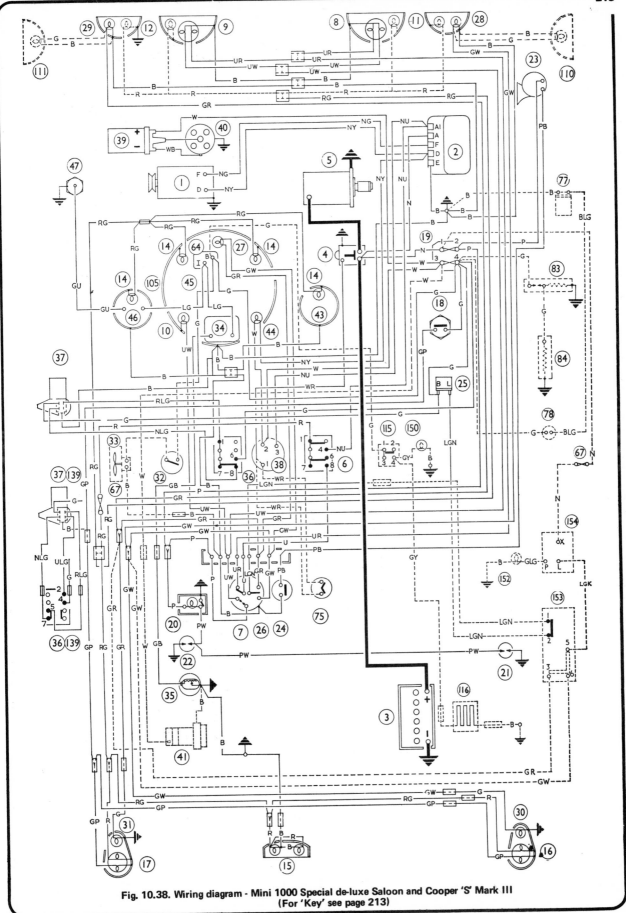

Fig. 10.38. Wiring diagram - Mini 1000 Special de-luxe Saloon and Cooper 'S' Mark III
(For 'Key' see page 213)

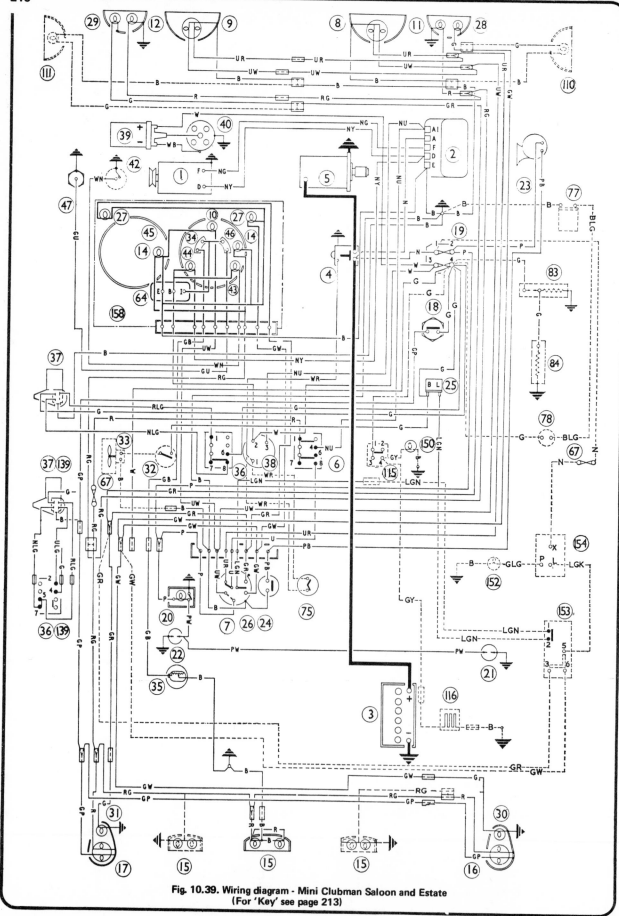

Fig. 10.39. Wiring diagram - Mini Clubman Saloon and Estate
(For 'Key' see page 213)

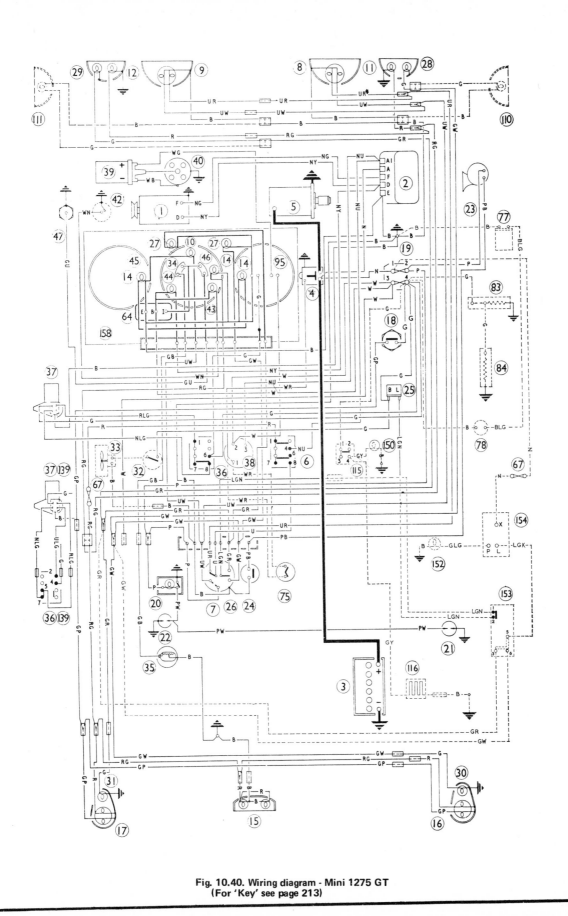

Fig. 10.40. Wiring diagram - Mini 1275 GT
(For 'Key' see page 213)

56 Fault diagnosis - electrical system

Symptom	Reason/s	Remedy
Starter motor fails to turn engine	Battery discharged	Charge battery.
	Battery defective internally	Fit new battery.
	Battery terminal leads loose or earth lead not securely attached to body	Check and tighten leads.
	Loose or broken connections in starter motor circuit	Check all connections and check any that are loose.
	Starter motor switch or solenoid faulty	Test and replace faulty components with new.
	Starter motor pinion jammed in mesh with ring gear	Disengage pinion by turning squared end of armature shaft.
	Starter brushes badly worn, sticking, or brush wires loose	Examine brushes, replace as necessary, tighten down brush wires.
	Commutator dirty, worn, or burnt	Clean commutator, recut if badly burnt.
	Starter motor armature faulty	Overhaul starter motor, fit new armature.
	Field coils earthed	Overhaul starter motor.
Starter motor turns engine very slowly	Battery in discharged condition	Charge battery.
	Starter brushes badly worn, sticking, or brush wires loose	Examine brushes, replace as necessary, tighten down brush wires.
	Loose wires in starter motor circuit	Check wiring and tighten as necessary.
Starter operates without turning engine	Starter motor pinion sticking on the screwed sleeve	Remove starter motor, clean starter motor drive.
	Pinion or ring gear teeth broken or worn	Fit new gear ring, and new pinion to starter motor drive.
Starter motor noisy or has excessively rough engagement	Pinion or ring gear teeth broken or worn	Fit new ring gear, or new pinion to starter motor drive.
	Starter drive main spring broken	Dismantle and fit new main spring
	Starter motor retaining bolts loose	Tighten starter motor securing bolts. Fit new spring washer if necessary.
Battery will not hold charge for more than a few days	Battery defective internally	Remove and fit new battery.
	Electrolyte level too low or electrolyte too weak due to leakage	Top up electrolyte level to just above plates.
	Plate separators no longer fully effective	Remove and fit new battery.
	Battery plates severely sulphated	Remove and fit new battery.
	Drive belt slipping	Check belt for wear, replace if necessary, and tighten.
	Battery terminal connections loose or corroded	Check terminals for tightness, and remove all corrosion.
	Dynamo not charging properly	Remove and overhaul dynamo.
	Short in lighting circuit causing continual battery drain	Trace and rectify.
	Regulator unit not working correctly	Check setting, clean, and replace if defective.
Ignition light fails to go out; battery runs flat in a few days	Drive belt loose and slipping, or broken	Check, replace, and tighten as necessary.
	Brushes worn, sticking, broken or dirty	Examine, clean, or replace brushes as necessary.
	Brush springs weak or broken	Examine and test. Replace as necessary.
	Commutator dirty, greasy, worn, or burnt	Clean commutator and undercut segment separators.
	Armature badly worn or armature shaft bent	Fit new or reconditioned armature.
	Contacts in light switch faulty	By-pass light switch to ascertain if fault is in switch and fit new switch as appropriate. Seek professional advice from BLMC garage.
Wiper motor fails to work	Blown fuse	Check and replace fuse if necessary.
	Wire connections loose, disconnected, or broken	Check wiper wiring. Tighten loose connections.
	Brushes badly worn	Remove and fit new brushes.
	Armature worn or faulty	If electricity at wiper motor remove and overhaul and fit replacement armature.
	Field coils faulty	Purchase reconditioned wiper motor.

Symptom	Reason/s	Remedy
Wiper motor works very slowly and takes excessive current	Commutator dirty, greasy, or burnt	Clean commutator thoroughly.
	Drive to wheelboxes too bent or unlubricated	Examine drive and straighten out severe curvature. Lubricate.
	Wheelbox spindle binding or damaged	Remove, overhaul, or fit replacement.
	Armature bearings dry or unaligned	Replace with new bearings correctly aligned.
	Armature badly worn or faulty	Remove, overhaul, or fit replacement armature.
Wiper motor works slowly and takes little current	Brushes badly worn	Remove and fit new brushes.
	Commutator dirty, greasy, or burnt	Clean commutator thoroughly.
	Armature badly worn or faulty	Remove and overhaul armature or fit replacement.
Wiper motor works but wiper blades remain static	Driving cable rack disengaged or faulty	Examine and if faulty, replace.
	Wheelbox gear and spindle damaged or worn	Examine and if faulty, replace.
	Wiper motor gearbox parts badly worn	Overhaul or fit new gearbox.

Chapter 11 Suspension and steering

Contents

Specifications

Rubber cone spring suspension

Front suspension:

Type	Independent by rubber cone springs and unequal length wishbones.
Castor angle	3º static unladen condition
Camber angle	1º positive to 3º positive. Static unladen condition
'King pin' inclination	9º 30' static unladen condition
Toe-out	1/16 in. (1.59 mm) static unladen condition
Dampers (shock absorbers)	Girling double acting telescopic type
Front hub bearings (standard)	Ball roller bearings
(Cooper 'S')	Timkin taper roller bearings.
Track: 3.50B wheels	47 7/16 in. (1.205 m)
4.5J wheels	48 17/32 in. (1.233 m)

Rear suspension:

Type	Independent by rubber cone springs and trailing radius arms
Camber angle	1º positive static unladen condition
Toe-in	1/8 in. (3.18 mm) static unladen condition
Radius arm bushes (reamed bore)	.8125 to .8130 in. (20.63 to 20.65 mm)
Dampers (shock absorbers)	Girling double acting telescopic type
Track: Standard	45 7/8 in. (1.164 m)
3.50B wheels - Cooper 'S'	46 5/16 in. (1.176 m)
4.5J wheels - Cooper 'S'	47 5/16 in. (1.202 m)

Steering:

Type	Rack and pinion
Steering wheel turns - lock to lock	2 1/3
Steering wheel diameter	15 3/4 in. (40 cm)
Steering lock angle of outer wheel	Inner wheel at 20º. Outer wheel 18 1/2º
Turning circle: Saloon	31 ft 7 in. (9.63 m)
Van, Countryman, Pick-up	32 ft 9 in. (9.983 m)

Wheels:

Type: All models except Cooper 'S'	3.50B x 10 ventilated disc
Cooper 'S' models	3.50B x 10 or 4.5J x 10 ventilated disc

Tyres:

Size: Standard	5.20 x 10 tubeless
Standard Cooper 'S' models	145 - 10SP or 5.20 - 10C41 tubed radial braced
Optional Cooper 'S' models	500L - 10 tubed

Pressures - crossply tyres	Front 24 lb/sq in. (1.7 kg/sq cm) Rear 22 lb/sq in. (1.55 kg/sq cm). Increase to 24 lb/sq in. (1.7 kg/sq cm) when fully laden
Pressures - radial tyres	Front 28 lb/sq in. (1.969 kg/sq cm) Rear 26 lb/sq in. (1.828 kg/sq cm)
Pressures - Denovo tyres	Front 26 lb/sq in (1.828 kg/sq cm) Rear 24 lb/sq in (1.7 kg/sq in)

Hydrolastic suspension

The suspension, dampers, and steering of hydrolastic models are identical to non-hydrolastic models with the following important exceptions:

Front suspension:	
Type	Independent by interconnected hydrolastic displacers and un-equal length wishbones
Dampers (shock absorbers)	None - suspension self damping
Rear suspension:	
Type	Independent by interconnected hydrolastic displacers and trailing radius arms
Dampers (shock absorbers)	None - suspension self damping
Hydrolastic operating data:	
Fluid pressure early models	263 lb/sq in. static unladen condition
Fluid pressure later models (December 1965 on)	282 lb/sq in. static unladen condition
Correct riding height early models	12¾ to 13¼ in. front 13¼ to 13¾ in. rear
Correct riding height later models	12 3/8 to 12 7/8 in. front 12 7/8 to 13 3/8 in. rear

Note: The riding height is determined by measuring the vertical distance from the centre of the wheel to the wheel opening above it.

Initial fluid pressure setting after displacer replacement ...	350 lb/sq in. for first 30 minutes

Torque wrench settings:

	lb f ft	kg fm
Front hub nut (drive shaft)	55 to 60	7.6 to 8.3
Front suspension upper arm pivot pin nut	26 to 28	3.6 to 3.9
Rear suspension stub axle nut	60	8.3 (align to next slot)
Road wheel nuts	42	5.8
Steering column/rack pinion clamp bolt	9 to 12	1.2 to 1.7
Steering lever to hub bolts	35	4.8
Steering lever balljoint nut (except Mini Cooper 997, 998 cc)	20 to 24	2.8 to 3.3
Steering knuckle ball pin bottom nut	35 to 40	4.8 to 5.5
Steering knuckle ball pin top nut	35 to 40	4.8 to 5.5
Steering knuckle ball pin retainer	70	9.6
Steering wheel nut	41	5.7
Brake caliper securing bolts	35 to 40	4.8 to 5.5
Steering lever balljoint nut	25 to 30	3.4 to 4.1
Radius arm pivot shaft nut	53	7.3
Driveshaft nut (disc brakes)	150	20.4
Driveshaft nut (drum brakes)	60	8.3
Wheelnuts	45	6.4

1 General description

On early models up to September 1964 the independent front suspension was of the rubber spring, lower wishbone and single upper link type. The rear suspension was also independent by trailing radius arms. Girling telescopic dampers are fitted and are attached to the upper link and wing valance at the front, and radius arm and bodyshell at the rear.

Later models with hydrolastic suspension made use of a special displacer unit at each wheel in place of the previous Moulton rubber spring. The front and rear displacer units are connected by tubes and piping.

Made from sheet steel and rubber, each displacer unit comprises a lower and upper chamber housing, and a nylon re-inforced rubber diaphragm which is connected to the top suspension arm by way of a strut and tapered piston. Damper valves in the top of the fluid separating chamber perform the function done by separate telescopic dampers on previous Minis.

The displacer units are fitted with a mixture of water, alcohol, and anti-corrosive additives and work in the following manner.

When either of the front wheels hit a bump the strut attached to the top suspension link forces the piston up, which displaces the diaphragm. This increases the pressure in the unit and so forces some of the fluid from the lower to the upper chamber.

This causes the rubber spring to deflect and to transfer some of the liquid, via the interconnecting pipe, to the rear displacer unit on the same side. As the fluid enters the rear top chamber it pushes down on the piston which results in the rear of the car being raised. This all occurs far more quickly than it takes to describe.

The same process happens when a rear wheel meets a bump, but in reverse, as the fluid is now forced into one of the front displacer units. In this way it is possible to obtain a very comfortable ride with the minimum of roll and pitching.

In November 1969 the standard models reverted back to the cone suspension system. The 1275 GT suspension continued up to June 1971, with the hydrolastic system, at which time it too reverted back to the cone type system.

Rack and pinion steering is fitted with 2 1/3 turns of the wheel from lock-to-lock, giving a 31 to 32 foot (9.3 - 9.6 metres) turning circle.

The rack and pinion steering gear is held in place against the engine bulkhead by a 'U' bolt at each end of the rack housing. Tie-rods from each end of the steering gear housing operate the steering arms, via both exposed, and rubber gaitered enclosed, ball joints. The upper splined end of the helically toothed pinion protrudes from the rack housing and engages with the splined end of the steering column. The pinion spline is grooved and the steering column is held to the pinion by a clamp bolt which partially rests in the pinion groove.

It is necessary to depressurise the system of later hydrolastic models if it is wished to overhaul the upper suspension arm, strut, or displacer unit, or to remove the front or rear subframes.

On reassembly it will be necessary to repressurise the system. This involves the use of special servicing equipment which most BLMC garage of any size possess.

A hydrolastic Mini can be driven for short distances with the

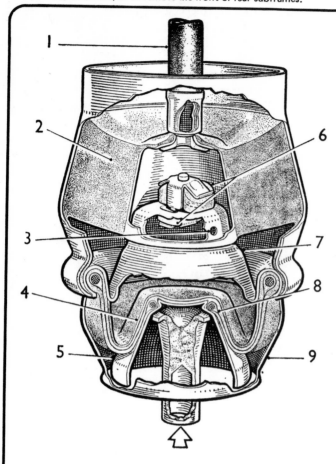

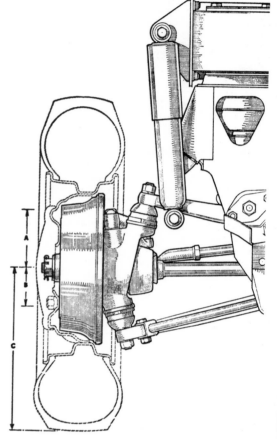

Fig. 11.1. Hydrolastic suspension displacer unit

1   Interconnecting pipe
2   Rubber spring
3   Damper bleed
4   Butyl liner
5   Tapered piston
6   Damper valve
7   Fluid separating member
8   Rubber diaphragm
9   Tapered cylinder

Fig. 11.3. Allowable suspension movement (rubber cone spring models)

The general arrangement of the front suspension:
A   Maximum upward deflection from normal (3.344 in. (85 mm))
B   Rebound maximum deflection from normal (2.281 in. (85 mm))
C   Normal distance above ground level

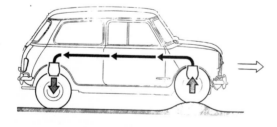

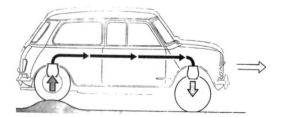

Fig. 11.2. Principle of hydrolastic suspension

(Left)   The rear rises in response to upward motion of the front wheel

(Right)   The front rises in response to upward motion of the rear wheel

system depressurised, providing it is driven slowly (ie 30 mph - 48.3 kph). It is therefore, quite feasible for the private owner to carry out repairs himself, providing his local BLMC garage is willing to depressurise and pressurise his hydrolastic system for him.

2 Suspension, steering and dampers - checking for wear

To check for wear in the outer ball joints of the tie-rods place the car over a pit, or lie on the ground looking at the balljoints, and get a friend to rock the steering wheel from side to side. Wear is present if there is play in the joints.

To check for wear in the rubber and metal bushes jack up the front of the car until the wheels are clear of the ground. Hold each wheel in turn, at the top and bottom and try to rock it. If the wheel rocks continue the movement at the same time inspecting the upper link bushes, and the rubber bushes at the inner ends of the wishbone for play.

If the wheel rocks and there is no side movement in the rubber bushes, then the swivel hub ball pins will be worn. Alternatively, if the movement occurs between the wheel and the brake backplate, then the hub bearings require replacement.

Sideplay or vertical or horizontal movement of the upper link relative to the body is best checked with the outer end of the link freed from the swivel hub. If play is present the bearings are worn and replacements should be purchased. How well the dampers function can be checked by bouncing the car at each corner. After each bounce the car should return to its normal ride position within 1 up, or down, movement. If the car continues to move up-and-down in decreasing amounts it means that the dampers are worn and must be replaced.

The dampers cannot be adjusted without special tools, and therefore must not be dismantled but exchanged with your local BLMC garage for replacement units (if available).

Excessive play in the steering gear will lead to wheel wobble, and can be confirmed by checking if there is any lost movement between the end of the steering column and the rack. Rack and pinion steering is normally very accurate and lost motion in the steering gear indicates a considerable mileage or lack of lubrication.

The outer balljoints at each end of the tie-rods are the most likely items for wear first, followed by the rack balljoints at the inner end of the tie-rods.

3 Front suspension rubber spring - removal and replacement

Removal of one of the rubber springs from the front suspension involves the use of a special rubber spring compressor. There is, unfortunately, no way round this, and as the tool is somewhat expensive to buy it is best to try to borrow or hire one from your local BLMC garage. (BLMC service tool "18G 574").

1 Undo the nuts securing the bonnet, and lift the bonnet off to give unrestricted working space.

2 Knock back the locking tabs from the two nuts (or bolts in the case of later cars) on the appropriate end of the engine bulkhead crossmember, remove one bolt, slacken the other sufficiently to move the washer plate to expose the hole which it covers.

3 Place the spring compression tool centrally over the hole in the crossmember. Oil the thread on the central bolt of the tool and screw the bolt into the thread in the centre of the rubber spring exactly nine turns.

4 Turn the ratchet handle so the centre nut makes contact with the body of the tool, and then, holding the centre screw to prevent it from rotating, turn the ratchet arm clockwise to compress the spring unit.

5 Slacken the road wheel nuts and then jack up the front of the car. Remove the road wheel and place an axle stand under the car. It should now be possible to withdraw the suspension strut. (Fig. 11.5).

6 Remove the bump rubber from the subframe tower by un-

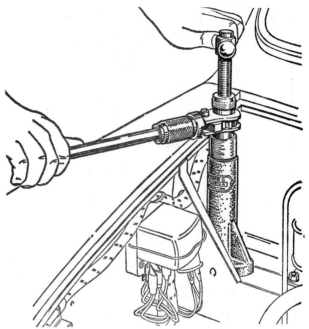

Fig. 11.4. Use of special tool to compress rubber cone spring DO NOT IMPROVISE THIS TOOL

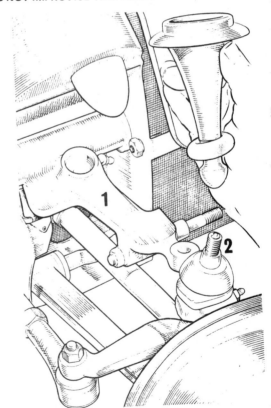

Fig. 11.5. Removal of suspension strut. Note how the upper arm (1) has been detached from the hub ball pin (2)

doing the retaining nut.

7 Undo the nut from the top swivel ball pin and disconnect the upper suspension arm from the ball pin shank.

8 Undo the nut securing the damper to the upper suspension arm; undo and remove the nuts from the pivot pin on which the

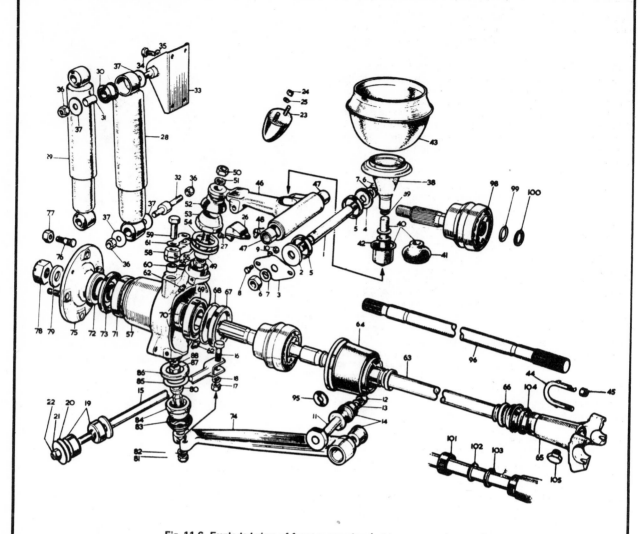

Fig. 11.6. Exploded view of front suspension (rubber cone spring type)

1 Upper support arm shaft	23 Bump buffer	49 Ball top pin	74 Lower wishbone arm
2 Thrust collar	24 Nut	50 Nut	75 Driving flange
3 Retaining plate	25 Spring washer	51 Spring washer	76 Wheel stud
4 Thrust washer	26 Rebound buffer	52 Dust cover	77 Wheel nut
5 Rubber sealing ring	27 Screw	53 Retainer	78 Castellated nut
6 Nut	28 Armstrong damper	54 Shim	79 Plain washer
7 Washer	29 Girling damper	55 Lockwasher	80 Lower ball pin
8 Screw	30 Rubber bush	56 Ball seat	81 Nut
9 Washer	31 Sleeve	57 Swivel hub	82 Spring washer
10 Nut	32 Anchor pin	58 Steering arm	83 Dust cover
11 Lower wishbone arm shaft	33 Right hand bracket	59 Screw	84 Ball pin retainer
12 Nut	34 Screw	60 Hollow dowel	85 Ball pin shim
13 Spring washer	35 Springwasher	61 Washer	86 Lockwasher
14 Rubber bushes	36 Nut	62 Grease nipple	87 Ball seat
15 Tie-rod	37 Washer	63 Drive shaft assembly	88 Ball seat spring
16 Tie-rod bolt	38 Strut	64 Rubber boot	98 Inner race
17 Nut	39 Strut washer	65 Flange	99 Inner circlip
18 Spring washer	40 Knuckle joint assembly	67 Oil seal	100 Outer circlip
19 Pad	41 Dust cover	68 Spacer	101 Dust cap
20 Washer	42 Ball socket	69 Inner bearing	102 Steel washer
21 Plain washer	43 Rubber spring	70 Distance ring	103 Cork washer
22 Nut	46 Upper arm assembly	71 Outer bearing	104 Circlip
	47 Needle roller bearing	72 Distance piece	105 Grease hole plug
	48 Lubricating nipple	73 Oil seal	

suspension arm hinges; remove the front thrust washer retaining plate, and remove the front and rear thrust washers. Carefully push the pivot pin forwards and then remove the upper suspension arm.

9 Free the compression of the rubber spring by holding the centre screw of the compression tool and, reversing the operation of the ratchet by turning the milled slave on the inner end of the handle, unscrew the central bolt from the centre of the rubber spring and remove the spring.

10 Replacement is a direct reversal of the removal sequence. Ensure that the rubber spring locates properly in the subframe tower and that the dust seal over the lip of the nylon seating in the upper arm is properly secured.

4 Front suspension strut - removal and replacement

The front suspension struts are located between the inner half of the upper suspension arm, and the rubber spring in the subframe tower.

2 In 1961 from car no. "44722" a circular section washer was fitted between the welded strut body and the knuckle shoulder. This served to raise the car about 1 in. (2.54 cm) over 1959 to 1960 models. Cars manufactured from 1962 onwards make use of a cast strut which was slightly longer, and dispensed with the need for the washer.

3 The ride height of 1960 models can be raised by fitting one washer to each of the four suspension struts. The knuckle shoulder is simply a push fit in the end of the suspension strut and adding the washer mentioned above is simplicity itself.

4 To remove a front suspension strut follow the sequence described in Section 3, paragraphs 1 to 5 inclusive.

5 Replacement is a straightforward reversal of the removal sequence.

5 Rear suspension rubber spring and suspension strut - removal and replacement

Compared with removal of the front springs, removal of the rear springs is relatively uncomplicated, and no special tools are required.

1 Open the boot and, if removing the left-hand spring take out the petrol tank as described in Chapter 3.

2 Undo the nut which secures the top of the right or left-hand rear dampers in place, depending on which spring is to be removed.

3 Slacken the road wheel nuts, and then jack up the rear of the car. Remove the roadwheel and place an axle stand under the rear subframe.

4 Pull the top of the damper free and pull the radius arm down so it is hanging in its lowest position. The suspension strut can now be pulled clear from the subframe, followed by the rubber springs. The nylon cup can be left in the arm, or, if wished, it can be removed by hand. If it is damaged and not fit for further service it will have to be prised loose.

5 Replacement is a straight reversal of the removal sequence. **Note:** Ensure when replacing the spring that the nylon cup is fitted to the strut ball end and that the rubber dust seal is fitted over the edge of the seal, prior to refitting the strut. Fit the strut **before** the spring. Ensure the strut and the spring are properly fitted on their spigots, and that they do not slip out of place while the radius arm is being raised so that the top of the damper can be reconnected to the body.

6 The same remarks concerning the fitting of the circular section washers to the front struts apply to those at the rear. Refer to Section 4 for full information.

6 Front damper - removal and replacement

1 Loosen the road wheel securing nuts, apply the handbrake and jack up the front of the car.

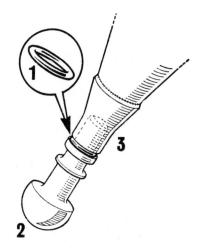

Fig. 11.7. The round section washer (1) fits between the knuckle joint (2) and the main body of the suspension strut (3). The joint (2) is a simple press fit in the strut (3)

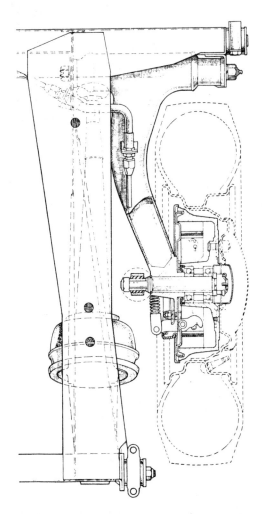

Fig. 11.8. Cross section view of rear hub and suspension assembly

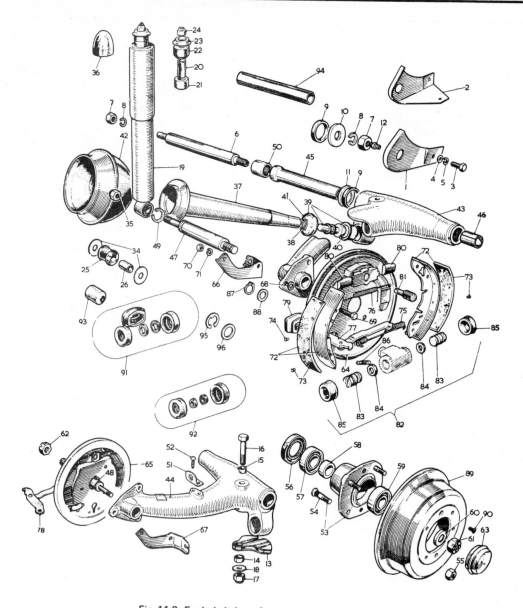

Fig. 11.9. Exploded view of rear brake and suspension assembly

1	Right-hand radius arm shroud
2	Left-hand radius arm shroud
3	Screw
4	Plain washer
5	Spring washer
6	Pivot shaft
7	Nut
8	Spring washer
9	Sealing ring
10	Thrust washer
11	Inner end thrust washer
12	Lubricator
13	Handbrake cable sector
14	Sector bush
15	Distance tube
16	Sector bolt
17	Nut
18	Plain washer
19	Damper
20	Ferrule
21	Lower mounting rubber
22	Top mounting rubber
23	Special washer
24	Nut
25	Ferrule
26	Sleeve
34	Retaining washer
35	Nut
36	Buffer
37	Strut
38	Strut washer
39	Knuckle joint
40	Ball socket
41	Dust cover
42	Rubber spring
43	RH radius arm
44	LH radius arm
45	Lubricating tube
46	Bush
47	RH stub shaft
48	LH stub shaft
49	Circlip
50	Needle roller bearing
51	Hose bracket
52	Screw
53	Hub assembly
54	Wheel stud
55	Wheel nut
56	Oil seal
57	Inner bearing
58	Bearing spacer
59	Outer bearing
60	Special washer
61	Nut RHT
62	Nut LHT
63	Cap
64	RH brake backplate
65	LH brake backplate
66	RH bracket
67	LH bracket
68	Packing washer
69	Bolt
70	Nut
71	Spring washer
72	Brake shoe
73	Brake lining
74	Rivet
75	Return spring
76	Adjuster end return spring
77	RH handbrake lever
78	LH handbrake lever
79	Wheel cylinder boot
80	Tappet
81	Wedge
82	Wheel cylinder assembly
83	Piston
84	Seal
85	Boot
86	Bleed screw
87	Circlip
88	Washer
89	Brake drum
90	Screw
91	Wheel cylinder repair kit
92	Wheel cylinder repair kit

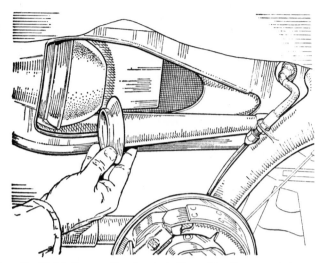

Fig. 11.10. Remove the rear strut after pulling it rearwards to free the ball end from the radius arm

2 Remove the wheel, place a support under the brake drum, and undo the securing nuts from the top and bottom mounting spigots.

3 Pull the damper away. Examine the condition of the rubber bushes in the mounting eyes, and renew them if worn. Keep the damper vertical all the time.

4 Note that, before refitting the damper, it is necessary to remove any air from the pressure chamber. Hold the damper vertical, and slowly compress and extend it fully about six times.

5 Keep the damper vertical while refitting, which is a direct reversal of the removal sequence.

7 Rear damper - removal and replacement

1 Open the boot (or doors on Van and Traveller models) and, if removing the left-hand damper, take out the petrol tank as described in Chapter 3.

2 Undo the nut which secures the top of the right or left-hand damper to the body, depending on which damper unit is to be removed, and remove the washer and rubber bush. If the body starts to turn as the nut is undone there is a flat on the shaft which can be held.

3 Loosen the road wheel securing nuts, place the car in gear, and jack up the rear subframe.

4 Remove the wheel and undo the lower mounting nut and washer.

5 Pull the top of the damper down, and free the bottom of the unit from the radius arm. Keep the damper vertical all the time.

6 Examine the condition of the rubber bushes and renew them if worn. **Note**: Before refitting the damper, it is necessary to remove any air from the pressure chamber. Hold the damper vertical, and slowly extend and compress it fully about six times.

7 Keep the damper vertical while refitting, which is a straight reversal of the removal sequence. Ensure the strut and springs are properly fitted on their spigots, and that they do not slip out of place while the radius arm is being raised to connect the top of the damper to the body.

8 Front hub - removal and replacement.

The front hubs are not adjustable and if wear is detected (play between the road wheels and swivel hubs) the hubs will have to be removed and new bearings fitted.

The inner hubs driving flanges are held in place on the splined outer ends of the drive shafts by castellated nuts. On all models except Cooper 'S' and 1275 GT models two single

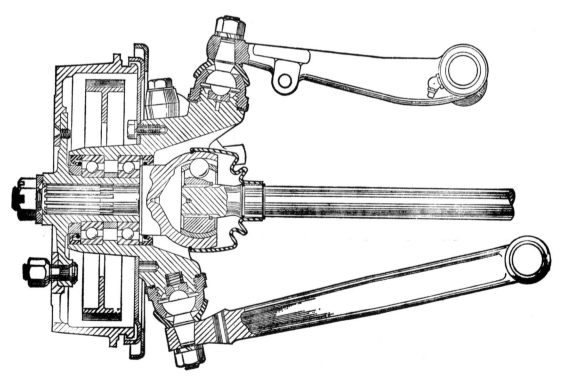

Fig. 11.11. Cross sectional view of front hub and suspension assembly (Mini range with front drum brakes)

row ball bearings are fitted between the swivel hub and the inner hub/driving flanges. On Mini Cooper 'S' models different hubs with taper roller bearings are used. In both cases no maintenance is required, and the bearings must always be renewed in sets. A new distance piece must **always** be used on Mini Cooper 'S' models.

1 Slacken the road wheel nuts, jack up the car, and remove the road wheel.

2 Lever off the hub cap, extract the split pin, and unscrew and remove the castellated nut and locating washer. It may be necessary to get a friend to hold the brakes on while the nut is undone.

3 In the case of drum-braked cars unscrew the two brake drum retaining screws and pull off the brake drum. In the case of disc-braked cars, remove the caliper assembly as described in Chapter 9 and support it on a block so the hydraulic hose is not stretched, which could lead to leaks.

4 Free the balljoint shank from the steering arm after knocking back the lockwasher and undoing the retaining nut.

5 Undo and remove the nut and spring washer from the top of the swivel hub and lift the upper suspension arm away from the ball pin. It may be necessary to use a balljoint extractor if the arm proves reluctant to free from the ball pin taper. Alternatively, strike in unison with two hammers the opposite sides of the suspension arm balljoint eye, to 'jar' the pin free.

6 Undo and remove the nut and spring washer off the rear end of the lower arm pivot pin, and drive the pin forwards so as to free the inner end of the the lower suspension arm. Remove the nuts and tie-rod bolt from the lower suspension arm and pull the tie-rod clear.

7 Mark the adjacent driveshaft and differential flanges so they can be replaced in their same relative positions. Undo the four outer nuts on the 'U' bolts of the inner rubber universal joint so it is left secured by the two remaining bolts to the differential flange.

8 Free the brake hose at the subframe and brake backplate on drum-braked models as described in Chapter 9 and plug the openings to prevent the ingress of dirt into the hydraulic system.

9 Remove the swivel hub unit, together with the lower suspension arm and the driveshaft.

10 Carefully drift the driveshaft out from the inner side of the swivel hub by tapping the outer end of the driveshaft with a hide faced hammer.

11 On drum-braked models arrange two robust wooden blocks (about 10 in. -254 mm - high) far enough apart for the drive flange to lie freely between them, with the brake shoes resting on the top faces of the blocks. Drift the drive flange out of the swivel hub. It is likely that the inner race of the outer bearing, together with the oil seal, and the outer bearing distance piece will come away with the flange. Carefully remove these items from the flange with the aid of a puller. It is necessary to drift the inner and outer inner races off the opposite ends of the hub, because of a raised lip which separates them and prevents them from being both removed from the same end.

12 On Cooper and Cooper 'S' models, after carefully drifting the drive flange and brake disc from the swivel hub, undo the four crosshead screws which hold the disc to the hub flange. **Note:** On 997 cc/998 cc Cooper models there is a spacer on the outer face of the hub. Ensure that on reassembly the chamfered face of this spacer is towards the hub drive flange. **Note:** On Cooper 'S' models inner and outer split tapered collars are fitted at either end of the drive flange. Drift out the bearings for both Cooper and Cooper 'S' models from each side of the hub as for 850 cc Minis.

13 Thoroughly clean all traces of old grease from the hub bore and take great care that none reaches the brake shoe linings. Make sure that any burrs or score marks in the hub bore or shoulder are carefully removed with the help of a scraper.

14 Pack the bearings with grease and ensure they are replaced hard against the raised lip in the centre of the hub. On Cooper 'S' models ensure the new distance piece which will have been supplied with new bearings, is inserted between the inner and outer bearings. These are supplied as a specially matched set and

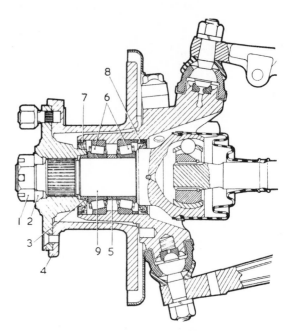

Fig. 11.12. Cross section view of front hub assembly (Cooper 'S' and 1275 GT models with disc brakes)

1	Driveshaft nut	6	Taper roller bearings
2	Outer taper collar	7	Outer oil seal
3	Inner tapered collar	8	Inner oil seal
4	Hub & disc assembly	9	Driveshaft
5	Bearing distance piece		

must never be fitted singly.

15 Fit the two grease retaining seals ensuring that the smooth rounded edge of each faces out from the centre of the hub. Fit the outer bearing spacer so the chamfered edge faces out. Drift the flange into position and reseat the inner bearing and grease seal if necessary.

16 On Cooper 'S' models assemble the hub on the driveshaft and fit the distance piece, outer bearing, and outer oil seal to the hub. Then fit the inner split taper collar, driving flange, and brake disc assembly, outer split taper collar and secure with the castellated driveshaft nut which must be tightened to a torque of 150 lb f ft (20.4 kg fm). Lock the nut with a split pin. Check the runout at the outer periphery of the disc. If more than 0.006 in. (0.15 mm) remove the disc and flange assembly and reposition on the driftshaft splines.

17 On all models other than Cooper 'S', carefully replace the swivel hub unit on the driveshaft, fit the driving flange washer with the chamfered edge facing inwards and refit the securing nut. If a vice is available place the driveshaft in it and tighten the nut to 60 lb f ft (8.30 kg fm). Lock with a split pin. Refit the swivel hub unit and driveshaft to the car.

18 Reconnect the brakes and bleed the hydraulic system. If a vice was not available and the driveshaft nut has not yet tightened, get a friend to hold the brakes on, while the nut is tightened to the correct torque.

9 Rear hub - removal and replacement

1 Loosen the appropriate rear wheel securing nuts, place the vehicle in gear, and jack up the rear of the car. Remove the wheel and prise off the hub cap.

2 Undo the screws which hold the brake drum in place, ensure the handbrake is off, and pull the drum away.

3 Pull out the split pin from the castellated nut and undo the latter from the stub axle.

4 Withdraw the hub assembly by judiciously levering it off with

the aid of two large screwdrivers, or similar. Alternatively, use a hub puller if available. In instances where the hub is very stubborn, refit the roadwheel, and pull the hub off together with the wheel actively shaking the wheel from side to side.

5 The inner grease seal should now be removed, and the ball races drifted outwards from the raised register in the hub.

6 Examine the ball races for wear, and thoroughly clean all traces of grease from the hub bore. Make sure that any burrs or score marks in the hub bore or shoulder are carefully removed with the help of a scraper.

7 Carefully grease both bearings and replace them in the hub bore so that the faces marked " thrust" face each other. Ensure the outer races are hard against the central shoulder and do not omit to fit the bearing distance piece.

8 Fit a new oil seal, with flatter side facing the radius arm and replace the hub assembly on the strut axle. Take particular care to ensure the bearing distance piece does not foul the end of the stub axle as the hub is pushed on.

9 Refit the thrust washer, chamfered side facing the bearing, replace the nut and tighten it to 55 to 60 lb f ft (7.6 to 8.30 kg fm) and lock it in place with a new split pin.

10 Replace the brake drum and rear wheel and lower the car to the ground.

10 Outer balljoint - removal and replacement

If the tie-rod outer balljoints are worn it will be necessary to renew the whole balljoint assembly as they cannot be dismantled and repaired. To remove a balljoint, free the balljoint shank from the steering arm and mark the position of the locknut on the tie-rod accurately to ensure near accurate "toe-out" on reassembly.

Slacken off the balljoint locknut, and holding the tie-rod by its flat with a spanner, to prevent it from turning, unscrew the complete ball assembly from the rod. Replacement is a straight reversal of this process. Visit your local BLMC garage to ensure that toe-out is correct.

11 Front suspension swivel hub balljoints - removal and replacement

The normal function of the king pin is undertaken on Minis by two balljoints, one at the top, and one at the bottom of each of the swivel hub units. To remove and replace the balljoints proceed as follows:

1 Compress the appropriate rubber spring unit using the special BLMC spring compressor as described in Section 3.

2 Loosen the wheel nuts, jack up the car, and remove the road wheel. Place a support stand under the front subframe.

3 Undo the nut from the bolt which holds the front tie-rod to the lower suspension arm.

4 Undo the nuts and washers from the ball pin shanks on the end of the upper and lower suspension arms. Use an extractor to free the arms from the ball pin taper. Alternatively strike in unison with two hammers the opposite sides of the suspension arm ball joint eyes to 'jar' the pin free.

5 Pull the arms away from the balljoints, remove the balljoint housing dust seal, take off the lubricator, knock up the tab of the lockwasher and unscrew the housing to release the ball and ball seat. **Note:** A spring is fitted underneath the lower ball seat joint.

6 Carefully clean all the component parts and examine them for excessive wear. Renew them as necessary. Normal wear can be taken up by shims.

7 Reassemble the ball seats, pins, and ball housings to the swivel hub without the lockwashers, or lower seat spring in position. Screw down the ball housings till there is no free movement between the ball seating and the ball, and then take a measurement with a feeler gauge in the gap between the housings and the swivel hubs.

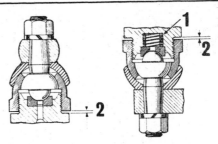

Fig. 11.13. Leave off the locking washers and the lower balljoint seat spring (1) and take feeler gauge measurements at (2) - see text

8 Dismantle the balljoints, pack with grease and then reassemble with the lockwashers, and lower seat spring. Add shims to the thickness of the feeler gauge measurement less the thickness of the washer. (Fig. 11.13).

9 Fully tighten the ball housing and ensure the joint is not too tight, or that play is present. If the initial gap was measured accurately the joint will be a perfect fit.

10 Knock up the housing washer to lock the housing in position.

11 Refit the dust seals, suspension arm, washers, and ball pin nuts and tighten the latter to a torque of 35 to 40 lb f ft. (4.8 to 5.8 kg fm).

12 Refit the tie-rod to the lower suspension arm, replace the wheel, and lower the car to the ground.

12 Radius arm - removal and replacement

1 Remove the rear damper as described in Section 7.

2 Loosen the wheel nuts, jack up the car, remove the road wheel and place a support under the subframe sidemember.

3 Remove the strut from the spring unit and the radius arm, as described in Section 5.

4 Undo the brake hose from the bracket and plug the end of the hydraulic pipe to prevent the loss of all fluid.

5 Undo the handbrake cable from the lever on the brake backplate, and, on early models, prise out the guide tube from its retaining clip on the arm, and, lifting the arm, pull the tube away from its anchorage hole in the arm boss. On later models undo the nut from the cable sector pivot and pull away the sector with the cable.

6 Undo the three set screws which hold the end finisher in place to give access to the radius arm pivot.

7 Unscrew the nut and washer from each end of the radius arm shaft which hold it to the subframe, and then remove the detachable bracket at the outer end by undoing the four securing bolts.

8 The radius arm can now be removed from the car together with the two thrust washers, and the rubber seal which fits between the arm and the sidemember.

9 Radius arm replacement is, generally speaking, a straightforward reversal of the removal sequence. The following additional points should be closely watched:

a) Pack the nylon cup and dust seal with 'Dextagrease Super GP' which is available from BLMC garages.

b) It is most important to refit the nylon cup, with the rubber dust seal lipped over it in the strut, before fitting the cup to the arm.

c) Ensure that the strut and the spring are properly fitted in their spigots, and that they do not slip out of place while the radius arm is being raised so that the top of the damper can be reconnected to the body.

d) Reconnect the brake pipe, and refit the handbrake cable, bleed the hydraulic system, replace the road wheel and lower the car to the ground.

13 Rear radius arm - dismantling, overhaul and reassembly

1 Pull out the shaft from the radius arm on which it rotates and

examine it carefully for wear. It will be quite evident if the shaft
has suffered from lack of lubrication by the amount of metal
worn away at each end.

2 The shaft runs in bronze bushes fitted to each end of the bore
in the radius arm. If the shaft is worn it is likely that the bushes
will be also. Their removal can be very difficult and it is recommended that the special BLMC service tool "18G 583" be
borrowed, or a BLMC garage requested to extract them. On no
account try to chisel or hammer them out, as this will not only
take several hours work but damage to the radius arm bore is
more than likely.

3 New bushes can be fitted with the aid of BLMC service tool
"18G 583" and they will then have to be reamed out considerably until the shaft fits perfectly. It is recommended that once
the radius arm is removed it is taken to your local BLMC garage
for the complete job of bush removal, replacement and
reaming.

4 On later models with the cast type of radius arm, a needle
roller bearing is fitted on the inner end instead of the bronze
bush (which is retained at the outer end). The needle roller
bearing is pulled out using BLMC service tool "18G 583B" and
replaced with the marked end of the bearing facing out, with the
aid of tool "18G 620". It is essential to remove the needle roller
bearing and the grease tube prior to reaming the bronze bush.

5 Generously grease the pivot and bushes and press the pivot
back into the radius arm.

14 Front upper suspension arm - removal and replacement

1 Compress the rubber spring with the aid of BLMC tool part
No. "18G 574B" as described in Section 3.
2 Loosen the wheel nuts, jack up the car, remove the roadwheel, and place a stand under the front subframe.
3 Remove the upper suspension arm from the swivel hub ball
joint, after undoing the nut from the ball pin shank. Use an
extractor to free the arm from the ball pin taper. Alternatively
strike the opposite sides of the suspension arm balljoint eye in
unison with two hammers to 'jar' the pin free.
4 Undo the nuts from the ends of the suspension arm pivot pin.
Undo the two nuts and bolts, holding the front thrust washer
plate in position and rmeove the plate and thrust washer.
5 Push the pivot pin forward, remove the rear thrust washer,
and ease the upper suspension arm out of the subframe.
6 Check the condition of the needle roller bearings fitted each
side of the inner end of the suspension arms. If worn remove
them with the aid of BLMC service tool "18G 581". Fit new
bearings with the aid of tool No. "18G 582A" so that the
marked ends face outwards. Replace the nylon cup in the suspension arm recess.
7 Pack the needle roller bearings with grease. Lubricate the
nylon cup and rubber dust seal with 'Dextagrease Super GP'. This
is available from BLMC garages.
8 Position the rear thrust washer against the pivot pin bore in
the suspension arm and secure it to the arm by its rubber dust
seal.
9 Stretch the front dust seal over the open bore of the suspension arm, and slip the pivot pin into the bore.
10 Ease the upper suspension arm into place on the subframe,
and fit the suspension strut to the arm. Slide the pivot pin into
its correct position.
11 Fit the front thrust washer followed by the retaining plate
(held by two nuts and bolts). Slip the dust seal over the thrust
washer, and fit the suspension strut to arm dust seal over the lip
of the nylon cup.
12 Refit the pivot pin washers and nuts and tighten down
securely.
13 Refit the suspension arm to the swivel hub balljoint, refit the
damper, and road wheel and lower the car to the ground.
14 Remove the special tool compressing the rubber spring.

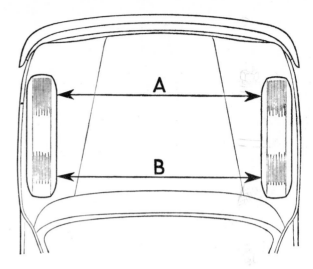

Fig. 11.14. Front wheel alignment
Dimension A must be 0.0625 in. (1.6 mm) greater than B

15 Front wheels - alignment

1 The front wheels are correctly aligned when they turn out at
the front 0.0625 in. (1.59 mm). It is important that this
measurement is taken on a 14.5 in. (368.3 mm) diameter on the
side wall of the tyre at a distance of 9.4 in (239 mm) above the
surface of the ground. Adjustment is effected by loosening the
locknut on each tie-rod balljoint, and the clips on the gaiters,
and turning both tie-rods equally until the adjustment is correct.
2 This is a job that your local BLMC garage must do, as
accurate alignment requires the use of expensive base bar or
optical alignment equipment.
3 If the wheels are not in alignment, tyre wear will be heavy
and uneven, and the steering will be stiff and unresponsive.

16 Front hydrolastic displacer unit - removal and replacement

1 Depressurise the hydrolastic system at your local BLMC
garage.
2 Loosen the appropriate wheel nuts, jack up the car, remove
the roadwheel, and securely support the subframe.
3 Free the displacer strut dust seal and remove the strut from
the displacer unit. Undo the displacer unit hose from its union
on the engine bulkhead. (Fig. 11.15).
4 Take off the upper suspension arm as described in Section 14.
5 Press the displacer unit up and undo the two screws inside the
subframe tower which secure the support bracket.
6 Free the lugs of the displacer unit by turning it anticlockwise. Pull the unit away from the subframe.
7 Replacement is a straightforward reversal of the removal
instructions. Always lubricate the strut ball end and seat with
'Dextragrease Super GP'. This is available from BLMC garages.

17 Rear hydrolastic displacer unit - removal and replacement

1 Depressurise the hydrolastic system at your local BLMC
garage.
2 Loosen the wheel nuts, jack up the car, remove the roadwheel, and securely support the subframe.
3 Remove the bump rubber from the subframe and free the
helper spring from the radius arm. Free the dust seal from the
displacer strut.
4 Free the flexible hose by undoing it from the union on the
rear end of the subframe.

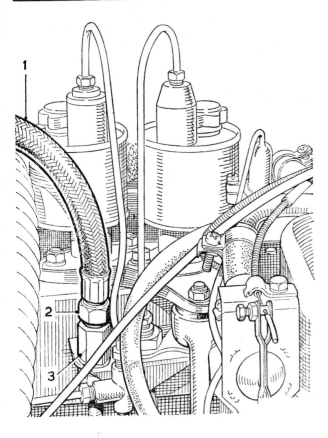

Fig. 11.15. Right-hand front displacer hose connector

1 Displacer hose
2 Hose nut
3 Connector

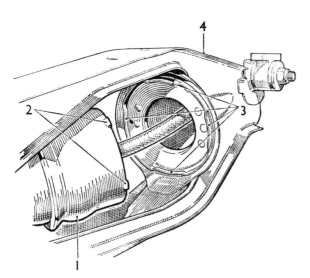

Fig. 11.16. Rear suspension displacer unit separated from locating plate

1 Displacer unit
2 Locating lugs
3 Locating plate
4 Subframe

5 Pull out the displacer strut. The displacer unit is held in position by four lugs which engage in four locating registers in the subframe. (Fig. 11.16).
6 Free the displacer unit by turning it anticlockwise.
7 Replacement is a straightforward reversal of the removal instructions. Always lubricate the strut ball end and seat with 'Dextragrease Super GP'. This is available from BLMC garages.

18 Steering wheel - removal and replacement

1 Unscrew the small screw from the side of the steering wheel boss where this is fitted, and prise off the motif cap from the centre of the steering wheel with a small screwdriver. With a suitable socket spanner, unscrew the nut which retains the wheel to the steering column.
2 Remove the nut, and on later models the retaining washer under it, and pull the wheel off the splines on the column. Replacement is a simple reversal of this process. Tighten the nut to 41 lb f ft. (5.7 kg fm).

19 Steering column bush - removal and replacement

If there is any play in the top of the steering column, it will be necessary to replace the felt, or nylon, bush which is fitted between the top of the inner and outer steering columns. The bush is replaced after removing the steering wheel and prising the old bush out. The new bush should be soaked in heavy oil and slid into place.

20 Steering column - removal and replacement

1 Disconnect the battery by removing the earth lead.
2 Disconnect the wires from the horn and the direction indicators at the snap connectors under the parcel shelf.
3 Undo the nut and bolt from the steering column support clip.
4 Unscrew the nut and remove the bolt from the clamp on the lower end of the steering column.
5 Pull the column assembly off the piston shaft splines and remove the column from inside the car.
6 Replacement is a straight reversal of this process. **Note:** The slot in the column clamp must be correctly located with the front wheels facing straight ahead. In order to bring the direction indicator cancelling lug into the right position the clamp should be underneath and horizontal to the column.

21 Rack and pinion steering gear - removal and replacement

The rack and pinion steering gear is held to the bottom of the turned up portion of the bodyshell floor by two 'U' bolts. It is sandwiched tightly between the floor and the front subframe. Before the steering gear can be removed it is necessary to lower the front subframe four of five inches to make enough room for removal of the 'U' bolts securing the rack. A good centre lift jack, several supports and a few load spreaders made from odd pieces of wooden plank are essential. Removing and replacing the steering gear will take about three hours.
1 Jack up the rear of the car, and place wooden blocks under the rear wheels. Remove the jack.
2 Loosen the front wheel securing nuts, and with the jack resting under the centre of the subframe jack the front of the car about 15 in. (381 mm) off the ground. Support the front subframe at each side with suitable chocks.
3 Take off the front wheels and undo the nuts which hold the lower ends of the dampers to the mounting spigots. Pull the lower end of the dampers off the spigots.
4 Remove the track rod ends from the steering arms, after undoing the securing nuts, by impact hammering.
5 From inside the car free the upper end of the steering column from its bracket on the front edge of the panel shelf, by loosening the transverse bolt. On late models remove the right-hand steering column cowl and loosen the column clip shear bolt by

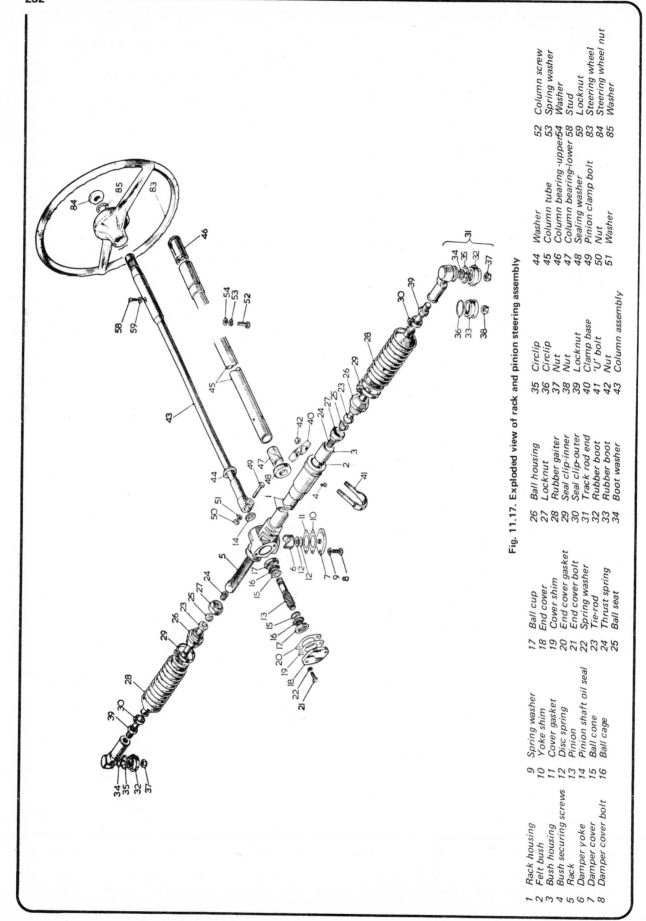

Fig. 11.17. Exploded view of rack and pinion steering assembly

1 Rack housing
2 Felt bush
3 Bush housing
4 Bush securing screws
5 Rack
6 Damper yoke
7 Damper cover
8 Damper cover bolt

9   Spring washer
10 Yoke shim
11 Cover gasket
12 Disc spring
13 Pinion
14 Pinion shaft oil seal
15 Ball cone
16 Ball cage

17 Ball cup
18 End cover
19 Cover shim
20 End cover gasket
21 End cover bolt
22 Spring washer
23 Tie-rod
24 Thrust spring
25 Ball seat

26 Ball housing
27 Locknut
28 Rubber gaiter
29 Seal clip-inner
30 Seal clip-outer
31 Track rod end
32 Rubber boot
33 Rubber boot
34 Boot washer

35 Circlip
36 Circlip
37 Nut
38 Locknut
39 Locknut
40 Clamp base
41 'U' bolt
42 Nut
43 Column assembly

44 Washer
45 Column tube
46 Column bearing -upper
47 Column bearing -lower
48 Sealing washer
49 Pinion clamp bolt
50 Nut
51 Washer

52 Column screw
53 Spring washer
54 Washer
58 Stud
59 Locknut
83 Steering wheel
84 Steering wheel nut
85 Washer

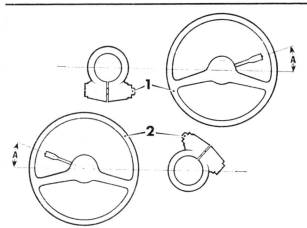

Fig. 11.18. Correct position of clamp bolt and direction indicator lever

$A = 20^o$
1   RHD models
2   LHD models

making a slot with a hacksaw and using a screwdriver. At the bottom of the steering column unscrew the pinch bolt which secures it to the serrated pinion shaft. Carefully pull the column off the pinion shaft so it just clears it.

6   Lift back the front carpet and undo the two nuts from each of the two 'U' bolts.

7   Remove the air cleaner and the bolts which secure the engine tie-rod to the block. Undo the two nuts from the bolts which hold the exhaust pipe to manifold clamp in position.

8   Free the speedometer cable from the rear of the speedometer and undo the two set bolts which hold the clutch slave cylinder to the top of the bellhousing.

9   From underneath the car undo the four bolts and nuts which hold the rear of the subframe to the bodyshell. Then free the exhaust pipe support from the lug on the gearlever extension.

10 A transverse cross member runs from side to side along the front bulkhead under the bonnet and terminates at each end in the suspension towers.

11 At the top of each tower are two bolts. (Studs and nuts on early models). Knock back the locking plate tabs and remove the bolts or studs.

12 Undo the two bolts behind the two holes for the front bumper, to release the front of the subframe.

13 Lowering the subframe is achieved by removing the chocks at each side of the subframe and replacing them under the body just behind the front wheel arches. Carefully lower the jack together with the subframe, and watch the brake pipe from the multi-way union on the nearside of the car. It may be necessary to disconnect it.

14 Remove the 'U' bolts from under the car. It may be necessary to prise the subframe down further by using a lever between the wing valance and the top of the tower to get sufficient clearance. Remove the rack and pinion from the driver's side of the car.

15 Replacement is a straightforward reversal of the removal operation but note the following points:

a)   Make sure the pinion shaft is in the centre of the hole in the toeboard, before fully tightening the 'U' bolts.

b)   Reconnect the track rod ends to the steering arms and make sure the wheels are facing straight ahead and the rack in the centre of its travel before fitting the column.

c)   Slacken the bolts holding the steering column bracket to the parcel shelf so the column can be easily centralised if necessary.

d)   Make sure the lower end of the steering column is pushed onto the pinion shaft sufficiently for the clamp bolt to enter the recess in the shaft, fully. Also ensure the split portion of the clamp lines up with the marked pinion spline. The clamp bolt should be tightened to 9 lb f ft (1.2 kg fm) torque.

e)   A new shear bolt must be fitted to the column clip and

tightened to 14 lbf/1.9 kgf m) .

f)   When refitting the exhaust and the engine support strut follow the instructions given in Chapter 1.

22 Rack and pinion steering gear - dismantling, overhaul and reassembly

It is not possible to make any adjustments to the rack and pinion steering gear unless it is removed from the car. With it removed it is as well to dismantle and examine the whole unit before making any adjustments. This will save having to remove the unit again later because of initial non-detection of wear. If wear is very bad it is best to fit an exchange reconditioned unit. All numbers in brackets refer to Fig. 11.17.

1   Mark the position of the locknuts (39) on the tie-rods (23) so that the 'toe-out' is approximately correct on reassembly.

2   Slacken the locknuts (39) and gripping the tie-rods firmly with a mole wrench screw off the trackrod ends (31).

3   The rack and pinion steering gear assembly is filled with oil. Ensure a 1 pint container is available before proceeding further.

4   Unscrew the clips (29,30) holding the rubber gaiters (28) to the rack housing (1) and tie-rods (23). Drain the oil from the housing and carefully remove the gaiters.

5   Unscrew the two damper cover bolts and spring washers (8.9) and remove the damper cover (7), gasket shims, springs and yoke (10,11,12,6). **Note:** Early models make use of a coil spring and plunger in place of the disc springs fitted to later models as illustrated.

6   Undo the two end cover bolts (21), and remove the endplate (18), shim (19), and gasket (20).

7   Carefully extract the lower ball bearing (15,16, 17) and then pull out the pinion. Access can now be gained to the upper ball bearing (15,16,17 nearest the rack housing 1) which can now be removed. If difficulty is experienced wait until the rack is removed from the housing. Extract the pinion shaft oil seal (14).

8   Each inner tie-rod balljoint is locked to a slot in the end of the rack (5) by means of tabs on a locknut (27) and also to the ball housing (26). Punch or prise up these tabs and then loosen the locknut (27). The ball housing (26) can then be undone so freeing the tie-rod (23), ball seat (25) and the thrust spring (24).

9   Pull the rack (5) out from the pinion end of the housing (1) so as not to damage the felt (plastic on later models) bush (2) fitted at the other end.

10 Undo the bush securing screws (4) from the housing (1) and carefully remove the bush (2) and metal housing (3) with the aid of a pair of long nosed pliers.

11 Thoroughly clean all the parts with paraffin. Carefully inspect the teeth on the rack, and also the pinion, for chipping, roughness, uneven wear, hollows, or fractures. Replace both components if either is badly worn.

12 Carefully inspect the component parts of the inner balljoints for wear or ridging and renew as necessary.

13 The outer trackrod joints cannot be dismantled and if worn must be renewed as a complete assembly. Examine the component parts of the damper and renew any that show signs of wear. Pay particular attention to the oil seals, and as a precautionary measure it is always best to renew them.

14 As it is very difficult to refill the rack and pinion assembly with oil once it is fitted to the car, make sure the rubber gaiters are sound before refitting them. If they are in the least torn or perished complete oil loss could occur later and they must be renewed.

15 If the steering gear is of the early type the felt bush in the end of the rack furthest from the pinion housing, must be replaced with a plastic bush and a new steel sleeved bush and spacer.

16 Push the spacer, plain end first (not shown in Fig. 11.17) into the end of the rack housing. Insert the plastic bush inside the steel sleeve (3) and slide the sleeve into the housing plain end first. **Note:** The flats on the plastic bush must be so positioned as to be offset to the retaining screw hole in the bottom of the rack housing.

17 Very carefully drill the bush through the retaining screw hole with a 0.109 in (2.7 mm) drill, Carefully clean all traces of swarf

away, liberally coat the threads of the retaining screw (4) with jointing compound and screw it into the retaining screw hole. Make sure that the screw does not break right through the bush into the bore.

18 Lubricate the upper ball bearing (15,16,17 nearest the rack housing) and it into place.

19 Push the rack (5) into the housing (1) from the pinion end and then fit the pinion (13) splined end first.

20 Lubricate the lower ball bearing (15,16,17) and fit in place on the lower end of the pinion shaft (13).

21 Fit the end cover (18) without any shims and gently tighten

down the two end cover bolts until all endfloat is taken up. Measure with a feeler gauge, the gap between the end cover (18) and the housing (1). (See Figs. 11.19, 11.20, 11.21 and 11.22). Remove the end cover.

22 Gather together packing shims (19) to the measurement of the feeler gauge less .002 in. (0.051 mm), treat the mating faces with shellac to make an oil tight joint, and refit the gasket (20), shims (19), and end cover (18). Ensure the spring washers (22) are refitted and tighten down the bolts (21).

23 Screw the ball housing locknuts (27) tightly into the ends of the rack (always use a new locknut). Refit the thrust spring (24)

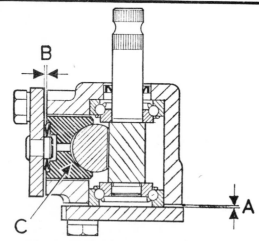

Fig. 11.19. Cross section view through rack and pinion steering damper (1st type)

A   Take a feeler gauge measurement and fit the pinion end cover with shims to the value of the measurement minus 0.001 to 0.003 in. (0.025 to 0.076 mm) before fitting the damper yoke (C)
B   Measure the gap and fit shims
C   Damper yoke

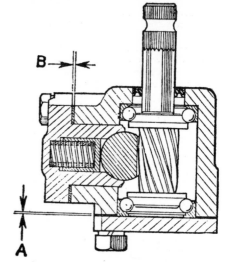

Fig. 11.20. Cross section through an early rack and pinion steering damper

Remove all packing shims and measure 'A' and 'B' with a feeler gauge

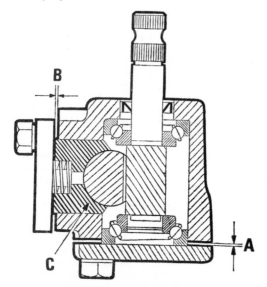

Fig. 11.21. Cross section through rack and pinion steering damper (2nd type)

A   Take a feeler gauge measurement and fit the pinion end cover with shims to the value of the measurement minus 0.001 to 0.003 in. (0.025 to 0.076 mm) before fitting the damper yoke (C)
B   Measure the gap and fit shims
C   Damper yoke

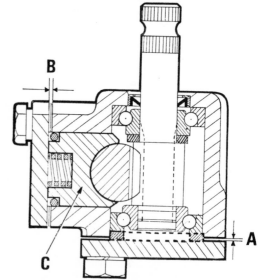

Fig. 11.22. Cross section through rack and pinion steering damper (Mk II models)

A   Take a feeler gauge measurement and fit the pinion end cover with shims to the value of the measurement minus 0.002 to 0.005 in. (0.05 to 0.013 mm) before fitting the damper yoke (C)
B   Measure the gap and fit shims
C   Damper yoke

ball seat (25), the tie-rod(23), and the ball housing (26).

24 Tighten up the ball housing (26) until the tie-rod (23) is firmly nipped and rotate the locking nut (27) to meet the ball housing (26).

25 Undo the ball housing an eighth of a turn and then tighten the locking nut (27) to a torque of 35 lb f ft (4.8 kg fm).

26 Test the balljoints by measuring the pull required to move them by means of a spring balance connected to the trackrod ends of the tie-rods. Between 2 to 4 lbs (0.90 to 1.8 Kg) should be all that is necessary to move the rods. If a heavier pull is required the ball housing has been overtightened and must be slackened off.

27 Punch the lips of the locking nut (27) into the slots in the rack and ball housing so the balljoint is held securely in place.

28 On early models fitted with a coil spring in the damper, assemble the damper plunger and then replace the damper cover (7), leaving out the spring and shims. On later models replace the damper cover (7) after fitting the yoke (6) *and* disc springs (12), also leaving out the shims (10).

29 With the damper cover (7) in place refit the two bolts (8), and ensure the rack is centralised (so both front wheels would face straight ahead if connected) (Fig. 11.23).

30 Tighten down the bolts until all backlash is taken up and it is just possible to turn the pinion by the splined end by rotating it between finger and thumb. Do not overtighten the bolts.

31 Measure, with a feeler gauge, the gap between the underside of the damper cover (7) and the rackhousing (1). (Measurement 'B' in Figs. 11.19, 11.20, 11.21 and 11.22). On early models add to the measured figure 0.002 in. (0.05 mm) and on later models subtract 0.001 to 0.003 in. (0.025 to 0.076 mm). The total figure represents the thickness of shims which must be fitted under the cover (7).

32 Remove the damper cover (7): in the case of early models refit the coil spring; fit the necessary gasket, shims, and cover and tighten the bolts and spring washer (21,22) securely. **Note:**

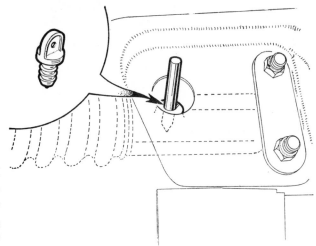

Fig. 11.23. Use of pin to centralise the rack
Inset shows plastic plug

It is sound practice to paint the cover joint to rack housing faces with shellac to ensure an oil tight joint.

33 Fit a new pinion shaft oil seal (14) and replace the rubber gaiters (28).

34 Tighten down the gaiter clips at one end of the assembly, turn the unit upright and pour in 1/3 pint (0.2 litre) of Extreme pressure SAE 140 oil through the free end of the upper gaiter. Tighten down all the gaiter clips securely (29,30).

35 Replace the locknuts (39), and the trackrod ends (31). Re-assembly is now complete.

23 Fault diagnosis - suspension and steering

Symptom	Reason/s	Remedy
Steering feels vague; car wanders and floats at speed	Tyre pressure uneven Dampers worn Steering gear balljoints badly worn Suspension geometry incorrect Steering mechanism free play excessive Front suspension and rear suspension pick-up points out of alignment	Check pressures and adjust as necessary. Test, and replace if worn. Fit new balljoints. Check and rectify. Adjust or overhaul steering mechanism. Normally caused by poor repair work after a serious accident. Extensive rebuilding necessary.
Steering stiff and heavy	Tyre pressure too low No oil in steering gear No grease in steering and suspension balljoints Front wheel toe-in incorrect Suspension geometry incorrect Steering gear incorrectly adjusted too tightly Steering column badly misaligned	Check pressures and inflate tyres. Top up steering gear. Clean nipples and grease thoroughly. Check and reset toe-in. Check and rectify. Check and readjust steering gear. Determine cause and rectify (usually due to bad repair after severe accident damage and difficult to correct).
Wheel wobble and vibration	Wheel nuts loose Front wheels and tyres out of balance Steering balljoints badly worn Hub bearings badly worn Steering gear free play excessive Front springs weak or broken	Check and tighten as necessary. Balance wheels and tyres and add weights as necessary. Replace steering gear balljoints. Remove and fit new hub bearings. Adjust and overhaul steering gear. Inspect and renew as necessary.

1 Drifting driveshaft through hub. Note castellated nut reversed

2 Steering tie-rod detachment from hub assembly

3 Detaching hub assembly from drive-shaft and upper and lower suspension arms

4 Drifting oil seal and bearing from hub

5 Drifting out race outer track

6 Oil seal correctly located. Note the spacer

7 Fitting spacer onto driving flange

8 Refitting drive flange to hub assembly

9 Correct fitment of brake shoe return springs

10 Refitting brake shoes

11 Brake shoe web correctly located on wheel cylinder

12 Driveshaft, suspension arms and tie-rod ready to accept hub assembly

13 Refitting hub assembly to lower suspoension arm

14 Refitting hub assembly to upper suspension arm

15 Suspension arm balljoint nuts and spring washers refitted

16 Refitting washer and castellated nut

17 Reconnect brake hose to rear of wheel cylinder ...

18 ... and to body mounted bracket (if removed)

19 Always use new split pins to lock castellated nut

Chapter 12 Bodywork and subframes

Contents

1 General description

Although the Mini has been produced in many forms since its introduction the principle of construction has remained the same.

The body and floor panels are of all welded steel construction which makes a very strong and torsionally rigid shell. Attached to the underside of the bodyshell are two subframes, the front one carrying the power unit and suspension assembly and the rear one the suspension assembly.

In the main, access to the various body attachments is good, although, in some cases can be a little time consuming.

The body has been designed to give as much interior space as possible. The sides of the car have been curved to give extra width at elbow and shoulder height. The doors are sufficiently wide to give plenty of room for entry and exit although they are rather low.

All Mini models, can be adapted, or already have, built in mounting points for the fitting of either static or inertia reel type seat belts.

On older cars there are several points that have to be watched carefully for corrosion. The rear subframe is liable to corrosion and this is a common cause for failure of the MoT test. Also watch the rear floor panels in the luggage compartment of all models. The author knows of an instance where the rear subframe burst through the floor into the luggage compartment!

2 Maintenance - body and underframe

1 The condition of the bodywork is of considerable importance as it is on this, in the main, that the second-hand value of the car will mainly depend. It is much more difficult to repair neglected bodywork than to renew mechanical assemblies. The hidden portions of the body, such as the wheel arches, the underframe and the engine compartment are equally important, although obviously not requiring such frequent attention as the immediately visible paintwork.

2 Once a year, or every 12,000 miles (20,000 km) it is advisable to visit a garage equipped to steam clean the body. This will take about 1½ hours. All traces of dirt and oil will be removed and the underside can then be inspected carefully for rust, damaged hydraulic pipes, frayed electrical wiring and similar maladies. The car should be greased on completion of this job.

3 At the same time the engine compartment should be cleaned in a similar manner. If steam cleaning facilites are not available, then brush 'Gunk' or a similar cleaner over the whole of the engine, and engine compartment, with a stiff brush, working it well in where there is an accumulation of oil and dirt. Do not paint the ignition system, and protect it with oily rags when the 'Gunk' is washed off. As the 'Gunk' is washed away it will take with it all traces of oil and dirt, leaving the engine looking clean and bright.

4 The wheel arches should be given particular attention, as under-sealing can easily come away here, and stones and dirt

thrown up from the road wheels can soon cause the paint to chip and flake, and so allow rust to set in. If rust is found, clean down the bare metal with 'wet-and-dry' paper. Paint on an anti-corrosive coating such as Kurust, or if preferred red lead, and renew the undercoating and top coat.

5 The bodywork should be washed once a week or when dirty. Thoroughly wet the car to soften the dirt, and then wash the car down with a soft sponge and plenty of clean water. If the surplus dirt is not washed off very gently it will in time wear the paint as surely as wet and dry paper. It is best to use a hose if this is available. Give the car a final wash down and then dry with a soft chamois leather to prevent the formation of spots.

6 Spots of tar and grease thrown up from the road can be removed by a rag dampened in petrol.

7 Once every three months, give the bodywork and chromium trim a thoroughly good wax polish. If a chromium cleaner is used to remove rust on any of the cars plated parts, remember that a cleaner also removes part of the chromium so use only when absolutely necessary.

8 On Countryman models with wooden battens, carefully inspect for signs of moisture penetration through the varnish which if evident should be rectified as described in Section 6.

3 Maintenance - upholstery and carpets

1 Remove the carpets or mats, and thoroughly vacuum clean the interior of the car every three months, or more frequently if necessary.

2 Beat out the carpets and vacuum clean them if they are very dirty. If the upholstery is soiled apply an upholstery cleaner with a damp sponge and wipe off with a clean dry cloth.

4 Bodywork repairs

See photo sequences on pages 246 and 247. Note: For body seam trim strip renewal see Section 41.

Repair of minor scratches in the car's bodywork

If the scratch is very superficial, and does not penetrate to the metal of the bodywork - repair is very simple. Lightly rub the area of the scratch with a paintwork renovator (eg. "Top-Cut"), or a very fine cutting paste, to remove loose paint from the scratch and to clear the surrounding bodywork of wax polish. Rinse the area with clean water.

Apply touch-up paint to the scratch using a thin paint brush; continue to apply thin layers of paint until the surface of the paint in the scratch is level with the surrounding paintwork. Allow the new paint at least two weeks to harden, then, blend it into the surrounding paintwork by rubbing the paintwork in the scratch area with a paintwork renovator (eg. "Top-Cut"), or a very fine cutting paste. Finally apply wax polish.

An alternative to painting over the scratch is to use Holts "Scratch-Patch". Use the same preparation for the affected area; then simply, pick a patch of a suitable size to cover the scratch completely. Hold the patch against the scratch and burnish its backing paper; the patch will adhere to the paintwork, freeing itself from the backing paper at the same time. Polish the affected area to blend the patch into the surrounding paintwork.

Where a scratch has penetrated right through to the metal of the bodywork, causing the metal to rust, a different repair technique is required. Remove any loose rust from the bottom of the scratch with a penknife; then apply rust inhibiting paint (eg. "Kurust") to prevent the formation of rust in the future. Using a rubber or nylon applicator fill the scratch with body-stopper paste. If required, this paste can be mixed with cellulose thinners to provide a very thin paste which is ideal for filling narrow scratches. Before the stopper paste in the scratch hardens, wrap a piece of smooth cotton rag around the tip of a finger. Dip the finger in cellulose thinners and then quickly sweep it across the surface of the stopper-paste in the scratch; this will ensure that the surface of the stopper-paste is slightly

hollowed. The scratch can now be painted over as described earlier in this Section.

Repair of dents in the car's bodywork

When deep denting of the car's bodywork has taken place, the first task is to pull the dent out, until the affected bodywork almost attains its original shape. There is little point in trying to restore the original shape completely, as the metal in the damaged area will have stretched on impact and cannot be re-shaped fully to its original contour. It is better to bring the level of the dent up to a point which is about 1/8 inch (3 mm) below the level of the surrounding bodywork. In cases where the dent is very shallow anyway, it is not worth trying to pull it out at all.

If the underside of the dent is accessible, it can be hammered out gently from behind, using a mallet with a wooden or plastic head. Whilst doing this, hold a suitable block of wood firmly against the outside of the dent. This block will absorb the impact from the hammer blows and thus prevent a large area of body-work from being 'belled-out'.

Should the dent be in a section of the bodywork which has double skin or some other factor making it inaccessible from behind, a different technique is called for. Drill several small holes through the metal inside the dent area - particularly in the deeper sections. Then screw long self-tapping screws into the holes just sufficiently for them to gain a good purchase in the metal. Now the dent can be pulled out by pulling on the pro-truding heads of the screws with a pair of pliers.

The next stage of the repair is the removal of the paint from the damaged area, and from an inch or so of the surrounding 'sound' bodywork. This is accomplished most easily by using a wire brush or abrasive pad on a power drill, although it can be done just as effectively by hand using sheets of abrasive paper. To complete the preparations for filling, score the surface of the bare metal with a screwdriver or the tang of a file, or alter-natively, drill small holes in the affected area. This will provide a really good 'key' for the filler paste.

To complete the repair see the Section on filling and re-spraying.

Repair of rust holes or gashes in the car's bodywork

Remove all paint from the affected area and from an inch or so of the surrounding 'sound' bodywork, using an abrasive pad or a wire brush on a power drill. If these are not available a few sheets of abrasive paper will do the job just as effectively. With the paint removed you will be able to gauge the severity of the corrosion and therefore decide whether to replace the whole panel (if this is possible) or to repair the affected area. Replace-ment body panels are not as expensive as most people think and it is often quicker and more satisfactory to fit a new panel than to attempt to repair large areas of corrosion.

Remove all fittings from the affected area except those which will act as a guide to the original shape of the damaged body-work (eg headlamp shells etc). Then, using tin snips or a hacksaw blade, remove all loose metal and any other metal badly affected by corrosion. Hammer the edges of the hole inwards in order to create a slight depression for the filler paste.

Wire brush the affected area to remove the powdery rust from the surface of the remaining metal. Paint the affected area with rust inhibiting paint (eg "Kurust"); if the back of the rusted area is accessible treat this also.

Before filling can take place it will be necessary to block the hole in some way. This can be achieved by the use of one of the following materials: Zinc gauze, Aluminium tape or Poly-urethane foam.

Zinc gauze is probably the best material to use for a large hole. Cut a piece to the approximate size and shape of the hole to be filled, then position it in the hole so that its edges are below the level of the surrounding bodywork. It can be retained in position by several blobs of filler paste around its periphery.

Aluminium tape should be used for small or very narrow holes. Pull a piece off the roll and trim it to the approximate size and shape required, then pull off the backing paper (if used) and stick the tape over the hole; it can be overlapped if the thickness of one piece is insufficient. Burnish down the edges of the tape with the handle of a screwdriver or similar, to ensure that the tape is securely attached to the metal underneath.

Polyurethane foam is best used where the hole is situated in a section of bodywork of complex shape, backed by a small box section (eg where the sill panel meets the rear wheel arch - most cars). The usual mixing procedure for this foam is as follows: Put equal amounts of fluid from each of the two cans provided in the kit, into one container. Stir until the mixture begins to thicken, then quickly pour this mixture into the hole, and hold a piece of cardboard over the larger apertures. Almost immediately the polyurethane will begin to expand, gushing frantically out of any small holes left unblocked. When the foam hardens it can be cut back to just below the level of the surrounding bodywork with a hacksaw blade.

Having blocked off the hole the affected area must now be filled and sprayed - see Section on bodywork filling and re-spraying.

Bodywork repairs - filling and re-spraying

Before using this Section, see the Sections on dent, deep scratch, rust hole, and gash repairs.

Many types of bodyfiller are available, but generally speaking those proprietary kits which contain a tin of filler paste and a tube of resin hardener (eg " Holts Cataloy") are best for this type of repair. A wide, flexible plastic or nylon applicator will be found invaluable for imparting a smooth and well contoured finish to the surface of the filler.

Mix up a little filler on a clean piece of card or board - use the hardener sparingly (follow the maker's instructions on the pack), otherwise the filler will set very rapidly.

Using the applicator, apply the filler paste to the prepared area; draw the applicator across the surface of the filler to achieve the correct contour and to level the filler surface. As soon as a contour that approximates the correct one is achieved, stop working the paste - if you carry on too long the paste will become sticky and begin to 'pick-up' on the applicator.

Continue to add thin layers of filler paste at twenty-minute intervals until the level of the filler is just 'proud' of the surrounding bodywork.

Once the filler has hardened, excess can be removed using a Surform plane or Dreadnought file. From then on, progressively finer grades of abrasive paper should be used, starting with a 40 grade 'wet-and-dry' paper. Always wrap the abrasive paper around a flat rubber, cork, or wooden block - otherwise the surface of the filler will not be completely flat. During the smoothing of the filler surface the 'wet-and-dry' paper should be periodically rinsed in water - this will ensure that a very smooth finish is imparted to the filler at the final stage.

At this stage the 'dent' should be surrounded by a ring of bare metal, which in turn should be encircled by the finely 'feathered' edge of the good paintwork. Rinse the repair area with clean water, until all of the dust produced by the rubbing-down operation is gone.

Spray the whole repair area with a light coat of grey primer - this will show up any imperfections in the surface of the filler. Repair these imperfections with fresh filler paste or body-stopper, and once more smooth the surface with abrasive paper. If bodystopper is used, it can be mixed with cellulose thinners to form a really thin paste which is ideal for filling small holes. Repeat this spray and repair procedure until you are satisfied that the surface of the filler, and the feathered edge of the paintwork are perfect. Clean the repair area with clean water and allow to dry fully.

The repair area is now ready for spraying. Paint spraying must be carried out in a warm, dry, windless and dust free atmosphere. This condition can be created artificially if you have access to a large indoor working area, but if you are forced to work in the open, you will have to pick your day very carefully. If you are working indoors, dousing the floor in the work area with water will 'lay' the dust which would otherwise be in the atmosphere. If the repair area is confined to one body panel, mask off the surrounding panels; this will help to minimise the effects of a slight mis-match in paint colours. Bodywork fittings

(eg chrome strips, door handles etc) will also need to be masked off. Use genuine masking tape and several thicknesses of newspaper for the masking operation.

Before commencing to spray, agitate the aerosol can thoroughly, then spray a test area (an old tin, or similar) until the technique is mastered. Cover the repair area with a thick coat of primer; the thickness should be built up using several thin layers of paint rather than one thick one. Using 400 grade 'wet-and-dry' paper, rub down the surface of the primer until it is really smooth. While doing this, the work area should be thoroughly doused with water, and the wet-and-dry paper periodically rinsed in water. Allow to dry before spraying on more paint.

Spray on the top coat, again building up the thickness by using several thin layers of paint. Start spraying in the centre of the repair area and then   using a circular motion, work outwards until the whole repair area and about 2 inches of the surrounding original paintwork is covered. Remove all masking material 10 to 15 minutes after spraying on the final coat of paint. Allow the new paint at least 2 weeks to harden fully; then, using a paintwork renovator (eg "Top-Cut") or a very fine cutting paste, blend the edges of the new paint into the existing paintwork. Finally, apply wax polish.

5   Major structural damage - general

1   Because the body is built on the monocoque principle and is integral with the underframe, major damage must be repaired by specialists with the necessary welding and hydraulic straightening equipment.
2   Although subframes are used front and rear they act, in the main, as supports and locations for the power units and suspension systems.
3   If the damage is severe, it is vital that on completion of the repair the body and subframes are in correct ailignment. Less severe damage may also have twisted or distorted the body or subframes although this may not be visible immediately. It is therefore always best on completion of repair to check for twist and squareness to make sure all is well.
4   To check for twist, position the car on a clean level floor, place a jack under each jacking point, raise the car and take off the wheels. Raise or lower the jacks until the sills are parallel with the ground. Depending where the damage occurred, using an accurate scale, take measurements at the suspension mounting points and if comparable readings are not obtained it is an indication that the body is twisted.
5   After checking for twist, check for squareness by taking a series of measurements on the floor. Drop a plumb line and bob weight from various mounting points on the underside of the body and mark these points on the floor with chalk. Draw a straight line between each point and measure and mark the middle of each line. A line drawn on the floor starting at the front and finishing at the rear should be quite straight and pass through the centres of the other lines. Diagonal measurements can also be made as a check for squareness.

6   Wooden battens - re-varnishing (Countryman and Traveller models)

In time the varnish finish on the wooden battening on Countryman models will deteriorate and water will penetrate into the wood. The first signs of this are varnish flaking and an area of wood darkening.

Regularly inspect the wood and if the previously mentioned symptoms exist immediate action should be taken. The recommended procedure is as follows:
1   Remove all traces of polish using methylated spirits .
2   Using a suitable scraper carefully remove the varnish from the area under repair and also about 1 inch (25.4 mm) further on to provide a lead in for the new varnish.
3   When scraping take care not to damage the paintwork accidentally.

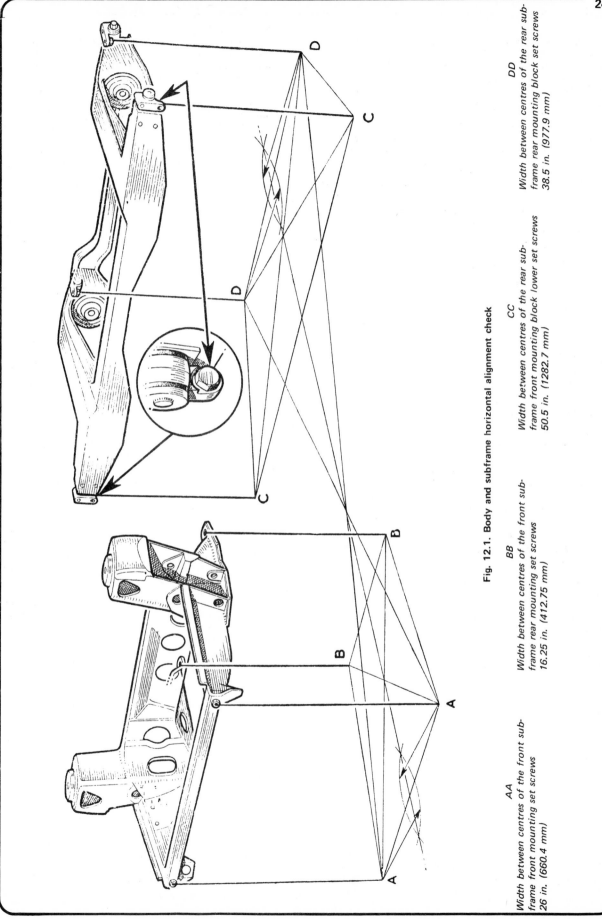

Fig. 12.1. Body and subframe horizontal alignment check

AA
Width between centres of the front sub-frame front mounting set screws
26 in. (660.4 mm)

BB
Width between centres of the front sub-frame rear mounting set screws
16.25 in. (412.75 mm)

CC
Width between centres of the rear sub-frame front mounting block lower set screws
50.5 in. (1282.7 mm)

DD
Width between centres of the rear sub-frame rear mounting block set screws
38.5 in. (977.9 mm)

4 If the wood has darkened but there are no signs of rotting then a wood bleach should be used. This may be obtainable from the local diy shop.

5 Remove all traces of dust and apply a thin coat of a good quality clean marine grade varnish.

6 When dry apply a further two coats and allow to dry throughly, before polishing.

7 Some Mini enthusiasts revarnish all the woodwork regularly every year because if the wood does rot it can be very expensive to have a new frame fitted, particularly to the sides.

   This is a specialist job at best left to the local BLMC Main Dealer. It is possible for the new door frames to be fitted as described in Section 29.

7 Maintenance - locks and hinges

   Once every 6,000 miles (10,000 Km) or 6 months the door, bonnet and boot hinges should be oiled with a few drops of engine oil from an oil can. The door striker plates can be given a thin smear of grease to reduce wear and ensure free movement.

8 Door rattles - tracing and rectification

1   The most common cause of door rattles is a misaligned, loose or worn striker plate but other causes may be;
a) Loose door handles, window wiper handles (late models) or door hinges.
b) Loose, worn or misaligned door lock components.
c) Loose or worn remote control mechanism (late models).
    or a combination of these.
2 Check that the door rattles are not emanating from the sliding door glass or catches as fitted to the earlier Mini models.

9 Doors - removal and replacement

1 Upon inspection it will be seen that each door is held in place by two hinges and a check strap.
2 To remove a door first unscrew and remove the two set screws and washers that secure the door check strap coupling bracket which is located on the inside of the door pillars. To gain access it will be necessary to ease back the side trim first.
3 Open the door carefully and on earlier models pull out the interior lining of the door. On later models it will be necessary to remove the door trim as described later in this chapter.
4 Undo and remove the crosshead screw and nut from the door side of each of the two hinges.
5 The door can now be lifted away from the body leaving the hinges still attached to the body.
6 Refitting the door is the reverse sequence to removal.

10 Door hinges - removal and replacement

1 Refer to Section 9 and remove the door.
2 Two nuts/bolts hold each hinge to the inside of the front wing. The heads of the nuts/bolts are very difficult to get at because they are surrounded at the top and bottom by the sides of the support brackets. This is particularly applicable to the top hinge, inside bolt.
3 Using a socket and universal coupling undo and remove the nuts and bolts and lift away the hinge.
4 If the head on one of the bolts has become so burred that the spanner will no longer fit and provide a positive grip very carefully examine a new hinge and decide on the exact position of the old bolt by comparision.
5 The old bolt can then be carefully drilled out from the outside of the hinge.
6 Refitting the door hinge is the reverse sequence to removal.

11 Door hinge pin - removal and replacement

1 If it is not wished to renew a complete hinge it is possible to drill out the old hinge pin and fit an oversize one. Obviously care must be taken not to damage the body when drilling out the old pin, if it is being done with the hinge still on the car.
2 If an oversize pin is not available use a suitable diameter rivet of dowel rod and peen over the ends.

12 Door hinge (concealed type) - removal and replacement

1   Refer to Section 16 and remove the door trim panel.
2   Ease back the door pillar to bulkhead trim panel to give access to the rear of the door pillar.
3   Undo and remove the two nuts and shakeproof washers and the long screws that secure each hinge to the door and door pillar.
4   Refitting the hinge is the reverse sequence to removal.

13 Rear doors (Van, Countryman and Traveller) - removal and replacement

1 Open both doors and disconnect the door support stays by undoing the nut, washer and bolt at the end of each stay.
2 Preferably have a friend hold the door, or place a support under it and then bend down the tab washer on each door hinge.
3 Undo and remove the nut, tab washer, hinge centre bolt, and the spherical bush from each of the door hinges in turn.
4 Replacement is a straightforward reversal of this operation.

14 Front door glass (early type) - removal and replacement

1   Locate the self tapping screws that secure the lower channel to the door waist panel.
2   Very carefully ease out the lower channel and glass from the door.
3   Refitting the door glass is the reverse sequence to removal.

15 Front door lock (early type) - removal and replacement

1 Undo and remove the screw that secures the lock to the inner panel.
2 Undo and remove the screw located at the end of the locking handle spindle.
3 Slacken the screw that clamps the inner lever and remove the handle and escutcheon.
4 Refitting the door lock is the reverse sequence to removal. When a cable is fitted instead of a metal handle ensure that the control cable lever is fitted upright.

16 Front door trim panel (later type) - removal and replacement

1 Remove the interior pull handle (photo), lock release handle (photo) and the window regulator handle (photos), note the position of the latter when the glass is up so that it may be refitted in its original position. Also, remove the private lock control surround (photo).
2 Using a knife or wide bladed screwdriver carefully detach the trim panel clips from the door panel.
3 The trim panel may now be lifted away (photo).
4 If it is wished to gain access to the door inner panel remove the waterproof covering (photo).
5 Refitting the door trim panel is the reverse sequence to removal. Ensure that the waterproof covering is in position.

16.1a Removal of interior pull

16.1b Lifting away interior lock release handle

16.1c Removing window regulator handle securing screw

16.1d Lifting away window regulator handle

16.1e Removing the private lock control surround

16.3 Lifting away interior trim panel

244

 16.4 Door interior panel showing locations of sealing tape

Fig. 12.2. Door lock assembly (later type)

Insets 1   Latch   *2   Interior locking control*   *3   Remote control*

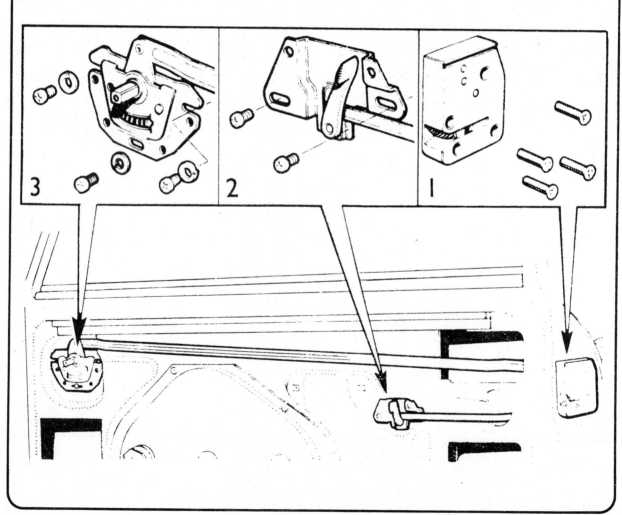

17 Door lock (later type) - general description

In place of the conventional mortice type latch and striker plate the latest models are fitted with striker loops on the door posts and the disc/claw type latch operated by push button on the door.

When the lock is set up correctly there should be no apparent 'drop' or 'lift' in the door from the free swinging to the closed position. Also when closed it should be possible to press it slightly against its seals, ensuring that the striker is not set too far in.

The interior locking control cannot be set in the locking position with the door open

18 Door lock push button plunger (later type) - adjustment

1   Referring to Fig. 12.3 this is set to provide 0.031 - 0.0625 in. (1-1.5 mm) of free movement (A) before touching the latch contactor and to release the striker loop before complete depression. The free movement is set by removing the door handle (see next Section) and screwing in or out the push button plunger (2). Care must be taken not to screw it too far in or the lock link will not operate.
2   The release of the striker loop before the push button is fully depressed is controlled by adjustment to the striker loop

19 Exterior door handle (later type) - removal and replacement

1   Refer to Section 16 and remove the front door trim panel.
2   Prise off the bottom of the key operated lock link from the latch locking rod. Ease the latch out from the door and remove the circlips attaching the interior handle link arm and locking link arm. The latch is now free and the interior handle and lock lever can be drawn out of the door.
3   The exterior handle securing screws may now be removed and the handle taken off (Fig. 12.4).
4   Reassembly of all the door handles and latch is a reversal of the foregoing porcedure. Take particular care that the link arm circlips are correctly and securely replaced and that the lock link and locking rod are reconnected properly

20 Striker loop (later type) - adjustment

1   Referring to Fig. 12.6 remove the over-travel rubber stop (2). Slacken the striker loop securing screws (1) so that the loop is attached firmly enough to lock and hold but can be moved if the door is pushed and pulled whilst it is in the closed position.
2   Close the door gently but firmly and push it in or out as required (moving the striker loop with it) until it lines up with the bodywork. Provided the door hinges have no slack in them the striker plate is now set (check that it lies horizontally). The securing screws can then be re-tightened. Refit the over-travel stop.
3   It is possible that the door appears to hang askew (even with firm hinges). If this is to be corrected the hinges must be re-aligned and the striker plate readjusted. With the newer concealed hinges the body mounting bolt nuts are readily accessible under the front wings. Under no circumstances try and force 'drop' or 'lift' on the door to align it on firm hinges by raising or lowering the striker loop. This will merely strain and impose excessive wear on the hinges and lock mechanism. In such circumstances it is advisable to leave the door as it is provided it does not leak. It does not profess to be an exact precision fit.

21 Window winder mechanism - removal and replacement

1   Refer to Section 16 and remove the front door trim panel.
2   Referring to Fig. 12.7 lift off the waist rail finishers (4 & 5)

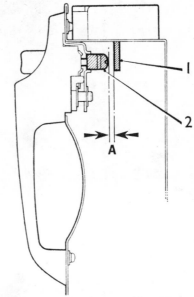

Fig. 12.3. Door handle push button plunger adjustment

1   Latch connector   *2   Push button plunger screw*
'A'   =   0.0313 - 0.0625 in. (1.0 - 1.5 mm)

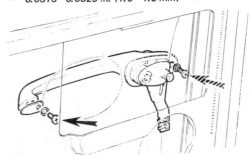

Fig. 12.4. Exterior door handle securing screws (arrowed)

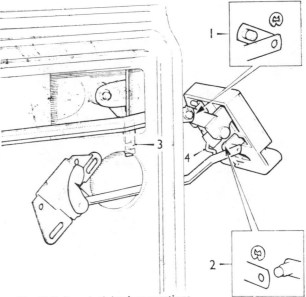

Fig. 12.5. Door lock latch connections

1   Remote control   *3   Exterior handle lock link*
2   Interior locking control   *4   Latch lock rod*

This sequence of photographs deals with the repair of the dent and scratch (above rear lamp) shown in this photo. The procedure will be similar for the repair of a hole. It should be noted that the procedures given here are simplified - more explicit instructions will be found in the text

In the case of a dent the first job - after removing surrounding trim - is to hammer out the dent where access is possible. This will minimise filling. Here, the large dent having been hammered out, the damaged area is being made slightly concave

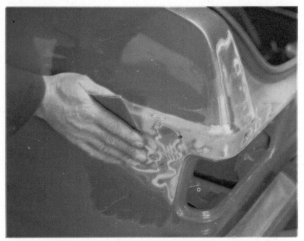

Now all paint must be removed from the damaged area, by rubbing with coarse abrasive paper. Alternatively, a wire brush or abrasive pad can be used in a power drill. Where the repair area meets good paintwork, the edge of the paintwork should be 'feathered', using a finer grade of abrasive paper

In the case of a hole caused by rusting, all damaged sheet-metal should be cut away before proceeding to this stage. Here, the damaged area is being treated with rust remover and inhibitor before being filled

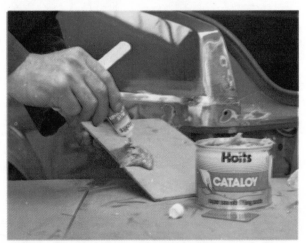

Mix the body filler according to its manufacturer's instructions. In the case of corrosion damage, it will be necessary to block off any large holes before filling - this can be done with zinc gauze or aluminium tape. Make sure the area is absolutely clean before ...

... applying the filler. Filler should be applied with a flexible applicator, as shown, for best results: the wooden spatula being used for confined areas. Apply thin layers of filler at 20-minute intervals, until the surface of the filler is slightly proud of the surrounding bodywork

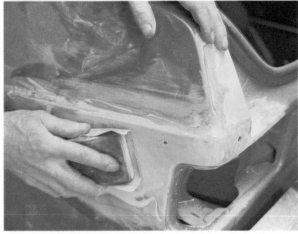

Initial shaping can be done with a Surform plane or Dreadnought file. Then, using progressively finer grades of wet-and-dry paper, wrapped around a sanding block, and copious amounts of clean water, rub-down the filler until really smooth and flat. Again, feather the edges of adjoining paintwork

The whole repair area can now be sprayed or brush-painted with primer. If spraying, ensure adjoining areas are protected from over-spray. Note that at least one-inch of the surrounding sound paintwork should be coated with primer. Primer has a 'thick' consistency, so will fill small imperfections

Again, using plenty of water, rub down the primer with a fine grade of wet-and-dry paper (400 grade is probably best) until it is really smooth and well blended into the surrounding paint-work. Any remaining imperfections can now be filled by carefully applied knifing stopper paste

When the stopper has hardened, rub-down the repair area again before applying the final coat of primer. Before rubbing-down this last coat of primer, ensure the repair area is blemish-free - use more stopper if necessary. To ensure that the surface of the primer is really smooth use some finishing compound

The top coat can now be applied. When working out of doors, pick a dry, warm and wind-free day. Ensure surrounding areas are protected from over-spray. Agitate the aerosol thoroughly, then spray the centre of the repair area, working outwards with a circular motion. Apply the paint as several thin coats.

After a period of about two-weeks, which the paint needs to harden fully, the surface of the repaired area can be 'cut' with a mild cutting compound prior to wax polishing. When carrying out bodywork repairs, remember that the quality of the finished job is proportional to the time and effort expended

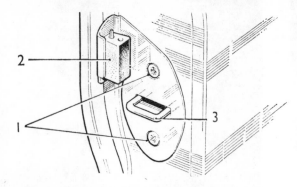

Fig. 12.6. Door lock striker unit (later type)

1 *Securing screws*   3 *Striker loop*
2 *Over-travel stop*

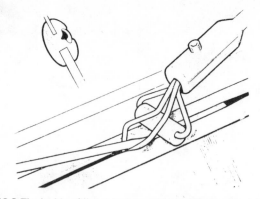

Fig. 12.8 The locking filler strip is best fitted with the aid of the glazing tool shown

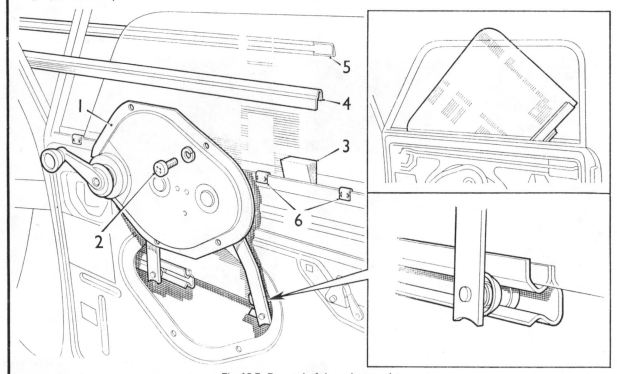

Fig. 12.7. Removal of door glass regulator
Inset shows regulator arms and position of door glass ready for removal

1 *Regulator unit*   3 *Wedge (to secure glass)*   5 *Waist rail finisher (outer)*
2 *Regulator securing screws*   4 *Waist rail finisher (inner)*   6 *Securing clips for finishers*

Fig. 12.9. The outside finishing strip in position

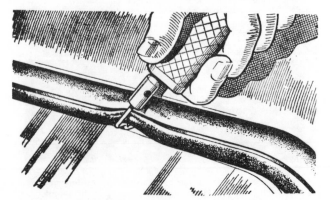

Fig. 12.10. Easing the rubber channel lip over the glass using a hook shaped service tool (18G 468)

taking care not to damage them when lifting away from the clips (6).

3 Wind the window approximately half way so that the two arms of the winder mechanism are as near vertical as they can be. With a piece of wood (3) wedge the window glass at the sill in this position.

4 Remove the winder mechanism securing screws (2).

5 Pull the regulator away from the door panel enough to move it forwards so that the rear arm comes out of the window channel. Then move the mechanism back to release the arm from the front channel and take it away.

6 Support the glass with one hand remove the wedge and tilt the forward edge down into the door so that the top rear corner of the glass comes inside the top of the window frame (A). The glass can then be lifted out.

7 Replace the window in reverse order with particular attention to the following:-

a) Make sure that the window is located snugly in the frame glazing channels before wedging it in the half-way postion.

b) Check that the waist rail finisher clips are evenly spaced before fitting the finishers back on. With the inner finisher, butt the forward end against the glazing channel rubber seal before fitting the rest.

c) Before screwing the winder mechanism back to the door panel apply a suitable mastic sealer (Seelastik) to the edge of the plate. This compensates for any irregularities in the panel stamping which could cause rattles. Ensure that the lip on the front edge of the plate is engaged inside the panel.

d) Put the adhesive sealing strips back where they came from using a good impact adhesive such as 'Bostik'.

22 Windscreen - removal and replacement

If you are unfortunate enough to have a windscreen shatter, fitting a replacement windscreen is one of the few jobs which the average owner is advised to leave to a professional. For the owner who wishes to do the job himself the following instructions are given:

1 Remove the wiper arms from their spindles using a screwdriver to lift the retaining clip from the spindle end and pull away.

2 The outside finisher strip can be removed and replaced quite easily by carefully working it out of its groove.

3 Then prise the end of the rubber locking filler and pull it away from its channel in the sealing rubber.

4 Press hard on one corner of the glass from inside the car until the glass forces the rubber away from the metal edge of the windscreen aperture. Ease the rubber out carefully.

5 Now is the time to remove all pieces of glass if the screen has shattered. Use a vacuum cleaner to extract as much as possible. Switch on the heater boost motor and adjust the controls to "Screen defrost" but watch out for flying pieces of glass which might be blown out of the ducting.

6 If the rubber surround has hardened or deteriorated in anyway, it is best to fit a new strip. This will also help prevent leaks round the edge of the glass.

7 Position the sealing rubber over the metal edge of the windscreen aperture. Lubricate the rubber channel into which the glass fits with soap and water and fit the glass to the bottom portion of the channelling.

8 With a small screwdriver, the end of which should be bent over 180º insert the end of the screwdriver under the lip of the rubber channel starting from one of the bottom corners and working all round the windscreen glass.

9 Generously lubricate the strip of rubber locking filler with soap and water and force it into the outside channel of the surround rubber. When the rubber filler has been fitted all round cut if off, leaving an overlap of 0.25 in (6.35 mm) so that the ends of the rubber are against each other under pressure.

23 Windscreen assembly (Moke) - removal and replacement

1 Refer to Chapter 10 and remove the windscreen wiper arm and blade/s.

2 Undo and remove the four securing nuts and screws.

3 Slacken the bottom securing screws.

4 The frame and glass assembly may now be lifted away from the vehicle.

5 Undo and remove the two screws securing the bottom channel and remove the glass from the frame.

6 Refitting the glass and frame is the reverse sequence to removal.

24 Rear window - removal and replacement

The rear window is removed, or the sealing rubber replaced in exactly the same way as the windscreen (described in Section 22)

25 Quarter light glass (fixed type) - removal and replacement

1 An assistant should support the exterior of the glass whilst a second person should firmly thump the top inside with the palm of the hand.

2 Carefully ease out the glass and rubber surround assembly.

3 Separate the rubber surround from the glass.

4 If the rubber surround has perished, hardened or cracked it should be renewed.

5 To refit first position the rubber surround on the glass.

6 Pass a length of thin but strong cord round the outer channel of the surround. Leave the ends hanging down on the inside of the glass.

7 Lubricate the body aperture with a little concentrated soap and water.

8 Hold the glass pressed in position, and lightly pull the cord from inside the car to draw the lip of the rubber over the edge of the body.

26 Quarter light glass (hinged type) - removal and replacement

1 Open the window and detach the catch from the body. It is secured with two crosshead screws.

2 Carefully ease up the seal on the body and locate the crosshead screws that secure the hinge to the body.

3 Undo and remove these screws and detach the glass assembly from the body.

4 The frame may be removed from the glass once the hinge screws at top and bottom are removed.

5 Refitting the quarter light glass assembly is the reverse sequence to removal.

27 Sliding glasses (Countryman and Traveller) - removal and replacement

1 Carefully remove the trim panel from above the sliding windows.

2 Remove the upper channels, support the inside and push the glass from the outside.

3 Refitting the sliding glass assembly is the reverse sequence to removal.

28 Rear door lock (Van, Countryman and Traveller) - removal and replacement

1 Undo and remove the four screws that secure the lock to the door.

2 Carefully detach the stays from their guides and lift away the complete lock assembly.

3 To remove the door handle, undo and remove the two nuts

and washers securing the handle to the door. Lift away the handle.

4 Refitting the handle and lock assembly is the reverse sequence to removal. Lubricate all moving parts.

29 Rear door wooden frame (Countryman and Traveller) removal and replacement

1 If the wooden frame condition has deteriorated it may be renewed as a complete assembly.

2 Refer to Section 13 and remove the rear door.

3 Undo and remove the two screws located at the centre of the inner door panel.

4 Carefully remove the door sealing rubber and retaining clips.

5 Undo and remove the self-tapping screws from the edge of the door.

6 The wooden frame assembly may now be lifted away from the door.

7 Clean off any sealer on the door and apply fresh. This may be obtained from your local BLMC dealer or diy shop.

8 Refit the frame and position all screws before finally tightening.

30 Bonnet - removal and replacement

1 Open the bonnet and support on its stay.

2 With a pencil mark the outline of the hinge on the bonnet to assist correct refitting.

3 An assistant should now take the weight of the bonnet. Undo and remove the bonnet to hinge retaining nuts, spring and plain washers at both hinges (photo). Carefully lift away the bonnet over the front of the car (photo).

4 Refitting is the reverse sequence to removal. Alignment in the body may be made by leaving the securing nuts slightly loose and repositioning by trial-and-error.

31 Boot lid - removal and replacement

1 Undo and remove the nut and bolt securing the boot lid stay wire. Suitably support the boot lid to prevent it opening too far.

2 Detach the number plate light wire from its terminal connection.

3 Undo and remove the nuts, spring and plain washers securing the boot lid to the hinge. Lift away the boot lid.

Bonnet removal - later type

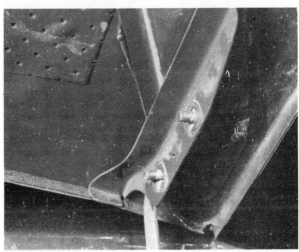

30.3a Hinge mounting bracket on bonnet lid

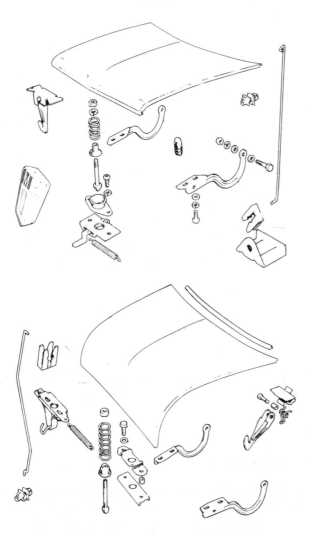

Fig. 12.11. Bonnet hinge and lock assemblies

30.3b Lifting bonnet over engine compartment

4 Refitting the boot lid is the reverse sequence to removal.

32 Front subframe - removal and replacement

To enable the front subframe to be removed it is best to remove the subframe assembly complete with power unit and then separate the two. Full information will be found in Chapter 1.

For information on stripping off the suspension from the subframe refer to Chapter 11.

33 Rear subframe - removal and replacement

If your Mini is more than 5 years old, it is a wise precaution to inspect the rear subframe for signs of excessive rusting (photos). Severe corrosion will substantially weaken the subframe - affecting the safety of the car. This problem is a common reason for MoT failure in Minis.

1 The rear subframe is held to the body by eight bolts. Its removal is sometimes difficult as with age the bolts may have become rusted in position.

2 On models having Hydrolastic suspension the system must be depressurised first. - see Chapter 11 for further information.

3 For safety reasons, disconnect the battery.

4 Empty the contents of the fuel tank; then remove the tank. This is not applicable for the Mini-Moke. See Chapter 3 for

Fig. 12.12. Boot lid hinge and lock assemblies

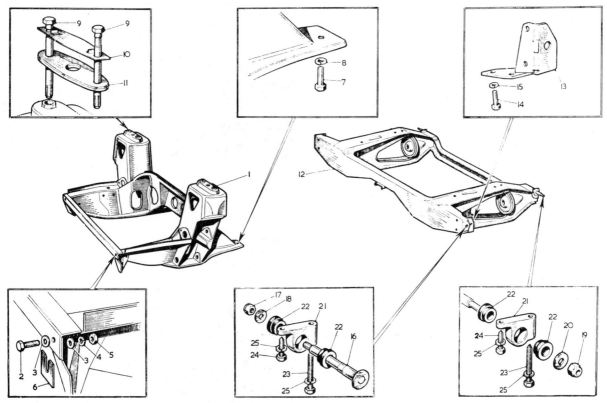

Fig. 12.13. Exploded view of the subframe assemblies

1 Subframe assembly - front	7 Screw - subframe to body	13 Bracket - outer radius arm	20 Washer for nut
2 Bolt - subframe to body	8 Washer for screw	14 Screw - bracket to frame	21 Mounting - support pin
3 Washer for bolt	9 Screw - tower to bulkhead	15 Washer for screw	22 Bush for support pin
4 Washer for nut	10 Washer for screw	16 Pin - front support	23 Screw for support pin
5 Nut for bolt	11 Pad - pressure - towers to	17 Nut for support pin	24 Screw for support pin
6 Packing - subframe to body	bulkhead	18 Washer for nut	25 Washer for screw
	12 Subframe - rear	19 Nut - rear support pin	

33.0a The Mini rear subframe is particularly prone to rust

33.0b If corrosion is allowed to go unchecked this is what can happen

33.0c This part of the subframe, although looking serviceable soon proved otherwise when probed with a screwdriver

33.15a Subframe front mounting. Note the grease nipple (arrowed)

33.15b Subframe rear mounting

33.15c The new subframe in position

further information.

5 *Models with an electric fuel pump (except Moke).* Disconnect the two wires from the fuel pump and then undo both the union nuts which hold the inlet and outlet fuel pipes in place.

6 The exhaust system should next be removed. The principle is the same for all models although the layout will be different. First release the manifold to downpipe clamp and then follow with the mounting attachments. Remove the exhaust pipe from under the car.

7 Undo the union nut securing the hydraulic pipe to the pressure regulating valve, which is mounted on the front of the rear subframe. Catch the contents of the brake hydraulic system in a jam jar or other suitable container.

8 Refer to Chapter 11 and detach the top of the dampers from the rear wheel arches. This is only applicable to models with telescopic dampers. **Note:** On Mini-Moke models this operation is carried out inside the rear part of the body.

9 *Hydrolastic suspension models.* Refer to Chapter 11 and detach the pipes from the hydrolastic pressure valves on the rear subframe.

10 Take off the two handbrake cable fairleads from the floor, undo the cables from the handbrake lever trunnion and pull the cables through the floor from under the car.

11 Undo and remove the eight bolts which hold the subframe to the body and with two strong men holding the body, one at each wheelarch, lift and pivot the body upwards so allowing the subframe to be drawn out from underneath.

12 The subframe mountings consist of a mounting bracket, rubber bushes and the mounting support pin. It is necessary to first remove the trailing arm before attempting to remove the front mountings.

13 For the front mountings, undo and remove the nut that secures the mounting support pin to the subframe, then pull off the support pin, rubbers and mounting block.

14 Refitting the rear subframe is the reverse sequence to removal

but the following additional points should be noted:

a) Take care to line up the mounting block holes with the tapped holes in the body when the subframe is positioned for refitting.

b) Do not forget to bleed the brake hydraulic system as described in Chapter 9.

c) When refitting the exhaust system make sure that the same number of packing washers are fitted between the lug on the exhaust pipe and the pick up on the transmission unit extension. This will ensure there is no strain on the system.

d) *Hydrolastic suspension models.* The car may be driven at a speed of not more than 30 mph (48 kph) on good quality roads to the local BLMC garage to have the system repressurised.

15 Photos 33.15a and 33.15b show the front and rear subframe mountings, respectively. Photo 33.15c shows a new subframe correctly fitted to an early Mini.

---

34 Heater assembly (recirculatory type) - removal and replacement

1 For safety reasons, disconnect the battery.

2 Refer to Chapter 2 and drain the cooling system.

3 Make a note of their relative position then disconnect the heater motor electric leads, at the terminal connecters.

4 Slacken the demister and water hose clips.

5 To prevent damage to the carpets or upholstery caused by rust contaminated water place polythene sheeting in the appropriate places on the floor and seating.

6 Undo and remove the screws that secure the heater unit to the panel shelf and carefully lift away the heater unit.

7 Refitting the heater unit is the reverse sequence to removal but the following additional points should be noted:

a) Open the heater tap on the rear of the engine and slowly refill the cooling system.

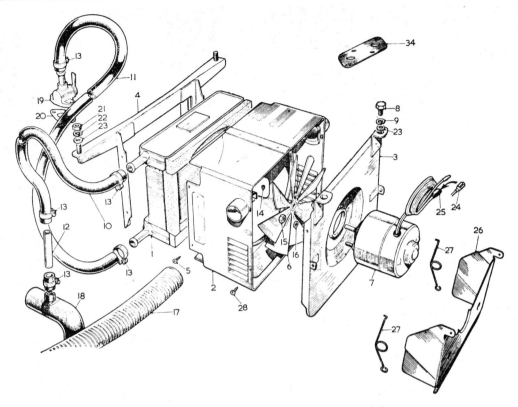

Fig. 12.14. Exploded view of recirculating heating and demisting system

1 Radiator	10 Outlet hose	19 Heat tap	28 Screw - cover plate to
2 Cowling	11 Inlet hose	20 Gasket for tap	cowling
3 Cover and motor	12 Connection for outlet	21 Nut - mounting bracket	29 Demister duct - LH
mounting plate	hose	fixing	30 Screw - demister duct to
4 Mounting bracket assembly	13 Hose clip	22 Spring washer	body
5 Screw - cowling to bracket	14 Screw - fan retaining	23 Plain washer	31 Demister duct - RH
6 Fan assembly	15 Nut - motor fixing	24 Lucar connector	32 Heater switch
7 Motor	16 Shakeproof washer	25 Rubber sleeve	33 Control knob - heater
8 Screw - heater fixing	17 Demister hose	26 Demister flap	switch
9 Spring washer	18 Hose - engine radiator to	27 Spring - demister flap	34 Sealing plate - hoses
	water pump		

b) If the heater does not warm up it is an indication that there is an air-lock. To clean: disconnect the return hose from the lower radiator hose and plug the hole. Now extend the return hose to reach the radiator filler neck. Start the engine and observe the flow of water from the return hose. When the bubbles cease, switch off the engine and reconnect the hose.

35 Heater assembly (fresh air early type) - removal and replacement

1 For safety reasons, disconnect the battery.
2 Refer to Chapter 2 and drain the cooling system.
3 Remove the front floor covering to avoid any damage through cooling water spillage as the pipes are disconnected.
4 Locate and disconnect the two electrical snap connections below the panel shelf and the blower switch connection from the ignition switch.
5 Remove the demister tube covers, detach the demister tubes and release the fresh air intake hose.
6 Slacken the heater water hose clips and pull the hose from the heater unit.
7 Slacken the nut that secures the rear of the heater unit to the mounting brackets (Fig. 12.15).

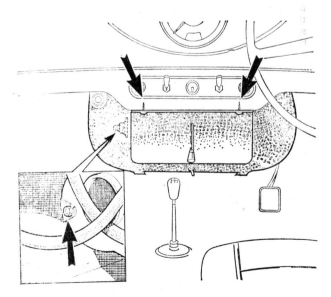

Fig. 12.15. Fresh air heater assembly securing points (early type)

8 Undo and remove the two screws, located beneath the panel shelf, that secure the front of the heater unit.

9 Carefully lift the heater unit from the slotted rear brackets, hold the fingers over the matrix pipe ends (or plug with corks) and lift the unit from the car.

10 Finally drain any remaining coolant from the unit.

11 **Note:** On some early models the heater unit is secured by four nuts. To gain access to these lift up the parcel shelf trimming. Undo and remove the nuts and lift away the heater, as described in paragraph 9. Note that distance pieces are fitted to the mounting studs.

12 Refitting the heater assembly is the reverse sequence to removal.

36 Heater assembly (fresh air early type) - dismantling and reassembly

Heater motor:

1 Remove the heater unit as described in Section 35.

2 Slacken the screws that secure the control panel, undo and remove the end cover screws and lift off the cover complete with blower motor (Fig. 12.16).

3 Using a suitable diameter drill remove the three 'pop' rivets that secure the motor unit to the end cover. Lift away the motor.

4 To fit the replacement motor locate in the end cover with the wiring positioned towards the top of the heater box when reassembled. Secure with three new 'pop' rivets.

5 Refitting the end cover is the reverse sequence to removal. Make sure that the flap valve is located on the end cover pivot and operates correctly before refitting the heater to the car.

Heater Matrix:

1 Remove the heater unit as described in Section 35.

2 Slacken the screws that secure the control panel, undo and remove the end cover screws and lift off the cover complete with the blower motor.

3 The heater matrix may now be lifted out of the casing.

4 Refitting the heater matrix is the reverse sequence to

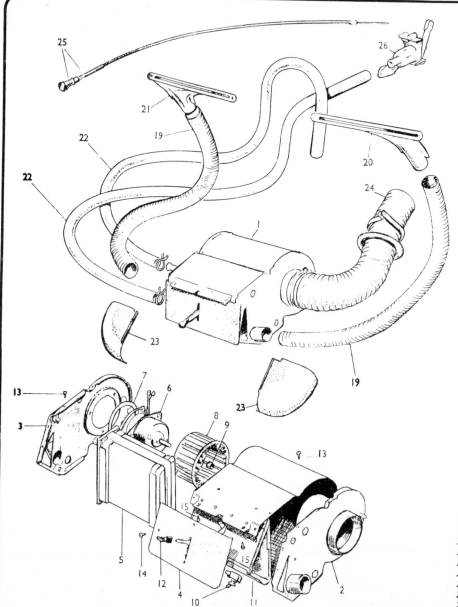

Fig. 12.16. Exploded view of heater assembly (fresh air, early type)

1   Heater unit
2   Cover
3   Cover
4   Control panel
5   Matrix
6   Motor
7   Seal
8   Fan
9   Fan securing ring
10 Blower switch
11 Flap valve
12 Control knob
13 Side cover securing screws
14 Control panel securing screws
15 Heater assembly securing screws
16 Heater assembly securing nut
17 Plain washer
18 Spring washer
19 Demister tubes
20 Right hand demister duct
21 Left hand demister duct
22 Water hoses
23 Demister tube covers
24 Air intake hose
25 Control cable
26 Water control valve

removal.

Heater blower switch:

1 Disconnect the battery, for safety reasons.

2 Remove the heater control panel and unscrew the switch securing nut.

3 Pull the flap valve outwards and withdraw the switch. Note the electrical connections and detach from the rear of the switch.

4 Refitting the switch is the reverse sequence to removal.

---

37 Heater assembly (fresh air later type) - removal and replacement

1 For safety reasons, disconnect the battery.

2 Refer to Chapter 2, and drain the cooling system.

3 Remove the front floor covering to avoid any damage through cooling water spillage as the pipes are disconnected.

4 Carefully pull the demister and air intake tubes out of the heater unit (Fig. 12.17).

5 Undo and remove the two screws that secure the front of the heater to the dash panel.

6 Slacken the nut that secures the rear of the heater to the body mounted bracket.

7 Make a note of the electrical connections to the blower motor

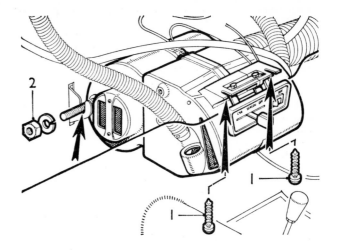

Fig. 12.17. Heater unit securing points

1 Securing screws
2 Nut and spring washer

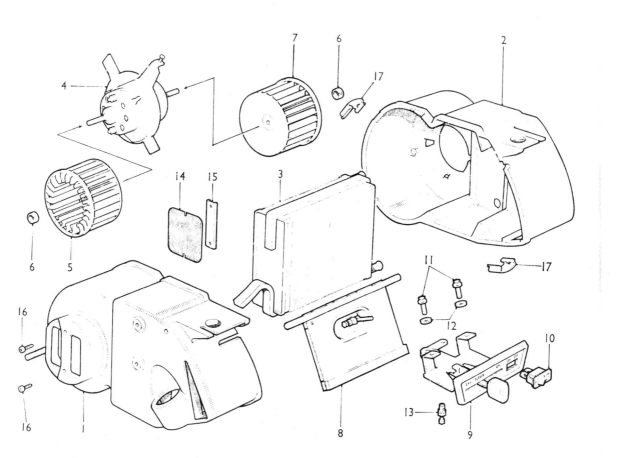

Fig. 12.18. Exploded view of the heater assembly (fresh air, later type)

1 Heater casing	6 Fan securing clips	11 Control panel to casing screws	14 One way valve
2 Heater casing	7 Air intake fan		15 Valve securing plate
3 Matrix	8 Air distribution fan	12 Washers	16 Valve securing screws
4 Blower motor	9 Heater control panel	13 Trunnion and screw - control	17 Heater casing joining clips
5 Recirculatory fan	10 Blower switch	lever to flap	

and switch, and detach.

8 Slacken the clips and disconnect the heater water hoses.

9 Carefully lift the heater unit from the slotted rear brackets, hold the fingers over the matrix pipe ends (or plug with corks) and lift the unit from the car.

10 Finally drain any remaining coolant from the unit.

11 Refitting the heater assembly is the reverse sequence to removal.

38 Heater assembly (fresh air later type) - dismantling and reassembly

Heater motor:

1 Remove the heater unit as described in Section 37.

2 Undo and remove the two screws securing the blower switch/air distribution panel. Lift away the panel (Fig. 12.18).

3 Carefully lever off the clips that secure the twin casing and separate the two halves of the heater unit.

4 Remove the motor assembly and withdraw each rotor from the motor.

5 Reassembling and refitting the heater motor is the reverse sequence to removal.

Heater Matrix:

1 Follow the instructions for removal of the heater motor paragraphs 1 to 3 inclusive.

2 Remove the matrix and clean away traces of dust and dirt. If it is leaking it may be repaired in a manner similar to the cooling system radiator (see Chapter 2).

3 Refitting the heater matrix is the reverse sequence to removal.

Heater blower switch:

1 It is possible to remove the blower switch without removing the heater unit from the car.

2 For safety reasons, disconnect the battery.

3 Working behind the blower switch/air distribution panel, pull off the electrical connections.

4 Using a pair of pliers press in the retainers on each side of the switch and manoeuvre the switch through the face of the panel.

5 Refitting the blower switch is the reverse sequence to removal.

39 Fresh air ventilation facia louvres - removal and replacement

1 Unscrew the louvre moulding retaining ring and lift away the moulding. Turn the ventilation louvre anticlockwise and withdraw it.

2 To remove the intake hoses, working under the wing carefully pull off both ends of the hose/s from their respective units and lift away the hose/s.

3 Refitting the louvres and hoses is the reverse sequence to removal.

40 Front grille - removal and replacement

1 This is a straightforward operation necessitating only the removal of the self-tapping screws from the outer edge and lifting the grille away (photo). On later models it is necessary to remove the headlight/grille extension panels (four screws securing each panel), then remove the grille panel securing screws and

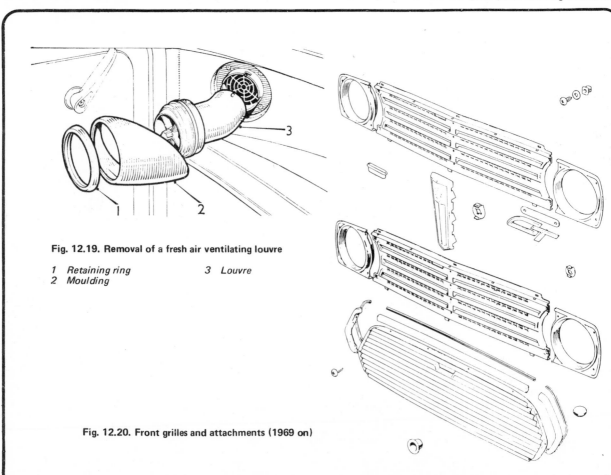

Fig. 12.19. Removal of a fresh air ventilating louvre

1   Retaining ring   3   Louvre
2   Moulding

Fig. 12.20. Front grilles and attachments (1969 on)

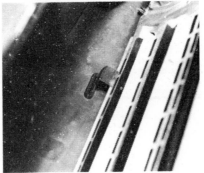

40.1a Lifting away front grille

40.1b Location for lower edge of front grille

Bodywork seam trim strip renewal (Section 41)

The horizontal and vertical finishing trims (they cover the welded body seams) are particularly prone to rusting on early Minis. New trims are available from BLMC

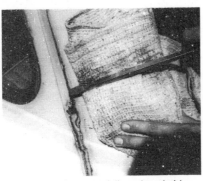

The trims are just a pushfit and are held in place with clips. On a badly rusted example like this the trim will need easing off with a screwdriver

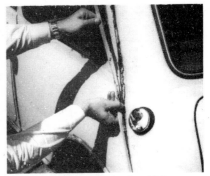

With the badly rusted trim freed it is quite easy to pull the rest of the trim away

The old clips which held the trim in place can now be eased off the seam by judicious levering with a screwdriver

The next step is to mask the surrounding paintwork. Use only proper masking tape as sellotape could lift off bits of paint when removed

The body seams suffer less from rust than the trims. Remove all loose rust with a wire brush or scraper. Clean down to the bare metal with emery paper

When the metal is reasonably clean and no loose rust is left protect it by brushing or spraying on an inhibitor such as Kurust

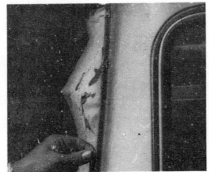

Also spray or paint the inside of the new trims and then fit six new clips at roughly equal distance up the seam

Then fit the trim, tapping it into place with a wooden mallet. Spray the trim to match the colour of the car and then remove the masking tape

lift the panel out of the locating holes in the lower grille panel (photo).

41 Bodywork seam trim strips - renewal

Refer to the photo sequence on page 257, which illustrates

and describes seam trim strip renewal. Although the trim being replaced in its sequence is a rear one, the procedure applies to all seam trim strips.

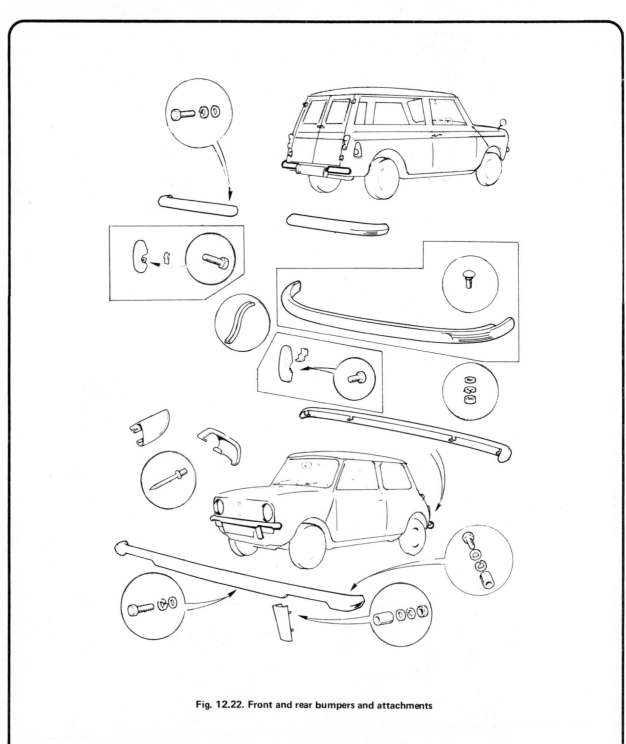

Fig. 12.22. Front and rear bumpers and attachments

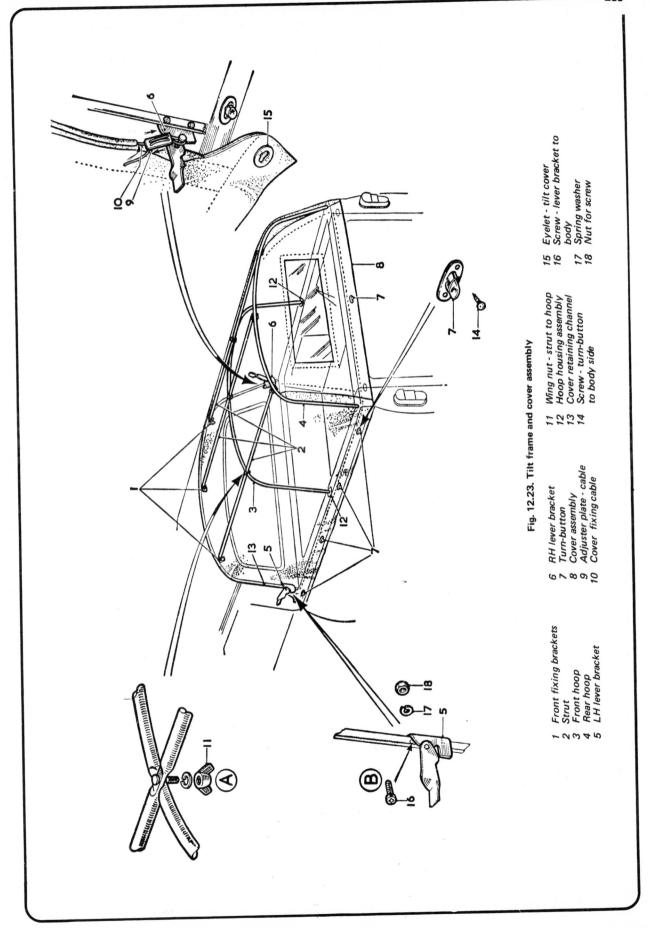

Fig. 12.23. Tilt frame and cover assembly

1 Front fixing brackets
2 Strut
3 Front hoop
4 Rear hoop
5 LH lever bracket

6 RH lever bracket
7 Turn-button
8 Cover assembly
9 Adjuster plate - cable
10 Cover fixing cable

11 Wing nut - strut to hoop
12 Hoop housing assembly
13 Cover retaining channel
14 Screw - turn-button
   to body side

15 Eyelet - tilt cover
16 Screw - lever bracket to
   body
17 Spring washer
18 Nut for screw

Chapter 13 Supplement

Contents

The information contained in this Chapter is intended to cover modifications to later models. It is additional or supplementary to the information contained in Chapters 1 to 12.

1 General Specifications

Engine

Specifications and data – Mini Clubman 1098 cc engine (Type 10H)
This engine is similar to the 8AM types, but with the following differences.

Engine (general)

Type	10H
Bore	2·543 in (64·59 mm)
Stroke	3·296 in (83·72 mm)
Capacity	1098 cc (67 cu in)
Compression ratio	8·5 : 1
Torque	60 lbf ft @ 2,450 rpm

Pistons

Type	Aluminium, solid skirt
Clearance of piston in bore:	
Top of skirt	0·0021 to 0·0033 in (0·05 to 0·08 mm)
Bottom of skirt	0·0005 to 0·0015 in (0·013 to 0·040 mm)

Gudgeon pins

Type	Fully floating, retained by circlips
Fit to piston and connecting rod	Hand push fit at 20°C (68°F)

Valves

Head diameter:	
Inlet	1·151 to 1·156 in (29·23 to 29·36 mm)
Exhaust	1·000 to 1·005 in (25·40 to 25·53 mm)
Valve guide length	1·531 in (38·89 mm)

Valve springs

Free length	1·96 in (49·7 mm)

Fitted length	1·34 in (33·0 mm)
Spring load with valves open	106 lbf (48·1 kgf)
Spring load with valves closed	70 lbf (31·8 kgf)

Valve timing

Inlet valve:	
Opens	5° BTDC
Closes	45° ABDC
Exhaust valves:	
Opens	51° BBDC
Closes	21° ATDC
Valve rocker clearance:	
Timing	0·021 in (0·533 mm)
Running (cold)	0·012 in (0·305 mm)

Carburettor

Mini 850 Saloon and variants

Type	SU HS4
Jet size	0·090 in (2.2 mm)
Needle	ADH
Piston spring	Red
Idle speed	750 rpm
Fast idle speed	1200 rpm
Exhaust emission	3% CO, or 3 to 4·5% CO with the FZX1064 carburettor specification

Mini 1000 and Clubman 1000
Specifications as for 850 Mini but with the following differences:

Needle	ADE
Idle speed	750 rpm
Fast idle speed	1300 rpm (manual) 1200 rpm (automatic)
Exhaust emission	3% CO, or 3 to 4·5% CO with the FZX1065 carburettor specification

Mini Clubman 1098
Specifications as for 850 Mini but with the following differences:

Needle	ABP
Exhaust emission	3% CO, with the FZX1066 carburettor specification

Mini 1275 GT
Specifications as for 850 Mini but with the following differences:

Needle	ABB
Idle speed	850 rpm
Fast idle speed	1300 rpm
Exhaust emission	3% CO, or 3 to 4·5% CO with the FZX1047 carburettor specification

Manual transmission

Clearances

Primary gear endfloat	0·003 to 0·006 in (0·076 to 0·15 mm)
Lay gear endfloat	0·002 to 0·006 in (0·05 to 0·15 mm)
First motion shaft endfloat	0·003 to 0·006 in (0·076 to 0·15 mm)
Intermediate gear endfloat	0·003 to 0·008 in (0·076 to 0·203 mm)

Ratios: 1275 GT (after July 1974)

	Top	Third	Second	First	Reverse
Gearbox	1.00	1·35	2·094	3·33	3·347
overall	3·44	4·654	7·203	11·46	11·15

Final drive ratio	3·44 : 1

Automatic transmission

Converter output gear endfloat	0·0035 to 0·006 in (0·09 to 0·15 mm)
Idler gear endfloat	0·004 to 0·007 in (0·10 to 0·18 mm)
Input gear pre-load	0·001 to 0·003 in (0·02 to 0·07 mm)

Brakes

Mini 850, 1000 and Clubman

Make	Lockheed
Footbrake	Hydraulic on all four wheels
Handbrake (rear wheels only)	Mechanical
Type of brakes:	
Front	Drum – 7 in (177·8 mm) diameter

Rear   . . . .   Drum – 7 in (177·8 mm) diameter
Lining material . . . .   Don 202

Mini 1275 GT

Make   . . . .   Lockheed
Footbrake   . . . .   Hydraulic on all four wheels
Handbrake (rear wheels only) . . . .   Mechanical
Types of brakes:
    Front   . . . .   Disc 8·4 in (213·4 mm) diameter
    Rear   . . . .   Drum 7·0 in (177·8 mm) diameter

Electrical system

Battery

Types   . . . .   Lucas A7, A9, A11/9
Capacity
    A7   . . . .   30 amp hour @ 20 hour rate
    A9   . . . .   40 amp hour @ 20 hour rate
    A11/9   . . . .   50 amp hour @ 20 hour rate

Fuses

Circuit 1 – 2   . . . .   17A
Circuit 3 – 4 and 5 – 6 . . . .   12A
Circuit 7 – 8   . . . .   8A
Radio   . . . .   1·5A

Torque wrench settings

	lbf ft	kgf m
Connecting rod big-end bolts	37	5·1
Connecting rod big-end nuts	33	4·6
Crankshaft pulley nut	75	10·3
Cylinder head nuts	50	6·9
Cylinder head nuts (emission control engine)	40	5·5
First motion shaft nut	150	20·7
Main bearing set bolts	63	8·7
Third motion shaft nut	150	20·7
Oil pump bolts	8	1·1
Oil pressure relief valve domed nut	43	5·9
Spark plugs	18	2·5
Water outlet elbow nuts	8	1·1
Coolant temperature transmitter	16	2·2

2 Engine

Cylinder head: 1275 GT models

1   On the 1275 GT range, the cylinder head differs in that it
has an additional head retaining nut (B) at the rear and an
additional retaining bolt (A) at the front as in Fig. 13.1. When
removing the cylinder head, these must be removed first, and
then the remaining retaining nuts for the rocker pedestal and
cylinder head can be progressively removed in the sequence
shown. Refit the cylinder head in the reverse order but tighten
the cylinder head bolt/nuts to the recommended torque in the
sequence shown.

Connecting rods and pistons: 1275 GT models

2   The connecting rod big-end journal on the 1275 GT is split
horizontally (as opposed to diagonally as on standard engines)
and its retaining nuts are multi-sided, there being no locking
tabs fitted as with the standard engines.
3   An interference fit gudgeon pin is used and this requires the
use of a special Leyland service tool number 18G 1150 with
adaptor 18G 1150A to remove and refit the pin. This tool is
shown in Fig. 13.2, and no attempt should be made to remove
the gudgeon pins without this tool. If you are able to procure
this tool and adaptor, they are used in the following manner:
4   Securely hold the hexagonal body in a firm vice and screw
back the large nut until it is flush with the end of the main
centre screw. Well lubricate the screw and large nut as they
have to withstand high loading. Now push the centre screw in
until the nut touches the thrust race.
5   Fit the adaptor number 18G 1150A onto the main centre
screw with the piston ring cutaway positioned uppermost. Then
slide the parallel sleeve with the groove end first onto the centre

screw.
6   Fit the piston with the 'FRONT' or 'V' mark towards the
adaptor on the centre screw. This is important because the
gudgeon pin bore is offset and irreparable damage will result if
fitted the wrong way round. Next fit the remover/replacer bush
on the centre screw with the flange end towards the gudgeon
pin.
7   Screw the stop nut onto the main centre screw and adjust it
until approximately 0.032 inch (0.8 mm) endplay ('A' in Fig.
13.2) exists, and lock the stop nut securely with the lock
screws. Now check that the remover/replacer bush and parallel
sleeves are positioned correctly in the bore on both sides of the
piston. Also check that the curved face of the adaptor is clean
and slide the piston onto the tool so it fits into the curved face of
the adaptor with the piston rings over the cutaway.
8   Screw the large nut up to the thrust race and, holding the
lockscrew, turn the large nut with a ring spanner or long socket
until the gudgeon pin is withdrawn from the piston.
9   To refit the pistons to the connecting rods proceed as
follows: Unscrew the large nut and withdraw the centre screw
from the body a few inches. Well lubricate the screw thread and
correctly locate the piston support adaptor.
10   Carefully slide the parallel sleeve with the groove end last
onto the centre screw, up as far as the shoulder. Lubricate the
gudgeon pin and its bores in the connecting rod and piston with
a graphited oil.
11   Fit the connecting rod and piston, side marked 'FRONT' or
'V' to the tool with the connecting rod entered on the sleeve up
to the groove. Fit the gudgeon pin into the piston bore up to the
connecting rod. Next fit the remover/replacer bush flange end
towards the gudgeon pin.
12   Screw the stop nut onto the centre screw and adjust the
nut to give a 0.032 inch (0.8 mm) endplay, ('B' as shown in Fig.
13.2). Lock the nut securely with the lock screw. Ensure that

Fig. 13.1. The 1275 GT cylinder head retaining bolt and nuts layout. The additional nut 'B' and bolt 'A' are clearly arrowed to show their position

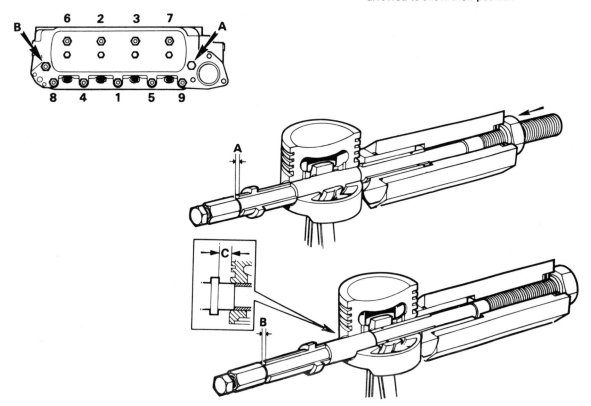

Fig. 13.2. Gudgeon pin removal showing special tools

A and B = 0.032 inch (0.8 mm)

the curved face of the adaptor is clean and slide the piston on the tool so that it fits into the curved face of the adaptor with the piston rings over the adaptor cutaway.

13 Screw the large nut up the thrust race. Adjust the torque wrench to a setting of 16 lbf ft (2.2 kgf m) if of the 'click' type which will represent the minimum load for an acceptable fit. Use the torque wrench previously set on the large nut, and a ring spanner on the lock screw. Pull the gudgeon pin into the piston until the flange of the remover/replacer bush is 0.032 inch (0.8 mm) from the piston skirt. It is critically important that the flange is NOT allowed to contact the piston. Finally withdraw the Leyland service tool.

14 Should the torque wrench not 'click' or reach 16 lbf ft (2.2 kgf m) throughout the pull, the fit of the gudgeon pin in the connecting rod is not within limits and the parts must be renewed.

15 Ensure that the piston pivots freely on the gudgeon pin and is free to slide sideways. Should stiffness exist wash the assembly in paraffin, lubricate the gudgeon pin with graphited oil and recheck. Again if stiffness exists dismantle the assembly and check for signs of ingrained dirt or damage.

Lubrication system

16 Late model cars with manual transmission are now fitted with a disposable cartridge type of oil filter, which screws directly onto the filter head on the crankcase.

17 To replace the cartridge, unscrew it from the filter head and discard it together with the seal. If the filter proves excessively tight obtain a strap wrench or alternatively pierce it with a screwdriver and tap it off. Smear the seal on the replacement

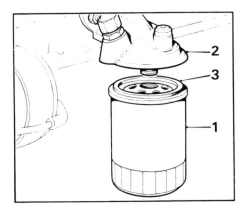

Fig. 13.3. The disposable cartridge type of oil filter now fitted to all manual transmission models

1   Cartridge
2   Filter head
3   Sealant ring

filter with a little clean engine oil and position it on the filter head, screwing it up firmly by hand. Do not overtighten with a spanner or strap wrench. Check for leaks on restarting the engine.

18 Cooper 'S' models are fitted with an oil cooler unit and should this ever need to be removed or serviced the front grille will have to be removed first to gain access to it. Check for leaks around the cooler unit at regular intervals and also after working on it when the engine is restarted.

Engine mountings

19 When removing the engine mounting on the right-hand side on the later models, it will be necessary to remove the solenoid from the wing valance and on the late 850 and 1000 models the coil must be removed from the cylinder head bracket.

Engine and manual transmission – removal

20 When removing the engine/transmission unit on cars fitted with the later type remote control gear change unit, first disconnect the engine tie rod from its location on the rear of the gearbox casing, loosen the bolt at the other end and swing it out of the way. Select reverse gear and then drive the roll pin from the remote control extension rod and selector shaft. Unscrew and remove the steady fork to the final drive housing. Then continue as described in Section 6 of Chapter 1, paragraph 14 onwards.

Engine and automatic transmission (later models) – removal

21 The following list of instructions is a revised version of Section 10 in Chapter 1 and includes information on the later models:

22 For safety reasons, disconnect the battery. Remove the bonnet by undoing and removing the two nuts and washers from each of the bonnet hinges on the bonnet side of the hinge. Carefully lift the bonnet off and place it somewhere safe where it will not be scratched or damaged.

23 Drain the cooling system (see Chapter 2) and disconnect the top, bottom and heater hoses and also the heater control valve cable.

24 Drain the oil and remove the oil filter unit.

25 Remove the air cleaner unit from the carburettor, then disconnect the vacuum pipe, petrol feed pipe and breather hose from the carburettor, and also the kickdown control rod.

26 Unscrew and remove the carburettor retaining nuts and carefully lift the carburettor from the inlet manifold, and place out of the way.

27 On those engines fitted with a mechanical fuel pump disconnect the petrol inlet hose.

28 Detach the exhaust down pipe from the manifold.

29 Disconnect the engine tie rod from the cylinder block and swing the rod away from the engine.

30 On Clubman models, disconnect and remove the ignition shield with brackets from the rocker cover.

31 Detach the HT leads from the spark plugs and ignition coil, but note the position of each lead for reassembly. Spring back the distributor cap retaining clips and lift away the cap with leads and place out of the way.

32 Make a note of the respective electrical connections to the engine and detach from the terminal connectors. Tuck the various cables out of the way of the engine.

33 On 1000 cc engine models, remove the horn.

34 On later models, disconnect the flexible air intake pipe from under the right-hand front wing and remove the intake from the wing valance. The starter solenoid can be inserted temporarily through the intake hole out of the way.

35 Disconnect the oil pressure gauge pipe hose from the cylinder block.

36 Unscrew the rocker cover retaining nuts and carefully lift away the cover.

37 Slacken the fixing clips on the heater fresh air tube connections on the grille (early models) and swing the tube clear of the engine.

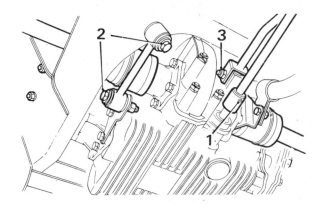

Fig. 13.4. View showing the selector rod (1), the tie rod (2) and the extension rod (3).

38 Jack up each side of the car in turn, placing supporting blocks under each side of the subframe. To give better access, remove the two front wheels. Alternatively, place the car over a pit or on a ramp.

39 Suitably mark the drive flanges at the inboard ends and then undo and remove the securing nuts.

40 Where a weather protection cover is fitted to the rear of the transmission unit this must next be removed. As an alternative a rubber sleeve may be fitted and in this case it should be pulled back.

41 Disconnect the gear selector cable by removing the clevis pin.

42 Slacken the yoke clamp nut and remove the yoke, nut, rubber ferrules and sleeve. Then remove the cable front adjusting nut from the outer cable and pull the cable clear of the transmission.

43 Remove the exhaust bracket from the final drive cover. Note that the larger nut is secured by a locking tab.

44 Working at the rear of the speedometer head disconnect the speedometer cable.

45 Place lifting brackets onto the rocker cover securing studs and then, using an overhead hoist or crane, suitably support the weight of the complete power unit.

46 Undo and remove the setscrews and washers that secure each engine mounting to the subframe.

47 Lift the complete unit sufficiently to release the drive shafts from the driving flanges.

48 Check that all attachments, hoses, cables and controls, have been disconnected and tucked out of the way and then lift the unit up through the engine compartment and away from the front of the car. Carefully lower to the ground.

---

3   Cooling system

Radiator drain plug

Late model cars do not have a drain plug fitted to the radiator and therefore, if the system is to be drained, the bottom hose to the radiator must be disconnected. When the radiator has been refilled, check that the bottom hose connection is satisfactory and that there are no leaks.

---

4   Carburettor

HS4 carburettor needle – removal and refitting

1   The HS4 type carburettor is basically the same as the HS2 and the instructions for removal and overhaul for both types are therefore similar. However, the HS4 differs in that it

incorporates a spring tensioned needle which is retained in a guide in the base of the piston, as shown in Fig. 13.5.

2   Removal of the needle assembly is the same as for the HS2 types, by simply unscrewing the guide locking screw in the side of the piston base.

3   Always check that the needle is of the correct type for your model; this is identified by the letters etched into the top of the needle.

4   To refit, first assemble the spring and guide to the shank of the needle, and carefully refit the assembly into the piston. The guide must be located so that it is flush with the base of the piston. Check that the guide etch mark on the needle is in line with the piston transfer holes, and then insert the guide locking screw, which should be renewed once removed.

5   Exhaust emission control system

General description

1   The exhaust emission control system as fitted to certain export market models, particularly those for the USA, has been modified and an illustration of the current layout can be seen in Fig. 13.6.

2   The air pump now has a built-in air filter. An air diverter valve is fitted and this is operational when the choke (mixture control) is activated. The air pressure from the pump is then shut off and re-directed into the atmosphere. The air cleaner unit for the carburettor incorporates an air temperature control and hot air duct and shroud.

3   It is generally recommended that any repairs to the emission control system components be entrusted to your nearest Leyland dealer. However, certain items may be removed to be renewed or for access to another component in the engine compartment. These are listed from paragraph 8 onwards.

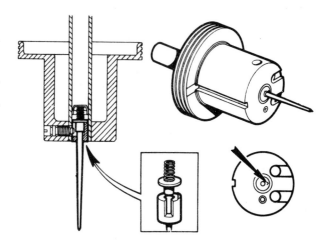

Fig. 13.5. The swinging needle fixing

Fig. 13.6. The exhaust emission control layout

1   Air pump
2   Air pump filter
3   Air pump relief valve
4   Air diverter valve
5   Check valve
6   Air manifold
7   Restrictor-gulp valve line
8   Gulp valve
9   Gulp valve signal pipe
10   Hot air duct and shroud
11   Air temperature control
12   Carburettor

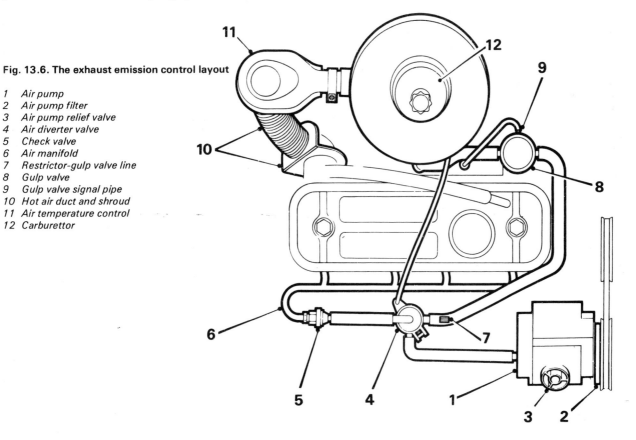

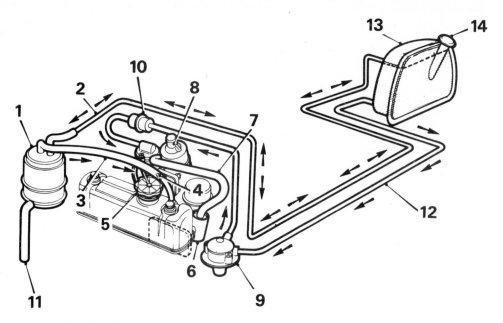

Fig. 13.7. The fuel evaporative loss and crankcase emission control system

1	Absorption canister	5	Sealed oil filler cap	9	Fuel pump
2	Vapour lines	6	The oil separator/flame trap	10	Fuel filter
3	Purge line	7	The crankcase purge pipe	11	Air vent hose
4	Restrictor connection	8	Carburettor	12	Fuel pipe

13	Fuel tank
14	Sealed filler cap

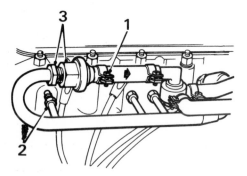

Fig. 13.8. The air manifold and check valve, showing the hose clip (1) the air feed pipes to the cylinder head (2) and the check valve (3)

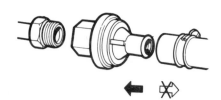

Fig. 13.9. The check valve showing the correct airflow direction

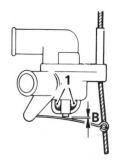

Fig. 13.10. The air diverter valve: check that the air silencer (1) is in position. Check the clearance at point 'B'

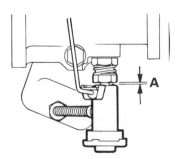

Fig. 13.11. Check the clearance between the jet housing and adjustment nut at point 'A'

The crankcase emission control/fuel evaporative loss system

4 The crankcase emission control system has been modified and, as can be seen from Fig. 13.7, now incorporates the fuel evaporative loss system. Briefly explained, the new system works in the following manner. An oil separator/flame trap (arrester) is attached to the cylinder side cover, and an interconnecting hose is fitted from the oil separator to the carburettor depression chamber. Blow-by fumes from the engine are directed from the separator to the carburettor and are mixed with purged air from the charcoal canister, which is part of the fuel evaporative loss system. These fumes, together with the ambient air induction through the carburettor air cleaner, are combined with the fuel mixture and drawn into the combustion chambers where they are burnt off.

5 The fuel evaporative loss control system operates as follows: When the engine is non-operational, the vapours from the fuel tank are directed to the special charcoal filled canister where they are absorbed. When the engine is in operation, the fuel vapours are directed to the crankcase emission control system and disposed of as described.

6 In order that the above systems can operate correctly both the oil filler cap on the rocker cover and the fuel filler cap are of the sealed type and it is important to see that they are fitted correctly and are in good condition.

7 The fuel tank is of a special design which allows for fuel displacement due to increased temperature, and the vapour vent to the charcoal canister is located so that any liquid fuel cannot enter the vapour pipe.

Air pump – removal and refitting

8 Detach the outlet hose from the pump. Unclip the number one spark plug lead, and unscrew and remove the spark plug. Loosen the pump unit adjustment bracket bolt and the alternator adjustment pivot bolt. Undo and remove the adjustment bracket to pump screw and the pump pivot bolt. The drivebelt and pump unit can now be removed. Refit in the reverse order but adjust the drivebelt so that it has a deflection of $\frac{1}{2}$ inch (13 mm) when hand pressure is applied at the midway point between the pulleys.

Air manifold and check valve – removal and refitting

9 Refer to Fig. 13.8. Unscrew and remove the number one spark plug. Unscrew the retaining clip (1) from the interconnecting hose between the check valve and the diverter valve (at the check valve end), and slide the clip to the middle of the hose.

The four air manifold feed pipe unions (2) to the cylinder head can now be disconnected, the check valve pulled from the hose and the air manifold removed. To disconnect the check valve (3), firmly support the air manifold and unscrew the valve from it.

10 Refit in the reverse order but ensure that the feed pipe unions are secure in the cylinder head and the hose connection to the check valve is good. Renew the hose if it is damaged, perished or suspect in any way.

11 If the check valve only is to be removed, then unscrew both of the interconnecting hose clips between the air manifold and the valve adaptor and move them to the middle of the hose. Support the air manifold and unscrew the check valve, then withdraw it from the hose. The check valve is easily checked by blowing by mouth (**not air line pressure!**) through each end. Air must only pass in one direction – from the air diverter valve side. If the air is able to pass through from the air manifold side, the check valve is faulty and must be renewed. Refit in the reverse order.

Gulp valve – removal and refitting

12 The gulp valve is retained to its bracket by two bolts. Undo these bolts, and loosen the respective hose clips. Detach the hoses and the vacuum tube and remove the gulp valve. Refit in the reverse order ensuring that the hose and vacuum tubes are secure.

Diverter valve – removal and refitting

13 Loosen the cable trunnion and detach the cable from the lever. Unscrew the respective hose clips and disconnect the hoses to free the diverter valve. Refit in the reverse order but ensure that the hose connections are secure and the adjustments are as given below.

Diverter valve – check and adjustments

14 Fiirst check that the diverter valve is in generally good condition and that the air silencer is in position – see Fig. 13.10. Pull the choke control knob (mixture control) so that the clearance between the jet housing and the adjustment nut on the carburettor, point 'A' in Fig. 13.11, is 0·010 to 0·015 in (0·25 to 0·38 mm), then lock the knob in this position. Now check the clearance between the valve stem and the operating lever of the diverter valve as shown in Fig. 13.10; point 'B' should be 0·0015 to 0·003 in (0·04 to 0·08 mm). If adjustment is necessary, loosen the trunnion and reposition the lever to suit, then retighten the trunnion.

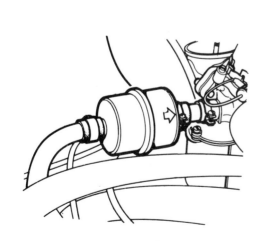

Fig. 13.12. The fuel line filter. Arrow shows direction of flow

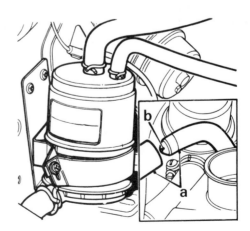

Fig. 13.13. The absorption canister. Inset shows purge hose 'a' and restrictor 'b'

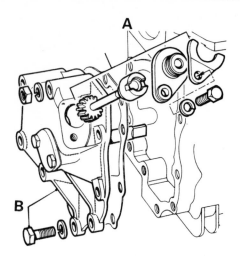

Fig. 13.14. Remove the speedometer drive pinion. 'A' - the drive pinion assembly. 'B' - Housing bolts

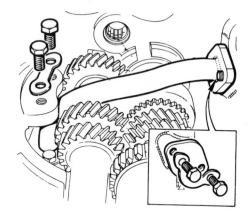

Fig. 13.15. The oil suction pipe

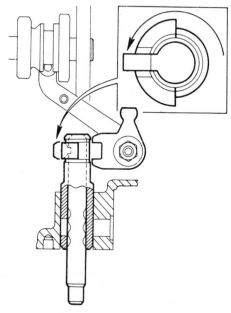

Fig. 13.16. Twist the selector shaft anti-clockwise (inset) to disengage from the operating stub and interlock spool

15 The valve can be checked for correct operation by detaching the hose from the check valve, then starting and running the engine at idle speed. A flow of air should be felt at the hose normally but when the choke is in operation, the air pressure at this point should be cut off completely. If, with the choke operated, there is an air supply at the hose then the diverter valve is faulty and should be renewed.

Emission control system – servicing

Every 12 000 miles or every 12 months
16 Renew the engine/transmission oil filler cap, ensuring that the correct type is fitted.
17 Inspect the various hoses and pipes in the air supply system. They must be in good general condition and securely retained with no leaks. Renew any that are at all suspect.
18 Renew the filter in the fuel line by loosening the inlet hose retaining clip and the outlet hose retaining clip. Pull the filter from the hoses and note the direction of flow arrow towards the carburettor. Ensure that the replacement filter is correctly positioned and that the hose clips are secure.
19 Renew the absorption canister as follows: Detach the vapour and purge hoses and also the air vent hose from the canister. Loosen the retaining bracket screw and withdraw the canister. Refit the new one in the reverse sequence but additionally detach the purge hose from the rocker cover elbow and inspect the restriction aperture. Use a piece of soft wire to clear any blockage, and reconnect the hose. Ensure that the hose connections are secure.
20 The gulp valve, check valve and air diverter valves must also be checked for efficiency of operation but this task is best entrusted to your local Leyland dealer. However, if necessary, with the exception of the gulp valve, which definitely requires specialised equipment for testing, the above items can be checked as described earlier.

Emission control system – fault finding
Poor or erratic engine performance is more likely to be caused by conventional engine faults. However, if it is decided that the fault lies in the emission control system, it should be checked through as follows.
21 Erratic running, with poor performance, if not a conventional defect is most likely to be the gulp valve.
22 If the engine stops after short periods it may be fuel starvation due to a blockage in the air lines to or from the absorption canister. This can be checked by quickly taking off the fuel filler cap as the engine fails, to listen for an intake of air.
23 If enrichment of the mixture is needed to get a correct exhaust emission reading there is likely to be an air leak to the crankcase, either on the engine itself, or the breather system piping.
24 If the exhaust temperature seems excessive check the air injectors for correct operation.
25 Leaks can often be located by listening with a plastic or metal pipe held with one end to the ear.
26 If the air pump is suspected of noise, run the engine with its belt removed to listen for the difference. This will also show how the characteristics of the engine are affected by loss of the air output from the pump.

6   Transmission

Manual transmission – dismantling and reassembly
Due to the various modifications made to the manual transmission over the many years of Mini production, the original dismantling and reassembly sections have been modified accordingly and are now in danger of outgrowing their original concept.
In order to simplify matters we have decided to segregate

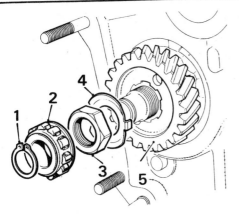

Fig. 13.17. The 1st motion shaft gear and shaft

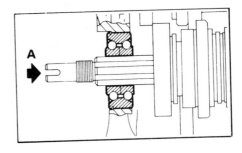

Fig. 13.18. Drive the shaft in direction of arrow 'A'

1 Circlip	4 Lockwasher
2 Bearing	5 1st motion shaft gear
3 Nut	

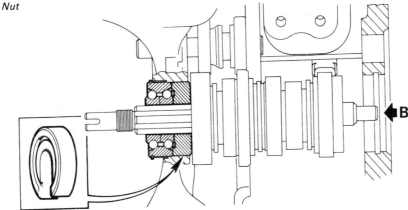

Fig. 13.19. Insert spacer between the gear and bearing and drive out in direction shown at point 'B'

the latest type manual gearbox dismantling and reassembly procedures and have detailed the instructions for the late type below. Removal of the gearbox and separation from the engine is still basically the same as for the earlier types, as are the inspection and overhaul procedures.

1   Unscrew the final drive end covers retaining screws, and remove the covers.
2   Withdraw the selector shaft detent ball and sleeve with spring.
3   Bend over the final drive housing retaining nut lockwasher tabs, unscrew the nuts and remove with washers. Withdraw the final drive housing, taking care not to damage the selector shaft oil seal.
4   Extract the final drive gear assembly and the speedometer drive pinion, having removed its retaining screw, spring washer and plate.
5   Remove the engine mounting adaptor housing and the speedometer drive housing.
6   Bend over the lockwasher tabs and unscrew the oil suction pipe retaining screws, and pull the pipe from the casing.
7   Using a suitable pair of circlip pliers, remove the circlip that retains the first motion shaft roller bearing. The roller bearing must now be withdrawn, and the best tool to use for this purpose is the Leyland service tool 18G 705 together with 18G 705C.
8   Bend over the first motion shaft retaining nut lockwasher tab and also the lockwasher tab on the third motion shaft final drive gear retaining nut.

9   Turn the selector shaft in an anti-clockwise direction and disengage the operating stub and interlock spool from the bell-crank levers.
10   Now lock the gears by engaging first and fourth gears simultaneously, and withdraw the lockwasher and final drive gear.
11   Unscrew the first motion shaft gear nut using a box spanner (wrench) and withdraw lockwasher and gear.
12   Locate the first and fourth gears in neutral, bend straight the lockwasher tabs retaining the third motion shaft bearing retainer bolts and unscrew and remove the bolts.
13   Withdraw the retainer and note the adjustment shims.
14   Remove the reverse lock plate and extract the layshaft.
15   Remove the laygear complete with small and large thrust washers.
16   With a pair of circlip pliers, remove the circlip retaining the first motion shaft bearing. Withdraw the first motion shaft complete with bearing from the gearbox casing using a suitable puller. If available, use Leyland service tools 18G 284 and 18G 284B for this purpose should the shaft and bearing prove difficult to remove.
17   To remove the third motion shaft assembly it is first necessary to extract the double row ball bearing. To do this proceed as follows:

a) Using a soft headed hammer, drive the shaft in the direction of the clutch but take care not to disengage the third/fourth synchronizer from its hub which in turn would cause the balls and springs to be released.

b) Insert a suitable spacer between the gear and the inside face of the bearing and drift the shaft back from the clutch end so that the bearing emerges from the casing aperture and can be removed from the shaft. The spacer can be fabricated from a block of hardwood or mild steel and should have a 'U' shaped cut-out section to fit over the shaft. The outside dimensions should not exceed the diameter of the bearing aperture. If available, of course, it is better to use the Leyland service tool 18G 1127 as shown in Fig. 13.19.

18 Remove the third motion shaft unit.

19 Withdraw the oil strainer and then extract the reverse gear and idler shaft. Drift the shaft through the casing and note which way round the gear is fitted when removing.

20 Remove the selector forks from the shaft. They are retained by roll pins which must be drifted out first before removal is possible.

21 To disconnect the bellcrank levers, first unscrew and remove the retaining nut and washer. Make a note of the lever positions before removing them with washers.

22 The interlock spool and selector shaft are now extracted from the casing, and if the O-ring seal is to be renewed, which is advisable, drift out the bellcrank lever hinge post.

23 The respective idler gear bearings can now be extracted if they are to be renewed, also the first motion shaft spigot bearing, which is retained by a circlip. The primary gear oil seal should also be removed and renewed in the flywheel housing.

24 With the gearbox fully dismantled the respective components should be cleaned and inspected for excessive wear and where necessary renewed. The mainshaft can be overhauled as described in Section 6 of Chapter 6. The reassembly procedure is as follows:

25 Refit the selector shaft into the interlock spool and insert into the gearcase, ensuring that the operating stub faces away from the hinge post.

26 Position the sleeve over the hinge post together with the bellcrank levers, ensuring that they are correctly fitted as noted when removed. Tighten the self-locking nut but the selector shaft and interlock spool must not be engaged with the bellcrank levers until the first and third motion shaft gear securing nuts are fitted and tightened to their respective torques.

27 Fit the third/fourth selector fork and also the first speed fork to the selector rod which is drifted through the casing and forks. Refit the roll pin to locate.

28 The reverse idler gear is now fitted and engages with the reverse bellcrank lever hinge and the shaft drifted into position.

29 Refit the oil strainer into position in the gearbox.

30 Lubricate the various components of the third motion shaft with clean engine oil and insert the complete unit into the gearbox to locate with the selector forks.

31 The third motion shaft bearing is now drifted into position in the gearbox aperture. If the special Leyland service tool 18G 579 is not available, use a piece of suitable pipe to drift the bearing squarely into position.

32 Lubricate and fit the first motion shaft into its location in the gear, then carefully drift the shaft unit into position in the gearbox. To retain in position refit the circlip that was originally fitted in the recess. If the gear casing has been renewed then a selected circlip must be fitted to suit the tolerance requirement of the new casing. Circlips are available in two thicknesses, as given below, and therefore, if the original circlip is to be renewed in the same housing, then ensure that one of the same type is obtained. Measure the circlip gap in the gearcase and select accordingly:

Gap size 0·096 to 0·098 in (2.43 to 2·48 mm)   =
circlip part no. 2A 3710
Gap size 0·098 to 0·100 in (2.48 to 2·54 mm)   =
circlip part no. 2A 3711

33 Fit the laygear needle roller bearing into position and lubricate, then refit the laygear shaft into position together with the selected thrust washers. The endfloat of the laygear should

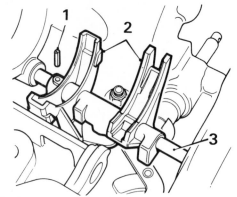

Fig. 13.20. The selector forks in position on shaft

1   Roll pin   3   Shaft
2   Selector forks

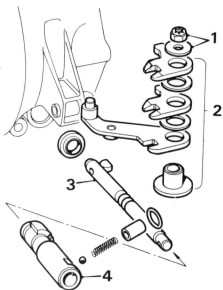

Fig. 13.21. The bellcrank lever and interlock spool assembly

1   Retaining nut/washer   3   Selector shaft
2   The bellcrank lever   4   Interlock spool

be 0·002 to 0·006 in (0·05 to 0·15 mm) and washers are available in thicknesses from 0·123 in (3·12 mm) to 0·131 in (3·32 mm) accordingly.

34 Having checked the endfloat, refit the layshaft and reverse shaft end plate, turning the shaft if required to correctly position the slots.

35 The third motion shaft bearing retainer is now fitted into position, less any shims, and the securing bolts lightly and evenly tightened. Using feeler gauges, check the amount of shims required to fit between the retainer and bearing. The shim requirements are as follows:

Gap	Shim requirement
0·005 to 0·006 in (0·13 to 0·15 mm)	0·005 in (0.13 mm)
0·006 to 0·008 in (0·15 to 0·20 mm)	0·007 in (0.18 mm)
0·008 to 0·010 in (0.20 to 0·25 mm)	0·009 in (0.23 mm)
0·010 to 0·012 in	0·011 in

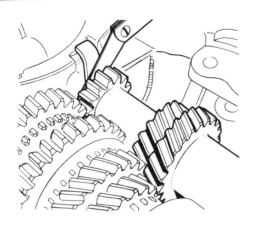

Fig. 13.22. Checking the laygear endfloat using feeler gauges

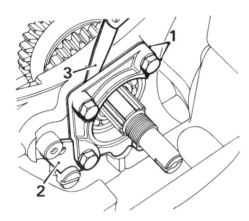

Fig. 13.23. Checking the third motion shaft bearing retainer to bearing clearance to assess the shim requirements.

1 Bearing retainer
2 Layshaft/reverse shaft lock plate
3 Feeler gauge check position

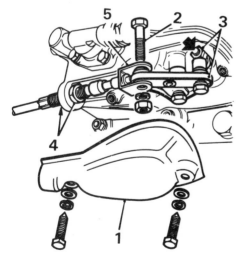

Fig. 13.24. Selector cable adjustment

1 Bellcrank cover plate
2 Clevis bolt
3 Transverse rod/bellcrank lever
4 Cable adjustment/ securing nuts
5 Clevis

(0·25 to 0·30 mm)	(0·28 mm)
0·012 to 0·014 in	0·013 in
(0·30 to 0·35 mm)	(0·33 mm)
0·014 to 0·015 in	0·015 in
(0·35 to 0·38 mm)	(0·38 mm)

Having found the requirement of shims, remove the retainer and fit the shims accordingly. Refit the bearing retainer and bolts using new lockwashers. Tighten the bolts to the specified torque and bend over the lockwasher tabs.

36 Lock the gears by engaging first and fourth simultaneously then relocate the final drive pinion together with a new locking washer and nut to the third motion shaft. Tighten the nut to the specified torque figure using a box spanner (box wrench), and bend over the lock tabs.

37 Relocate the first motion shaft gear with lockwasher and securing nut. Tighten the nut to the specified torque and bend over the lock tabs of the washer.

38 The first motion shaft roller bearing is now fitted into position and retained with its circlip.

39 Relocate the fourth and first gears to the neutral position, then turn the selector shaft and interlock spool so that it engages with the bellcrank levers.

40 Refit the oil suction pipe to the strainer; then, using a new joint washer and locking tabs, locate and tighten the flange screws followed by the pipe bracket screws. Bend over the lock plate tabs.

41 The speedometer drive housing is now fitted using a new joint washer, and the retaining nuts and screws tightened to the specified torque. Relocate the speedometer drive pinion with a new washer.

42 The engine mounting adaptor housing is now refitted and the final drive gear fitted and adjusted as described in Chapter 8.

Automatic transmission – adjustment

Selector cable adjustment of the latest type of transmission is carried out as follows:

43 With the car securely raised on chassis stands, on ramps or over an inspection pit, unscrew and remove the bellcrank cover plate screws from underneath.

44 Undo the cable clevis fork nut and bolt. Withdraw the bolt from the bellcrank lever. Pull out the transverse rod to its fullest extent, then push in the rod to the second detent position.

45 Loosen the cable adjustment/securing bolts to the gear casing and locate the cable fork so that the bellcrank pivot bolt can be located through the fork and lever, and retighten the retaining nut.

46 Retighten the cable adjusting nuts and check the selection positions as follows:

With the selector in 'N' start the engine and move the selector to 'R' position, and ensure that the gear is engaged then slowly return the lever to the 'N' position. The reverse gear should disengage just before or as the lever reaches the 'N' position. Repeat this procedure but engage first gear instead.

47 Assuming the gear selection to be in order (if not, further adjustment is required), refit the bellcrank cover plate and lower the car.

---

7 Braking system

Bleeding – split braking system

1 The basic principle for bleeding the brakes on late models fitted with the split braking system is identical to that described in Chapter 9, Section 3 except that the order of bleeding differs. Referring to Fig. 13.25A it can be seen that bleeding commences on the rear wheels first starting at 'A' and finishing on the front wheels at point 'D'.

2 On completion of bleeding the brake test switch and warning light must be checked for operation as follows:

a) Apply a firm pressure to the brake pedal. The warning

272

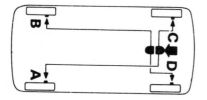

Fig. 13.25A. Sequence for bleeding the brakes on models
fitted with split braking system (Sec. 7)

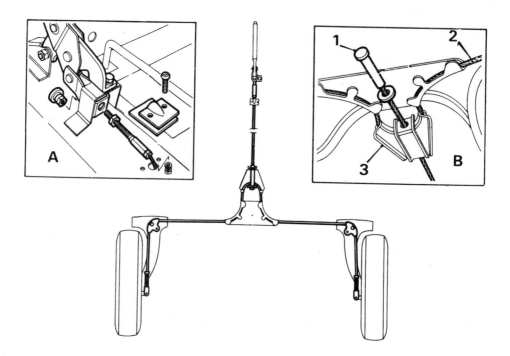

Fig. 13.25B. The latest handbrake cable layout showing
inset 'A' the handbrake lever cable connection and 'B' the
compensator (3) showing the front (1) and rear (2) cables

Fig. 13.26. The latest type fuse box showing the wiring
colour codes:

W   – white
N   – brown
LGW – light green/white
R   – red
G   – green
P   – purple
LGO – light green/orange
RG   – red/green

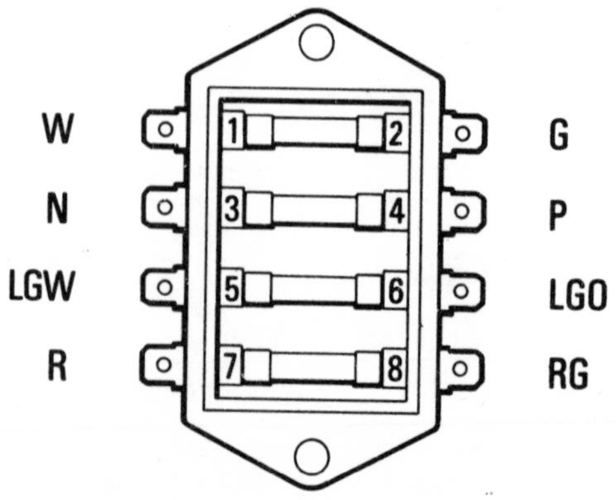

W   1   2   G
N   3   4   P
LGW   5   6   LGO
R   7   8   RG

light should go out and on releasing the pedal pressure, stay out. Should the light stay on it indicates uneven pressure in the brake system. Otherwise, possibly the pressure differential warning actuator or failure switch are faulty, and must be rectified as soon as possible. Re-bleed the system to check the pressure.

b) *If the light is already off, then check its operation by pressing the test push, when the light should glow – if not check the bulb and/or electrical connections.*

Handbrake cable

3   The layout of the handbrake cable on the late models differs slightly from the earlier type. Referring to Fig. 13.25B it can be seen that instead of having a separate cable from the handbrake lever trunnion to each rear wheel, there is now a single cable which is interconnected to the respective rear brakes. This cable is located in the same manner (by round corner pivot segments) and attached via a clevis pin to the operating lever – but differs in that it is guided centrally round a compensator unit.

A single cable from the handbrake lever is connected at its rear end to the compensator and this cable is adjusted at the lever by means of adjusting nuts as were the previous cables. The adjustment instructions are therefore as described in Section 12 of Chapter 9, except that there is now only one cable to adjust.

To remove and refit the handbrake cables of the later type proceed as follows:

Front cable

4   With the front seats hinged forward, fold the rear floor mats out of the way and loosen the cable locknut.
5   Unscrew and remove the adjusting nut from the cable and then remove the cable guide plate screws. Detach the guide plate and seal pad.
6   From underneath the vehicle, pull the cable through the floor and release from the compensator.

Rear cable

7   Remove the front cable as described above.
8   Withdraw the split pin and extract the clevis pin from each rear brake backplate lever.
9   Free the cable from each abutment bracket on the back-plates and prise back the flange on each sector corner that retains the cable. Prise open the subframe guide plate tags sufficiently to release the cable and remove it complete with compensator.
10 Refitting of both cables is the reverse of the removal procedure but be sure to clean out the guide slots, lubricate the pivot points and use new split pins for the clevis pins. Renew the clevis pins if they are worn. Re-adjust the handbrake as described in Chapter 9.

8   Electrical system

Fuses

1   The fuse box on the latest models now has two extra fuse circuits incorporated in it. As with the earlier fuse box there are two spare fuses retained in the lid. Removal of the fuses is identical to the earlier type – simply prise the fuse free of the retainers. The layout of the latest fuse box is shown in Fig. 13.26 together with a colour code for the wiring.

Lights

Front indicator – 1000 cc models (export only)

2   The front direction indicator light on certain 1000 cc export models is now as shown in Fig. 13.27. The lens is retained by two screws. To remove the lamp complete remove the lens, then undo the two securing nuts on the inner wing panel and pull the light unit forward from the body. Carefully pull the rubber seal back and disconnect the wiring connectors, then withdraw the lamp unit. Refit in the reverse order ensuring that the wiring connections are clean and secure.

Number plate lamp – late model saloons

3   The rear number plate lamp on all saloon models is now as shown in Fig. 13.28. The unit is retained by three screws which are accessible from inside the luggage compartment lid.

Front side/flasher lamp – 1275 GT and Clubman

4   The front side light and direction indicator lights on the 1275 GT and Clubman models are now as shown in Fig. 13.29 in a combination unit. To remove the lens for bulb renewal, simply unscrew the two lens retaining screws from the front. If the complete unit is to be removed, first disconnect the lens as mentioned, then detach the wires to the rear of the lamp from the engine compartment. Note the wire connection positions. Unscrew the four lamp unit retaining nuts from the inner wing panel and withdraw the lamp. Refit in the reverse order but ensure that the sealing gasket around the body aperture is in good condition – renew if damaged or perished.

Ignition and starter switch (late models) – removal and refitting

5   To remove the latest type of ignition/starter switch, (see Fig. 13.30) first, disconnect the battery, then remove the cowl to steering column retainer screws and withdraw the cowl. Detach the multi-wiring connector plug. Unscrew and remove the screw securing the switch unit in position and carefully pull the switch from the steering lock unit. Refit in the reverse order.

Panel switch – removal and refitting

6   The latest panel switches are of the 'rocker' type as shown in Fig. 13.31. To remove, first loosen the nut to the rear of the heater, then unscrew and remove the two screws retaining the

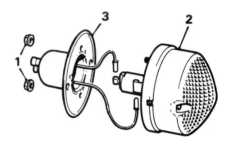

Fig. 13.27. The front indicator light now fitted to certain export model 1000 cc cars

1   Retaining nuts   *3   Rubber seal*
2   Lens

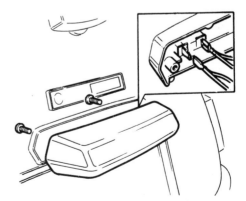

Fig. 13.28. Late model rear number plate light

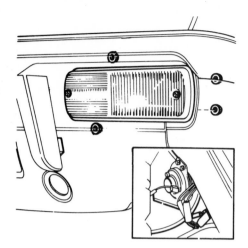

Fig. 13.29. The front side light/flasher light as fitted to the 1275 GT and Clubman

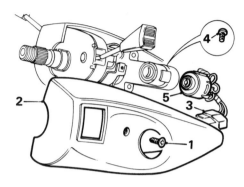

Fig. 13.30. The latest ignition starter switch

1 and 2   *Cowl and retaining screw*
3   *Multi-wiring connector*
4   *Switch securing screw*
5   *Switch*

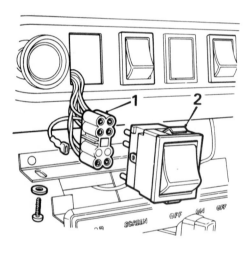

Fig. 13.31. The panel switch (late type) showing multi-connector (1) and switch retaining tabs (2)

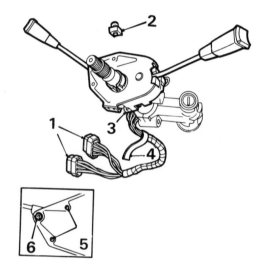

Fig. 13.32. The combination horn/direction indicator and main beam control switch

1 *Multi-connectors*	4 *Insulating tape*	
2 *Cancelling ring drive block*	5 *Rivet positions*	
3 *Clamp screw*	6 *Screw*	

heater. The heater can now be lowered from the facia panel and this gives access to the rear of the switch. Compress the switch retaining tabs at the rear of the panel and push the switch out. Detach the multi-connector and remove the switch. Refit in the reverse order.

Combination horn/direction indicator/main beam control switch and wiper/washer switch – removal and refitting

7   Remove the steering wheel as described in Chapter 11, Section 18. Detach the multi-connection plugs to the switches.

Remove the cancelling ring drive block from the indicator (see Fig. 13.32), and loosen the switch clamping screw. The switch can now be withdrawn from the column. To remove the wiper/washer switch from the indicator switch mounting plate, unwind the insulating tape and separate the respective switch wiring harnesses. Drill the two rivets out that secure the washer/wiper switch to the plate and undo the screw. Remove the switch.

Refit in the reverse order but check that the nylon switch striker dog centre is in alignment with the direction indicator switch stalk.

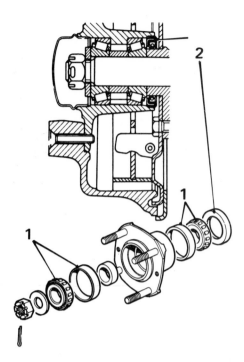

Fig. 13.33. The rear hub unit – 1275 GT models

1   Roller bearing, cup and cone
2   Oil seal – lip facing away from the bearing

---

9   Suspension and steering

Rear hubs – 1275 GT models

The rear hubs on the 1275 GT models differ from the standard versions in that they have tapered roller bearings in place of the normal ball bearing types – see Fig. 13.33. With this type of bearing fitted it is not necessary to use a puller to remove the hub unit from the hub shaft. If either the inner or outer (or both) roller bearings are to be renewed, the bearing cups must be extracted from the hub. It should also be noted that the oil seal is positioned with its lip away from the bearing.

10 Bodywork

General

Various cosmetic changes were made to the Mini range in August 1977. These included such items as a new style steering wheel, automatic reversing lights incorporated in the revised tail light clusters (not 850 model or Estate), tinted glass on the Clubman and 1275 GT models and body coachline side trim (not 850 models or Estate).

These trim changes should not affect the basic procedures described elsewhere in this manual.

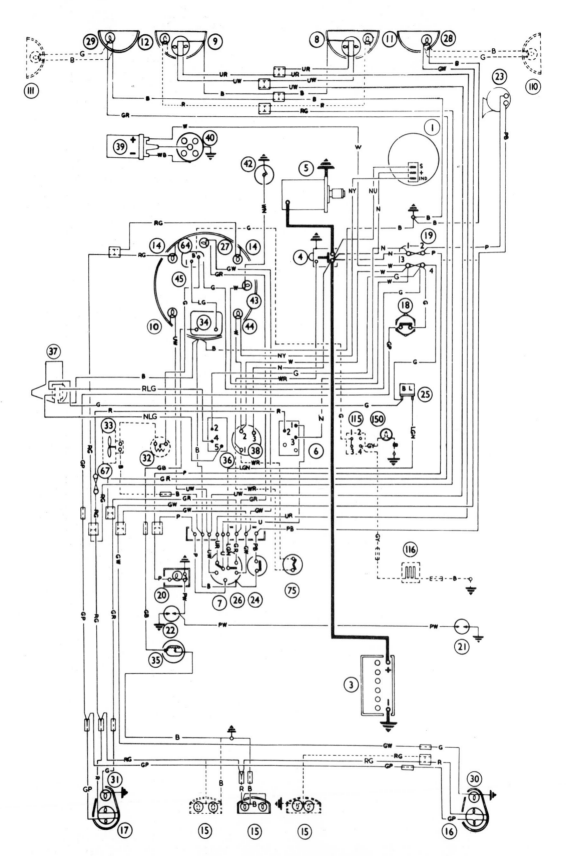

Fig. 13.34. Wiring diagram – Mini 850 De-luxe Saloon, Van and Pick-up (with alternator and rocker type switches) - Pre-1976. For key see page 213.

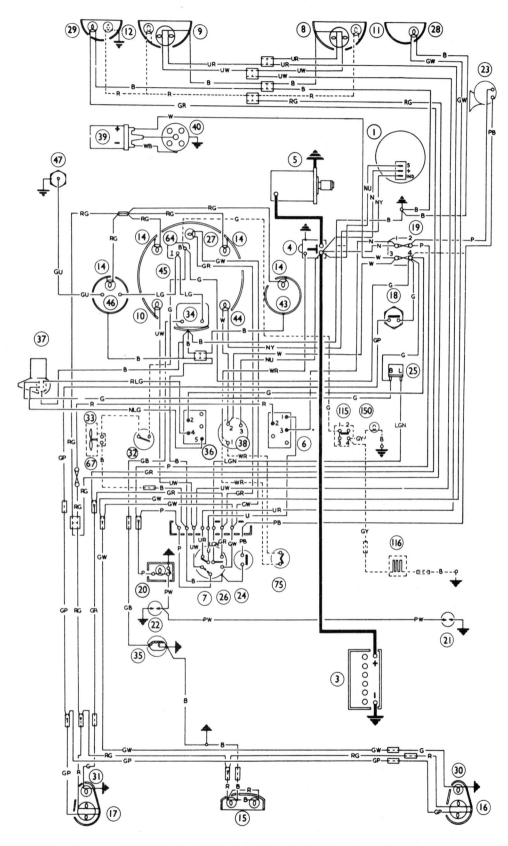

Fig. 13.35. Wiring diagram – Mini 1000 Special De-luxe Saloon (with alternator and rocker type switches) –
Pre-1976. For key see page 213.

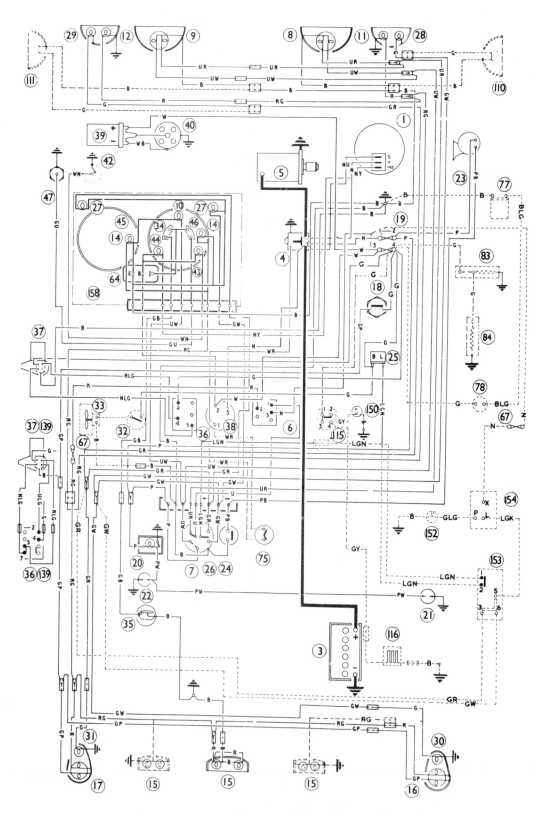

Fig. 13.36. Wiring diagram – Mini Clubman Saloon and Estate (with alternator and rocker type switches) – Pre-1976
For key see page 213.

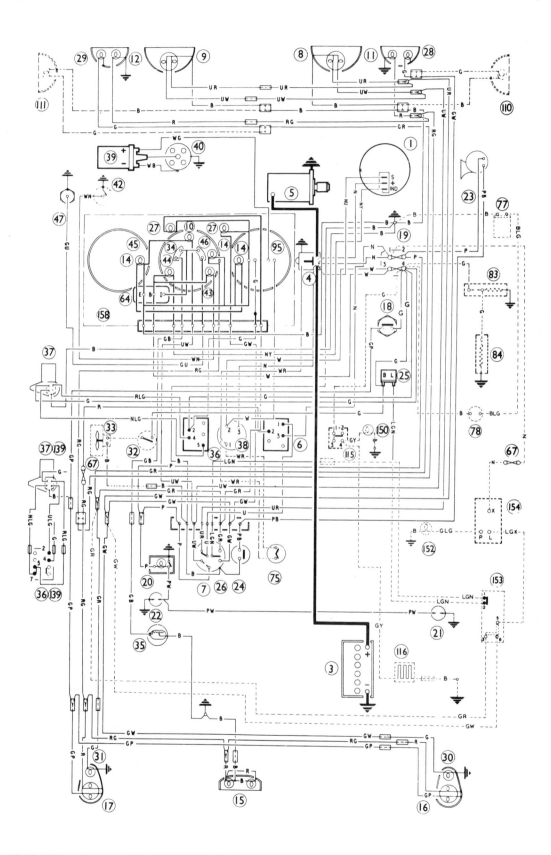

Fig. 13.37. Wiring diagram – Mini 1275 GT (with alternator and rocker type switches) - Pre-1976. For key see page 213.

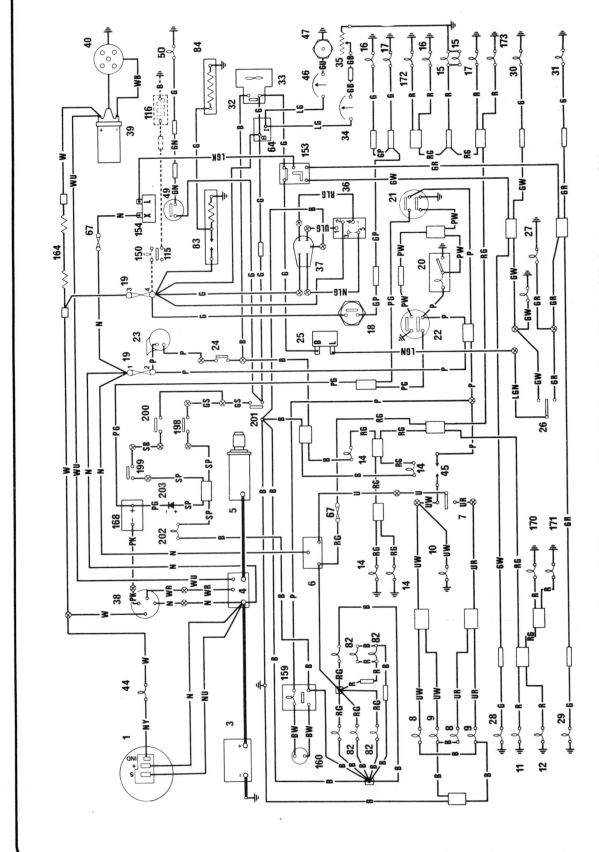

Fig. 13.38. Wiring diagram — Mini 1000 Saloon (Canada) - Pre-1977. For key see page 213.

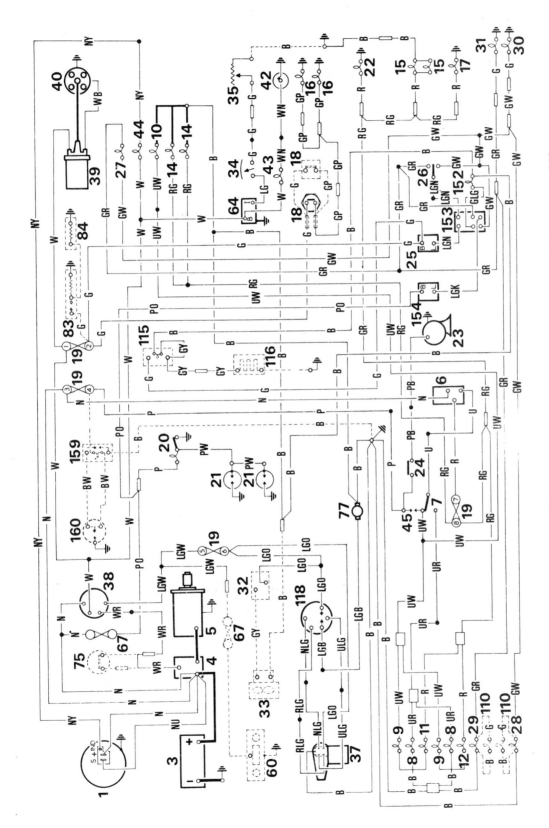

Fig. 13.39. Wiring diagram – Mini 850 Saloon, Van and Pick-up – 1976 onwards. For key see page 282.

Master key to wiring diagrams
(Figures 13.39 - 13.43 inclusive)
Some of the components listed in this key may not be fitted to certain models

1	Alternator
3	Battery
4	Starter solenoid
5	Starter motor
6	Lighting switch
7	Headlamp dip switch
8	Headlamp dip switch
9	Headlamp main beam
10	Main beam warning lamp
11	Sidelamp - RH
12	Sidelamp - LH
14	Panel illumination lamps
15	Number plate illumination lamps
16	Stop lamps
17	Tail lamp - RH
18	Stop lamp switch (hydraulic)
18	Stop lamp switch (mechanical)
19	Fuse box
20	Interior lamp
21	Interior lamp switch (door)
22	Tail lamp - LH
23	Horn
24	Horn-push
25	Indicator flasher unit
26	Indicator switch
27	Indicator warning lamp
28	Front indicator lamp - RH
29	Front indicator lamp - LH
30	Rear indicator lamp - RH
31	Rear indicator lamp - LH
32	Heater switch
33	Heater motor
34	Fuel level indicator
35	Fuel level indicator tank unit
37	Windscreen wiper motor
38	Ignition switch
39	Ignition coil
40	Distributor
42	Oil pressure switch
43	Oil pressure warning lamp
44	No charge warning lamp
45	Headlamp flasher switch
46	Water temperature indicator
47	Water temperature transmitter
49	Reverse lamp switch
50	Reverse lamp
60	Radio
64	Voltage stabilizer
67	Line fuse
75	Automatic gearbox ignition inhibitor switch
77	Windscreen washer motor
82	Switch illumination lamp
83	Induction heater and thermostat
84	Suction chamber heater
95	Tachometer
110	Indicator repeater lamps
115	Heated rear screen switch
116	Heated rear screen
118	Combined windscreen washer and wiper switch
132	Brake warning lamp
150	Heated rear screen warning lamp
152	Hazard warning lamp
154	Hazard warning flasher unit
158	Printed circuit instrument panel
159	Brake failure test switch and warning lamp
160	Brake pressure differential switch
164	Resistive cable
165	Handbrake switch
166	Handbrake warning lamp
168	Ignition key warning buzzer
169	Buzzer door switch
170	RH front side marker lamp
171	LH front side marker lamp
172	RH rear side marker lamp
173	LH rear side marker lamp
198	Driver's seat belt switch
199	Passenger's seat belt switch
200	Passenger seat switch
201	Seat belt warning gearbox switch
202	Seat belt warning light
203	Blocking diode - seat belt warning
210	Panel illumination theostat
211	Heater control illumination
291	Brake warning relay

CABLE COLOUR CODE

B	–	Black
G	–	Green
K	–	Pink
LG	–	Light Green
N	–	Brown
O	–	Orange
P	–	Purple
R	–	Red
U	–	Blue
W	–	White
Y	–	Yellow
S	–	Slate

When a cable has two colour code letters the first denotes the main colour and the second denotes the tracer colour.

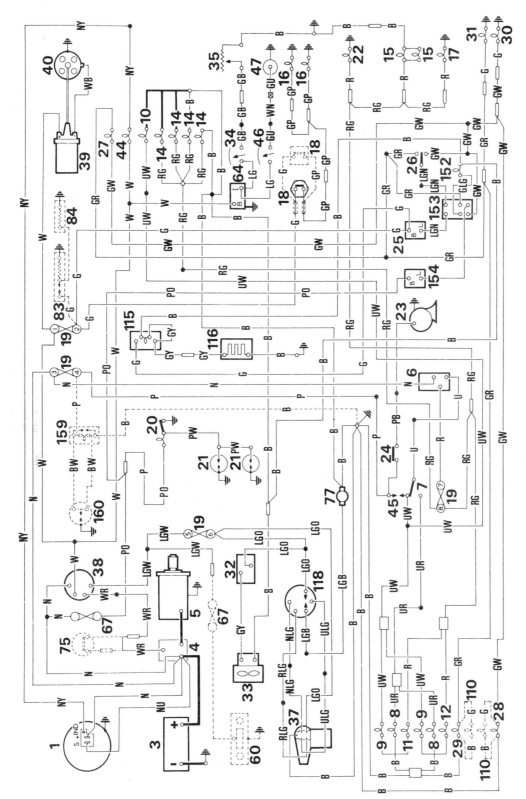

Fig. 13.40. Wiring diagram – Mini 1000 Saloon (Triple instrument facia) – 1976 onwards (UK, Europe and Sweden). For key see page 282.

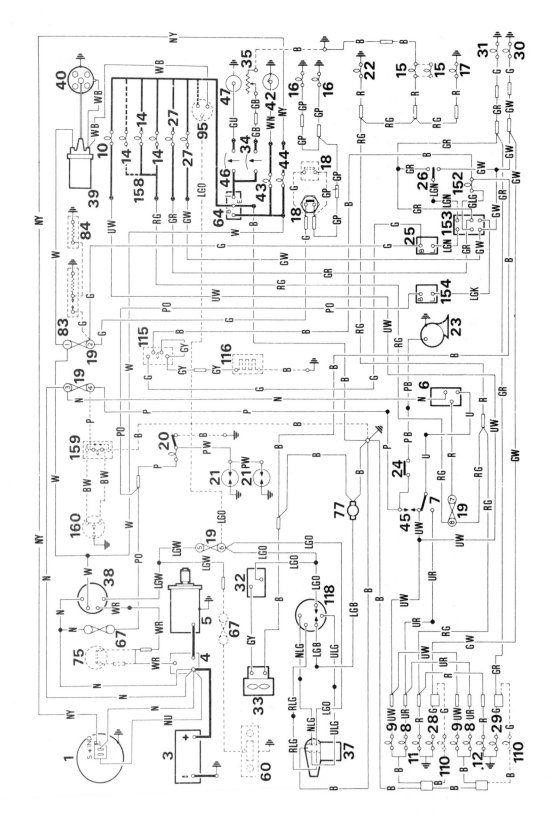

Fig. 13.41. Wiring diagram – Mini Clubman, Estate and 1275 GT - 1976 onwards. For key see page 282.

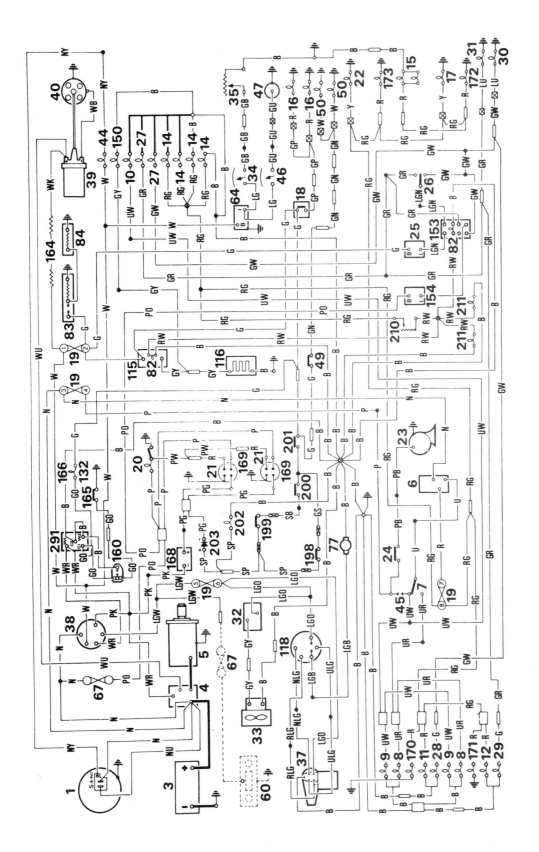

Fig. 13.42. Wiring diagram -- Mini 1000 (Canada) - 1977 onwards. For key see page 282.

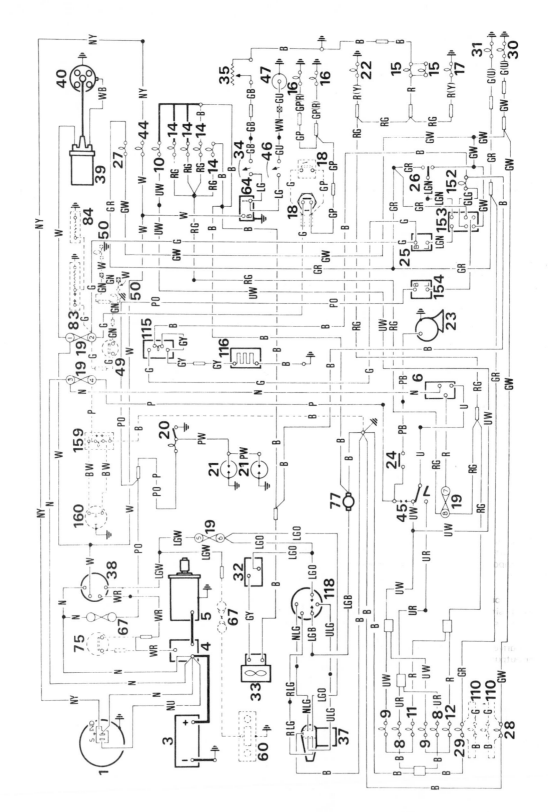

Fig. 13.43. Wiring diagram – Mini Special – 1976 onwards. For key see page 282.

List of illustrations

Chapter 7/Driveshafts and universal joints

Chapter 8/Differential unit

Chapter 9/Braking system

Index

**Printed by
Haynes Publishing Group
Sparkford Yeovil Somerset
England**